November 1966   ALEX. D. SHE

27 GILMO

EDI

SCOTLAND.

70/-

WALKER

on

THE SCOTTISH LEGAL SYSTEM

THE SCOTTISH LEGAL SYSTEM

AN INTRODUCTION TO THE
STUDY OF SCOTS LAW

BY

DAVID M. WALKER

M.A., LL.B.(Glas.), LL.B.(Lond.), Ph.D., LL.D.(Edin.)
One of Her Majesty's Counsel in Scotland,
of the Middle Temple, Barrister-at-Law,
Regius Professor of Law, formerly
Professor of Jurisprudence, in
the University of Glasgow

SECOND EDITION, REVISED

EDINBURGH
W. GREEN & SON LTD.
LAW PUBLISHERS
1963

First Edition . . . 1959   By D. M. Walker
Second Edition . . 1963   „   „

Printed in Great Britain by The Eastern Press, Ltd., London and Reading

PREFACE

THIS book has been written primarily to provide a textbook for the introductory course in the legal curriculum of Glasgow University, which is designated Scottish Legal System. Nevertheless I hope that it may prove of interest and utility to other persons concerned to obtain a general conspectus of the subject.

That course, and consequently this book, is intended not as a first or general introductory course on Scots Law itself, but as an attempt to tackle the problem of teaching the novice law student how to go about the study of law and an attempt to equip him to do so. It is an introduction to the *study*, not to the law itself. The traditional method of plunging the law student at once into the subject-matter of various branches of the law is quite unsatisfactory, because he does not at that stage have the knowledge or skill necessary to study law with understanding and effect. This book is therefore not an elementary book on the principles of Scots Law but an attempt to acquaint the student at the very outset of his studies with the legal materials and the methods of working, with the basic knowledge and the background requisite to enable him intelligently and profitably to pursue legal studies.

The study of this book is not intended to supersede the necessity for later, closer and more detailed study of each of the topics it covers, as well as of the doctrinal principles of the substantive law. Every topic discussed herein has been deliberately treated in a preliminary and elementary way, and many details, qualifications, subtleties and difficulties have been glossed over. Considerations of space and expense have further severely limited or even prevented altogether the discussion of many points.

I have deliberately avoided the detailed treatment and the full citation of authority which might be expected in a more advanced book, and much bibliographical material has been mentioned in footnotes not so much to vouch the statements in the text as to indicate the sources of further information.

This second edition has been completely revised to take account of developments in the law since the first edition and in the hope of clarifying some of the difficulties.

I am deeply indebted to my wife, who assisted me at every stage of the book, to the publishers for undertaking the preparation of the Tables of Statutes and of Cases, and to the printers who have taken such pains and trouble over this book. I have tried to take account of all developments down to the date of this Preface.

D. M. W.

THE UNIVERSITY,
GLASGOW, W.2.
1st February, 1963.

CONTENTS

vii

TABLE OF CASES

ix

Pollok School *v.* Glasgow Town Clerk, 1946 S.C. 373; 1946 S.N. 55; 1946 S.L.T. 365; 1947 S.C. 605; 1947 S.N. 127; 1948 S.L.T. 45 324
Portobello Magistrates *v.* Edinburgh Magistrates (1882) 10 R. 130; 20 S.L.R. 92 298
Powell *v.* Kempton Park Racecourse Co. [1899] A.C. 143; 68 L.J.Q.B. 392; 80 L.T. 538; 63 J.P. 260; 47 W.R. 585; 15 T.L.R. 266; 43 S.J. 329; 19 Cox C.C. 265 293
Power *v.* Central S.M.T. Co., 1949 S.C. 376; 1949 S.L.T. 302 247
Poyser *v.* Minors (1881) 7 Q.B.D. 329, 333 137
Proprietary Articles Trade Association *v.* Att.-Gen. for Canada [1931] A.C. 310; 100 L.J.P.C. 84; 144 L.T. 577; 47 T.L.R. 250 135
Public Trustee *v.* I. R. C. [1960] A.C. 398; [1960] 2 W.L.R. 203; [1960] 1 All E.R. 1; 104 S.J. 68 310
Pugh *v.* Golden Valley Ry. (1880) 15 Ch.D. 330; 49 L.J.Ch. 721; 42 L.T. 863; 28 W.R. 863 317
Purden's C.B. *v.* Boyd, 1962 S.L.T. 180 331
Purves *v.* Landell (1845) 12 Cl. & F. 91; 8 E.R. 1332 226
Purves' Trustees *v.* Purves (1895) 22 R. 513; 32 S.L.R. 379; 2 S.L.T. 627 335

QUALCAST (WOLVERHAMPTON), LTD. *v.* Haynes [1959] A.C. 743; [1959] 2 W.L.R. 510; 103 S.J. 310; [1959] 2 All E.R. 38 300
Queensbury Case (D. of Buccleugh and Queensbury *v.* Hyslop) (1824) 2 Sh.App. 43 87
Quinn *v.* Leathem [1901] A.C. 495; [1901] W.N. 170 321

R. *v.* Bourne [1939] 1 K.B. 687; 108 L.J.K.B. 471; [1938] 3 All E.R. 615 337
—— *v.* Cade [1914] 2 K.B. 209; [1914] W.N. 48; 110 L.T. 624; 30 T.L.R. 289; 58 S.J. 288; 10 Cr.App.R. 23 312
—— *v.* Condon (1952) 96 S.J. 531; 36 Cr.App.R. 130 193
—— *v.* Denyer [1926] 2 K.B. 258; 95 L.J.K.B. 699; 134 L.T. 637; 42 T.L.R. 452; 28 Cox C.C. 153; 19 Cr.App.R. 93 312
—— *v.* Edwards (1884) 13 Q.B.D. 586; 53 L.J.M.C. 149; 51 L.T. 586; 49 J.P. 117 317
—— *v.* Ettridge [1909] 2 K.B. 24; 78 L.J.K.B. 479; 100 L.T. 624; 73 J.P. 253; 25 T.L.R. 391; 53 S.J. 401; 22 Cox C.C. 101; 2 Cr.App.R. 62 ...... 312, 318
—— *v.* Fulham, Hammersmith and Kensington Rent Tribunal [1951] 2 K.B. 1; [1951] 1 T.L.R. 423; 115 J.P. 132; 95 S.J. 237; [1951] 1 All E.R. 482; 49 L.G.R. 275 313
—— *v.* Gray's Inn (1780) 1 Doug.K.B. 353; 99 E.R. 227 200
—— *v.* Houghton [1952] W.N. 304; [1952] 1 T.L.R. 1507; 96 S.J. 398; 36 Cr.App.R. 98 193
—— *v.* Jackson [1891] 1 Q.B. 671; 60 L.J.Q.B. 346; 64 L.T. 679; 39 W.R. 407; 7 T.L.R. 382; 55 J.P. 246 317
—— *v.* Keyn (1876) 2 Ex.D. 63; 46 L.J.M.C. 17; 41 J.P. 517; 13 Cox C.C. 403 273
—— *v.* Labouchere (1884) 12 Q.B.D. 320; 53 L.J.Q.B. 362; 50 L.T. 177; 48 J.P. 165; 32 W.R. 861; 12 Cox C.C. 415 301
—— *v.* London County Council [1893] 2 Q.B. 454; 63 L.J.Q.B. 4; 69 L.T. 580; 58 J.P. 21; 42 W.R. 1; 9 T.L.R. 601; 37 S.J. 669; 4 R. 531 272
—— *v.* Millis (1844) 10 Cl. & F. 534 310
—— *v.* Minister of Agriculture and Fisheries, *Ex p.* Graham; R. *v.* Agricultural Land Tribunal (South Western Province), *Ex p.* Benney [1955] 2 Q.B. 140; [1955] 2 W.L.R. 872; 99 S.J. 275; [1955] 2 All E.R. 129; 53 L.G.R. 281 316
—— *v.* Minister of Health, *Ex p.* Yaffe. *See* Minister of Health *v.* R., *Ex p.* Yaffe.
—— *v.* Norman [1924] 2 K.B. 315; 93 L.J.K.B. 883; 131 L.T. 29; 88 J.P. 125; 40 T.L.R. 693; 68 S.J. 814; 27 Cox C.C. 621; 18 Cr.App.R. 81, 119 ... 312

TABLE OF STATUTES

Table of Statutes

xxxi

ABBREVIATIONS

A.J.C.L.	American Journal of Comparative Law.
A.J.I.L.	American Journal of International Law.
A.P.S.	Acts of the Parliaments of Scotland (Record Edition, 12 vols.).
B.J.A.L.	British Journal of Administrative Law.
B.Y.I.L.	British Year Book of International Law.
Can.B.R.	Canadian Bar Review.
C.L.J.	Cambridge Law Journal.
C.L.P.	Current Legal Problems.
C.L.Y.	Current Law Year Book.
Col.L.R.	Columbia Law Review.
H.L.R.	Harvard Law Review.
I.C.L.Q.	International and Comparative Law Quarterly.
J.Crim.L.	Journal of Criminal Law.
J.R.	Juridical Review.
J.S.P.T.L.	Journal of the Society of Public Teachers of Law.
L.Q.R.	Law Quarterly Review.
M.L.R.	Modern Law Review.
N.I.L.Q.	Northern Ireland Law Quarterly.
N.Y.U.L.Q.R.	New York University Law Quarterly Review.
Pub.L.	Public Law.
S.H.R.	Scottish Historical Review.
S.L.R.	Scottish Law Review.
S.L.T.	Scots Law Times.
Yale L.J.	Yale Law Journal.

CHAPTER 1

LAW AND OTHER STUDIES

THE field of human knowledge and inquiry is roughly divisible into three
areas, known as the humanities, the social sciences, and the natural
sciences (or the physical and biological sciences, or simply " science ").[1]
These areas of knowledge and inquiry comprise respectively the studies
which consider, discuss, criticise and evaluate the products of human
reasoning, speculation and imagination,[2] which examine, analyse and
seek to explain particular facets of the conduct, attitudes, interaction and
interrelations of human beings living and working together in organised
and civilised society,[3] and those which investigate the universe and
the phenomena, creatures and things which are found in it.[4] It is only
since the Renaissance that these different areas of thought and study
have come to be thus divided, and further subdivided into branches
and subjects of study; in ancient and medieval times the polymath could
know something of all.[5] To Plato philosophy embraced almost the whole
field of knowledge. But division and subdivision, with their necessarily
concomitant specialisation and compartmentation of knowledge, are
inevitable consequences of the enormous and continuing growth in the
extent, complexity and detail of knowledge in every field and of thinking,
investigation and writing thereon, though this increasingly tends to
give rise to the division between the Two Cultures, of Arts (and Social
Sciences) and of Science,[6] in which persons knowledgeable in one field
are frequently largely ignorant in the other.

This tripartite distinction is, however, not rigid and the areas are
not strictly defined or self-contained; many subjects of study partake

[1] Universities frequently recognise this general division in the form of the distribution of subject-matter of study between Faculties of Arts (or Letters), of Social
Sciences, and of Science, though in many the social sciences are included in
the Faculty of Arts. Other Faculties are specialised offshoots of these main
groups, related particularly to the studies relevant to certain major professions.
[2] e.g., philosophy in its various branches, languages, literature, fine art.
[3] e.g., politics, economics, history, sociology, anthropology. The humanities
and the social sciences are together sometimes spoken of as dealing with super-
organic phenomena.
[4] e.g., physics, chemistry, geology, astronomy (physical sciences dealing with
inanimate nature and inorganic phenomena); botany, zoology, physiology,
biochemistry (biological sciences dealing with living creatures, plants and organic
phenomena).
[5] Encyclopaedia of the Social Sciences, Introd. II—The Social Sciences as Disciplines
(Vol. I, 231 et seq.).
[6] See Encyclopaedia of the Social Sciences, Introd. I—The Development of Social
Thought and Institutions (Vol. I, pp. 8–228).

1

of elements from different areas and are therefore difficult to classify,[7] and many more run into one another, but it is a generally accepted and useful division, and does also correspond to differences in the methods of study and research. The humanities are studied chiefly by study of written texts, close examination of arguments, reasoning, verbal disputation and criticism; the social sciences by observation, examination and analysis of recorded instances of human behaviour, and deduction of conclusions therefrom; and the physical and biological sciences by observation of natural phenomena, classification, measurement, the tabulation and comparison of the results of experiments, the induction of hypotheses which explain the results and observed phenomena, and experimental verification, correction and amplification of these hypotheses.

Each one of these branches of study, moreover, has its own body of theory and philosophy, its own course of historical development, and its own body of recognised principles, constantly being modified in the light of changing conditions and progressive research and criticism; each one also has its more theoretical and abstract side, in which it is regarded primarily as a more or less coherent body of knowledge and studied with little or no regard to its utility, and its more practical and applied side, in which it is considered mainly as a system of useful principles capable of application to practical needs and ends, to solving actual problems and surmounting real difficulties.

In this general pattern legal science, or the study of law in its most general sense, falls to be grouped with the social sciences [8]: it deals, that is, with one aspect of the relations and interactions of individuals living in society, namely, with the institutions, machinery and principles which particular societies have developed for the purposes of defining the claims and liabilities of persons against one another in various circumstances, and of providing means for vindicating just claims and peaceably resolving their disputes and controversies in accordance with the principles accepted as fair and right in the particular community at a given time.[9] Moreover, the content of law is influenced and even determined by the views of society, and it has important consequences

---

[7] Thus psychology is partly derived from introspection and reasoning, partly from observation of human and animal conduct, partly from planned experiments; geography is partly social science, dealing with human activities, partly physical science, dealing with the characteristics of the world inhabited by man; architecture is partly a fine art, partly an applied science; and so on. Many studies, such as psychology, moral philosophy, geography, medicine, biology, linguistics and others have important social implications quite apart from their own substance and technicalities.

[8] Cf. *Encyc.Soc.Sc.*, I, 3, defining social sciences as "those mental or cultural sciences which deal with the activities of the individual as a member of a group."

[9] Patterson, *Jurisprudence*, 50, points out that so far as jurists deal with precepts for conduct which *ought to be* followed, law is not a social science but a philosophic discipline.

for society and individuals. The existence of a legal order in society is furthermore presupposed by most other social sciences, so that law and the other social sciences are interdependent and, as studies, overlap.

Law is, indeed, a part of human culture, of " that complex whole which includes knowledge, belief, art, morals, law, custom and any other capabilities acquired by man as a member of society." [10] It is both a product of civilisation, in that wherever groups of individuals have attained that stage of organisation and of control over their environment which we call civilisation, some kind of legal ordering of society is found,[11] and it is also an essential of the continuance and development of civilisation, in that without a legal order to regulate conflicting claims and to resolve differences, civilisation would slip back into anarchy. The intimate connection between the legal system and the general culture of our society is well illustrated by the extent to which legal institutions are pictured in English literature [12] and legal phraseology has penetrated into common speech.[13]

Law a True Science

Law, moreover, is truly a science,[14] that is, a systematic body of coherent and ordered knowledge about the institutions, principles and rules regulating human conduct in society.[15] It is "an organised

[10] Tylor, *Primitive Culture*, 1.
[11] Thus, highly developed legal systems existed in ancient Mesopotamia (see Driver and Miles, *The Babylonian Laws*, 2 vols.; *The Assyrian Laws*), Asia Minor (see Neufeld, *The Hittite Laws*), Palestine (see Kent, *Israel's Laws and Legal Precedents*) and elsewhere.
[12] See, *e.g.*, Underhill, *Shakespeare's England*, Chap. 13; Keeton, *Shakespeare and His Legal Problems*; Holdsworth, *Charles Dickens as a Legal Historian*; McNair, *Dr Johnson and the Law*; Marshall, *Sir Walter Scott and Scots Law*; Cardozo, " Law and Literature " in *Selected Writings*, 339; Holdsworth, " Literature in Law Books " in *Essays in Law and History*, 219; Lord Macmillan, " Law and Letters " and " Law and Language " in *Law and Other Things*; Windolph, *Reflections on the Law in Literature*; Collins, *Dickens and Crime*.
[13] See, *e.g.*, Simon, " English Idioms from the Law " (1960) 76 L.Q.R. 283, 429; (1962) 78 L.Q.R. 245.
[14] The word " science " is not confined, or appropriate only, to natural science; it is applicable to the systematised knowledge of any subject of intellectual inquiry.
[15] Lord Atkin once said: " That law is a scientific subject, I suggest, cannot be disputed. I think it was Burke who said that law is one of the finest and noblest of human sciences: a science which does more to quicken and invigorate the understanding than all the other kinds of learning put together." (" Law as an Educational Subject " (1932) J.S.P.T.L. 27.) Stair (*Institutions*, I, 1, 17) affirmed that law could, and should, be handled as a rational discipline, having principles from whence its conclusions may be deduced. Alexander Bayne (Professor of Scots Law at Edinburgh, 1722–37) in *A Discourse on the Rise and Progress of the Law of Scotland*, annexed to his edition of Hope's *Minor Practicks* (1726), wrote that the Science of the Law was of the highest character among the humane sciences, the most useful to mankind, and best entitled to first place among them. Similarly Blackstone (*Commentaries on the Laws of England*, I, 34) wrote: " Law is to be considered not only as a matter of practice, but also as a rational science." (On Blackstone see further: Boorstin, *The Mysterious Science of the*

and critically controlled body of knowledge both of legal institutions and
legal precepts and of the legal order, that is, the legal ordering of
society . . . a science of achieving social control by means of or with the
aid of laws . . . a science of the adjustment of human relations through
the public administration of justice, or, more specifically, a science of
the securing of interests in civilised society by means of an ordered
judicial and administrative adjustment of relations." [16]   Legal science,
or jurisprudence (in the wider sense of that word), includes all thinking
and writing about and systematic study and knowledge of the making,
exposition and analysis, development and transmission of law, and
also legal dogmatics, or the study of the actual content of the legal
system, of the body of propositions, precepts, doctrines, principles and
rules accepted in a particular community and of their applications.[17]
Law in a modern community does not consist of a great mass of particular,
specific, unrelated rules which have to be looked up, as in a telephone
directory, and the study of law does not consist in memorising, or even
in learning how to look up, such a directory.   The scientific element
in law consists in that a system of law comprises a body of reasonably
consistent principles and rules, susceptible of arrangement under heads
and sub-heads and of systematic study, defining consequences and
standards of conduct in particular kinds of circumstances, which can
be applied to an infinite number and variety of problem-situations,
whether known or foreseeable or not, and can solve them in accordance
with overriding principles of justice, in the same way as propositions
and formulae about the triangle can be applied to any actual triangle.[18]
Furthermore law can be studied by scientific methods just as can any
other science.   Experiment, or the observation of phenomena under
conditions controlled by the investigator, is possible only to a very limited
extent,[19] but observation, classification, analysis and synthesis, inductive
and deductive inference, and comparison and analogy are all applicable

Law and Hanbury, *The Vinerian Chair and Legal Education.*) *Cf.* also Pollock,
First Book of Jurisprudence, 46; Langdell, Introduction to *Cases on the Law of
Contract* (1886).
[16] Pound, *Jurisprudence*, I, 16–17.
[17] *Cf.* Kantorowicz, *The Definition of Law*, 11–13; Schulz, *History of Roman Legal
Science*, 1.
[18] *Cf.* Fraser Tytler's *Memoirs of Lord Kames*, I, 114: " The examination of various
cases which turn upon one common *ratio decidendi*, familiarises the mind, in
all points of doubt to recur immediately to a principle; and this habit of reference
will not only be found of the utmost benefit when any abstruse or intricate question
is the subject of discussion; but it tends from the agreeable and vigorous exercise
it affords to the intellectual powers, to give to jurisprudence that dignity as a
science which it merits, and to render the study of the laws, instead of a servile
drudgery, the manly employment of a philosophic mind."
[19] It is possible to some extent in such contexts as trying different methods of treatment of criminals, or different methods of control of anti-social activities, such
as gambling.

to legal problems as much as to those of other sciences. Observation
and classification in particular are clearly illustrated by the common and
centuries-old legal practice of having interesting cases noted or reported
under legal headings, so that jurists can subsequently read what the
courts have done and said in solving particular problems,[20] and can
classify and study together cases relating to similar problems. Analysis
involves the breaking down of a legal problem or reported decision
into its elements, into the particular factors which constitute it, so as
to discern what is unknown or different from other comparable cases,
while synthesis is the building up of the legal elements involved in a
factual situation which go to impose liability or provide a valid defence
or justify a legal remedy in the particular circumstances. Inductive
inference consists in drawing a general principle from a number of
similar observed instances; deductive inference is the process of applying
general principles to suitable particular instances. Both are illustrated
repeatedly in the way the courts handle previous reported decisions to
help them solve a new problem before them.[21] Comparison and analogy
involve the recognition of greater or lesser degrees of similarity between
one case and another or others, and again these are techniques regularly
resorted to in legal reasoning.[22]

Law must not be thought of solely or even primarily as a body of
professional knowledge, the stock-in-trade of the practitioners of certain
professions, or as purely a practical or applied science. It is primarily
a social science, a pure science, a branch of the field of studies of men's
relations with one another. The knowledge gained from that study
can of course be used to understand and to solve actual everyday problems;
to that extent it forms part of the background knowledge employed by
several professions, but the same is true of economics, physiology and
many other subjects. The evident utility and manifold applications of
the knowledge should not be allowed to obscure the status of the subject
as a major department of the social sciences, indeed one of the most
ancient of them, and one which has in every age and country attracted
the attention and devotion of some of the ablest minds of the time.

The Methods of Legal Science

The full understanding of a legal system or any branch of it requires
study from four standpoints; these are the analytical, breaking down

---

[20] " Case law has a scientific aim, namely, the prediction of events by means of
past experience ": Pollock, " The Science of Case Law " in *Essays in Jurisprudence
and Ethics*, 237, and in *Jurisprudence and Legal Essays*, 169.

[21] *Cf.* the inductive inference in *Donoghue* v. *Stevenson*, 1932 S.C.(H.L.) 31, of the
general principle implicit in various particular earlier decisions, and the deduction
from that general principle of the particular decision in *Lockhart* v. *Barr*, 1943
S.C.(H.L.) 1.

[22] See further Levi, *Introduction to Legal Reasoning*.

the problem-situation and ascertaining what elements compose it and what rules are applicable to each part of the subject and its problems; the historical, ascertaining how and why these rules have come to be accepted and to take their modern form; the philosophical, considering whether those rules are consistent with the needs of society, and with accepted ideas of right and justice; and the comparative, seeing how other societies at a similar stage of civilisation face up to the same or corresponding problems. For proper appreciation, that is, one must find out what the rules are here and now, what they were and how and why they have come to be what they are, whether they are satisfactory judged by an ideal standard, and how they appear compared with the rules which are accepted elsewhere.[23]

Relations of Law with other Studies

Legal science deals with only one facet of human conduct and of the relations of people in society, and cannot ignore those other sciences which study other facets of the same relations.[24] One particular piece of conduct may be of interest to the students of many disciplines; an assault by one man on another is to the sociologist a deviation from normal conduct, to the psychologist a problem of motivation, to the philosopher a problem of right and wrong, to the psychiatrist a possible manifestation of a diseased mind, and to the lawyer a breach of a legal duty which is punishable. The relations between law and the principal other social sciences are so close and important as to justify more detailed individual examination.[25]

Law and Politics

The relationship in this case is obviously close. Politics is the study of the organisation of the members of a society living in a defined area for their own government in the general interest of peace and order.[26] The framework of the political organisation of a community, its constitution, is set out in legal terms and legal forms and secured by legal means, and the subordinate standards, such as the structure and powers of the legislative assembly, the rights and liberties of citizens, the powers and duties of officials, the position of the police and their powers, the system of taxation and so on, are all defined by law. Even in a dictatorial régime, the dictator commonly secures his powers by law; in a democracy

[23] Bryce, " The Methods of Legal Science " in *Studies in History and Jurisprudence*, II, 607.
[24] *Cf.* Lord Kames's Preface to his *Elucidations respecting the Law of Scotland*: " Were law taught as a rational science, its principles unfolded, and its connection with manners and politics, it would prove an enticing study to every person who has an appetite for knowledge."
[25] See generally Cairns, *Law and the Social Sciences.*
[26] See further Heller, " Political Science " in *Encyc.Soc.Sc.*, XII, 207.

every power, control and regulation is a matter of law and effected by legal forms.

Conversely, the political structure of a society has as one of its primary purposes and duties the maintenance of a legal system, of law and order in the community, and in most modern organised societies the modification and reformation of the law in the interests of the community, or possibly of the politically dominant group thereof, is the prerogative of the legislative assembly, which is a part of the political framework, while the application to particular cases and enforcement of the legal principles is the function of other branches of the political organisation. It is clear therefore that the nature and content of a legal system may be largely determined by the views of those politically dominant at any given time.

As studies jurisprudence and politics are interdependent and almost indistinguishable in origin, and the most profound thinking on the theoretical side, such as Aristotle's *Politics*, is common to both. In practice the studies of law and politics are inextricably enmeshed and inseparable.[27]

Law and Economics

Law and economics similarly overlap at many points. Economics is the study of human action in relation to the production, exchange and distribution of wealth, or of "social phenomena centring about the provision for the material needs of the individual and of organised groups."[28] Much law springs from the necessity of regulating economic relations and exists for that purpose, while economic activity, such as buying and selling, transport, manufacture and financial transactions can flourish only within a régime of law and order and are shaped materially by the legal forms recognised in the community. Associations, such as companies and trade unions, are formed in legal ways and subject to legal regulation for economic ends. The salient economic relations such as sale, hiring, transport and employment are effected within a legal framework. The ancillaries which facilitate such relations, such as credit, bills, cheques, money and other modes of payment, securities for payment and insurance against loss, are all regulated by law. Monopolies,[29] restrictive trading agreements, hire-purchase transactions and the protection of consumers from defective quality, are spheres in which law and economics are increasingly interacting. General concepts, such as contract, property and succession on death, taxation and many more, can profitably be studied from both standpoints. Not merely

---

[27] See further Pound, *Jurisprudence*, II, 283; Bryce, *Studies in History and Jurisprudence*, Essay X.

[28] Seligman, " Economics " in *Encyc.Soc.Sc.*, V, 344; and see Robinson, " Law and Economics " (1938) 2 M.L.R. 257.

[29] See, *e.g.*, Lewis, " Monopoly and the Law " (1943) 6 M.L.R. 97.

those engaged in industry or commerce but every individual every day enters into numerous transactions which have both legal and economic significance, the law determining whether it is permissible and in what form it may or must be effected, what its legal effect and consequences are and what can be done to enforce performance, and considerations of economics determining whether that transaction should be entered into or deferred or abandoned, on what terms, and whether completion will give satisfaction or not.

As a study economics emerged from ethical, legal and political thinking. Adam Smith lectured and wrote on ethics and legal theory as well as on economics, and only in the nineteenth century did economics become distinct.[30]

Law and Sociology

Sociology is the study of society, social groups, social phenomena, the forms of social institutions, social relationships, social structure, social change and development,[31] and it therefore deals with much that is the background to, and the justification for and explanation of, the legal system. In its study of the interaction and relationships of individuals and groups it deals with the same subject-matter as does the law, but from a different standpoint. Social institutions, such as the family, marriage and inheritance are in fact regulated in large part by legal rules and are legal institutions as well as sociological.[32]

To the sociologist law is necessarily a matter of interest because law is, like custom, habit, morals, taboos and fashion, one of the forces of social control which tend to regulate conduct and impose uniformities of behaviour, and is moreover the most widespread and powerful of these forces.[33] Law is also largely a product of social requirements and changes, and of custom and accepted social practices, and develops to take account of such social changes; if it does not, it becomes out of date, out of touch with the requirements and the feelings of the community and to that extent fails to serve its purpose.[34] In the present century

---

[30] Adam Smith's work includes *The Theory of Moral Sentiments* and *Lectures on Justice, Police, Revenue and Arms* as well as the *Wealth of Nations*. See further Scott, *Adam Smith as Student and Professor*; Fay, *Adam Smith and the Scotland of His Day*; Cooke, " Adam Smith and Jurisprudence " (1935) 51 L.Q.R. 326; and, more generally, Gide and Rist, *History of Economic Doctrines*; Roll, *History of Economic Thought*. See also Jones, *Historical Introduction to the Theory of Law*, Chap. 10—" Law and Economic Theory."

[31] See generally MacIver, " Sociology " in *Encyc.Soc.Sc.*, XIV, 232.

[32] See generally MacIver and Page: *Society, an Introductory Analysis*; Johnson, *Sociology, a Systematic Introduction*; Ogburn and Nimkoff, *Handbook of Sociology*; Ginsberg, *Essays in Sociology and Social Philosophy*, 3 vols.; Michael and Adler, *Crime, Law and Social Science*; Glueck and Hall, *Crime, Theft and Society*.

[33] See Pound, *Social Control Through Law*; " Sociology and Law " in Ogburn and Goldenweiser, *The Social Sciences* (1921) 319.

[34] See further Friedmann, *Law in a Changing Society*; Ginsberg (ed.), *Law and Opinion in England in the 20th Century*.

there has indeed developed a branch of study called sociology of law, studying law as a specialised phase of the study of society.[35]

To the student of law, sociology explains much of the society in which his legal system works and for which it exists.[36] It enables him to take account of social facts in the framing of new legislation or the enforcement of existing rules, and requires him to reconsider time-honoured rules or institutions in the light of changed conditions. What is social disorganisation to the sociologist includes what are to the lawyer also problems, such as of crime, divorce, illegitimacy, racial discrimination, street and industrial accidents, and town planning. Sociology both helps to explain the institutions of the legal order, and itself assumes them in its own studies.

Law and History

History involves not only the tracing of the order of past happenings but elucidating the causal factors which helped to determine these happenings, and their effects and influence on every facet of the life of the society or institution whose history is being studied.[37] The connection of law with history is very close. In the first place every branch of law, international, supra-national and national, has its own history and course of development which can be traced, and which alone can in many cases provide the explanation for the existence today of apparently peculiar or irrational rules. In the second place that history itself is only one facet of the general development of international and supra-national institutions and relations, of the growth of the structure and organisation of the particular nation-state, and of the communities therein, and has to be related to the other facets, social, political, economic, religious and so on, of that history. Legal history is moreover not merely a facet but largely a product of the more general history of the particular society and may repeatedly have been powerfully influenced by important events in other sectors of the general history of the community.[38] Thus in Scottish legal history important legal changes have been brought about by such events as the struggle for independence, the religious Reformation, the political unions with England under the Commonwealth

[35] See Timasheff, *The Sociology of Law*; Ehrlich, *Fundamental Principles of the Sociology of Law*; Gurvitch, *Sociology of Law*; sociology of law is closely related to sociological jurisprudence, which is rather the " applied " aspect of the relations of law and society, examining the legal system functionally, as it works and operates in society. On the latter see Pound, *Jurisprudence*, I, 291 *et seq.*

[36] John Millar, Professor of Law in Glasgow University 1761–1801, wrote on *The Origin of the Distinction of Ranks*, which is important as an early sociological study. It is reprinted with a valuable introduction in Lehmann, *John Millar of Glasgow* (1961). See also Lehmann, " John Millar " (1961) 6 J.R.(N.S.) 218.

[37] See generally Berr and others, " History and Historiography " in *Encyc.Soc.Sc.*, VII, 357 *et seq.*

[38] See further Pound, *Interpretations of Legal History*.

and Protectorate and since 1707, the industrial revolution, the two world wars and so on.[39]

Historical study of law is of particular importance not only because it can frequently explain what is rationally inexplicable, but because it makes clear that particular rules cannot always be considered as immutable, or as embodying eternal or universal principles; they may proceed only from the prejudices or the exigencies of a particular time; their history explains them but does not justify them, leaving them open to criticism on other grounds.

Two other branches of study, which stand partly in the sphere of social studies and partly in that of biological science, deserve mention.

Law and Anthropology

Anthropology is the study of man as a social being as he is found in different environments in the world, and of this one aspect is social anthropology which deals with the life of primitive peoples living in primitive conditions at the present day, and studies their conduct, habits, institutions, and attitudes, their beliefs, taboos, marriage customs, trading relations, reactions to wrongdoing and so on. Such studies provide important indications of the origins and bases of modern social institutions and the patterns of conduct of civilised peoples. They serve to stimulate, illustrate and modify thinking about law and its origins and nature rather than to influence it today or to provide material to which it is applicable. From such studies it is apparent that means of social control, some approximating in substance to law, can exist without writing or lawyers, without force or formal procedure, in such communities.[40]

[39] On these points, see further Chap. 3, *infra*. *Cf.* Kames, *Historical Law Tracts*, preface, where he says: " Law in particular becomes then only a rational study, when it is traced historically, from its first rudiments among savages, through successive changes, to its highest improvements in a civilised society." See also Fraser Tytler's *Memoirs of Lord Kames*, I, 208: " There cannot indeed be a more pleasing exercise for the understanding, nor any that affords a greater scope for ingenuity, than the reciprocal elucidation of Law and of History, by the aids which they borrow from each other. Every law is a key to the history of the times in which it was framed, and may, in most instances, be traced up to the political emergency which required its enactment."

[40] See further, generally, Boas, " Anthropology " in *Encyc.Soc.Sc.*, II, 73; Chappel and Coon, *Principles of Anthropology*; Piddington, *Introduction to Social Anthropology* (2 vols.); Lowie, *Primitive Society*; and, on points of legal interest, Hartland, *Primitive Law*; Diamond, *Primitive Law*; Malinowski, *Crime and Custom in Savage Society*; Hogbin, *Law and Order in Polynesia*; Gluckman, *The Judicial Process among the Barotse of Northern Rhodesia*; Llewellyn and Hoebel, *The Cheyenne Way*; Hoebel, *The Law of Primitive Man*; see also Robson, *Civilisation and the Growth of Law*; Cairns, " Law and Anthropology " (1931) 31 Col.L.R. 32.

Law and Psychology

Psychology is concerned with investigating the mental processes of the individual, his instincts, beliefs, emotions, means of perception, feeling, remembering and thinking.[41] In legal contexts it is frequently material to determine such facts as the intention of a party, whether he could have or should have known something, the motive for his conduct, and so on. While the courts normally are content to ignore the underlying mental processes and draw inferences from facts external to the individual, the individual's mental state may be acutely important, as where issues of insanity or diminished responsibility arise in criminal cases, and psychology may be valuable as giving insight into the springs of the conduct under investigation. In another context, psychology can cast light on the value or fallibility of human evidence and on the ways by which judges think.[42]

Social psychology is the study of persons' conduct in their interactions with one another with reference to the effects of this on their thoughts, feelings, emotions and habits. It stems from both psychology and sociology. Social conduct, and the person and the group's prejudices, convictions, attitudes, frames of reference and values may all be highly relevant to law and help to explain facts giving rise to legal issues.[43]

The Theoretical and Practical Sides of Legal Science

Like the other main social sciences, legal science has two sides to its study; there is the theoretical and philosophical study, seeking to classify, rationalise, explain, restate, criticise and evaluate the existing principles of law, to trace their origins, examine their consistency one with another, compare them with those accepted at earlier periods or in other contemporary societies, to relate them to their philosophical bases and evaluate them by ideal standards, and to give consideration to their amendment and reform. This side is concerned with such questions as why the law is what it is, what it has been, what it is elsewhere, how its terms are used, and its rules classified and arranged, whether it is fair or not and whether it should be otherwise. Secondly there is the study of law as a coherent and reasonably systematic body of principles and rules capable of practical application to the affairs of men in everyday life, to the defining of their claims and liabilities in particular circumstances and to the resolution of their controversies and

---

41 See Jastrow, " Psychology " in *Encyc.Soc.Sc.*, XII, 588; Bernard, " Social Psychology " in the same, XIV, 151.

42 See Frank, *Law and the Modern Mind* and *Courts on Trial*.

43 See further Thouless, *General and Social Psychology*; McDougall, *Introduction to Social Psychology*; Newcomb, *Social Psychology*; Kimball Young, *Handbook of Social Psychology*; Jones, *Historical Introduction to the Theory of Law*, Chap. 7— " The Psychological Theories."

the decision of disputes. This side is concerned with what the existing law prescribes, permits or forbids, and with its application to specific people in particular circumstances. Sir Frederick Pollock once distinguished between the practice of law as an art, and the study of law as a science. So, too, law has been called " social engineering " by analogy with the way in which principles of physical science can be used by engineers for useful ends. In the university, the emphasis is naturally on the study of law as a science; in everyday life, the emphasis is on law as a practical art.

This distinction is sometimes drawn in some other studies by a distinction in names, such as that between theology and religion, economic theory or science and applied economics, political theory or philosophy and political science or politics, social theory or philosophy and sociology or social science, moral philosophy and moral science, pure (natural) science or natural philosophy and applied science, and so on, though the terminology is not always consistent and there is no clear or sharp line of division between any two. In legal studies this same distinction is sometimes drawn, between jurisprudence [44] or legal theory and philosophy and law or legal principles or legal dogmatics or even legal science (in a narrower sense of that phrase), though the term Law is more commonly used for both sides of legal science. In every case the pure or more theoretical and philosophical study and the applied or more practical overlap and their problems constantly run into one another. A problem of practical application may require for its answer a thorough examination of the theoretical basis of the principle to be applied. But it is important to note that law is not only, or even primarily, a body of rules or formulae for practical application to the solution of concrete problems. This is the obvious, the common, aspect of law but not by any means the whole of law as a science or as a study, since the theory and the abstract principles underlie every particular rule and application.

[44] The term jurisprudence may accordingly be used, firstly, as earlier in this chapter, in its widest and most general sense, as *juris prudentia* or *juris scientia*, for legal science, or the science of law; secondly, for that branch of legal science which deals with general problems of the theory of law, particularly with the examination of the concepts and terminology of law, " the comparative anatomy of developed systems of law," and sometimes including also problems of the philosophy of law (on this sense see further p. 14, *infra*); and occasionally, thirdly, as a grandiloquent synonym for the dogmatic principles of one legal system or a branch thereof, *e.g.*, Scottish jurisprudence, medical jurisprudence. In France *la jurisprudence* means what we call case-law (on which see Chap. 8). Jurisprudence in its second sense is an important element in legal studies, just as is Law, *i.e.*, the dogmatic exposition of accepted principles. The terminology is further complicated by the fact that some writers speak of " the science of jurisprudence " (in the second sense), or call jurisprudence (in the second sense) the " science of law," as distinct from dogmatic exposition of law, which itself is sometimes called " legal science " (in the narrower sense of that phrase). These words and phrases do not have completely fixed or settled usages or meanings. See further Campbell, " A Note on the Word ' Jurisprudence ' " (1942) 58 L.Q.R. 334.

Law and Philosophy

On its theoretical side the study of law, as of other social sciences, inevitably impinges on various aspects of philosophy.[45] For centuries law and politics had a common philosophic foundation,[46] while economics and sociology emerged later from this same body of thought. Only in the nineteenth century did law tend to be divorced from politics and economics, but a counter-movement, starting in the latter half of the nineteenth century, urged the unification of the social sciences, stressing the interrelation and interaction of all and their common background of philosophical thinking. The study of law, as of all the other social sciences, inevitably leads to questions of the rightness or wrongness of conduct, the ends sought to be attained, the justifiability of means and ends, the problem of justice, the validity of reasoning, the meanings of the terms used and the proper use of terminology, and so on, all of which are essentially philosophic problems. The philosophy of law, or the critical examination of the propositions, presuppositions and underlying ideas of legal systems in the light of philosophical ideas and methods is an important part of jurisprudence (in the narrower sense of that word).

Of the recognised branches of philosophy three, logic and scientific method, semantics, and moral philosophy, are vitally important, for the light they cast on problems of law and the study of law in relation to and in the light of these branches forms legal philosophy or philosophy of law.

Logic and scientific method serves an important purpose by clarifying ideas as to thinking and reasoning, and as to the validity of inferences drawn from initial propositions.[47] Law has many logical characteristics; it is a body of general propositions, forming a more or less systematic structure, and legal principles and problems can be classified, defined and distinguished. While logic does assist in legal thinking, it does not by itself ensure legally correct or just answers. At most it tests the correctness of thinking, but the basis for the reasoning may still be legally inaccurate,[48] and the final determination may be a matter of policy or discretion,[49] not determined by logic at all. Logic does not provide, or guarantee the correctness of, the bases for reasoning. Thus

---

[45] See Dewey, " Philosophy " in *Encyc.Soc.Sc.*, XII, 118.

[46] See Cairns, *Legal Philosophy from Plato to Hegel*; Cohen, " Philosophy and Legal Science " (1932) 32 Col.L.R. 1103.

[47] " No science affords more opportunity for exerting the reasoning faculty than that of law ": Kames, *Elucidations*, preface.

[48] Thus logically valid conclusions in a particular case could be drawn from an initial premiss such as: In Scotland a wife can divorce her husband for incompatibility of temperament, though that premiss is legally unsound.

[49] *e.g.*, the appropriate sum to award as damages, the appropriate penalty, whether to give custody of a child to one parent or the other.

a judge's finding that one spouse has committed adultery is a basis for logical reasoning to a legal conclusion, but cannot itself be checked or controverted by logic.[50]

Semantics is the study of the theories as to the meanings and mental influences of words and other symbols used in communication. The results of semantic study are particularly important in legal thinking, writing and argument, since so many of the terms and concepts used in law and legal books are inherently vague and capable of conveying different ideas in different circumstances; such words as " right," " wrong," " negligence " are susceptible of different meanings in different contexts.

It is fatal to legal study to think that any such words have a fixed meaning; they all have many shades of meaning in different contexts and when used for different purposes, and even have uses other than pure communication; thus such a word as " agitator " has a strong emotional flavour.[51]

Ethics or moral philosophy studies human conduct with reference to its goodness or badness, rightness or wrongness, and accordingly evaluates conduct by reference to some such criterion as whether it promotes the general happiness or could without absurdity be generalised into a universal rule of conduct.[52] Its overlap with law is obvious; both study and approve or censure human conduct, but using different standards. Acutely difficult but interesting problems arise as to whether, and how far, law should seek to promote and secure ethical values; should it, for example, punish conduct which is morally objectionable but may be harmless to the general community? How far can a child of five be held " responsible " for wrongdoing? How far, again, are a person's motives and intentions relevant to his moral guilt, and to his legal guilt? Legal phenomena are also moral phenomena.[53] In some respects the law treats of matters ethically neutral, as when it lays down the rule of the road and the rules as to authentication of deeds, where there has to be a rule, though the rule currently adopted in Scotland can hardly

---

[50] On the place of logic in law see further Cohen, " The Place of Logic in the Law " (1915) 29 H.L.R. 622; Dewey, " Logical Method and Law " (1924) 10 Cornell L.Q. 17; Lloyd, " Reason and Logic in the Common Law " (1948) 64 L.Q.R. 468; Guest, " Logic in the Law " in *Oxford Essays in Jurisprudence*, 176; Castberg, *Problems of Legal Philosophy*, Chap. 3.

[51] The standard books on semantics are Ogden and Richards, *The Meaning of Meaning*, 8th ed., and Carnap, *Philosophy and Logical Syntax*. See also Cohen and Nagel, *Introduction to Logic and Scientific Method*; Chase, *The Tyranny of Words*; Hexner, *Studies in Legal Terminology*; Jensen, *The Nature of Legal Argument*; Wasserstrom, *The Judicial Decision*; Hart, " Definition and Theory in Jurisprudence " (1954) 70 L.Q.R. 37.

[52] The literature is enormous; a good modern introduction is Lillie, *An Introduction to Ethics*. See also Sidgwick, *History of Ethics*.

[53] Miller, *Lectures on the Philosophy of Law*, 9.

be said to be good or bad in comparison with the alternative, but many matters raising legal issues also raise moral issues.[54] The concept of justice and the relations between human law and ideal justice are other topics of common interest to law and ethics.

The examination of moral problems inherent in legal issues leads on in some cases to metaphysical problems such as, for example, the status and existence of universal propositions, such as that all persons should obey the law, or what a rule of law, in the most general sense, is, or to the examination of the most abstract general ideas, such as Right, Freedom or Liability. One point at which everyday law touches metaphysics is when we speak of an accident " causing " injuries and are driven to inquire what is really meant by " cause " and " causation." [55] So too deep study of legal issues leads on into theology, to such questions as human and divine justice, crime and sin, the dissolubility of Christian marriage, and the legal attitude to life and death.[56] All these and similar problems go to make up that part of jurisprudence known as philosophy of law.

Conclusion

Legal science, or jurisprudence (in its broad sense), or Law in its most general sense, is a body of knowledge akin to and related to politics, economics, history and other studies of human behaviour; like them it has an historical aspect, a theoretical and philosophic aspect (jurisprudence in the narrow sense [57]) and a dogmatic aspect, dealing with the actual content of specific legal systems, international, supra-national and national, which sets out the currently accepted principles and rules. The present book seeks to deal with some of the main elements in the historical and theoretical aspects of the Law of Scotland and of its most general doctrines

---

[54] See among many books, Pound, *Law and Morals*; *Introduction to the Philosophy of Law*; *Jurisprudence*, II, 215; Stone, *Province and Function of Law*, Chap. 16; Friedmann, *Legal Theory*; Cahn, *The Moral Decision*; Goodhart, *English Law and the Moral Law*; Lloyd, *Public Policy*; see also Ames, " Law and Morals " (1909) 22 H.L.R. 97; Winfield, " Ethics in English Case Law " (1931) 45 H.L.R. 112, and *Select Legal Essays*, 266; Cohen, " Philosophy and Legal Science " (1932) 32 Col.L.R. 1103, and in *Law and the Social Order* (1933), 219; Cohen, " Law and Scientific Method " in the same, 184; Cohen, " Moral Aspects of the Criminal Law " (1940) 49 Yale L.J. 987; Hart, " Positivism and the Separation of Law and Morals " (1958) 71 H.L.R. 593; Fuller, " Positivism and Fidelity to Law," *ibid.*, 630.

[55] See Hart and Honore, *Causation in the Law*; Castberg, *Problems of Legal Philosophy*, Chap. 4.

[56] Books casting interesting light on such problems are Williams, *The Sanctity of Life and the Criminal Law*, and Stevas, *Life, Death and the Law*. See also Daube, *Studies in Biblical Law*; Bryce, " The Relations of Law and Religion " in *Studies in History and Jurisprudence*, II, 638; Lord Devlin, " The Enforcement of Morals " (British Academy Maccabaean Lecture, 1959).

[57] Some books on jurisprudence are mainly concerned with legal theory (classification, terminology, etc.), others with legal philosophy (ideals, justice, etc.), but the two branches are not separable and the titles of books on jurisprudence frequently use the terms " theory " and " philosophy " indifferently.

and structure as an introduction to the detailed study of its dogmatic content and of the applications thereof to particular problems, and ultimately to the study of the philosophy of law.

FURTHER READING

Law as a University Study

Brown: " Purpose and Method of a Law School " (1902) 18 L.Q.R. 78, 192.
Brownlie: " Legal Education in the Scottish Universities " (1955) 67 J.R. 26.
Cardozo: " Law and the University " (1931) 47 L.Q.R. 19.
Denning: " The Universities and Law Reform " (1949) 1 J.S.P.T.L.(N.S.) 258.
Gavit: *Introduction to the Study of Law.*
Goodhart: " The Vocational Teaching of Law " (1950) 1 J.S.P.T.L.(N.S.) 333.
Gower: " English Legal Training " (1950) 15 M.L.R. 137.
Hamson: " The Teaching of Law " (1952) 2 J.S.P.T.L.(N.S.) 19.
Hanbury, *The Vinerian Chair and Legal Education.*
Hughes Parry: " Some Reflections on Legal Education " (1949) 1 J.S.P.T.L.
  (N.S.) 249.
Jones: " Modern Discussions of the Aims and Methods of Legal Science "
  (1932) 47 L.Q.R. 62.
Kennedy: " A Project of Legal Education " 1937 S.L.T.(News) 1, 17, 21.
Llewellyn: *The Bramble Bush.*
Montrose: " Law, Science and the Humanities " (1957) 4 J.S.P.T.L.(N.S.) 61.
Smalley Baker: " The Teaching of Law as one of the Social Sciences " (1947)
  1 J.S.P.T.L.(N.S.) 69.
Stallybrass: " Law in the Universities " (1948) 1 J.S.P.T.L.(N.S.) 157.
Vanderbilt (ed.): *Studying Law.*
Wade: " Legal Education; the Changing Scene " (1951) 1 J.S.P.T.L.(N.S.) 415.
Walker: " Law as a Liberal Education " 1956 S.L.T.(News) 57.
  " Legal Studies in the Scottish Universities " (1957) 2 J.R.(N.S.) 21.
Williams: *Learning the Law.*
Wright: " The Study of Law " (1939) 54 L.Q.R. 185.

Law and the Social Sciences

Arnold: *The Folklore of Capitalism.*
Cairns: *Law and the Social Sciences.*
Carlston: *Law and the Structures of Social Action.*
Cohen: *Law and the Social Order.*
Cohen and Cohen: *Readings in Jurisprudence and Legal Philosophy*, Part 4.
Commons: *Legal Foundations of Capitalism.*
Diamond: *The Evolution of Law and Order.*
Dicey: *Law and Public Opinion in England in the Nineteenth Century.*
Friedmann: *Law in a Changing Society.*
Ginsberg (ed.): *Law and Opinion in England in the Twentieth Century.*
Gregg: *Social and Economic History of Modern Britain.*
Gurvitch: *Sociology of Law.*
Hall: *Readings in Jurisprudence*, Part 3.
Ogburn and Goldenweiser (eds.): *The Social Sciences and their Interrelations.*
Patterson: *Jurisprudence.*
Pound: *Social Control through Law.*
Renner: *The Institutions of Private Law and their Social Functions.*

Robson: *Civilisation and the Growth of Law.*
Stone: *The Province and Function of Law*, Part 3.
Ullman: *The Mediaeval Idea of Law.*
    Principles of Government and Politics in the Middle Ages.
Welford: *Society: Problems and Methods of Study.*
Wootton: *Social Science and Social Pathology.*

Law and Philosophy
Barker: *Principles of Social and Political Theory.*
Berolzheimer: *The World's Legal Philosophies.*
Cahn: *The Moral Decision.*
Cairns: *Legal Philosophy from Plato to Hegel.*
    Theory of Legal Science.
Cohen: *Ethical Systems and Legal Ideals.*
Cohen and Cohen: *Readings in Jurisprudence and Legal Philosophy*, Part 3.
D'Entreves: *Natural Law.*
Friedmann: *Legal Theory.*
Friedrich: *Philosophy of Law in Historical Perspective.*
Goodhart: *English Law and the Moral Law.*
Hall: *Readings in Jurisprudence*, Part 1.
    Studies in Jurisprudence and Criminal Theory.
Hamburger: *Morals and Law—Aristotle's Legal Theory.*
Jones: *Historical Introduction to the Theory of Law.*
Lamont: *Principles of Moral Judgement.*
Micklem: *Law and the Laws.*
Morris: *The Great Legal Philosophers.*
Patterson: *Jurisprudence.*
Pound: *Law and Morals.*
    Introduction to the Philosophy of Law.
Radin: *Law as Logic and Experience.*
Stone: *The Province and Function of Law*, Parts 1 and 2.

CHAPTER 2

THE STUDY OF LEGAL SCIENCE

LEGAL science is the systematised knowledge of law in the most general sense of that word. What then is law? A full study of the nature of law is an important branch of jurisprudence and legal philosophy and it is a topic of much complexity. But it is desirable at an early stage in legal studies to formulate a provisional idea of the general nature of law which can be corrected and refined in the light of later study. It is necessary at once to put aside such uses of the term " law " as " law of gravitation " or the other " laws " of the natural sciences, physical or scientific laws, since these are generalisations explaining various uniformities in the phenomena of nature, describing what *happens* in certain defined circumstances,[1] and also such uses as " natural " or " moral " law, which expresses an ideal standard of conduct to which rules of positive law, *i.e.*, the law laid down in particular communities, ought to conform so as to make human conduct be in accordance with moral beliefs as to right and wrong. This latter use of the term " law " is, however, nearer to the jural significance in that it has the connotation of a rule for human conduct which is absent from the former, purely descriptive use.

In the sense which is of jural significance the law consists of a body of rules for the regulation of social conduct, recognised as obligatory, and enforceable. Different jurists emphasise different aspects of this body of rules. Thus some [2] stress the fact that those rules which are termed " law " are based on the will and force of the organised political community, the state, and define law as the commands of superior authority. This serves to distinguish rules of law from customary practices and rules voluntarily agreed upon and observed by particular groups, from conduct merely habitual or accepted by reason of moral or religious belief.

Others emphasise the end to be attained by those rules of social conduct, defining it, for example, as " the body of principles recognised and applied by the state in the administration of justice " [3] or " the expression of the idea of right involved in the relation of two or more human beings," [4] or " the sum of the rules of justice administered in a

---

1 Salmond, *Jurisprudence*, 11th ed., 24; Holland, *Jurisprudence*, 13th ed., 17.
2 *e.g.*, Hobbes, Bentham, Austin, Amos, Markby, Holland.
3 Salmond, *Jurisprudence*, 41.
4 Miller, *Philosophy of Law*, 9.

state and by its authority " [5]; and these views reflect the very prevalent belief that law is and should be related to right and justice, that it does not exist merely to regulate life or resolve controversies but to do so in a manner consistent with justice.

In recent times law has been regarded and defined largely by reference to its function in society, sometimes with an emphasis on the way in which it is applied by the courts. For example: " The prophecies of what courts will do in fact and nothing more pretentious, are what I mean by the law " [6]; " What these officials [judges or sheriffs or clerks or jailers or lawyers] do about disputes is, to my mind, the law itself " [7]; " A body of social rules prescribing external conduct and considered justiciable." [8] Other definitions emphasise that its function is to resolve conflicts of claims and interests of individuals and groups and to harmonise their differing desires with the minimum of disagreement. Thus: " The legal order is a régime of adjusting relations and ordering conduct through the systematic and orderly application of the force of a politically organised society, in order to prevent friction in human use and enjoyment of the goods of existence and eliminate waste of them." [9] Stress also is laid on the fact that the legal order of society is more than the abstract rules. The law is " the body of precepts and received ideals and the technique of using them, established or recognised by organised human society for the delimitation and securing of interests" (an interest being a demand or want or desire which human beings either individually or in groups seek to satisfy and of which the ordering of human relations in civilised society must take account).[10]

Law as Social Control

The legal system of a country is simply a form of social control, that is, a body of principles and rules regulative of human conduct in society, persuading persons to do some things and constraining them from doing others.[11] It is thus intimately related to the social functions that are the subject-matter of the other social sciences and to the regulative influence of religious and moral beliefs. The main bodies of rules which exist and operate as social controls in this way are law, religion, morals,

---

[5] Pollock, *First Book of Jurisprudence*, 17.
[6] Holmes, " The Path of the Law " (1897) 10 H.L.R. 457, 461.
[7] Llewellyn, *The Bramble Bush*, 3.
[8] Kantorowicz, *The Definition of Law*, 79.
[9] Pound, " Introduction to American Law," in Vanderbilt, *Studying Law*, 379.
[10] Pound, " Theory of Social Interests," in Hall, *Readings in Jurisprudence*, 238; see also Pound, " A Survey of Social Interests " (1943) 57 H.L.R. 1, reprinted in Vanderbilt, *Studying Law*, 439, and *Jurisprudence*, III, Chaps. 14 and 15.
[11] On social controls generally see MacIver and Page, *Society*, 137 *et seq.*; 175–181. The concept is a sociological one and an example of the influence this science has had on the study of law. See further Everett, " Social Control," *Encyc.Soc.Sc.*, IV, 344; Pound, *Social Control through Law*.

custom, fashion, convention, etiquette, and club, trade or union rules. Each has its distinctive forms of sanction brought to bear on one who transgresses the rules. In many particular sets of circumstances several of these social controls may all be operating simultaneously on an individual and influencing his conduct. Thus conscience pricks him for doing wrong, religious feeling causes remorse for sin, custom and habit of society frown on his conduct and may result in his being shunned, despised or ostracised, while the legal order may cause him to be fined or imprisoned or forced to pay compensation for what he has done.

State law, however, differs from the other social controls in that it is more widespread, extending to and covering far more activities than does any other form of control, its rules are more fixed and definite, being frequently prescribed in a strict verbal form, its operation extends in general to all persons subject to the state's authority, its authority is greater in that it may override and cancel the prescriptions of other social controls, and, lastly, it alone may be enforced by the whole authority of the state by means of fines, imprisonment or the taking of property. Law is accordingly a very important form of social control, of regulative influence, over practically every form of human conduct.

The concept of law as social control is one which provides a readily comprehensible idea of the notion of law in general, and the other definitions quoted may be treated as simply more particularised statements, emphasising respectively the fact of enforcement by the state, the aim of securing justice, and the mode of functioning of the law.

Law and the Legal System

The application of the controlling factor in society which is called "law" to various sets of circumstances requires the intervention of a legal system, which comprises an establishment of courts and judges, a coherent body of particular principles, doctrines and rules of law, with means for amending, restating and adding to them, and an apparatus of procedure whereby individuals may bring controversies and conflicts of claims before the courts for resolution. It is this legal system in any particular country which individualises the general conception of law into specific rules and applies them to the determination of specific controversies.

Law and the State

The precise organisation of the legal system and the content of the rules of law vary from one country to another. These elements are closely connected with the form of human association known as the state, which is the organisation or association of all the persons living within a demarcated extent of territory and organised into a distinct political community.[12] It is possibly the most important form of human association and an essential basis for peace, order, civilisation and good government. One of the main functions of the state as a political and legal organisation is to establish and maintain for its subjects a legal order, and to enforce a system of law and order. The identification of a legal system with a particular state is not, however, invariable in that within the territory of one political state there may exist simultaneously several distinct legal systems, each in a distinct portion,[13] or even for different classes of individuals in the same area,[14] while one system of law might in theory be applied throughout several political states.

A second main function of the state is the maintenance of its own existence and integrity, its freedom and that of its inhabitants from external aggression and domination; and this is a prerequisite of the maintenance of its own system of law and order.

The adequate performance of these main functions has required each state to set up a taxing apparatus to obtain the revenue required and a legislative, judicial and administrative system, so that the principles on which justice is to be administered and the territory governed may be decided, and those principles applied and worked out in detail in specific cases. There is further implied in the performance of these functions that this association of persons should have a definite organisation, a determinate and systematic form, structure and organisation, and not be merely a temporary or casual union. The organisation of a modern state is of great complexity and embodies a great mass of legal rules and principles.

In modern times an important group of functions has been added to the responsibilities of the state. It provides a postal system, highways and bridges, engages in scientific research, controls building and the use of land; it has assumed the duties of providing for the health, welfare, education and well-being of its citizens,[15] and to a considerable extent the conservation of national natural resources,[16] as well as the management and regulation of enterprises,[17] public utility services,[18] and industries,[19] which are of paramount importance for the national economy. This tendency towards an extension of state organisation and control

---

[12] See further Sidgwick, *Elements of Politics*, 217; MacIver, *The Modern State*, 22; Salmond, *Jurisprudence*, 10th ed., 129; Field, *Political Theory*, 54–56; Barker, *Principles of Social and Political Theory*, 3; Vinogradoff, *Historical Jurisprudence*, I, 85; and see generally Pound, *Jurisprudence*, II, 283.

[13] As in the United Kingdom and U.S.A.

[14] *e.g.*, Hindu and Mohammedan law in the former British India.

[15] Thus in Britain the Education Acts, National Health Service Acts, National Insurance Acts, Factory Acts, Children Acts, etc.

[16] *e.g.*, Petroleum Acts, work of the Forestry Commission.

[17] *e.g.*, B.B.C., I.T.V. Authority.

[18] *e.g.*, the railways under the Transport Acts, electricity and gas.

[19] *e.g.*, coal-mining.

leads to a great increase in the volume of legal rules regulating the conduct of individuals and groups of individuals and restricting their freedom of action in various respects in the interest of what is conceived to be the general welfare.[20]

The Scottish Legal System

Within the territorial limits designated as Scotland the state has developed a body of principles, rules and precepts, an organisation of courts and legal practitioners, and a body of knowledge and thinking about law which amounts to the Scottish legal system. It is largely indigenous, having grown and developed naturally within the country rather than having been imposed from without, yet it is not narrowly parochial, having shared in drawing something from the legal systems of antiquity, nor yet insular, having strong historical connections and logical affinities with legal systems of and derived from continental Europe. It is unitary in that it has grown as a body rather than been formed by aggregation or merging of substantially different elements; it is reasonably simple in being remarkably free from anomalies, absurdities and historical survivals which have outlived their usefulness and their justification; and it is firmly rooted in general principles, so that much can be explained as deduction from, or detailed working out of, great overriding principles based on reason and justice. Accordingly, the main elements in the Scottish legal system which will require detailed examination are the history and systematic structure of the law, the organisation of courts, and the personnel of the law, and the principles and rules applicable to various sets of circumstances. But several further preliminary matters remain to be discussed.

Elements in a Legal Situation

The legal situations which arise, which the judge or lawyer has to deal with, are not all matters of pure law. At every stage there are four elements; there are principles and rules of law, which are abstract and general, facts, which are concrete and specific, persons, who are complex, possibly irrational and unpredictable, and the physical, social, intellectual, economic, political and other environments which form the background to the acts and events spotlighted for investigation and inquiry in the particular situation which has arisen. Of these elements two require special attention, though the others remain factors which cannot be ignored: those two are facts and law.

Facts and Law

In all legal discussion the distinction between fact and law has to be kept in mind, for it is a distinction of fundamental importance in many

---

[20] The legal monopolies of coal-mining, broadcasting, generation of electricity, etc. prevent individuals commencing business enterprises in these fields.

connections.[21] A question of fact concerns the existence in past or present
time of some act or event or state thereof, cognisable or ascertainable
by the senses; a question of law concerns the applicability of some
doctrine, rule or principle of the legal system. Thus, for example, what
A said, what B heard, whether C's car was going fast at the moment of
impact, whether D intended to kill E, whether F warned G of his danger,
whether lamps were lit, questions of time, place, speed, direction, colour,
temperature, visibility, mental state, identity, and generally anything
cognisable by the senses, or by inference from sense-data, are questions
of fact. On the other hand whether J's conduct was legally reckless,
whether K's departure from his wife amounted in law to desertion,
whether L's killing amounted legally to murder or not, whether M's vehicle
was a " trailer " within the meaning of the Act, and so on, are questions
of law, which cannot be decided by the senses but only by determination
of whether or not the fact in issue falls within the verbal terms of some
doctrine, principle, rule, category or standard of law, from which certain
legal consequences will follow, such as entitlement to some remedy
or liability to some penalty. A question of law, that is, concerns the
applicability of a precept of law to certain circumstances. Thus whether
S is liable in damages for defamation depends on (a) what he said, and
the circumstances in which he said it (fact), and (b) whether these words
in these circumstances are defamatory (law). So too other legal controversies and problems can be resolved into factual and legal elements,
though it should be remembered that either the factual or legal element
may be admitted on all sides, or be so clear as to be beyond argument.
Thus it may be admitted that X struck the blow, but be argued that in
the circumstances it was not murder but culpable homicide, or it may
be admitted that the killing of Y was murder but be disputed whether X
was the person who did it. The proper meaning or interpretation of
statutes and documents, or statements made, is always a question of law.

Certain consequences of this distinction must also be borne in mind.
A question of fact has to be determined, if disputed, by evidence, by
proof of what happened, what was said, or seen, or heard, or done and
so on. Questions of law on the other hand are determined not by
evidence [22] but by legal argument, by adducing cases, statutes and statements in books of authority which persuade the judges or other persons

[21] See further Corbin, " Legal Analysis and Terminology " (1919) 29 Yale L.J.
163 and in Hall, *Readings in Jurisprudence*, 471.
[22] An exception to this principle arises in the cases where the law of *another* country
is in issue, *e.g.*, a matter of English law in a Scottish court, and vice versa. In
such cases the foreign law is treated as a question of fact (since the court does
not have judicial knowledge of a foreign system) and its rules must be proved by
evidence, as by producing as witnesses practitioners of the other systems involved,
e.g., English barristers, as in *Rosses* v. *Bhagvat Sinhjee* (1891) 19 R. 31, or by
remitting to the courts of the other system for a statement on their law.

concerned with making the decision to the view that the facts which
have been proved amount to circumstances having a particular and
prescribed consequence in law. A court or other tribunal is presumed
to know the law of its own country; accordingly one need not, and
must not, seek to prove the law to it, but must simply seek to persuade
it by legal argument as to which particular rule should be applied in
the circumstances. But one must enlighten a court as to the facts in
issue by leading evidence of them, unless those facts are admitted or
not in dispute.

While these are the fundamental distinctions between questions of
fact and questions of law, subsidiary meanings of the terms are also
found. Thus in the determination of certain litigated controversies a
jury has a part to play and matters which are for the decision of the jury
are rather arbitrarily called questions of fact, and matters reserved for
the decision of the presiding judge are called questions of law, and this
nomenclature persists notwithstanding that certain of the matters which
are committed to the judge may be in their nature questions of fact.[23]
This difficulty is not so apparent in cases decided by a judge sitting alone
since he has to decide issues both of fact and of law.

Again a question of law may be any question which is determined by
some rule of law, such as the punishment for treason, as distinct from
a question of fact, which depends on the facts and circumstances of
the case,[24] or which is determined by the exercise of the judge's discretion.[25]

Lastly, a question of law may be a question as to what the true rule
of law is, applicable to a particular matter. Thus in special cases and
stated cases [26] certain admitted or proved facts are set before the court
and a question of law formulated, raising a problem of the applicability
or otherwise of some rule or principle of law, whether a statutory provision applies, or whether a particular doctrine deduced from case-law
governs the case thus presented, or what effect a particular rule has
in the circumstances.

Transformation of Fact into Law

As the law develops and grows in complexity there is in some circumstances a tendency for matters which in their nature are truly matters

---

[23] Thus in a case of damages for malicious prosecution, the pursuer must prove that
the defender initiated the prosecution maliciously and without probable cause.
It is a question for the judge whether facts have been proved which suffice to imply
malice and lack of probable cause, even though this is factual in nature.

[24] Thus under the Sale of Goods Act, 1893, unsatisfactory goods must be returned
" within a reasonable time " and what is a reasonable time is a question of fact,
i.e., it has to be decided in the circumstances of each case. There is no rule laid
down as to what is a reasonable time, no rule that a week or a month is reasonable.

[25] Thus in a divorce case the judge has a discretion to which parent to give custody
of the children and he is not bound by law to give to one rather than the other.

[26] As to these, see Chap. 7, *infra*.

of fact to be treated as matters of law and determined by rules of law accordingly. Thus in some cases legal presumptions arise by virtue of which the law deems some state of fact to exist, whether in truth it exists or not. For example, there is a legal presumption that children under ten are incapable of committing crime, which applies despite any indications of capacity or intention in fact; no contrary proof can countervail. Again certain conduct may by a legal fiction be " deemed to be " fraudulent or criminal with the result that it will be so in law whatever it may have been in fact. A further class of presumptions exists, whereby certain factual circumstances have certain legal validity and consequences, unless the presumption is rebutted, that is, unless it can be shown that in fact and in truth the circumstances were otherwise: thus every man is presumed sane, every man is presumed innocent, and so on. Again once it has been decided in one case that certain facts amount to cruelty or adultery or culpable homicide or such other legal category, similar facts arising subsequently will have the same effect as a matter of law, by the operation of the doctrine of judicial precedent.[27]

In all these cases the circumstances of fact have ceased to be purely factual in that certain legal force and effect necessarily attaches to them by operation of law from the mere fact of their existence.

Questions of Discretion

Matters of judicial discretion are matters which are not of pure fact in that they are not wholly determinable or ascertainable by evidence or proof, nor yet are they determinable by the application of a rule of law, but they are questions of moral judgment in which the court must try to determine what is good or reasonable or fair or equitable or right or just. The tendency is, as the legal system progresses and develops, to convert questions of discretion into questions of law since a body of decisions on prior similar sets of facts grows up, tending to limit and define the ways in which and the extent to which the judicial discretion should be exercised.[28] " In respect of questions as to what is just, right, and reasonable, the purpose and effect of a system of law is to exclude and supersede to a very large extent the individual moral judgment of the courts, and to compel them to determine these questions in accordance with fixed and authoritative principles which express the established and

[27] On judicial precedent see further Chap. 8, *infra.*
[28] Consider the body of decisions which has grown up as to the exercise of judicial discretion on such questions as: to which parent is custody of a child to be given? In what circumstances can one apply for a winding-up order under the " just and equitable " clause—Companies Act, 1948, s. 222 (*f*)? In these and other cases the judge's discretion is not free but limited by earlier decisions, which tend to harden into rules that in cases like X something must be done, and in cases like Y the reverse must be done.

permanent moral judgment of the community at large." [29]　While this tendency is constantly at work statute or judicial decision may sometimes overrule the growth of such a body of limiting rules and restore freedom of judicial discretion.

Mixed Questions of Fact and Law

Questions frequently arise in which elements of fact and of law are both present and intermixed.　These arise in two forms: the problem may be really a composite one depending both on the existence of a state of fact and also on the sufficiency of these facts for some legal purpose. Thus the question whether partnership exists between two persons depends on the terms of the agreement entered into by them (fact) and also on the sufficiency of an agreement in those terms to constitute what the law will recognise as a partnership (law).　Very many questions which arise are of this type, such as whether A had murdered B, whether C had slandered D, whether E had married F, whether G had wrongfully imprisoned H, and so on, and a very common fault in pleading before a court is to make statements of this composite kind which beg the question whether the facts are truly legally sufficient to justify the use of the term having a legal connotation.　Thus to state that " by letters of 1st and 2nd May the pursuer and the defender *contracted* to . . ." begs the question whether the letters (the existence and terms of which are facts) did, as interpreted by the court, truly constitute a contract, which is a matter of law.

Secondly, mixed questions of fact and law may arise where a judicial discretion may be exercised only within legally determined limits.　Many powers of imposing fines and imprisonment are of this kind and in such cases the question for the court is one of fact so far as concerns the appropriate measure of punishment to be imposed in any particular case in the exercise of its discretion, and one of law so far as concerns the limits within which the discretion may operate.[30]

Again the questions set to juries and answered by their general verdicts are frequently problems of mixed fact and law.　When a jury returns a verdict that the prisoner is guilty of culpable homicide they are truly reporting two things: that in their view the prisoner had done certain things (fact), *and* that these happenings amounted in the circumstances to culpable homicide, as that legal category has been explained to the jury by the presiding judge in his charge to the jury (law).

---

[29] Salmond, *Jurisprudence*, 11th ed., 71.

[30] In such a case there is, of course, frequently a prior mixed question of fact and law on the matter of liability, *e.g.*, was the accused guilty of reckless driving? before the question as to punishment arises.　The latter question alone would arise if the accused pleaded guilty or were convicted.

Difficulties as to Facts or Law

The preceding discussion must not obscure the difficulty that in many cases matters of fact or of law or of both remain doubtful or disputed till in the end the final decision in a litigation reaches a conclusion which binds the parties. Facts in a textbook problem or a reported case are set down as matters fixed and established but in practice much remains in doubt. The judge or jury in hearing evidence is trying to reconstruct what really happened, as in a detective novel, from fragmentary, misleading and inaccurate clues. What emerges may be not a finding of what happened, but of what the judge or jury *think* must have happened, as being the sequence of happenings most consistent, in their view, with the bulk of the testimony.[31] The facts finally held to have been " proved " are at the mercy of witnesses who cannot be found, who did not notice, who cannot remember, of parties who have failed to keep letters, who cannot recall where or when, who did not think something was worth mentioning to the lawyer, of cars which do not stop, workmen who have left no address, bystanders who did not give their names, and so on. Accordingly the facts disclosed by a client to his legal adviser frequently contain gaps and uncertainties, and they almost certainly and invariably conflict with some of the evidence adduced by the opposing party. Frequently much of this arises from the fact that something happens quickly and suddenly and is all over before anyone has had a chance to observe what was happening. The human senses are in any event fallible recorders of events and may be very inaccurate.

Difficulties as to facts and discrepancies in evidence arise far more from faulty observation, or inattention, or forgetfulness, than from dishonesty by witnesses.

Similarly, even if and when some state of facts is " found " by the court to have " happened," it may still be uncertain precisely which principle or rule of law, or what precise verbal formulation of it, falls to be applied. It may not be at all clear what rule applies, or whether any existing rule can be applied, or whether resort must be had to analogy, to formulating a new rule or modifying an old one to cover the case, because principles and rules of law are frequently much vaguer and less precise than the exact and categorical prescriptions which laymen think of as rules of law.

Even thereafter much may depend on the temperament of the judge. Where he has to apply a flexible standard of law, such as " reasonable care," the answer to the problem whether reasonable care was in fact taken in the circumstances held to have happened depends not on any

---

[31] On the uncertainty of judicial fact-finding see Frank, *Courts on Trial* (1949), and " What Courts do in Fact " in Hall, *Readings in Jurisprudence*, 1103.

fixed touchstone but on whether that judge *thinks* that reasonable care was taken. Another judge might think differently.

The Expression of Legal Precepts

The precepts of the law which have to be applied to different sets of facts are not all of the same form, and the form they take in particular cases does not depend on their source, that is, whether the precepts in question are laid down by statute or developed in cases. There are four distinguishable kinds of legal precepts, namely, principles, rules, concepts and standards, and it is through these forms that legal ideas are expressed.

Principles are the broad formulations of reason which underlie particular rules. They are broader than rules and justify and explain various particular rules. Principles may be so broad as to be indefinite and uncertain, yet they can frequently be expressed concisely and accurately, embracing within them numerous particular rules and yet harmonising these rules. They are the authoritative starting-point or basis for legal reasoning wherever legal provision must be made for a situation not governed by a strict or precise rule of law. Principles are not commonly laid down by statute or case, but more commonly arrived at inductively by jurists from consideration of the particular rules of various cases and then set out in textbooks; they are sometimes hinted at or even tentatively formulated by judges in particular cases,[32] though such formulations may subsequently be found in the light of criticism and other cases to be too wide or too narrow, or otherwise to require correction or reformulation.

Thus it is a principle that a person should not be allowed to profit from another's loss when there was no intention to confer benefit. This principle explains, connects into a coherent body, and justifies such specific rules as that a payment made when it was not due may be recovered, that payment made on the faith of an agreement which later fails is recoverable, and that work done voluntarily in emergency on behalf of an absent person should be recompensed. Moreover, from a principle it is possible to deduce other particular rules applicable to circumstances hitherto unrecognised so that one great merit of a legal principle is that it has not been exhausted by the deduction of other specific rules from it but remains a reservoir of future rules. It is largely through principles that the law grows and develops and keeps in touch with the feelings and beliefs of the community; principles need to be elastic and flexible yet not wholly formless.

---

[32] *e.g., Hadley* v. *Baxendale* (1854) 9 Ex. 341, restated in *Victoria Laundry* v. *Newman* [1949] 2 K.B. 528; *Rylands* v. *Fletcher* (1868) L.R. 3 H.L. 330, restated in *Read* v. *Lyons* [1947] A.C. 156; *Donoghue* v. *Stevenson*, 1932 S.C.(H.L.) 31.

Rules are categorical precepts attaching a distinct, definite and detailed legal effect or consequence to follow on definite prescribed facts. They are more specific and detailed than principles. Thus it is a legal rule that a person convicted of treason is punishable by death, that a formal deed must be signed and attested by two witnesses, that the evidence of one witness must be corroborated, unless in certain exceptional cases. Rules may be laid down by statute, by the decision of a court, or set out in an authoritative book. Such rules may be rigid, or may be flexible, as where they confer a measure of discretion; thus the rule is that if a person has been injured by the negligence of another, the other must pay such damages in compensation as the court may think reasonable to award. The advantage of a rule is that it is definite and certain, but it may on that account be unadaptable to new conditions or changing circumstances [33]; it may become out of date and obsolete though these dangers are less likely if the rule contains within it a standard rather than a fixed measure or confers a discretion rather than prescribes consequences.

Both legal principles and legal rules are built up of and stated in terms of legal concepts; a legal concept is the name given to a category of legal thought or classification, the title given to a set of facts and circumstances which satisfies certain legal requirements and has certain legal consequences. It is an authoritatively defined category into which facts may be put in order that definite principles or rules may be applicable thereto. Thus marriage, contract, negligence, culpable homicide, partnership, duty, tenure, and many more terms are legal concepts. These are the terms of legal thought and expression, in that rules and principles are built up of them and legal consequences attach to them. The connotations of the words convey complex and abstract legal ideas, and one task of jurisprudence is to analyse the constituents and requisites of particular legal concepts, to see how the words are used and what they mean in different contexts and different branches of the law. Endless controversy, for example, has raged over the concept of " possession." British law is in some ways deficient in legal concepts in that some ideas are not clearly formulated in a legal concept and statutes frequently establish their own definitions for the purpose of that statute only, rather than generally. Some legal concepts, such as those of corporate personality, property, and future interests in land are highly abstract and not always easy to explain or to comprehend. The definition of a " crime," for example, has given rise to much thought, discussion and writing and probably no concise yet comprehensive description of the indicia and characteristics of a crime has yet been made.

---

[33] Thus, *e.g.*, a rule formulated in the days of horse-drawn traffic may be unsuitable for mechanised traffic.

Two of the commonest and most important concepts deserve mention, rights and duties. Principles and rules sometimes confer legal rights, that is, state what one party is legally entitled to claim as against another, or impose legal duties, that is, state what the party affected is legally obliged to do. Both concepts are frequently misused and there is a considerable literature on the uses of these terms.[34]

It has to be noticed particularly that legal concepts do not always coincide in connotation with the everyday uses of the same verbal form. Thus not everything which in common speech is called " negligence " truly amounts to negligence in law, nor is every " contract " or " crime " truly such in law. In each department of the law considerable attention must be paid to discovering the constituent elements of the concepts used so that legally accurate uses of the word may be distinguished from instances which have apparent similarities. Statutes frequently contain long interpretation sections defining particular terms in special, frequently very extended, ways, so that such words as " factory," " development " and " family " may become legal concepts with meanings materially different from the everyday meaning in the context of these statutes and cases thereon and with important legal consequences. So, too, in decided cases concepts may be explained and in the course of time refined and modified.

Sometimes principles and rules do not prescribe specific or definite legal consequences but prescribe standards of conduct or evaluation. A legal standard is a measure for conduct, to be applied according to the circumstances of each individual case. The standard is the main means whereby both legal rules and principles maintain flexibility. Where the standard is employed rules and principles are usually expressed not in absolute but in relative terms and this enables the court in a particular case to consider the precise circumstances of that case and to determine whether the conduct falls short of or comes up to the desired level. The law is full of expressions of such standards as " the reasonable man," " the prudent trustee," " the *bonus paterfamilias*," " fair rent," " reasonable precautions," " the normally skilful practitioner." The use of such standards enables account to be taken of individual circumstances; consider how much more flexible is the rule " unsatisfactory goods must be returned within a reasonable time " than such a rigid rule as " . . . within seven days." The former gives room for discretion and allows account to be taken of difficulties; the latter might be very unfair in particular cases. Sometimes the law does impose fixed rather than relative standards, as where it prescribes a speed limit of thirty miles per hour in built-up areas.

---

[34] See, *e.g.*, Salmond, *Jurisprudence*, 11th ed., Chaps. 10–11; Kocourek, *Jural Relations*; Hohfeld, *Fundamental Legal Conceptions*; Pound, *Jurisprudence*, IV, 39; Hall, *Readings in Jurisprudence*, Chap. 11.

In practice the formulation of the law on any topic may utilise all four forms of expression. Thus it is a *principle* that a person injured by the fault of another is entitled to recover compensation from him, and one *rule* derived from this is that a person who causes injury to another by driving *without reasonable care* (*standard*) is liable in damages for *negligence* (*concept*). But it is not always easy to say whether a particular decision of a case lays down a rule or merely applies a wider principle to particular facts or merely holds that they fall within or without the standard set up by a principle or rule. Every case must be interpreted on its own, regard being had to the language used, to the definiteness or vagueness, to the presence or absence of detail, and to the reference to a standard or otherwise, in the formulation of the legal precept. In legal study, important though specific rules are, the main task of the jurist and the student of law must be to ascertain the general principle involved, relate the rules and specific cases thereto, and to examine, evaluate and criticise the principles as elements in a systematic body of principles of social regulation.

The term doctrine is sometimes used for the most general systematic fitting together of principles, rules, concepts and standards relating to particular situations or fields of the legal order. These are almost entirely the work of the jurists and found in their textbooks, through which they influence legal reasoning and decisions.[35]

Language and Words

Since the legal order consists of the regulation of conduct by the application of various kinds of principles and rules to various sets of factual circumstances the enormous importance in legal connections of language and words must not be overlooked. For the rules and principles and precepts of law are formulated verbally in statutes and orders, in judicial and administrative decisions, and in books of authority, and the circumstances of fact to which rules of law are to be applied are frequently expressed in verbal form in contracts, agreements, wills, deeds, dispositions and other writings, are brought before courts by way of written pleadings, indictments or complaints, while oral evidence of facts is given in verbal form. It is apparent then that an important part of the study and application of law consists of the correct appreciation and understanding of the uses and meanings of words, the accurate formulation of thought in words so as to convey precisely the meaning intended, and the nice analysis of language used so as to extract from it the precise connotations and implications inherent in it.[36] Attention to

---

35 See further Pound, "Hierarchy of Sources and Forms" in Hall, *Readings in Jurisprudence*, 661; Pound, *Jurisprudence*, II, 124 *et seq.*
36 See Sapir, "Language," in *Encyc.Soc.Sc.*, IX, 158.

word-meaning and usage is of practical importance in legal study and accordingly good textbooks devote considerable attention to the analysis of the legal terms and words relevant to their subject-matter, while this analysis is also pursued in jurisprudence.[37]

It has to be admitted that many terms used in legal connections, and many more in social, ethical and political studies, are vague and do not necessarily cause the hearer immediately to have in mind the same thing as the speaker had in mind. Thus such phrases as " reasonable care," " unreasonable restraint of trade," " satisfied beyond reasonable doubt," leave room for differences of opinion and do not refer to a concrete measurable criterion. This is even more so in the case of such words as " just," " wrong," " unconstitutional " which are sometimes used emotionally and with no clear significance at all. It is this vagueness which can easily permit judges to differ in opinion as to the decision of a case even though the facts may be established and the law well settled. Thus if the law is that rejected goods must be returned to the seller " within a reasonable time " and they have in fact been returned in ten days, one judge may consider that ten days was reasonable in the circumstances of the case and another that it was not reasonable but unduly delayed.

Again many words have several senses or meanings which require to be carefully distinguished since the word is not always used with the same connotation in all legal discourse. Thus " malice " may mean simply the deliberate doing of a legally wrongful act, or it may mean malevolence, spite or ill-will; " property " may mean the legal rights of proprietorship[38] or may mean the actual object to which these legal rights relate.[39]

There are again numerous words which have two or more distinct senses, one or more in ordinary everyday speech and one with a particular and rather different meaning in legal discourse. Thus " negligence " in ordinary speech means carelessness, whereas in law it means a failure to fulfil the duty of care imposed in the circumstances by the law, whether or not that be carelessness in the common sense.

This category of words is again distinct from the category of words

[37] A valuable discussion of this topic in legal connections is Williams, " Language and the Law " (1945) 61 L.Q.R. 71, 179, 293 and 384; (1946) 62 L.Q.R. 387. See also Corbin, " Legal Analysis and Terminology " (1919) 29 Yale L.J. 163; Chafee, " The Disorderly Conduct of Words " (1941) 41 Col.L.R. 381.

The student interested in pursuing this topic should make the acquaintance of such works as Fowler's *Modern English Usage* and *The King's English* and make frequent reference to both legal and standard English dictionaries. The study of literature and other languages does much to develop the sensitive weighing and handling of words.

[38] Thus in the Sale of Goods Act there are rules for the passing or transference of the " property," which is quite a distinct matter from the transfer of the goods sold.

[39] As in the estate agent's phrase " a desirable property."

which have definite legal meanings only and which are seldom, if ever, used in everyday discourse at all, words such as " vitious intromitter, " " bailee." English law was formerly rich in words peculiarly legal but many have now disappeared. Scots law has not so many peculiarly legal terms, and all British law is weak in accurate technical terminology as compared with medicine or engineering.

This close attention to words and the verbal form of statutes, deeds and other legal expressions must extend to the commonest and most ordinary parts of speech since it may be of crucial importance whether " or " or " and " be used, " may " or " shall," " among " or " between," and every indication of meaning which can be gathered from a grammatical shift may be important. Again the precise position of the word " only " in a sentence may be crucial.

Closely connected with this topic is the body of guiding principles and presumptions which have been developed by the courts to assist them in the difficult task of statutory interpretation,[40] a problem which perplexes courts and legal advisers precisely because the communication of ideas by words can never be achieved with complete accuracy and perfect freedom from ambiguity.

FURTHER READING

The Nature of Law

Cohen and Cohen: *Readings in Jurisprudence and Legal Philosophy.*
D'Entreves: *Natural Law.*
Hall: *Readings in Jurisprudence.*
Hart: *The Concept of Law.*
Kantorowicz: *The Definition of Law.*
Lloyd: *Introduction to Jurisprudence.*
Morris: *The Great Legal Philosophers.*
Pound: *Jurisprudence*, Vol. 2.
Stone: *The Province and Function of Law.*

Law and Fact

Cardozo: *Nature of the Judicial Process*; (also in *Selected Writings of Benjamin N. Cardozo*, 107).
Dowling, Patterson & Powell: *Legal Method.*
Salmond: *Jurisprudence*, Chap. 3.
Wigmore: *Principles of Judicial Proof.*

Language and the Law

Chase: *The Tyranny of Words.*
Hohfeld: *Fundamental Legal Conceptions.*
Hexner: *Studies in Legal Terminology.*
Kocourek: *Jural Relations.*
Lloyd: *Introduction to Jurisprudence.*

---

[40] These principles are discussed in Chap. 8, *infra*.

Philbrick: *Language and the Law.*
Pollock and Wright: *Possession in the Common Law.*
Williams: " Language and the Law " (1945) 61 L.Q.R. 71, 179, 293, 384;
(1946) 62 L.Q.R. 387.
" International Law and the Controversy concerning the word Law "
(1945) 22 B.Y.I.L. 146, and in Laslett (ed.) *Philosophy, Politics
and Society*, 134.

CHAPTER 3

THE SCOTTISH LEGAL TRADITION

THE modern Scottish legal system and the complex body of doctrines, principles and rules which it utilises has not been the creation of a single edict, but represents the present state of a long and slow process of development and evolution, in which numerous factors have played a part, social and economic developments, political and governmental changes, the effects of war, religious upheaval, constitutional moves and so on. At different times different influences have been predominant. Not only does an outline of the historical development of the Scottish legal system show how that system has come to take its present shape, but it helps to explain numerous practices and rules which survived long after the conditions which gave rise to them had passed away, and some of which still survive to upset the simplicity and symmetry of the law and sometimes to cause confusion and even injustice.

Early times

Very little is known of legal institutions in Scotland prior to the year A.D. 1000 and nothing from any earlier period can be shown to have exercised any material or permanent influence on the development of the modern law. For present purposes accordingly the story starts after that date.[1] In particular it should be noted that the introduction of Roman law into Scotland was not effected by the Roman occupation of the South of Scotland.

I.—THE FEUDAL PERIOD

Introduction of Feudalism

After the victory of Carham over the Northumbrians in 1018 the Scottish kingdom reached its present boundaries by the incorporation of the northern part of Northumbria.[2] Northumbrian influence had penetrated into Lothian prior to then though it was long before the more outlying parts of the kingdom were assimilated and lost their previous characteristics. Civilisation was confined to the Lothians and the coastal plain round to the Moray Firth, and particularly the districts near the burghs and baronial and ecclesiastical centres.

---

[1] Rait and Pryde, *Scotland*, 13; Ritchie, *Normans in Scotland*, xiii. Traces of Celtio law are discussed in Cameron, *Celtic Law*. See also Levie, " Celtic Tribal Law and Custom in Scotland " (1927) 39 J.R. 191.
[2] On the formation of the Kingdom see also Dickinson, *Scotland to 1603*, Chap. 4.

In the Gaelic Highlands the populace probably lived under the influence of Celtic customs, traces of which are found in the Senchus Mor and the Book of Aicill. In the Britons of Strathclyde there was a point of contact with the traditions of early Welsh Law while in Galloway traces of customary law persisted as late as 1384. Orkney, Shetland, the Western Isles and large tracts of land north of Dingwall had been occupied by Scandinavians and long remained independent.

The Norman Conquest of England in and after 1066 influenced Scotland less immediately and directly than it did England, but gradually it permeated and influenced Lowland Scottish society and institutions and southern influences were potent in Scotland for many years. Normans began to come to Scotland from about 1050 and by 1150 " Scotland was Normanised beyond recall. Normans held the chief offices in Church and State. Land and power had largely passed into Norman hands. The old feudal system had been changed to Norman-feudal. A French aristocracy had been established, a French civilisation implanted." [3]

An important factor in the assimilation of Anglo-Saxon influences was the marriage of Malcolm III (Canmore) (1057–93) to the Saxon princess Margaret about 1070. The queen had great influence on her husband and used it to strengthen the Anglo-Saxon influences on church and state. In the course of the next two centuries the population of the Lowlands became converted into an English-speaking community with life organised on the model of the Anglo-Saxon-Norman Kingdom of England, and spiritually more akin to England than to Gaelic Scotland.[4]

Prior to 1124 Norman feudalism [5] had probably made some headway in the south of Scotland but was not generally accepted.[6] The process of Anglicisation or Anglo-Normanisation was definitely accepted in the reign of David I (1124–53) [7] and the law as much as the court and the Church was subjected to English influence. David, trained as a knight under Henry I of England, did much to reproduce in his own realm the pattern of feudal government and institutions prevailing in Norman England, at least in the southern third of the kingdom.[8] The features of this system, at once a social, military and legal one, were castle-building,

3 Ritchie, *Normans in Scotland*, xv. For Celtic opposition to Anglo-Norman feudalism see Dickinson, *op. cit.*, 57. See further Gardner, " Historical Survey of the Law of Scotland prior to the reign of David I " (1945) 57 J.R. 34, 65.
4 Rait and Pryde, *Scotland*, 13; Ritchie, *op. cit.*, xiii.
5 On feudalism in general see Ganshof, *Feudalism* (trs. Grierson); Barrow, *Feudal Britain*, 1066–1314, *passim*: Vinogradoff, " Origins of Feudalism," 2 Camb.Med. Hist., Chap. 20; *idem.*, " Feudalism," 3 Camb.Med.Hist., Chap, 18.
6 Hume Brown, *History of Scotland*, I, 73; Ritchie, *op. cit.*, 67–83, 160–175; Barrow, " Beginnings of Feudalism in Scotland " (1956) 29 Bull.Inst.Hist.Res. 1.
7 On his reign see generally Innes, *Scotland in the Middle Ages*, Chap. 4; Dickinson, Chap. 9; and generally, Cooper in *Introduction to Scottish Legal History* (Stair Society) Chap. 1.
8 Ritchie, *op. cit.*, 179–190.

the use of professional cavalry, church-building and monastic development, the grant of land in knights' fees to be held in knight-service for the provisions of one or more knights,[9] and the requirement of homage and fealty from tenants. Under Malcolm (1153–65) and William the Lion (1165–1214) military feudalism became more intensive.

The feudal system of land tenure whereby land was held by a " vassal " from a lord in return for certain services, the grant being confirmed by written charter, was introduced into Scotland in the twelfth century. The system was by this time well developed in England and on the Continent. After 1153 the practice seems to have been to grant tracts of land in return for the service of a knight or even of a part of a knight, for the Scottish barons were men of lesser substance than their English counterparts.[10] There were, however, large estates held by military service and within them a fairly systematic process of subinfeudation, that is, of giving smaller areas of land to a sub-vassal to be held by him of his lord by the performance of feudal duties.

The characteristics of the system were that it was at once a decentralised method of government and administration, a social and economic system and a system of land tenure. In all these aspects its introduction had lasting importance and influence in Scotland, and the land law is still fundamentally feudal. Moreover a grant of land to be held in feudal tenure naturally conveyed with it the right to hold a court for the feudal tenants and civil and criminal jurisdiction over them, the extent of jurisdiction varying with the rank of the grantee.[11]

This system seems to have fitted quite well into the previously existing Celtic method of land tenure under which land was held by the chief and his near kindred and there seems to have been little racial displacement or dispossession of existing holders of land.[12] Land and the accompanying jurisdiction over the population were conferred by royal charter both upon the king's Anglo-Norman friends and on native Scottish chiefs who had their customary rights confirmed and enlarged by the grant of feudal jurisdiction.[13] By the end of the thirteenth century old Celtic institutions had been feudalised as far as the Moray Firth and in some more remote areas where, however, Celtic custom in the main lasted for several more centuries.[14]

The institution of this land system was the basis of the family in

[9] Neilson, " Tenure by Knight-Service in Scotland " (1899) 11 J.R. 71, 173; see also Neilson, " Scottish Serjeanties " (1899) 15 L.Q.R. 405.
[10] Barrow, *op. cit.*, 15.
[11] Dickinson, *op. cit.*, 84–93; Milne, in *Introduction* (Stair Society), Chap. 13; see specimen charter in Dickinson and others, *Source Book of Scottish History*, I, 90–94.
[12] Rait and Pryde, *op. cit.*, 19.
[13] *Ibid.*, 20; Ritchie, *op. cit.*, 237–242.
[14] Skene, *Celtic Scotland*, III, 287 *et seq.*

Anglicised Lowland Scotland as much as was the clan system in the
Celtic Highlands and extensive grants of land were made in David's
lifetime to men of Saxon, Norman or Danish extraction and, particularly
in Strathclyde, Lothian and Fife, castles were planted and feudal communities developed, with land held by vassals and sub-vassals of the
king, which greatly strengthened the royal authority.[15] So too the trading
burghs developed and from the deliberations of the Four Burghs,[16]
originally Berwick, Roxburgh, Edinburgh and Stirling, sprang the *Leges
Quatuor Burgorum*, a code of municipal regulations, partly copied and
adapted from English models.

Feudal Administration

Feudalism introduced the idea that the king was lord of the whole
land and the fountain of all justice.   The king's court could hear appeals
from lower courts and cases relating to important persons or matters.
The king sat with the officers of his household and such great men as
were with him at the time.   Later he began to summon other tenants-in-
chief and those regularly called to give the king counsel became his council.
In time this council began to sit in various capacities, for finance, for
justice, for affairs of state.   By the end of the thirteenth century a sitting
for discussion, a *parliamentum*, had become primarily a sitting of the
council as supreme court which laid down the law or changed it.   Parliament was primarily a court of law, while a council, strengthened by
summoning additional persons, called a general council, was primarily
a deliberative body.[17]

David I also introduced the political officers and institutions of the
feudal monarchy, such as the chancellor, chamberlain, justiciar, constable
and steward.[18]   A network of sheriffdoms began to spread over the
whole country, under sheriffs who were the king's representatives and
charged with the maintenance of order and the collection of the revenue
in the king's name.[19]   Periodically the chamberlain held an ayre or court
in each royal burgh, at which all the burgesses had to be present, to
ensure that the king had his dues from trade and also that there were no
breaches of trading or commercial relations.   A court was held in the
burghs fortnightly, presided over by the king's bailie.

---

[15] Hume Brown, I, 89–90.
[16] The association of these burghs is the genesis of the still-surviving Convention
of Royal Burghs.
[17] Dickinson, *op. cit.*, 106–107.
[18] Dickinson, *op. cit.*, 103–104; Ritchie, *op. cit.*, 184; Innes, *Scotch Legal Antiquities*,
74–85; Duncan, in *Introduction to Scottish Legal History* (Stair Society) Chap. 23.
[19] Rait and Pryde, *op. cit.*, 21; Hume Brown, I, 88; Dickinson, *op. cit.*, 101; see also
Vary Campbell, " The Sheriff in Scotland " (1900) 12 J.R. 15; Ferguson, " The
Sheriff in Scotland " (1910) 22 J.R. 105.   See also *Sheriff Court Book of Fife*,
ed. Dickinson (S.H.S.), Appx. D.

The performance of important services to the king passed into office by invisible steps. A man of importance [20] had rights and privileges and land to support him: he tended to acquire powers, military, administrative, or judicial in a definite area so that his service came to be in effect an office under the crown, and both office and district came to be called a barony and both passed to his heir after confirmation by the king.[21]

A great council of the realm or *Curia Regis* was established on the English model. In theory it consisted of all tenants-in-chief and the chief ecclesiastical dignitaries.[22] The burgesses did not appear till later.

The Justice-Ayres

Under David the justiciars appear as important officials.[23] This office is also of Norman origin. The justiciar or justice-general was originally the king's delegate for the administration of justice. He had originally supreme jurisdiction both in civil and criminal matters and the general administration of justice seems to have been entrusted at an early date to two justiciars, one for the north and one for the south of the kingdom, under whom various inferior judges exercised subordinate and delegated jurisdiction. A third justiciar is also known of.[24] Their office was to dispense justice in civil and criminal cases not dealt with by the king's court and they had to hold justice-ayres or circuit-courts in spring and autumn for that purpose, though in times of trouble the ayres were irregular. They had further to supervise the sheriffs. At this time the office was not hereditary.[25]

While Edward I had Scotland temporarily subjugated he appointed eight justiciars and Robert Bruce seems to have maintained five.[26] The office of justice-general, however, later became hereditary and remained so till 1836 when on the death of the Duke of Montrose, the then holder of the office, it was united with that of Lord President of the Court of Session. After the institution of the College of Justice in 1532 the justiciar never judged in civil matters. In 1672 [27] the supreme criminal court was reformed and constituted the High Court of Justiciary.

The limited power of the crown at this time and the inadequate central machinery of government combined with feudal theory to effect

[20] In Norman-French " baron " was simply a man, later a man of importance in battle or council.
[21] Ritchie, 222–223. In this way primogeniture became accepted as the rule of succession in heritage.
[22] Dickinson, *op. cit.*, 105; Rait and Pryde, 21; Ritchie, 208–209; Rait, *Parliaments of Scotland*, 1.
[23] See generally Dickinson, in *Introduction to Scottish Legal History* (Stair Society) Chap. 31, and on procedure, *ibid.*, Chap. 33.
[24] See list in Cooper, *Select Scots Cases of the Thirteenth Century*.
[25] Mackinnon, *Constitutional History of Scotland*, 128.
[26] Tytler, I, 248; Dickinson, 161.
[27] Act 1672, c. 16.

a wide dispersion of judicial functions and powers among men and families of importance all over the country, which powers were linked to landholding and readily became not merely territorial but hereditary.[28]

Rise of the Burghs

About the time of David I there began to develop the burghs, which were inhabited places, usually adjacent to a royal castle, latterly, if not originally, possessing charters which granted the burgesses privileges, such as of holding a fair, or freedom from tolls.[29] Burghs were fundamentally economic organisations acting as market-centres for the sheriffdoms, and they tended to attract foreigners and merchants to settle there but they also served as colonies, outposts of political control.[30] The weekly market in the burgh was the regular occasion for local trade and burghs were frequently granted the monopoly of trade in a particular area, which was known as its "liberty." [31] So, too, burghs were the exclusive centres of foreign trade and the trades of the burgh had an exclusive right in craft work. The burgesses soon acquired the right to elect their own provost, bailies and other officers.

These privileges were granted in consideration of liability to provide a share in any grant of money to the king, at first one-fifth and, later, one-sixth of the total. The apportionment of this among the individual burghs was the work of the Convention of Royal Burghs, a body of uncertain origin which comes into the limelight in the sixteenth century.[32]

Apart from these royal burghs with royal charters there were established from early times burghs dependent on ecclesiastical magnates, burghs of barony, and burghs of regality which were erected by lords of baronies or of regalities. Burghs of barony were founded as early as royal burghs, with similar commercial privileges, and were frequently ecclesiastical foundations. They were always erected by a subject-superior under licence from the king.[33] Many such burghs were erected in the fifteenth, sixteenth and seventeenth centuries. The administration of burghs of barony depended on the superior or on agreement with him and consequently varied from one town to another.

A lord of regality had within his lands a jurisdiction as wide as that of

---

[28] Hill Burton, II, 54 *et seq.*
[29] The model was Norman, as with most of David's introductions: Dickinson, 111; Ritchie, *Normans in Scotland*, 323. See also Pryde, " Origin of the Burgh in Scotland " (1935) 47 J.R. 271; " Burghal Administration," in *Source Book of Administrative Law*, 1–11; " The Scottish Burghs " (1949) 28 S.H.R. 155; Innes, *Scotland in the Middle Ages*, Chap. 5; and specimen burgh charters in *Source Book of Scottish History*, I, 102–105.
[30] Mackenzie, *The Scottish Burghs*, 1–50.
[31] *Ibid.*, 66.
[32] *Ibid.*, 76; Ritchie, *op. cit.*, 327–330.
[33] *Ibid.*, 79–80; Dickinson, 112; see also Ferguson, "The Barony in Scotland " (1912) 24 J.R. 99.

the king, including jurisdiction in the crimes normally reserved to the
royal courts, the pleas of the Crown, and such a lord might create a
burgh, though his exceptional jurisdiction did not make a corresponding
extension of the burgh's commercial powers. That might, however, be
done by special arrangement.[34] Burghs of barony or of regality might
be raised to royal rank.

Guild Merchants and Burgh Courts

In many burghs a merchant guild was formed and craftsmen were
generally admitted to it, and this was probably the first official recognition
of self-control as against control by the superior of the burgh. An Act of
Parliament in 1593 approved the power and jurisdiction of the Dean
of Guild and his council in burghs to deal with actions between merchants
or between merchant and mariner.[35] This gradually fell into desuetude
but from about the sixteenth century the Dean of Guild was recognised
as having a common law jurisdiction over buildings, nuisances and
questions of neighbourhood, and this still survives in the form of jurisdiction to regulate streets and buildings.[36]

Apart from the guild every burgh tended to develop a court to enforce
its regulations and settle disputes, which tended in turn to assume powers
of administration. All burgesses, unless excused, had to attend the three
head courts of the year (Yule, Easter and Michaelmas). The burgh
bailies may have had power to try all crimes except the four pleas of the
Crown but this was early attenuated to dealing with boundary disputes,
failure to use proper weights and measures or observe the market rules,
and various offences such as encroaching on another's land or allowing
animals to trespass on another's fields.[37] The competence of the burgh
courts was cut down by the rise of the Court of Session and the justices
of the peace, so that the bailies came to be limited to trivial cases and
petty disputes.[38]

The Chamberlain had some supervisory functions over burghs. In
his annual ayre or circuit he dealt with appeals from the burgh court,
decided disputes between burghs, and investigated the mode in which
the bailies had been discharging their functions. From 1292 the *Curia
Quatuor Burgorum* met under the presidency of the Chamberlain to hear
appeals from the burgh courts and from the ayre [39] and to lay down the
law of the burghs which may have been influenced by the *Leges Quatuor*

---

[34] *Ibid.*, 78.
[35] Mackenzie, 100–105; McKechnie, in *Source Book of Administrative Law*, 95–104;
Pryde in *Introductionto Scottish Legal History* (Stair Society) Chap. 29.
[36] McKechnie, *loc. cit.*, 100–101; Pryde, in *Introduction* (Stair Society) Chap. 29.
[37] Pryde, in *Source Book of Administrative Law*, 4; Dickinson, 114–115.
[38] Pryde, in *Source Book*, 8.
[39] Pryde, in *Source Book*, 5; Dickinson, 118–119; *Source Book of Scottish History*,
I, 228–230.

Burgorum [40] borrowed from Newcastle. The Chamberlain's power disappeared in the fifteenth century and the *Curia* vanished about 1500.

Only in the fourteenth century, under the necessity of financial stringency, did the great burghs obtain representation in Parliament and from the informal discussions of the burgh commissioners to Parliament there arose the Convention of Royal Burghs (1552) with legislative, executive and financial jurisdiction.[41]

Barony and Regality Courts

The term baron in early feudal law included any considerable tenant but later came to be restricted for the most part to those who held lands direct of the king, which had been erected by the grant *in liberam baroniam*.[42] Barony tenure was characterised by being a unity, a unit for administration and law, and possessing its own officers and baron-bailie, and when lands were granted *in liberam baroniam* the charters included a clause granting certain rights of public justice. The barony always had a legal *caput* which was inseparable from it and wherein was centred the jurisdiction. The baron by accepting the barony accepted responsibility to the king for ordinary public justice within the lands included in the barony; he had power of pit and gallows, *fossa et furca*.[43] Hence a grant of barony excluded to that extent the king's officers, and in time this exclusion grew greater so that certain barons received all rights of public justice including even the four pleas of the Crown [44] and other royal rights so that they became holders *in regalitatem*. A regality was a barony with fuller jurisdictional and administrative rights, the precise rights depending on the charter of erection.[45] The only right excluded was the right to try treason. Regalities were in fact so much petty kingdoms that the realm was divided into royalty and regality.

Barony jurisdiction appears to have been granted from the twelfth century and such grants were common in the later Middle Ages.[46] The baron usually held court at the *caput baroniae* at various intervals as need arose.[47] It might be presided over by the baron or by his bailie, or by both, or by two bailies, and the judges of the court were the suitors, that is, those tenants who held land by suit of court, for whom attendance

---

[40] Printed in A.P.S. I. 329. The four burghs were at first Berwick, Edinburgh, Roxburgh, and Stirling, and later Edinburgh, Stirling, Lanark and Linlithgow.
[41] Dickinson, *op. cit.*, 186–187.
[42] Dickinson, *op. cit.*, 91–92; *Barony Court Book of Carnwath* (ed. Dickinson), xiv. See also Ferguson, "The Barony in Scotland" (1912) 24 J.R. 99.
[43] *Ibid.*, xx–xxvi.
[44] Murder, arson, rape and robbery.
[45] *Ibid.*, xxxix–xl.
[46] On the details of barony jurisdiction see Innes, *Scotch Legal Antiquities*, 54–60; McIntyre, in *Introduction to Scottish Legal History* (Stair Society) Chap. 28.
[47] *Cf.* Ritchie, *Normans in Scotland*, 311.

at court was a feudal burden attached to the holding of their land,[48] and the sentence or doom was pronounced by the dempster or doomsman.[49] The court had civil jurisdiction in matters of debt, possession, lawburrows,[50] breach of arrestment, bloodwite [51] and deforcement,[52] and criminal jurisdiction in theft and slaughter.[53]

In time these jurisdictions tended to fall into disuse with the development of centralised institutions and courts. By the seventeenth century only regalities or earldoms might still punish capitally and baron courts had given up this jurisdiction. They disappeared with the abolition of the heritable jurisdictions in 1747.

The Sheriff Courts

The establishment of the office of sheriff in Scotland is probably to be attributed to David I [54] and many areas were erected into sheriffdoms in the twelfth and thirteenth centuries.[55] England supplied the model, where the Norman kings had introduced their own officer, the *vicecomes* or shire-reeve. The Scottish sheriffdom seems to have been an artificial unit which did not coincide with previous divisions of the land or natural boundaries, and was frequently dependent on a castle.[56] The sheriffs were appointed from among the Scoto-Norman barons and gradually royal sheriffs were established over the whole kingdom, showing the power of the central government. The sheriff was the king's judicial, financial, administrative and military officer and gradually the office became almost uniformly heritable.[57] The office had to be fitted into the existing system and it is uncertain how the office compared with that of the mair, who continued to sit as an assessor in the sheriff's court.[58]

The sheriff court was originally held at the castle and was the king's court of the sheriffdom, which consisted of the lands which owed court duty and military service to the castle.[59] Head courts were held thrice a year and lesser courts at intermediate times at irregular intervals, which

[48] On the suitors of the court see also Hamilton-Grierson in (1917) 14 S.H.R. 1 and Dickinson in *Sheriff Court Book of Fife*, Introd., lxxii.
[49] *Barony Court Book of Carnwath*, lxxx.
[50] Surety for keeping the peace.
[51] Fines for bloodshed.
[52] *Ibid.*, civ.
[53] *Ibid.*, cvii.
[54] Dickinson, *op. cit.*, 101; *Sheriff Court Book of Fife* (ed. Dickinson, S.H.S.), 347. See also Philip in *Source Book of Administrative Law*, 74–80; Malcolm, " The Office of Sheriff in Scotland " (1923) 20 S.H.R. 129, 222, 290; Milne, *Introduction to Scottish Legal History* (Stair Society) Chap. 25.
[55] *Ibid.*, 347–368.
[56] *Ibid.*, 384; Ritchie, 319.
[57] *Ibid.*, xxxi–xxxiii. See specimen sheriff's account in *Source Book of Scottish History*, I, 96–99.
[58] Ritchie, *op. cit.*, 321.
[59] *Ibid.*, 372. *Cf. ibid.*, 311.

probably averaged six weeks. Head courts were courts held at the seat
of the sheriffdom, attended by the full complement of those who owed
the duty of suit of court [60] and presided over by the sheriff in person; at
them all the more important business was transacted. The lesser courts
might be held at different places in the sheriffdom. As burghs tended to
grow up beneath the walls of the castle, the burgh became the *caput* of
the sheriffdom, and by the sixteenth century all courts were held in the
tolbooth of the head burgh of the shire.[61]

The sheriff court was the king's baron court and within the sheriffdom
the sheriff administered both civil and criminal justice. He might not deal
with cases involving the four pleas of the Crown nor exercise jurisdiction
over any ecclesiastical person. Nor, of course, had he jurisdiction
within stewartries, where the king's steward was the sole competent
judge, nor within regalities, nor within burghs, since burgesses claimed
to be heard only before their own courts or the Chamberlain's ayre.
Personal exemptions were also sometimes granted.[62] In civil matters
the sheriff could deal with actions of molestation, removing, ejection,
spuilzie, and all kinds of personal actions.[63] The sheriff was the presiding
officer in the court, controlling procedure, and instructing the suitors in
the law, but the judgment was that of the suitors.

The sheriff had also an oversight of the proper administration of
justice in inferior courts within the sheriffdom and his court was the
court of appeal against decisions of baron courts within the sheriffdom.[64]
He had to uphold the Church courts, search for and pursue rebels put to
the horn, to guard prisoners, arrest idle men, issue tokens to beg, keep
the castles in repair, supervise the efficiency of the arms and the holding
of the wappinschaw, execute royal writs and letters and carry out many
more administrative duties.[65]

Ecclesiastical Courts

In the medieval kingdom the clergy and the religious houses were of
great importance.[66] They were favoured by David I and grew rich and
powerful under him. Not least they imported into the kingdom an
element of scholarship and of the canon law of the Roman Church and
it was probably through this infusion of canon law that Roman law
came first to influence Scottish procedure.

[60] See *Source Book of Scottish History*, I, 101.
[61] *Sheriff Court Book of Fife*, xi–xx.
[62] *Ibid.*, xxvii.
[63] *Ibid.*, xxxviii and Appx. B.
[64] *Ibid.*, xxxix.
[65] *Ibid.*, xl–xlv.
[66] See generally Dickinson, *op. cit.*, 120–124; Easson, *Scottish Religious Houses*;
Dowden, *Mediaeval Church in Scotland*; Innes, *Scotch Legal Antiquities*, 161–208;
and on the Church courts, Donaldson in *Introduction* (Stair Society) Chap. 27.

A great volume of the litigation in the thirteenth century, even involving laymen, took place before ecclesiastical tribunals, particularly before judges-delegate, usually three in number, who were constituted an *ad hoc* tribunal by mandate from the Pope or papal legate with instructions to carry out specified procedure. These mandates were obtained by the prospective pursuer in the action.[67] The judges-delegate might carry the case to conclusion without further reference to Rome, or refer back for instructions and guidance in case of difficulty, or even report the facts to Rome for final hearing and decision there. Appeals might be made to Rome at any stage. The judges-delegate dealt with a great variety of cases, claims to money, lands, for damages or specific implement, for reduction of a decree arbitral or even for an award of sequestration.[68]

As the thirteenth century proceeded there was increasing resort to lay tribunals [69] and cases were heard before the King in Council or in Parliament, the justiciar, and the sheriff. The justiciars numbered usually two and never more than four, and the sheriffs numbered from twenty to thirty so that the judicial establishment of the country was inadequate. The system of papal judges-delegate lost most of its importance by the time of the War of Independence but the Courts Christian remained.[70]

Law books—
Regiam Majestatem and Quoniam Attachiamenta
    The principal source of knowledge of Scoto-Norman law in later times is the book called, from its opening words, *Regiam Majestatem.*[71] It probably describes law and practice as they were under Alexander II rather than under David I or later and was probably privately and unofficially compiled about 1225. It is not original or distinctively Scottish but is based on Glanvill's [72] *De Legibus et Consuetudinibus Angliae* (1187) but with amendments, adaptations to Scottish conditions and variations on the original, since by 1225 Scots law had progressed beyond the stage described by Glanvill. But Glanvill was the basis as providing an account of the main features of the system which Scotland was developing. There is also heavy drawing on the early Scots statutes and the primitive laws of the Brets and Scots, which probably survived

[67] Cooper, *Select Scottish Cases*, xxvii.
[68] *Ibid.*, xxxi–xxxii.
[69] *Ibid.*, xxxvii.
[70] Donaldson, " Church Courts " in *Introduction to Scottish Legal History* (Stair Society) Chap. 27.
[71] Edited with a valuable introduction by Lord Cooper for the Stair Society. See also Duncan, " Regiam Majestatem : A Reconsideration " 1961 J.R. 199.
[72] While this book is called Glanvill, it was probably written not by Glanvill (Henry II of England's Justiciar) but by his nephew Hubert Walter: see further Plucknett, *Concise History of the Common Law*, 5th ed., 256–257.

in Galloway into the fourteenth century, and on Roman and canon law, particularly the *Corpus Juris*, the *Summa* of Azo, the *Decretum* and probably the *Panormia* of Ivo of Chartres, and possibly the *Decretum* and *Decretals*. It attempts to cover the whole field of civil and criminal law and procedure from the standpoint of the royal courts. The arrangement, following Justinian's *Institutes*, is in four books.

The subsequent history of the *Regiam* has been chequered. It was repeatedly chosen as part of the basis for intended revisions of the laws,[73] was condemned by Stair as " no part of our law," accepted by others and yet was still being cited in court in the twentieth century. The modern view is that it is quite authentic, an attempt, founded on Glanvill, probably made by an unknown cleric about 1225, to set out the existing law of Scotland.

The *Quoniam Attachiamenta*, usually printed along with the *Regiam*, belongs to the fourteenth century and is exclusively Scottish. It is essentially a systematic manual of procedure in feudal courts based on experience gained in practice. It includes styles and forms and even practical hints and utilises a new technical vocabulary. Nothing is known of the author. It may fairly be described as the earliest purely Scottish legal work.[74]

Procedure

In the period before the foundation of the College of Justice the primary procedural writ was the brieve, a short writ issued from the Chancery, in the form of a command in the king's name, requiring an official, a commissioner or a party to take some action which justice was thought to require.[75] Sometimes the brieve had to be " retoured," in which case the verdict was returned to the Chancery. The system contributed greatly to the development of a uniform system of law common to the whole country. This system was in operation in the thirteenth century, though not fully developed, and was extended by James I after his return from captivity in 1424.[76]

Scottish brieves were undoubtedly founded on English models though papal practice probably also had some influence. English forms were, however, often discarded or modified and Scotland had fewer and more adaptable basic writs than the great multiplication of writs in the English

---

[73] In 1425, 1469, 1566 and 1649. See Mackay, *Memoir of Stair*, 42–43. Projects of 1574 and 1628 did not expressly refer to *Regiam Majestatem*.

[74] Cooper, Introd. to *Regiam Majestatem*, 47–50.

[75] Dickinson, *op. cit.*, 107. See generally McKechnie, *Judicial Process upon Brieves*, 1219–1532; Lord Cooper, Introd. to *Register of Brieves* (Stair Society); Innes, *Scotch Legal Antiquities*, 222–240; Hamilton-Grierson (ed.), Bisset's *Rolment of Courtis*, III, 41; Maxwell, in *Introduction to Scottish Legal History*, Chap. 32.

[76] For specimens and the procedure thereunder, see Innes, *op. cit.*, 233–237, and *Source Book of Scottish History*, I, 95–98.

register.[77] After 1532 brieves tended to give way to other forms of initial writs in litigation; the brieve passed into the summons under the signet and fell into desuetude as a means of initiating litigation.

The brieve had also other uses. In its widest sense a brieve covered any kind of formal writ issued by the king, administrative or judicial. Other brieves were used as a means of obtaining the factual answer to problems. Such were the brieves of succession, terce and tutory. Very important was the brieve *de recto* by which the title to heritage could be determined.

Modes of Trial—the Jury

The common modes of trial in early times were battle, compurgation, whereby a man could clear himself by the oath of a prescribed number of oath-helpers or compurgators that they believed his oath to be true, or the ordeal by water or by hot iron.[78] The fourth Lateran Council of 1215 prohibited clerical assistance at ordeals and the withdrawal of religious sanction contributed to its disappearance: it seems to have vanished by 1230. Proof by writ or by witnesses is little heard of in the twelfth and thirteenth centuries and seems to have developed first in the burgh courts.

The jury system came to Scotland in the wake of feudalism and by 1230 it is possible that the jury had definitely superseded the ordeal but at first it was difficult to distinguish the jury from sworn witnesses or from compurgators. The jury was frequently chosen by the pursuer in conjunction with the officers of court. For long there was no settled number for a jury and the rule that the number should be odd was arrived at only gradually and later.[79]

The jury disappeared in nearly all civil cases after 1532 though retained for some special kinds of cases, but remained in criminal cases, though latterly a greatly increased number of criminal cases have been allowed to be heard summarily. In 1815 the jury was imported afresh for civil cases.

Private Law in the Feudal Period

It is difficult to obtain or to present in brief compass a general picture of private law at this early period. Much early law was local and customary.[80] Predominantly it was concerned with complaints against

---

[77] On the English register see Pollock and Maitland's *History of English Law*, I, 150, 195; Plucknett, *Concise History*, 276–277.

[78] Innes, *Scotch Legal Antiquities*, 209–222; *idem, Scotland in the Middle Ages*, 182–189; Neilson, *Trial by Combat*. As late as 1567 Bothwell, when suspected of Darnley's death, offered to prove his innocence by battle. Compurgation is last mentioned in 1622.

[79] Dickinson, *op. cit.*, 108; Dickinson, *Sheriff Court Book of Fife*, Introd. lxxxvi.

[80] See *Source Book of Scottish History*, I, 114–118.

violence and wrongdoing and included much which in later times would have been classed as criminal. The oldest laws describe a system of combined fines and compensation for murder and personal injuries, which represents the beginnings of the commutation of the blood-feud into judicial remedy. There were elaborate tariffs of fines and compensation varying with the status of the injured man and the gravity of his injuries. Wrongs predominate and there is little of contract while testamentary law was within the jurisdiction of the Church.

Accordingly, in the period immediately before the War of Independence, Scots law appears to have closely resembled Anglo-Norman law but even then to have had distinct differences. There had been borrowing, not wholesale, nor indiscriminate, but critical, with adaptations and simplifications. Scots law and English law were recognisably different, though bearing many marks of close relationship.[81] Canon law had also established itself in many spheres. " Development as compared with England proceeded not on parallel, but on gradually diverging, lines— the divergence being due in part to the inability of Scotland to keep abreast with the rapid progress made in England from Glanvill, through Bracton, to the Edwardian law, and in part to Scotland's deliberate refusal, under the influence of the Romano-canonical tradition, to absorb the more technical and artificial features of the Bractonian law. By the end of the [thirteenth] century the divergence was already marked, not only in the rejection of much that England had introduced, and in the adoption of ideas and expedients which Scotland did not owe to England but in a general effort towards greater simplicity, flexibility and directness." [82]

This early period of Scottish legal development was abruptly terminated by the deep division of the War of Independence, though some of the customary and Roman and canon law survived to a later period.

II.—THE MEDIEVAL PERIOD

The War of Independence and After

During the English occupation of Scotland Edward I appointed eight justiciars in 1305 and he took action with a view to establishing an Exchequer on the English model, and possibly also a Chancery, at Berwick.[83] He increased the number of sheriffs while twenty commissioners drew up an Ordinance for the Government of Scotland,[84] but in a few months this existed on paper only.

---

[81] Cooper, " Scottish Legal Tradition " in *Selected Papers*, 175.
[82] Cooper, Introd. to *Register of Brieves*, 25.
[83] Cooper, *Select Scottish Cases of the Thirteenth Century*, xlv. See also 25 S.H.R. 27.
[84] A.P.S. I, 119: It was sometimes thought that *Regiam Majestatem* was a product of this commission.

The period from 1329 to about 1600 is the Dark Age of Scottish legal history,[85] a period of political strife and economic troubles which was an unkindly background for the development of law. Yet even in this period there were enacted a few statutes which are even yet of fundamental importance. If satisfactory judicial machinery had been established the Scoto-Norman law which had already been developed might have continued to evolve steadily as did English law. But by reason of the absence of a powerful central court and settled government no such development could take place and despite many attempts it was not till 1532 that the requisite court was created.[86] This was the period when Scots Law as a science and a philosophy reached its nadir, yet even so the evidence is that there was plenty of law and plenty of lawyers.

After Bannockburn there followed a period of reconstruction; a great reform and consolidation of the system of land tenure was carried through, probably devised by Bernard de Linton, abbot of Arbroath and Chancellor of the kingdom. Under it the basic unit of land held from the crown was the barony, usually held by knight service or archer service but sometimes for payment of money or in frankalmoign. The reorganisation was designed to strengthen both defence and the administration of justice.[87]

Many of the provisions of the reforming measures passed at this time assume the existence and use of Anglo-Norman forms of procedure and amend them to an extent which shows that Scotland had progressed considerably towards the construction of an independent legal system.[88]

The feudal pattern of society steadily tended to dissolve and effective power tended to become concentrated in fewer and larger units, though the judicial power continued dispersed, and consequently inefficient, for too long. Yet the period does not lack legal interest. In 1326 there was convoked at Cambuskenneth the first Parliament, so far as known, at which burghal representatives were present. The fifteenth and sixteenth centuries witnessed the passing of much statute law of great immediate and permanent importance. Among the most notable of these statutes are the Act 1449, c. 17 which gave a tenant a real right against a purchaser of the land from the landlord; the Act 1469, c. 28 and later Acts establishing the long negative prescription; and the Act 1573, c. 55, which long regulated divorce for desertion. A number of the statutes of this period are still in force. " Had it not been for these statutes, modern Scots law

---

[85] On this see generally Cooper, " The Dark Age of Scottish Legal History," in *Selected Papers*, 219; Paton, in *Introduction to Scottish Legal History*, Chap. 2; and Levie, " Place of the War of Independence in Scottish Legal History " (1943) 55 J.R. 121.

[86] *Ibid.*, 226–227.

[87] Rait and Pryde, 33–34; Dickinson, 173–174.

[88] Cooper, *Select Cases*, xlii.

would have been an entirely different thing in many respects, and their enactment is proof positive of the existence of legal statesmanship of a high order at the time when they were passed." [89]

After Bruce's death in 1329 Edward III of England revived the attempt to subjugate Scotland and warfare ensued. Edward Balliol was crowned as vassal of Edward III in 1332 and in 1334 ceded much of the Lowlands to Edward but most of the ceded territory was recovered by 1341; about this time common enmity towards England gave France and Scotland a common interest and in 1346 David II was captured while invading England and remained a prisoner till 1357; part of the exorbitant ransom was never paid but the extraordinary efforts required of an impoverished kingdom to meet the ransom resulted in important constitutional developments. Meetings of Parliament and of the general council became frequent and burgesses came to attend the former certainly from 1366 and the latter from 1357, since their concurrence in the levying of taxation and the quadrupling of the great custom was thought essential. But the economic drain also militated against the enforcement of law and order. [90]

About this time too there was adopted the practice of delegating parliamentary powers to committees, one which became in time a salient, but regrettable feature of the Scottish Parliament. [91] One was the Committee of Articles. Out of another, the Committee for Causes, and similar judicial committees, there eventually evolved the Court of Session. [92] Parliament alone was competent to deal with some matters, in particular " falsed dooms " which were brought up from court to court, possibly originating in a baron court and advancing through the court of a sheriff or lord of regality and coming up to Parliament via the justice-ayre. Resort to the king's council could not be had unless due order had been infringed at some stage or the form of law not observed. But questions of unusual character or importance might be remitted to Parliament by the royal Ministers. [93]

The Beginnings of Parliament

Parliament is first referred to in Scotland in the latter years of the thirteenth century [94] and seems to have originated earlier in that century, springing from a reinforced meeting of the King's Council. Two forms

[89] Cooper, *Selected Papers*, 227.
[90] Dickinson, *op. cit.*, 185; see also *Source Book*, I, 184–188; 194–203.
[91] Hume Brown, I, 181; *Source Book*, I, 204.
[92] On the judicial committees see *Acta Dominorum Concilii, II* (ed. Neilson and Paton) Introd.; Rait, *Parliaments of Scotland*, 458 *et seq.*; Hamilton-Grierson, " Judicial Committees of the Scottish Parliament, 1369–70 to 1544," (1924) 22 S.H.R. 1.
[93] Hannay, *College of Justice*, 2–3.
[94] On earlier assemblies see Innes, *Scotch Legal Antiquities*, 99–103.

of this larger body are distinguishable, namely, Parliament and General Council. The distinction lay in that Parliament was the supreme court of law and, unlike General Council, it was summoned publicly and in accordance with judicial procedure.[95] Both bodies were competent in legislation and finance but Parliament alone had jurisdiction in cases of treason and appeals from subordinate courts, the latter by the process of " falsing of dooms." About 1530 the term Convention of Estates seems to have superseded that of General Council though Conventions do not seem at first to have claimed parliamentary powers.[96]

From the mid-fourteenth century the presence of burgesses was normal and, following French practice, Parliament came to be referred to as the assembly of the three Estates, or the Estates.[97] The three Estates were clergy, tenants-in-chief, and burgesses, though at a late date tenants-in-chief were superseded by Lords of Parliament and commissioners of shires (who were representatives of tenants-in-chief of lower rank than Lords of Parliament) while in its last years, apart from some Officers of State, it was composed of two groups which represented the original estate of tenants-in-chief and of one group which represented the original estate of burgesses.[98] The three Estates met separately for deliberation and discussion as well as in a single chamber for the disposal of business.

An important characteristic of the Scottish Parliament was its practice of delegating functions to committees. A committee of auditors was regularly appointed to hear judicial business and after 1424 the practice developed of appointing a committee known as the Lords of the Articles to discuss the " articles " or proposals of the Crown, probably prepared beforehand by the Council, which reported back to the final meeting of Parliament which passed the proposed legislation. In consequence in the sixteenth and seventeenth centuries sessions of Parliament were brief.[99]

Parliament as Supreme Court

It is quite apparent that from the first Parliament was a meeting of the Estates exercising judicial functions. In 1398 the regular holding of Parliaments was ordained so that the king's subjects might be " servit of the law." [1] It was both a court of first instance and a court of appeal and had jurisdiction in both civil and criminal causes.

---

[95] Rait, *Parliaments of Scotland*, 128.
[96] *Ibid.*, 130–164.
[97] Dickinson, *op. cit.*, 189–190.
[98] *Ibid.*, 165–166. The franchise Act of 1587, largely re-enacting an Act of 1428, regulated the county franchise till 1832: Dickinson, *op. cit.*, 214, 363.
[99] *Ibid.*, 357–374; Dickinson, *op. cit.*, 216–217. See also *Source Book*, II, 37–44; III, 234–246.
[1] A.P.S. I, 573.

As a court of first instance it was specially concerned with cases of treason, most other criminal matters falling to the justiciars and later the High Court of Justiciary. In civil matters there were constant efforts made to limit the judicial functions of the Estates but even after the establishment of the Court of Session, special circumstances or private influence might bring cases directly to Parliament.[2]

As a court of appeal the most important jurisdiction was the " falsing of dooms " in civil cases.[3] Appeals were allowed from baronial courts to the sheriff, from burgh courts to the court of the Four Burghs and from the sheriff court to the justiciar.

Judicial authority in Parliament belonged to the whole Parliament and to every Estate thereof, but very early came to be exercised by committees. Committees of the Great Council had been appointed to discharge judicial functions even before the War of Independence. In 1341 two auditors were appointed *ad audiendum et terminandum supplicationes et querelas* after the end of the parliamentary session and judicial commissions were again appointed in 1369 and 1370. These auditors had to hear the cases and probably suggest suitable disposal for them, the final decision being pronounced in Parliament. Thereafter the practice of appointing Lords Auditors was regular.[4]

Ecclesiastical Courts

Before the Reformation the bishop of each diocese had his own consistorial court, presided over by a judge known as the official, who was skilled in the canon and frequently also in the civil law. From his decisions there was normally no appeal to the bishop.[5]

The ecclesiastical courts were chiefly occupied with matrimonial cases, questions of legitimacy and illegitimacy and of dowry, with causes relating to testacy and intestacy, and the interpretation of wills, and with cases of slander. The canon lawyers also tried to extend the jurisdiction of the Church courts to all cases of contract which had been fortified by the oaths of the parties. They also had to deal with disputes as to patronage, or tithes, or concerning Church property, and petty cases of assaults on ecclesiastics or brawling in sacred places. In addition much business came before the bishop's court by consent of parties.[6]

The majority of the matrimonial causes were instituted with a view to obtaining a declaration of the nullity of a pretended marriage.

2 Rait, *Parliaments of Scotland*, 456.
3 A.P.S. II, 246, 254.
4 Rait, *op. cit.*, 459–460.
5 Dowden, *Medieval Church in Scotland*, 288; Donaldson, in *Introduction to Scottish Legal History*, Chap. 27.
6 *Ibid.*, 287. For specimens of the work of the courts see *Liber Officialis Sancti Andree* (ed. Innes, 1844), and Dowden, 295–298.

Marriage was considered indissoluble so long as the spouses lived and the only divorce granted was separation *a mensa et thoro*, which did not permit remarriage of the parties.[7]

Apart from the body of ecclesiastical legislation which formed the canon law and was the general law of the Church throughout Western Christendom, there was a substantial amount of legislation by provincial synods peculiar to Scotland.[8] Much of this was drawn from the statutes of English councils. Some dealt with clerical duties and conduct but a great deal concerned the laity also.

The Auld Alliance

The period from 1329 to the death of James II in 1460 was also the really significant period of the alliance with France. By 1460 the English had been finally expelled from both Scotland and France and France was now on the threshold of developing into a great European power. Neither any longer needed the alliance but its tradition persisted long after 1460 and led Scotland into disastrous adventures.[9]

The influence of France on Scottish civilisation in these and later years was considerable and it replaced that of England in the legal and administrative as in most other spheres.[10] A number of Scottish practices appear to owe their origin to French influence such as the sitting of the king *pro tribunali*, analogous to the *Lit de Justice* of the French kings, the institution of the Scottish parliamentary auditors, analogous to the *maitres des requêtes*, about 1341, shortly after David II returned from France, the provision of counsel for the poor, found in France in 1400 and 1414 and instituted in Scotland in 1424, the development of a body of practitioners inferior to counsel, *les solliciteurs*.[11] Apart from direct influence, both countries were influenced by feudalism and Scottish students resorted regularly to Orleans, Bourges and Louvain prior to the Reformation and the French connection was the channel through which particularly in the medieval period the Roman and feudal laws were received into Scotland.

The Origins of the Session

Warfare, invasion and rebellion continued to be the rule till about 1424 when James I (1406–37), who had been captured at sea in 1405 on

7 *Ibid.*, 290.
8 *Ibid.*, 224–239. They may be found in *Statutes of the Scottish Church* (ed. Patrick, S.H.S.).   9 Rait and Pryde, 40.
10 *Ibid.* See also Smith, " Influence of the Auld Alliance on the Law of Scotland," 1961 S.L.T.(News) 125.
11 Neilson and Paton, Introduction to *Acta Dominorum Concilii*, II. See also Gardner " French and Dutch Influence," in *Sources and Literature* (Stair Society), 226; Walton, " Relationship of the Law of France to the Law of Scotland " (1902) 14 J.R. 19; " Influence of France on Scots Law " (1895) 3 S.L.T. 189; Ross, *Lectures on Conveyancing and Diligence*, I, 180, 235, 414, 420.

his way to refuge in France, was ransomed and released. He returned to Scotland determined to introduce law and order, " to make the key keep the castle and the bracken bush the cow " and set about repressing disorder. He tried to apply to Scotland many ideas learned during his captivity in England. Parliament was summoned frequently and many measures taken to improve the machinery of government.[12]

James early tried to reform the ordinary courts which were always giving cause for complaint by an Act ordaining that there be made officers and ministers of law through all the realm to give law to the king's commons. The attempt failed and the king tried another method. An Act of 1426 [13] accordingly decreed that the chancellor and certain discreet persons chosen from each Estate should sit three times a year and determine complaints and causes.[14] Nine members were usually chosen, three from each Estate, with the Clerk Register in attendance. This was modelled on the auditorial committee of Parliament but distinct therefrom and was intended to relieve the council of business and administer justice more regularly than could be done in connection with Parliament. There is little information on the working of the new institution but it flourished sufficiently to acquire the name of " the session " and survived to about 1468 or 1470 when this model of session seems to have been abandoned.[15]

Another Act of 1426 directed all freeholders of the Crown, both great and small, to attend Parliament and general council in person, but in 1428 it was laid down that only the greater tenants-in-chief would be summoned by writ, but the other freeholders need not attend but might be represented by two commissioners from each shire and these were to elect a speaker on the English model. Neither Act seems to have been operative.[16]

Yet another facet of the urge to establish settled government and to enforce law and order was the appointment of a commission in 1425 to examine the books of law, that is *Regiam Majestatem* and *Quoniam Attachiamenta*, and amend the laws that needed mending. But nothing seems to have come of this.[17] An Act of 1426 provided that all the king's subjects were to be governed by the king's laws, not by particular laws or privileges. Thus there was to be a common law of the realm.[18]

There was also a considerable volume of well-intentioned social

[12] *Source Book*, II, 10, 13.
[13] A.P.S. II, 11.
[14] Rait and Pryde, 37; Hannay, *College of Justice*, 5–7; and generally Balfour-Melville, *James I*. See also Duncan, in *Introduction to Scottish Legal History*, Chap. 23; *Source Book*, II, 45–46.
[15] Hannay, 8; Dickinson, 213.
[16] Rait and Pryde, 38; Hume Brown, I, 218–219; Dickinson, 214–215.
[17] Cooper, *Regiam Majestatem* (Stair Society), 1.
[18] Dickinson, *op. cit.*, 212.

and economic regulation, such as the regulation of dress and prices, the prohibition of football and poaching, and the exhortation to hunt wolves and sow peas and beans.[19] It is clear that the executive was inadequate to enforce these Acts.

In 1456 the Estates themselves chose nine judges, three from each Estate, to sit in three sections after the General Council which appointed them had dispersed, to hear and decide cases. In 1458 the Estates provided that the Session was to be continued till the next Parliament and the Lords of Session were to hold three sittings of forty days each at Edinburgh, Perth and Aberdeen. Three of each Estate were appointed for each sitting. This was supplementary both to the local courts and the parliamentary auditors. Further Sessions seem to have been appointed in 1460, 1464–65 and 1468 but the Parliament of 1467 appointed auditors in two divisions, *ad querelas* and *ad judicia contradicta* with the provision that causes undecided during the parliamentary session should be decided by the Lords of Council.[20] This "continuing" of cases from Parliament to council became regular after this time.

While Parliament continued to meet frequently during the reign of James III (1460–88) the Lords of the Articles were the virtual masters of the country and their existence was detrimental to the development of a strong and effective Parliament.[21]

In 1471 it was made possible to make direct complaint to the council in respect of an error at the trial and in 1487 a summons of reduction was recognised as an alternative to falsing a doom as a mode of appeal. Falsing survived for the better part of another century but the tendency was to facilitate access to the council.[22] In the late fifteenth century it was apparent that the council could not avoid responsibility for civil justice, though it was frequently interrupted by affairs of state.

In 1469 or 1487 there was a revival of the project of revising the law, the king's laws, *Regiam Majestatem*, Acts, statutes and other books, but again nothing came of it and the administration of justice languished during the reign.[23] Sessions of the council for civil causes, as distinct from sessions of the Lords Auditors, began at least as early as 1478,[24] and the council found itself increasingly committed to dealing with civil causes.

In 1488 the king was slain in the course of a rebellion and it is significant of the increased prestige of the monarchy that the rebels deemed it necessary to obtain parliamentary approval of their conduct

[19] Rait and Pryde, 38.
[20] A.P.S. II, 88.
[21] Hume Brown, I, 289.
[22] Hannay, 10–11.
[23] Dickinson, *op. cit.*, 226–227.
[24] Hannay, *College of Justice*, 22.

and sought to explain to the people and to foreign countries that they had not been guilty of rebellion.[25]

Under James IV (1488–1513) there was material improvement in the administration of justice and the king personally took an active part in holding the justice-ayres all over the kingdom.[26]

In 1491 the Chancellor was ordained to sit with certain lords of council or else the lords of session for the disposal of civil causes, three times a year, during the terms which James I had fixed for the auditorial sessions.[27] At first there was no clear distinction between judicial business and General Council business and the personnel were always mixed, partly officers of state, partly members of the privy council and partly others brought in to be lords of session.

In 1495 an attempt was made to settle a " table " or distribution of summonses, in fact, a court roll, and the experiment was tried of disposing of session business in conjunction with that of the justice-ayres. This was unsuccessful as was an attempt in 1503 to group the shires so that cases might come up in order and litigants be aware of approximate dates.[28]

In 1504 the privy council proposed the institution of a council to sit continually in Edinburgh and decide all civil matters, apparently to fill the gaps between sessions but not to supersede the customary sittings of council. This body was set up, but was to be itinerant and to have the same power as the lords of session, and it came to be known as the " daily council " and in 1505 the lords of session and the king's council sat concurrently on civil business. The term " session " was applied indiscriminately to both, but the association of the lords of session with the Chancellor and the fact that they sat in Edinburgh warrants the conclusion that the Court of Session had now evolved.[29] The whole of the fifteenth century is accordingly a period of experiment, false starts and struggle against arrears of judicial business and the detail of the story is not clear. The burgh courts continued to exercise both civil and criminal jurisdiction in their own spheres and to deal with much legal work of everyday concern.[30]

The College of Justice

The foundation of the College of Justice is legally the most important event in the reign of James V (1513–42).[31] In the early years of the reign

---

[25] Rait and Pryde, 41.
[26] Hume Brown, I, 340–341; Hannay, 15–16; Mackie, *King James IV of Scotland*, 57–58, 192–193.
[27] A.P.S. II, 226.   [28] Hannay, 16–18.
[29] *Ibid.*, 19–21.
[30] Dickinson, *op. cit.*, 250–251.
[31] See generally Irvine Smith, " The Transition to the Modern Law " in *Introduction to Scottish Legal History* (Stair Society) Chap. 3.

there was a growing tendency for the session to become a specialised branch of the council's work. Thus in 1526 eight persons were added to the lords of secret council to sit on the next session and nearly all seem to have been experienced in law.[32] By 1527 eleven of those subsequently appointed senators of the College of Justice in 1532 were already acting.[33] But some settled remuneration was needed if judges were to be permanent and this was still lacking. The king badly needed money and approached the Pope who in July 1531 imposed a tithe on the Scottish Church for three years as a subsidy for the defence of the realm. It probably owed something to pressure on the Pope by the Emperor arising from enmity towards Henry VII of England. In September a further bull was issued, narrating the king's desire to establish a college of judges,[34] and requiring the prelates to contribute a large sum annually for this purpose. The project of the College of Justice seems to have been extemporised as a pretext for obtaining the subsidy.[35] The prelates sought to offer a composition for the perpetual tax and, pending settlement of this issue, a President and fourteen others were named to sit in the interval until the college might be established. No scheme had really been thought out and it was difficult to fit the contemplated college of judges into the pattern of lords of council and session.

It was provided also that the Chancellor, if present, might occupy the presidential chair, and that the king might nominate three or four lords of his great council to take part in the judicial business as extraordinary lords. The president and half of the fourteen judges were to be clerics. Negotiations over the ecclesiastical subsidy and preoccupation with defence caused delay and it was not until 1535 that the Pope granted the bull creating the College of Justice.[36] In 1541 Parliament confirmed the first institution of the college in 1532, ratified the papal bull, and ordained that the college should remain perpetually for the administration of justice to the lieges of the realm.[37] It also gave the senators power to make Acts for the ordering of process and the expedition of justice. The importance for the development of the law and the proper administration of justice of having a permanent supreme court was immense.

At first the court sat as a collegiate body but by about 1554 there is

---

[32] Hannay, 29–30.

[33] *Ibid.*, 35.

[34] The view that the College was founded on the model of the Parlement of Paris is a mistake. If it had any model it was the Collegio dei Giudici of Pavia. Hannay, *op. cit.*, 49; McKechnie in *Common Errors in Scottish History* (Historical Assocn., 1956). See also J. S. H(enderson), " The Scottish College of Justice in the 16th century " (1934) 50 L.Q.R. 120; " Connection between the Parlement of Paris and the Court of Session " (1897) 5 S.L.T. 72, 74.

[35] Hannay, 50–54; Dickinson, 308.

[36] Hannay, 56–61.

[37] A.P.S. II, 371; *Source Book*, II, 48–52.

evidence of lords proceeding to the outer tolbooth to hear witnesses and before 1600 it seems to have become settled practice to have two or three ordinary lords sitting in the outer house dealing with bills and witnesses.[38]

Legal Consequences of the Reformation

Anti-Catholic religious doctrines had been making headway in Scotland for some time before 1546 when the Reformation flared into life with the murder of Cardinal Beaton in St. Andrews castle. The new religious opinions made steady progress despite attempts at repression. In 1559 direct action was resorted to and much ecclesiastical property was damaged.[39]

When the Estates met in 1560 Knox's Confession of Faith [40] was ratified and the national Church abolished, along with the papal authority, the mass, and all practices contrary to the new creed. An Act of that year also abolished all papal jurisdictions and brought to an end the courts of the Officials in the dioceses and appeals therefrom to Rome.

Consistorial cases and all matters formerly competent in the ecclesiastical tribunals were determined by the Court of Session from 1560 to 1563 though the kirk sessions in various parts of the country constituted themselves consistorial courts. In 1563, however, there was established the commissary court of Edinburgh, with four judges authorised to determine all causes formerly competent in the courts of the Roman Officials, and jurisdiction over all Scotland in matters of marriage, divorce and bastardy.[41] The office of Commissary was held by some learned lawyer but the slowness of the court's proceedings gave rise to general dissatisfaction. Appeal lay to the Court of Session. Despite the change the consistorial law of the old courts, based on the canon law of the pre-Reformation provincial councils of the Scottish Church, continued to be observed, except in so far as expressly altered by the reformers.[42]

The previous marriage law was defective in having excessively extended the forbidden degrees of relationship for marriage [43] which resulted in much uncertainty whether persons were married or not and much ingenuity in finding grounds on which marriages might be declared null.

In 1567 Parliament annulled all laws, acts and constitutions, canon,

---

[38] Hannay, 91–98. See also Cooper, " The King versus the Court of Session " (1946) 58 J.R. 83, and *Selected Papers*, 116; and Cooper " The Central Courts after 1532 " in *Introduction* (Stair Society) Chap. 24.

[39] Hume Brown, II, 20–70; Dickinson, 323–331.

[40] Printed in his *History of the Reformation in Scotland* (ed. Dickinson) II, 257.

[41] This court was created by royal charter and ratified by Parliament in 1592.

[42] See further *Introduction to Scottish Legal History* (Stair Society) Chaps. 6, 7 and 8.

[43] Hay Fleming, *Reformation in Scotland*, 477–502; Dowden, *Medieval Church in Scotland*, 251. See also Fraser on *Husband and Wife*, 2nd ed., 104–134.

civil or municipal, contrary to the reformed religion, and later provided that marriage should be open to all related in the second degree or more remotely.[44]

The most material change was, however, in the introduction of judicial divorce. Prior to the Reformation separation only was recognised in accordance with the general canon law of the West. Immediately after the Reformation, however, the courts held that divorce for adultery was competent at common law.[45] In 1573 divorce for malicious desertion, persisted in for four years,[46] was introduced by statute, although the statute narrates that since 1560 it had been the law that divorce was allowed for desertion, and divorces on both grounds were regularly granted from that time onward.[47]

Medieval legal literature—Practicks

The establishment of the Court of Session gave rise to a new kind of legal literature, notes of judgments made privately by judges for their own use, passed from hand to hand and frequently copied. The collections came to be known by the names of their compilers. Two kinds of practicks [48] developed, those which contained only notes of decisions usually in chronological order, and those others which included abstracts of statutes and other sources, such as passages from *Regiam Majestatem*, as well as notes of cases and practical observations, and were usually digested under alphabetical subject-headings. The best-known examples of the latter kind are the *Practicks* of Balfour,[49] Spotiswoode [50] and Hope,[51] and this kind of *Practicks* is the forerunner of the modern textbook or encyclopaedia, while the former kind is the forerunner of the modern law reports. Balfour's *Practicks* in particular is regarded as authoritative and is of the greatest importance for the law of Scotland down to 1579 since it preserves matter from earlier collections now lost and covers the whole field of Scots law. Collections of *Practicks* continued to be made well into the seventeenth century until the decision-Practicks were superseded by the early published reports and the digest-Practicks by the treatises of Craig and Stair.

---

[44] Hay Fleming, 503; Fraser, 112.   [45] Fraser, 1141.
[46] Reduced to three years in 1938; the other grounds of divorce are also modern.
[47] Judicial divorce, as distinct from divorce by Act of Parliament, was not permitted in England till 1857.
[48] See McKechnie " Practicks " in *Sources and Literature* (Stair Society), 25. " Practick " means a decision or precedent, and hence in the plural a collection of decisions.
[49] Published 1754; reprinted by the Stair Society, 1962–63; see McKechnie, " Balfour's Practicks " (1931) 43 Jur.Rev. 179; McNeill, " Sir James Balfour of Pittendreich " (1960) 5 J.R.(N.S.) 1.
[50] Published 1706.
[51] Published by the Stair Society in 1937–38 in two volumes as Hope's *Major Practicks*. A slighter collection by the same Hope was published in 1726 as Hope's *Minor Practicks*.

Private Law, 1328–1600

If informality and lack of precision characterised procedure at this time the substantive law was in no better state. The records contain specimens of many kinds of actions, usually exhibiting the common tendency of undeveloped law " to conceive of any legal question as one of wrongdoing and its suppression." [52] " With insignificant exceptions one and all of them are envisaged simply as the infliction of a wrong by the defender upon the pursuer, as if the only chapter in the law of Scotland were one devoted to delicts or torts. Irrespective of whether the action is one for breach of contract, or for payment of a debt or the price of goods sold, or for damages, or for specific implement, or for delivery, or for warrandice of title, or for reduction of a challenged transaction, or for half a hundred other things, the pursuer simply takes objection to the ' wrangous ' detention and withholding of something, or the ' wrangous ' occupation and labouring of certain lands, and so on; and the common form of judgment is one which simply finds that the defender did ' wrang ' or did ' na wrang,' as the case may be. It is hardly an exaggeration to say that each pursuer eventually presented himself before the tribunal in the guise of ' an infant crying in the night, and with no language but a cry ' and that the whole of Scots law had been compressed into a single commandment: ' Thou shalt do na wrang '." [53]

While this was the case with litigation, in this same period land law was being developed to a high degree and charters evidence a considerable measure of skill in conveyancing.

III.—THE UNION AND AFTER

The Union of the Crowns brought many changes; it greatly increased the prestige of the monarchy and also removed the king from personal participation in the government of Scotland. James utilised the Tudor device of government by council and the Privy Council became the main executive and, to some extent, the legislative body. He also managed Parliament by utilising the committee of the Lords of the Articles, whose composition was not unlike that of the Privy Council. Even the General Assemblies were convened by him and their work prearranged. The business of government was mainly effected by the great officers of state who were the leading members of the Privy Council and their supervision extended to every branch of the national administration.

James had ordained (1587) that justice-ayres should be held twice a year in every shire, with eight persons specially commissioned to conduct them.[54] In 1609 he imported from England the office of justice

---

[52] Daube, " The Scales of Justice " (1951) 63 J.R. 124.
[53] Cooper, " Dark Age," in *Selected Papers,* 219.
[54] A.P.S. III, 458; *Source Book,* III, 283–285.

of the peace to exercise the functions of a local magistracy. A sufficient number was to be appointed for every shire, those of lesser rank to be paid for their services, and they were endowed with all the duties of magistracy, save that capital offenders and those of high rank were to be referred to the Council, and the powers of provosts and bailies of burghs were also saved.[55] In 1611 Norse law and customs were abolished in Orkney and Shetland and the isles were annexed to the Crown in 1612.[56]

In 1604 a project for the complete union of Scotland and England, a matter urged by the king in his first speech to the English Parliament, resulted in the appointment of commissioners to discuss the issue. The project broke down on account of the English refusal to concede parity to the Scots on account of their greater wealth and resources.[57] The furthest James was able to go was to obtain from the English Parliament the repeal of the Acts which treated Scotland as a hostile country, and the decision [58] that Scots born after his accession to the English throne were not aliens in England. A similar concession was made by the Scottish Parliament for the king's English subjects.[59] Beyond that his scheme for an incorporating union failed. James also assumed by proclamation the title of King of Great Britain,[60] while he also gave Scottish trade a measure of commercial freedom in England.

James meanwhile steadily pursued his ecclesiastical policy, directed towards the full restoration of episcopacy in Scotland. Bishops had been restored and their powers extended while in 1610 the king imposed on the country two Courts of High Commission (united in 1615) for the punishment of ecclesiastical offences.[61] Each was under an Archbishop and had authority over the whole populace in life or religion, and they came to be a byword for arbitrary action, wide and indefinite powers, unreasonable severity and tyranny.[62]

Mounting Opposition under Charles I
The reign of Charles I opened with trouble. He secured the passage in October 1625 of a very comprehensive Act of Revocation which threatened the resumption by the Crown of all grants of land made by it since 1542, including most of the gifts of old Church lands.[63] This

---

[55] Hume Brown, II, 277–278; Pryde, *Scotland from 1603*, 5; *Source Book*, III, 278–282.
[56] Pryde, *op. cit.*, 5.
[57] Hume Brown, II, 246; Hill Burton, V, 401–408; Rait and Pryde, 60–61. Sir Thomas Craig was one of the Scottish Commissioners and his arguments are printed in *De Unione Regnorum Britanniae Tractatus* (ed. Sanford Terry, S.H.S.). See also *Source Book*, III, 456–461.
[58] *Calvin's Case*, or the case of the *post-nati*: (1608) 2 St.Tr. 459; 7 Co.Rep. 6a.
[59] Hill Burton, V, 409–410; Pryde, *op. cit.*, 3.
[60] Rymer, XVI, 603.
[61] Hume Brown, II, 249; *Source Book*, III, 58–60.
[62] *Ibid.*, 250.
[63] Rait and Pryde, 63; Hume Brown, II, 286–289.

attempt to take back the bulk of the property of the pre-Reformation church alienated most of the nobles, since most of them had acquired some of the former Church lands, and they tended to ally with the Presbyterians against the king. Charles, however, pushed through his policy in the face of opposition.

In the following year the king initiated legal proceedings for annulling many titles to ecclesiastical lands and teinds or tithes, which had come to be largely in the hands of lay owners, other than the heritors or owners of the lands, and known as titulars, since he planned the provision of a reasonable maintenance for the clergy from the teinds.[64] Only in 1629 was he able to pronounce a final deliverance settling the composition for which the heritors were entitled to purchase their teinds from the titulars. While the plan was sensible and put ministerial stipends on a sure basis, the king's actions antagonised many of the nobles and lords.

Charles even sought to revive one of his father's institutions known as the Commission for Grievances, with enlarged powers which would have virtually made it a Scottish Star Chamber, but strenuous opposition made him desist.[65]

Through control of the Lords of the Articles Charles secured much legislation of the kind he desired, including Acts relative to religion which made clear his intention to make the Church of Scotland conform to the Laudian pattern of the Church of England. This body of legislation excited both attention and hostility and in 1635 a new Book of Canons was imposed, while a new Court of High Commission with more extensive powers was established to secure the operation of the new canons.[66] In 1637 the attempt to impose Laud's Liturgy led to riots, the National Covenant and the Glasgow Assembly of 1638 which swept away all the traces of episcopacy and abolished the Court of High Commission.[67] Then followed the Bishops' Wars and the quarrels between king and Parliament in England which resulted in the Civil War. The struggle between king and Parliament took place mainly in England but not without intervention by the Scottish army. The last stages of Charles's reign and his execution were, however, wholly the acts of his English subjects. During the years 1638–49 the Parliament and the General Assembly had played a larger part than ever before in the affairs of the country, and had made real advances in the government of the country. At the same time the parishes and burghs advanced in importance and the system of shires was extended and completed.[68]

[64] Rait and Pryde, 63; Hume Brown, II, 286–289; *Source Book*, III, 66–77.
[65] Hume Brown, II, 285.
[66] Hume Brown, II, 298–299.
[67] See *Source Book*, III, 90–115.
[68] Pryde, *op. cit.*, 10–12.

Commonwealth and Protectorate

Scotland espoused the cause of Charles II and came to blows with the English in consequence. Cromwell defeated the Scottish royalist forces at Dunbar (1650) and Worcester (1651) and proceeded to the subjugation of the country. The Estates were captured at Alyth, the royal robes and public records sent from Stirling to London and arrangements made for the government of the country. Eight commissioners were entrusted with the task. The first idea had been to convert Scotland into a province of England, but more generous conditions were proposed later. Scotland and England were to be made into one Commonwealth with all convenient speed, liberty of worship secured, and compensation paid for damage caused to England by the resistance on Charles's behalf.[69] The representative of the shires and burghs had no option but to acquiesce. Deputies had further to be chosen to go to London not so much to discuss the proposed union as to supply information for the Bill to effect it. Scotland sent thirty members to the Commonwealth and Protectorate Parliaments, twenty representing the thirty-three shires and ten representing fifty-seven of the burghs; some of the features of this system of representation such as double-county seats and districts of burghs appeared in much later schemes of parliamentary representation.[70] The representation allotted in 1651 was in fact ridiculously inadequate and many of the members were English officers, mere ciphers of the government.[71]

The Privy Council and Court of Session ceased to function on Cromwell's invasion in 1650 and the Commonwealth appointed seven Commissioners, of whom four were English, to administer justice.[72] Their efficiency and impartiality contrasted favourably with their dilatory predecessors. The court sat as a body, each judge acting as president for a week in rotation. The heritable jurisdictions were abolished and the judges went on circuit. The Outer House was abolished but restored in 1655.[73] Scotland benefited on the whole from the firm rule of the Protectorate in matters of administration and justice.

Consideration of union was still proceeding when Cromwell dissolved Parliament and was appointed Protector by the Instrument of Government (1654). Later in that year the Council produced the

---

[69] Hume Brown, II, 365–366. The detailed story is traced in *The Cromwellian Union* (ed. Terry, S.H.S.). See also *Source Book*, III, 146–151.

[70] Pryde, *op. cit.*, 14–15.

[71] Rait and Pryde, 67–68; *Source Book*, III, 248–251; 462–468.

[72] Mackay, *Memoir of Stair*, 58–59. The Scots were Sir John Hope of Craighall, Colonel William Lockhart and John Swinton of Swinton. See also Cooper, " Cromwell's Judges and their Influence on Scots Law " (1946) 58 J.R. 20 and in *Selected Papers*, 111.

[73] *Ibid.*, 60–62. Stair was raised to the bench in 1657, but the courts were closed from Cromwell's death in 1658 till the Restoration.

Ordinance of Union which provided that Scotland was henceforth to make one Commonwealth with England and to send thirty members to the Union Parliament. The Protectorate Parliament was however dissolved before it could confirm the Ordinance of Union.

In 1656 the Commissioners for the government of Scotland were replaced by a Council of State of eight while seven were appointed to supervise the administration of justice, and in the following year the Ordinance of Union was approved by the second Protectorate Parliament but within a year the Long Parliament was restored and the whole question of union reopened.[74] The restoration of the Stuarts put an end to hopes of union and to the English domination yet it has to be conceded that peace and order had been better maintained under the Protectorate than ever before.

The Restoration

The Scottish Parliament met again in 1661, but it was a carefully selected body of members and passed a large volume of subservient legislation, restoring the nearly absolute monarchy of the days of James VI.[75] A general Rescissory Act declared null and void the proceedings of every Parliament since 1633. The Privy Council now proceeded to restore episcopacy and from 1662 onwards the Privy Council was the effective government of the country. The Court of High Commission was even revived in 1664 to enforce royal ecclesiastical policy, but was so detested that it fell into abeyance within a couple of years.[76]

The Court of Session was restored, Stair being one of the judges and from 1661 he was named Vice-President [77] but in 1664 he resigned, having refused to take the Declaration that it was unlawful for subjects to enter into Leagues and Covenants, but was then readmitted by the king's personal intervention.[78]

Free trade with England came to an end at the Restoration and Scottish trade began again to suffer from the English Navigation Acts. Charles II was unable to secure for Scotland the privileges obtained by James VI and I. Negotiations in 1667 for a commercial treaty came to naught, but consequent on that failure Commissioners were again appointed by both Parliaments to treat of union.[79] The Commissioners met at Westminster for two months in 1670 and adjourned but did not reassemble. The conference failed on the refusal of the English to accept

---

74 Hume Brown, II, 374–375.
75 Gray, " The Parliaments of Scotland: Judicial Proceedings, 1660–88 " (1924) 36 J.R. 135.
76 Hume Brown, II, 385–393; *Source Book*, III, 152–160.
77 Mackay, *Memoir of Stair*, 70–71.
78 *Ibid.*, 74–79.
79 Lord Stair was one of the Commissioners. For the negotiations see *The Cromwellian Union* (ed. Terry, S.H.S.), Appx.

the Scottish demand that the existing number of members of the Scottish Parliament should sit in a Parliament of Great Britain, and over the difficulty of appeals to Parliament, the Scottish Commissioners being insistent that no appeals could lie from Council and Session to the proposed Parliament of Great Britain.[80] Four years later this problem gave rise to the secession of the Bar.

In a litigation between Lords Dunfermline and Callendar in the Court of Session the defeated party sought to appeal to the Estates of Parliament, and the counsel for the appellants were suspended from their profession. This was taken as an insult to the whole Bar and some fifty members of the Faculty of Advocates seceded and remained out for two years until the matter was compromised in 1676.[81]

The Privy Council continued to govern Scotland in a bitter atmosphere of religious antagonism and repression of Presbyterianism until 1679 when the Duke of York (later James VII) became Royal Commissioner. In 1681 he convened a Parliament which passed a Test Act, prescribing a test to be taken henceforth by all holding offices of trust in Church and State.[82] Stair, Lord President of the Court of Session, and others resigned rather than take the Test. The Privy Council governed for the rest of the reign and persisted in seeking the repression of Covenanters, a task in which Sir George Mackenzie, the Lord Advocate, distinguished himself as a fanatic for the prerogative.[83]

In 1685 James VII succeeded his brother; tyranny and persecution continued. His attempts to grant indulgence to Catholics further roused opposition and by 1688 Scotland as much as England was looking to William of Orange for deliverance. He duly landed at Torbay and James fled to France. A Convention Parliament assembled and in April 1689 made a declaration that James had forfeited the Crown and that the throne was now vacant, and they offered the Crown to William and Mary, bringing to an end the period from 1603 during most of which Scotland had been governed autocratically and repressively.

The High Court of Justiciary [84]

From the feudal period there had existed the institution of justiciars for Scotland and by the middle of James V's reign the office of justice-general was apparently exercised by one individual with various deputes. Down to the sixteenth century the office was not hereditary but it then became hereditary in the family of Argyll. Argyll in 1628 resigned

---

[80] Rait and Pryde, 75–76; Mackay, *Memoir of Stair*, 90.
[81] See further Mackay, *Memoir of Stair*, 113–116; Hill Burton, VII, 194–195; Sir George Mackenzie's *Memoirs*, 267 *et seq.*
[82] *Source Book*, III, 185–189.
[83] Hume Brown, II, 141–221.
[84] See further Dickinson in *Introduction* (Stair Society), Chap. 31.

the office into the hands of Charles I but reserved his rights as justice-general for Argyll, Tarbet and the Isles. In 1587 Parliament had again to enact that justice-ayres should be held by the justice-general and his deputes commissioned for the purpose.

In 1672 the office of justice-depute was abolished and the High Court of Justiciary created, consisting of the Justice-General, Justice-Clerk [85] and five [86] judges of the Court of Session as Commissioners of Justiciary, for the trial of criminal causes in Edinburgh.[87] The office of Lord Justice-General became a sinecure post and not till 1808 was it provided that on the death of the existing holder (the Duke of Montrose), which happened in 1837, the office should be held by the Lord President. The same Act divided the kingdom into three districts and appointed circuit courts to be held each spring, a system which with modifications still survives.

The Public Registers of Deeds

The Scottish registers are in some cases of great antiquity, that of the Great Seal being extant since 1306, but of greatest importance for the land law was the institution in 1617 of the General Register of Sasines, which maintains from henceforth a continuous record of all transactions relating to or affecting landed property, the existence and accuracy of which has been of the greatest value in ensuring the validity and security of such transactions, since search of the Sasine register for the appropriate county will reveal previous transactions with the land and many of the burdens affecting it.[88] In 1672 the system was developed by the requirement of keeping a minute-book recording those in whose favour charters and writs were granted, while permission was given for writs and charters to be written book-wise.

Development of Private Law in the Seventeenth Century

Despite civil war and religious persecution, private law was greatly developed and improved in the seventeenth century.[89] Much legislation

---

[85] He was originally clerk of the justiciar's court, later acted as assessor, and did not become a judge till the seventeenth century: see Ersk. I, 3, 26; Hannay, " Office of Justice Clerk " (1935) 47 J.R. 311.

[86] Only in 1887 by the Criminal Procedure Act did all judges of the Court of Session become Lords Commissioners of Justiciary also.

[87] Mackinnon, *Constitutional History of Scotland*, 260–261; Ersk. I, 3, 26; *Source Book*, III, 283–287.

[88] 1617, c. 16; *Source Book*, III, 565. There had been earlier attempts in 1425, 1469, 1555 and 1587. Registration is now governed by the Land Registers (Scotland) Act, 1868. Other registers include the Register of Deeds (since 1554) in which, *inter alia*, wills are now registered, the Registers of Inhibitions and Adjudications, of Hornings, of Service of Heirs and others. There are now fourteen registers in all, mostly of considerable antiquity and all of great legal and historical value. See further Milne, *The Scottish Office*, 190–192.

[89] See further Irvine Smith, " The Rise of Modern Scots Law, 1660–1707," in *Introduction to Scottish Legal History*, Chap. 4.

of fundamental and permanent importance was passed such as the statutes of prescription,[90] the foundation of the law of entail,[91] new regulations for the conduct of business in the Court of Session,[92] an Act nullifying alienations in defraud of creditors,[93] regulating the execution of deeds,[94] settlement of the law of tithes, rules for the division of commonties and runrig lands, which were complementary to the statutes for the encouragement of agriculture, the statutory recognition of the fundamental principles of bankruptcy, and many other important pieces of legislation. Trading enterprise flourished and many joint-stock companies were established.[95]

It is remarkable that at this time, despite, apart from the disturbances, the extent of royal and other authority and the weakness of Parliament, so many measures of such importance and beneficial character were passed. It is apparent that the leading lawyers and statesmen must have had profound knowledge of the law and also a strong desire to develop and improve the legal system and the judicial institutions.[96]

The Seventeenth-Century Jurists

In the seventeenth century flourished a considerable number of jurists of great importance for the development of the law whose works are still of importance and authority.[97]

Sir Thomas Craig of Riccarton (1540–1607), justice-depute in 1564, was the first systematic writer on law, as distinct from a collector of decisions and statutes.[98] His *Jus Feudale* (1603, pub. 1654) deals with the origin of law and traces the progress of the civil, canon and feudal laws. His exposition of the feudal law makes the work the first·Scottish institutional text. He also wrote on the succession to the English throne, a treatise on the Union of the Kingdoms of Scotland and England [99] and much Latin verse.

Sir John Skene (?1549–1611), Lord Advocate and later Lord Clerk Register, was the first great legal antiquary, somewhat erratic and inaccurate, but deserving of great credit for his work. He first edited the *Regiam Majestatem* and *Quoniam Attachiamenta* in 1609 and produced

---

[90] Acts, 1617, c. 12; 1669, c. 9.
[91] Act 1685, c. 22.
[92] Act 1672, c. 16.
[93] Act 1621, c. 18.
[94] Act 1681, c. 5.
[95] Pryde, *op. cit.*, 31.
[96] See also Gibb, "International Private Law in Scotland in the 16th and 17th Centuries" (1927) 39 J.R. 369.
[97] See generally Cooper, "The Scottish Lawyer's Library in the Seventeenth Century," in *Selected Papers*, 276, and *Introduction* (Stair Society), Chap. 3.
[98] See Fraser Tytler's *Life of Sir Thomas Craig of Riccarton, passim*, and Law, "Craig's *Jus Feudale*" (1898) 10 J.R. 177.
[99] Published by the Scottish History Society.

in *De Verborum Significatione* an invaluable glossary of ancient legal terms.

Sir Thomas Hope of Craighall (?1580–1646), Lord Advocate and father of three judges, is said to have been the most eminent advocate of his time. He compiled the *Major Practicks* [1] and the *Minor Practicks*.[2] He acted for Charles I in the famous revocation of grants of Church lands in 1625, which led to the law of teinds being put on a satisfactory footing. He was a partisan of the Solemn League and Covenant and responsible for the legal side of much of the Covenanters' activities.

Other notables of the Bar about this time were Sir Robert Spotiswoode, author of the *Practicks*,[3] Sir Thomas Nicolson, Sir John Gilmour, who defended Montrose in 1641 and held office as Lord President from 1660 to 1670, and Sir John Nisbet, who was the last to combine the offices of Lord Advocate and Lord of Session, which he did in 1664. He wrote *Doubts and Questions in the Law* [4] which were answered many years later by Sir John Steuart, Lord Advocate under Queen Anne.

Sir John Lauder of Fountainhall (1646–1722) was concerned in most of the great causes of the time. He left voluminous manuscripts and two volumes of printed decisions, too infrequently referred to, since they contain much interesting and entertaining matter about the law, the courts and the personalities of the times, and cast much light on the history and state of Scotland in the middle of the century.

Stair

Born in Ayrshire in 1619, James Dalrymple, later (1664) baronet and (1690) first Viscount Stair, graduated at Glasgow, served with Glencairn's Horse in the Bishops' War and was a regent in philosophy in Glasgow University (1641–47) before passing advocate in 1648. In 1657 he became a judge under the Protectorate, being continued in office at the Restoration, but retired from office in 1663 to avoid taking the " declaration " abjuring the right to take up arms against the king. In the following year he resumed office having made a modified declaration.

In 1671 he was appointed Lord President of the Court of Session and was sworn of the Privy Council and in 1672 was largely responsible for a series of revised regulations governing jurisdiction and procedure,[5] while in the following year he advocated a more clement policy towards the Covenanters.

In 1681 he was ejected from his post for failure to take the Test and

---

1 Edited by Lord Clyde, Stair Society, Vols. 3 and 4, 1937–38.
2 Published 1726 and 1734.
3 Published in 1706.
4 Known as Dirleton's *Doubts*. (His judicial title was Lord Dirleton.)
5 Mackay, *Memoir of Stair*, 94–100. See also Thomson, " The First Viscount Stair " (1924) 36 J.R. 33; Duncan, " Viscount Stair " (1934) 46 J.R. 103.

later retired to Leyden whence he published his *Decisions* (two volumes, 1684 and 1687), the first series of reports published in Scotland.[6] In 1688 he returned with William of Orange and in the following year was readmitted as President, which office he held until his death in 1695.

The publication of Stair's *Institutions* in 1681 (second edition, revised and enlarged, 1693) marked the creation of modern Scots law. It is " an original amalgam of Roman law, feudal law and native customary law, systematised by resort to the law of nature and the Bible, and illuminated by many flashes of ideal metaphysic." [7] It is not a compendium of municipal law but an essay in historical and comparative jurisprudence. Rules are classed analytically and deduced from principles with frequent reference to the philosophic bases of the positive law.[8] " Its outstanding feature is the emphasis consistently laid upon first principles, and the systematic development of these principles in harmony with the most enlarged and comprehensive views of comparative jurisprudence. The *Institutions* are no mere compendium of Scots Law; for Stair made the whole science of jurisprudence his province." [9]

Mackenzie

Sir George Mackenzie of Rosehaugh,[10] born in 1636, came to the Bar in 1656 and early distinguished himself. In 1677 he became King's Advocate and won his sobriquet of " Bloody " Mackenzie by relentless persecution of the Covenanters. In 1686 he was removed from office for refusal to concur in the exercise of the dispensing power in favour of Catholics, was restored briefly in 1688 and retired to Oxford in 1689 where he pursued literary work till his death in 1691.

His writings include *Aretina*, an early specimen of prose fiction, moral essays, political writings in support of the prerogative, and many legal works, a treatise on criminal law, one on actions, observations on the statutes, commentaries on the bankruptcy Act and the entail Act, and a *Science of Heraldry* and *Institutions of the Law of Scotland* (1684). This is, however, a slight work and quite overshadowed by Stair's *Institutions*. As much as anything he will be remembered for the foundation of the Advocates' Library, now the National Library of Scotland, which he inaugurated with a notable oration.

---

[6] Durie's *Decisions* relate to an earlier period but were not published till 1690.
[7] Cooper, " Scottish Legal Tradition," in *Selected Papers*, 177.
[8] See further Campbell, *The Structure of Stair's Institutions*.
[9] Cooper, " Some Classics of Scottish Legal Literature," in *Selected Papers*, 39, 43.
[10] See Lang, *Sir George Mackenzie of Rosehaugh*; article in D.N.B.; Young, " Sir George Mackenzie of Rosehaugh " (1907) 19 J.R. 266; Brown, " Sir George Mackenzie of Rosehaugh " (1902) 9 S.L.T. 1, and " Mackenzie's Institutions " (1901) 8 S.L.T. 105, 113, 130, 138, 145, 154, 157; 9 S.L.T. 9.

The Movement Towards Union

In 1689 yet another attempt was made to effect a union of the Parliaments. The Scottish Convention appointed commissioners to treat of complete union, except in Church government, and offered to accept King William as arbiter in any dispute about the terms of union. The English Parliament refused, however, to appoint commissioners though William was himself favourable. No further progress could be made during William's reign since he had become personally unpopular and anti-English feelings had been aroused by the massacre of Glencoe and the failure of the Darien Scheme.[11]

In 1700 at the height of the Darien controversy William again recommended to the English Parliament the appointment of commissioners to discuss union, but while the Lords agreed, the Commons declined the royal recommendation. The Lords discussed the matter again in 1701, and in 1702 William renewed his request and it was endorsed by Anne on her accession later in the year. Accordingly a commission sat from October 1702 till February 1703 but again proved fruitless, the insuperable objection being that of the English to free trade between the two countries.[12]

Further consideration of union between the two countries was provoked by the question of the succession to the throne which arose sharply after the death of all Queen Anne's children. The English Parliament in 1701 by the Act of Settlement limited the succession to the English crown on the house of Hanover, but the Scottish Parliament had taken no action and English statesmen feared the possibility of a restoration of the Stuarts, which might endanger the Protestant succession in England and the system of limited constitutional monarchy established in 1688. Hence union became politically desirable for England though there was still great unwillingness to concede the equal privileges of trade with England and the English colonies.[13] The Scottish Parliament sought to take advantage of the Queen's difficult situation and her entanglement in the war of the Spanish Succession against Louis XIV. In 1703 an Act was passed to the effect that no future sovereign should have power to make war or peace without the consent of the Scottish Parliament.[14] Anne consented to this but refused assent to the bill entitled the Act of Security under which, on the death of Anne without issue, the Scottish Estates were to name a successor from the Protestant descendants of the old royal line of Scotland, but this was not to be the same person as the designated successor to the throne of

11 Rait and Pryde, 76–77; Pryde, *op. cit.*, 48. See also *Source Book*, III, 337–344; Pratt Insh, *The Company of Scotland trading to Africa and the Indies.*
12 Rait and Pryde, 79; Hume Brown, III, 83–84.
13 Rait and Pryde, 79–80.
14 *Source Book*, III, 472.

England unless there were such conditions of government settled and enacted as might secure the honour and sovereignty of the kingdom, the freedom and power of Parliament, the religion, freedom and trade of the nation from English or foreign influence.[15] The Act was passed the following year by dint of Parliament refusing supply for the first time in its history.[16] This and other measures were not designed to force a union since the Country Party had in mind complete separation from England and in this had the support of the Jacobites who wished to avoid the recognition of the Electress of Hanover and her line as heirs to the Scottish crown.[17]

The English Parliament recognised the danger of allowing a settlement to wait till Anne's death. By the Aliens Act of 1705 [18] they again authorised the Queen to negotiate with any commissioners who might be appointed by the Scots and provided further, as a counterweight to the Act of Security, that from Christmas 1705 until the Scottish Parliament should have passed an Act settling the Crown of Scotland upon the designated successor to the Crown of England, every native of Scotland, with a few exceptions, should be an alien in England and that, apart from a few exceptions, trade between England and Scotland should be prohibited.[19]

The debates of the Scottish Parliament that summer were heated and of crucial importance for the future; they took place in an atmosphere of confused excitement and amid popular agitation against union. In September, however, Parliament resolved that commissioners should be nominated not by itself but by the Queen to treat of union, a resolution with the practical consequence that the Scottish commissioners would be selected from advocates of union. In November the English Parliament repealed the threatening clauses of the Aliens Act.[20]

The joint commission met in London in April 1706 and early agreed on three main points, an incorporating union, guarantees by the English of complete freedom of trade, and an undertaking by the Scots to recognise the Electress of Hanover and the heirs of her body, being Protestants, as successors to Anne as Queen of Scotland. Agreement was also reached on taxation and the jurisdiction of the Scottish courts but the sharpest difference arose over the number of Scottish representatives in the new Parliament of Great Britain. The Scots asked for fifty members in the House of Commons but the English suggested thirty-eight and later proposed forty-five with sixteen representative peers in

[15] *Source Book*, III, 473–477.
[16] Clark, *Later Stuarts*, 275–276; Hume Brown, III, 88–94.
[17] Rait and Pryde, 81.
[18] *Source Book*, III, 477–478.
[19] Clark, 276; Hume Brown, III, 94.
[20] *Source Book*, III, 480.

the House of Lords,[21] and agreement was reached on this basis. These numbers were unsatisfactory and inadequate on the basis of population though they were liable to produce great unsettlement of the balance of political forces in the new chambers and they did result during Anne's later years in policy being influenced by the Scottish members. Each country ceased to have exclusive control of its own political affairs, a state which has, however, resulted in the long run in far more English influence on Scotland than the other way.

The English gave up their exclusive commercial privileges, a great sacrifice according to the economic notions of the times which did not foresee the ultimate advantages of an extension of the free-trade area, and paid a sum of £398,085 to the Scottish exchequer as an " Equivalent " for the share of the national debt which Scotland was to assume. The Scots accepted the principle that taxation and trade regulation should be uniform in the two countries in future, though this was made acceptable by substantial tax concessions.[22]

The commissioners completed their work in three months and the articles of union were ratified by the Scottish Estates in January 1707 [23] in the face of many protests and indications of popular disapproval, rioting in Edinburgh and accusations of bribery. They were ratified by the English Parliament in March [23a] and came into force on May 1, 1707; in October of that year the first Parliament of Great Britain met at Westminster.[24] The Estates at the same time passed an Act for the Security of the Church of Scotland as an essential part of the union settlement.[25]

The Preservation of Scots Law by the Union

The continuance of Scots law and the Scottish courts was provided for by the Treaty of Union by provisions (Art. XIX) that the Court of Session and Court of Justiciary should continue in all time coming, that the Court of Admiralty should always be continued in Scotland, and that no causes in Scotland should be " cognoscible by the Courts of Chancery, Queen's Bench, Common Pleas or any other court in Westminster Hall " and that there should be a Court of Exchequer in Scotland after the union for deciding questions concerning the revenues of customs and excises. Heritable offices, superiorities and jurisdictions were preserved (Art. XX) and also the rights and privileges of the royal

[21] On these see Fergusson, *The Sixteen Peers of Scotland.*
[22] Hume Brown, III, 100–110; Pryde, *The Treaty of Union*, 20–24; *Source Book*, III, 480–489.
[23] A.P.S. XI, 406, c. 7.
[23a] 6 Anne, c. 11.
[24] Rait and Pryde, 82–83; Clark, 276–278; Hume Brown, III, 110. See also Smith, " The Union of 1707 as Fundamental Law " [1957] Pub.L. 99.
[25] *Source Book*, III, 489–492.

burghs (Art. XXI). Laws concerning regulation of trade, customs and excises were to be the same in both countries after the union but all other laws in use in Scotland were after the union and notwithstanding it to remain in force as before " but alterable by the Parliament of Great Britain with this difference betwixt the laws concerning publick right policy and civil government and those which concern private right that the laws which concern publick right policy and civil government may be made the same throughout the whole United Kingdom But that no alteration be made in laws which concern private right except for evident utility of the subjects within Scotland " (Art. XVIII). The right of the House of Lords to continue to hear appeals from England and to hear appeals from Scotland was simply evaded by the Treaty since the House of Lords was not another " court in Westminster Hall."

Nevertheless among the first measures of the new Parliament of Great Britain were the abolition of the Scottish Privy Council,[26] the setting up of a system of Justices of the Peace, and the establishment of a Court of Exchequer in Scotland. A year later in defiance of the Treaty the Government put through an Act applying one law of treason, the ancient English one, to both countries, and a commission of Oyer and Terminer superseded the High Court of Justiciary in this field of law.[27]

IV.—THE EIGHTEENTH CENTURY

In the early years of the eighteenth century there was much dissatisfaction with the union, particularly over questions of taxation and in particular the malt tax of 1713, which was inequitable and technically contrary to the treaty.[28] In that year a motion for the repeal of the union was lost in the House of Lords by only four votes.[29] The growing practice of taking appeals from the Court of Session to the House of Lords seems to have excited little popular discontent or excitement though ecclesiastical feeling was offended by the decision in *Greenshields'* case which tolerated the Episcopal Church in Scotland, and more so by the Act of Toleration in 1712 which sanctioned episcopacy and prescribed unacceptable oaths for the clergy both Presbyterian and Episcopalian.[30] It appears that initially union was in one way or another distasteful to a majority of both peoples and only made acceptable by the pressure of events.[31]

Serious grievances appeared during 1707–08 during the passage

26 *Source Book*, III, 495.
27 Hume Brown, III, 143–144; Hill Burton, VIII, 210–216.
28 Clark, 280–281.
29 Hume Brown, III, 152–153.
30 Stephen, *History of the Scottish Church*, II, 468; Grub, *Ecclesiastical History of Scotland*, III, 361–367; Pryde, *op. cit.*, 94–95.
31 Rait and Pryde, 86.

of the Act for abolishing the Scottish Privy Council and increasing the powers of the justices of the peace though the objections must be discounted at least in part as those of parties interested in maintaining the instrument for controlling elections.[32]

Again in 1708 Parliament, following a threatened Jacobite landing in the Forth, substituted the English law of treason for that of Scotland and united all the Scottish parties into an unsuccessful opposition, though the motives of some of the peers for the opposition were rather mixed. In 1711 the House of Lords ruled in the case of the Duke of Hamilton and Brandon that no British title could confer on a Scottish noble the right to a seat in the House of Lords and this was deeply resented as a national insult and proof of England's twisting of the Union to its own advantage.[33] In the following year the restoration of lay patronage to ecclesiastical livings aroused fear and anti-union feeling among the Presbyterians. The Act in question [34] was a clear breach of the Treaty both in letter and in spirit.[35]

In 1715 the first Jacobite rebellion broke out. The government sought to preserve the loyalty of Scotland by an Act commonly known as the Clan Act, by which every Crown vassal was to forfeit his lands if found guilty of treasonable correspondence with the Pretender, while entails and settlements in favour of children or other heirs were made void from August 1, 1715, in all time coming. This threat hung over the heads of all lords who might think of departing from allegiance to the Hanoverian dynasty.[36]

The rebellion was a military failure and two Acts followed, one appointing a Commission to deal with estates forfeited during the rebellion and the other for disarming the Highlands as a means of securing the peace of the country.[37] In breach of the Treaty of Union many prisoners were removed from Scotland to Carlisle for trial under the treason law. This caused much bad feeling among all classes in Scotland. Though attempts were made to enforce the new treason law, it is questionable if any instances occurred of punishment by the courts of criminal justice for concern in the insurrection. The penal retributions were inflicted through English tribunals, and were thus treasured in the Scots mind as a national aggression and injury.[38] The proceedings of the Forfeited Estates Commissioners [39] were equally loathed; their actings were hindered by the Scottish Court of Exchequer

[32] Rait and Pryde, 86.
[33] *Ibid.*, 87.
[34] 10 Anne, c. 12.
[35] Rait and Pryde, 87; Hume Brown, III, 143–144.
[36] Hume Brown, III, 162–163.
[37] *Ibid.*, 189.
[38] Hill Burton, VIII, 331–338.
[39] Hill Burton, VIII, 348–350.

and the Court of Session and few would buy the forfeited estates until the York Buildings Company, which had been founded to supply London with water from the Thames, came forward as chief purchaser.[40] Further resentment attended the proceedings of a commission of Oyer and Terminer sent to Scotland to take proceedings in absence against Jacobites who had fled. Its failure was proof not of Jacobite sympathies but of Scottish resentment and bitterness at English interference.

Dissatisfaction with the Government was also shown in the resistance of the Faculty of Advocates in 1722 to the Crown's appointment of Patrick Haldane, one of the commissioners on the forfeited estates, as a Lord of Session. The court held that Haldane had not made out his qualification to be received as a judge, but this decision was, it need hardly be said, reversed by the House of Lords. The government, however, withdrew the nomination but by statute abolished the court's veto on nominees, leaving the privilege of subjecting the presentee to an examination, and also the extraordinary Lords of Session.[41]

In 1725 an Act for Disarming the Highlands was passed and a serious attempt made to bring the country within civilisation. General Wade began to erect barracks and forts and make roads throughout the Highlands to check cattle-lifting and the gathering of troops,[42] while a little later the Highland regiments began to be raised.

House of Lords Appeals

There was no express provision in the Treaty as to whether any appeal was to be permitted to the House of Lords of the Parliament of Great Britain. In England appeal to the House of Lords by writ of error had become established by the seventeenth century. In Scotland it was an obscure and still uncertain question how far any appeal lay from the Scottish courts to the Scottish Parliament. The Treaty avoided the difficulty but its silence on the matter left open the possibility of appeal.

In 1711 an Episcopalian clergyman, James Greenshields, was imprisoned in Edinburgh for openly using the Anglican form of service and the Court of Session upheld the action of the presbytery and the magistrates. Appeal was taken to the House of Lords and the Lords reversed the Court of Session and ordered Greenshields' release.[43] The decision caused great alarm in Scotland but since then the House of Lords has continued to entertain appeals from Scotland and the practice, however erroneous, is now settled.

---

[40] Hume Brown, III, 190–193.
[41] Hill Burton, VIII, 352.
[42] Hill Burton, VIII, 368–378; Hume Brown, III, 211–212. On the roads see further Salmond, *Wade in Scotland*.
[43] There were earlier appeals in 1708, but *Greenshield's* case attracted more attention.

Central Government

After the abolition of the Scottish Privy Council in 1708 the government of Scotland was till 1746 sometimes in the hands of a third Secretary of State but was frequently entrusted to one or other of the joint Secretaries of State. In the intervals Scottish affairs were managed by a Scottish noble or by the Lord Advocate. Responsibility fell to the northern Secretary of State till 1782 and thereafter to the Home Secretary assisted by the Lord Advocate. The management consisted largely of control of elections and the dispensing of patronage. The most successful manager was Henry Dundas, later Viscount Melville, during the years 1783 to 1806.

Local Government

At the time of the Union the functions of local government were distributed among six agencies which had developed with little reference to each other and at different periods. The sheriffs and the burghs had arisen in the twelfth century, baronies and regalities in the fourteenth, kirk sessions in the sixteenth and justices of the peace and commissioners of supply in the seventeenth.

The administrative functions of the sheriff had formerly been the collection of Crown dues, execution of royal writs, publishing of statutes and latterly making the return of the shire members. These functions were, however, restricted as the sheriffships became heritable in the hands of the great families and administrative power was curtailed while legal jurisdiction increased.[44]

The royal burghs had each a constitution or " sett " which entrusted power to a provost, bailies and self-elective town councils and they remained into the nineteenth century self-contained agencies of local government frequently enjoying substantial revenues. The merchant guilds and crafts in the burghs had numerous exclusive privileges which legally survived till 1846 though they had been largely abandoned by then. Measures for the control of the burghs were enacted from time to time, notably in 1822, but this was too late and the courts refused to enforce them.[45]

The baronies and regalities had formerly enjoyed substantial jurisdictional rights but by 1707 these had very largely fallen into abeyance. Their executive duties, however, continued; these were to preserve common lands, pastures, woods and mosses, dykes and ditches and to keep the assizes of bread and ale. After the abolition of heritable jurisdictions in 1747 even their administrative functions fell into desuetude though particular instances survived till much later.[46]

[44] Rait and Pryde, 177–178.
[45] Rait and Pryde, 178.
[46] Hill Burton, VIII, 517–518; Rait and Pryde, 178.

The kirk sessions established at the Reformation acted under the general guidance of the commissioners of supply and, in burghs, in co-operation with the town council. Expenditure required the sanction of the heritors of the parish, *i.e.*, the heritable proprietors appearing on the valuation roll of the parish.[47] The kirk session managed the parish schools, paid small allowances to the poor, aged and indigent and distributed charitable relief in case of need. It was permissible to lay assessments on the parish after 1663, half on owners, half on occupiers but these were unpopular and infrequently resorted to and most funds came from church collections and mortifications for the poor. The poor law system was, however, disintegrating and badly needed reform by the nineteenth century.[48]

In Scotland the justices of the peace never enjoyed either the powers or the prestige of their English counterparts. After 1708, however, they did enjoy considerable administrative powers, having jurisdiction over the settlement of disputes as to work and wages, weights and measures; they had to suppress riots, support customs officers and supervise prisons and almshouses and, from 1718, in conjunction with the commissioners of supply, to see to the maintenance of country roads and bridges.[49]

The commissioners of supply were recognised by statute in 1667 but had existed on a customary basis before then. They were a country committee of wealthy landowners appointed to allocate the monthly cess or land tax, and their organisation made it convenient to entrust them with other duties such as the enforcement of the Education Act of 1696 and, with the justices, the control of vagabonds and the upkeep of roads.[50]

Break-up of the Clan System and the Heritable Jurisdictions

The measures adopted to restore and ensure internal peace after the defeat of the second Jacobite rebellion at Culloden provoked considerable dissatisfaction. The chief constitutional change was the abolition, in breach of the Treaty of Union, of heritable jurisdictions in 1748.[51] Compensation amounting to £152,000 was paid, of which £21,000 went to the Duke of Argyll in compensation for his right of justiciary over Argyll and the Western Isles. Thereafter the power and prestige of the sheriff courts advanced steadily and in 1787 the office of sheriff-substitute was recognised and made a salaried office. So too the

---

[47] The meaning of the term is discussed at length in Black's *Parochial Ecclesiastical Law of Scotland*, 4th ed., p. 44.
[48] Rait and Pryde, 179; Ferguson, *Dawn of Scottish Social Welfare*, Chap. 7.
[49] Hill Burton, VIII, 210; Rait and Pryde, 179.
[50] Rait and Pryde, 180.
[51] Pryde, *op. cit.*, 65; Omond, *Lord Advocates of Scotland*, II, 32–38, 41–42; Dickson, " Heritable Jurisdictions " (1897) 9 J.R. 428.

holding of land in return for military service was abolished and lands thus held converted to ordinary feudal tenure.[52]

The measures for disarming the Highlands and breaking up the clan system were probably unnecessarily severe. The tartan and the pipes were proscribed as military and badges of sedition and not legalised again till 1782 while suppression and persecution contributed materially to the great emigration to North America about the middle of the century.[53]

An Act of 1752 disposed of the estates which had been forfeited after the rebellion and devoted their revenues to the improvement of Highland farms, the establishment of schools and the planting of forests.[54] The Act had beneficial results and many areas were greatly improved. A few years later followed another beneficial measure in the Act for the better preservation of turnpike roads under which dues were levied from vehicles and spent on the maintenance of the public roads, while in 1770 Montgomery's Entail Act empowered heirs of entail in possession to grant leases for substantial periods on certain conditions, a provision which greatly tended towards the agricultural improvement of the country.[55]

In 1782–84 the Act prohibiting the wearing of the Highland dress was repealed, and the forfeited estates restored to the legal heirs but on condition that debts charged on them were to go to the public benefit and particularly towards the expense of completing the Forth and Clyde canal and of making roads in the Highlands.[56]

Heritable Jurisdictions and the Inferior Courts

The abolition of the heritable jurisdictions affected not only rights of jurisdiction held by virtue of grants of barony or regality but the office of sheriff all over the country.

The office of sheriff had early tended to become hereditary in the line of a powerful Crown vassal and by 1747 twenty-three out of thirty-three sheriffs held thus. But since about 1357 there had been a growing practice for the sheriff to appoint a qualified depute to perform the judicial work. In 1747 the qualified depute everywhere replaced the hereditary officer and became the sheriff of the county.[57]   In 1828 the name Depute was dropped and he became the modern Sheriff, commonly called Sheriff-Principal. The Sheriff-Depute in turn appointed sheriffs-substitute and from 1825 it was provided that the sheriff-substitute should

52 Hill Burton, VIII, 503–504; Hume Brown, III, 330.
53 Hume Brown, III, 328–329.
54 Rait and Pryde, 97; Hume Brown, III, 337–338; Pryde, *op. cit.*, 153.
55 Hume Brown, III, 345.
56 *Ibid.*, 352–353; Pryde, 155.
57 For list of the first sheriffs see Omond, *Lord Advocates*, II, 43–44. See also Malcolm, in *Introduction* (Stair Society), Chap. 26.

be a trained lawyer while in 1877 that office became a distinct Crown appointment.

Private Law in the Eighteenth Century
The later eighteenth century was the classical age of the Scottish common law, developed and brought to maturity by Erskine and not yet debased or defiled by inconsidered statutes, uncritical following of English principles or ignorant interference by an English House of Lords.[58] It largely coincided with the great days, the golden age, of Edinburgh and the efflorescence of the arts and letters and of the Scottish School of philosophy. Material prosperity advanced and the law had to take account of more settled conditions, developing agriculture, industry and commerce, and a more complicated social and economic order.

Legal Literature—Bankton, Erskine and Kames
The eighteenth century saw some very distinguished lawyers and judges. On the bench the work of Forbes, Dundas and Ilay Campbell was outstanding. But now among the jurists the academic is becoming for the first time prominent. William Forbes, professor of Law at Glasgow (1714–46) wrote books on *Bills of Exchange, Tithes* and *Justices of the Peace* as well as a small *Institutes of the Law of Scotland.*[59]

In 1751 there appeared the *Institutes* of Andrew McDouall, Lord Bankton, a work still of considerable authority and value and notable for its extensive comparisons with the law of England, but overshadowed by the work of Erskine.

John Erskine of Carnock[60] was born in 1695 and passed advocate in 1719. In 1737 he became professor of Scots Law at Edinburgh, which chair he held till he retired in 1765. In 1754 he published his *Principles of the Law of Scotland* for use as the textbook of the class, a function which in repeated editions it performed until well into the twentieth century. His larger work, the *Institute of the Law of Scotland,* was not published in his lifetime but appeared posthumously in 1773, and soon achieved a place second only to Stair's *Institutions* in juristic regard. Erskine displays classical Scots law, deduced from principle and considered in leisurely prose, not yet overwhelmed by the citation of difficult or even contradictory decisions or by masses of barely comprehensible statutory amendment. It is as the final and authoritative exponent of the older law of Scotland, resting on the Roman law and the feudal customs, that Erskine stands supreme. His work lacks the philosophic breadth of Stair and the bold insight of Bell, and he probably failed to

---

[58] See further Paton, " The Eighteenth Century and Later," in *Introduction to Scottish Legal History*, Chap. 5.
[59] See also Stein, " Legal Thought in Eighteenth Century Scotland " (1957) 2 J.R.(N.S.) 3.
[60] See Grant, *Story of the University of Edinburgh*, II, 372, and D.N.B.

appreciate that, even when he wrote, the centre of interest in legal studies was shifting from the law of property to commercial law. His treatment is academic, cautious, exact and workmanlike rather than inspired, but yet worthy of the highest admiration and respect. John Millar, professor of Law at Glasgow from 1761 to 1801,[61] was the most celebrated and successful law teacher of his time; his writings included *The Origin of the Distinction of Ranks*, an interesting early sociological study, and *An Historical View of the English Government*, the first constitutional history of Britain. He was a notable supporter of the liberties of the subject and an outspoken advocate of parliamentary reform. Also in the eighteenth century appeared some of the collections of styles of deeds, which are the beginning of modern conveyancing practice.[62]

Of the judiciary Henry Home, Lord Kames (1696–1782), was among the most notable. He passed advocate in 1723 and was raised to the Bench in 1752. His literary output was considerable and diverse, collections of decisions,[63] essays on legal subjects, antiquities, on morality and natural religion, literary criticism, farming and education. The works still of most interest and value are the *Historical Law Tracts* (1757) and the *Principles of Equity* (1760), the latter of which examined, with much comparative reference to English law, the principles on which rules of law might be modified in application by an overriding equitable discretion. In this connection he conducted extensive correspondence with Lord Hardwicke and Lord Mansfield in England. " We moderns are hardly enough aware of how much the Scotch lawyer is indebted to Henry Home, Lord Kames. His versatile and truly philosophical mind neglected nothing. He enriched the law of Scotland by his collections of remarkable decisions, by his abridgment of the Statutes, and by a large body of ingenious speculations and criticisms upon law and legal decisions." [64]

The eighteenth century practically saw the end of the old intimacy between Scotland and the Continent and of the practice of young men resorting, formerly to France and later to Holland, for study of the Roman law as expounded by the commentators and the great civilians. Craig, Mackenzie, Spotiswoode and Fountainhall had studied at Orleans, Poitiers, Bourges or Paris. In the seventeenth and eighteenth centuries it is known that about 1,600 Scottish lawyers studied at Leyden alone. Stair

---

[61] See further Lehmann, *John Millar of Glasgow*; and " John Millar " (1961) 6 J.R.(N.S.) 218.

[62] See Macmillan, " The Old Scots Conveyancers " (1898–99) 10 J.R. 425; 11 J.R. 41.

[63] *Remarkable Decisions*, 1716–28, continued later, 1730–52; *Select Decisions*, 1752–68 (pub. 1780); *Dictionary of the Decisions of the Court of Session* (completed by Woodhouselee, 4 vols., 1741).

[64] Innes, *Scotch Legal Antiquities*, 10. On Kames see also Fraser Tytler's *Memoirs of the Life and Writings of Henry Home of Kames*; Brown, " Kames's Principles of Equity " (1903) 10 S.L.T. 94, 111, 127, 159, 173, 181; Brown, " A Master of Equity " (1904) 20 L.Q.R. 308; Brown, " Equity " (1914) 26 J.R. 338.

was there in exile from 1682 to 1688 [65]; Lord President Forbes studied there and Lord President Dundas at Utrecht. Most cogent evidence of the link can be seen in the older books of the Advocates' Library, founded in 1681, of which the great majority are Continental treatises, mostly from France, Holland and Northern Germany, but some drawn from further away. " From their sojourn in Holland the aspirants to practice in the Parliament House brought back with them not only the principles which they had imbibed from the masters of the Roman-Dutch law but also the treatises with which the law schools of the Dutch Universities were so prolific. No Scots lawyer's library was complete in those days which did not contain the works of Grotius, Vinnius, the Voets, Heineccius and other learned civilians. Collections of decisions of the Scottish judges were few and inaccessible, and the Court of Session, with its predilection for principle rather than precedent, heard many arguments, adorned with citations of the Roman law and its Dutch commentators." [66] Scots law has still, for this reason, an affinity with the Roman-Dutch law of South Africa.

V.—THE MODERN PERIOD

The keynotes of the period since the Napoleonic wars have been reform, the increasing volume and importance of public and especially administrative law, the growing bulk and complexity of statutory law, and the increase of English influence and the tendency to assimilate Scots law to English. Constitutionally it has been a period of constant reform and movement towards democracy.

The Movement for Reform

In 1792 the Society of Friends of the People was formed and branches spread over Scotland and England. The doctrines of liberty found ready acceptance. The government became alarmed and prosecutions were initiated. The first in Scotland was of Thomas Muir of Huntershill, a young advocate and champion of reform, who was unfairly tried and sentenced to transportation.[67] Further trials, public excitement and government fears continued but calm was restored by 1795. But the movement for reform continued and grew in strength.

After Waterloo there was a severe economic depression which gave rise to a spirit of unrest and the founding of revolutionary societies. Sedition was feared, especially in Glasgow, and a number of weavers

[65] On Stair's familiarity with Continental jurists, see Campbell, *The Structure of Stair's Institutions.*
[66] *Stewart* v. *L. M. S. Ry.,* 1943 S.C.(H.L.) 19, 38, *per* Lord Macmillan.
[67] Hume Brown, III, 381–382; Craik, *Century of Scottish History,* II, 149–154; Meikle, *Scotland and the French Revolution, passim.*

were tried in 1818 but general opinion had changed since Muir's trial and the prosecutions mostly failed.[68]

Discontent and agitation for reform continued throughout the 1820s; fruits of the movement were found in the reforms of the Court of Session in 1808 and 1825 and a measure of 1822 giving jurisdiction over burgh accounts to the Court of Exchequer.

The Scottish Reform Bill was passed in 1832 raising Scottish representation from 45 to 53, redistributing seats and extending the franchise, and the following year saw the reform of the burghs, putting an end to the self-election of the magistrates.[69]

Conflict between Church and State and the Disruption

The courts and the General Assembly of the Church came into sharp conflict in the 1830s. In 1834 the Assembly passed the Veto Act whereby the dissent of a majority of male heads of families was to prevent the presentation of a minister to a charge by the patron of the living. In 1835 the Presbytery rejected a presentee to the church of Auchterarder under the Veto Act. The Court of Session held [70] that the Veto Act (of Assembly) was contrary to the Patronage Act (of Parliament) of 1711 and this view was upheld by the House of Lords. The difficulties were also apparent in the Lethendy case [71] and the Strathbogie [72] and other cases, which resulted in the Assembly defying the court and the court interdicting the Assembly. The controversy continued; appeals to Parliament failed of effect and in 1843 a large body of ministers and laity seceded from the Church and formed the Free Church of Scotland.[73] Patronage was abolished in 1874 but the breach between the Church and the Free Church was healed only in 1929 and then not completely.

Central Government

In the second half of the nineteenth century criticism began to be directed against the system whereby the Lord Advocate under the loose control of the Home Secretary administered Scotland. This administration consisted very largely in the management of elections and the dispensing of patronage. It was brought to its peak of perfection by

[68] Craik, II, 284–291.
[69] Ibid., II, 365–371; Pryde, 192–196.
[70] Earl of Kinnoull v. Fergusson (1841) 3 D. 778; (1842) 1 Bell 662; (1843) 5 D. 1010.
[71] Clark v. Stirling (1839) 1 D. 955.
[72] Presbytery of Strathbogie (1839) 2 D. 258, 585, 1047, 1380; Edwards v. Cruickshank (1840) 3 D. 283; Presbytery of Strathbogie (1842) 4 D. 1298; Edwards v. Leith (1843) 15 Sc.Jur. 375.
[73] Hume Brown, III, 423–431; Pryde, 184–186; Taylor, " Church and State in Scotland " (1957) 2 J.R.(N.S.) 121, 125 et seq. See also Crabb Watt, John Inglis, 60–73; Craik, Century of Scottish History, Chap. 22; Grub, Ecclesiastical History of Scotland, IV, 203–235; Cunningham, Church History of Scotland, II, 450 et seq.; Burleigh, Church History of Scotland, 334.

Henry Dundas, later Viscount Melville, between 1783 and 1806. From 1827 till the creation of the Secretaryship for Scotland in 1885 the Home Secretary was the Minister nominally responsible though *ad hoc* bodies tended to be set up to exercise some administrative functions. Such were the Board of Supervision (for Poor Law) in 1845 and the Prison Commissioners in 1877.[74]

Under the third Reform Act (1884–85) Scotland for the first time was given her proper share of representatives according to population, with 72 members, while the grievance over the maladministration of Scottish affairs was to a small extent remedied by the creation of an under-secretaryship of Home Affairs, with Scotland as the special charge and only a year later was the office of Secretary for Scotland created.[75] About this time too the troubles in Ireland caused many of the Scottish Liberal members [76] to speculate on the need to review the terms of the Union and speak of devolution within the United Kingdom.[77] In 1894 a concession was made to the demand for devolution which from 1889 to 1895 underlay a perennial motion in favour of a separate parliament for Scotland by the establishment of the procedure whereby all Scottish members were included in a Scottish Grand Committee for the consideration of a Bill.[78] It was revived in 1907 as a concession to nationalist sentiment and became a standing committee, while in 1912 the House of Commons approved a resolution to grant equal treatment in the matter of devolution to Scotland and Ireland. Irish affairs, however, were more pressing.[79] Nationalist sentiment ran strongly in the years 1945–53, stimulated largely by the growth of centralised government in London and in part in consequence of this the Scottish Grand Committee was in 1948 granted power to discuss the estimates and given some real control of Scottish legislation, while in 1952 a Royal Commission was appointed to review the exercise of government in relation to Scotland.[80] So too in 1899 the Private Legislation Procedure (Scotland) Act took much Scottish Private Bill legislation from Parliament and transferred it to the Scottish Office to be dealt with by provisional orders.

The tendency of the twentieth century has been to increase the direct responsibility of the Secretary of State for Scottish administration and to bring under his control matters formerly entrusted to distinct Boards

---

[74] See the tracing of the development of the office of Secretary of State for Scotland in Milne, *The Scottish Office*, Chap. 2.
[75] On this see further Mure Mackenzie, *Scotland in Modern Times*, 267–269. A list of the holders of the office can be found in Milne, *The Scottish Office*, 216.
[76] The Liberals consistently held most of the Scottish seats from 1833 to 1900.
[77] Rait and Pryde, 121; Mure Mackenzie, 270.
[78] *Ibid.*, 124; Mure Mackenzie, 273–275.
[79] *Ibid.*, 127, and see p. 128 as to the Government of Scotland Bill sought to be introduced in 1913 and 1914, and p. 133 as to home rule bills between 1919 and 1927. See also Mure Mackenzie, 392–398.
[80] Report: Cmd. 9212/1954.

and Commissions. There has also been an increasing and salutary tendency to assign to the Scottish Secretary matters on which there is a
distinctive tradition or body of law or pattern of administration, or where
Scottish conditions are notably different from those in England and Wales.

The Reorganisation of Offices (Scotland) Act, 1939, brought together
the several Scottish Departments which had formerly existed under the
control of the Secretary of State for Scotland and these now became
branches of the Scottish Office, having their principal home in Edinburgh
and a liaison office in London. They are the Scottish Home and Health
Department dealing with prison and Borstal services, police, fire and
civil defence, public order and safety, national health, welfare services,
fisheries administration; the Department of Agriculture for Scotland
which supervises the Agricultural Executive Committees and deals with
agriculture, forestry and drainage; the Scottish Education Department
responsible for training colleges and schools and guiding the thirty-five
local education authorities; and the Scottish Development Department
whose responsibility extends to local government, rating, electricity, roads,
housing, town and country planning and economic development.[81]

In 1951 the group of Ministers responsible for Scottish affairs was
increased by the appointment of a Minister of State, Scottish Office, and
a third Under-Secretary of State which, with the Lord Advocate and
Solicitor-General, bring up to seven the group in the government available
for the direction of Scottish affairs. The salient defect which remains
is that all these are primarily politicians, members of a United Kingdom
party, and Scottish requirements and interests have to conform to national
ones, while legislation is made when London wishes it, too frequently
to a pattern settled in London, and discussed in an assembly dominated
by party political considerations in which seven-eighths of the members
have little knowledge of or interest in Scotland.

Local Government
The reform of local government [82] began with the Acts of 1833 whereby
the magistrates and town councils of the sixty-six royal and thirteen
parliamentary burghs were to be elected by the £10 householders.

A whole series of statutes authorised royal burghs and burghs of
barony (1833), parliamentary burghs (1847) and other populous places
(1850, 1862) to adopt a uniform code of " police," covering watching,
lighting, paving, cleansing and water supply, and thereby to become
" police burghs." In the police burgh authority was entrusted to police

---

[81] Till 1962 the departments were Scottish Home Department, Department of
Health, Department of Agriculture and Scottish Education Department; as to
these see Milne, *The Scottish Office, passim.*
[82] See generally Pryde, *op.cit.,* 188–190, and " Burghal Administration," in McLarty
(ed.) *Source Book of Administrative Law,* Chap. 1.

magistrates and police commissioners who might or might not be the same as the bailies and councillors and this dual administration lasted to the end of the nineteenth century. Minor reforms included the abrogation of the exclusive rights of guildry and craft and burgess-ship, the abolition of petty customs, transfer to the county council of the duty of maintaining a police force, and authority to appoint a stipendiary magistrate.

This trend culminated in the Burgh Police (Scotland) Acts, 1892 and 1903, and the Town Councils (Scotland) Act, 1900, under which over two hundred towns administer their own machinery for preserving order, health and good government.

In the counties [83] a regular, paid police force made its appearance under Acts of 1839 and 1857, its administration being entrusted to the commissioners of supply.[84] The justices of the peace also had administrative functions, particularly in connection with roads and bridges.

In 1845 parochial boards were established to take over administration of the poor law; they were composed of elected members, kirk session delegates, heritors and burgh magistrates. The whole of Scotland was supervised by a Board of Supervision of nine members. These parochial boards were given further duties later, in connection with registration (1854) and public health and water supply (1867).[85]

In 1853 the Forbes Mackenzie Act commenced the system of licensing of public-houses, while 1854 saw the introduction of compulsory registration of births, deaths and marriages, and in 1872 popularly elected school boards were set up in each burgh and parish with power to levy a local rate for education and to compel attendance up to the age of thirteen.[86]

In 1878 county road trustees assumed responsibility for all roads and bridges, superseding the older statute-labour roads and turnpike trusts.[87]

In 1889 a substantial reform of local government was effected by the establishment of comprehensive authorities in the shape of popularly elected county councils.[88] They took over the functions of commissioners of supply, justices of the peace and county road trustees, administered the police in smaller burghs and public health services. They were authorised to levy a consolidated rate in place of the former separate assessments. In the larger shires district committees were to act as their agents in matters of roads and public health. As regards police and capital

---

[83] On the counties see Slevin, "Rural Administration," in McLarty (ed.) *Source Book of Administrative Law*, Chap. 2.
[84] Rait and Pryde, 180.
[85] Slevin, "Rural Administration," in McLarty (ed.) *Source Book of Administrative Law*, Chap. 2; Ferguson, *Dawn of Scottish Social Welfare*, Chap. 8.
[86] Rait and Pryde, 181.
[87] Rait and Pryde, 181; Pryde, *op. cit.*, 207.
[88] Rait and Pryde, 123–124.

works the final say was given to the standing joint committee composed of seven county councillors and seven commissioners of supply with the sheriff as chairman.[89]

In 1894 popularly elected parish councils were set up in lieu of the old parochial boards and charged with the administration of poor relief and all local matters, with a Local Government Board to co-ordinate their activities.[90] District committees composed of county councillors for the district, and one parish councillor from each parish and from any burgh within the district formed a link between county and parish.[91]

The Local Government (Scotland) Act, 1929, recast the whole system, sweeping away the older and *ad hoc* authorities, and substituting county, town and district councils to which all powers and functions were entrusted. This pattern was amended only in detail in 1947. Burghs were divided into three categories, counties of cities, a small number of large burghs and a larger number of small burghs. The Act provided an admirable scheme but it has been found in practice to remove most power to the larger authorities and to increase reliance on the central government, a tendency visible in other fields of administration also. Various functions have since 1945 been transferred from local to national organisations and dependence on the Exchequer for money is heavy, which tends to effect also a transfer of control.

Special Authorities

In the Highlands high rents and ejections among the crofters produced much bad feeling and hardship and some outbursts of violence when in 1886 the Crofters' Holdings Act sought to fix fair rents, guarantee security of tenure, enlarge existing holdings and allow compensation for improvements. The Crofters Commission was appointed with executive and judicial functions and toured the northern counties seeking to settle disputes and alleviate difficulties.[92] In 1897 a Congested Districts Board was set up for the settlement of land scheduled as suitable for new holdings and small farms. In 1911 its work was passed to the Board of Agriculture and in 1912 the Crofters Commission gave place to the Scottish Land Court.[93] In 1955, however, a new Crofters Commission was appointed charged with the reorganisation, development and regulation of crofting in the crofting counties.[94]

The House of Lords and Scots Appeals

In the first half of the nineteenth century the reputation of the House of Lords as an appeal court from Scotland, never high, touched its nadir.[95]

[89] *Ibid.*, 181; Slevin, *loc. cit.*, 17–19.
[90] Rait and Pryde, 124.
[91] *Ibid.*, 181; Slevin, *loc. cit.* 17–19.
[92] Rait and Pryde, 124; Mure Mackenzie, 294.
[93] Mure Mackenzie, 294–295.
[94] Laird, in *Source Book of Administrative Law*, 90–91.
[95] See Gibb, *Law from Over the Border*, Chap. 3.

Some Lord Chancellors frankly confessed their ignorance of Scots law on the matter under appeal, others merely showed it in their judgments, which frequently reversed the Court of Session, while judgments were regularly and normally thought and sometimes spoken in terms of English law and not even translated into the terms of art of Scots law. It is not surprising that decisions of the Lords continued to be worthless as statements of Scots law and, so far as influential, to be seriously detrimental to the principles of Scots law. Repeatedly Lords, in complete ignorance of the principles, asserted that the law of Scotland *must* be the same as the law of England.[96] An infamous example, which fastened on Scots law the wickedly unjust rule of common employment,[97] is *Bartonshill Coal Co.* v. *Reid* [98] where Lord Cranworth, having discussed the English cases, said: " But if such be the law of England on what ground can it be argued not to be the law of Scotland? " In cases of doubt moreover the Lords sometimes consulted the judges, but the *English* judges,[99] and this practice persisted in isolated cases as late as 1904.[1]

By 1866 the position had become intolerable. " For at least a century there had been intense dissatisfaction in Scotland with the constitution of the House of Lords as Court of Appeal. Scottish lawyers in particular felt aggrieved because they had to plead before a foreign tribunal which had to be instructed in the elements of their system . . . the House of Lords, as a bench of competent judges, had thus to a great degree lost the confidence of the profession in Scotland. Lawyers naturally thought the administration of Scots law in the court of last resort could not be entrusted to men who were conversant only with a foreign system, and who showed little or no consideration for the opinions of Scotch judges— at least not that deference accorded to them in the days of Mansfield and Erskine. There were other reasons for the discontent. In many cases—for example, the *Douglas*, the *Roxburghe* and the *Queensberry* cases—property to the value of half a million had been involved. These were great causes and attracted wide notice. But hundreds of others had stood in the same position as far as the feebleness of the House of Lords as the ultimate judicature, constituted without a Scotch judge, was concerned. It was esteemed a radical defect, as indefensible as absurd, that the judges knew little or nothing about the law they had to administer. Even the English members of the bench from time to time kicked against the pricks. Some of them, like Lord Redesdale, who officiated in the

---

96 Gibb, *op. cit.*, 57.
97 Abolished by statute in 1948; the rule was *not* previously part of Scots law.
98 (1858) 3 Macq. 266, 285.
99 *e.g.*, *Baillie* v. *Grant* (1832) 6 W. & S. 40.
1 In *Free Church of Scotland* v. *Overtoun* (1904) 7 F.(H.L.) 1: this appears from the *Memoirs of Lord Salvesen* (ed. Andorsen, 1949), pp. 66–67. Salvesen was one of the counsel in the case.

Queensberry cases (1819) openly confessed that they had to divest themselves of English prejudice before studying a Scotch case. . . . Scotch
lawyers have resented the interposition of an English mixture into the
solid body of their Roman system." [2]

Accordingly, so as to have someone in the House who knew something
about Scots law, and to be a counterpart in the Upper House as expositor
of Scottish measures to the Lord Advocate in the Commons, Lord
President McNeill was raised to the peerage as Lord Colonsay in 1866.

In 1873 the Judicature Act abolished the jurisdiction of the House of
Lords but this provision never came into force and in 1876 the Appellate
Jurisdiction Act provided for salaried Lords of Appeal in Ordinary with
life peerages. While this jurisdiction is still doubtfully satisfactory it is
at least less objectionable than before 1867.[3] At least since 1876 the
House has never lacked at least one Scottish Law Lord [4] though it is
still the case that Scottish appeals are decided by a tribunal all of whom
may be, and the majority of whom almost invariably are, English lawyers.

The consequence of this strange jurisdiction has been the introduction
of much English law into Scotland, much of it then or subsequently misunderstood, and the assimilation of much Scots law to English usually
to the detriment of the native rule. Opinions still differ as to the merits
of the practice of an appeal to Westminster and it is significant that the
Scottish criminal law, where no such appeal has ever been permitted, has
developed on quite satisfactory lines without the influence of appeal to
the Lords. Since the time of Watson, however, Scots law has at least
been represented by distinguished jurists in the House and contributed
something to its judgments.

The Superior Courts

The pattern of the Court of Session remained substantially unchanged
from its foundation till after 1800.[5] It remained a unitary court, sitting
and deliberating as a whole though two or three judges might at any time
be on duty in rotation in the Outer House acting as Lord Ordinary, dealing
with witnesses, oaths and the preliminary stages of actions, or in the Bill
Chamber authorising the initiation of exceptional forms of actions, but
such judges were delegates of the whole court rather than independent
judges. The system had, however, ceased to be satisfactory by the early
nineteenth century and the first third of the century saw a flood of reports

---

[2] Crabb Watt, *John Inglis*, 256–257.
[3] See modern cases discussed by Gibb, *op. cit.*, Chap. 4.
[4] The succession has been Lords Gordon, Watson, Robertson, Shaw of Dunfermline, Dunedin, Macmillan, Thankerton, Normand, Reid, Keith of Avonholm
and Guest, while other Scottish judges who were peers, such as Lords Kinnear
and Shand, have also sat occasionally.
[5] See generally Cooper, " The Central Courts after 1532 " in *Introduction to Scottish
Legal History*, Chap. 24.

of commissions and committees, pamphlets and memoranda urging change.

In 1808 the Inner House was divided into the First and Second Divisions, consisting respectively of the Lord President and seven Lords Ordinary, and the Lord Justice-Clerk and six Lords Ordinary. In 1810 the three junior judges of the First Division and the two junior judges of the Second Division became permanent Lords Ordinary sitting only in the Outer House. Further adjustment was necessary and in 1825 the court was settled on the basis of an Inner House of two Divisions, each of four judges (including the Lord President and Lord Justice-Clerk in the First and Second Divisions respectively) and an Outer House of seven Lords Ordinary. In 1830 the Outer House was allowed to diminish to five and the total to thirteen but in 1948 the traditional number of fifteen was again authorised and appointments in 1949 and 1954 completed the number. A sixteenth judge, authorised in 1956, was appointed in 1961, and two more were authorised in 1963.

An important change in procedure was made in 1850 by the Court of Session Act of that year.[6] Hitherto litigation had been conducted largely by written pleadings, learned and voluminous,[7] but thereafter it was incompetent to order " cases or minutes of debate or other written argument to be prepared by the parties." " These minutes of debate gave employment to scores of men who could not address a judge without blushing or stammering—honest, able worms that burrowed away their lives amid the parchment, the print, and the moths of Voet and Heineccius, of Stair and Erskine, of the Jus Feudale and the Pandects . . . from 1850 forward Vinnius and the Corpus Juris vanished into obscurity."[8] Written pleadings became much briefer and oral argument thereon became normal.

Even after the Act of 1850 reform of procedure was sadly required, for the mills of justice ground slowly. The Distribution of Business Act of 1856 gave some relief and the Court of Session Act of 1868, though attacked as anglicising, instituted an improved and expeditious procedure.

A factor which made for expedition was the change in the method of taking proofs. Down to the beginning of the century the depositions of witnesses were taken by the Lord Ordinary in his week of duty in the Outer House. They then resorted to the device of appointing commissioners to hear witnesses, write down the gist of their testimony and report, but neither commissioner nor judge reported on the import of the evidence or the credibility of the witnesses. This continued till 1866

---

[6] See further Maxwell in *Introduction* (Stair Society), Chap. 32.

[7] A specimen of this style at its best is Thomas Thomson's memorial on Old Extent, written for the case of *Cranstoun* v. *Gibson*, May 16, 1818, F.C., 511 and printed by the Stair Society in 1946.

[8] Crabb Watt, *John Inglis*, 54–55.

when it was provided that in all ordinary cases proof should be led before the Lord Ordinary but the success of the change was due largely to the adoption of the practice of having shorthand notes taken, which was first sanctioned by the Conjugal Rights Act of 1861. At first the judges dictated the evidence to the shorthand writer but this was later given over and shorthand notes became competent in all civil cases in 1866. Some judges, however, such as Inglis, always took the notes themselves.

In 1913 much of the mass of Acts of Sederunt regulating practice was consolidated into the Consolidating Act of Sederunt and this in turn was superseded in 1936 by Rules of Court made under the authority of the Administration of Justice (Scotland) Act, 1933. The principal excrescence on a reasonably simple and direct system of procedure was and is the persistence of civil jury trial, an expensive time-wasting alien imposition and an unsuitable mode of trial to boot, which was nevertheless recommended for retention in a restricted sphere by a departmental committee in 1961.[9]

The Admiralty Court

In the sixteenth century [10] the Court of Admiralty sat to exercise the judicial functions of the Admiral of Scotland and but for the opposition of the other courts would probably have captured most of the commercial litigation by reason of the suitability of its jurisdiction and procedure. It had jurisdiction in maritime causes, civil and criminal, over the whole of Scotland. It administered the customary law of the sea, particularly the Laws of Oleron. But the Court of Session and the Court of Justiciary were jealous of this rival and stole business from it despite attempts at parliamentary protection.[11] In 1825 the jurisdiction in prize was transferred to the English Court of Admiralty [12] and in 1828 a jurisdiction in criminal causes, cumulative with that of the Admiralty Court, was conferred on the Court of Justiciary. Finally in 1830 the civil jurisdiction of the Admiralty Court was transferred to the Court of Session and to the sheriffs and thereafter the criminal jurisdiction was merged in that of the Justiciary Court and of the sheriffs.

The Jury Court

The jury as a tribunal for determining disputed issues of fact in civil matters had vanished by the sixteenth century. In 1810, however, a Royal Commission suggested the introduction of civil juries on the English

---

9 Report of the Committee on Civil Jury Trial in Scotland (Cmnd. 851/1959).
10 See further *Acta Curiae Admirallatus Scotiae*, ed. Wade, Stair Society, Vol. 2; Baty, " The Judge Admiral of Scotland " (1916) 28 J.R. 144; McMillan, " The Scottish Court of Admiralty " (1922) 34 J.R. 38, 164.
11 Acts 1609, c. 22 and 1681, c. 82.
12 A violation of Art. XIX of the Treaty of Union.

model and in 1815 this was put into effect by the creation of a separate tribunal, first of three and later of five judges, entitled the " Lords Commissioners of the Jury Court in Civil Causes." [13] The Chief Commissioner was William Adam who, though a Scot, had practised only in England. This court had no original jurisdiction but acted only on remit from the Court of Session or Admiralty Court. The experiment never seems to have been much of a success and subsequent statutes limited the causes in which jury trial was requisite.

In 1830 the powers and duties of the Jury Court were transferred to the Court of Session and the court abolished. The Royal Commission of 1868 reported that the institution of civil jury trial had not given general satisfaction but it has nevertheless survived, despite constant criticism and the withering away of civil jury trial in England on the model of which it was established.[14]

The Court of Exchequer

This court was created in 1708 pursuant to the Treaty of Union and consisted of the High Treasurer of Great Britain,[15] a Chief Baron,[16] and four ordinary Barons[16] of Exchequer. The court sat in Edinburgh and was concerned mainly with questions of customs, excise, revenue and Crown debts. During the nineteenth century the functions of the court were curtailed by various statutes and in 1856 it was merged in the Court of Session. Revenue cases coming before the Court of Session continue, however, to be designated Exchequer causes.

The Commissary Courts

The Reformation left undischarged the functions formerly attaching to the courts of the Officials in each diocese by abolishing all jurisdiction depending on papal authority. In 1563 a new Commissary Court was created for Edinburgh and commissaries named for each diocese.[17] The chief court consisted of four with a jurisdiction over the bishopric of Edinburgh and a general jurisdiction over the whole of Scotland in matters of marriage, divorce, legitimacy, status and the moveable succession of

---

[13] For the reasons underlying the introduction of jury trial see Gibb, *Law from Over the Border*, 45 *et seq.*

[14] For criticisms see Sidgwick, *Elements of Politics*, 491 *et seq.*; Lord Cooper, " Trial by Jury in Scotland " in *Selected Papers*, pp. 58–70, and "The Scottish Legal Tradition," *ibid.*, pp. 172–200. As to England see Jackson, " Incidence of Jury Trial during the past Century " (1937) 1 M.L.R. 132, and " Jury Trial Today " (1938) 6 Camb.L.J. 367; Glanville Williams, *The Proof of Guilt*, Chap. 10.

[15] The office of Treasurer has been entrusted since 1714 to a commission consisting of the First Lord of the Treasury, the Chancellor of the Exchequer and the junior Lords of the Treasury.

[16] From Norman-French *baron*, a man; they were not in any sense peers.

[17] Donaldson, " The Church Courts " in *Introduction to Scottish Legal History*, Chap. 27.

Scottish subjects dying abroad or not subject to another jurisdiction. Down to the nineteenth century the commissaries nearly monopolised jurisdiction in actions affecting status and succession, both at first instance and on intermediate appeal, and despite the Reformation continued to develop the law largely in reliance on Continental jurists, canonists and civilians.

In 1823 the inferior commissaries became merged in the Sheriff Courts, though they were not formally abolished till 1876 and the name still survives in the designation of executry business as " commissary business," just as matrimonial causes are still designated " consistorial causes." The Commissary Court of Edinburgh was abolished in 1836, since when its functions have been performed by the common law courts.

The Teind Court

An Act of 1708 transferred to the Court of Session in the capacity of Commission for the Plantation of Kirks and Valuation of Teinds work relating to parish churches and manses, stipends and teinds previously entrusted to various *ad hoc* commissions. The court in this capacity continued to perform numerous administrative and judicial functions, both those of the older commissions and further duties imposed by later legislation. From 1839 the Lords Commissioners of Teinds comprised the judges of the Inner House together with the second junior Lord Ordinary, any five of whom, it was provided in 1868, should form a quorum. Most of the now much diminished work is today done by the second junior Lord Ordinary as Lord Ordinary on Teinds.

The Bill Chamber

The Bill Chamber originated in an Act of Sederunt of 1532 as a Vacation Court, but in addition acquired a special jurisdiction, granting leave to issue certain kinds of privileged summonses and to use certain kinds of diligence. Down to 1933 it retained control of the processes of suspension or suspension and interdict, and in the nineteenth century statute conferred on the Bill Chamber miscellaneous special jurisdictions, particularly in relation to bankruptcy, entails and judicial factories. The Bill Chamber was, during session, under the junior Lord Ordinary and had its own office and staff and a great deal of peculiar and detailed procedure. In 1933 it was merged with the Court of Session and its jurisdiction became ordinary Outer House jurisdiction.

The Legal Profession

The Faculty of Advocates maintained its position as a learned and influential society as well as one of the most honourable professional bodies; its ranks included not only the most distinguished lawyers but wits, scholars, politicians and men of letters.

The Faculty for long differed from the English Bar in having no formal differentiation between senior and junior [18]; a man " gave up writing " (pleadings) when of sufficient age and experience, but the absence of a distinct status placed the senior advocate in an invidious position when appearing before the House of Lords or meeting English counsel. In 1857–58 the problem of precedence was much discussed and was settled by according ex-law officers precedence postponed only to the Lord Advocate, the Dean of Faculty [19] and the Solicitor-General. In 1892 a petition craving Her Majesty to create a roll of Queen's Counsel in Scotland was granted, since when a formal distinction between senior and junior counsel has subsisted.

The status of the solicitors' profession was immensely promoted by the Law Agents Act of 1873 which for the first time demanded the passing of examinations as a requirement for admission to practice. The former requirement of apprenticeship continued and continues, but since 1873 a significant feature has been the steadily increasing number of apprentices who have graduated in one of the universities. Equally significant has been the increasing number of solicitors employed in local government and in industry.

In 1949 the Law Society of Scotland was established by statute, so that the profession had for the first time a national body including all solicitors. The former societies and the local bodies however continued. It acquired further statutory powers in 1958 and exercises a wide authority over the qualification and professional conduct of solicitors. It was set up partly to administer the legal aid scheme introduced in 1949, which is done through a central and a number of local committees.

Legal Literature—Hume and Bell

Since the early nineteenth century the greatest contributions to the literature of the law have come from the academic lawyers. David Hume (1756–1838), a nephew of the philosopher of the same name, Professor of Scots Law at Edinburgh from 1786 to 1822, published the *Commentaries on the Law of Scotland respecting Crimes* in 1797, a book which has always been accepted as of the highest authority on the subject. He also published a valuable volume of *Decisions* and his academic lectures were highly regarded and frequently cited. They have subsequently been published by the Stair Society.[20] Hume was promoted

---

[18] King's Counsel are known in English law from the sixteenth century; Bacon did much to define their position and secure their privileges.

[19] A list of the Deans of Faculty in the nineteenth century will be found in Crabb Watt, *John Inglis*, 111, and lists of Deans since 1698 and Vice-Deans since 1754 in 1958 S.L.T.(News) 241.

[20] ed. Paton, 6 vols., 1939–57.

a Baron of Exchequer in 1822. He had also been a Principal Clerk of Session contemporaneously with Sir Walter Scott.[21]

George Joseph Bell (1770–1843), his successor as Professor of Scots Law (1822–1843), took an active part in promoting improvements in Court of Session Procedure but made his name as a jurist with his *Commentaries on the Law of Scotland and on the Principles of Mercantile Jurisprudence*, which set out to systematise the principles of the law merchant and to reconcile them with the fundamental principles of Scots law, and the *Principles of the Law of Scotland*, published originally as a textbook for students, and later revised and enlarged. He contributed immensely not only to the exposition but to the creation of mercantile law and to the harmonisation of Scots law on the topic with the decisions of English and other courts. Bell became a Principal Clerk of Session in 1832 and Lord Advocate Jeffrey would have made him a judge had there been a vacancy. Bell's successor, John Schank More (1784–1861), Professor 1843–61, published the standard, modern, annotated edition of Stair in 1832. His *Lectures* were posthumously published.[22]

The Bench and Bar in the early nineteenth century continued the tradition of scholarship not confined to the law.[23] Francis Jeffrey was among the brilliant group who founded the *Edinburgh Review*, Henry Cockburn wrote those *Memorials* which are still the finest evocation of the Edinburgh of his young days, while Walter Scott wrote the *Waverley Novels* in the intervals of duty as Principal Clerk of Session and Sheriff-Depute of Selkirk. Thomas Thomson, as depute Clerk Register, laboured to organise and publish many of the invaluable public records, and through the Bannatyne Club published many more volumes of immense historical interest and value.

On the bench Lord President Inglis set out in classic judgments many principles of the steadily developing law while Lord McLaren wrote the standard book on *Wills and Succession* and Lord Fraser authoritative books on *Husband and Wife*, *Parent and Child*, and *Master and Servant*.

In the twentieth century Lord Dunedin [24] and Lord Cooper [25] were outstanding on the Bench while Professor Gloag's book on *Contract* won a high reputation for its breadth and grasp of principle. The foundation

---

[21] See further Paton's *Life of Hume*, in Vol. 6 of the Stair Society edition of the *Lectures*.   [22] Edited by McLaren, two volumes, 1864.

[23] It is noteworthy that the two greatest biographies in the English language, Boswell's *Life of Johnson*, and Lockhart's *Life of Scott*, were written by advocates. At the end of the century R. L. Stevenson was an advocate but did not practise.

[24] " Dunedin, the greatest master of the principles of Scots Law in our time ": *per* Lord Macmillan, *Stewart* v. *L. M. S. Ry.*, 1943 S.C.(H.L.) 19 at 38.

[25] See Smith, " The Contribution of Lord Cooper of Culross to the Law of Scotland " (1955) 67 J.R. 249 and in Lord Cooper's *Selected Papers*, xxix.

of the Stair Society in 1934 showed a quickening interest in Scottish legal history, while the Law Faculties of the Universities began to concern themselves as much with the theory, history, philosophy, analysis and criticism of law, and with its wider implications as with its dogmatic exposition and practical applications, and the foundation of the Scottish Universities Law Institute in 1960 marked the beginning of a major undertaking in restating Scots law in modern form.[26]

Developments in Private Law

The two factors which most influenced the development of Scots law since 1800 have been increasing statutory modification of common law doctrines and increasing reliance on English rather than Roman law as a source for borrowing.[27] Hardly any branch of common law has escaped statutory modification, while many topics of entirely statutory creation have developed. Most of these changes reflect changes in public opinion, in prevailing social, political and economic philosophy, and in conceptions of the functions and responsibilities of the state, or the changes wrought by two world wars, which necessitated an unparalleled amount of state control and interference with matters of private concern.[28] Industrial law and social welfare legislation[29] are both almost entirely modern statutory creations.

The nineteenth century was a great period for the formulation and working out of legal principles in cases and judicial decisions, and in many branches of the law the basic modern formulation of the principles is still to be found in nineteenth-century cases. In contrast the twentieth century since 1914 has been concerned increasingly with the interpretation of statutory provisions, and comparatively few common law decisions of really outstanding significance have been pronounced. *Donoghue* v. *Stevenson*[30] is undoubtedly the principal decision of the century to date with the most profound influence on the development of the law.

In nearly all branches of law references to the *Digest* and the civilians have come to be replaced by reference, usually uncritical and too frequently mistaken, to English law and English books.[31] Much unsuitable

---

[26] See 1961 S.L.T.(News) 97.

[27] See also *Introduction to Scottish Legal History*, 53–63.

[28] See generally Dicey, *Lectures on the Relation between Law and Public Opinion in England in the Nineteenth Century*; Ginsberg (ed.) *Law and Opinion in England in the Twentieth Century*; Friedmann, *Law in a Changing Society*; Walker, " Law and Opinion in Britain since 1900 " (1956) 1 J.R.(N.S.) 117, 213.

[29] See generally Ferguson, *Dawn of Scottish Social Welfare*; *Scottish Social Welfare*, 1864–1914; Marwick, *Economic Developments in Victorian Scotland*; Mackinnon, *Social and Industrial History of Scotland*; Hutchins and Harrison, *History of the Factory Acts*. [30] 1932 S.C.(H.L.) 31.

[31] See Henderson, " English Cases as Scots Authorities " (1900) 12 J.R. 304; Burn-Murdoch, " English Law in Scots Practice " (1908–9) 20 J.R. 346; 21 J.R. 59, 148.

or misunderstood law has thereby infiltrated into Scotland and warnings have been uttered from the Bench as to the dangers of ignorant use of non-native sources of law. Students, practitioners, judges and the House of Lords have all on various occasions been decoyed by the similarity of result attained by the two systems into saying that the principle is the same in both countries or into relying on English authorities or more up-to-date English textbooks.

Statute has effected numerous and far-reaching reforms, especially in property law. The fetters which bound entailed property and rendered it unsaleable and unburdenable with debt had subsisted since Sir George Mackenzie's Act of 1685, relieved only by the Act of 1746, which authorised the sale of entailed lands to the Crown for public purposes, and the Montgomery Act of 1770, which further authorised leasing, powers extended by the Rosebery Act of 1836. The Aberdeen Act of 1824 and the Rutherford Act of 1840 conferred wider powers on the heir of entail, the latter legalising under certain conditions the alienation of the estate. Acts of 1875 and 1882 led up to the Act of 1914 which prohibited the creation of future entails.

The feudal system of landholding was simplified and shortened by a series of Acts leading up to the Consolidation Act of 1868 while Gordon's Act of 1874 made further sweeping changes in the direction of simplifying land transfer, a process continued in the present century in 1924 and 1938.[32]

In the Highlands the proprietors in the late eighteenth and early nineteenth centuries transformed much of the interior of the West and North Highland counties into large sheep-farms, clearing out the crofters and settling them in crofting townships on patches of ground near the coast. When sheep-farming became less profitable owing to wool and mutton coming from Australia and New Zealand, large sheep-farms were turned into deer forests. Population had increased despite emigration but migration and depopulation followed the clearances and the ruin of the kelp industry. The middle years of the nineteenth century were years of great hardship and destitution. The government remedy was emigration, suggested by a commission in 1841: friction and unrest resulted, evictions for non-payment of rent were common and there were instances in the 1880s of violence, resistance to ejection measures and clashes with the police and the military. A Commission of Enquiry was set up in 1883 which resulted in the Crofters' Holdings Act of 1886 which conferred security of tenure on certain conditions, fixed fair rent, compensation for improvements and gave facilities for the enlargement

[32] See further Monteath in *Introduction* (Stair Society), Chap. 14.

of holdings. It set up the Crofters' Commission which performed executive and judicial functions until superseded by the Land Court under the Small Holders Act of 1911.[33] A new Crofters' Commission was set up in 1955 to reorganise and develop crofting in the crofting counties.

In the law of persons two of the common law forms of irregular marriage were abolished in 1939 and civil marriage introduced, while the grounds of divorce were widened in 1938 and this, combined with the disturbance to family life effected by the War and a changed social attitude to divorce, made divorce a common form of litigation. Many statutory changes ameliorated the position of the illegitimate child, while changes in guardianship made the welfare of the child the paramount consideration.[34]

During the nineteenth century contract increased in importance as commerce flourished. Towards the end of the century there were passed the Mercantile Law Amendment Act of 1856, designed to assimilate in large measure the laws of Scotland and of England in business matters and the forerunner of the Sale of Goods Act, 1893, and other pieces of partial codification, and the Bankruptcy Act of 1856, later superseded by the Act of 1913, and the Merchant Shipping Act, 1894.[35]

Conditions contributed very much to the development of the law of reparation. More settled conditions and greater willingness to abide the law reduced the number of cases of spuilzie and deliberate wrong-doing. At the same time increasing use of machinery and the coming of railways and later of road traffic brought more into prominence wrongs of negligence, particularly personal injuries, arising out of travel and industrial accidents. The increasing congestion of the roads similarly gave rise to the large number of traffic offences dealt with in the summary criminal courts.[36]

From early in the nineteenth century legislation strove to improve the position of factory workers and increasingly to make provision for their safety, health and welfare. The common law claim of an injured employee for damages for injury was reinforced by recognition of his claim for breach of statutory duty, and by his claims, independently of proof of fault on the employer's part, under the Employers' Liability Act, 1880, and subsequently to workmen's compensation (1897) and then to industrial injuries benefit (1946). Trade unions were recognised as lawful institutions and collective bargaining, conditions of work fixed by statute, arbitration or independent bodies largely replaced individual contracts of employment.[37]

---

[33] Mackinnon, *Social and Industrial History of Scotland from the Union*, 74.
[34] See further *Introduction* (Stair Society) Chaps. 8–11.
[35] *Ibid.*, Chap. 19.
[36] *Ibid.*, Chap. 20.
[37] See further Smith, in *Introduction* (Stair Society), Chap. 12, and " Master and Servant: Further Historical Outlines " (1958) 3 J.R.(N.S.) 215.

The great extension, enlargement and development of industrial enterprises in the nineteenth century made for conditions with which the private individual and the partnership could not cope. "After 1720, the foundation of joint-stock companies was controlled by the so-called ' Bubble Act ' of that year, a panic measure passed by Parliament as a direct consequence of the public scandal caused by the collapse of the South Sea Company. This law prohibited the formation of new joint-stock companies unless sanctioned by private Act of Parliament or Crown charter. The law stood unrepealed till 1825. It never affected the continuance of those aristocrats among the older public companies, the East India Company (founded in 1600) or the Hudson's Bay Company (founded in 1670), or the Bank of England. Long before it was repealed as the need for collective capital increased, the ingenuity of lawyers and business men got round the Act by promoting the formation of unincorporate joint-stock associations." [38]   This expedient allowed a considerable growth of company enterprise in certain fields such as insurance. But the old law of partnerships in an age of business instability and enterprise on larger scales frequently brought ruin owing to the absence of limitation on liability.[39] Partnership or unincorporated enterprise was manifestly unsuitable for the great investment in railways after 1840 [40]; it had the economic advantages of combined capital but the members' liability for the debts of the concern was unlimited as in partnership, and legal proceedings by or against the concern were apt to be intricate and laborious. In 1837 it was provided that the privilege of incorporation might be obtained not only by private Act or Crown charter but by letters patent and by the Registration Act of 1844 any company might register by a simple process and thereby become incorporated as a single entity in law. In 1856 limited liability was extended to all registered companies. A consolidating Act in 1862 extended the new facilities to insurance companies, and codified the law. Banks were for long excluded from limited liability and for long were also reluctant to take advantage of the privilege, and in consequence the failure of the joint-stock but unlimited City of Glasgow Bank in 1878 caused widespread ruin.[41] In 1879 the legal difficulties in the way of

---

[38] Court, *Concise Economic History of Britain from 1750*, 84; see also Brown, " The Genesis of Company Law in England and Scotland " (1901) 13 J.R. 185; Roberton Christie, " Company Law: Joint Stock Enterprise in Scotland before the Companies Acts " (1909) 21 J.R. 128.

[39] *Cf.* the ruin of Sir Walter Scott in the failure of Ballantyne's in 1825, and the cases arising out of the failure of the City of Glasgow Bank in 1878.

[40] On the development of Scottish railways see Mackinnon, *Social and Industrial History of Scotland from the Union*, 131–143; Pryde, 239–40.

[41] The directors were tried for fraud in the High Court and received various terms of imprisonment. The call on the shareholders of the bank was very heavy and this gave rise to much litigation in the next few years, mainly by shareholders

adoption by the banks of limited liability were removed. The law of companies has several times subsequently been consolidated afresh, each time incorporating new provisions designed to protect the investor from fraud, duplicity or misrepresentation.

Criminal law continued to develop with only small statutory interference, but methods of treatment and reformation of criminals were very largely altered in the twentieth century. Procedure was greatly rationalised by the Criminal Procedure Act of 1887 which greatly simplified indictments, a development extended to the summary criminal courts by the Summary Jurisdiction Act, 1907.

In the civil courts procedure was simplified by the Consolidating Act of Sederunt of 1913, itself superseded by the Rules of Court of 1936 (now 1948) while the Sheriff Courts Act of 1907 continued the same process for the sheriff court.

In the twentieth century conscious reform of the law has become increasingly recognised. The Statute Law Committee established in 1859 cleared away much dead wood from the statute book; this committee supervises the publication of the periodical editions of the Statutes Revised and the annual volumes of statutes and the indexes and tables thereto.[42]

In 1934 a Law Revision Committee was set up in England. After the War it was reconstituted in 1952 as the Law Reform Committee and a separate [English] Criminal Law Revision Committee in 1959. There is also a Private International Law Committee established in 1952. All these consider and report on topics of law referred to them for consideration.[43] In Scotland the Law Reform Committee for Scotland was established in 1954 and has done useful work in reporting on topics referred to it by the Lord Advocate; some of the reports have resulted in amending legislation.[44] There have also been numerous *ad hoc* committees on particular subjects, such as the Mackintosh Committee on the Law of Succession in Scotland.[45]

VI.—SOME FACTORS IN SCOTTISH LEGAL HISTORY

It is desirable finally to abstract some elements which have been powerful factors at different times in shaping Scottish legal history.

seeking to have their names removed from the list of shareholders, and thereby to escape contribution. See also Kerr, *History of Banking in Scotland*; Mackinnon, *Social and Industrial History*, 154.
[42] See also Carr, " The Statutes Revised " (1951) 67 L.Q.R. 482.
[43] See Winfield, " Law Reform " (1928) 44 L.Q.R. 289; Foster, " Law Revision " (1938) 2 M.L.R. 14; Wade, " The Machinery of Law Reform " (1961) 24 M.L.R.1; Hutton, " The Mechanics of Law Reform " (1961) 24 M.L.R. 18.
[44] *e.g.*, The Occupiers' Liability Act, 1960.
[45] Report, Cmd. 8144, 1951.

Feudal Law

The medieval feudal law which came from Normandy through England has been the source and is still the basis of the land law and of heritable property and succession.[46] In Scotland, particularly since the War of Independence, it has developed on its own lines and Scotland at once preserved a feudal system simpler and closer to the original than did England, and also avoided the complications imported into England by the premature rigidity of the common law, the consequent rise of equity and the growth of a dual system of legal and equitable interests in property.[47]

Canon Law

The pre-Reformation canon law of the Roman Church, in Scotland as elsewhere, has had a lasting influence on the law of the personal and domestic relations, marriage, separation and divorce, wills and succession. But the canon law has also had its influence on contract and on the form of deeds and writs.[48] In most branches, however, its influence is largely spent and the canonical principles have been overlaid by legislation and a native tradition of decisions. Nevertheless even in the twentieth century its force cannot be ignored and resort may still have to be had to the texts and commentaries thereon.

Roman Law

Roman law was profoundly influential in the times of the institutional writers and its force is not yet exhausted.[49] It has been a quarry of principles, terminology and examples, was accepted as decisive in countless cases, the traditional fundamental training in legal science, and a constant subject of study and source for principles to supplement indigenous doctrines. It was never " received " or adopted entire in Scotland as it

---

46 *Cf.* Farran, *Principles of Scots and English Land Law.*
47 See further Girvan, " Feudal Law " in *Sources and Literature of Scots Law* (Stair Society), 193.
48 In 1775 Lord Hailes said (*Maxwell* v. *Gordon,* Hailes' Decisions, 624) " The Canon Law is not the Law of Scotland, but the law of Scotland contains much of the Canon Law. This is so certain that, in many cases, we determine according to the Canon Law, without knowing it." On canon law influence see further Baird Smith, " Canon Law " in *Sources and Literature of Scots Law* (Stair Society), 183; Hermand's *Consistorial Decisions,* ed. Walton (Stair Society), *passim.*
49 See Goudy, *The Fate of Roman Law North and South of the Tweed,* 1894; Dove Wilson, " Historical Development of Scots Law " (1896) 8 Jur.Rev. 217; *idem,* " The Reception of Roman Law in Scotland " (1897) 9 Jur.Rev. 361; Miller, " Reception of Roman Law in Scotland " (1923) 35 J.R. 362; Baird Smith in *Sources and Literature of Scots Law* (Stair Society) 171; Campbell, " The Romanisation of Scottish Law " (1942) 22 Boston Univ.L.R. 581; Fisher, " Scotland and the Roman Law " (1947) 22 Tulane L.R. 13; Stein, " Influence of Roman Law on the Law of Scotland " (1957) 23 *Studia et Documenta Historiae et Juris,* 149; Smith, " Strange gods: The Crisis of Scots Law as a Civilian System " (1959) 4 J.R.(N.S.) 119.

was in Germany, but woven into the texture of the native law, and no statement of the law of Scotland can avoid reference to it. It is the basis of Scots law on pupils and minors, tutors and curators, moveable property, securities, servitudes, succession to moveables, contract, quasi-contract and delict. Since 1800, however, it has declined in importance and is not now a major force in development of the law. It would, however, be advantageous if there were more tendency today, in default of immediate authority, to look to the Roman law than to the English common law for guidance.

The Law Merchant

The law merchant was the embodiment of customs and usages established by general convenience and a common sense of justice for the carrying on of trade, gradually and continuously recognised, first locally and eventually internationally. The trading relations of Scotland with the Continent necessitated and stimulated the adoption of customary rules widely accepted abroad, and strengthened the legal connections with these principles common to Western Europe, to the countries of which, in consequence, Scots law in these branches shows close affinities.

The principles of mercantile law have always been to some extent international, having been developed by the trading intercourse of mercantile communities largely independently of their national systems of law.[50]

The origins of mercantile law probably go back to the commercial usages of ancient Sumeria which extended to Greece and Egypt, were adopted by the Phoenicians and spread to Greece, Carthage and Rome. In the Middle Ages these usages were continued and developed by the Arabs and the Italians and progressively incorporated into the legal systems of Western Europe. But for long at commercial towns and ports on the great natural highways the mercantile community had a measure of independence of the national law and disputes were decided by consuls or merchants in accordance with customs of great antiquity or according to one or other of the compilations of mercantile customs. In mercantile law accordingly more than in most other topics Scots law is like, and may draw on the books and decisions of, England and other foreign jurisdictions.

Bell wrote [51]: " The Law-merchant is universal. It is a part of the law of nations, grounded upon the principles of natural equity, as regulating the transactions of men who reside in different countries, and carry on

---

[50] See generally Bewes, *Romance of the Law Merchant*; Lord Murray " The Law Merchant " in *Sources and Literature of Scots Law* (Stair Society), 241 and for England, Holdsworth, *History of English Law*, V, 60; VIII, 99; XII, 524; *Select Cases concerning the Law Merchant* (Selden Society, 3 vols.).

[51] *Commentaries*, Preface. The whole preface is of interest and value.

the intercourse of nations, independently of the local customs and municipal laws of particular states. For the illustration of this law, the decisions of courts, and the writings of lawyers in different countries, are as the recorded evidence of the application of the general principle; not making the law but handing it down; not to be quoted as precedents, or as authorities to be implicitly followed, but to be taken as guides towards the establishment of the pure principles of general jurisprudence.

" This general Law-merchant is in England said to form part of the common law; . . . the English books afford valuable aid in cultivating the subject of Mercantile Law." Similarly in Scotland the institutional writers recognised that the principles were given effect to from the earliest times, and they are now recognised as part of the common law.

The development of commercial law in the last two centuries has been greatly stimulated by the industrial revolution and the development of Britain as a great commercial and trading community with commercial interests and connections all over the world. The courts steadily developed mercantile customs and incorporated them into the general body of law, but there was and is no distinct and self-contained body of commercial rules, as in some foreign codes and legal systems.

The Maritime Law

The general maritime law of Europe was also of a largely international character in the Middle Ages and was administered in local courts like the law merchant. Gradually the great maritime codes [52] were recognised as authoritative and much Roman principle came to be incorporated. Later the Court of Admiralty developed the principles as does its successor, the Court of Session. From the seventeenth century maritime law in Scotland and England developed on similar lines and in both it was absorbed into the general body of the common law and it is now common to the United Kingdom. [53]

English Law

Since 1800 English law has been a most powerful factor, not so often imported on its merits as taken over and applied by mistake, in ignorance, through reliance on English books or cases, frequently without appreciation of the subtle differences between the two systems of law, and by

---

[52] The most important of these were the Rhodian Sea-Law (*c.* A.D. 600–800, but originating a thousand years earlier) on which see Ashburner, *The Rhodian Sea-Law;* the Consolato del Mare of Barcelona (*c.* 1340); the Laws of Oleron (*c.* 12th century) of Guienne, and the Laws of Wisby of the Baltic and Hanseatic towns. The Laws of Oleron in particular influenced English customs. See also Bell, *Commentaries,* I, 546–551.

[53] McMillan " Admiralty and Maritime Law " in *Sources and Literature of Scots Law,* (Stair Society) 325; see also *Acta Curiae Admirallatus Scotiae* (ed. Wade) (Stair Society); *Select Pleas of the Court of Admiralty* (ed. Marsden, Selden Society, 2 vols).

subordination to a single Parliament often ignorant and careless of Scottish conditions, traditions and sentiment, composed of men sometimes more concerned with party than with country, and by the existence of an ultimate appeal in civil causes to a court composed as to a majority of English lawyers with no necessary knowledge of, qualification in, or sympathy with, the principles of Scots law. In most branches of public law, mercantile and industrial law, and delict, English influence has been powerful; its influence has been least in land law. No branch of law has escaped the influence of legislation, frequently imbued with an English spirit and cast in English models of terminology and procedure, albeit sometimes " translated " for Scotland, while too often Scottish appeals to the House of Lords have been judged from the standpoint of what English law would sanction. The warnings of Bell and some of the greatest Scottish judges against the promiscuous citation, acceptance and following of English authorities have constantly to be borne in mind, of the danger of spoiling Scots law by misunderstanding and misapplying English law.[54]

The Threat to the Scottish Legal Tradition

The greatest threat today to the Scottish legal tradition lies in Scotland, in the apathy and ignorance of Scotsmen, in their failure to study, cherish, conserve, restate and develop their traditional principles. Facile acceptance of English books and judgments, acceptance of English legal training as of value in Scotland, ignorance of everything but narrow practicalities, unwillingness and inability to search far back for a true principle consistent with the traditional development of the native law, have all militated against the vigorous survivance of Scots law. So too the growth in parliamentary powers and the ubiquity of legislation have accompanied a decline in the quality of Parliament and an interest in power, and in party and class advantage rather than in good legislation and government.

Scots law is in danger not least because it lacks a provincial legislature to effect the necessary amendments; its amendment and restatement is left to be fitted into, and more often left out of, the programme of a national legislature heavily overburdened with national, Commonwealth and international affairs and in any event little interested in Scotland and Scots law, and in which Scots law has little or no voice.

Beyond that the Scottish legal tradition is in danger, like so many other national and traditional institutions, from the modern tendency to amalgamate the smaller into and identify it with the larger, to prescribe from the centre a dead uniformity and to obliterate individual characteristics, to abolish the solid old for the flashy new, and from modern

---

[54] See Brodie-Innes, " Some Outstanding Differences between English and Scots Law " (1914–16) 26 J.R. 396; 27 J.R. 28, 175, 312; 28 J.R. 62.

ignorance of the value of the native law. Such tendencies spell the end
of what is left of Scotland's independent life and culture, her law included.
" The Scottish legal tradition is a thing to be prized both in Scotland and
beyond its borders, and the public of Scotland should be more conscious
of the fact. It is in a very real sense a typical product of the Scottish
ethos, and has attracted to its enthusiastic service some of the greatest
figures in our country's history. . . . The truth is that law is the reflection
of the spirit of a people, and so long as the Scots are conscious that they
are a people, they must preserve their law." [55]

FURTHER READING

The general histories of Tytler, Hill Burton, Hume Brown, Andrew Lang,
Agnes Mure Mackenzie and Dickinson and Pryde give the background. More
specifically legal are:
Atlay: *The Victorian Chancellors*, 2 vols.
Brunton and Haig: *Historical Account of the Senators of the College of Justice.*
Campbell: *Lives of the Lord Chancellors*, 10 vols.
Lord Campion (ed.): *British Government since 1918.*
Cockburn: *Life of Lord Jeffrey.*
   Memorials of his Time.
   Journal.
   Circuit Journeys.
Cooper (Lord): *Selected Papers.*
Cowan: *The Lord Chancellors of Scotland*, 2 vols.
Crabb Watt: *John Inglis.*
De Foe: *History of the Union between England and Scotland.*
Dicey and Rait: *Thoughts on the Union between England and Scotland.*
Dove Wilson: " Historical Development of Scots Law " (1896) 8 J.R. 217.
   " Reception of Roman Law in Scotland " (1897) 9 J.R. 361.
Ferguson: *Dawn of Scottish Social Welfare.*
   Scottish Social Welfare, 1864–1914.
Fisher: " Scotland and the Roman Law " (1947) 22 Tulane L.R. 13.
Forbes Gray: *Some Old Scots Judges.*
Fraser Tytler: *Memoirs of the Life and Writings of Henry Home of Kames*, 2 vols.
Gibb: " Interrelation of the Legal Systems of Scotland and England " (1937)
   53 L.Q.R. 61.
Goudy: *Fate of Roman Law North and South of the Tweed*, 1894.
Grant: *The Faculty of Advocates in Scotland*, 1532–1943 (Sc. Record Society).
Hannay: *The College of Justice.*
   Early History of the Scottish Signet, in revised *History of the Society
   of Writers to H.M. Signet.*
Howden: "History of the Scottish Constitution" (1898–9) 10 J.R. 64; 11 J.R. 209.
Hume Brown: *Union of England and Scotland.*
Innes: *Scotch Legal Antiquities.*
   Scotland in the Middle Ages.
   Sketches of Early Scotch History.

[55] Cooper, " Scottish Legal Tradition," in *Selected Papers*, 197–198, 199.

Kames: *Historical Law Tracts.*
Keir: *Constitutional History of Modern Britain since 1485.*
Lang: *Sir George Mackenzie of Rosehaugh.*
Mackay: *Memoir of Sir James Dalrymple, First Viscount Stair.*
Mackinnon: *Union of England and Scotland.*
          Constitutional History of Scotland.
          Social and Industrial History of Scotland from the Union.
McLarty (ed.): *Source-book and History of Administrative Law in Scotland.*
Maidment: *Court of Session Garland.*
Marshall: *Sir Walter Scott and Scots Law.*
Menary: *Life and Letters of Duncan Forbes of Culloden.*
Milne: *The Scottish Office.*
Mitchell: " Royal Prerogative in Modern Scots Law " [1957] Pub.L. 304.
Murray: *Early Burgh Organisation in Scotland,* 2 vols.
          Legal Practice in Ayr and the West of Scotland.
Neilson: *Trial by Combat.*
Omond: *The Lord Advocates of Scotland,* 3 vols.
Pitcairn: *Scottish Criminal Trials,* 1488–1625, 3 vols.
Pryde: *The Treaty of Union.*
Rait: *The Parliaments of Scotland.*
Rait and Pryde: *Scotland.*
Riddell: *Inquiry into the Law and Practice in Scottish Peerages,* 2 vols.
Scott-Moncrieff: *Record of the Proceedings of the Justiciary Court,* 1661–78,
          2 vols.
Seton: *Memoir of Chancellor Seton.*
Speirs: " Catalogue of Senators of the College of Justice, 1834–1957," in 1958
          S.L.T. (News) 241.
Stair Society: *Sources and Literature of Scots Law.*
          Introduction to Scottish Legal History.
Terry: *The Scottish Parliament,* 1603–1707.
W.S. Society: *History of the Society of Writers to Her Majesty's Signet.*
Wight: *Inquiry into the Rise and Progress of Parliament, chiefly in Scotland.*

See also publications of the Stair Society, Scottish History Society, Scottish Burgh Records Society, Scottish Text Society, Maitland, Bannatyne and Spalding Clubs, Proceedings of the Society of Antiquaries in Scotland, and of local antiquarian and historical societies, and articles in periodicals, particularly the *Juridical Review* and *Scottish Historical Review.*

CHAPTER 4

THE SYSTEMATIC STRUCTURE OF THE LAW

IT conduces to convenience and economy of statement, effectiveness of study and completeness of understanding of legal science to divide up the whole body of legal science into a number of fairly distinct subjects and branches.[1] No division of the subject-matter of legal studies is wholly satisfactory [2] and however it be done, some topics are difficult to classify while others again fall logically into more than one class. There is necessarily overlapping at the edges in any such classification but this is no bad thing since it emphasises that the whole of legal knowledge is ultimately a unity which in turn has very indefinite frontiers with other fields of knowledge. Moreover legal controversies not infrequently involve issues pertaining to several of the branches so that the convenience of such a division should not be allowed to lead to mental compartmentation. To decide that a particular controversy or problem pertains to the law of persons does not mean that problems of evidence and international law may not also be involved. Proper classification of legal problems may also be of practical importance with regard both to finding the law, and correct application of the rules.

The fundamental division of legal science is into (a) background subjects, some of which are, at least in part, not peculiar to any system of law but common to legal science as developed and studied in any country; (b) international law, or the body of law existing as between independent sovereign states and political communities; (c) supranational law, or the law of regional organisations; and (d) the various bodies of state or national law operating within these various states and communities and within the provinces thereof which have distinct legal systems, differing from each other in greater or less extent. Each of these heads may be further subdivided into distinct branches of study.

Since there are numerous distinct and independent political communities in the world each having and enforcing its own legal system or systems it is unfortunately true that legal science is not a unified body of

---

[1] The student should observe that the division into subjects does not necessarily correspond in number, name or scope with the subjects of a university degree curriculum.

[2] For other divisions see Salmond, *Jurisprudence*, Appx. III; Keeton, *Elementary Principles of Jurisprudence*, Chap. 17; Markby, *Elements of Law*, Chap. 7. Erskine, I, 1, 7, divides law into the law of nature (*i.e.* roughly jurisprudence), the law of nations (*i.e.*, international law), and civil or municipal law. So too Mackenzie, *Inst.*, I, 1, 3.

knowledge like medical or engineering science which, learned in one country, is valid everywhere. While there are affinities between various legal systems there is a greater or lesser measure of distinctness so that one state's legal system differs from every other at least in details and sometimes in fundamentals too. For practical purposes accordingly students of law must confine themselves to an intimate knowledge of one or two systems of law with, at most, a general knowledge of some others, and an understanding of those elements of legal thought common to many, if not all, actual systems of law, and of the international law which holds as between the distinct political communities themselves.

I.—THE GROUP OF BACKGROUND SUBJECTS

This group includes a number of subjects of great interest and importance, though their immediate practical relevance may not always be obvious, which have in common that they relate to the sources, development and foreign relations of law rather than to its dogmatic content. Their importance consists in examining and showing the origins, bases and development of rules and principles of law, in seeking the justification and true reason of the rules, in analysing the terms, ideas and presuppositions of the rules, in bringing out anomalies and difficulties by comparison with other systems of law, and in seeking out the ultimate aims and purposes of the legal system.

Some of these topics are peculiar in parts to a particular state and system of law, such as legal history, though this has wider and more general importance in so far as it deals with the influence of foreign law and of borrowing and imitation therefrom, or elucidates common origins or elements in diverse systems, while others, particularly jurisprudence, are common to all legal systems though the precise scope of the study, the problems examined, and the answers favoured, tend to vary from one country and legal system to another.

JURISPRUDENCE OR LEGAL THEORY AND PHILOSOPHY

The topic of jurisprudence [3] is variously defined as the " examination of the precepts, ideals and techniques of the law in the light derived from present knowledge in disciplines other than the law " [4] or " the body of theories of and about law," [5] " the study and systematic arrangement of the general principles of law in its widest sense," [6] " the science of the

---

[3] On the meaning of the word itself see Campbell, " A Note on The Word Jurisprudence " (1943) 58 L.Q.R. 334.
[4] Stone, *Province and Function of Law*, 25.
[5] Patterson, *Jurisprudence: Men and Ideas of the Law*, 1.
[6] Keeton, *Elementary Principles of Jurisprudence*, 4.

first principles of the civil law . . . those more fundamental conceptions and principles which serve as the basis of the concrete details of the law." [7]

It is concerned with such problems as the nature of law, its historical origins and development from primitive times, its relationship with theories of morality and of the state, the sources of the law and their interpretation, the relation between law and justice and the manner in which law maintains justice, the examination of the judicial process and the elucidation of the meaning, significance and use of such fundamental legal conceptions as the terms right, duty, obligation, ownership, possession, malice, intention, motive, liability and so on, but different jurists at different times have approached these and kindred problems from very different angles and have evolved very different and contradictory theories. The one general element in all jurisprudence is the attempt to analyse and discover the general principles and theory underlying various sets of actual rules of law. [8]

The literature of jurisprudence is enormous, frequently voluminous and obscure and in every language, while its pursuit frequently draws heavily on disciplines, such as logic, philosophy and psychology, sociology and political theory, relatively unfamiliar to the legal student but which help to cast light on central problems of legal studies.

Furthermore, the approach of different jurists and different books is very diverse, [9] some dealing in a most abstract way with the most general notions and problems, and having little apparent connection with the legal system applied in any country, while others deal almost exclusively with specific systems of law to such an extent as to be in many respects little more than generalised accounts of that legal system, examining general notions entirely in the light of one particular system of law.

Broadly speaking there are three main schools of jurists, or approaches to jurisprudence [10]; the first, the oldest and most voluminous, is philosophical jurisprudence.[11]   It deals with such topics as the concept of justice, and its relations with law; the distinction, if any, between the spheres of law, morality and other factors of social control; the ethical significance and validity of fundamental legal conceptions and principles;

---

[7] Salmond, *Jurisprudence*, 2. See further Allen, " Jurisprudence—What and Why," in *Legal Duties*, 1; Pound, *Jurisprudence*, I, Chap. 1.

[8] It is sometimes denied that any principles can be discovered at all: see, *e.g.*, Harvey, " A Job for Jurisprudence " (1944) 7 M.L.R. 42, and the reply, Kennedy " Another Job for Jurisprudence " (1945) 8 M.L.R. 21.

[9] See Vinogradoff, " The Study of Jurisprudence," in *Collected Papers*, II, 205, and " Aims and Methods of Jurisprudence," *ibid.*, 319; Allen, " Jurisprudence— What and Why," in *Legal Duties*, 1.

[10] Stone, *Province and Function of Law*, Chap. 1, pp. 182–187.

[11] Some leading figures of this school are St. Thomas Aquinas, Grotius, Bentham, Kant, Hegel, Jhering, Lorimer, Stammler, del Vecchio, Geny, Duguit.

the criticism of legal institutions and problems of legal reform. This approach has been favoured more on the Continent than in Britain and frequently by scholars who were philosophers primarily rather than jurists, whose theories of law reflect their philosophical positions.

The second is analytical jurisprudence, which has found greatest favour in the English-speaking countries.[12] It has been profoundly influenced by its founder John Austin,[13] and since his time analytical jurisprudence has usually been regarded in English-speaking countries as the main topic of juristic speculation. It proceeds mainly by seeking to resolve a legal system into its fundamental conceptions, such as rights, obligation, possession, and subjecting these to close examination. Accordingly it rests largely on logic and semantics. But disregard of the moral and social implications of law tends to reduce purely analytical jurisprudence to arid formalism so that it cannot usefully be pursued alone and the later followers of Austin have not avoided all questions of the rightness of law and its relation to justice.

The third is sociological jurisprudence, which has been developed very largely in America in the present century.[14] It studies particularly the interaction between social forces and the law, and the ways in which law works and gives effect to the different claims, interests, rights and duties of men interacting in society. This school of jurisprudence has to a large extent superseded and taken over from the nineteenth-century school of historical jurisprudence[15] which was primarily concerned with the manner of growth of legal systems, their evolution and organic development, and the evaluation of the various sources and influences which had contributed to their forms and characteristics.[16]

The importance of jurisprudence cannot be overestimated. It is the fundamental branch of legal study, though too frequently it receives inadequate attention, and legal study generally pays too much attention to dogmatic rules of law. " This neglect of legal theory and philosophy, added to a concentration on the substantive rules of law, must inevitably lead to a failure by the general body of lawyers, to appreciate not only the nature and purpose of law but also the place of law among the other social sciences.

[12] Leading figures include Austin, Markby, Holland, Salmond.

[13] 1790–1859: Professor of Jurisprudence at University College, London, 1826–32; *The Province of Jurisprudence Determined* was first published in 1832. On Austin see further the article in D.N.B., Vol. II, by Sir John Macdonell; Sarah Austin's Memoir in fifth edition of his *Lectures on Jurisprudence*, and the Introduction to the 1954 edition of the *Province* (ed. Hart) in the Library of Ideas.

[14] Leading figures are Pound, Frank, Llewellyn and Stone.

[15] Some writers treat the historical school as a distinct, fourth, school of jurisprudence.

[16] See further Kantorowicz, " Savigny and the Historical School of Law " (1938) 53 L.Q.R. 326. Leading figures are Savigny, Puchta, Maine, Bryce and Vinogradoff.

" We have entered upon a period of profound social and legal adjustments—particularly in the department of social legislation. Yet the general body of English lawyers is wholly untrained in legal science." [17]

It is true that law is a practical matter, but " the law is not identical with the science of the law. Every science is essentially theory; at the very basis of every action, however practical, is always theory, and no science is possible without philosophy." [18] " Philosophy of law lies at the base of all divisions of legal science." [19]

LEGAL HISTORY

Legal history differs from Historical Jurisprudence in that the former, unlike the latter, seeks simply to follow out, record, explain and understand the changes and developments which have taken place in the evolution of each particular system of law, to discover the causes of the specific changes which have taken place and to disclose the historical origins, bases and justifications of modern rules. It follows that there is a body of historical knowledge relative to every distinct system of law, though in the earlier periods one system tends to resemble and overlap other related systems,[20] and the influence of, and deliberate borrowing from, other systems are factors always to be kept in mind. Historical jurisprudence, on the other hand, studies the origins and development of legal institutions and ideas generally, of law as a factor in human society.

Legal history necessarily overlaps with constitutional history though the latter subject is more particularly concerned with tracing the origins and development of governmental institutions, such as the legislative body, the superior executive body, the Council of Ministers or Cabinet and so on, which are matters of public law, while legal history is alone concerned with the development of rules of private law such as contract and succession. Both legal and constitutional history are concerned with such topics as the development of the courts and the rights of the subject, though even there a difference of emphasis is usually discernible, the one study being more concerned with the legal aspects and the other with the political aspects. So too legal history necessarily overlaps with social, political, religious and economic history since these studies

---

[17] Parry, " Economic Theories in English Case Law " (1932) 47 L.Q.R. 183, 186. Note that the terms legal science and science of law are sometimes used, as here, in the narrow sense of legal theory or jurisprudence. *Cf.* Friedmann, " Legal Theory and the Practical Lawyer " (1941) 5 M.L.R. 103.

[18] Kunz, " The American Science of International Law " in *Law: A Century of Progress,* II, 166 at 182.

[19] Kocourek, *An Introduction to the Science of Law,* 3.

[20] Thus in the period prior to the War of Independence Scottish legal development very much resembles that of England. So too all the European systems deriving from Roman law have marked affinities in the medieval period.

relate to and cast light on the background in which the legal system developed and frequently provide the explanation for purely legal changes. Law does not develop in a vacuum, sealed off from other facets of the development of the society it relates to; it is an integral part of society and changes with it.

The study of legal history necessarily depends on the discovery, examination and interpretation of records and archives and in most countries legal societies exist for the purpose of bringing to light, editing and publishing material from public and private collections of historical material [21] but diligent search and a discerning eye can find information of legal importance in every kind of historical material, charters, rent-rolls, taxation lists, memoirs, letters, parish registers and similar records. In Scotland the study of legal history has hitherto been inadequately pursued and a great deal of research still remains to be done.

CIVIL OR ROMAN LAW

The Civil or Roman law is in the first place the law of the ancient city of Rome and the Roman empire from the foundation of the city (traditionally 753 B.C.) to the fall of the Western empire in the fifth century A.D. and even thereafter till the fall of the Eastern empire with the capture of Constantinople by the Turks in 1453. The system really begins [22] with the adoption of the Laws of the Twelve Tables about 450 B.C. which established a system of law for Roman citizens only (*jus civile*) characterised by rigidity and formality.

In 242 B.C. the increase of foreigners at Rome made it necessary to appoint a special judge, the peregrine praetor, to deal with causes in which a foreigner was involved, and he and the urban praetor, who dealt with cases involving only citizens, both issued edicts defining the circumstances in which they would give particular remedies, and these edicts became important sources of new and revised law which came to be known as *jus praetorium* or *jus honorarium*. In the late republican period, from about 150 B.C. to 27 B.C., this was the chief reforming factor in Roman law. Also in this period the *jus gentium* came to be of importance; this was the body of law applicable equally to Roman citizens and to foreigners, a system based on common principles of the Mediterranean peoples with

---

[21] In Scotland the Stair Society exists for this purpose, but much legal material has been published by the Scottish History Society, the Scottish Text Society and the Scottish Burgh Records Society and by such older clubs as the Maitland and Bannatyne Clubs and the Spalding Club. In England the great legal-historical society is the Selden Society.

[22] For the history, see Muirhead, *Historical Introduction to the Private Law of Rome*, 3rd ed.; Jolowicz, *Historical Introduction to the Study of Roman Law*, 2nd ed. For the law, see Buckland, *Text-book of Roman Law from Augustus to Justinian*; Girard, *Manuel Élémentaire de droit romain*, 8th ed.

a strong Roman flavouring but free from formalistic elements, and it was later applied to Roman provincials also. It came to be connected with the theoretical idea of a law common to all peoples and dictated by nature, a notion taken over by the Romans from Greek philosophy.

In the early empire (27 B.C. to A.D. 100) legal literature developed [23] and the praetors' edicts tended to become fixed and carried on from year to year, as is evidenced by the growing practice of writing commentaries on the edict. In or about A.D. 131 the emperor Hadrian had the jurist Salvius Julianus revise and settle the edicts, which thereafter became fixed and alterable only by the emperor. The classical age of the law was reached in the second century and the first half of the third, considerably later than the classical age of Latin literature, and it is marked by extensive juristic writing and the detailed working out of principles. The great age was short and soon over: Papinian was killed in 212, Ulpian in 228, and Ulpian's pupil Modestinus was the last of the great jurists. By A.D. 300 jurisprudence was stricken with sterility. The most important work surviving in its original form from this period is the *Institutes* of Gaius, a student's textbook written about A.D. 161, which subsequently formed the basis of Justinian's *Institutes* and is of unique importance as evidence of the state of the law in the classical period.

While the law did not stand still there was a falling off in legal literature after 235; new ideas were introduced, especially from the East, while the law was also influenced by the growing importance of the eastern half of the empire with its capital at Constantinople. More and more law-making had become the function of the emperor, and in the third and later centuries attempts were made to collect the mass of imperial constitutions. Two unofficial collections are known, the *Codex Gregorianus* and the *Codex Hermogenianus*. They may have been made in the East, for the tendency was for the imperial centre to shift eastwards and Constantine in 326–328 removed the imperial court to Byzantium, now renamed Constantinople, while in the fourth century the seat of the Western government was removed first to Milan and then to Ravenna. In 438 the *Codex Theodosianus* was promulgated: it was an official collection of imperial statutes beginning with Constantine I, a collection rather than a code, but by the time it was issued the barbarians were already striking at the empire.[24]

Fall of the Western Empire

In the fourth and fifth centuries the encroachments of barbarian tribes on the empire increased and twice the empire was divided into

---

[23] On this see Schulz, *History of Roman Legal Science*.
[24] A valuable summary of the later days of the Roman empire is in *The European Inheritance*, I, 222–249. For fuller account, see *Cambridge Medieval History*, Vol. IV, esp. Chap. 21. See also Bryce's *Holy Roman Empire*, Chaps. II and III; Bury's *Invasion of Europe by the Barbarians*, passim.

East and West portions for ease of administration and defence. The weakness of successive Western emperors culminated in the capture and sack of Rome by the Visigoths under Alaric in 410. The Franks and Burgundians founded kingdoms in northern Gaul, the Visigoths in southern Gaul, while the Vandals passed through Spain and conquered North Africa. Rome was again sacked in 454, by the Vandals, and the empire in the West came to an end in 476 when the last puppet emperor was deposed. The Eastern half was, however, to stand for another thousand years until the Turks captured Constantinople in 1453. The two halves had never become completely unified or integrated and remained Greek and Latin though united politically. By the end of the fifth century Germanic kingdoms, superficially romanised, had been established all over Western Europe, Visigoths in south-west Gaul and Spain, Burgundians in south-east Gaul, Ostrogoths in Italy, Vandals in Africa. Rather later the Franks established themselves between the Rhine and the Somme, the Alemanni on the upper Rhine and Danube, the Bavarians on the Danube and in the Alps, the Angles, Jutes and Saxons in South Britain.

Roman Law in the West

The Western provinces of the former Roman Empire adhered to the former law summed up in the *Codex Theodosianus* of A.D. 438. There was legislation by the emperors down to that date, fragments of older legislation contained in the private collections known as the *Codex Gregorianus* and the *Codex Hermogenianus*, numerous *Novellae* of early fifth-century emperors and a great volume of older jurisprudence laid down in opinions and treatises going back to the classical age. The temporary reconquering of part of Italy by Justinian's troops in the sixth century had no legal or permanent consequences and his legislation was ineffective there. But other law was beginning; the barbarians had been writing down their customs and barbarian kings had begun to issue law-books for their Roman subjects while books of ecclesiastical law were also being compiled.

Roman law in the provinces had become a debased body of rules by the fifth century when many races of foreigners were within the Empire, and occupying posts of authority and importance in the civil and military administration. For such peoples in the provinces various state- ments of barbarised Roman law were prepared in the late fifth and early sixth centuries. The principal were the *Edictum Theodorici* for the Ostrogothic kingdom (*c.* A.D. 500), the *Lex Romana Burgundionum* (*c.* A.D. 500) and the *Lex Romana Visigothorum*, also known as the *Breviarium Alaricianum* (A.D. 506), of which the last became the standard source of Roman law in Western Europe during the first half of the Middle Ages. It was a more or less complete code for the use of the Roman populace in France and Spain, comprising the enactments of the later Empire with interpretations of the text designed to make the sense of the laws as clear as possible, and consisted of three main portions, an introductory survey for beginners, legal and jurisprudential doctrines laid down by authorities and a body of enactments by recent emperors.[25] But the most important event for the subsequent history and influence of Roman law happened in the East after the fall of the Western Empire.

Justinian

When Justinian became emperor at Constantinople in 527 he set out to collect, codify and reform the mass of law which had grown up over the centuries. His efforts resulted in the promulgation of (a) *The Old Codex*: a new collection of imperial constitutions superseding the older ones and including later legislation; (b) *The Fifty Decisions*: a collection of fifty constitutions settling matters of dispute and abolishing some institutions and distinctions no longer of practical importance; (c) *The Digest or Pandects*: a collection of excerpts from the works of jurists, amended and omitting obsolete or superfluous matter, arranged in fifty books according to subject-matter; the Digest preserved the writings of the classical jurists who were really responsible for the greatness of the Roman law; (d) *The Institutes*: this was a systematic new book for the elementary instruction of students based on Gaius' Institutes, and on other elementary works; (e) *The New Codex*: this was a revision of the Old Codex in the light of the Fifty Decisions and other later constitutions; (f) *The Novels* (Novellae Constitutiones) or later legislation. The Institutes, Digest, (new) Code and Novels together form the *Corpus Juris Civilis*.[26]

After Justinian's time Greek versions of parts of the *Corpus Juris* were made in the East and selections published modifying some of the enactments particularly to make the law more consonant with Christian principles. Under Leo the Wise (886–911) was prepared the *Basilica* [27] in which are fused, in sixty books, all the parts of Justinian's compilations, in Greek versions of the sixth and seventh centuries, with some changes. This remained the law of the Eastern Empire until the fall of Constantinople in 1453. There was some revival of legal studies in the

25 For a valuable comparison of the Breviary with Justinian's *Corpus Juris* see Vinogradoff, *Roman Law in Medieval Europe*, 2nd ed., 18–21, where he shows how much the Breviary evidences intellectual decay. See also Roby, " Roman Law," 2 *Camb.Med.Hist.*, Chap. 3.

26 The standard edition is the Berlin one edited by Krueger, Mommsen and Schoell in three volumes: The parts are cited by book, title, and paragraph or fragment: thus Inst. I, iii, 3; D. (or Dig.) IX, 2, 7, 1; C.I, xviii, 12; the *Novels* are cited by number, *e.g.*, Nov. 118.

27 See further Lawson, " The Basilica " (1931–32) 46 L.Q.R. 486; 47 L.Q.R. 536; Collinet, " Byzantine Legislation," *Camb.Med.Hist*, IV, Chap. 20.

eleventh century and later, and about 1345 the *Hexabiblos* was compiled at Thessalonica. This still had a measure of authority in Greece until the promulgation of the modern Civil Code in 1946.

The West after Justinian

Justinian's *Corpus Juris* was long accepted and even known only in the East and in parts of Italy. The *Breviarium Alaricianum* still comprised the Roman law for the West and legal knowledge decayed seriously in the Dark Ages. The *Lex Romana Curiensis* of the late eighth century, a statement of legal custom for the population of Eastern Switzerland, and used also in the Tyrol and Northern Italy, testifies to even greater decadence and is little more than custom flavoured by Roman law.

In the Dark Ages and early Middle Ages law was essentially personal and local rather than territorial, since no state was strong enough to enforce a legal order or system of its own. Moreover the entry of Goths, Franks and Lombards into the former Roman provinces had not involved the disappearance of Roman inhabitants and their special legal status was allowed to continue and relations between them were governed by their own racial law. So, too, men of each nation, such as Burgundians or Bavarians or Salian Franks, lived under their own law, which raised difficulties when members of different nationalities wished to enter into legal transactions. This system of national laws gave rise to problems of conflict of laws.[28]

Moreover in most districts local customs arose to regulate the ordinary dealings of the people and these tended to take their colouring from the prevailing national majority and to modify any surviving traces of Roman law. Thus legal customs were built on a basis of Roman law in Southern Italy till the advent of the Saracens and Normans, where the Byzantine Empire still held sway, in the Romagna, and in Southern France and Northern Spain where the *Breviarium Alaricianum* was applied.[29]

In other districts, Northern France, Germany and England, the barbarian laws applied but Roman institutions and legal customs still had influence, particularly since the clergy still followed Roman law. Roman influence was strongest in the case of the Ostrogoths of Northern Italy and Austria and of the Visigoths of Spain and France who adopted Roman enactments wholesale quite apart from Imperial Roman law codified for Roman fellow-citizens.[30]

Legal learning did not, however, entirely disappear in these times and

---

[28] In a famous letter from Bishop Agobard of Lyons to Ludwig the Pious about 850 it is narrated that " It often occurs that five men walking or sitting together are each of them living under a different law," and it became customary for the parties to a deed or action to make an express declaration of which system they lived by.
[29] Vinogradoff, *op. cit.*, 28.
[30] *Op. cit.*, 30.

still survived in part and can be found in medieval salvage of the wreckage
of antiquity such as in Bishop Isidore of Seville's *Etymologiae* and in
clerical abstracts and glosses or explanations of older texts.[31]

The Corpus Juris in the West

In the West, Justinian's law was rediscovered in Italy in the eleventh
century.[32] The study centred on Bologna [33] where Irnerius began the
succession of Glossators,[34] or scholars who wrote glosses on the text,
settling its form, explaining it, resolving contradictions, deducing maxims
and discussing concrete cases, becoming in the end a commentary. The
men who administered local laws and customs were trained in the *Corpus
Juris* and its more civilised rules influenced the natural growth of the law
of developing communities. The *Summa* of Azo (*fl. c.* 1190) was an
indispensable text while the Gloss of Accursius (*ob. c.* 1260) was a standard
commentary on the text.

About 1300 there arose the school of Commentators [35] of whom the
greatest were Bartolus of Sassoferrato (1314–57) and his pupil Baldus
(1327–1400). They sought to make the Civil Law applicable to the
practice of their time, adapting it to living conditions, and to harmonise
it with the feudal, Germanic or canon laws then in force. They transformed it and made it living law but at the cost of casuistry, pedantry
and voluminous confusion. " The great achievement of the Commentators, the Post-Glossators, was in fact the transformation of the Roman
law into a medieval Italian law. They created a literature in Romano-
Italian law which not only possessed authority in Italy itself, but played
a role of great importance in the legal and political life of Europe as
a whole. Thus it was the living Romano-Italian law of the Commentators,
and not the pure Roman law of Justinian, which crossed the Alps into
Germany in the age of the Reception." [36]

During this period from 1100 to 1500 the Roman law became the
basis for legal science throughout Western Europe and its importance

---

[31] *Op. cit.*, 37–41; see also Jenks, *Law and Politics in the Middle Ages*, Chaps. 1, 2.
[32] The great authority on the later Roman law is Savigny's *Geschichte des Römischen
    Rechts im Mittelalter* (1822); see also *Continental Legal History Series*, Vol. I,
    for a general survey.
[33] Provence, Pavia and Ravenna were also early centres of the revival.
[34] See Vinogradoff, *Roman Law in Medieval Europe*, 2nd ed., Chap. 2; Hazeltine,
    " Roman and Canon Law in the Middle Ages," *Camb.Med.Hist.*, V, 697; Hazeltine,
    " Glossators," in *Encyc.Soc. Sciences*, VI, 679; Hazeltine, Introd. to Ullman,
    Medieval Idea of Law; Kantorowicz and Buckland, *Studies in the Glossators of
    the Roman Law.*
[35] See Hazeltine, " Commentators," in *Encyc.Soc. Sciences*, III, 679; Woolf,
    Bartolus of Sassoferrato.
[36] Hazeltine, Introd. to Ullman, *Medieva Idea of Law*, xix; see also Hazeltine, *Camb.
    Med.Hist.*, V, 697, and on the legal and political theories of the Glossators and
    Commentators, see Carlyle, *History of Medieval Political Theory in the West*,
    Vols. II and VI.

and influence spread rapidly. Moreover in this period great political and economic changes were taking place, towns were developing, commerce, trade, agriculture, fairs, and the older customary law, gradually elaborated to regulate the relations of men living by agriculture, became inadequate for a populace depending on industry and commerce. Roman law was looked to for its embodiment of the old Roman cultural ideal and as carrying an aura of the old Roman glory and unity, but particularly since it contained principles capable of solving many of the problems of the more cultivated society which was arising and of the developing trade and commerce. It made important contributions to the solution of specific problems and became the basis for much development.

The study spread [37] to France where in the south, the *pays du droit écrit*, it gradually superseded the older Roman law books as the law of the land, modified only by local custom. In northern France, the *pays du droit coûtumier*, it was mingled with the traditional customs in the thirteenth century, and it was freely used in Philippe de Beaumanoir's *Coûtumes de Beauvaisis* (*c.* 1280).

The third great school of Roman law studies is that of the Humanists, which rose following the decline of the Commentators about the beginning of the fifteenth century. They had a historical sense and began to try to reconstruct the classical law from the amended passages found in the Digest by detecting the interpolations made in the texts included in the *Corpus Juris* by the compilers. This movement was very strong in France and is represented by such jurists as Cujacius (Jacques Cujas, 1520–90), Donellus (Hugues Doneau, 1527–91) and Faber (Antoine Favre, 1557–1624), while Jacobus Gothefredus (Jacques Godefroy, 1587—1652) published a great edition of the Theodosian Code, with commentary. Rather later Pothier [38] in France published in 1748 his *Pandectae Justinianae in novum ordinem digestae*, recreating the correct order of the text, and on that foundation, wrote a series of treatises on aspects of French law, such as the *Traité des Obligations* (1761).

In Germany it began to oust the native tribal law in the later Middle Ages, facilitated by the theory of continuity of the Holy Roman Empire with the older Empire of the West,[39] and by the lack of political unity among the Germanic states. About the fourteenth century there took place the " Reception " in Germany of civil and canon law, which were widely studied in the universities. While in theory the *Corpus Juris* was accepted only as subsidiary and its rules to be applied if Germanic law were silent, in practice Germanic law was to a large extent superseded.

---

[37] On the extension see Munroe Smith, *Development of European Law*; *Continental Legal History Series*, Vol. I, General Survey; " Law," by Vinogradoff, le Bras and Meynial in *The Legacy of the Middle Ages*.
[38] On Pothier see Macdonell (ed.) *Great Jurists of the World*, 447.
[39] For an account of this see Bryce, *The Holy Roman Empire*.

The central Imperial court adopted Roman law for its guidance as the common law of the Empire in 1495 and it exercised considerable influence on the legal institutions of all the states of the Empire so that the " Reception " spread. Roman law remained a main source of Germanic law until the German Civil Code of 1900 and in the nineteenth century Savigny and his successors created an elaborate, highly systematic body of law (*Pandektenrecht*) on the basis of the *Corpus Juris*. So, too, until the promulgation of the Code Napoleon in 1804 the customs, particularly of Paris, influenced and supplemented by Roman law, constituted the law of France.[40] These codes in turn have been copied repeatedly in codes all over the world.

In Holland resort was had to the Roman law to supplement the in-adequacies of general and local customs and Roman law was " received " in all the provinces in varying degrees from the fifteenth to the seventeenth centuries; in Holland also there flourished many great jurists whose writings on law, particularly on Roman law, have been very important and influential.[41] The law of Holland was carried to South Africa by the early Dutch settlers there, though in Holland itself it was superseded by the French civil code during the Napoleonic wars. But in South Africa it took root, developed and survived as the Roman-Dutch law.

Roman law probably entered Scotland [42] initially through the church and the canon law but by the sixteenth century it had come frequently to be referred to in supplement of native customary or common law. Knowledge of Roman law was increased by the long association of Scotland with France and the works of the French jurists of the fifteenth and sixteenth centuries were well known to Scottish students who flooded to such universities as Bourges. Some doctrines of Roman law were introduced by legislation. In the seventeenth century the writings of French and Dutch civilians were well known and when Stair wrote his *Institutions* he naturally turned to Roman law, as developed by these civilians, to fill gaps and harmonise differences. In the seventeenth and eighteenth centuries Scottish students frequented the Dutch universities and the citation of the Dutch and German commentators can be traced in the earlier Scottish collected decisions. The Roman law which was adopted and introduced was generally a simplified form, ignoring

---

40 On France see Brissaud, *Manuel d'Histoire du Droit Français*; Esmein, *Histoire du Droit Français*; Olivier-Martin, *Histoire du Droit Français*.
   On Germany see Hubner, *Institutionen des deutschen Privatrechts* (trans. in *Continental Legal History Series*); Fehr, *Deutsche Rechtsgeschichte*.
41 In this connection the long-standing practice of Scottish advocates studying in Holland must be remembered since Holland is the channel through which much Roman law came to Scotland.
42 See further Baird Smith, " Roman Law," in Stair Society, *Sources and Literature of Scots Law*, and references there.

elaborate refinements, accepted on its merits and for its reason and equity, not as of binding force. After the Union of 1707 English influence tended to grow and this has been more pronounced with the passage of time. Simultaneously reliance on Roman law has tended to decline and in the twentieth century it is seldom referred to except in matters previously adopted from the Roman law, while reference to the older French, Dutch and German commentators is rare.

The Roman law never became a constituent element of English law but it was influential when legal doctrines were being formulated in the twelfth and thirteenth centuries and was continuously studied in the universities [43] and in particular topics it has been a direct source of English rules. Hence also Roman law has been less influential in the parts of the world settled from England. Thus, apart from Quebec and Louisiana, North America has taken its law initially and fundamentally from England. But, largely through the French and German codes, principles stemming originally from Roman law have spread all over the world.

Permanent Importance of Roman Law

The Roman law is still a material subject of legal study for several reasons; in the first place, the development and working out of their great system of law by the Roman jurists over a thousand years is an excellent example of the modes of growth and development of a legal system; furthermore this development was one of the great intellectual achievements of antiquity and Roman law is entitled to be placed with Greek philosophy and Jewish religious thought as one of the most important and powerful intellectual forces in European civilisation inherited by the modern from the ancient world.[44] " Roman law, next to Christianity, was the greatest factor in the creation of modern civilisation, and it is the greatest intellectual legacy of Rome." [45]

Secondly, the rules, doctrines, conceptions and terminology of the Roman law were closely studied everywhere in Europe from the end of the Dark Ages till modern times and have powerfully influenced legal thinking and terminology and the actual content of many modern systems of law. Roman law has unique significance as a common source of legal conceptions. " Roman law is still the foundation for the liberal

[43] Vinogradoff, *op. cit.*, 97 *et seq.*; Winfield, *Chief Sources of English Legal History*, Chap. 4; Scrutton, *Influence of Roman Law on the Law of England* in *Essays in Anglo-American Legal History*, I, 208; Potter, *Historical Introduction to English Law*, 4th ed., 631; Plucknett, *Concise History of the Common Law*, 5th ed., 294; Powell, " Roman Law in Common Law Courts," 1958 Curr.Leg.Prob. 19.
[44] This point is well brought out in de Burgh, *Legacy of the Ancient World*, esp. Chaps. 7, 8 and 11. See also Vinogradoff, " The Work of Rome " in *Collected Papers*, Vol. I, 222; Meynial, *Roman Law* in *The Legacy of the Middle Ages*, 364; Bryce, Inaugural Lecture, in *Studies in History and Jurisprudence*, II, 860.
[45] Buckland (1931) J.S.P.T.L. 25.

education of a lawyer, the training and the sharpening of his logical equipment. The methods of reasoning of the Roman jurists, their way of approaching a legal problem we still follow today." [46] " It may be said that the Romans have fixed for all time the categories of juristic thought." [47]

Thirdly, the rules of Roman law have been a material source of rules accepted and applied in modern systems and to the Roman law modern systems have frequently turned for rules to apply to new sets of circumstances. By acquaintance with Roman law the English-speaking legal student gains a key to the understanding of the many modern systems of law which derive ultimately from Rome, of French law, German law and the many systems based on these systems, of the Roman-Dutch law of South Africa, international law and of much of jurisprudence. Roman law is thus fundamental to jurisprudence and comparative legal study. Roman law and English law between them cover a large part of the civilised and most of the uncivilised world.[48] The reception of Roman law created a great body of continental law which served along with the feudal law, canon law, and the law merchant to unify the diverse legal system of much of western Europe.[49]

Fourthly, Roman law was taken as the basis of international law by Grotius and his successors. The founders of international law turned unhesitatingly to Roman law for the rules of their system whenever the relations between ruling princes seemed to them to be analogous to those of private persons. The international rules as to territory are still in essentials the Roman rules of property.

" From the purely academic point of view we cannot afford to neglect a branch of legal learning which has had so large an historical effect, a branch of learning which is still so necessary to a scientific study of law. From the purely practical point of view we cannot afford to neglect a branch of learning which is necessary to the proper understanding of international law, and of foreign Codes de Commerce." [50]

The debt of Scots law to Roman law is very great and Roman law must continue to be studied in Scotland as a material source of the living law of Scotland.[51] Scotland, unlike England, " received " the Roman law and it had great influence from the mid-sixteenth to the mid-eighteenth centuries. Mackenzie, Stair, Bankton and Erskine all consider that in default of native statute or custom great weight attaches

---

[46] Meynial, in *The Legacy of the Middle Ages*, 399.
[47] Cuq, *Institutions juridiques des Romains*, 2nd ed., I, xxiv.
[48] Bryce, *Studies in History and Jurisprudence*, I, 74.
[49] Munroe Smith, *General View of European Legal History*, 3, 28.
[50] Holdsworth, *Sources and Literature of English Law*, 235.
[51] Baird Smith in Stair Society, *Sources and Literature*, p. 177; Smith, *Short Commentary on the Law of Scotland*, 19–24; Mackintosh, " Our Debt to Roman Law " (1926) 38 J.R. 327. *Cf. Stewart* v. *L.M.S. Ry.*, 1943 S.C. (H.L.) 19, 38.

to the Roman law, and the courts constantly referred to continental treatises on the Roman and canon law. Since about 1800 this influence has been less but it remains a fact that Roman law was a factor of major importance in the formative period of modern Scots law, with particular influence on the law of moveable property and obligations, and its influence is not yet wholly spent.[52]

CANON LAW

Canon law is the body of laws framed by an ecclesiastical body for its own regulation, and particularly the law of the Roman Church.[53] In the early centuries of the Christian Church there was no general legislation but the various communities framed rules themselves and in time collections were made in the East of decisions by councils and bishops and rather later in the West. The Churches of Britain tended to remain outside the centralising movement. In the Middle Ages the canon law was a common law for Europe sharing in the authority conceded to the Roman law on which, along with Holy Scripture, it was based. The Roman law was the temporal law of the clergy and councils and Popes drew inspiration therefrom. The canon law, like the Roman, was a principal branch of university study down to the Reformation.

The principal sources of medieval canon law were the New Testament, canons or decrees of councils, oecumenical, national or provincial, and the custom of the Church. Collections of these were made, into which forged documents sometimes found their way.

About 1148 Gratian, a monk of Bologna, published the treatise at first called the *Concordia discordantium canonum* and later the *Decretum* in which he brought together and tried to make into a coherent juridical system the vast body of texts of different periods, furnished by earlier collections. Gratian drew on the existing collections, the works of the fathers and the ecclesiastical councils, and the Roman law, as well as later councils, and recent decretals down to the Lateran council of 1139 and fitted the texts into a treatise. The Decretum was a work of only private authority but it has subsequently been the basis of instruction in canon law in all universities, been commented on by the most illustrious canonists, and having been cited, corrected and edited by the popes has obtained an authority recognised and accepted by the Roman Church.

[52] " The Roman law, though interesting, is only of service as showing the foundation on which the Scots law rests. The real question must always be what is the law of Scotland." *Cantiere San Rocco* v. *Clyde Shipbuilding Co.,* 1923 S.C.(H.L.) 105, 123, *per* Lord Dunedin.

[53] For the history see *Continental Legal History Series,* Vol. I, 705–724; Munroe Smith, *Development of European Law,* 191–212.

The disciples of Gratian collected later papal decretals into five large compilations which were condensed into a single collection by Raymond of Pennaforte in 1234 under the orders of Gregory IX (*Decretales Extravagantes, i.e., extra Decretum vagantes*). Two official collections followed, one prepared by a committee of canonists under Boniface VIII and published in 1298. Since it followed the five books of Gregory IX it was called the *Liber Sextus*. The other collection was called the *Clementinae*, from Pope Clement V, and promulgated in 1314. There are also two later collections of private authority, the *Extravagantes* (*i.e., extra collectiones publicas*) of John XXII and the *Extravagantes communes* of several popes down to Sixtus IV in 1484. These various collections complete the body of law known as the *Corpus Juris Canonici*.[54] After the Council of Trent pontifical constitutions continued to appear and a revised Codex of Canon Law was promulgated by Benedict XV in 1917.[55]

In addition the canon law included bodies of local canons, bodies of state law on ecclesiastical matters and the decisions of the Tribunal of the Rota and of the Congregations of Cardinals, while an enormous and valuable literature of commentaries grew up round the texts and decisions.

The canon law in Scotland [56] prior to the Reformation was generally that of the Continent of Europe and the usages of the Church were similar to those in France rather than in England. In the twelfth century Robert, Bishop of St. Andrews, with the consent of David I promulgated to his clergy the *Exceptiones Ecclesiasticarum Regularum*, the lineage of which has been traced to the Decretum of Ivo of Chartres. Canon law was not automatically authoritative in Scotland since in the canons of her national provincial councils she possessed a canon law of her own which was recognised by parliament and the popes, and enforced in the courts. Much of it was doubtless borrowed from the *corpus juris canonici* and English provincial canons but these portions derived their authority from the Scottish Church, by adoption and not by original promulgation, and the general canon law was received only according to equity and expediency except where it had been acknowledged by parliament or decision of the courts.

In the Middle Ages the Church courts exercised wide civil jurisdiction,

---

54 This title is met with from the twelfth century. It was obviously suggested by the *Corpus juris civilis*. The best edition is by Friedberg (2 vols., Leipzig, 1879–81).
55 On the modern canon law see Willock " A Civil Lawyer looks at The Canon Law " (1962) 11 I.C.L.Q. 89.
56 For Scotland see Baird Smith, "Canon Law," in *Sources and Literature of Scots Law*, Stair Society; Mylne, *Canon Law*; *Statuta Ecclesiae Scoticanae* (ed. Robertson); *Statutes of the Scottish Church* (ed. Patrick); Stair, I, 1, 14; Fraser on *Husband and Wife*, Introduction.
See also Mortimer, *Western Canon Law*; Maitland, *Roman Canon Law in the Church of England*; Galante, "The Modern Study of Canon Law," in *Essays in Legal History* (ed. Vinogradoff).

including all matters of marriage, legitimacy and succession, with a possible ultimate appeal to Rome. At the Reformation the canon law of marriage, legitimacy and succession was taken over by the Scottish secular courts and survived almost unimpaired as part of the common law on these subjects.[57]

In Catholic countries the canon law of the Roman Church has had a continuous influence on the legal and social system, and in practically every system of law stemming from Western Europe it has been influential to some extent. " Decretals and canons of a date earlier than the fifteenth century still govern the administration of the best disciplined and, from the point of view of numbers, the greatest of all monarchies— that of the Sovereign Pontiff—and regulate the religious and social life of the three hundred millions of the faithful of whom it is composed. . . . The principles developed by the Church and applied by her during the period when no one disputed her control over all civil matters in which the salvation of souls was concerned, still underlie a considerable portion of the common law of the West, and are predominant in large provinces such as those of marriage or of obligations." [58]

From the renaissance of legal studies in the eleventh century the civil law and canon law were principal subjects of study in the universities of Europe [59] and the pre-Reformation Scottish universities were founded to study and teach, *inter alia*, civil and canon law.[60] Though since the Reformation the study of canon law has been largely abandoned in Britain, its historical importance was considerable and reference to the canonists as ultimate sources of some of the principles of modern law may still on occasion be required.[61] Public law and the law of nations, criminal law and procedure, civil law and procedure of Western Europe all owe something to canonist principles.

COMPARATIVE LAW

Despite its name comparative law is neither a body of law nor a branch or department of the law of any country.[62] Rather is it a method of study

---

[57] *Cf.* the list of authorities cited in Fraser on *Husband and Wife*, vol. II, p. xxxiv; see also *Collins* v. *Collins* (1884) 11 R.(H.L.) 19, 31, *per* Lord Watson.

[58] Le Bras, *Canon Law* in *Legacy of the Middle Ages.*

[59] Rashdall, *The Universities of Europe in the Middle Ages, passim.* See further Mackie, *The University of Glasgow*, 7, 27, 232–234; Grant, *Story of the University of Edinburgh*, I, 35, 63, 123, 167.

[60] Hence the degree in Law (LL.B.) is still *baccalaureus utriusque juris* (*i.e.*, both civil and canon laws).

[61] See, *e.g.*, *Kerr* v. *Martin* (1840) 2 D. 752; *Annan* v. *Annan*, 1948 S.C. 532. Notice too the reliance on canonists in Lord Fraser's treatise on *Husband and Wife.*

[62] The best general introduction to the subject is Gutteridge, *Comparative Law*, 2nd ed., 1949. See also Buckland and McNair, *Roman Law and Common Law*, 2nd ed. by Lawson; Lawson, *A Common Lawyer looks at the Civil Law*, 1955;

and research originating from the facts that different countries have different systems and rules of law, applying different legal solutions to very similar problems, and that it is enlightening and stimulating to see what these other solutions are, so as not to fall into the easy error of thinking that the solution propounded by one's own legal system is the best or the natural or the only one.[63] This involves obtaining at least a general acquaintance with the judicial structure and the sources, literature and main principles of some foreign systems of law. Not only complete legal systems but any major branches of several legal systems can usefully be compared: thus study may be directed to comparative constitutions, comparative law of contract, of delict, of matrimonial property or of criminal procedure.[64] The function of comparative legal study is variously said to be the ascertainment of principles common to all civilised systems of law, or the discovery of the causes which underlie the development and extinction of legal institutions, or the promotion of unification of legal rules followed in civilised communities, but in fact the comparative method is sufficiently elastic to embrace all activities concerned with the study of foreign law, the resemblances and differences between different legal systems and the results achieved by different legal methods, techniques and principles applied to fundamentally similar problems.[65] This study may have practical as well as cultural value as the increase in international intercourse today more frequently requires some appreciation of foreign legal doctrines and conceptions, or at least awareness of the salient characteristics of the other systems involved. So too comparative study may suggest ways of law reform or a solution for problems not hitherto determined in the student's own system. Traditionally Scots law has been developed and studied comparatively, and the institutional writers, particularly Stair and Bankton, have a strongly developed comparative approach.[66]

Most of the world's developed legal systems fall conveniently into two families, those which are derived ultimately from the Civil or Roman law, or have absorbed it as a principal ingredient in their modern developed system, and those based on the Common Law, which, Germanic in origin, was developed from the eleventh century by the English courts and spread

---

Schmitthoff, " The Science of Comparative Law " (1939) 7 C.L.J. 95; Lord Cooper, " The Importance of Comparative Law in Scotland," in *Selected Papers*, 142; Lord Macmillan, " Scots Law as a subject of Comparative Study " (1933) 48 L.Q.R. 477.

[63] *Cf.* Lepaulle, " The Function of Comparative Law " (1922) 35 H.L.R. 838, 858; Gutteridge, " The Value of Comparative Law " (1931) J.S.P.T.L. 26.

[64] *Cf.* Hazeltine, " The Study of Comparative Legal History " (1927) J.S.P.T.L. 27.

[65] *Cf.* Walton, " The Study of Foreign Laws " (1934) 46 J.R. 1; Gutteridge, " Comparative Law and the Law of Nations " (1944) 21 B.Y.I.L. 1.

[66] *Cf.* Lord Cooper, " The Importance of Comparative Law in Scotland," in *Selected Papers*, 142.

over the world with the English people and language.[67] The former is the foundation or a principal element in the law of modern continental Europe, Central and South America, Quebec, Louisiana, South Africa, Ceylon and Scotland,[68] and French, Dutch, Spanish and Portuguese colonies and settlements; the latter is the basis of the law of England and Wales, Ireland, the United States (except Louisiana and Porto Rico), Canada (except Quebec), Australia and New Zealand, of the former British India (except over Hindus and Mohammedans as to inheritance and family law) and generally in British colonies. While there is this familial distinction, some systems, basically of the Roman law family, have been and are being much influenced by common law conceptions and methods, as in the cases of Scotland, Louisiana and South Africa.[69] Since 1945 the system of law developed since 1917 in Russia has been extended as a concomitant of military occupation to all the countries of Eastern Europe and has transformed their legal systems into systems on the Russian model [70] while Communist China has also radically changed its legal system in the same general direction and made it an agency for changing its society.[71] The Scandinavian countries have distinct legal systems which embody features characteristic of both civil law and common law countries.[72] Islamic law, based on the Koran, is a powerful influence in North Africa and the Middle East,[73] and former colonial territories in Africa, on gaining independence commonly develop legal systems incorporating elements of Islamic or tribal law and of civil or common law from the legal system of the former governing European power.

[67] See Schlesinger, *Comparative Law; Cases and Materials, passim*; von Mehren, *The Civil Law System*, Chap. 1; Symposium on " The Migration of the Common Law " (1960) 76 L.Q.R. 41. See also Wigmore, *Panorama of the World's Legal Systems*, 3 vols.

[68] Réné David, *Introduction à l'Etude du Droit privé de l'Angleterre*, 164, characterises Scots law as " très different du droit anglais " and Levy Ullman, " The Law of Scotland " (1925) 37 Jur.Rev. 370, described it as " absolutely Roman in character."

[69] Amos, " The Common Law and the Civil Law in the British Commonwealth of Nations " (1937) 50 H.L.R. 1249. *Cf.* Lawson, *Rational Strength of English Law*, 5; Jolowicz, " The Civil Law in Louisiana," 1954 *Curr.Leg. Problems*, 1; Hahlo and Kahn, *South Africa: the Development of Its Laws.*

[70] See further Gsovski and Grzybowski, *Government, Law and Courts in the Soviet Union and Eastern Europe*, 2 vols.

[71] Buxbaum, " Preliminary Trends in the Development of the Legal Institutions of Communist China " (1962) 11 I.C.L.Q. 1.

[72] Orfield, *The Growth of Scandinavian Law*; Gomard, " Civil Law, Common Law and Scandinavian Law " (1961) 5 *Scand. Studies in Law*, 27.

[73] Anderson, *Islamic Law in Africa.*

II.—PUBLIC INTERNATIONAL LAW

Legal rules regulating international relations and the practices of states *inter se* have existed from a very early period [74] but modern international law is a product of the turbulent sixteenth and seventeenth centuries which witnessed the break-up of the medieval community of mankind under the Pope and the Emperor and the emergence of independent nation-states, each administered by a separate government with its own particular law, as part of the turmoil produced by the Renaissance and the Reformation.[75] Thus there grew up a body of " rules which determine the conduct of the general body of civilised states in their mutual dealings." [76] The name International Law was invented by Jeremy Bentham in 1780.[77] It may now be described as " the body of customary and conventional rules which are considered legally binding by civilised states in their intercourse with each other " [78] or " The body of rules and usages which among civilised independent states are recognised as binding upon their several governments in their dealings with one another and with each other's subjects," [79] or " The principles and rules of conduct declaratory thereof which states feel themselves bound to observe, and, therefore, do commonly observe in their relations with each other." [80]

The modern system dates from the publication in 1625 of Hugo Grotius' *De Jure Belli ac Pacis* [81] though the system had been taking shape in the works of such jurists as Vitoria, Suarez, Ayala and Gentilis in the previous century. The immediate source of his work was to be found in the barbarities of the European Wars of Religion and particularly of the Thirty Years War (1618–48). The first result of the Peace of Westphalia which ended that war was the formal recognition of a society of independent nations occupying defined territory, equal before the law, and transacting with one another as principal parties without reference to Pope or Emperor. Since that time general congresses of states, the practice of establishing embassies and legations at

---

[74] See, *e.g.*, I Samuel xv, 18; II Samuel xii, 31; Greek and Roman instances cited in Holland, *Lectures on International Law*, 10–15; Vinogradoff, " Historical Types in International Law," in *Collected Papers*, II, 248; and generally Walker, *History of the Law of Nations*; Nussbaum, *Short History of the Law of Nations*; Butler and Maccoby, *Development of International Law*.
[75] Lawrence, *Principles of International Law*, Chap. 2; Pollock in 12 Camb.Mod. Hist., Chap. 22.
[76] Lawrence, *Principles of International Law* (7th ed.), 1.
[77] *Principles of Morals and Legislation*, Chap. xvii, s. xxv.
[78] Oppenheim, *International Law*, I, 4.   [79] Pollock in 12 Camb.Mod.Hist., 703.
[80] Hyde, *International Law*, I, 1; see further Lauterpacht, *The Function of Law in the International Community*.
[81] Hugo de Groot or Grotius: 1585–1645: scholar and jurist; Grand Pensionary of West Friesland and Holland; Swedish ambassador to France, 1634–44. See Lauterpacht, " The Grotian Tradition in International Law," 1946 B.Y.I.L. 1; and Oppenheim, *International Law*, I, 79 *et seq.*

the courts of other states, and diplomatic, commercial and legal relations between states have become formalised. International law accordingly has come to be the body of rules which regulates the actions of civilised states in their dealings with one another, defining the essentials of state personality, the conditions under which states are recognised as coming into existence or disappearing, their rights, duties and privileges *inter se* in time of peace and war, as amicable partners, as belligerents and as neutrals.

This body of law was built up largely from the writings of jurists, such as the followers of Grotius, men such as Pufendorf,[82] Thomasius,[83] Burlamaqui,[84] Wolff,[85] Vattel,[86] Bynkershoek [87] and von Martens.[88] They based their work originally largely on Roman law, theology, canon law and the concept of a " law of nature," and, later, on developing usages.

It must be remembered that it is disputable how far international law is properly called law in the strict sense of that word in respect that it lacks some of the usually accepted criteria of law.[89] Thus there is no legislative body which promulgates rules of law, authoritatively declaring the true rule and altering previous rules; there is only a rudimentary and frequently ineffective system of sanction or compulsion in case of disobedience; and the jurisdiction of international tribunals is limited and their decisions are frequently flouted or ignored, and are not enforceable to anything like the same extent as those of domestic tribunals. To a large extent international law is still the custom and practice of nations, a body of rules binding so far as accepted, and for that reason it is still commonly defined in terms of rules and standards of conduct rather than of law.

Thus Hall [90] defines international law as consisting in " certain rules of conduct which modern civilised states regard as being binding on them in their relations with one another with a force comparable in nature and degree to that binding the conscientious person to obey the laws of his country, and which they also regard as being enforceable by appropriate means in case of infringement." In fact, however, this

---

82 1632–94; Professor of the Law of Nature and Nations at Heidelberg, 1661; Professor of Jurisprudence at Lund, 1670; *De jure naturae et gentium*, 1672; historiographer at Stockholm, 1677 and at Berlin, 1688.
83 1655–1728; Professor at Leipzig and later at Halle; *Fundamenta juris naturae et gentium*, 1705.
84 1694–1748; *Principes de droit naturel*, 1747.
85 1679–1754; *Institutiones juris naturae et gentium*, Halle, 1750.
86 1714–67; *Le droit des gens*, 1758.
87 1673–1743; *De dominio maris*, 1702; *De foro legatorum*, 1721; *Questionum juris publici libri duo*, 1737.
88 1756–1821; *Précis du droit des gens modernes de l'Europe*, 1788.
89 See also Ago, " Positive Law and International Law " (1957) 51 A.J.I.L. 691.
90 *Treatise on International Law*, 8th ed., I.

controversy is academic and international law is increasingly and now usually regarded as law, though still underdeveloped in comparison with state law in respect of definiteness and enforcement, and it is being increasingly accepted expressly as binding on states. " The best evidence for the existence of international law is that every actual state recognises that it does exist and that it is itself under an obligation to observe it. States may often violate international law just as individuals often violate municipal law; but no more than individuals do states defend their violations by claiming that they are above the law." [91]

In modern times the practice and custom of states, treaties, alliances and conventions, ordinances of particular states, opinions of jurists to their governments and decisions of international tribunals and courts have added substantially to the volume of law recognised, while more recently the growth and development of international institutions and agencies has also contributed a large volume of new law.[92] The Hague Conferences of 1899 and 1907 reduced to written form many of the rules hitherto unwritten, such as the rights and duties of neutral states. The League of Nations and the United Nations Organisation and their respective subsidiary organs, including the Permanent Court of International Justice (1921) and the International Court of Justice (1946), have made much new law,[93] while increasing international intercourse has continually raised fresh problems.

International administrative, social and economic organisations have developed enormously in the last century and such bodies as the Universal Postal Union (1878) and the International Labour Organisation (1919) have added great volumes to the body of international agreement, while the growth of population, science, industry, commerce, foreign trade and investment in recent times have made international relations even more complex and more in need of legal regulation.[94] The body of law relating to international organisations and peaceful relations now greatly outweighs the subjects of war and neutrality which bulk so largely in the older books. But international law is still a long way short of the developed state attained by the municipal law of the more advanced countries.

Moreover in modern times international law is ceasing to be primarily a body of law between states but " increasingly includes cross-frontier-relationships of individual organisations and corporate bodies which call

---

[91] Brierly, *Outlook for International Law*, 5; see also Fitzmaurice, " Foundations of the Authority of International Law and the Problem of Enforcement " (1956) 19 M.L.R. 1; McNair, " General Principles of Law Recognised by Civilised Nations " (1957) 33 B.Y.I.L. 1.
[92] See Lauterpacht, *The Development of International Law by the International Court.*
[93] See also Lauterpacht, *Private Law Sources and Analogies of International Law*, and " Decisions of Municipal Courts as a Source of International Law " (1939) 16 B.Y.I.L. 65.   [94] See generally Ball and Killough, *International Relations*.

for appropriate legal regulation on an international basis,[95] problems of economic and technological interdependence requiring the regulation on the basis of common rules of matters which do not *per se* involve inter-state relations in any real sense, and rights designed to protect the individual, and in some cases organisations, with a measure of protection against the individual member states of the international community." [96] Most modern international law is treaty law, indeed international legislation, and increasingly it deals with trade, commerce, finance, and trans-frontier aspects of topics of private law,[97] while the influence of juristic writing in developing international law is diminishing.

III.—SUPRANATIONAL LAW

Supranational law arises where states, without entering into any kind of federation or union, have created new institutions and transferred part of their national sovereign powers thereto; these institutions are not properly international, but only regional and limited in membership, yet their organisations and its law are above and wider than national law; it is intermediate in generality between international and national law.[98]

Since 1945, particularly in the face of the Russian threat to the independence of Western European countries, there has been a developing movement for the integration of these countries, towards a goal described by Sir Winston Churchill in 1946 as a " United States of Europe." The first European organisation was created by the Brussels Treaty of 1948 between Britain, France and the Benelux countries, followed closely by the Organisation for European Economic Cooperation in response to the American Marshall Plan to aid the recovery of Europe. In 1949 the Council of Europe was set up by these five countries along with Italy, Ireland and the three Scandinavian countries, with a Committee of Ministers and a Parliamentary Assembly which can, however, only recommend to member governments. In 1954 the Brussels Treaty Organisation was enlarged and converted into Western European Union, a defence organisation, itself largely superseded since 1955 by NATO. In 1960 a convention for the formation of the Organisation for Economic Cooperation and Development was signed; this included the U.S.A. and Canada and converted OEEC into an Atlantic Organisation (OECD).

[95] *e.g.*, the International Civil Aviation Organisation.
[96] Jenks, " The Scope of International Law " (1954) 31 B.Y.I.L. 1.
[97] Jennings, " The State of International Law Today " (1957) 4 J.S.P.T.L.(N.S.) 95; see also Jennings, " The Progressive Development of International Law " (1947) 24 B.Y.I.L. 301.
[98] For the meaning of the term " supranational " see Robertson, *European Institutions*, pp. 105–108. See also Efron and Nanes, " The Common Market and Euratom Treaties: Supranationality and the Integration of Europe " (1957) 6 I.C.L.Q. 670.

The Assembly of the Council of Europe promoted a European Convention for the Protection of Human Rights and Fundamental Freedoms in 1950 [99] to be guaranteed by a European Court of Justice,[1] and a European Commission of Human Rights, while a separate European Social Charter, dealing with social and economic rights, was signed in 1961, and in 1952 the Assembly adopted a recommendation for the establishment of a European Court of Justice and a European Act for the peaceful settlement of disputes, but later the International Court was put in place of the proposed European Court.

In 1951 France, Germany, Italy, Belgium, Holland and Luxembourg successfully formed the European Coal and Steel Community (ECSC) to pool their resources of iron, steel and coal in a single market without frontier barriers, and in 1957 they signed the Treaty of Rome [2] and thereby established the European Economic Community (EEC), (the Common Market), planning an area in which goods, persons, services and capital could move freely without hindrance at national frontiers by tariffs or import restrictions, and the European Atomic Energy Community (Euratom).

These three communities have each a High Authority (ECSC) or Executive Commission (EEC and Euratom) as executive, a Council of Ministers, and one European Parliamentary Assembly and one Court of Justice for all three, and all, like some other international organisations, report to the Assembly of the Council of Europe. So too does such a body as the International Institute for the Unification of Private Law. Outside the Common Market the United Kingdom took the lead in forming the European Free Trade Association (EFTA), to establish a free market between its members. Greece and Turkey subsequently sought to be associated with EEC and in 1961 the United Kingdom announced its intention to seek to join EEC and, in 1962, also to join ECSC and Euratom. Ireland and Denmark also sought membership, while other countries have sought association with EEC.

The institutions thus set up are supranational and the EEC itself has personality under international law. The Council of Ministers, which acts as executive, takes the policy decisions and seeks to coordinate the policies of the national governments and those of the Community as a whole, the European Parliament meets at Strasbourg, to which the

---

[99] This is distinct from the United Nations Universal Declaration of Human Rights (1948) on which see Lauterpacht, *International Law and Human Rights*, Chap. 17. See further Robertson " The Legal Work of the Council of Europe " (1961) 10 I.C.L.Q. 143.

[1] See Waldock " The European Convention for the Protection of Human Rights and Fundamental Freedoms " (1958) 34 B.Y.I.L. 356; Robertson " The European Court of Human Rights " (1959) 9 A.J.Comp.L. 1.

[2] The text of the Rome Treaty is printed in Campbell and Thompson, *Common Market Law*, pp. 206–383.

executive Commissions of the ECSC, EEC and Euratom report, and the Court of Justice of the Community, sitting at Luxembourg, has to decide whether decisions of the executives and of the Council of Ministers must be annulled and other problems of the legal interpretation of the various treaties. The judgments of the court have the force of law in the community and are directly enforceable on individuals, firms, governments and the European Executives. There are also various consultative committees, *e.g.*, on transport or monetary problems.

A declared object, as well as a practical necessity, of the developing European Community is the approximation of national systems of law, starting with the protection of industrial property and the development of a European law of patents, trade-marks, designs and models, and the development of a common law on bankruptcy, companies, the enforcement of judgments, and so on. British membership would also have constitutional significance in involving constitutional limitations on the sovereign powers of Parliament. The political implications of these developments indicate that the developing economic unification of Europe is only a stage towards greater political unification or federation. Thus there is clearly developing a body of law within the European Community distinct from International Law and also from the national systems of the constituent states. It will come increasingly to affect the legal relations of individuals and the legal systems of the countries. The increasing intercourse between the countries will also give rise to a sharply increased number of problems of international private law, while domestic courts will also have to apply Community Law in certain circumstances since the Treaty of Rome makes Community Law a part of the municipal law of each member state. An understanding of the salient principles and general structure of the domestic legal systems of other Community countries will similarly become of increasing importance.[3]

IV.—STATE OR MUNICIPAL LAW

The body of state, national, domestic, civil or municipal law [4] comprises the whole body of doctrines, principles and rules laid down, applied and enforced in a particular state or political community; it is

---

[3] See generally Robertson, *European Institutions*; Robertson, *The Law of International Institutions in Europe*; Gaudet, *The Common Market and the Law* (Information Services of the European Community, 1961); Campbell and Thompson, *Common Market Law*; Frank, *The European Common Market*; Hahn " Euratom— The Conception of an International Personality " (1958) 71 H.L.R. 1001; Bebr " The Relation of E.C.S.C. Law to the Law of Member States " (1958) 58 Col.L.R. 767.

[4] State law is sometimes called civil, as being enacted by a *civitas* or state, or municipal, which originally connoted laws binding *municipia*, or dependent states, but was later extended also to laws enacted by sovereign states: Ersk. I, 1, 18.

what is commonly called the law of the particular country.[5] Every state and territory recognised as a political entity possesses a whole apparatus of state law which may differ very substantially from that in an adjacent state; indeed many states, such as the United Kingdom, have several distinct bodies of municipal law in force in different parts of the one state. The similarities and differences were in practice formerly dictated by the origins, sources and historical borrowings of the legal system in the state in question and by the existence in many cases of federal or common legislative bodies and final courts of appeal. In modern times differences are dictated more by different social and economic conditions and the different policies pursued by the political superiors in the state in question.

The Subject-Matter of Municipal Law

The subject-matter of these doctrines, principles and rules is rights and duties, that is, those claims, powers, privileges, immunities and other advantages conferred on persons over and against other persons, and those burdens, liabilities and disabilities which are imposed and incumbent on persons in relation to other persons. These rules of law are binding on all persons in the country under the common authority of the state and are administered by the courts, being invoked as need arises, sometimes by a public official, sometimes by an aggrieved individual seeking redress. Thus if A enters a shop and buys a book, the law confers on him a right to obtain delivery of the book, which right it will enforce at his instance, if need be, and imposes on him a duty to pay the agreed price, which duty it will enforce, if need be, at the instance of the bookseller, and it imposes on the bookseller a duty to hand over the book and a right to recover the price.[6] In the majority of cases, of course, people implement their legal rights and duties without compulsion or resort to the courts. The classification, analysis and examination of these concepts of rights and duties is an important element of jurisprudence, but cannot be pursued further here.[7]

It is important to appreciate the scientific analytical arrangement of the legal principles in force in one community. It reveals that the body of law is an ordered system with a coherent logical structure. The mass of legal principles may be classified in various ways [8] and the method and accuracy of classification may be of great practical importance. The

---

[5] *Cf.* Mackenzie, *Inst.* I, 1, 6; " Civil or Municipal Laws are the particular Laws and Customs of every Nation, or People, who are under one Sovereign Power."

[6] Pollock, *First Book of Jurisprudence*, Chap. 4.

[7] See further Holland, *Jurisprudence*, 13th ed., Chap. 7; Salmond, *Jurisprudence*, 11th ed., Chaps. 10–11; Dias and Hughes, *Jurisprudence*, Chap. 9.

[8] See Paton, *Textbook of Jurisprudence*, 2nd ed., Chap. 11; Pound, " Classification of Law " (1924) 37 H.L.R. 933, and *Jurisprudence*, V, 3–75; Kocourek, " Classification of the Law " (1934) 11 N.Y.U.L.Q.R. 319. The same classification is not appropriate in detail to all national systems of law because terminology varies

choice of remedy, or of which court should be approached to grant it, may depend on whether the claim is classified as of one kind or another. Classification is important as facilitating study, as showing the logical structure of the legal system and permitting scientific examination of its doctrines and principles, and is specially important where legal problems involving a foreign element are present.[9]

Public Law and Private Law

State law may be divided firstly into Public Law and Private Law.[10] While the distinction has been current since the time of the classical Roman law at least and is commonly accepted and generally understood, its basis is difficult to define and different jurists distinguish the two bodies of law in different ways, while there is not complete agreement as to whether certain topics should be placed under the one head or the other. According to Stair [11]: " Rights . . . are divided into public and private rights. Public rights are those which concern the state of the commonwealth. Private rights are the rights of persons and particular incorporations, . . ." Erskine [12] wrote: " The public law is that which hath more immediately in view the public weal and the preservation and good order of society; as laws concerning the constitution of the State, the administration of the government, the police of the country, public revenue, trade and manufactures, the punishment of crimes, etc. Private law is that which is chiefly intended for ascertaining the civil rights of individuals." Again it is said that the division corresponds to the twofold activity of the state, in providing an organisation of government and means for the maintenance of order and the repression of disorder, and on the other hand providing machinery for the settlement of disputes and the resolution of conflicts of interest between private persons.[13] Questions between the state and the individual, however, give rise to some difficulty of classification.

Again it is generally true that a mark of public law is that the state

and historical factors have sometimes affected classification. The classification here adopted as appropriate for Scots law is, however, subject to variations in terminology, applicable also to English and most Anglo-American systems of law. Civil law systems commonly divide private law into separate bodies of civil and commercial laws; thus French law has separate codes for civil and commercial law, as well as for criminal law, civil procedure and criminal procedure. In Scotland and England the law merchant has long been absorbed in the common law, so that division between civil and commercial laws is neither necessary nor desirable.

[9] Hence in international private law (conflict of laws) careful classification of the problem-situation is essential.

[10] On this see further Jones, *Historical Introduction to the Theory of Law*, 139–163; Jolowicz, *Roman Foundations of Modern Law*, Chap. 7.   [11] I, 1, 23.

[12] I, 1, 29; the distinction is also found in Art. 18 of the Articles of Union of 1707, and is used by William Forbes in his *Institutes* (1722) and Gilbert Stuart's *Observations concerning the Public Law of Scotland* (1779).

[13] Keeton, *Elementary Principles of Jurisprudence*, 2nd ed., 227–228.

or a state department is a party to the legal relationship or controversy, while private law applies as between private individuals.[14] But this test is not by any means invariable since in many legal relationships the state and its agencies are submitted to the ordinary principles of private law, as in owning property and making commercial contracts. Hence " public law comprises the rules which specially relate to the structure, powers, rights and activities of the state. Private law includes all the residue of legal principles. It comprises all those rules which specially concern the subjects of the state in their relations to each other, together with those rules which are common to the state and its subjects." [15] Markby,[16] in explanation of the distinction drawn in Justinian's *Institutes*,[17] wrote: " Public law is that portion of law in which our attention is directed mainly to the state; private law is that in which it is mainly directed to the individual. I do not think that it means that these topics are capable of exact separation; but that our attitude changes in regard to them. And, according as we assume one attitude or the other, we call law public or private." Pollock [18] expressed the view: " No rule of law can be said, in the last resort, to exist merely for the benefit of the state or merely for the benefit of the individual. But some departments of legal rules have regard in the first instance to the protection and interests of the commonwealth, others to those of its individual members. . . . The topics of public and private law are by no means mutually exclusive."

This division is not accordingly wholly clear-cut and there is no essential or inherent difference in nature between the two kinds of law; both may be relevant in particular cases and both come before the same courts; accordingly some would deny the existence of the division, though its general convenience causes it usually to be retained.

Civil and Criminal Law

Another division is that into civil [19] and criminal law.[20] This distinction is fundamentally one of procedure since the classification of

---

[14] This was the view of Holland, *Jurisprudence*, 13th ed., 128–129.
[15] Salmond, *Jurisprudence*, 506.
[16] *Elements of Law*, 151.
[17] Inst. I, 1, 4. *Jus publicum est quod ad statum rei Romanae spectat, jus privatum quod ad singulorum utilitatem pertinet.*
[18] *First Book of Jurisprudence*, Chap. IV, reprinted in *Jurisprudence and Legal Essays.*
[19] The uses of the term " civil law " are numerous and confusing. The main ones are (i) the Civil Law of Rome as opposed to the Canon Law—*Corpus Juris Civilis* and *Corpus Juris Canonici*, the twin subjects of legal study in the Middle Ages; (ii) the civil law of Rome as opposed to the praetorian law—*jus civile* and *jus praetorium*; (iii) civil law as opposed to martial or military law; (iv) civil law as opposed to criminal law; (v) civil law as opposed to common law, with reference to the main families of legal systems; (vi) civil (or municipal or state) law as opposed to international law.
[20] See further on this distinction Salmond, *Jurisprudence*, 507.

any conduct depends on whether infringements and infractions of the rules are pursued in civil courts by civil procedure or in criminal courts by criminal procedure. In fact most legal relationships give rise to remedies in the civil courts only. In the sphere of wrongs there is no universal touchstone by which one can classify some wrongs and injuries as essentially offences against the state or the community at large, or merely against private persons, dealt with respectively in criminal courts by criminal procedure and by civil courts under civil procedure. Some wrongful acts may be either, and pursued in either or even in both ways; many others are one or other only but the only guidance which can be given as to whether or not a particular course of conduct is a crime, and therefore of concern to the criminal law, is to discover whether or not it is conduct which the state power on behalf of the community has determined to repress and punish by fine and imprisonment.[21] If not, if it is left to the individual to work out a remedy himself by action in the civil courts, the conduct is not criminal nor of concern to the criminal law.

The volume of civil law is enormously greater and more hetero- geneous than the criminal law and for this reason this division is not very helpful since it merely segregates the criminal law from the whole mass. Of greater interest is the issue whether the body of criminal law should be grouped with the public or private spheres of law. It may be classified with private law [22] on the basis that most criminal wrongs are done to individuals, albeit pursued and punished by the state, or with public law [23] on the basis that criminal wrongs, even though done directly to indi- viduals, are indirectly detrimental to the peace and order of the com- munity; moreover they are dealt with by state agencies on behalf of the community and today an increasing number of crimes and petty offences are not done against any individual at all but are declared criminal and repressed simply because of their injurious tendency to the communal interest, to the national economy, or to people generally. Moreover many fundamental public rights are frequently in issue in criminal cases.

Criminal law is particularly appropriately classified as public rather than private law in Scotland since the prosecution of criminal charges

---

[21] Kenny, " The Nature of a Crime," in his *Outlines of Criminal Law*, 16th ed., Appendix I; Allen, " The Nature of Crime " in *Legal Duties*, 220; Hall, *General Principles of Criminal Law*, Chaps. 5–7; Williams, " The Definition of Crime " 1955 *Cur.Leg.Problems*, 107. *Cf. Pty. Articles Trade Assocn. v. Att.-Gen. for Canada* [1931] A.C. at p. 324.

[22] This view is taken by Salmond, *Jurisprudence*, 507.

[23] As by Holland, Markby and Pollock.

is almost invariably carried through in Scotland by officials acting in the public interest and not by wronged individuals. In England on the other hand private prosecution is commoner. The view here adopted is accordingly that criminal law is a branch of public law,[24] while civil (*i.e.*, non-criminal) comprises the rest of public law and all of private law.

Common Law and Statute Law

The distinction of common law [25] and statute law depends on the source of the particular rules in question and this distinction is met with in civil and criminal, public and private law. Common law was originally the body of law common to the whole country, based on ancient customs and worked out and built up in the courts by the process of authoritative declaration of the rules and their application in specific cases. Statute law or legislation, enacted by Parliament, was long thought of as an alien source of rules breaking in upon the established doctrines of the law. In consequence rules and principles tend to be distinguished according as their source is in case law worked out and declared by the courts on the basis of ancient custom and practice, or in the statutes of the legislative body. This distinction corresponds to that mentioned in older books between consuetudinary and statutory, or unwritten and written law.[26]

In consequence of this distinction mention will be found in the books of common-law crimes and statutory crimes or offences, common-law rights and statutory rights, and so on.[27] The difference is not merely in the origin and source of the crime or right in question but in that in the former case the definition and conditions attaching to the right or claim or power in question have to be gathered mainly from the decisions in which the courts recognised, defined and restated the right or claim in question, while in the latter the definition and conditions are laid down in authoritative form in the statute, though subsequent decisions may be

---

[24] *Cf.* Ersk., I, 1, 29 " . . . That part of the public law that relates to crimes . . ."
[25] The term " common law " is used in various senses with different counterparts. Of these the principal are (i) the common-law or Anglo-American system of law as contrasted with civil law systems, deriving from the law of Rome; (ii) common law (in England) as distinct from equity; (iii) common law of the realm as distinct from particular local or customary law; (iv) common law as contrasted with statute law, as here discussed. See further Salmond, *Jurisprudence*, 81–99; Ersk., I, 1, 28.
[26] Ersk., I, 1, 30 and 43. *Cf.* Mackenzie, Inst. I, 1, 9–10.
[27] Thus the claim of one person to damages for the loss caused by the death of a spouse, parent or child, is a common-law claim, in that it has no other origin than ancient custom, recognised and defined in authoritative decisions of which the leading case is *Eisten* v. *N.B. Ry.* (1870) 8 M. 980. The claim of a person to Industrial Injury Benefit is statutory in that it was conferred by and is obtainable only under conditions specified in the National Insurance (Industrial Injuries) Act, 1946, as amended by later Acts and amplified by subordinate legislation made thereunder. Again, murder is a common-law crime; to be in charge of a vehicle while under the influence of drink is a statutory crime.

of value in showing the interpretation put by the courts on the verbal formulation adopted in the statute.

Substantive and Adjective Law

Another distinction of great materiality which runs through all the topics of state law is that between substantive law and adjective law (or procedural law), although at many points the dividing line is difficult to draw. Broadly speaking substantive law defines the rights and claims, liberties and privileges, duties and liabilities of persons, while adjective law defines the procedure whereby, the circumstances in which, the qualifications under which, these rights can be vindicated or these duties enforced.[28] Adjective law covers procedure, remedies, evidence, the enforcement of decrees and related topics. There is accordingly a body of adjective law attaching to each of civil and criminal law and their respective sets of courts, while a rather indefinite body of adjective law also attaches to administrative law and its tribunals. The distinction is sometimes put briefly as that between "right" and "remedy" but this is a very approximate division, and in many respects the two are inextricably intertwined. The method by which a right can be enforced sometimes determines to some extent the nature or content of the right. On the other hand the distinction is at some points quite clear, and accurate delimitation of the two areas may be of crucial importance, as in some problems of conflict of laws.[29] And it is a distinction not without practical importance,[30] for unless adjective or procedural law works quickly, cheaply and efficiently, substantive law might as well not exist.[31]

IVA.—PUBLIC LAW

Public law is generally considered to consist of the bodies of principles and doctrines grouped under the heads of Constitutional Law and Administrative Law,[32] while most British jurists [33] also include Criminal Law and Procedure. These topics have greatly increased in importance

---

[28] Procedure has been described as " The mode of proceeding by which a legal right is enforced, as distinguished from the law which gives or defines the right, and which by means of the proceeding the court is to administer—the machinery as distinguished from its product ": *Poyser* v. *Minors* (1881) 7 Q.B.D. 329, 333.

[29] See, *e.g.*, *McElroy* v. *McAllister*, 1949 S.C. 110.

[30] Thus, *e.g.*, in Scots law it is a rule that loan of money may be proved by writ or oath only. If I lend money and seek to recover it, but have lost the debtor's written acknowledgment, is my right gone, or only my remedy barred (ignoring, for the sake of argument, the question of the debtor's oath)? What happens, on either of these views, if I later find the debtor's writ?

[31] *Cf.* Harvey, " A Job for Jurisprudence " (1944) 7 M.L.R. 42, 49; Lord Cooper, " Defects in the British Judicial Machinery " in (1953) 2 J.S.P.T.L.(N.S.) 91 and *Selected Papers*, 244.

[32] *e.g.*, Salmond.

[33] *e.g.*, Holland, Markby, Pollock, Keeton, Paton. *Cf.* Ersk., I, 1, 29, quoted *supra*.

```
                              ┌─General Part
                              │    Sources and literature
                              │    Authority and interpretation of sources
                              │    Fundamental concepts—the rule of law, separa-
                              │       tion of powers
                              ├─Constitutional law
                              │    The Crown
                              │    The executive—Privy Council and Cabinet
                              │    The legislature—Parliament
                              │    The judicial system, courts of general and special
                              │       jurisdiction
                              │    The civil service
                              │    The armed forces; courts-martial
                              │    Established churches; ecclesiastical law
                              │    Public revenue and taxation
                              │    Nationality and citizenship
                              │    Rights and liberties of citizens
                              │    Commonwealth, colonial and foreign relations
                              ├─Administrative law
                              │    Powers and functions of central departments
                              │    Powers and functions of local authorities
                ┌─PUBLIC ──  │    Powers and functions of public corporations
                │    LAW     │    Delegated legislative powers
                │            │    Delegated judicial powers—administrative tri-
                │            │       bunals
                │            │    Control of powers by Parliament and courts
                │            └─Criminal law
                │                 Sources and literature
                │                 Jurisdiction of criminal courts
                │                 Investigation and prosecution of crime
                │                 Nature of crime generally
                │                 Principles of liability in general
                │                 Liability in special cases
                │                 Constituent elements of various specific crimes
                │                 Criminal procedure
                │                 Evidence in criminal cases
                │                 Punishment and treatment
                │                 Appeal, commutation of sentence and pardon
                │            ┌─General Part
                │            │    Sources and literature
                │            │    Authority and interpretation of sources
                │            │    Fundamental concepts—personality, rights,
                │            │       duties
                │            │    General principles—good faith, public policy
                │            │    Effect of time on rights
                │            ├─International Private Law
                │            │    Preliminary concepts and classification
                │            │    Jurisdiction of Scottish or foreign court
                │            │    Choice of law
                │            │    Effect of foreign judgments
                │            ├─Law of persons
   LAW OF       │            │    Natural persons—status and capacity
   SCOTLAND─    │            │       in domestic relations—husband and wife
                │            │                              parent and child
                │            │                              guardian and ward
                │            │       in extra-domestic relations
                │            │    Unincorporated associations
                │            │       unestablished churches
                │            │       partnerships
                ↓            ↓       trade unions
```

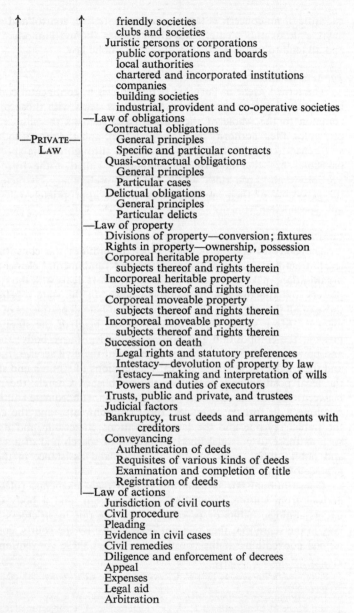

friendly societies
clubs and societies
Juristic persons or corporations
    public corporations and boards
    local authorities
    chartered and incorporated institutions
    companies
    building societies
    industrial, provident and co-operative societies
—Law of obligations
    Contractual obligations
        General principles
        Specific and particular contracts
    Quasi-contractual obligations
        General principles
        Particular cases
    Delictual obligations
        General principles
        Particular delicts
—Law of property
    Divisions of property—conversion; fixtures
    Rights in property—ownership, possession
    Corporeal heritable property
        subjects thereof and rights therein
    Incorporeal heritable property
        subjects thereof and rights therein
    Corporeal moveable property
        subjects thereof and rights therein
    Incorporeal moveable property
        subjects thereof and rights therein
    Succession on death
        Legal rights and statutory preferences
        Intestacy—devolution of property by law
        Testacy—making and interpretation of wills
        Powers and duties of executors
    Trusts, public and private, and trustees
    Judicial factors
    Bankruptcy, trust deeds and arrangements with
        creditors
    Conveyancing
        Authentication of deeds
        Requisites of various kinds of deeds
        Examination and completion of title
        Registration of deeds
—Law of actions
    Jurisdiction of civil courts
    Civil procedure
    Pleading
    Evidence in civil cases
    Civil remedies
    Diligence and enforcement of decrees
    Appeal
    Expenses
    Legal aid
    Arbitration

—PRIVATE—
LAW

in the present century on account of the greatly increased and still
increasing power and influence of the state and the greater extent to which
it controls, supervises and interferes in matters with which it previously

had little or no concern. State regulation, initiative, control and management, state or public enterprises and agencies abound in modern Britain and all tend to increase the importance of public law.

The General Part

The term " General Part " is better known in continental codes than in uncodified British law. The General Part deals with those principles common to the whole of the Public Law, such as the sources of the principles, their authority and interpretation, and the most fundamental and general concepts and ideas which run through all the specific and particular branches and rules. Salmond [34] called it the Introductory Portion—" all those rules which by their preliminary character or of the generality of their application cannot be appropriately relegated to any special department."

Constitutional Law

The body of legal principles which determines the constitution or legal structure of a state, the essential and fundamental elements of its organisation, make up its constitutional law.[35] It deals with the structure, powers and functions of the supreme power in the state together with those of all the more important of the subordinate departments of government.[36] More specifically it deals with the head of the state and his powers; the composition and powers of the legislative body; the status and powers of Ministers, the executive and of the civil service; the courts and their judges; the armed forces; the relations of Church and state and the legal position and powers of the established Church; the relations between central government and local or subordinate authorities; relations with foreign countries, the Commonwealth and the colonies; the public revenue and the law of taxation; citizenship and its rights, such as those to personal liberty, freedom of speech and of association, and public duties, such as of jury service and assistance in the maintenance of order.[37]

Constitutional law is made up of two main elements, rules of law derived from statute, decided cases and custom, and a body of rules, understandings, habits or practices which are not in strictness rules of law, in the sense that they will not be enforced by the courts, commonly termed conventions of the constitution.[38] Yet these conventional rules

---

[34] *Jurisprudence*, Appx. III.

[35] Salmond, *Jurisprudence*, 138; *cf.* Dicey, *Law of the Constitution*, 9th ed., Chap. 1.

[36] *Ibid.*, 506.

[37] Hood Phillips, *Constitutional Law*, 8–9. The whole of Chap. 1, " The Nature and Scope of Constitutional Law," is enlightening. The subject-matter of constitutional law can be discerned also from the bibliography in Chap. 9.

[38] The term was invented by A. V. Dicey in his *Law of the Constitution* (1885, 9th ed. 1939) and has been generally accepted since. See his discussion of the distinction at pp. 24–30.

and practices, while of very particular interest to the historian and political scientist, cannot be ignored by the lawyer in that they complete the structure, the bare bones of which are supplied by the law. Without the conventions the constitutional machinery would probably be unworkable, while many of the conventions could be ignored or flouted only at the expense of causing sooner or later a breach of the law or the breakdown of the machinery of government. Hence constitutional law has been defined as: " the rules of law, including binding conventions, which regulate the structure of the principal organs of government and their relationship to each other, and determine their principal functions." [39]

Constitutional law, possibly more than any other branch of law, requires to be studied with constant reference to its history and development. Many of its institutions and fundamental rules can be explained only by reference to the past circumstances which gave rise to them or caused the evolution to take a particular course. In consequence constitutional, legal and political history must regularly be prayed in aid for explanation, while many of the problems of the constitutional lawyer are equally pressing problems of the political scientist, because the organisation of the state is both a legal and a political conception and form of association or institution. The very haphazard historical development of the British Constitution, coupled with the fact that it has never been reduced as a whole to writing in the form of a single comprehensive legal document, as is customary in other countries, is one reason for the tangled and illogical nature of many of the rules of constitutional law. The close connection between law and politics in the sphere of constitutional law may be seen from the fact that the working of the British Constitution must be explained not merely in terms of rules of law but also of practices or conventions of political origin.

Administrative Law and Procedure

Administrative law has been recognised as a distinct branch of law and topic of legal study in Britain only in the last fifty years or so, owing to the enormous growth of its manifestations during that period, though the subject is really much older. There is no rigid line between it and constitutional law since the difference is mainly one of convenience and degree, constitutional law dealing with structure and with the broader rules which regulate function, while the details of function are left to administrative law.[40]

It is that part of public law which describes the nature of the activities of the executive and administrative portions of government, the powers and duties of executive departments, agencies and officials and their

[39] Wade and Phillips, *Constitutional Law*, 2.
[40] Maitland, *Constitutional History*, 526–539.

relations with individuals, the forms and instruments in and through which the lower ranges of government operate.[41]

Thus it deals with the organisation and functions of the various departments of the central government, such as the Treasury and the Scottish Office, the various authorities of local government, such as county councils, which exercise functions within particular limited areas only, and of the public corporations and statutory bodies, set up by the state yet not departments thereof, for the exercise of various specific social or economic functions, such as the National Coal Board, Regional Hospital Boards, Agricultural Marketing Boards, the British Broadcasting Corporation. The first execute the policy of Parliament, under the direction of the Ministers of the Crown, the second the policy of representatives elected by local government electors within the framework set by Parliament, but the third are neither government departments under the control of Ministers of State nor are they elected by the electorate.[42] The functions of central departments, local authorities and public corporations are very numerous and the law is bulky and complicated: it covers such matters as police and fire services, public utilities, roads and bridges, public education, housing, social services, public health, licensing, town and country planning, the regulation of industry, trade and agriculture, supervision of factories and mines, valuation and rating, compulsory purchase of land and compensation therefor, and all the great variety of circumstances in which the state exercises control or guidance over people's lives in the general interest, or, directly or indirectly, provides some benefit or service for them.

Departments, local authorities and public bodies, moreover, have delegated to them by Parliament certain limited legislative powers, of making rules binding within limited spheres only in the form of rules, orders, by-laws, and so on, and the scope of and limitations on these powers also fall to be studied.

While administrative agencies and officials work to some extent through the ordinary civil and criminal courts and processes, of great importance are the special administrative courts, tribunals and procedures frequently set up to determine matters of controversy arising in the course of administering some particular service or body of administrative controls, so that to some extent along with each branch of the public administration one must study the particular machinery provided for

41 Salmond, *Jurisprudence*, 506–507; *cf.* Jennings, *The Law and the Constitution*, 3rd ed., 194. See also Chap. 9, *infra*.
42 See generally Campion (ed.) *British Government since* 1918; Greaves, " Public Service Boards " (1944) 7 M.L.R. 25; Friedmann, " The New Public Corporations and the Law " (1947) 10 M.L.R. 233, 377; Wade, " The Constitutional Aspect of the Public Corporation," 1949 *Current Legal Problems*, 172; Robson, " The Public Corporations in Britain To-day " (1950) 63 H.L.R. 1321; Robson, *Nationalised Industry and Public Ownership*; Friedmann, *Law and Social Change*, Chap. 9.

enforcement or the resolution of disputes in connection therewith. Thus the system of National Insurance set up in 1948 brought into existence not merely a new Ministry, and a mass of new legal rights and duties, but a special system of tribunals for determining disputes concerning entitlement to a payment of National Insurance benefits.

The problems of administrative law are amongst the most interesting of the present day, not least because they are frequently politico-economic-legal and not purely legal, in that they raise fundamental problems of social policy and of government as well as of pure law. The salient problems of administrative law can probably be said to be:

(1) The extent to which and the powers under which Ministers and departments of state enjoy authority delegated by Parliament to make rules, regulations and orders, filling in with details the gaps left by skeleton legislation, and the control of this delegated legislative power by the courts.[43]

(2) The extent to which and the ways in which the individual may, either through the ordinary civil courts or by administrative means, inquire into, question and challenge the exercise of administrative powers and in some cases check and limit such executive action.[44]

(3) The extent to which the ordinary courts can review and control the proceedings of administrative tribunals and officials exercising a judicial power or right to determine disputes.[45]

(4) The way in which adequate supervision and control of public corporations may be exercised by Parliament in the interests of the consumer and taxpayer, while allowing the authority freedom from detailed control and avoiding excessive centralisation.[46]

(5) Special rules relative to litigation against executive officials and departments, a topic sometimes conveniently entitled Crown Proceedings.[47]

Administrative law exhibits equally with constitutional law the defects of unplanned historical development, lack of coherent system, and a welter of individual cases, each facet of public administration having a system of

---

[43] See generally Carr, *Delegated Legislation*; *Concerning English Administrative Law*; Allen, *Law and Orders*; *Law in the Making*; Sieghart, *Government by Decree*; Kersell, *Parliamentary Supervision of Delegated Legislation*; Report of the Committee on Ministers' Powers (Cmd. 4060, 1932).

[44] The above books and Report of the Committee on Administrative Tribunals and Enquiries (Cmnd. 218, 1957).

[45] See Griffith and Street, *Administrative Law*; Allen, *Law and Orders*; de Smith, *Judicial Review of Administrative Action*.

[46] See Morrison, *Government and Parliament*, Chap. 12; Friedmann, *Law and Social Change in Contemporary Britain*, Chap. 9.

[47] See Bickford Smith and Middleton, *The Crown Proceedings Act*, 1947; Glanville Williams, *Crown Proceedings*.

its own.[48] The law is developing rapidly and is constantly undergoing change, though much remains to be done to fashion it into a coherent body of doctrine. Public dissatisfaction with aspects of it has twice given rise to investigations of aspects of the subject by strong committees [49] which recommended many changes, not all of which have been carried into effect.[50] It is in the sphere of administrative law more than any other that the rights and liberties of the subject are involved in modern times and most of the important cases illustrate one facet or another of the constant struggle between the state and the individual, between government and freedom.

Criminal Law and Procedure

While constitutional and administrative law overlap and run into one another, criminal law stands rather apart from the rest of Public Law with a considerable literature of its own. The criminal law consists of the body of rules relative to crimes and offences, that is, to such human acts and omissions as the supreme authority in the state wishes to prevent and consequently declares wrong, deserving to be repressed, and punishable. The distinction between wrongs which are criminal and those which are rated by the legal system as merely civil wrongs or delicts depends not on the essential nature of the act or omission in question but simply on whether the government policy of the time deems the activity to deserve repression by punishment on the ground that its doing or repetition would be harmful to the community. Some wrongful conduct, such as assault, may be both a crime and a delict; conversely, adultery was once a crime and is now only a delict [51]; while modern social policy requires many kinds of conduct to be made criminal and repressed though they were previously innocent. Accordingly the main distinguishing mark of criminal law is that the state rather than an individual initiates proceedings, which have as their object the punishment of the wrongdoer and the repression of such conduct, rather than compensation for a person harmed.

So, too, classification as criminal does not necessarily follow from the inherent wrongness or wickedness or immorality of an act; thus it is no crime to commit fornication, nor, in general, to let a person drown

---

[48] The principal discussions, analyses and criticisms are Allen, *Law and Orders*; Robson, *Justice and Administrative Law*; Schwarz, *Law and the Executive in Britain*; Carr, *Concerning English Administrative Law*.

[49] Committee on Ministers' Powers (Donoughmore Committee), 1931–32 (Report—Cmd. 4060), and Committee on Administrative Tribunals and Enquiries (Franks Committee), 1955–57 (Report—Cmnd. 218).

[50] See Tribunals and Inquiries Act, 1958.

[51] The confusion between criminal wrongs and civil wrongs (delicts) is very marked in early systems of law; see, *e.g.*, Maine's *Ancient Law*, Chap. 1; Walker, " The Development of Reparation " (1952) 64 J.R. 101; Robson, *Civilisation and the Growth of Law*, Chap. 8.

unassisted. Unless the activity has been condemned by common law or statute as criminal it may be done with impunity so far as the criminal law is concerned.

A distinctive characteristic of those activities declared criminal is that they are dealt with by legal proceedings of a special kind, in distinct courts and by distinct procedure and for practical purposes an important classification of crimes is into those triable by a judge and jury in the superior criminal courts, carrying a heavy penalty, and those triable by a sheriff or magistrate, without a jury, in the inferior criminal courts and carrying only a limited penalty. There is also a substantial area of overlap between the two in that some crimes may according to circumstances be dealt with either in the superior or inferior courts.

In the study of criminal law there are three main topics for consideration: there is the general problem of criminal liability, that is, the question of what physical acts or omissions and what concomitant mental states will import criminal liability [52]; secondly, there is the problem of variations in liability, that is, of what differences from the normal rules of liability exist in the case of individuals who are in some respect abnormal, either temporarily or permanently, as by reason of youth, insanity, intoxication, pregnancy or amnesia. Lastly, there is the problem of what factual and mental elements are required to constitute various specific and individual types of crimes: this is really the application in detail of the general conditions of criminal liability to particular crimes. When dealing with these specific crimes they are frequently conveniently grouped into crimes against the state, such as treason and breach of the peace, which are harmful to the peace and order of the community, crimes against the person, such as murder, rape, and assault, which are infringements of some individual's personal integrity, and crimes against property, such as arson, malicious damage, theft and reset.[53]

In criminal procedure the main topics are the constitution and competence or jurisdiction of the different courts dealing with criminal cases, the means of investigating crimes, of apprehension of suspects, and of initiating criminal proceedings, the steps which have to be gone through before, at and after trial, the course of procedure at trial, specialties of the rules of evidence in criminal cases, the protection of the accused, the provision for appeal and the modes of punishment or treatment of the convicted which may be ordered in different circumstances.[54]

---

[52] See further Allen, " The Nature of a Crime," in *Legal Duties*, 221; Kenny, " The Nature of a Crime," in his *Outlines of Criminal Law*, 16th ed., Appx. I; Hall, *General Principles of Criminal Law, passim*; Williams, *The Criminal Law— The General Part. Cf.* also Hall Williams, " The Proper Scope and Function of the Criminal Law " (1958) 74 L.Q.R. 76.

[53] Crimes against property are by far the most numerous.

[54] See further Chap. 9, *infra*.

The discussion of the purposes of punishment and treatment and of the most appropriate methods for various kinds of criminals and crimes is so important as to be a subject in itself, and one nowadays attracting greater attention more commensurate with its importance.

Criminology and Penology

The body of criminal law and procedure is necessarily closely connected with those other branches of social studies which are concerned with the volume of socially harmful conduct in the community.[55] The criminal law and its procedure is the instrument of the criminal policy of the state in its task of repressing and punishing socially harmful conduct. That policy leans heavily on criminology, the study of the causes of crime and criminality, both those causes which may be traced to the mental and physical constitution or abnormalities of the delinquent, such as his heredity and innate defects of character, and those which may be ascribed to the effects of social environment, such as bad housing, evil companions, poverty or unemployment, poor conditions of work and so on. " Criminology is the body of knowledge regarding crime as a social phenomenon. . . . The objective of criminology is the development of a body of general and verified principles and of other types of knowledge regarding this process of law, crime, and treatment or prevention." [56]

The discovery of the causes of crime will naturally lead to the study of suitable measures to remove or neutralise them and also, so long as criminal conduct continues to take place, study must similarly be devoted to methods of education, deterrence, repression and punishment, the suitability of particular sanctions for particular individuals, the institutions in which offenders should be treated and the methods of training and reformation which can best be employed to bring home to the offender the wrongness of his conduct and lead him on release to live an honest life.[57] This is the science of penology, which increasingly influences state criminal policy.

While neither criminology nor penology is a branch of law in the strict sense, both are so bound up with criminal law that the study of the latter inevitably leads to the former and it is from the criminal policy of the country, informed by the discoveries of criminology and penology, that guidance can be found for the reform and development of criminal law.[58]

---

[55] See Radzinowicz and Turner, " The Meaning and Scope of Criminal Science," in *Modern Approach to Criminal Law* (1948), 12 *et seq.*
[56] Sutherland and Cressey, *Principles of Criminology*, 6th ed., 3.
[57] See further Fox, *English Prison and Borstal System.*
[58] A good general introduction to this subject are the volumes of the *English Studies in Criminal Science* (now *Cambridge Studies in Criminology*) series, especially Vol. I: *Penal Reform in England*; Vol. II: *Mental Abnormality and Crime*; and Vol. IV: *Modern Approach to Criminal Law.*

These sciences in turn lean heavily on sociology, statistics, psychology and psychiatry.

IVB.—PRIVATE LAW

Private law is the other main branch of state or municipal law, dealing in the main with the legal relations of individuals with other individuals or with state departments and agencies in matters wherein the latter have no special privileges, but only the rights and powers, duties and liabilities of private individuals. It defines what interests, claims or demands are recognised and protected by rules of law and how they may be vindicated against other individuals. Despite the growth of state intervention it is the private law which is of greatest concern to the layman and his legal adviser and most of the personal and economic relationships a man has with other men are regulated by private law.

The fundamental and best-known division of private law is still that of the Roman lawyers,[59] into law of persons, law of things, and law of actions, and this, with its subdivisions, is the basis for most later classifications. Another classification formerly employed was into personal rights, that is, claims against another individual only, and real rights, that is, claims enforceable against some object of property such as a man's house.[60] The division here adopted, based on the Roman one, is convenient for study and understanding as well as for practical purposes.

The General Part

For academic purposes it is again useful to segregate for separate study the most general ideas which apply throughout the whole of private law, such topics as the recognised sources of law,[61] their respective authority and the accepted principles for their interpretation, the most fundamental conceptions, such as legal personality, status, rights and duties, obligation, and so on, principles of wide general application such as good faith, public policy and personal bar, and the effect of lapse of time on rights as by cutting them off, altering the rules of proof, or limiting the right to sue on those rights. These general ideas have to be gathered from their piecemeal examination in books on diverse specific topics and in Scots and common law systems are largely relegated to books on jurisprudence, whereas in civil law systems they belong to the General or Introductory Part of the Civil Code.[62]

---

[59] Inst., I, iii, 12. Omne autem jus quo utimur, vel ad personas pertinet, vel ad res vel ad actiones. *Cf.* Ersk., I, 2, 1.
[60] See, *e.g.*, Ersk., IV, 1, 10.
[61] For the term " sources of law," see Chap. 8, *infra.*
[62] These topics are to some extent dealt with in the opening sections of the works of the institutional writers: see, *e.g.*, Stair, I, 1; Erskine, I, 1.

International Private Law

It has been pointed out already that in general every state or national territory has a distinct system of law, and the courts and other agencies for enforcing that law. It follows that a group of facts raising a legal problem may involve a foreign element, in that one of the parties may live under another legal régime or that some material fact, such as the performance of a contract, may take place in a foreign country.[63] In recent years the extension of business and commercial relations throughout the world, of foreign travel and service abroad, of intermarriage and migration, have increased this tendency and swelled the number of cases in which a foreign element arises. Accordingly in every case three preliminary problems fall to be determined, namely, what country's courts have jurisdiction, or the legal power of determining this controversy; secondly, once that has been decided, what system of law falls to be applied to determine the controversy; and, thirdly, what effect is to be given to any foreign judgment in existence on the matter in issue.[64]

The rules which exist for resolving these preliminary problems are the rules of international private law, conflict of laws, or private international law. All three names have found support yet none is specially felicitous.[65] The first is probably best as indicating what the topic truly covers, namely, private law so far as it has an international or extra-national character or has to take account of extra-national factors.

It is to be noted that, despite the similarity of names, these rules have no connection with, or even similarity to, Public International Law,[66] and that unlike that body of law, the rules of international private law are not common to all or many legal systems, but are bodies of rules which are part of each particular legal system and vary from one state to another as do the other parts of the several legal systems. International private law or private international law is therefore that part of the private law of a particular state which determines, in a case involving a foreign element, whether the courts of that state have jurisdiction to determine the issue

---

[63] Notice that for the purposes of the Scottish rules of International Private Law, England is a foreign country as much as France or Peru. The converse is equally true.

[64] While logically the possibility that a problem raises an issue of International Private Law has in every case to be considered first, it is in fact convenient to postpone the study of the principles of International Private Law to a late stage in legal studies, dealing with cases having a foreign element only after the principles applicable to cases not thus complicated have been studied.

[65] The name "conflict of laws" is supported by the Bills of Exchange Act, 1882, s. 72; see also *Ewing* v. *Orr-Ewing* (1885) 13 R.(H.L.) 1.

[66] See further Stevenson, "Relationship of Private International Law to Public International Law" (1952) 52 Col.L.R. 561; Gutteridge, "Comparative Law and the Conflict of Laws" (1944) Trans. Grotius Society, 119; Schmitthoff, "The Science of Comparative Law" (1939) 7 Camb.L.J. 107; Starke, "The Relation between Private and Public International Law" (1937) 52 L.Q.R. 395; Beckett, "What is Private International Law?" (1926) 7 B.Y.I.L. 73.

and, if so, what system of law falls to be applied, and what effect given to any foreign judgment there may be. It is in a sense a series of appendices to the main subjects of private law, in that a question of conflict of laws may arise in any and every branch of private law.[67] Thus marriage is a matter of private law: if it involves a foreign element, *e.g.*, is celebrated abroad, the international private law rules relative to marriage come into play. So too there are conflict of laws rules applicable to contracts, property, and so on. Moreover, it is noteworthy that the rules of international private law do not solve the actual problems which arise, but simply answer the preliminary questions which will enable the courts to decide whether it is their duty or not to decide the case, by directing them to deal with or to decline to handle the controversy, and in the former case, to apply Scots law or another system, as may be required in the circumstances. It is then for the rules of the Scots law or other system chosen to determine the rights and duties of the parties.

It further follows that in some cases the appropriate answer given by one country's rules of international private law will be that that country's courts have no jurisdiction to deal with the case, or that they have jurisdiction but must apply another country's rules of private law to the matter in issue; it is therefore not in every case that a country's courts will adjudicate upon a case brought before them, or will apply their own system of private law to that case. The justification for this possible declinature of jurisdiction or application of another country's rules of law by a court is fundamentally the interests of justice, and the general practice of civilised countries in recognising, by the comity of nations, and giving effect to, rights acquired under another legal system or properly enforceable by other courts. Difficulties may arise, however, as to the determination of what foreign rules may be applied by a state since the domestic private law of some states might be unsuitable for application or recognition by another state. The tendency is to recognise all rights acquired under the law of another country unless their recognition is flatly contradictory of fundamental principles of British law.[68]

Law of persons

Law deals with the rights and duties of legal persons, and duties and rights attach to legal persons. But there are " persons " in law who are not individual human beings, who are groups of individuals collectively personified by law as artificial or juristic persons and also groups which are treated as entities for some purposes yet not fully recognised as

---

[67] Such questions do not arise in public law since it is concerned only with transactions within the frontiers of the country in question.

[68] On the history of the subject see Yntema, " The Historic Bases of Private International Law " (1953) 2 Am.Jo.Compar.L. 297; Sack, " Conflict of Laws in the History of English Law," in *Law, A Century of Progress*, III, 342.

legal persons. Personality is in law the attribution by the legal system of legal existence, of the ability to have legal rights and to be subject to legal duties, and it is for the law itself to lay down what kinds of human beings, of groups of beings and of institutions, have legal personality.[69]

The law of natural persons deals with all the rights, privileges and powers which attach by law to an individual as such, independently of rights acquired by contract or rights arising from the possession of property. It relates first to the recognition of an individual's legal personality, or his existence in the eyes of the law, and of his legal status and capacity, as being a minor or a person of full age or an incapax, and as having various rights, powers and immunities, and being subject to various duties, liabilities and disabilities.[70]

Secondly, the law of persons deals with the law of domestic relations, those legal rules which affect an individual by reason of his membership of a family group and govern his interactions with others of that group. This branch falls into three main topics concerned respectively with relations flowing from marriage, parenthood, and guardianship, frequently called the law of husband and wife, parent and child, and guardian and ward respectively.[71] In each of these spheres one is concerned with the constitution and termination of the relationship, the mutual rights and duties which flow from it during its subsistence, and the regulation of the matrimonial or family property rights of the parties.

At the centre of all these relationships lies the cardinal social, moral and religious institution of marriage of which the root conception is a lasting and permanent, though possibly not lifelong, union of one male and one female for cohabitation, as distinct from a merely temporary association.[72] This idea of lasting union has been recognised by every legal system in varying degrees; in Christian countries monogamous marriage alone is fully recognised though polygamous or potentially polygamous marriages contracted under other legal and religious régimes are not necessarily wholly devoid of recognition and effect.

The nature of marriage and the conditions under which it may be contracted and under which, if indeed at all, it may be dissolved, is a difficult modern social, moral and religious as well as legal problem.[73]

---

[69] On the concept of personality see further Salmond, *Jurisprudence*, Chap. 15.

[70] Much of the detail of this branch of the law of persons is, for reasons of convenience, discussed also in connection with constitutional law (*e.g.*, the right to become an M.P. or a naturalised subject), or contract (*e.g.*, power to make a contract), or reparation (*e.g.*, rights to liberty, reputation and freedom from harm), or property (*e.g.*, right of landowner to cut timber).

[71] The name " Family Law " is being increasingly given to this branch of the subject, as a convenient compendious term for its main topics.

[72] On marriage generally see Westermarck's *History of Human Marriage*; James, *Marriage and Society*; Lecky, *History of European Morals*.

[73] See Report of the Royal Commission on Marriage and Divorce (Cmd. 9678, 1956).

The rules of law on the subject at any time can only be those which commend themselves as a compromise solution to a large proportion of the community. The legal rules, it should be noted, are those of the state and not of the individual's Church, so that the state law may permit a person to do what his religious beliefs and his Church will not permit him to do, and conversely. The legal rules are those which seem best, having regard to marriage primarily as a social institution, though they naturally tend to correspond fairly closely with the general view of the principal Churches. But there are many matters on which the law is silent and the Churches may exert their influence unhindered on their own members.

It follows that there are bodies of legal rules regulating the contracting of marriage and the dissolution of marriage and the consequences which result in various departments of law from the fact that two individuals are husband and wife. Formerly, the fact that a woman was married placed her under numerous and serious legal disabilities, but over the last hundred years the movement has been towards the emancipation of women and these disabilities are now greatly diminished.[74]

In the same way legal consequences, mutual rights and duties, follow from the birth of children, and these differ according as the children are legitimate or illegitimate, while there must also be considered the third, intermediate, category of those who are adopted by individuals as their children though not born as such.

The last topic of family law, guardianship, arises from the natural incapacity of young persons and persons of defective mental capacity to look after themselves or exercise the judgment required in legal transactions. Accordingly there is a body of rules laying down the extent of legal incapacity of various categories of persons too young or mentally too weak to be allowed to act on their own behalf and prescribing what persons may act on their behalf and by what means the appropriate person may be selected and appointed and authorised to act on behalf of the ward, and what the mutual rights and duties of guardian and ward shall be.

Guardianship, it should not be overlooked, is not merely a matter between the parties, but is today of increased social importance as part of the complex legal machinery for the care and protection of children and others unable to look after themselves, and it is now regarded as increasingly important that these persons should have as good opportunities as other individuals of growing up and developing their potentialities.

The law of natural persons also covers the capacities and powers of

---

[74] See *A Century of Family Law*, 1857–1957 (ed. Graveson and Crane). The details belong to English law only, but the general parts apply substantially to Scotland also.

individuals in extra-domestic relations, that is, vis-a-vis persons outside the family, the status, capacity and powers of exceptional persons such as aliens, bankrupts, convicts, and persons of unsound mind, in their relations with other persons, and the special capacities and powers attaching to persons by virtue of professional qualifications.

It has been pointed out that legal persons include not only human beings or natural persons; there are also groups of persons who come together for particular purposes and form voluntary associations. These associations are to some extent and for limited purposes treated by the law as legal entities, but are unincorporated, *i.e.*, not fully recognised as legal persons in themselves.[75] The device of association is rather a collective name for the group of members, though in some cases such associations come very close to being legal persons or corporations. Of this kind are churches other than the legally established church, friendly societies, trade unions, partnerships, trustee savings banks and many clubs, societies and professional bodies.

Thirdly, however, there are those other cases where the groups formed by the association of individuals for specific purposes are treated by the law as themselves legal entities or juristic persons, with legal powers and capacities, liabilities and duties, quite independent and separate from those attaching to the persons who form the group. This arises only where the group is incorporated in a manner recognised by law; the corporation, not the members, owns the property, sues and is sued, can contract, do wrong, and even commit crime, and it will still exist if all the members die.[76] The main examples of juristic persons are public corporations incorporated by statute, such as the National Coal Board, and municipal corporations, both considered in their private capacities, *e.g.* as employers or buyers of goods, chartered bodies such as Universities, Royal Colleges and professional institutions, companies incorporated under the Companies Acts, building societies, and industrial and provident societies.

In the cases of voluntary associations and of corporations the law of persons defines the way in which the association or corporation comes into being, its powers and capacities, its duties and liabilities, the relations between the body and its members and outsiders, the position of the representatives who act in its name, and the way in which the association or corporation may be ended and dissolved. While in many respects associations and corporations can act like natural persons in other respects

[75] See generally Lloyd, *Unincorporated Associations*.
[76] See further Geldart " Legal Personality " (1911) 27 L.Q.R. 90; Wolff, " On the Nature of Legal Persons " (1938) 54 L.Q.R. 494; Gray, *Nature and Sources of the Law*, Chap. 2; Hallis, *Corporate Personality*; Salmond, *Jurisprudence*, Chap. 15; Maitland " Trust and Corporation " in *Collected Papers*, III, 321, and *Selected Essays*, 141. See also Gower, *Modern Company Law*, 2nd ed., Chaps. 1–3 and 11.

they cannot, nor are the different kinds of associations and of corporations all alike.[77]

Law of Obligations

The law of obligations covers all those sets of circumstances when two persons come to be so placed that the law imposes a legal link or bond between them from which flow rights, duties, liabilities, privileges, disabilities and powers as between one another.[78] This department of law again falls into three branches.

The first is the law of contract, which deals with the rules whereby individuals may contract or agree in legal and binding form to create certain rights and duties, claims and liabilities between themselves and exigible from each other only. Thus where A and B agree, the one to buy and the other to sell, there is a legal contract of sale, and the law imposes duties on one to deliver the goods and on the other to pay the price, or grants remedies for defective performance or non-performance. The law of contract deals generally with the capacity of individuals to contract, the form requisite for contracts, the effect of such factors as error or fraud on the making of a valid contract, the illegality of some contracts, performance, and remedies for breach of contract. The general principles of the law of contract have been determined inductively by jurists from the examination of the particular cases. This branch also includes the particular and specific kinds of contracts which, as well as being regulated by the general principles applicable to all or at least most kinds of contracts, have frequently specialties and peculiarities applicable only to contracts of those particular kinds. In many cases, too, there are statutory provisions applicable to particular kinds of contracts only. The main specific contracts are agency, banking contracts, cautionry and guarantee, carriage by land, by sea, and by air, custody, deposit, employment or service, hire, hire-purchase, insurance, lease, loan, moneylenders' contracts, partnership, pledge, sale of goods, of land, and of incorporeal rights, and of works such as building and engineering contracts.

The second branch of obligations, usually known as quasi-contract or restitution, covers various miscellaneous cases of obligation which are neither truly contractual, despite the name, not truly delictual, but which resemble contract in that they might have arisen from contract and may even fictionally be supposed to have done so, and resemble reparation or delict in that the obligation is imposed by force of the general law rather than undertaken by agreement of the parties. The circumstances giving rise to a quasi-contractual obligation all have the

---

[77] See further bibliography in Chap. 9, *infra*.
[78] *Cf.* Inst. 3, 13, *pr.* Obligatio est juris vinculum, quo necessitate adstringimur alicuius solvendae rei, secundum nostrae civitatis jura.

common element that, if the law did not impose in these circumstances
an obligation to make restitution, one party would benefit unjustifiably
and the other would lose. Thus quasi-contractual obligations of restitution are imposed by law where one man pays by mistake money which
he did not owe, or where one comes into possession of another's property
not intended for him.

The third branch of obligations is the law of reparation or delict,
whereby the law by its own force and independently of any agreement
imposes on one individual a legal obligation to make compensation for,
or otherwise to remedy, a legal wrong he has done to another, which has
constituted an infringement of a legal right vested in that other person by
a general principle of law. Thus the law invests individuals generally
with a right to freedom from bodily harm; if X injures Y the law creates
an obligation of reparation, imposing on X the duty to compensate Y,
and giving Y a right of legal action to recover reasonable reparation from
X for his injuries. The law of reparation defines the circumstances in
which and conditions under which such a claim to reparation arises.
There is again a body of general principles applicable generally to all or
at least most delicts, dealing with such matters as title to sue, the liability
of one person for another, the general grounds of liability, defences and
exemptions from liability, the effect of insurance and contributory
negligence, the remedies, and so on. In addition there are principles
applicable to specific delicts, to harm done in particular ways. The main
specific delicts recognised are assault, damage to property, defamation,
fraud, negligently causing personal injury or death, infringement of
copyright or patent rights, nuisance, passing-off, trespass, and wrongful
imprisonment or use of legal process, but the list is not closed and new
modes of wrongs may yet call for recognition and remedy.

These bodies of law are of enormous practical importance. Contract
is obviously of great importance in business and trade, and commercial
undertakings engage every day in numerous contracts, of employment
of men, of hiring of plant, of purchase of material, of sale of finished
products, of carriage of goods to consignees, and so on. The individual
likewise enters into and performs contracts every time he buys a newspaper, travels on public transport, orders coal, instructs the plumber
to repair his water-taps and so on. Reparation or delict is similarly of
widespread and everyday importance. Every accident in the street or at
work may give rise to a claim of damages in reparation for the breach
of duty, i.e., the legal duty or obligation, imposed on each of us by the
legal system, not unjustifiably to injure or do harm to our neighbour.
Quasi-contract or restitution is much less common or important yet
arises not infrequently.

The law of obligations in one branch or another accordingly regulates a great deal of our relations with one another in the normal life of society and it covers a very extensive body of principles and rules of law. It is important to remember that the number of cases of breach of contract or cases where contracts fail of their intended effect are enormously outnumbered by the cases where legal contracts are made, duly performed on both sides, and terminated to the complete satisfaction of both parties, all in accordance with the rules of the law of contract, but without the legal system being formally invoked at all. So, too, in the great majority of cases persons avoid doing unjustifiable harm to others and avoid coming under the duty to pay damages in compensation for wrong, that is, they manage to observe the legal obligation not to do wrong to others.[79]

Law of Property

The law of property [80] consists of all the rules conferring, defining and regulating legal rights vested in individuals over material and immaterial things, rights of ownership, possession, use, alienation, and disposal. It is a large and important subject of law because of the great number, importance, utility and value of the kinds of property recognised, and of the number and variety of the kinds of legal rights which may be exercised in relation thereto. For various reasons, partly historical, partly rational, various kinds of property have special sets of rules applicable to them. Moreover, in modern times legislative intervention in property law has been common, the underlying notion being to limit or prevent the use of property for personal or selfish ends and to encourage and even require its use in the interest of the general welfare. Thus disposal on death is limited by death duties and the rules of succession, and use during life is regulated by requirements of licences, planning permission, requisition or compulsory purchase by public authorities and so on.

Property, however, takes many forms and a distinction must be drawn at once between heritable and moveable property,[81] which, in general, relate respectively to land and buildings on the one hand and to goods, such as clothes, furniture and vehicles, on the other hand. This distinction, moreover, is close to but does not quite coincide with the physical distinction between immoveable and moveable property, which is a distinction

---

[79] See further bibliography in Chap. 9, *infra*.

[80] Note that the word " property " may mean either some thing over which legal rights subsist (*e.g.*, " desirable property situated at . . . "), or the legal right of property, of holding, using and disposing of a thing.

[81] This corresponds, in general though *not* exactly, to the distinction in English law between real and personal property; land is real property, books, money and shares personal property. In neither system does the distinction correspond *exactly* to that between moveables and immoveables. Note also that " moveable " in this connotation is spelled with an " e." On the distinction between heritable and moveable property, see further Erskine, *Inst.* II, 2; Bell's *Commentaries*, II, 1–10.

important where problems of conflict of laws arise. This is not a distinction drawn entirely on logical grounds but stems from the dualism of rules of succession on death whereby for reasons explicable only by legal history some property (heritable property) descends to the person designated by the law as heir, and some (moveable property) descends to the persons designated by the law as next-of-kin. Difficult questions sometimes arise as to whether some thing is in the circumstances heritable or moveable, and it must be noted that a thing may shift from one category to the other: thus trees are heritable, but when cut the timber is moveable.

Cutting across this division into heritable and moveable property is the distinction of corporeal and incorporeal property, according as there is a corporeal, visible and tangible object over which the property-rights subsist, such as land, buildings or goods, or only an incorporeal right, such as patent rights and copyrights, shares in companies, leases or servitudes. In the latter case all that exists is the legal right, which may, however, be represented by some tangible object such as a deed, certificate or other piece of paper; but in such a case the paper is evidence only of the right, and is not itself the object of the proprietary right.

A further distinction of importance applicable to all kinds of property is that between *jura in re propria*, or the rights which an individual may exercise over or in relation to objects of his own property, whether material or immaterial, such as enjoying, using, selling or bequeathing them, and *jura in re aliena*, or those rights which an individual may possess and exercise in or over the property of another, whether material or immaterial, such as using a servitude or holding a security right over it, or enjoying a lease of it. The rights, *jura in re propria* or proprietary rights, which a man has over his own property are those of ownership and possession. The full rights of ownership include the power to use the property, deal with its fruits or produce or earnings, and to use up or consume or destroy; the power to possess in person or by another; the power to sell or to give or burden as security for debt; and the power to bequeath or give by will.

These rights are not by any means unqualified; thus the common law rules of nuisance limit the uses to which land may be put while statutory regulations restrict building or development, and the power of bequest is restricted by the doctrine of legal rights.[82] The modern tendency is to limit very much by statute the exercise of the rights of ownership in the general interest of the community. Social and political theory and the economic exigencies of modern times have played havoc with property rights and there is as much law, and more complicated law, dealing with

[82] See under Succession, *infra.*

what one is not now allowed to do than with what one may do at common law.

Jura in re aliena, on the other hand, are created by the transfer by an owner to another of certain of the mass of rights which he enjoys by virtue of his ownership; in consequence the other party comes to have certain defined and limited rights in property which he does not himself own. *Jura in re aliena* are always incorporeal. The commonest forms of such rights are first, the taking of a lease of land or buildings, whereby a tenant acquires the right to possess and occupy certain property for a defined period and on conditions defined partly by the general law, both of statute and of common law, and partly by the terms of the lease or tenancy agreement. The comparable transaction in moveable property is that of letting on hire. The second important kind of *jus in re aliena* consists of the transfer of property, heritable or moveable, to another in security for the repayment of money borrowed by the owner from that other. This has various forms, some applicable to heritable property [83] and some to moveable property [84]; in some the title is transferred to the lender [85] but in others, particularly of moveable property, only possession and not full title of ownership is transferred.[86] The third main item under this heading is the servitude or right of another to put an owner's property to a certain class of definitely limited uses [87] or to prevent the owner from putting it to a certain class of determined uses.[88] A servitude right is normally real, *i.e.*, attaching to and exercisable over a piece of land, but there is a small class of personal servitudes, of which the only important example is liferent, or the right of one person to occupy or use certain property during his lifetime only, and not as absolute owner, and for that period to be a burden or encumbrance on the rights of the owner. The last kind of *jus in re aliena* is the trust where the holder of property as trustee has his rights qualified by the claims of the beneficiary, for whose benefit he holds the property.[89]

These distinctions may be summed up in tabular form [90]:

---

[83] *e.g.*, bond and disposition in security (*i.e.*, bond to repay and disposition of heritable property in security for repayment), or disposition and back-letter (acknowledging the loan and promising reconveyance on being repaid).

[84] *e.g.*, pawn or pledge; assignation in security (for incorporeals).

[85] *e.g.*, in disposition or assignation in security.

[86] *e.g.*, in pledge.

[87] *e.g.*, right of way, *i.e.*, right to pass over X's land by a determined path.

[88] *e.g.*, right *altius non tollendi*, to prevent X's raising his building higher and thereby cutting off light and air.

[89] On trusts see further p. 160, *infra*.

[90] The items of property listed in the two columns are examples of each class only, not a complete enumeration.

PROPERTY

		Heritable	*Moveable*	
Jura in re propria	over material things	land, buildings, woods,	goods, vehicles, furniture,	Corporeal property
	over immaterial rights	arms, dignities, titles of honour	patents, trade-marks, debts, claims for damages	
Jura in re aliena	over material things	liferents, leases, servitudes, some dispositions in security	trusts, liens, some dispositions in security	Incorporeal property
	over immaterial rights	reversionary rights under entail	assignations in security	

Accordingly, the law of property falls naturally into a preliminary part and four main branches. The preliminary part deals with the classification of things and rights as heritable or moveable, corporeal or incorporeal, with " fixtures," that is, with the circumstances in which a thing moveable by nature may be treated in law as so affixed to heritage as to be heritable, and with the doctrines of conversion and reconversion, that is, with the circumstances in which a claim to heritable property may be changed in law to a claim to moveable property and vice versa, as where, for example, land bequeathed by will has been converted into money before the will takes effect. The four branches are (i) corporeal heritable property, such as land, buildings, growing timber and crops; (ii) incorporeal heritable property, such as titles and rights to arms, leases of land, servitudes over land and some security rights secured over land; (iii) corporeal moveable property, such as vehicles, furniture, books, animals, trading stock and machinery; and (iv) incorporeal moveable property, such as claims of debt or for damages, patents and trade-marks, commercial goodwill, shares in companies and some security rights. The rules of law are not always the same for the four branches: thus sale of land differs in certain respects from sale of goods, such as vehicles, and the mode of taking security over land for the repayment of money differs from the mode of taking security over trading stock or company shares. Under each of the branches have to be considered the kinds of property covered, the rights (*jura in re propria*) conferred by ownership and possession of that kind of property, the rights (*jura in re aliena*) which others may enjoy in that kind of property, and the circumstances in which and the legal modes by which the various rights in that kind of property can come into being, can be transferred voluntarily or by operation of law, outright or in security for debt, and can be extinguished.

Succession

An important branch of the law of property, both heritable and moveable, consists of the rules of succession, which determine the way in which property devolves on other persons on the death of its owner. It falls into three sections. In the first place there are certain claims existing at common law in Scotland known as " legal rights," conferring on certain relatives of a deceased rights to succeed to specified proportions of the heritable and moveable property of the deceased. There are also certain statutory preferences under which in particular cases relatives have preferential claims on the property of the deceased. These claims are of the nature of debts against the estate and may be claimed whatever the deceased may have wanted or prescribed by his will and even against his wishes. Accordingly it is not possible in Scotland completely to disinherit the relatives protected by these provisions.

Secondly, there is the body of rules of intestate succession, which apply in the cases where there is no will, or no will which is valid and effectual, or where any will left has failed in part or has left part of the estate undisposed of; these rules prescribe to what persons and in what proportions the estate should be distributed. Separate sets of rules exist for heritable property and for moveable property and further rules deal with the interaction of the two sets of rules where the deceased left both kinds of property.

Thirdly, there are the rules of testate succession, covering the case where the deceased leaves a will. These rules prescribe the requirements for the form and validity of a will or testamentary declaration by the owner how he wishes his property to devolve or be distributed on his death, and there are various principles of construction and presumptions which have been developed to assist the courts in interpreting the various forms of written expressions which are found in wills.

A pendant to the law of succession is the body of rules governing the rights and duties of executors, who are the individuals appointed by the deceased, or by the court, to ingather the deceased's estate, pay his debts, and distribute it according to his will or the rules of succession.

Succession is in practice materially affected by the incidence of estate duty (which now incorporates legacy duty and succession duty) prescribing what percentage of a deceased person's estate falls to the government on his death. This is itself a substantial body of statutory law and of the interpretations placed on the various statutory provisions in particular circumstances, and the effect of estate duty has always to be considered in framing wills and settlements of property.

Trusts

A further branch of the law of property is the law of trusts. A trust is the legal relationship which arises when property is owned by two persons at the same time, one the trustee, having legal title to the property and formal ownership, but being under an obligation to use his ownership for the benefit of the other, the beneficiary, who has the beneficial owner-ship and is entitled to the benefit of the trust property. " When a person has rights which he is bound to exercise on behalf of another or for the accomplishment of some particular purpose he is said to have those rights in trust for that other or for that purpose and he is called a trustee." [91]   The purposes of the trust operate as limitations on the trustee's ownership and powers of disposal and are commonly declared in a deed or will under which the truster creates the trust.[92]

The trust conception has many and varied uses; it has been and is of social importance in protecting inexperienced, absent or incapable owners whose property is held and managed by trustees on their behalf. It is the normal way in which endowments for charitable, religious and educational purposes are held and administered. Again, the property of unincorporated groups and communities such as some clubs, churches, trade unions, is commonly held by trustees on behalf of their body of members. In the international sphere the concept has been applied to the protection and supervision of less developed communities by more advanced ones.[93]

Private law trusts are classified as private or public, private where the property is held for individuals, public where it is held for charitable, educational or other public purposes. There is a great mass of law dealing with trustees' powers and duties in different circumstances, the most striking feature of which is the strict insistence by the court that the trustee must always take care, be diligent in his duties, and never make any personal profit from his trusteeship or otherwise permit a conflict to arise between his personal interests and those of the funds under his care. Trusteeship is an onerous responsibility, but the high standards exacted have played a considerable part in the maintenance of public morality, probity and honour, while the courts have extended this by treating company directors and others having charge of property not their own as trustees, and thus enforced a generally high standard of commercial morality.

The Judicial Factor is a kind of trustee; he is appointed by the court

---

[91] Maitland, *Lectures on Equity*, 44.
[92] Bell, Prin. s. 1991. The trust has been greatly developed in English law: a classic passage is Maitland's *Lectures on Equity*, lects. III-IV. But history and practice in Scotland have not followed English models entirely.
[93] The Trusteeship Council of the United Nations operating under the United Nations Charter, Chaps. 11-13.

and answerable thereto, but his functions are similar to those of the trustee in that they normally consist in holding, administering or otherwise dealing with property on behalf of another, who is absent, or incapax, or bankrupt or otherwise cannot be allowed to handle it himself. While he is an officer appointed by the court he is usually an accountant or other man of business and is not a permanent court official.

Bankruptcy

Bankruptcy is the proceedings taken to declare bankrupt a person who cannot pay his debts, to take his property, heritable and moveable, out of his hands and administer it for the benefit of his creditors, distributing it rateably among them. The court may in appropriate circumstances sequestrate the estates of an insolvent person and appoint a trustee in bankruptcy to administer the property. The debtor is bound to assist in the realisation and distribution of his estates and, when he is discharged, he is freed from liability for his debts. As an alternative to going through the procedure of bankruptcy, an insolvent person may voluntarily sign a trust deed, making over his property to a trustee who administers it for behoof of the creditors, or make an arrangement with his creditors, called a composition contract, whereby he agrees to pay each so much in the pound of his debt.

Conveyancing

The topic of conveyancing is an adjunct to the law of property. " Conveyancing is the art which deals with the transfer of property by writing . . . transfer includes every kind of right in and over property which can be originated, conveyed, or extinguished by writing." [94] It accordingly covers the requisites of deeds in general and the form of the particular deeds appropriate to create, transfer or extinguish all the different kinds of rights which may subsist in and over the various kinds of property, in particular their transfer on sale or by succession from one person to another. Rules of the law of property define what rights may subsist in various kinds of property and who may hold them and what the incidents of his enjoyment of those rights are: conveyancing law and practice prescribe how the rights may be created, transferred or extinguished. Hence conveyancing covers the examination of the written title-deeds to land to ascertain a seller's rights therein and the framing of the disposition requisite to convey those rights to the buyer, the preparation of dispositions in security, wills, leases, and similar documents affecting property rights.

The handling of conveyancing occupies a large part of the time and

---

[94] Wood, *Lectures on Conveyancing*, 1; *cf.* Bell's *Law Dictionary*, *s.v.*; Jowitt's *Dictionary of English Law*, *s.v.*

attention of many solicitors, and it involves drafting and practical techniques and rules of professional practice as well as law and requires practical instruction as much as study.[95]

Law of Actions

The law of actions prescribes the circumstances in which and the manner in which actions may be brought in the different civil courts. It is plain that it is of no advantage to a man to have a legal right or claim against another if he cannot in case of necessity vindicate that right speedily and cheaply, and the importance of a simple and inexpensive method of bringing disputes before a court and having them determined and enforced can hardly be stressed too much. It is equally true that for the legal practitioner knowledge of procedure is important so that he will know in what way best to obtain the remedy required by his client.

The law of actions accordingly comprises rules prescribing the competence or jurisdiction [96] of the various civil courts in different kinds of civil cases, the kinds of claims which may be made in different circumstances, the steps to be taken to initiate the claim and the stages it must or may go through before hearing, the course of events at the hearing, and the rules regulating appeals. Procedure is constantly in danger of being treated as an end in itself rather than as merely a means to facilitate the ascertainment of rights and the adjudication of disputes. It is today less possible than it formerly was to lose a good case through mistakes in procedure but mistaken procedure may still waste much time and money.

Closely connected with procedure are the rules prescribing what litigants may be granted Legal Aid, *i.e.*, financial assistance from public funds to litigate, and the principles of expenses, defining who must bear the cost of particular steps of litigation. Diligence deals with the various ways of enforcing a decree obtained against a defender and is a topic of some size and complexity.

An adjunct of civil procedure is the art of pleading,[97] of framing properly and accurately the written statements which are necessary steps

---

[95] See further bibliography in Chap. 9, *infra*.

[96] Notice that jurisdiction means (1) the *power* of issuing an enforceable decree or order, and also (2) the *area* within which a particular court may issue valid and enforceable decrees or orders. Thus the Court of Session alone has jurisdiction in divorce cases (sense 1) but actions for debt may be brought in Edinburgh Sheriff Court only against individuals residing within the jurisdiction thereof (sense 2).

[97] The art of advocacy or oral pleading and argument is a further more remote adjunct, which is, however, almost completely unrestrained by rules of law, depending almost entirely on the arts of rhetoric and logic, yet requiring an extensive underlying knowledge of procedure and evidence as well as of law. It is a subject by itself, best learned by experience and following good exemplars. See further Munkman, *The Technique of Advocacy*.

in litigation. This is something of an art in itself, requiring an extensive knowledge of law and of procedure, a ready pen, and a subtle and even crafty insight into the strategy and tactics of litigation. In the past pleading has sometimes been practised rather as an intellectual exercise for its own sake than for its proper function, which is to bring before the court as shortly and accurately as possible the litigant's version of what events happened, his contentions as to what legal result should follow, and to afford his opponent fair notice of the case the latter has to meet.

The law of evidence is likewise intimately connected with procedure and pleading. Evidence comprises the facts, documents and testimony which may legally be adduced at a judicial inquiry to prove or disprove the existence or happening of some matter in dispute. The principles of the law of evidence define, first, what matters the judge is expected, as an intelligent and educated man, to know,[98] and in what cases the judge must [99] or may [1] presume some fact. Then there are principles regulating the admissibility or competency of particular kinds of evidence, as whether certain persons may give evidence, whether oral evidence may be given or only written, whether evidence of what the witness was told by another may be given and so on; there are other principles relating to the relevancy of evidence, or its pertinency to the matter under inquiry, such as whether previous incidents similar to that under investigation may be adduced as evidence, or whether actings or statements should be proved as tending to establish intention or other state of mind, and principles regulating the mode of proof of particular kinds of facts, such as that trust may be proved only by writing or the defender's admission on oath.

There are numerous other topics important to evidence such as oaths and affirmations, questions of onus of proof, identification of persons, authentication of documents, sufficiency of evidence and corroboration, and the weight of evidence and its evaluation.

While pleading and procedure may tend to be technical and somewhat arid, the study of evidence is valuable for developing the logical and reasoning faculties, and is of great importance in legal practice since points of evidence frequently crop up and, if objection is not taken instantly, some damaging statement may be made.

Arbitration is the determination of a dispute, not by resort to the courts, but by an arbiter or arbiters. Any matter, except an issue relating

---

[98] *e.g.*, the main facts of geography, history, physical science, social and commercial life, etc.

[99] *e.g.*, that a child under ten is incapable of committing crime; in such cases no evidence to the contrary is allowed.

[1] *e.g.*, that a person confined in an asylum for five years is incurably insane; presumptions of this latter kind may be rebutted by evidence to the contrary.

to the status of an individual or of a criminal nature, may be referred to arbitration. In some cases statute directs that certain disputes are to be referred to arbitration. Arbitration may be preferable to litigation in some circumstances, as being quicker, informal and more private, and permitting the parties to choose an arbiter familiar with the technicalities of the subject in dispute. Commercial contracts frequently provide for the settlement of disputes by arbitration in accordance with rules framed by a trade association. The London Chamber of Commerce maintains a Court of Arbitration which has great experience in settling commercial disputes.[2]

Mercantile law; Industrial law; Agricultural law

In Scots law, as in Anglo-American legal systems generally, mercantile or commercial law is not a distinct branch of law applicable to a particular class of persons or transactions, but is only a name for a group of topics of the general law of the land.[3] The same is true of industrial law and agricultural law.[4] Any special rules applicable to merchants or traders under the law merchant or the general maritime law have long since been absorbed into the general body of the law,[5] and the legal principles applicable to sale, insurance, cheques, patents, bankruptcy and so on apply equally to all persons, whether merchants or not, whether in any particular kind of business or not, whose activities or transactions fall under that legal heading.

These names therefore do not denote distinct branches of law or logical divisions of the legal system, but are at most cross-divisions, merely convenient compendious names for groups of specific topics selected from all the recognised branches of law and brought together

---

[2] See further Bibliography in Chap. 9, *infra*.
[3] Pound, *Jurisprudence*, V, 73; Keeton and Lloyd, *The British Commonwealth—England*, 232, 347; Paton, *Jurisprudence*, 216–217; Keeton, *Jurisprudence*, 228, 416. It is otherwise in French, German and some other systems of law founded closely on the Roman law, which have separate commercial codes, the rules based on the law merchant not having been absorbed into the general law. Hence French private law is divisible into *droit civil* and *droit commercial*, but there is a movement to integrate commercial law with *droit civil*. See further Schlesinger, *Comparative Law*, 186; Van Mehren, *The Civil Law System*, 43–54.
[4] The same is also true of business law, banking law, engineering law, medical, dental, veterinary and nursing law (commonly miscalled "medical jurisprudence," etc.), and any other similar collection of legal principles relevant to the work of a particular profession.
[5] For England see Holdsworth, *History of English Law*, V, 60; VIII, 99; Plucknett, *Concise History of the Common Law*, 657. For Scotland see Bell's *Commentaries*, Preface, where he says: "The same principle operates as in England; and our courts are daily in the habit of proceeding on this Law-merchant as fully authoritative in Scotland, and of allowing the decisions of courts and the writings of lawyers to be cited in illustration of it. . . . The English books afford valuable aid in cultivating the subject of Mercantile Law." But Bell's *Commentaries* was not meant to be, and is not, a treatise on mercantile law alone.

because of common relevance to particular professions and aspects of business life. Books bearing these titles are manuals only, usually for persons whose concern is only with the topics of law relevant in their particular business or profession; the lawyer finds his law applicable to commercial or industrial relations under the general branches and analytic headings of the law and in the detailed treatises on particular heads thereof.[6] In consequence the scope and boundaries of these groups are very vague and indefinite.

Books on mercantile law usually deal with partnerships and companies (from the law of persons), contract generally and the specific contracts of sale, carriage and insurance (from the law of obligations), moveable property, including bills and cheques, securities and bankruptcy (from the law of property), and arbitration (from the law of actions).

In modern times the law on various mercantile topics has been restated and modified by statute but the statutes have been more concerned to achieve a settled formulation of the rules than to innovate so that reference is still frequently necessarily made to older cases and practice.[7] The law of companies is, however, entirely a modern statutory creation. Prior to the nineteenth century trading enterprises were either partnerships or set up by Royal Charter,[8] private Act of Parliament [9] or by contract between the members.[10] Private Act became common but was expensive and inconvenient and the principle of limited liability, that each shareholder was to be liable to the amount of the nominal value of his shares and no more, was conceded in 1862. The law has been periodically restated and modified since then with increased stress on the disclosure of information to the public and the present or prospective shareholder.

Characteristics of topics included in mercantile law have been relative informality, a large degree of freedom to the parties to make what bargains they chose, and steady change and development. Thus in recent years carriage by air and the financing of transactions by commercial credits have developed very much. The volume of commercial transactions taking place in the United Kingdom and with persons abroad is large

---

[6] Such headings as mercantile law, industrial law and so on are not found in encyclopedias, digests of cases, or other reference books; the particular branch of law in question must be looked for.

[7] Some of the principal statutes are the Bills of Exchange Act, 1882; the Partnership Act, 1890; the Sale of Goods Act, 1893; the Merchant Shipping Acts, 1894–1960; the Marine Insurance Act, 1906; the Bankruptcy (Scotland) Act, 1913; the Carriage of Goods by Sea Act, 1924; the Carriage by Air Act, 1932.

[8] *e.g.*, The Bank of Scotland, The East India Company.

[9] *e.g.*, The Royal Bank of Scotland, early railway companies.

[10] The standard work is W. R. Scott, *Constitution and Finance of English, Scottish and Irish Joint Stock Companies to 1720* (3 vols., 1910–12); see also Carr, *Select Charters of Trading Companies* (Selden Society); Causton and Keane, *Early Chartered Companies, 1296–1858*; Davis, *Corporations* (2 vols.); Formoy, *Historical Foundations of Modern Company Law*; Hunt, *Development of Business Corporation in England, 1800–67.*

and the problems which arise are numerous, frequently involving large sums of money and great commercial reputations, and interesting, while every change in commercial practice or technique is liable to react on the law.[11]

The study of industrial law commonly covers trade unions and industrial associations (from the law of persons), contract generally and the specific contract of employment (traditionally known as the law of master and servant), and the employer's delictual liability for wrongs by or to the employee (from the law of obligations), industrial property, such as patents and trade-marks (from the law of property), and arbitration and the settlement of industrial disputes (from the law of actions). The fundamental topic is the contractual relationship of master and servant,[12] employer and employee, a relationship which gives rise to numerous contractual and delictual rights between the parties and between them and third parties. On this stem there has been grafted since 1800 an enormous growth of statute law and subordinate legislation regulating wages and holidays, hours and conditions of work, and providing in great detail for the safety, health and welfare of the employee. The complexity of modern industry requires separate provisions for many particular kinds of industrial enterprises. In modern times, as part of the national system of social security,[13] there have developed provisions for unemployment insurance [14] and for insurance against the loss caused by industrial injuries.[15] Again, one of the significant modern social and economic developments has been the development of freedom to associate in trade unions for the purpose of collective bargaining [16] and the legal aspects of trade union activity, industrial disputes and their settlement are of profound importance. Elements of public law, such as the control of monopolies may also be considered in the context of industrial law, and some relevant elements in the total situation such as collective bargaining between employers and trade unions are very little regulated by law at all.

Agricultural law deals with contract generally, the particular

---

11 See Lord Devlin, "Commercial Law and Commercial Practice," in *Samples of Lawmaking*, 28.

12 In the older books the law of master and servant was usually dealt with as part of the law of persons, or of domestic relations, but this treatment is appropriate only to domestic servants now.

13 The history, background and development of this may be studied in the (Beveridge) Report on Social Insurance and Allied Services, 1942 (Cmd. 6404) Appx. B.

14 National Insurance Acts, 1946–60, superseding legislation which originated with the National Insurance Act, 1911.

15 National Insurance (Industrial Injuries) Acts, 1946–60, replacing the Workmen's Compensation Acts, 1897–1943.

16 This can be studied in such books as Cole's *Short History of the British Working Class Movement, 1789–1947*, and in books on social and economic history such as Gregg's *Social and Economic History of Britain, 1760–1955*.

contracts of sale, hiring and employment, delictual liability to and for employees and for animals, the law of landownership, leases and small-holdings, compensation and arbitration. It may include partnerships and even companies and many topics of public law such as farm subsidies, and taxation.

These titles accordingly connote functional selections of topics which are useful for particular groups of students and particular professions, but the student of the law and of the legal system as a whole must regard them as divisions cutting across the logical and analytical classification of the law and not as distinct branches of law. In the same way books can bring together all the principles of law relevant to the theatre, or engineering operations, or any other species of activity.[17]

Forensic Science, Medicine and Psychiatry
    These subjects are not branches of the law at all, but are applications of science, medicine and psychiatry to the purposes of the law and the ends of justice. In many sets of circumstances, both in civil but even more so in criminal law, the lawyer has to call on the scientist, doctor [18] or psychiatrist for assistance in the elucidation or interpretation of facts, particularly where difficult issues as to the state of mind or body of some person arise for determination. Thus scientific knowledge is called on in questions involving forgery, poisons and weapons, medical knowledge in cases of wounding, homicide, sexual offences and the like, and psychiatric knowledge in regard to cases of mental deficiency or abnormality, diminished responsibility and other difficult mental states. There is no good reason why there should not equally be subjects of forensic engineering or forensic architecture where equally the knowledge of experts in other branches of learning must be called on to assist legal purposes, but the three branches referred to have legal importance with particular frequency because the law is always dealing with human

17 It is noteworthy also that the institutional writers and main text-writers deal with the topics sometimes brought under the headings of mercantile, industrial or agricultural law in the context of their general expositions of the private law as a whole. Thus, *e.g.*, Bell's *Principles* deals with all the different kinds of commercial contracts in Book First, with industrial property in Book Second, and with bankruptcy in Book Fifth. So, too, do Erskine's *Principles*, Hume's *Lectures* and More's *Lectures*. Furthermore the study of law under such titles as commercial and industrial law is overlapping and very repetitive, and it is not possible on any such basis to construct a convenient or satisfactory classification of the whole legal system, because much of the law would have to be restated for each of the types of human relations. Similarly the grouping of cases or rules under topic-headings arranged alphabetically, as in legal encyclopedias, and other reference works, is useful only to the person who understands the analytical arrangement. For purposes of exposition, study and understanding, analytical classification remains the only satisfactory basis.
18 Forensic medicine is sometimes called Medical Jurisprudence but, despite the name, it has no connection at all with Jurisprudence in the sense of legal theory.

beings and their actings, and has so often to answer the questions Who, When, How and Why, about these human beings before it can seek to apply a legal rule. These branches of knowledge, and indeed all expert testimony from persons skilled in sciences other than law, supply evidence of states of fact and the bases for inference of fact, so that they are adjuncts of the law of evidence. They do not themselves answer problems of law. Much of the confusion and dispute between legal and medical approaches to insanity would be avoided if it were remembered that the function of the forensic physician or psychiatrist is to supply expert evidence from which a judge or jury may, as tribunal of fact, determine whether or not the person under examination is insane within the legal definition thereof, which is concerned with liability to punishment, rather than with insanity in a medical sense.

Scots Law and English

Having now surveyed the main departments of the law it may be of value, in view of the proximity of English law and of its constant tendency to encroach on Scots law, to consider the points of contact and distinctness between the two systems. It is too often assumed that Scots law is much the same as English, or a pale reflection, or substantially the same with different terminology, or with a few minor variations.[19] In fact it is radically different,[20] has developed differently under the influence of different agencies and frequently arrives at results not dissimilar to those of English law but from very different premises and by a very different train of reasoning.[21] It is all too common to find in judgments, even of the highest courts,[22] statements or assumptions that the laws of Scotland and of England are the same on the matter in issue; these are frequently unjustified and frequently made by persons with no real qualification to say so.

Quite apart from terminology and procedure of enforcement the principles and content of the rules of Scots law are different from English. This is most noticeable in property law where the two systems are poles apart in their land law.[23] The differences are lesser in family law, in reparation and in contract, and least in mercantile and industrial topics. In public law, the difference is quite substantial in constitutional and

---

[19] Lawson, *The Rational Strength of English Law*, persistently underestimates the differences.

[20] René David, *Introduction à l'Etude du Droit Privé de l'Angleterre*, 164, considers Scots Law as " très différent du droit anglais."

[21] Untold harm has been done to Scots law by lawyers and judges, even of the House of Lords, who have assumed that because Scots and English law both give a remedy for the same wrong, they do so for the same reasons. See further Walker, " Some Characteristics of Scots Law " (1955) 18 M.L.R. 321.

[22] Gibb, *Law from Over the Border, passim.*

[23] See Farran, *Principles of Scots and English Land Law.*

administrative law, very material in criminal law, and at its least in taxation. Pleading and procedure are quite different in both civil and criminal matters, but evidence rather less so, though not by any means the same in the two systems.

In its reliance on broad principles the Scots law shows affinity with civil law systems of the Continent rather than with the Anglo-American common law. " The civilian naturally reasons from principles to instances, the common lawyer from instances to principles. The civilian puts his faith in syllogisms,[24] the common lawyer in precedents. . . . The civilian thinks in terms of rights and duties, the common lawyer in terms of remedies. The civilian is chiefly concerned with the policy and rationale of a rule of law, the common lawyer with its pedigree. The instinct of the civilian is to systematise. The working rule of the common lawyer is *solvitur ambulando.* . . . The differences in methods are fundamental and far more significant than the apparent similarity of the end products of widely different processes of thought." [25]

Accordingly while Scots law operates in an environment very similar to that of English law and is subject to a common court of final appeal [26] and a common legislative body and higher executive, it is, in varying degrees in different topics, a distinct system with principles and methods of legal thought of its own which are not necessarily inferior to English. It can never safely, and should never, be assumed that any principle or rule of English law either is or should be the law of Scotland, and the Scottish rule should always be sought independently.

FURTHER READING

Classification and Arrangement

Hall: *Readings in Jurisprudence*, Chap. 14.
Holland: *Jurisprudence*, Chap. 9.
Paton: *Jurisprudence*, Chap. 11.
Pound: *Jurisprudence*, Vol. V.

Jurisprudence

Cohen and Cohen: *Readings in Jurisprudence and Legal Philosophy.*
Friedmann: *Legal Theory.*
Hall: *Readings in Jurisprudence.*
Jones: *Historical Introduction to the Theory of Law.*
Lloyd: *Introduction to Jurisprudence.*
Morris: *The Great Legal Philosophers.*
Pound: *Jurisprudence*, 5 vols.

[24] On this mode of legal reasoning in Scotland see Walker, " The Theory of Relevancy " (1951) 63 J.R. 1.
[25] Cooper, " The Common and the Civil Law—A Scot's View " (1950) 63 H.L.R. 468, 471.
[26] Except that no Scottish criminal appeals go to the House of Lords.

Simpson and Stone: *Cases and Readings on Law and Society*, 3 vols.
Stone: *Province and Function of Law.*

Legal History
Continental Legal History Series: Vol. I—*General Survey.*
                                   Vol. II—*Great Jurists of the World.*
                                   Vol. X—*Progress in the Nineteenth Century.*
Diamond: *Evolution of Law and Order.*
Jones: *Law and Legal Theory of the Greeks.*
Munroe Smith: *Development of European Law.*
Plucknett: *Concise History of the Common Law.*
Stair Society: *Introduction to Scottish Legal History.*
Ullman: *The Medieval Idea of Law.*

Roman Law
Bryce: " Extension of Roman and English Law throughout the World," in
         Studies in History and Jurisprudence, I, 72.
Buckland: *Textbook of Roman Law.*
Buckland and McNair: *Roman Law and Common Law.*
Jolowicz: *Historical Introduction to the study of Roman Law.*
          Roman Foundations of Modern Law.
Lawson: *A Common Lawyer looks at the Civil Law.*
Lee: " Modernus Usus Juris Civilis " (1947) 22 Tulane L.R. 135.
Mackintosh: *Roman Law in Modern Practice.*
Schulz: *Classical Roman Law.*
         Roman Legal Science.
Vinogradoff: *Roman Law in Mediaeval Europe.*

Canon Law
Maitland: *Roman Canon law in the Church of England.*
Mortimer: *Western Canon Law.*
Mylne: *Canon Law.*

Comparative Law
Amos and Walton: *Introduction to French Law.*
Arminjon, Nolde and Wolff: *Traité de Droit Comparé.*
David: *Traité Elémentaire de Droit Civil Comparé.*
David and De Vries: *The French Legal System.*
Foreign Office: *Manual of German Law*, 2 vols.
Gsovski: *Soviet Civil Law.*
Gutteridge: *Comparative Law.*
James: *Introduction to English Law.*
Lee: *Introduction to Roman-Dutch Law.*
Pound: " Comparative Law in Space and Time " (1955) 4 A.J.C.L. 70.
Schlesinger: *Comparative Law.*
Van Mehren: *The Civil Law System.*
Vyshinsky: *Law of the Soviet State.*
Yntema: " Roman Law as the Basis of Comparative Law " in *Law: A Century
         of Progress*, II, 346.

Public International Law
Lauterpacht: *Function of Law in the International Community.*
             International Law and Human Rights.

Schwarzenberger: *Manual of International Law*, 2 vols.
Starke: *Introduction to International Law.*
United Nations Yearbook.
Wright: *The Role of International Law in the Elimination of War.*

Supranational Law
Campbell and Thompson: *Common Market Law.*
European Yearbook, 1953–
Frank: *The European Common Market.*
Robertson: *European Institutions.*
Law of International Institutions in Europe.

State or Municipal Law
Carter: " Early History of the Law Merchant in England " (1901) 17 L.Q.R. 232.
Dicey: " Development of Administrative Law in England " (1917) 31 L.Q.R. 148.
Dove Wilson: " Historical Development of Scots Law " (1896) 8 J.R. 217.
    " Reception of Roman Law in Scotland " (1897) 9 J.R. 361.
Dunedin: *Divergencies and Convergencies of English and Scots Law*, Glasgow Univ. Publications, 1935.
Fisher: " Scotland and the Roman Law " (1947) 22 Tulane L.R. 13.
Gibb: " Interrelation of the Legal Systems of Scotland and England " (1937) 53 L.Q.R. 61.
Goudy: *Fate of Roman Law North and South of the Tweed*, 1894.
Holdsworth: " Reception of Roman Law in the Sixteenth Century " (1913) 27 L.Q.R. 387; (1914) 28 L.Q.R. 39, 131, 236.
Keith: *The Spirit of the Law of Scotland* (Holdsworth Club, Birmingham, 1957).
Levy-Ullman: " The Law of Scotland " (1925) 37 J.R. 370.
Lovat-Fraser: " Some Points of Difference between English and Scottish Law " (1895) 10 L.Q.R. 340; 11 L.Q.R. 1.
Macmillan: " Two Ways of Thinking " in *Law and Other Things.*
Normand: *Scottish Judicature and Legal Procedure* (Holdsworth Club, 1941).
Radbruch: " Anglo-American Jurisprudence through Continental Eyes " (1937) 52 L.Q.R. 530.
Smith: *British Justice: The Scottish Contribution.*
    " English Influence on the Law of Scotland " (1954) 3 Am.Jo.Compar.L. 522.
    " The Common Law Cuckoo," 1956 *Butterworth's South African Law Review*, 147.
    " Strange Gods: The Crisis of Scots Law as a Civilian System " (1959) 4 J.R.(N.S.) 119.
    " Scots Law and Roman-Dutch Law " (1961) 6 J.R.(N.S.) 32.
Stein: " Influence of Roman Law on the Law of Scotland " (1957) 23 *Studia et Documenta Historiae et Juris*, 149.
Walker: " Some Characteristics of Scots Law " (1955) 18 M.L.R. 321.

CHAPTER 5

THE MODERN JUDICIAL SYSTEM

THE judicial system consists of all the agencies which exist to adjudicate on disputes, to resolve controversies as to legal rights and conflicts of interests and claims, and to enforce legally recognised claims in case of recalcitrance or refusal to conform to law.

The salient features of the modern administration of the law are the existence of separate sets of courts and tribunals for civil, criminal and administrative business, though in fact all Scottish judges may at different times sit in either civil or criminal courts and many English judges may do so too. The civil and criminal courts are mainly of considerable antiquity but many of the administrative courts and tribunals are much more modern and they have not yet attained anything like the settled nature, composition or system exhibited by the civil and criminal courts. It is impossible in modern times to confine the judicial system, the organs for the decision of disputes and the resolution of controversies, to the traditional courts of law. In modern Britain many kinds of issues are justiciable and by many different kinds of persons and bodies.

It is accordingly necessary to consider individually the various civil, criminal, administrative and other tribunals which exist and to ascertain generally their spheres of competence and the limitations on their powers. In respect of the administrative tribunals it is difficult, if not impossible, to enumerate or describe them all, since they are constantly changing and developing.

The Judicial Function

A notable characteristic of litigation in Scotland is that it is contentious rather than inquisitorial. The function of the judge is not to act as inquisitor and himself to make an investigation, or even to inquire into a claim or complaint initiated by a party, but to preside at a forensic contest between two parties, to ensure that the rules of law are applied and followed and to arbitrate between the contending cases. The contentious nature of proceedings is further indicated by the fact that in criminal proceedings the Crown may drop a charge at any stage and that the judge may not pronounce sentence on a finding of guilt unless the prosecutor moves him to do so, and that in civil proceedings it is for the aggrieved party to determine whom to pursue, on what ground of law, on what issues of fact the action is to be fought, whether the action is to be compromised or settled, and whether any of the rules of evidence or of procedure are to be waived. Above all, in both civil and criminal proceedings, the overriding rule is that it is for the parties to determine what evidence they will produce and elicit from witnesses; the judge will not summon other or fresh witnesses or examine them himself, apart from sometimes putting a few supplementary questions to clear up a matter on which he is still in doubt. But his task is to supervise the contending parties and to arrive at a decision on the facts submitted to him, not to engage himself in the search for truth and justice.

The judicial function is not, however, by any means wholly passive, since the judge may take notice of principles of law even though they are not brought to his notice by the parties. He can, for example, dismiss an action founded on an illegal contract even though the parties take no notice of the fact. " In the system of trial which we have evolved in this country, the judge sits to hear and determine the issues raised by the parties, not to conduct an investigation or examination on behalf of society at large, as happens, we believe, in some foreign countries. Even in England, however, a judge is not a mere umpire to answer the question ' How's that? ' His object, above all, is to find out the truth, and to do justice according to law." [1]

The existence of the jury system is another element indicating the contentious character of litigation. Where there is a jury,[2] the parties set out to convince the jury and the judge has merely to explain the relevant law to the jury, take their answer to the questions of fact and law raised by the case, and give effect to their verdict.

I.—SCOTLAND

CIVIL COURTS

The J.P. Small Debt Court

Justices of the Peace were instituted in Scotland by James VI in 1587, on the model of the local unpaid magistrates in England. He believed that the institution would be a valuable method of achieving his avowed object of bringing peace, order and good government to the disturbed realm. Subsequent statutes confirmed the institution. From 1707 to 1955 the Lord Chancellor was responsible for nominating them but this responsibility has now been transferred to the Secretary of State for Scotland.

The institution has not, however, taken root and the justices have

---

[1] *Jones* v. *N.C.B.* [1957] 2 W.L.R. 760.
[2] Jury trial is confined to criminal trials on indictment and certain kinds of civil claims, so that 90 per cent. of cases are tried without a jury.

never enjoyed the jurisdiction, powers, influence, nor the respect, which have fallen to the justices in England. It may be that the fault lay in never giving the justices sufficient jurisdiction or business to enable them to develop into a useful court, but probably the main cause is the long-continued power of the sheriffs, officials whose judicial functions in England atrophied, whereas in Scotland they grew and multiplied. The justices at one time had considerable administrative powers and duties but most of these have been transferred to local authorities, the most important remaining one being in relation to the licensing of premises for the sale of excisable liquors.[3]

In practice the civil jurisdiction of the justices is confined to actions for the recovery of debts not exceeding £5. The quorum of the court is two and no legal practitioner may appear before them.

If a decree is pronounced in the absence of the defender (the debtor), the case may be reheard before the justices at their next court but a decree pronounced *in foro* is final, though it may be reduced by the Court of Session at any time within one year on the ground of malice or oppression.[4]

The justices have no power to decide cases involving a question of the right to heritable property,[5] and this court is of trivial importance.

The Sheriff Court

The most generally useful and important civil court is the sheriff court.[6] Scotland is divided into twelve sheriffdoms based on groupings of the thirty-three counties.[7] Each has a sheriff-principal who is a senior member of the Bar; in two cases [8] the appointment is a full-time one but in other cases the holder of the office may continue in practice at the Bar, visiting the sheriffdom periodically, chiefly to hear appeals from decisions of the sheriffs-substitute. The office is one of great antiquity and prestige. The modern sheriff (principal) is the successor of the sheriff-depute, who was the trained deputy appointed by the former hereditary sheriffs and who became the permanent functionary when

---

[3] See generally Philip in *Source-Book of Administrative Law in Scotland*, 78–79.
[4] Small Debt (Scotland) Act, 1825.
[5] *Wales* v. *Wales* (1888) 16 R. 164.
[6] Sheriff Court, *not* Sheriff's court. An idea of the amount of business can be gathered from the annual *Civil Judicial Statistics*.
[7] The groupings have been changed several times: at present the sheriffdoms are: (1) Caithness, Sutherland, Orkney and Zetland; (2) Inverness, Moray, Nairn, and Ross and Cromarty; (3) Aberdeen, Kincardine and Banff; (4) Perth and Angus; (5) Fife and Kinross; (6) Renfrew and Argyll; (7) Stirling, Dunbarton and Clackmannan; (8) Ayr and Bute; (9) Lanarkshire (including Glasgow); (10) Lothians and Peebles (including Edinburgh); (11) Dumfries and Galloway; (12) Roxburgh, Berwick and Selkirk.
[8] Lanarkshire, and Lothians and Peebles.

the hereditary and titular sheriffs were replaced in 1747.[9] The sheriffs-depute formerly appointed sheriffs-substitute at their own hand but since 1825 the sheriff-substitute has had to be a lawyer and since 1877 the office is a separate Crown appointment. The sheriff still retains, in addition to judicial functions, considerable administrative powers and duties.[10]

Each sheriffdom has a force of several sheriffs-substitute who are qualified lawyers of experience permanently resident in the principal towns of the sheriffdom, the number varying according to the place and the amount of business.[11] As a rule they hold court only in one place but in some cases they hold courts in more than one town.[12] The sheriff may still, however, appoint a few honorary sheriffs-substitute, either laymen or lawyers, partly as an honour and partly to assist with the work in case of need. Apart from the appellate jurisdiction and the administrative powers of the sheriff, the powers of sheriff and sheriff-substitute are the same.

In civil business the sheriff court is both a court of first instance and a court of appeal, in that cases heard first by a sheriff-substitute may be appealed to the sheriff-principal. This provision for appeal from a single judge to another single judge is anomalous but it does provide for an appeal being heard locally without undue expense, and, though sometimes abused by being used merely for delay, the system gives general satisfaction.

Jurisdiction

The civil jurisdiction of the sheriff court is wide. It extends to actions of debt or damages *without any pecuniary limit whatever* so that cases involving thousands of pounds may be and regularly are dealt with by the sheriff-substitute. Neither party can require a case to be remitted to the Court of Session on account of the magnitude of the sum involved, except in cases of actions involving questions of heritable right or title, divisions of commonty or division of common property, where the amount

---

9 See further Philip in *Source-Book of Administrative Law*, 74–76; McDonald, " The Sheriff Court and its Judges," 1952 S.L.T.(News), 121; Malcolm, in *Introduction to Scottish Legal History*, Chap. 26.
10 *Ibid.*, 76–78, and Dobie, *Sheriff Court Practice*, Chap. 25.
11 Thus Glasgow has twelve (with assistance from Paisley and Lanark); Edinburgh three (one shared with Linlithgow, and with assistance from Haddington); Aberdeen, Dundee, Hamilton, Paisley and Ayr two each, while such places as Lanark, Banff, Dumbarton, Airdrie, Inverness, Oban and Dumfries have one each.
   Sheriffs, both principal and substitute, are addressed as " My Lord " in court and " sheriff " when off the Bench.
12 *e.g.*, Linlithgow and Falkirk, Perth and Dunblane, Forfar and Arbroath, Stirling and Alloa, Elgin and Nairn, Dingwall, Tain and Dornoch, Dunoon and Rothesay, Cupar and Kirkcaldy. In some cases the towns are in different sheriffdoms so that appeals will lie to different sheriffs. For a full list see the *Parliament House Book*.

involved exceeds £1,000 or £50 per annum.[13] The sheriff court also deals with many other kinds of cases, such as landlord and tenant, rent restriction, separation, affiliation and aliment, contract, succession and so on.

At the other end of the scale the sheriff's jurisdiction is exclusive and his decision final in cases where the value of the cause does not exceed £50.[14] Special procedure applies to claims not exceeding £20 brought under the Small Debt Acts and the sheriff's decision can in this case be reviewed only by the High Court of Justiciary on the ground of corruption, incompetency, malice or oppression.

The subjects excepted from the sheriff's jurisdiction and reserved to the Court of Session are actions involving status (marriage, divorce and legitimacy), reductions, petitions for the winding up of companies whose paid-up capital exceeds £10,000, and actions for proving the tenor of a lost document.

Trial is normally by the sheriff-substitute alone but actions of damages brought by workmen against employers for personal injuries may be tried by a jury of seven.[15]

The sheriff court also exercises important administrative functions, such as dealing with petitions for adoption of children and bankruptcy proceedings. The commissary offices are departments of the sheriff-clerks' offices which deal with the inventories of the estates of deceased persons and issue confirmation of appointments of executors. The office of commissary clerk, formerly separate, is now merged in that of sheriff clerk, except in Edinburgh, though even there they are held by the same person. The Sheriff Court of Chancery has functions in respect of the completion of title to land by the heirs of deceased persons. The office of Sheriff of Chancery is now held by the sheriff of the Lothians.

Appeals

Appeal lies in civil matters from the sheriff-substitute to the sheriff-principal, or to the Inner House of the Court of Session, or to the sheriff-principal and then from his decision to the Inner House of the Court of Session. This multiplicity of possible appeals is theoretically undesirable though the system works satisfactorily in practice. The tendency is for defenders to take the long course where delay is of value, as in the case of a tenant's appeal from an order for possession under the Rent Restriction Acts. The appeal does not involve a rehearing of the evidence, but only argument on a transcript of the evidence already heard and on the relevant law. The sheriff may affirm, vary or reverse the decision of the sheriff-substitute.

---

[13] Sheriff Courts (Scotland) Act, 1907, s. 5.
[14] *Ibid.*, s. 7.   [15] For criticism of this see 1954 S.L.T.(News) 25, 57.

The Court of Session

The Court of Session, the supreme civil court, is likewise both a court of first instance and a court of appeal. It is, however, notionally still a unitary collegiate court; all judges have the same rank and title.[16] It sits only in Edinburgh, in the Parliament House,[17] and judges do not take civil business when on circuit.[18] From 1532 to 1808 the court sat as a group—the " haill fifteen "—but one or two of the judges went out in turn, a week at a time, to hear the preliminary stages of cases in the Outer House. In 1808 the court was divided into two Divisions, presided over by the Lord President and the Lord Justice Clerk respectively, and in 1825 the junior judges became permanent Lords Ordinary sitting only in the Outer House.

The Outer House—The Lords Ordinary

The Outer House consists of the eight junior Lords of Session, who sit singly,[19] sometimes with, sometimes without, a jury of twelve, to determine cases at first instance. The jurisdiction is extensive and extends to all kinds of civil claims unless jurisdiction is expressly excluded. In particular it extends to actions of contract and debt, reparation, property and personal status, such as divorce, various kinds of petitions, the appointment of trustees, judicial factors and curators and many matters of succession and trusts.

The Outer House is exclusively a court of first instance in which most Court of Session business is initiated and adjudicated on for the first time. Much of the business does not proceed any further in that the parties rest content with an Outer House judgment; this is particularly so in the case of undefended divorce and other uncontested actions. Apart from the cases in which the Court of Session has exclusive jurisdiction, such as actions involving status, the pursuer has the choice of initiating his claim in the appropriate sheriff court or in the Court of Session and the choice may be determined by such factors as the value or importance of the cause, the availability of jury trial, or the desire to obtain a more authoritative ruling on the issue in dispute than that of a sheriff-substitute. The Outer House judges also deal with many

---

[16] The judges are designated Senators of the College of Justice and sometimes Lords of Council and Session, titles reflecting the origin of the Court. They wear dark blue worsted robes with maroon facings and scarlet crosses on the facings.

[17] An interesting illustrated account of the Parliament House is in *The Pictorial History of Parliament House, Edinburgh* (Pitkin, " Pride of Britain " Books); see also Malcolm, in *Introduction to Scottish Legal History*, Chap. 34.

[18] For circuits, see p. 184, *infra*.

[19] Until the Administration of Justice Act, 1933, a pursuer might choose his judge and his Division for appeal, which produced some remarkable inequalities between the rolls of different judges, as can be traced in the periodical reports in the *Scots Law Times* (News) prior to that Act.

petitions of an administrative nature, such as for the appointment of new trustees, or a judicial factor, for sequestration or for the winding up of a company.

Jury trial,[20] despite extensive criticism, is still utilised in certain classes of cases, mainly claims of damages for injuries occurring in industrial or street accidents. While favoured by speculative litigants it is an uncertain and doubtfully just mode of trial, and many jury verdicts seem questionably satisfactory. In certain cases actions commenced in the sheriff court may be remitted to the Court of Session for jury trial in the Outer House.

The Inner House

The Inner House consists now of two divisions, the First and the Second Division, of equal authority, importance and jurisdiction. The Lord President and three Lords of Session comprise the First Division while the Lord Justice-Clerk and three Lords sit in the Second Division. Decisions are by a majority and the presiding judges have one vote only and no casting vote, so that in the event of equal division, a rehearing is necessary, usually before a larger court. In each Division three judges are a quorum, except in certain exceptional cases.[21] When hearing motions for the allowance of a new trial against the verdict of a jury it is the practice for the judge who presided at the trial, if not a member of the Division, to sit and vote with it. Either Division may call in a judge from the Outer House or from the other Division to make up a quorum. Any three judges may be constituted by the Lord President an Extra Division to assist in dealing with Inner House business; in such a case the senior judge of the Extra Division presides. In cases of importance and difficulty the two Divisions may sit together as a Court of Seven Judges, or may even summon additional judges to make a fuller court.

While in practice certain kinds of cases are sometimes appropriated to one Division rather than the other, the two are of co-ordinate authority and there is no formal distinction between the sphere of the one and that of the other. Nor can the litigant now [22] choose to which Division to carry his case.

The Inner House is a court of first instance in respect of special

---

20 A committee set up in 1957 under the chairmanship of Lord Strachan to examine the question of the retention or abolition of jury trial recommended, by a majority, that it be retained in a limited sphere.

21 Hence when there is pressure of business one judge of the Division can, and frequently does, sit in the Outer House to deal with business there. Similarly the absence of one judge on criminal circuit does not upset the working of the Division.

22 He could prior to 1933.

cases,[23] certain petitions, revenue stated cases, and various particular appeals against decisions of tribunals and committees, but it is also and is mainly a court of appeal, reviewing judgments of the sheriff court and of the Lords Ordinary in the Outer House.

Only exceptionally is evidence heard in a case before the Inner House, in which case it is heard before one judge of the Division: normally Inner House business is disposed of by consideration of the transcript of evidence heard in a lower court and by hearing argument thereon, while much of the business involves only argument on law applicable to proved or admitted or undisputed facts and no question of hearing evidence arises.

The House of Lords

The House of Lords as an appellate body exercises the jurisdiction to deal with appeals to the Queen in Parliament, and in theory appeals are heard by the whole House.[24] In modern practice, however, appeals are heard only by the legally qualified members of the House, namely, the Lord Chancellor, the Lords of Appeal in Ordinary [25] and peers who hold or have held high judicial office. There is a convention that peers who are not legally qualified should not sit at the hearing of appeals.[26] The quorum is three [27] but appeals are frequently heard by five and sometimes, in cases of importance, by seven Law Lords; decision is by a majority. In modern times it has been customary to have two of the Law Lords at any time of Scottish origin [28] while other Scottish judges who were peers have from time to time assisted with the hearing of appeals.[29] There is, however, no rule that a Scottish Law Lord, still less a majority of Scottish Law Lords, must be present to hear a Scottish appeal, so

[23] A special case is a written case setting forth certain facts as admitted and not in controversy and seeking a decision of the legal difficulty raised by those facts. It is frequently adopted in cases of disputes on the interpretation of a will or trust instrument.

[24] The Judicature Act, 1873, abolished the House of Lords as final court of appeal. The operation of the Act was suspended till 1875 and this provision was repealed before it took effect.

[25] The Appellate Jurisdiction Acts, 1876–1947 authorise the appointment of at first two, later four, later (1929) seven, and now (1947) nine Lords of Appeal in Ordinary. They are entitled to sit in the House of Lords, at first during their tenure of office, and since 1887 for life. They must be barristers or advocates of fifteen years' standing or persons who have for two years held high judicial office.

[26] *O'Connell* v. *The Queen* (1844) 11 Cl. & Fin. 155: see also Lord du Parcq in (1949) *Current Legal Problems* 5, and Megarry, *Miscellany-at-Law*, 11–13.

[27] In *Rylands* v. *Fletcher* (1868) L.R. 3 H.L. 330 only two Law Lords are reported as being present: see [1945] K.B. 242. Since 1960 two Committees of Law Lords may sit simultaneously to hear appeals, and this happened in the autumn of 1962.

[28] The Scottish Law Lords since 1876 have been Lords Gordon, Watson, Robertson, Shaw of Dunfermline, Dunedin, Macmillan, Thankerton, Normand, Reid, Keith of Avonholm and Guest.

[29] *e.g.*, Lords Shand, Kinnear and Alness.

that in the last resort Scottish appeals may be decided by judges a majority (or even all) of whom have no training in or experience of Scots law.[30]

By a legal fiction the House of Lords, as the final Court of Appeal from England, Scotland and Northern Ireland, has judicial knowledge of all the legal systems involved so that it can take cognisance of points of the law of each of these systems even though they have not been pleaded or established by evidence before it.[31] This is, however, the sheerest fiction, to ascribe to members of the English Bar and bench, on their promotion to be Lords of Appeal, a sufficient knowledge of Scots law to correct the judges of the Court of Session.[32] In the past there have been some remarkable confessions of ignorance in the House and some scandalous impositions of foreign law on Scotland.[33] The House of Lords has been responsible for some of the worst misunderstandings and confused law in the Scottish books; over and over again English doctrines have been forced into Scots law by English Law Lords who did not know or realise the fundamental differences of principle and reason which frequently underlie apparent similarities of result, as where remedies are granted in circumstances similar to those justifying the corresponding remedy in English law.

Appeal to the House of Lords is competent both on fact and on law though appeals on fact are not regarded favourably and great weight is attached by the House to the views on the evidence of the trial judge who saw and heard the witnesses.[34] If the case originated in the sheriff court the right of appeal is limited to questions of law. Appeal may be taken against final judgments of the Inner House, which dispose of the action, or against interlocutory judgments, which dispose of some part or stage of the action, if the Court of Session has given leave to appeal, or if the judges were not unanimous, and in certain other cases. In view of the delay and expense of an appeal to the House of Lords such appeals are usually taken only where a large sum or an important issue is at stake, or where an important or difficult point of law is in issue. Only a dozen or so cases are appealed from Scotland to the House of Lords in a year, and the majority of Scottish cases do not go beyond the Inner House.

---

30 Thus *A/B Karlshamns Oljefabriker* v. *Monarch SS. Co.*, 1949 S.C.(H.L.) 1, was heard by five English Law Lords, and *Grant* v. *Sun Shipping Co., Ltd.*, 1948 S.C. (H.L.) 73 by four.

31 *Elliot* v. *Joicey*, 1935 S.C.(H.L.) 57.

32 The converse is, of course, true in the case of Scottish Law Lords sitting in English appeals with the difference that the Scots are most unlikely to be in a majority, if indeed they sit at all. It is fair, however, to add that Lord Watson, a Scot, won golden opinions for his judgments in English cases while Lord Birkenhead delivered some outstanding judgments in Scottish cases. See also (1956) 19 M.L.R. 95.

33 Gibb, *Law from Over the Border, passim.*

34 *Thomas* v. *Thomas*, 1947 S.C.(H.L.) 45.

CRIMINAL COURTS

Criminal jurisdiction is divided into Solemn and Summary jurisdiction, the former being trial on indictment before a judge or sheriff sitting with a jury of fifteen,[35] and the latter trial on complaint by sheriff or magistrate alone, or by a bench of justices of the peace. The determination whether a case is to be prosecuted under solemn or under summary procedure depends on any statutory prescription which is applicable to the offence in question and on the gravity of the offence. If statute is silent the prosecutor has a discretion but that discretion is limited by the fact that procedure in magistrates' and the sheriff's summary court is regulated by the Summary Jurisdiction (Scotland) Act, 1954, which excludes from the jurisdiction of these courts a number of the more serious crimes, and limits the powers of these courts to punish offenders. Furthermore it is a general principle that justices and burgh magistrates cannot deal with statutory offences unless jurisdiction is conferred on them expressly or by implication in the statute in question.[36] There are accordingly four modes of trial: (i) judge of the High Court and jury; (ii) sheriff [37] and jury; (iii) sheriff alone (summary offences); and (iv) magistrate or bench of justices alone (summary offences).

The prosecution of crimes and offences is almost exclusively in the hands of the Lord Advocate in the High Court and of procurators-fiscal acting on instructions from the Lord Advocate in the sheriff court. Private prosecution, though possible, is practically unknown,[38] and while certain officials, such as factory inspectors, may prosecute summary offences in their own names, they do so in the public interest. The police do not prosecute in any circumstances in Scotland. Crimes are reported to the procurator-fiscal in the first place and he decides, in serious cases in consultation with the Crown Office in Edinburgh, whether to prosecute and in what form. In High Court cases the indictment is settled by the Lord Advocate, the Solicitor-General or one of the advocates-depute appointed by the Lord Advocate, and one of these conducts the case for the Crown in the High Court and in important

---

35 Notice that the Scottish criminal jury numbers fifteen, the Scottish civil (like the English) jury twelve.

36 *Macpherson* v. *Boyd*, 1907 S.C.(J.) 42. The sheriff's summary court is accordingly the commonest forum for prosecutions in Scotland. Magistrates in burghs deal principally with petty breaches of the peace.

37 Sheriff principal or sheriff-substitute.

38 *J. & P. Coats* v. *Brown*, 1909 S.C.(J.) 29; *McBain* v. *Crichton*, 1961 J.C. 25. The concurrence of the Lord Advocate must be sought though the High Court may permit the prosecution without his concurrence. It is wholly incompetent for a private prosecutor to prosecute on indictment in the sheriff court: *Dunbar* v. *Johnston* (1904) 7 F. 40.

cases in the sheriff court. In other sheriff court cases and in summary offences the procurator-fiscal conducts the prosecution case.[39]

The J.P. Court

A court consisting of two or more justices of the peace has a criminal jurisdiction extending to all breaches of the peace and certain petty charges under statute and extending over the county for which the justices are appointed. The sheriff has jurisdiction within his sheriffdom concurrent with the justices in regard to all offences triable by them. Prosecutions are conducted by the Justice of the Peace Fiscal and procedure is summary, there being no jury. Special panels of justices are sometimes employed as juvenile courts to deal with juvenile offenders.[40]

Appeal lies to quarter sessions,[41] *i.e.*, a meeting of all the justices of the county, held once a quarter, which rehears the whole case on both fact and law. At least three justices must hear the appeal. It also lies to the High Court of Justiciary by way of a stated case, which sets out the facts admitted or proved and raises a question of law only, or by bill of suspension. As a criminal court the J.P. Court is very much less important in Scotland than in England, it deals only with the most ordinary cases and not even with the bulk of them, and the appeal to quarter sessions is now unknown and obsolete.

Burgh Police Courts

Under the Burgh Police Acts, 1892 and 1903, under various local and personal Acts relating to particular burghs, and, in the case of royal burghs,[42] at common law, the burgh magistrates[43] have a civil and criminal jurisdiction analogous to that of the J.P.s. Any town councillor who has held the office of magistrate of any burgh having a police court may be appointed, under the name of Judge of Police, to be a judge of the police court of the burgh.[44] The jurisdiction of this court extends to breaches of the peace and in practice large numbers of " drunks " and disturbers of the peace are dealt with in these courts. Prosecution is in

---

[39] See further Milne, *The Scottish Office*, 206–208; Gordon, in *Source Book of Administrative Law*, Chap. 5. For statistics see the annual *Criminal Statistics, Scotland*.
[40] Special juvenile courts exist only in Aberdeen and the counties of Ayr, Fife and Renfrew. Elsewhere juveniles are dealt with by the sheriff acting under juvenile court rules, and the sheriff court has concurrent jurisdiction even where there is a juvenile court: *Weir* v. *Cruickshank*, 1959 J.C. 94.
[41] The procedure is found in the Scots Act, 1661, c. 38. See also *List* v. *Pirie* (1867) 6 M. 185; *Allice* v. *Scott* (1863) 1 M. 406.
[42] *i.e.*, burghs given burghal status by royal charter prior to 1707; examples are Rothesay, Dingwall.
[43] Provost (or Lord Provost in the case of cities) and the bailies.
[44] Local Government (Scotland) Act, 1947, s. 36. For details as to Glasgow see *Third Statistical Account of Scotland*, Vol. 5, " Glasgow," pp. 658–659.

the hands of the Burgh Prosecutor and appeals lie to the High Court by stated case and bill of suspension. Procedure is always summary, without a jury.

A town council has power [45] to secure the appointment of a stipendiary magistrate, who must possess the qualifications requisite for appointment as a sheriff-substitute and who may exercise the same jurisdiction as the magistrates. Only in Glasgow has this power been used, where a stipendiary sits in the Central Police Court.

The powers of punishment of these courts are strictly limited so that numerous but not serious cases only are brought before them.

The Sheriff Court

As in civil matters, the sheriff court is the most generally important lower criminal court. In criminal cases no distinction need be taken between the sheriff (principal) and the sheriffs-substitute since their powers are co-extensive and no appeal lies from the one to the other. The sheriff or sheriff-substitute may, sitting alone, deal with cases brought under the Summary Jurisdiction Act, 1954, and when sitting with a jury of fifteen, deal with cases prosecuted on indictment. In the latter case the procedure followed is identical with that followed in the High Court of Justiciary. In either case the prosecution is prepared and conducted by the procurator fiscal or one of his deputes, though in difficult cases an advocate-depute may appear for the Crown. Counsel may always, and frequently do, appear for the accused. As compared with the High Court, however, the sheriff's power of punishment is limited to two years' imprisonment in cases on indictment and to three months' imprisonment in summary cases unless there are previous convictions or a particular statute confers wider powers. The sheriff court has concurrent jurisdiction with other lower courts within the sheriffdom in regard to all offences which can be tried in such courts and its jurisdiction is practically universal in that it need not be expressly conferred by the statute creating the offence, but it is limited in that the most serious crimes of all, such as murder and rape, may be tried only in the High Court, and by the fact that its powers of punishment are limited. Nevertheless the sheriff court, either summarily or on indictment, deals with an immense number of offenders and with practically every kind of crime and offence, and it is by far the most important of the inferior criminal courts.

An appeal lies from the sheriff sitting summarily to the High Court of Justiciary by way of stated case or bill of suspension and, from the sheriff sitting with a jury under solemn procedure, to the High Court of Justiciary in its capacity as Court of Criminal Appeal under the Criminal Appeal (Scotland) Act, 1926.

[45] Burgh Police (Scotland) Act, 1892, s. 455.

The High Court of Justiciary

The High Court was established in 1672, replacing the Court of the Justiciars, and consisted till 1887 of seven judges—the Lord Justice-General, Lord Justice-Clerk and five Lords Commissioners of Justiciary. The office of Lord Justice-General was long hereditary, becoming vested in the sixteenth century in the Dukes of Argyll. In 1628 the Duke resigned this office to the King, retaining the office of Justice-General for Argyll and the Isles. The office of Lord Justice-General was held from 1628 to 1836 by various noblemen, but since 1836 has been held by the Lord President of the Court of Session.

The Lord Justice-Clerk was originally the clerk of the criminal court but became the normal president since the Act of 1672 provided that he should preside when the Lord Justice-General did not sit, which regularly happened down to 1836, while the latter office remained honorary.[46]

Since the Criminal Procedure (Scotland) Act, 1887, the court consists of the Lord Justice-General, Lord Justice-Clerk, and all the other (fourteen) Lords of Session [46a] as Lords Commissioners of Justiciary.[47]

It has jurisdiction over all Scotland and in respect of all crimes, unless its jurisdiction is expressly or impliedly excluded by the terms of a statute. It has exclusive jurisdiction to try the most serious crimes, such as treason and murder, and in practice deals with all the more serious cases of crime even though some of these might also have been tried by sheriff and jury.

The High Court as Court of Trial

The High Court is both a court of first instance and a court of appeal. As a court of first instance sittings of the High Court are held in Edinburgh and also on circuit as required. Scotland is divided into four circuits, Home, West, North and South, and courts are held for these districts at (i) Edinburgh; (ii) Glasgow, Stirling and Oban (formerly Inveraray); (iii) Inverness, Aberdeen, Dundee and Perth; and (iv) Dumfries, Jedburgh and Ayr. Sittings are not, however, restricted to these towns and a sitting may be held in any town which is convenient to or near the locality of a crime. Sittings on circuit are appointed to be held quarterly but no circuit need be held if there is no business.[48] On the other hand

---

[46] See further Introduction to Scottish Legal History, Chap. 31.

[46a] Two more judges have been authorised by the Criminal Justice (Scotland) Act, 1963.

[47] This gave rise in H.M.Adv. v. Sugden, 1934 J.C. 103, to the interesting question whether a decision of a Full Bench of 1773 of seven judges could be overruled by that of a Full Bench of 1934 consisting of twelve judges (the total strength being then thirteen, and one being absent). It was held that it could. When sitting as Lords Commissioners of Justiciary the judges wear scarlet robes faced with white, decorated with scarlet crosses.

[48] Lord Cockburn's Circuit Journeys gives a delightful picture of the circuit system in the early nineteenth century.

the volume of business at Glasgow frequently requires extra circuits there. As a rule only one judge needs to go on circuit but in Glasgow two courts sit concurrently and two judges go on the West circuit. They may be replaced at a convenient stage in the sittings by colleagues. As a rule only one judge sits at a trial but in cases of difficulty or importance two or more, usually three, may sit.[49] Procedure is always solemn (on indictment) and with a jury.

The jurisdiction of the court extends to all cases of crime except where its jurisdiction has been excluded by statute and it is exclusive in the case of the most serious crimes, such as treason, murder and rape. In practice, all the most serious cases are tried in the High Court, particularly since its powers of punishment are greater than those of any inferior courts.

The prosecution is invariably conducted by one of the Law Officers or one of the Advocates-Depute, and the accused is invariably defended by counsel (unless, as sometimes happens, he refuses or dismisses counsel).

The High Court as Appellate Court

Appeals from courts of summary criminal jurisdiction lie to the High Court of Justiciary in Edinburgh and are heard by three or more Lords Commissioners of Justiciary. The normal modes of appeal are by way of stated case or bill of suspension.

In a stated case the sheriff or other judge of the inferior court is requested to prepare a statement of the facts found admitted or proved and to formulate a question or questions of law raising the issue the accused wishes to have argued. The appeal is thus only on points of law and in this way authoritative rulings are given on many points, particularly of the interpretation of statutes and instruments creating offences. Thus the phrase, " in charge of " a vehicle, has been elucidated several times, when the High Court has held in stated cases that a sheriff was or was not entitled in particular circumstances to hold that an accused was " in charge of " a vehicle, so as to render him liable to certain penalties. The question in such a case is not whether the inferior court was *correct* in its decision, which is a matter for it on the evidence, but whether the lower court was *entitled in law* to do what it did. Questions of evidence and matters of fact and the inferences therefrom are for the inferior court and cannot be raised in a stated case.

Appeal by bill of suspension is appropriate to raise an issue of jurisdiction, incompetency of proceedings or another matter extrinsic to

---

[49] *e.g.*, trial of Madeleine Smith, where L.J.C. Hope, Lords Handyside and Ivory all sat. Three or more judges also sit to dispose of any difficult or important point raised before trial, for deciding points raised at trials on circuit and certified to the High Court (see, *e.g.*, *H.M. Advocate* v. *Bickerstaff*, 1926 J.C. 65), and for disposing of petitions to the *nobile officium* of the court.

the complaint or the facts adduced, or where the appeal is an attack on the judicial character of the proceedings, such as an allegation of oppression, or irregularity or radical defect in the proceedings. A Bill is prepared by the accused's advisers, narrating the conviction and the objections to it and served on the procurator-fiscal as respondent; he usually lodges written answers and appears by counsel at the hearing to uphold the conviction. The High Court may pass the Bill and suspend the sentence, or refuse the Bill, or amend the conviction and sentence.

Down to 1926 no appeal lay to the High Court from trials on indictment (*i.e.*, under solemn procedure, with a jury, whether before a judge or a sheriff), but in that year in consequence of the miscarriage of justice in the case of Oscar Slater [50] the Scottish court of criminal appeal was established. It consists of three or more [51] judges of the High Court of Justiciary and is consequently another aspect of the appellate work of the High Court.[52] Appeal may be brought against conviction on a question of law, or against conviction on a question of fact or of mixed fact and law if the appellant obtains the leave of the High Court or the certificate of the judge who presided at the trial, or against conviction on any other ground which appears to the High Court or to the trial judge to be a sufficient ground of appeal. Appeal may further be taken against the sentence, unless it is one fixed by law,[53] with the leave of the High Court. The appellant, or counsel on his behalf, may present argument and a law officer or advocate-depute will appear for the Crown.

The Court may allow the appeal if it thinks the verdict of the jury was unreasonable and cannot be supported having regard to the evidence, or that there was improper admission or rejection of evidence, or misdirection of the jury by the court or that on any ground there was a miscarriage of justice. In such a case the conviction is quashed. Or the court may refuse the appeal, or may modify the sentence.

There is also provision for the Secretary of State referring a case to the High Court or referring a point to the court for their opinion.[54] No further appeal lies from the High Court to the House of Lords, so that this court has final responsibility, and has given many judgments of great importance and value for the development of Scottish criminal law.

---

[50] See *Trial of Oscar Slater*, ed. Roughead (Famous Trials Series) and *Slater* v. *H.M. Advocate*, 1928 J.C. 94.

[51] *e.g.*, in *H.M. Advocate* v. *Kirkwood*, 1939 J.C. 36, thirteen judges sat.

[52] In practice what usually happens is that every three or four weeks either the First or the Second Division of the Court of Session does not sit as such but three of its members (the Lord President or Lord Justice-Clerk and two others) don their justiciary gowns and sit as the High Court and then, having disposed of the criminal appeal roll, sit on for disposal of the justiciary roll, *i.e.* appeals from summary cases. The fourth judge of the Division may be absent or unwell or on circuit, but, if available, is usually set to assist the Outer House judges in civil business.   [53] *e.g.*, the penalty of death for treason.

[54] For an example, see *Gallacher* v. *H.M. Advocate*, 1951 J.C. 38, footnote to p. 49.

COURTS OF SPECIAL JURISDICTION

The Court of the Lord Lyon

The Lord Lyon King of Arms is one of the Officers of State of the Kingdom of Scotland, and the Queen's counsellor in matters armorial, genealogical and ceremonial. The office is very ancient but appeared in its modern form in 1318. He exercises the whole Crown jurisdiction in armorial matters, enforces the laws of arms, and adjudicates in questions of name, family representation and chiefship. He is official adviser to the Secretary of State for Scotland in matters relating to the Scottish Honours and ceremonial and, as controller of messengers-at-arms, is head of the department of Scots law relative to execution and diligence.[55]

The Court of the Lord Lyon[56] exercises both a civil and criminal jurisdiction, both at common law and under statute, and almost all heraldic business is conducted therein on judicial lines, legal representation being allowed though not usually necessary. The court is concerned with the establishment of rights to arms and pedigrees which when established are recorded in the Public Register of All Arms and Bearings in Scotland or in the Public Register of All Genealogies and Birthbrieves in Scotland, and with protecting the rights of individuals and of the Crown in Scottish armorial bearings, and over messengers-at-arms. Lyon has, however, no jurisdiction to determine rights of precedence,[57] nor a disputed question of chieftainship.[58] The Lyon Court has a procurator-fiscal who acts as public prosecutor, and has powers of fine and imprisonment, power to erase unwarrantable arms, to break unwarrantable seals and to seize goods on which arms are unwarrantably represented. It may also interdict usurpers of arms.[59] Appeal lies to the Court of Session and to the House of Lords,[60] since arms are incorporeal heritable property.

Lyon also enforces Royal Warrants of Precedency in Scotland, makes Royal Proclamations and acts as Secretary of the Order of the Thistle. He is assisted by Lyon Clerk, three heralds and three pursuivants.

The Scottish Land Court

The Land Court was established in 1911 in succession to the Crofters Commission set up in 1886.[61] Its work is entirely linked with agriculture

---

[55] Innes of Learney, *Scots Heraldry*, revised ed., Chap. 2, and references therein.
[56] It sits in H.M. Register House, Edinburgh. See also *Introduction to Scottish Legal History*, pp. 397–398.
[57] *Royal College of Surgeons* v. *Royal College of Physicians*, 1911 S.C. 1054.
[58] *Maclean of Ardgour* v. *Maclean*, 1938 S.L.T. 49; 1941 S.C. 613.
[59] Innes of Learney, *supra*. See also Adam, *Clans, Septs and Regiments of the Scottish Highlands* (ed. Innes), *passim*; Milne, *The Scottish Office*, 189–190. Reports of selected cases in Lyon Court are published in the *Scots Law Times*.
[60] *e.g.*, *Stewart Mackenzie* v. *Fraser Mackenzie*, 1922 S.C.(H.L.) 39.
[61] A new Crofters Commission was set up in 1955 with duties of reorganising and developing crofting in the crofting counties. The judicial functions of the old Commission (1886–1911) were transferred to the Land Court.

and the members of the court, other than the chairman, are practical agriculturists. The chairman is an experienced lawyer having the status and tenure of a judge of the Court of Session. The court makes an annual report which is laid before Parliament.

Its jurisdiction is entirely statutory [62] and has been greatly extended by the increased modern statutory control of agriculture, so that it has to decide a great variety of questions of considerable scope and value relative to agriculture. Some of its administrative duties have now been transferred to the (new) Crofters Commission.[61]

Resort may also be had to it, by agreement of parties, instead of to an arbiter, to decide questions arising between landlord and tenant, to deal with questions of valuation of sheep stocks, payment of grants under the Hill Farming Act, 1946, and sundry war-time provisions. It is also the only court of appeal against certain decisions of the local Agricultural Executive Committees, giving or withholding consent to the dispossession of the occupier of a farm.

A party to a dispute decided by the Land Court may require a case to be stated on a point of law to one of the Divisions of the Inner House of the Court of Session.

Lands Valuation Appeal Court

This is a court consisting of three judges of the Court of Session which is constituted as and when necessary to dispose of appeals against the determination of the local Valuation Appeal Committees (which are established in each county and county of city) as to the value to be set on heritable property for the purpose of the raising of local rates.[63] The appeal is taken by way of a stated case setting out the facts held by the Committee to be established and the questions of law in issue, and argument is heard on the principle of law in issue. The actual monetary valuation set on a building or set of premises by the assessor is not usually challenged, but problems of statutory interpretation frequently arise, such as whether certain premises are a " retail shop " and entitled to be treated as such,[64] questions of whether certain subjects should be entered in the valuation roll at all or not, and problems of the proper principle to be applied in arriving at a valuation. This court is final and there is no appeal to the House of Lords.

---

[62] Small Landholders (Scotland) Act, 1911. See further Lamb: " The Scottish Land Court," 1958 S.L.T.(News) 129.
[63] Decisions are reported in *Session Cases* and *Scots Law Times* and there is a considerable volume of case-law. Some of the older authorities are superseded by the Valuation and Rating (Scotland) Act, 1956, which made revolutionary changes in the system. On older bases of valuation see McKechnie, in *Source-Book of Administrative Law*, 213–219.
[64] *Perth Assessor* v. *Shields Motor Car Co.*, 1956 S.C. 186.

Court of Exchequer

The jurisdiction of the Court of Exchequer in Scotland, remodelled in 1708,[65] was in 1856 transferred to the Court of Session, but that court sits as Court of Exchequer in Scotland when dealing with revenue cases and for long exchequer causes were subject to procedural specialties.[66] The business consists chiefly of appeals on law by way of stated case from the determination of the Special Commissioners of Income Tax on issues of liability to tax. A further appeal lies to the House of Lords.[67]

Registration of Voters Appeal Court

An appeal on a matter of registration as a parliamentary elector lies from the registration officer to the sheriff and from him to a court of three judges of the Court of Session, whose decision is final. Business rarely arises for this court.

Election Petition Court

Petitions presented against the election of Members of Parliament on the ground of illegality or improper practices at the election are heard by a court of two judges of the Court of Session whose decision is final. This court also rarely requires to be constituted.

Court of Teinds

The Court of Teinds is in fact merely a function of the Court of Session, since in statutes the judges have been nominated as Lords Commissioners of Teinds, but having distinct procedure and a separate Teind Clerk. The court now consists of the eight Inner House judges along with the second junior Lord Ordinary, five, including the last-named, to be a quorum. Teinds were originally the tenth part of the fruits of land and labour assigned for the maintenance of church and clergy.[68] In recent years the whole basis and substance of teind law has been much changed and the business of the court is almost entirely formal and carried through by the Lord Ordinary and the Teind Clerk, without opposition.

---

[65] See further Clerk and Scrope's, *Historical View of the Court of Exchequer in Scotland* (1820).

[66] See *Inland Revenue* v. *Hood Barrs*, 1959 S.C. 273; and Bennett Miller, " Certiorari and the Scottish Courts " (1962) 25 M.L.R. 423.

[67] For an example see *Inland Revenue* v. *Glasgow Police Athletic Association*, 1952 S.C. 102, reversed by H.L., 1953 S.C.(H.L.) 13.

[68] See further Bell's *Law Dictionary*; Black and Christie, *Parochial Ecclesiastical Law*, 395–446, 523–534; Church of Scotland (Property and Endowments) Act, 1925. The development of the law is traced in *Galloway* v. *Earl of Minto*, 1920 S.C. 354; 1922 S.C.(H.L.) 24.

Ecclesiastical Courts [69]

Since there is no Church in Scotland established as part of the state, Church courts have jurisdiction only over their own members and in matters affecting church discipline, ritual and membership. But the courts of the Church of Scotland are legally established courts of the realm within their own field whereas courts of other Churches have jurisdiction only so far as conferred by their own constitutions and the adherence of their members.[70]

The constitution and powers of the courts of the Church of Scotland are founded on the Act 1592, c. 116, confirmed by the Act 1690, c. 7, which in turn was ratified by the Act of Security which is incorporated into the Treaty of Union with England. These courts are supreme, and independent of the civil and criminal courts in matters ecclesiastical and spiritual,[71] so that no claim of damages lies against a Church court for a judgment in a proper case of discipline duly brought before it.[72] The civil courts are bound to assist the Church courts in making their decrees effectual, but cannot review their decisions in matters falling within their jurisdiction.

The courts of the Church are the Kirk-Session, composed of the minister and elders of the parish, which has a general power of discipline over members; the Presbytery, which consists of all the ministers of parishes within its bounds and an elder from each kirk-session and has a general supervisory responsibility, power to censure, suspend or depose ministers after due trial, and the duty of hearing appeals and references from inferior courts; the Synod, which consists of the members of the several presbyteries within its bounds and hears appeals and complaints against decisions of inferior courts; and the General Assembly.

The General Assembly is both the legislature [73] and the Supreme Court of the Church. It consists of ministers and elders elected by presbyteries, universities and royal burghs. It is presided over by the Moderator, who is elected annually, and the Queen is represented by a Lord High Commissioner who has no voice in the deliberations of the Assembly

---

[69] See further Donaldson, " The Church Courts " in *Introduction to Scottish Legal History*, Chap. 27; Cox, *Practice and Procedure in the Church of Scotland*, 4th ed.; the *Church of Scotland Year Book*; Taylor, " Church and State in Scotland " (1957) J.R. 121; King Murray, " Constitutional Position of the Church of Scotland " (1958) Pub.L. 155.

[70] *McMillan* v. *General Assembly of the Free Church of Scotland* (1859) 22 D. 290; (1861) 23 D. 1314.

[71] *Lockhart* v. *Presbytery of Deer* (1851) 13 D. 1296; *Wight* v. *Presbytery of Dunkeld* (1870) 8 M. 921.

[72] *Sturrock* v. *Greig* (1849) 11 D. 1220.

[73] The legislation is printed in the Acts of Assembly. *The Booke of the Universall Kirk of Scotland* (Peterkin, 1839) contains many Acts 1560–1616. Other volumes contain Acts of Assemblies of 1638–49, 1690, 1692, 1694–1895 while the printed Acts of each year are maintained in many libraries.

but is the official medium of communication between the Sovereign and the Assembly.

The judicial functions consist of hearing and deciding appeals and complaints from inferior courts and adjudicating on petitions from members and congregations. Legal representation is permitted. Forms of libels in the Church courts are similar to those of indictments in the High Court. The procedure is regulated by Acts of Assembly.[74]

Courts-Martial and the Courts-Martial Appeal Court

Offences against naval, military or air force law are dealt with either summarily, by the accused's commanding officer, or in more serious cases by courts-martial constituted under the several codes of discipline for the various forces.[75] The offences in question are mostly " service " ones, such as mutiny, desertion or other breach of discipline, but include also offences punishable by the ordinary law,[76] though the most serious crimes, unless committed on active service, must not be tried by a court-martial if they can with reasonable convenience be tried by an ordinary court.[77]

While it is no doubt desirable to have a common code of service law for all personnel, it is unfortunate that the code adopted is based entirely on English criminal law, which may cause difficulties for Scottish counsel or solicitors defending and may give rise to problems of great difficulty on appeal, since Scottish judges do not profess to know English criminal law.

If preliminary investigation within the unit discloses a prima facie case, a court-martial will be convened by an authorised convening officer.

In the Army and Royal Air Force there are General Courts-Martial, consisting of not fewer than five officers, which try officers and also other ranks in the most serious cases, and District Courts-Martial, consisting of not fewer than three officers, which try other ranks. The president is usually of the rank of colonel or brigadier and the members are drawn, so far as possible, from different corps and units. Women officers must be represented on the court if a member of the women's forces is being tried. No member of the court need have any legal experience but must have certain minimum periods of commissioned service. On service the Field General Court-Martial, consisting of three officers, is the usual tribunal.

---

[74] Acts of Assembly, 1707, XI and 1889, XIX.
[75] Naval Discipline Act, 1957; Naval Disciplinary Courts (Procedure) Orders, 1958; Army Act, 1955; Rules of Procedure (Army), 1956; Air Force Act, 1955; Rules of Procedure (Air Force), 1956. See further Halsbury's *Laws of England*, tit. " Courts."   [76] *i.e.*, the criminal law of *England*.
[77] Thus murder or assault in Britain, especially if perpetrated on a civilian, would be tried by the ordinary criminal courts. But murder committed on a foreign station would be tried by court-martial at that station; *e.g.*, *R*. v. *Page* [1953] 3 W.L.R. 895.

The prosecution is conducted by an officer but counsel [78] may be instructed on his behalf, and the accused may be represented by an officer or by counsel or solicitor. A judge-advocate [78a] must, in the case of general courts-martial, and in other cases may, be appointed by the Judge Advocate General of the Army and Air Force to attend to advise the court on law, procedure and powers of punishment. He sums up the evidence and advises the court before it deliberates on its finding. Courts-martial normally sit in public and the procedure, which is based on English criminal procedure, is largely regulated by the printed form used to record the proceedings, which sets out the stages of the trial. Findings and sentence are subject to confirmation by the convening authority.

In the Navy, commanding officers of ships have very extensive powers of summary punishment and there is only one type of court-martial— Naval Court-Martial—which deals with all offences under the Naval Discipline Act which cannot be dealt with summarily. The Naval Discipline Act does not extend to the W.R.N.S. The minutes of every defended court-martial and any legal questions of importance are always referred to the Judge-Advocate of the Fleet, who advises the Board of Admiralty as to the validity of procedure, evidence, finding and sentence, whereupon the Board decide whether to uphold or quash the conviction and to uphold or reduce the sentence. An officiating judge-advocate is appointed at each court-martial to advise on law and procedure and to protect the accused.

The Courts-Martial (Appeals) Act of 1951 constituted a Courts-Martial Appeal Court consisting, in Scotland,[79] of such Lords Commissioners of Justiciary as the Lord Justice-General may nominate, being uneven in number and not less than three. A person convicted by court-martial in any of the services may, with the leave of the Appeal Court, appeal against his conviction. The court's decision is final unless the Appeal Court certifies that a point of law of general public importance is involved and that it is desirable in the public interest that the point be considered by the House of Lords.

A person convicted by court-martial may petition the confirming or reviewing authority to quash or vary his conviction or sentence before

---

[78] In this context " counsel " includes Scottish advocates and solicitors, and they may appear wherever the trial be held; *e.g.,* a Scottish advocate may appear at Aldershot.

[78a] Judge-advocates are advocates or barristers employed whole-time in the legal branches of the services.

[79] When this court sits in England the judges are the Lord Chief Justice and the puisne judges of the High Court (of England), and when it sits in Northern Ireland the judges are such of the judges of the High Court of Justice in Northern Ireland as the Lord Chief Justice of Northern Ireland may nominate. The Act also makes provision for " such other persons, being persons of legal experience, as the Lord Chancellor may appoint " being appointed judges of the court for such term as may be determined by the Lord Chancellor.

or even after confirmation and in some cases the proceedings may be submitted to Her Majesty or to the Army Council. Apart from these prerogative petitions a convicted person must petition to have his conviction quashed before he may apply for leave to appeal; he is entitled to apply for leave to appeal within ten days of the dismissal of his petition or the end of the period for disposing of his petition.

The practice of the High Court of Justiciary sitting as Court of Criminal Appeal is followed [80] and the powers of the court are similar except that it has no jurisdiction to deal with sentences. The court will allow an appeal if it thinks that the finding of the court-martial is unreasonable or cannot be supported having regard to the evidence, or involves a wrong decision on a point of law, or that on any ground there was a miscarriage of justice, but the court may dismiss an appeal on a technical point if in the circumstances no substantial miscarriage of justice has occurred.

Restrictive Practices Court

This court was established by the Restrictive Trade Practices Act, 1956. It consists of five judges, one being a judge of the Court of Session nominated by the Lord President,[81] and not more than ten other persons (laymen) holding office for not less than three years. It may sit as a single court or in two or more divisions, in Scotland, England or Northern Ireland. The quorum is three, including at least one judicial member. Proceedings may be taken in this court by the Registrar of Restrictive Trading Agreements to have certain restrictions, which have been disclosed to and registered with him, found to be contrary to the public interest and the relevant agreement held void to that extent. Restrictions are presumed to be contrary to the public interest unless the court is satisfied that certain general conditions are satisfied. An appeal from the decision of this court will lie, in Scotland, to the Court of Session.[82]

Dean of Guild Court

The Dean of Guild was originally the head of the Merchants' Guild which had a practical monopoly of trade and commerce in the Scottish

---

[80] See *R.* v. *Houghton* [1952] C.L.Y. 159; *R.* v. *Condon* (1952) 36 Cr.App.R. 130; *Hendry*, 1955 S.L.T.(Notes) 66.

[81] The other judicial members are three judges of the High Court in England, nominated by the Lord Chancellor, and one judge of the Supreme Court of Northern Ireland nominated by the Lord Chief Justice of Northern Ireland. The Lord Chancellor nominates one of the judicial members to be President of the court. See further Grunfeld and Yamey, " The Restrictive Trade Practices Act, 1956 " (1956) 1 Pub.L. 313; Korah, " The Restrictive Practices Court " (1959) 12 C.L.P. 76.

[82] Cases are reported in the ordinary series of reports and also in Law Reports Restrictive Practices series (1958–   ).

burghs.[83]   Nowadays the Deans of Guild of Edinburgh, Glasgow, Aberdeen, Dundee and Perth sit in their respective town councils *ex officio* but in other burghs the office of Dean of Guild is held by a member of the town council.   The Dean and his Council originally had an extensive jurisdiction in mercantile and maritime disputes but this jurisdiction gradually fell into disuse.   The Dean also had at common law a jurisdiction over buildings, nuisances and questions of neighbourhood, and under it he granted or withheld permission to erect or alter buildings, but this has now come to be principally the regulation and control of building operations within the burghs to prevent obstruction or encroachment on private or public property, to ensure conformity with local and general legislation, and to promote public health and safety, so that now no building operations can be undertaken without a warrant of the Dean of Guild Court.

The court, though a civil one,[84] may impose fines for such offences as deviating from plans approved by the court or building without a warrant of the court.

The court sits periodically, usually fortnightly in the larger burghs, to deal with applications which are contained in "petitions for lining." Much of the jurisdiction is formal, simply approving proposals and plans submitted and of which notice has been given to adjacent proprietors and any other parties having an interest.   In the event of opposition answers are lodged by the objectors to the petition and a record made up as in the sheriff court, after which procedure follows much as in the sheriff court.   The court has jurisdiction to deal with questions of nuisance and to determine the true interpretation of its statutory powers but cannot decide issues as to title to land or buildings.[85]

There is a procurator-fiscal of the court who acts in the public interest in bringing matters or offenders before the court [86] and he is assisted in technical matters by the burgh master of works.   There is also a legal assessor who advises the court on points of law.   An appeal lies to the Court of Session.[87]

Licensing Courts

The sale of excisable liquors may be effected only in premises licensed for that purpose.[88]   Licensing courts consist of the magistrates in a

---

[83] See generally Irons, *Law and Practice of the Dean of Guild Court*; Murray, *Early Burgh Organisation in Scotland*; Mackenzie, *The Scottish Burghs*; McKechnie in *Source Book and History of Administrative Law in Scotland* (ed. McLarty), 95; *Introduction to Scottish Legal History*, pp. 390–392.
[84] *Fraser* v. *Downie* (1901) 3 F. 881; *Jeffrey* v. *Angus*, 1909 S.C. 400.
[85] *Macandrew* v. *Dods*, 1908 S.C. 51.
[86] *Heatly* v. *McQueen*, 1956 S.C. 123.
[87] *Stewart* v. *Marshall* (1894) 21 R. 1117; *Saltoun* v. *Edinburgh Magistrates* (1896) 23 R. 956; *Smith* v. *Rennie*, 1919 S.C. 705; *Heatly* v. *McQueen*, 1956 S.C. 123.
[88] For the whole law see Purves, *Scottish Licensing Laws*.

burgh or, in a county, of a body elected as to half by the county justices of the peace and half by the county council. Two half-yearly meetings of the licensing court are held. There are different kinds of licences, for hotels, for public-houses, and for grocers or dealers, and the court may also modify the licensing hours in certain cases, within statutory limits. Under the Licensing (Scotland) Act, 1959, a community can, if so minded, determine by poll to terminate or restrict the sale of liquor in its area.

Appeals from a decision of a licensing court and applications for confirmation of new certificates are heard by burgh and county courts of appeal, differently composed from the court which dealt with the application. Courts of Appeal meet half-yearly after the meeting of the licensing court.

ADMINISTRATIVE COURTS AND TRIBUNALS

The development of administrative law in Britain has been empirical and unsystematic and this is reflected particularly in the tribunals which adjudicate on claims and disputes. Their composition, jurisdiction and procedure are varied and individualistic and there is no clear hierarchy of authority or line of appeal. All that can be done is accordingly to discuss various important and representative tribunals, subject to the general observations that the powers, composition, functions and procedure of every tribunal depend on the statute which created it,[89] and that changes are frequent.

The function of so-called administrative tribunals is in fact not administrative but judicial, consisting in the resolution of conflicts and disputes which arise incidentally out of the functioning of public administration, usually between the citizen and a state department or agency, and in many cases resort to the tribunal is itself an appeal from the preliminary adjudication by the official dealing with the case or the claim in the first instance. Their practical importance can be appreciated from the fact that in 1960 at least 122,000 cases were decided by administrative tribunals.[90]

It is difficult to classify these tribunals and impossible to describe them all.[91] They can be classified functionally, according to the subject

[89] The best modern short account is Allen, " Administrative Jurisdiction " (1956) 1 Pub.L. 1. See also the Report of the (Franks) Committee on Administrative Tribunals and Enquiries (Cmnd. 218, 1957) and the Annual Reports of the Council on Tribunals, 1959– .
[90] Council on Tribunals, *Report*, 1960, p. 1. (In 1960 civil proceedings before the Court of Session and sheriff courts totalled about 45,000, together with 150,000 small debt cases, but the great majority of these cases were uncontested or did not go to trial.)
[91] A detailed list of tribunals is given in the Council on Tribunals, *Report*, 1960, Appx. B.

dealt with, or by their nature and composition. The latter method would merely indicate an infinite gradation of types from formality and procedure similar to that of a court in the ordinary sense to considerable informality and lack of method.

Another grouping would be into cases justiciable by a committee or tribunal, cases justiciable by a permanent legally qualified official, and cases determinable by a Minister of the Crown himself. In some cases appeal lies from one kind of body to another. Moreover there are differences as between England and Scotland and some bodies have different counterparts in the other country.

The Tribunals and Inquiries Act, 1958, which put into effect some of the recommendations of the Franks Committee, made some badly needed reforms in a chaotic situation. Since 1959 the chairmen of various tribunals have been selected from panels of persons appointed by the Lord President and the removal of members of certain tribunals requires his concurrence. Appeal to the courts on a point of law is now permitted from a large number of tribunals and many are required on request to give reasons for their decisions.

The Council on Tribunals

This body was constituted by the 1958 Act to exercise a general supervision over tribunals and inquiries and it keeps under review the constitution and working of some 2,000 bodies. It consists of 10 to 15 members, with a Scottish Committee of 2 or 3, with 3 or 4 non-members added, and has power over the whole United Kingdom. Its functions are purely advisory and consultative, and are confined to the constitutional and procedural aspects of the work of tribunals. It is not an appellate body. It must be consulted before procedural rules are made for specified tribunals, or for any statutory inquiry, and members visit tribunals to watch their operation. It also issues a valuable Annual Report.

Social Services Tribunals

Within the National Health Service [92] the twenty-five Executive Councils which are responsible for providing general medical, dental and other services in their areas have also to deal with complaints referred to them by the various Services Committees, which are investigated in private and informally, and they have wide disciplinary powers over practitioners, with a right of appeal to the Secretary of State for Scotland.

At the national level, apart from advisory and other committees, there is a Medical Practices Committee charged with the proper distribution of practitioners throughout the country, from which appeal lies to the Secretary of State, and a National Health Service Tribunal which deals

[92] For a general description, see Milne, The Scottish Office, 105 et seq.

only with disciplinary matters and serious complaints, usually referred to it by an Executive Council. There is again an appeal to the Secretary of State. The Secretary of State has these, and other, appellate duties, but from him no appeal lies to any court. The whole apparatus of tribunals is governed by a great mass of subordinate legislation, and is very complicated, so as to have incurred considerable criticism as " tribunalism run mad." [93]

In the sphere of National Insurance a dissatisfied claimant for benefit may resort to a local appeal tribunal of three. The procedure is very informal and legal representation, though allowed, is not usual. There is no appeal to the courts but instead to the National Insurance Commissioner or one of his deputies. These persons are full-time, legally qualified officers, and they issue reasoned judgments some of which are published and which are tending to develop into a body of case-law on the subject. [94] Some justiciable issues are, however, reserved for the determination of the Minister of Pensions and National Insurance himself.

Under the National Insurance (Industrial Injuries) Acts, which have replaced the Workmen's Compensation Acts and are concerned with insurance against death or disablement caused by injury or industrial disease arising out of and in the course of employment, a claim is made in the first place to the local insurance officer, from whom appeal lies to local tribunals [95] and to the Industrial Injuries Commissioner and his deputies, [96] who are permanent and legally qualified experts. Certain matters may be appealed to the Minister himself and such a question may be referred or appealed to the Court of Session. There are also Medical Boards, consisting of two or more medical practitioners, which deal with disablement cases and make provisional assessments of disablement benefits, [97] and from these appeal lies to Medical Appeal Tribunals, [98] which consist of a legally qualified chairman and two medical practitioners, with a further appeal on a point of law to the Commissioner. Cases before local appeal tribunals or the Commissioner will generally be heard in public. There are elaborate provisions for the review of decisions on the emergence of fresh evidence or on a change of circumstances.

Disputed claims under the Family Allowances Acts are decided by the Minister of Pensions and National Insurance, from whom appeal lies to the National Insurance adjudicating authorities. [99] Certain issues are reserved for decision by the Minister.

---

[93] Allen, *Administrative Jurisdiction*, 8; *cf.* Robson, *Justice and Administrative Law*, 3rd ed., 143.
[94] Safford, " The Creation of Case Law under the National Insurance and National Insurance (Industrial Injuries) Acts " (1954) 17 M.L.R. 197.
[95] National Insurance (Industrial Injuries) Act, 1946, s. 43.
[96] *Ibid.*, s. 36 (2).   [97] *Ibid.*, s. 36.   [98] *Ibid.*, s. 38.
[99] Family Allowances and National Insurance Act, 1959, s. 1.

The National Assistance scheme managed by the National Assistance Board is administered by local officers, from whom appeal lies to a local tribunal of three, from which there is no further appeal.

Tribunals relating to Land [1]

Since 1947 all planning, use and development of land is ultimately controlled by local planning authorities.   Development plans and applications give rise to numerous *ad hoc* inquiries but final adjudication is retained in the hands of the Secretary of State.   The same is true of the Housing Acts with their provisions for slum clearance, demolition and redevelopment, though there is a limited appeal to the courts from orders in such cases.

In respect of valuation for rating purposes mention must be made of the local Valuation Appeal Committees, which deal with appeals against the valuation of buildings and land for local rates, and from which appeal lies to the Lands Valuation Appeal Court.

The relationship of landlord and tenant of house-property falls within the jurisdiction of the sheriff court so far as relating to disputes about rent and ejection, but local authorities have the semi-judicial power of issuing certificates of disrepair which prevent an increase of rent being allowed, while in respect of furnished houses there are Rent Tribunals, sometimes of entirely non-legal composition, from which there is appeal only on a point of law to the Court of Session.

In the case of agricultural land, County Agricultural Executive Committees have executive and semi-judicial functions.   Appeal lies to the Scottish Land Court,[2] with a further appeal on a point of law to the Court of Session.[3]

The growth of marketing boards and governmental regulation of agriculture has given rise to numerous bodies to deal with complaints, applications, inquiries and so on.   Thus a producer of wool has it valued by a marketing board appraiser and, if aggrieved by his decision, has a right of appeal to a tribunal of five members.[4]

Transport

The grant of licences for passenger road services and for goods vehicles [5] is in each area [6] in the hands of three Traffic Commissioners,

---

[1] See generally Franks Committee Report, Chap. 13.
[2] In England appeal lies to an Agricultural Land Tribunal, with an appeal on a point of law to the High Court.
[3] Decisions on these matters can be found in the *Scottish Land Court Reports.*
[4] *Barrs* v. *British Wool Marketing Board,* 1957 S.C. 72.
[5] These licences are required as part of the regulation of services and are quite distinct from (*a*) vehicle excise licences; and (*b*) driving licences.   See Road Traffic Act, 1960, Part IV, and Kahn-Freund, *Law of Inland Transport,* 3rd ed., Chaps. 10 and 11.
[6] Scotland constitutes one area of the 11 in the U.K.

the chairman of whom is a permanent official and the other two are drawn from panels nominated by local authorities. They sit in public and legal representation is permitted and common. The three commissioners sit as Licensing Authority for Public Service Vehicles and issue Public Service Vehicle Licences, Road Service Licences and the Drivers' and Conductors' Licences which are specially required for public service vehicles. Appeal lies from a refusal to the Minister of Transport, or, in the case of a driver's or conductor's licence, to the sheriff court.

The chairman sits alone as Licensing Authority for Goods Vehicles and may issue A, B or C licences according as the vehicle is to be used for road haulage, for either road haulage or the carriage of the applicant's goods, or only for the carriage of the applicant's goods, and also the necessary Heavy Goods Vehicle Driver's Licence. Objections may be raised and the Licensing Authority may hold any inquiries necessary. An aggrieved person may appeal to the Transport Tribunal (which since 1947 has replaced the Railway and Canal Commission and the Railway Rates Tribunal). The Tribunal consists of five permanent whole-time officers, two experienced in transport, two in commerce and finance and one, the president, in law. It sits in two divisions, the London Fares and Miscellaneous Charges Division and the Road Haulage Appeals Division, each consisting of the president and two members. The president may appoint a person from a special panel, alone or with a member of the Road Haulage Appeals Division, to deal with the Division's business.[7] The Tribunal is a court of record, determines all matters of fact and law, and works in accordance with settled procedure regulated by rules. Appeal lies from it on questions of law to the Court of Appeal in England or to the Court of Session in Scotland.

The Air Transport Licensing Board is responsible for granting licences to BEA, BOAC and independent air-lines for the operation of air services. Its decisions are subject to appeal to the Minister of Aviation. An Air Registration Board makes recommendations to the Minister for the issue or renewal of certificates of airworthiness and conducts the examinations for the licensing of pilots and engineers.

The Industrial Court

The Industrial Court was set up in 1919[8] as a standing body, partly of independent persons, partly of representatives of employers and of employees, appointed by the Minister of Labour. Any trade dispute may be reported to the Minister by or on behalf of the parties, and he may, with the consent of the parties, refer the matter for settlement by the Industrial Court, or to arbitration, or for settlement by a Board of Arbitration.

---

[7] See further Kahn-Freund, *op. cit.*, 58–66; Transport Act, 1962, s. 57.
[8] Industrial Courts Act, 1919. See further Flanders and Clegg, *System of Industrial Relations in Great Britain*, 87–91; Sharp, *Industrial Conciliation and Arbitration in Great Britain*, 347–360.

The Minister may also refer other matters to the Industrial Court for advice. Where, however, there are arrangements in a trade for conciliation or arbitration, the Minister may bring the matter before the Industrial Court only by the consent of both parties and if the existing arrangements have failed to produce a settlement.

Commissioners of Income Tax

The Special Commissioners of Income Tax[9] are officials of the Inland Revenue Department, usually two in number, appointed by the Treasury to hear appeals against assessments for income tax and surtax. The General Commissioners of Income Tax[9] are unpaid laymen who also have a limited appeal jurisdiction in income tax assessments. The findings of the commissioners are final as to the facts but appeal lies by way of case stated on points of law to the Inner House of the Court of Session and thence to the House of Lords.[10]

DOMESTIC TRIBUNALS

The various organisations and associations established by individuals for various purposes, social, economic, intellectual, professional and otherwise, may, and frequently do, establish their own adjudicating and disciplinary bodies to regulate the rights and duties of members *inter se* and, in some cases, also *vis-à-vis* the outside world. The law in general permits such organisations to manage their own affairs, but sometimes interferes where the individual member's rights, which are at stake, are of vital importance to him. Again some domestic jurisdictions are almost entirely internal, while others are recognised by statute and even provision made for appeal to the courts.

The bodies exercising most completely " internal " domestic jurisdiction are the Faculty of Advocates and the Inns of Court which each have jurisdiction over their members in matters of discipline and professional conduct to the extent, if need be, of disbarring counsel. At least in England there is, by custom, an appeal to the judges.[11] So too the committee of the London Stock Exchange is complete master over the members. But in all these cases it is likely that the courts would

---

9 Income Tax Act, 1952, Part II.

10 For examples, see any recent volume of *Session Cases*. Decisions are also reported in a special series, *Reports of Tax Cases*, 1875 to date, and in various privately published reports.

11 *Re Marrinan* [1957] C.L.Y. 2747; see also *R. v. Gray's Inn* (1780) 1 Doug.K.B. 353. In 1874 E. V. H. Kenealy, Q.C., was disbenched and disbarred by Gray's Inn. In 1961 Mr. Victor Durand, Q.C., was suspended from practice for three years by the Benchers of the Inner Temple. On appeal five judges reduced this to one year. See further Halsbury's *Laws of England,* tit. " Barrister."

interfere to ensure that the requirements of natural justice [12] are complied with, though not further.

In the case of disciplinary committees of trade unions and associations to which the individual submits himself contractually by joining the body in question, the courts may interfere only on an issue of natural justice, and provided the association acts within its own constitution and rules, the interpretation of which is a matter for the courts.[13]

But in other cases the disciplinary body is set up by statute, and there may even be prescribed appellate procedure. Thus the General Medical Council has disciplinary jurisdiction in respect of infamous professional misconduct, with an appeal to the Privy Council.[14] Solicitors are subject, in England, to the Disciplinary Committee, with an appeal to three judges, and subsequently, by leave, to the Court of Appeal and the House of Lords. In Scotland solicitors are subject to the Solicitors' Discipline Committee and it may censure or fine or suspend the solicitor from practice or order his name to be struck off the roll of solicitors.[15] An appeal against the decision of the Discipline Committee lies to the Court of Session.

Similar disciplinary bodies have been established under statute for architects,[16] dentists,[17] pharmacists,[18] midwives,[19] registered nurses,[20] and veterinary surgeons,[21] and some other professions. All partake of some of the characteristics of courts, with defined procedures and, in some cases, statutory rights of appeal.

AD HOC TRIBUNALS

Public Inquiries [22]

A public local inquiry is required under many statutes for many different purposes but commonly to ascertain facts and local opinion,

[12] The requirements of natural justice are vague and undefined, but certainly cover the requirements that the person charged should be acquainted with the charge against him, be allowed to hear the evidence against him, and be heard in his own defence, and that the members of the tribunal be not biased or personally interested in the outcome of the dispute.
[13] See further Morris, " The Courts and Domestic Tribunals " (1953) 69 L.Q.R. 318; *Lee* v. *Showmen's Guild* [1952] 2 Q.B. 329; *Birch* v. *N.U.R.* [1950] Ch. 602; *Baker* v. *Jones* [1954] 1 W.L.R. 1005.
[14] Medical Act, 1956, s. 20 (this was first established by the Medical Act, 1858); and see *G.M.C.* v. *Spackman* [1943] A.C. 627.
[15] See further Solicitors' Discipline (Scotland) Committee Rules in *Parliament House Book.* See also *Solicitors' Discipline (Scotland) Committee* v. *B.,* 1942 S.C. 293; *X.* v. *Y.,* 1948 S.L.T.(Notes) 72; *E.* v. *T.,* 1949 S.L.T. 411.
[16] Architects Registration Act, 1938.
[17] Dentists Act, 1956.
[18] Pharmacy Act, 1954.
[19] Midwives (Scotland) Act, 1951.
[20] Nurses (Scotland) Act, 1951.   [21] Veterinary Surgeons Act, 1948.
[22] See further Robson, " Public Inquiries as an Instrument of Government " (1954) 1 B.J.A.L. 71.

objections and grievances, so that a particular Minister or Department may be fully conversant with the state of local feeling in relation to certain proposals, such as a housing, town planning or development scheme, or with the opinions in a particular industry or trade, such as a proposed marketing scheme for some commodity.[23]

In Scotland the person appointed to hold the inquiry is usually an experienced member of the Bar. Legal representation is allowed and evidence is led and submissions made very much as in a court of law. In England such inquiries are usually held by an official of the Department concerned. Hitherto the reports of the persons holding such inquiries have not been published.[24]

Tribunals of Inquiry

The Tribunals of Inquiry (Evidence) Act, 1921, empowers Parliament, by resolution of both Houses, to establish an *ad hoc* tribunal to investigate any matter of urgent public importance. The purpose of such an inquiry is to investigate and report its findings, it being for Parliament to take any action thought fit. Such a tribunal has most of the powers of a court; it usually sits in public and legal representation is allowed, and its report is usually published.[25]

Departmental Inquiries

A Minister may at any time institute an inquiry, frequently by a committee, into any matter which seems to him to require special investigation. The report is usually published. Thus the Secretary of State for Scotland set up a Departmental Committee to inquire into the law of succession in Scotland and propose changes, and this committee produced a valuable report [26] on which Parliament took no action.

Fatal Accidents Inquiries

One of the commonest of the *ad hoc* tribunals is the Fatal Accidents Inquiry held to inquire into cases of death of a person engaged in any industrial employment or occupation due, or reasonably believed to be due, to accident occurring in the course of the employment or occupation,[27] and cases of sudden or suspicious death.[28] The inquiry is held before a sheriff or sheriff-substitute and a jury of seven, and the evidence is collected and presented by the Procurator-Fiscal. Persons interested

23 Whether the Minister is affected by anything in the report of the inquiry may be doubtful: see *Franklin* v. *Minister of Town and Country Planning* [1948] A.C. 87.
24 See the observations of the Franks Committee on this (Report, paras. 344–345) and the Tribunals and Inquiries Act, 1958, s. 12. Statutory inquiries are also under the supervision of the Council on Tribunals.
25 See, *e.g.*, the " Lynskey " Inquiry into Budget leaks (Cmd. 7616, 1949) and the " Parker " Inquiry into leakage of information about Bank rate (Cmnd. 350, 1958), and generally Keeton, *Trial by Tribunal*.
26 Cmd. 8144, 1951.   27 Fatal Accidents Inquiry Act, 1895.
28 Fatal Accidents and Sudden Deaths Inquiry Act, 1906.

may appear personally or by counsel or solicitor, take part in and lead evidence at the inquiry. These include the deceased's relatives, employer, fellow-employees, trade union representatives, and inspectors of mines or of factories. The inquiry is held in public and conducted on the lines of a criminal jury trial, the evidence being recorded. Parties may address the jury and the sheriff usually delivers a short charge indicating the form of verdict desired, after which the jury deliberate and return their verdict, by a majority or unanimously. The verdict may not be used in evidence or founded upon in subsequent civil or criminal proceedings arising out of the same accident and no witness may be required to answer questions tending to show him guilty of any crime or offence. Verdicts are usually in fairly formal terms and seldom include any finding of fault against anyone. They may include riders or recommendations as to the adoption of safety measures in future.

Board of Trade Shipping Inquiries

A sheriff may also have to hold an inquiry into the circumstances attending a shipping casualty [29] to answer questions raised by the Board of Trade. The sheriff sits with one or more nautical assessors, and parties may appear by counsel or solicitor. Board of Trade witnesses are heard, the questions in regard to the casualty and the conduct of the ship's officers on which the Board of Trade desires the court's opinion stated, and each party may be heard on the questions, and lead evidence thereon, the witnesses being subject to cross-examination and re-examination. After the evidence parties may address the court and then the Board of Trade representative may be heard in reply on the whole case. The judgment of the court is given in the form of answers to the questions proposed by the Board of Trade. Ship's officers, if in fault, may be penalised by having their certificates cancelled or suspended, and the sheriff reports his findings to the Board of Trade, with a confidential annexation setting out the circumstances, the court's opinion of the cause of the casualty and of the conduct of persons involved. A party found in fault may appeal to either Division of the Court of Session, which hears the appeal with nautical assessors, in the same way as an ordinary appeal from the sheriff court, and in certain circumstances the Board of Trade may direct a rehearing before the same court, or before a wreck commissioner or a judge of the Court of Session.

An analogous inquiry may be held by the sheriff with two assessors, sitting as a Court of Survey, in a dispute between a Board of Trade surveyor and a shipowner as to whether a passenger vessel is so constructed as to be entitled to a passenger certificate.[30] The court may

---

[29] Merchant Shipping Act, 1894, ss. 466 (12), 479; Shipping Casualties Rules, 1923.
[30] Merchant Shipping Act, 1894, ss. 274–275.

uphold or refuse the appeal and in either case reports to the Board of Trade.

Inquiry may also be ordered by the Board of Trade into the conduct of ship's officers, their incompetency, misconduct or failure in duties, and this may be held by a sheriff, or a person designated, or the local Marine Board.[31] The procedure is as in the case of an inquiry into a shipping casualty, and there is a report to the Board of Trade.

II.—ENGLAND

While the courts and legal system of England have no direct or immediate jurisdiction over transactions or legal problems arising entirely in and affecting Scotland only, the Scot may frequently have to consider whether legal action should or must be taken in England while the references to English courts and procedure in legal books, documents and statutes are so common that he must be cognisant of the main features of the English system of courts and their respective competence in broad outline.[32]

CIVIL COURTS

Justices of the Peace

A court of summary jurisdiction consisting of two or three justices of the peace has limited civil as well as substantial criminal jurisdiction [33] and may make maintenance orders in bastardy cases, grant judicial separation between husband and wife, grant a wife a maintenance order as well as exercising many ministerial functions particularly with regard to licensing. Domestic proceedings are heard separately from other business and the public is excluded.

County Court

The main local courts for small causes are the county courts instituted in 1846.[34] England and Wales are divided into sixty-three circuits each with one or more county court judges.[35] These are full-time salaried judges who have had considerable experience at the Bar. They hold courts regularly in the principal towns of the circuit.[36] They may sit with, but nearly always sit without, a jury of eight and have jurisdiction in actions founded on contract or tort where the claim does not exceed £400, and in certain other cases, and in cases under the Housing,

---

31 *Ibid.*, s. 471.
32 On these see generally Halsbury's *Laws of England*, tit. " Courts."
33 The principal statute is the Magistrates' Courts Act, 1952.
34 For the modern jurisdiction see County Courts Act, 1959.
35 The full title is His Honour Judge X, and they are addressed as Your Honour.
36 For the circuits, judges and court towns, see the annual (English) *Law List*.

Landlord and Tenant, and Rent Restriction Acts. They have no divorce or criminal jurisdiction.

Appeal lies to the Court of Appeal on a matter of law, or, in cases involving the larger sums of money, on matters of fact or law. The amount of work dealt with in the county courts is very great, as procedure is relatively simple and inexpensive. Both solicitors and counsel have the right of audience in county courts.

In addition to the ordinary county courts there are a few local courts, survivals from medieval times, with somewhat similar jurisdiction. The most important are the Mayor's and City of London Court, the Liverpool Court of Passage and the Salford Hundred Court.[37]

High Court

The superior civil courts are the High Court of Justice and the Court of Appeal which are both branches of the single Supreme Court of Judicature.[38] The High Court in 1875 replaced, and assumed the jurisdiction possessed by, the former separate Courts of King's Bench, Common Pleas, Exchequer, Chancery, Admiralty, and Probate, Divorce and Matrimonial Causes,[39] together with that of certain others, such as the Assize Courts and the Courts of Common Pleas at Lancaster and Durham. The High Court was for convenience divided in 1875 into five Divisions, Queen's Bench, Common Pleas, Exchequer, Chancery and Probate, Divorce and Admiralty Division; in 1881 the first three were amalgamated into the Queen's Bench Division. All Divisions are empowered to grant all remedies and to try all kinds of actions, but certain matters were assigned to each Division, corresponding roughly to the jurisdiction of the courts they had replaced, and in practice work is distributed among the Divisions according to subject-matter, the Queen's Bench dealing with actions of contract and tort, the recovery of land and commercial litigation, the Chancery Division with trusts, mortgages, wills and estates, partnership, companies and bankruptcy and the wardship of infants, and the Probate, Divorce and Admiralty Division dealing with the probate of wills, divorce and nullity of marriage, ship collisions and wrecks.[40] There are no minimum or maximum pecuniary limits to High Court jurisdiction. The Divisions are staffed by judges [41] under the

---

[37] For details see the (English) *Law List* and Halsbury's *Laws of England*, tit. " Courts."

[38] The main Acts are the Judicature Acts, 1873–75, substantially re-enacted by the Supreme Court of Judicature (Consolidation) Act, 1925, and later amended in detail.

[39] This is why pre-1875 English reports are of cases decided in one or other of these courts.

[40] The so-called Commercial Court is not a separate court, but only the practice of assigning commercial cases to a particular list to be dealt with by a particular judge in a simple and expeditious manner in which pleadings are discouraged.

[41] The proper title is, *e.g.*, Mr. Justice Smith, notwithstanding that on appointment they receive knighthoods, and the printed contraction is Smith J. The plural is,

presidency respectively of the Lord Chief Justice of England (Q.B. Division), the Lord Chancellor (who very seldom sits in the High Court at all) (Chancery Division), and the President (P.D. and A. Division).

Assizes

When judges of the Queen's Bench Division visit the principal towns of the country on circuit [42] part of the time is devoted to trying civil cases but criminal business has priority. Judges of the Probate Division may also go on circuit for the disposal of divorce cases but judges of the Chancery Division do not go on circuit.[43] Divorce cases are also heard, both at Assize towns and in other " Divorce towns," by county court judges and senior members of the Bar specially commissioned (" Divorce Commissioners ") to try such cases.

Divisional Courts

A Divisional Court of the Queen's Bench Division is a tribunal of two or more judges of that Division which has a jurisdiction partly original and partly appellate. Its original jurisdiction includes the issue of the writ of habeas corpus and orders of certiorari, mandamus and prohibition, which are important in the judicial control of certain administrative bodies,[44] and the appellate jurisdiction covers the decision of questions of law raised by cases stated by Quarter Sessions and Petty Sessions,[45] the decision of appeals from the justices of the peace in landlord and tenant cases and certain other appeals from a judge sitting in chambers. The work of the Queen's Bench Divisional Court is, however, mainly criminal or administrative rather than civil.[46] A Divisional Court of the Chancery Division deals with appeals from county courts in bankruptcy matters and a similar court of the Probate, Divorce and Admiralty Division hears appeals from courts of summary jurisdiction in bastardy, affiliation, separation and maintenance orders and in certain other civil cases.

In all these civil cases there is an appeal from the Divisional Court to the Court of Appeal, and, with leave, to the House of Lords. There is no appeal from a decision on an application for a writ of habeas corpus

e.g., Smith and Jones JJ. Judges other than the heads of the three Divisions are known as " puisne " (pronounced " puny ") judges. The maximum number is now (1962) fifty-three. For the current number and names of the judges, see the (English) *Law List*.

[42] For the circuit and Assize system, see p. 211, *infra*.

[43] There are Chancery Courts of Lancaster and of Durham, survivals of ancient courts, which have a jurisdiction limited in area, but otherwise virtually equivalent to that of the Chancery Division.

[44] See Griffith and Street, *Principles of Administrative Law*, 2nd ed., 229–241.

[45] For these courts see *infra*, pp. 209–210.

[46] Till 1934 a Divisional Court heard appeals from county courts.

or one of the other prerogative orders if the application arises out of a criminal cause or matter.

The Court of Appeal

The Court of Appeal consists, apart from certain *ex officio* judges who rarely sit, of the Master of the Rolls and eleven Lords Justices of Appeal [47] sitting normally in four divisions each of three judges; the divisions all have the same powers and are not related to particular subject-matter. A judge of the High Court may sit to make up a quorum and conversely a Lord Justice may sit as an extra judge in the High Court. The jurisdiction extends to hearing appeals from all Divisions of the High Court, assizes in civil matters and county courts.[48] Further appeal lies to the House of Lords, but only with the leave of the Court of Appeal or of the House of Lords. For the great majority of cases the Court of Appeal is the final stage and its judgments command great respect as authoritative statements of the law of England.

House of Lords

The House of Lords as the supreme court of appeal from English courts in civil business is the same court and constituted in the same way as the House sitting as the supreme court of appeal from Scottish courts in civil business, and it acts subject to the same rules and conventions. Scottish Lords of Appeal may sit even for the hearing of English appeals.[49]

CRIMINAL COURTS [50]

The essential distinction is into courts which may deal only with petty offences punishable on summary conviction (without a jury) and indictable offences, tried on indictment before a jury. Most criminal offences are of one kind or the other, but in some cases an offence may be tried either on indictment or by summary proceedings. Magistrates' courts deal with summary proceedings only and superior courts with

---

[47] The titles are, *e.g.*, Lord Blank, Master of the Rolls, abbreviated as Blank M.R., and Lord Justice Smith, printed as Smith L.J. The plural is, *e.g.*, Smith and Jones L.JJ. They are appointed by the Queen on the recommendation of the Prime Minister and are sworn of the Privy Council. For the current names of the judges, see the (English) *Law List*.

[48] On the work of the courts, see Lord Evershed M.R., *The Court of Appeal in England*; Asquith L.J. "Some Aspects of the Work of the Court of Appeal" (1950) 1 J.S.P.T.L.(N.S.) 350; Cohen L.J., "Jurisdiction, Practice and Procedure of the Court of Appeal" (1951) 11 Camb.L.J. 3.

[49] This gives rise to the complaint among English lawyers that Scottish Lords have sometimes mishandled the law of England. But it has to be remembered that the Scottish Law Lords are hardly ever in a majority in the House, particularly when dealing with English appeals, so that the chance of their ever affecting English law detrimentally is small.

[50] See generally Wilshere's *Criminal Procedure*, Chap. 4.

indictable offences and with appeals. Judged by the number of cases dealt with, the magistrates' courts are by far the most important in the country, though the more serious crimes can be tried only by higher courts.

Magistrates' Courts

Justices of the peace are appointed in every county, county borough and certain large boroughs in England and Wales and the counties are divided into petty sessional divisions.[51]   Certain persons are also *ex officio* justices. One such magistrate sitting alone has very limited powers; he may grant a prisoner bail, act as " examining justice " to determine whether to commit a prisoner for trial on indictment, and discharge him if there is insufficient evidence to justify committing him for trial, but he may not act as a court of trial. The function of the examining justice or justices is to conduct a preliminary inquiry to decide whether or not there is sufficient evidence against the accused to justify committing him for trial, and the justices must commit for trial if there is evidence on which a reasonable jury could convict. Only if there is no such evidence can the justices discharge him.

A petty sessional court as a court of trial is constituted by from two to seven justices of the peace, one of whom acts as chairman, and tries criminal cases of minor importance, such as road traffic offences. The power of punishment is in general limited to six months' imprisonment and to a fine of £100. If the offence charged carries a maximum penalty of more than three months' imprisonment the accused must be given the option of being tried on indictment by jury at quarter sessions. Conversely some indictable offences may be dealt with summarily if the accused consents.

Juvenile courts are specially constituted magistrates' courts dealing with young persons charged with crimes other than homicide, needing care or protection, or truants, or beyond control. They sit separately from other courts and publicity for their proceedings is limited.

Stipendiary and Metropolitan Magistrates

Counties and boroughs may obtain the appointment of a legally qualified stipendiary magistrate who, sitting alone, has all the powers of a petty sessional court. He may also sit with, and act as chairman of, a bench of justices. In London there are a number of metropolitan magistrates who sit in the various courts while additional acting magistrates may be appointed when there is pressure of business.

---

[51] The office of justice dates from 1361 in England, and is now regulated by the Justices of the Peace Act, 1949. Jurisdiction and procedure are regulated by the Magistrates' Courts Act, 1952, and rules made thereunder.

Appeals from Petty Sessions

Appeal lies at the instance of the accused from petty sessions to quarter sessions; this is a rehearing of the whole case before an Appeal Committee of Quarter Sessions, consisting of from three to twelve justices, or, in boroughs with their own quarter sessions, before the Recorder of the borough as sole judge, and questions of both fact and law may be reviewed. There is a further right of appeal to the Queen's Bench Divisional Court by way of case stated, which sets out the findings of fact made by the justices and seeks a determination of any question of law raised thereby. Alternatively appeal lies direct from petty sessions to the Divisional Court by way of case stated.

Court of Quarter Sessions

The court of quarter sessions is both a court of first instance or trial court, and a court of appeal. In counties it is a meeting of county justices held every quarter for judicial business. As a court of trial it consists of from two to nine justices, one of whom, as chairman, decides questions of evidence and sums up to the jury, though in truth all are equally judges in the case. Formerly the chairman might be a layman, or a person legally qualified, and in the latter case the court had more extensive jurisdiction.[52] Since 1962 a person elected chairman of a county quarter sessions must be legally qualified. The office is frequently held by retired judges, county court judges, or persons of comparable experience. A legally qualified chairman may, if no other justice is available and delay is undesirable, deal with a case himself. Quarter sessions are in larger counties usually held in several towns in succession and two courts may be held concurrently, the second one presided over by a deputy chairman who also is often legally qualified.

Where a borough has its own quarter sessions, they are held four times a year but the sole judge is the Recorder of the borough, who, usually a practising Queen's Counsel, is appointed and paid by the Crown to visit and hold the court for a few days each quarter.[53] An assistant recorder may also be appointed so that a second court may sit concurrently. The judicial functions are similar to those of county quarter sessions and the Recorder has the wider jurisdiction appropriate to a court with a qualified chairman. If a borough does not have separate quarter sessions, the work is done by county quarter sessions.

Greater London is served by County of London Sessions (twenty-four sessions a year), Middlesex Sessions (monthly), both with qualified and salaried chairmen and deputy chairmen, and by the quarter sessions of the adjacent counties.

[52] For a list of chairmen see the (English) *Law List*. Many chairmen are in fact judges of the Supreme Court or county courts.
[53] For a list of Recorders see the (English) *Law List*.

Quarter sessions may deal with nearly all indictable crimes and they handle a large volume of cases and impose heavy sentences. Both county and borough quarter sessions hear cases only on indictment (with a jury).

Appeal lies from decisions of quarter sessions as a court of first instance to the Court of Criminal Appeal under certain conditions.

As a court of appeal quarter sessions hears appeals both on matters of fact and of law from the decisions of a court of summary jurisdiction (*i.e.*, stipendiary magistrate or justices in petty sessions), except that a person who pleaded guilty can appeal only against sentence. The appeal, which is heard by the Recorder in boroughs, or by an Appeal Committee of Quarter Sessions in counties, in each case without a jury, is by way of a complete rehearing of the case. Either party to such a case, or any person aggrieved, may require the court to state a case on a point of law for the decision of a Divisional Court of the Queen's Bench Division on the ground of error in law or excess of jurisdiction, and the Divisional Court may affirm, amend or reverse the decision. This is, in effect, a further appeal on law only.

Queen's Bench Divisional Court

A Divisional Court of the Queen's Bench Division exercises appellate jurisdiction in respect of the proceedings of magistrates' courts by hearing and deciding cases stated on points of law (*a*) by quarter sessions on an appeal from a magistrates' court, or (*b*) by a magistrates' court. The Divisional Court may reverse, affirm or amend the determination of the lower court in respect of which the case was stated, or remit the matter to the justices with the court's opinion thereon, or make such other order as may seem just. In criminal matters the decision of the Divisional Court may be appealed by either party to the House of Lords, with the leave of that court or of the House of Lords, if a point of law of general public importance is involved in the decision and it appears that the point ought to be considered by the House.

Queen's Bench Division

The Queen's Bench Division of the High Court, as the successor of the old Court of Queen's Bench, has now a limited jurisdiction in cases where the High Court has directed that an indictment or inquisition is to be tried at bar, *i.e.*, before at least three judges, in the Queen's Bench Division, or where a criminal information *ex officio* has been filed by the Attorney-General. The High Court may now order that in the former case it shall be tried at the Central Criminal Court before three judges of the Queen's Bench Division. This jurisdiction is not commonly exercised.

Assize Courts

England and Wales are divided into seven circuits,[54] and groups of two or three judges of the Queen's Bench Division go on circuit regularly from London visiting several important towns in each county on the circuit, generally three times a year, and there holding courts, primarily for criminal but also for civil business, for a few days, before proceeding to the next town on the circuit. Except in a few large towns the autumn assize is confined to criminal cases; at winter and summer assizes civil and criminal business may be taken. Assizes is a court of trial only and does not hear any appeals. The judges sit, not by virtue of being judges of the High Court, but as commissioners appointed under the four commissions of Assize, of Oyer and Terminer, and of Gaol Delivery, and experienced county court judges or Queen's Counsel may be included in the commission as Commissioners of Assize to help with the business, but all equally have all the powers of a judge of the High Court with unlimited criminal jurisdiction, and they may try any type of indictable case. Cases which might be tried by quarter sessions but are of particular difficulty or importance are usually reserved for assizes. The visits of assizes to the various towns are the main means of dealing with serious crimes throughout England. The judges of the Queen's Bench Division spend a substantial part of their time on circuit and groups of counsel attach themselves to the different circuits and attend at the towns thereof as required to handle the business to be dealt with there.

Central Criminal Court

Sessions are held at the Old Bailey in London once a month, or more frequently if necessary, for the disposal of criminal cases from Greater London. The Lord Mayor and Aldermen of London are still theoretically judges of this court but cases are tried by one of the judges of the Queen's Bench Division, the Recorder of London, the Common Serjeant or one of the judges of the Mayor's and City of London Court, always with a jury, though to form the necessary quorum the Lord Mayor or an alderman sits beside the judge. The court has the power of a court of assize and also acts as quarter sessions for the City of London.

Crown Courts

At Liverpool and Manchester there are Crown Courts which take the place of the criminal assizes and quarter sessions for their areas. They are presided over by full-time Recorders who hold sessions of the courts at

---

[54] The circuits are (i) Northern, (ii) North-Eastern, (iii) Midland, (iv) South-Eastern, (v) Oxford, (vi) Western, (vii) Wales and Chester. On the circuit system see also Halsbury's *Laws of England*, tit. " Barrister."

least eleven times a year, but a case may be held over to be tried before a judge of the High Court.[55]

Court of Criminal Appeal

This court, created in 1907 and superseding the former Court for Crown Cases Reserved, consists of the Lord Chief Justice and all the judges of the Queen's Bench Division. The court is constituted by three or a greater uneven number of judges; it may sit in two divisions. Appeal may be brought by a person convicted on indictment at quarter sessions, assizes, the Central Criminal Court or the Crown Courts against conviction, on any question of law, or under certain conditions on a question of fact, or a mixed question of fact and law, or against sentence. The Crown cannot appeal against an acquittal. The practice is for only one judgment to be delivered by the court and many of these judgments are of great importance. The court acts also as Courts-Martial Appeal Court for England and Wales.

House of Lords

Any case brought on appeal to the Court of Criminal Appeal may be appealed by either prosecutor [56] or defendant to the House of Lords with the leave of the court below or of the House of Lords, if it is certified by the court below that a point of general public importance is involved and it appears to that court or to the House that the point is one which ought to be considered by the House.[57] The House is constituted as for the hearing of civil appeals.

English Special Courts and Administrative Tribunals

Some of the special courts and many of the administrative tribunals found in Scotland are found also in England. In some cases there is no parallel and in other matters England has special courts of her own. These include a number of anomalous survivals of old local courts, distinct ecclesiastical courts, the jurisdiction of which is now limited to causes affecting the Church of England, and Coroners' Courts, which deal principally with ascertaining the causes of sudden deaths. Most of the Scottish administrative tribunals, domestic and *ad hoc* tribunals, have their English counterparts with corresponding jurisdiction.[58]

---

[55] Criminal Justice Administration Act, 1956.
[56] Thus in *D.P.P.* v. *Beard* [1920] A.C. 479 the Court of Criminal Appeal reduced a conviction of murder to one of manslaughter and the House of Lords restored it to one of murder. (The death penalty was not carried out.)
[57] Cases heard under this provision include *Joyce* v. *D.P.P.* [1946] A.C. 347 (the trial of Lord Haw-Haw). Till 1960 appeal required the certificate of the Attorney-General that the decision involved a point of law of exceptional public importance. This was not always granted as a matter of course.
[58] For further information see Hood Phillips, *Constitutional Law*, 2nd ed.; Wade and Phillips, *Constitutional Law*, 6th ed., and the (English) *Law List*.

III.—NORTHERN IRELAND

CIVIL COURTS

The courts are in general organised on the English model. Resident magistrates hold courts for minor civil cases but the main inferior court is the county court which has a limited jurisdiction in common law, equity and probate matters. There are no juries. Appeals may be taken by way of civil bill appeal to a visiting judge of assize, when the case is reheard, or appeal may be made on a point of law to a Divisional Court of the Supreme Court.

The Supreme Court of Judicature of Northern Ireland consists of the High Court and the Court of Appeal.[59] The High Court is divided into a Queen's Bench Division, which also has probate, divorce and admiralty jurisdiction, and a Chancery Division. Further appeal lies from the Court of Appeal to the House of Lords, and there is also an appeal on the constitutionality of a Northern Ireland statute to the Judicial Committee of the Privy Council, whose decision on such a point is binding on the House of Lords.

CRIMINAL COURTS

The resident magistrates, like stipendiary magistrates, try summary offences at petty sessions and also act as examining magistrates in more serious crimes. Lay magistrates have no criminal jurisdiction. Appeal lies from the petty sessional court to the county court. The county court judge in counties and the recorder in boroughs is also the chairman of quarter sessions and, as such, sits with a jury to try all but the most serious indictable offences.

The judges of the Supreme Court go on circuit to hold assizes (at which appeals from county courts are also heard) for the trial of serious crimes; appeal from assizes lies to the Court of Criminal Appeal, which consists of all the judges of the Supreme Court, with a further appeal to the House of Lords.

IV.—JUDICIAL COMMITTEE OF THE PRIVY COUNCIL

This body [60] consists of all Privy Councillors who hold or have held high judicial office in the United Kingdom together with certain

---

[59] The High Court consists of the Lord Chief Justice of Northern Ireland and two puisne judges, and the Court of Appeal of the Lord Chief Justice and two Lords Justices of Appeal. The two puisne judges may be called on to serve as extra judges of the Court of Appeal, and the two Lords Justices of Appeal frequently sit in the High Court and go on assize. See further MacDermott, " The Supreme Court of Northern Ireland—Two Unusual Jurisdictions " (1954) 2 J.S.P.T.L.(N.S.) 201, and " Law and Practice in Northern Ireland," 10 N.I.L.Q. 47.

[60] See also Normand, " Judicial Committee of the Privy Council " (1950) 3 C.L.P. 1.

distinguished colonial judges. In practice the Lords of Appeal in Ordinary sit so that the judicial composition of this body is very much the same as that of the House of Lords. The Committee is still in theory a branch of the Privy Council so that its decisions are tendered, not as judgments, but in the form of humble advice to Her Majesty to allow or dismiss an appeal, and one opinion only is given.

It is not a court of appeal in the usual way from the United Kingdom but only in certain matters from the English ecclesiastical courts, from the Probate, Divorce and Admiralty Division of the High Court in prize cases, from the courts of the Channel Islands and the Isle of Man, and in certain constitutional matters from Northern Ireland. Any other disputed matter may be referred to it by the Crown for hearing and opinion.

As an appellate court it hears appeals from the Dominions and Colonies, a jurisdiction now considerably reduced since many parts of the Commonwealth, on attaining independence, have abolished appeals to the Privy Council from their own Supreme Courts. Nevertheless in view of the personal eminence of its judges, decisions of the Judicial Committee are entitled to careful consideration in so far as they seem relevant to any matter of United Kingdom law. Their authority is, however, never more than highly persuasive.

V.—ARBITRATION

Arbitration is the submission by parties of any controversy or matter in dispute between them to the decision of a third party.[61] Reference to arbitration is commonly contractual, where the parties bind themselves by contract to refer disputes of any particular kind arising between them to the decision of a particular third person. The reference may also be made by a statutory provision that disputes arising in certain specified circumstances are to be determined not by resort to the courts but by arbitration. Thus the Workmen's Compensation Acts provided for disputes as to compensation between employer and employee being decided by the sheriff-substitute as arbitrator. Under the Agricultural Holdings (Scotland) Act, 1949, questions and differences between landlord and tenant of an agricultural holding arising out of the tenancy fall to be determined by arbitration. Again the reference may be made by deed, expressing the agreement of parties to have their dispute decided by a person as arbiter rather than by the ordinary courts.

---

[61] Questions of crime, personal status and issues involving the public interest cannot be the subject-matter of arbitration. Apart from that practically any issue can be referred to arbitration, though contractual and commercial issues are the commonest topics.

The advantages of arbitration are that in many cases the reference may be to an expert in the subject-matter of dispute, the procedure can be less formal and suited to the controversy, and not bound by rules of court procedure, that the issue may be determined more quickly than in the courts, and in private. The expense, however, may be greater in that the arbiter and his clerk have to be remunerated, while counsel and solicitors are required as for a court and witnesses may have to be called as to a court. Nevertheless commercial men frequently prefer quick arbitration by an expert to the lengthy process of a court action and various chambers of commerce and professional and trade associations have established arbitration panels to deal with disputes arising in their trade or business.

Effect of Submission
The effect of the contractual or statutory submission of any matter to arbitration is that the jurisdiction of the ordinary courts is excluded as to that matter, and if one party does appeal to the courts, the other may object; the court will decline to consider the merits of the dispute and will sist the action to await the result of the arbitration.[62] In case of doubt as to the interpretation of the reference, it is for the court to decide,[63] as a problem of the interpretation of the deed or statute in question, whether the dispute is one covered by the reference to arbitration or not, in which case the court may proceed to deal with the merits of the dispute. The scope of the submission depends on the terms used; it may be to specified or incidental matters only or to all questions arising between those parties out of their contract. If one party repudiates the contract completely, that does not exclude the jurisdiction of the arbiter if there was a reference to arbitration of all questions that may arise under the contract, and it will be for the arbiter to say whether the repudiation was justified or not. But the arbiter's jurisdiction will be excluded if the contract referred only specified matters to arbitration.[64]

Who may Arbitrate
Parties may submit their disputes to the arbitration of whomever they care to name. It is competent[65] in the contract to provide for arbitration by a specified and named person, or by the holder for the time being of a particular office, or by a person nominated by the holder for the time being of a particular office, or by a person designated in any similar way. Sometimes the reference is to a sole arbiter, or to two

---

[62] *Hamlyn* v. *Talisker Distillery* (1894) 21 R.(H.L.) 21.
[63] See, *e.g., Brodie* v. *Ker,* 1952 S.C. 216.
[64] *Sanderson* v. *Armour,* 1922 S.C.(H.L.) 117; *Heyman* v. *Darwins* [1942] A.C. 356; *Mauritzen* v. *Baltic Shipping Co.,* 1948 S.C. 646.
[65] Prior to the Arbitration (Scotland) Act, 1894, the rule was that reference to an unnamed arbiter was not binding.

arbiters, one chosen by each party, in which case the two arbiters have power, unless there is provision to the contrary, to appoint an oversman. If the parties cannot agree as to the choice of a single arbiter, or if one party does not nominate an arbiter where the reference is to two, the court may make an appointment on the application of any party interested.[66] So too the court may appoint an oversman if the two arbiters cannot agree in nominating one.[67] The person designated must be fair and unbiased, and have no interest in the subject-matter in dispute or in the outcome of the arbitration. He may stipulate for a fee and a man acting in a matter involving his professional knowledge and experience is in practice recognised as entitled to a fee.

Powers of Arbiter

In statutory arbitrations the powers of the arbiter, including any matter of appeal to the courts from his decision, are regulated by the relevant statute. In non-statutory arbitrations the decision of the arbiter, or of the oversman if two arbiters differ, is final both on questions of fact and of law. An arbiter has no power to find either party liable in damages unless there is express provision for that,[68] and he has no power to enforce his decision by civil diligence, though it is usual to insert in deeds providing for arbitration a clause consenting to the registration for preservation and execution of the award, and diligence may in such a case proceed on an extract of the award from the register. If there is no such clause, an action in court for decree conform is necessary. An arbiter has an implied power to award expenses.

Procedure

The procedure in an arbitration is such as the parties may agree, and the degree of formality or informality will depend largely on whether issues of fact or of law bulk larger in the case. Counsel or solicitors may be instructed, there may be pleadings, written or oral argument, a proof, an inspection of the premises or subject-matter of dispute or otherwise as may be required. The arbiter may consult an expert, such as an engineer, if such assistance is necessary.

The arbiter may submit a draft award or proposed findings to the parties, and allow them to lodge, and be heard on, representations regarding these proposed findings. He may also make an interim award. The final award or decree arbitral narrates the circumstances, the submission, and the procedure which followed, and then makes the final finding and decree, which, once issued and delivered to the parties, is beyond recall and binding on them and their successors.

---

[66] Arbitration (Scotland) Act, 1894, ss. 1–3.
[67] Ibid., s. 4.
[68] Mackay & Son v. Leven Police Commissioners (1893) 20 R. 1093.

Appeal to the Courts

By accepting arbitration parties voluntarily exclude the jurisdiction of the courts. In statutory arbitrations there may be an appeal to the courts by case stated.[69] Apart from that the courts will not interfere on the merits, however wrong the arbiter's decision may appear to be in fact or in law or in both, and there is no appeal. The whole object of arbitration is to exclude resort to the courts.

An arbiter's award may however be reduced by an action of reduction in court on the ground that he had an interest, unknown to one party, in the case, or if he proceeds *ultra fines compromissi*, that is, deals with a point beyond the scope of the reference to him, or if he has mistaken the point in issue, or has not exhausted the questions submitted to him, or if there has been corruption, bribery or falsehood, or such a serious error in procedure as amounts to a denial of a principle of natural justice, as, for example, failing to hear one party.

FURTHER READING

Scottish Courts
Dobie: *Sheriff Court Practice.*
Gibb: *Law from Over the Border.*
Hannay: *The College of Justice.*
Mackay: *Practice of the Court of Session.*
Maclaren: *Court of Session Practice.*
Renton and Brown: *Criminal Procedure.*

English Courts
Archer: *The Queen's Courts.*
Devlin: *The Criminal Prosecution in England.*
    Trial by Jury.
Halsbury's *Laws of England*, tit. " Courts."
Holdsworth: *History of English Law*, Vol. 1.
Jackson: *The Machinery of Justice in England.*
Kiralfy: *The English Legal System.*
Plucknett: *Concise History of the Common Law.*
Potter: *Historical Introduction to English Law.*
Radcliffe and Cross: *The English Legal System.*

Special Courts and Administrative Tribunals
Allen: *Law and Orders.*
    Administrative Jurisdiction.
Denning: " Courts and Tribunals " (1954) 1 B.J.Adm.L. 107.
Forster: " The Industrial Court " (1954) 1 B.J.Adm.L. 35.
Hene: " Domestic Tribunals of Great Britain " (1956) 2 B.J.Adm.L. 24.
Mitchell: " Domestic Tribunals and the Courts " (1956) 2 B.J.Adm.L. 80.
Robson: *Justice and Administrative Law.*

[69] *e.g.*, under the Agricultural Holdings (Scotland) Act, 1949; see, *e.g.*, *MacNab of MacNab* v. *Willison*, 1960 S.C. 83; *Forsyth-Grant* v. *Salmon*, 1961 S.C. 54.

CHAPTER 6

THE PERSONNEL OF THE LAW

THE College of Justice in Scotland, established in 1532, comprises the judges of the Court of Session, who are designated Senators of the College, and advocates, Writers to the Signet, and others, who are members of the College.[1] The judges are invariably, and sheriffs and sheriffs-substitute are usually, chosen from among the senior advocates, but on appointment to the Bench, apart from part-time appointments as sheriff (principal), members of the judiciary become public officers and cease to be practising members of the legal profession, though they do not relinquish their membership of their professional organisation.

The judiciary

The office of judge is one of great honour and dignity as well as of immense constitutional and legal importance, and calls for the noblest moral and mental qualities and the highest standards of intelligence, scholarship and diligence.

Appointment to the Court of Session bench is made [2] by selection from the practising bar, frequently of a Law-Officer or senior Advocate-Depute or the Dean or Vice-Dean of the Faculty of Advocates.[3] The person appointed has usually had previous judicial experience as a sheriff-principal; there seem, at least in modern times, to be no instances of the promotion of a sheriff-substitute, still less of an academic jurist.[4] The judges are not peers,[5] nor are they knighted on appointment, but are accorded the courtesy title of Lord ——, the title being either taken from their estates or, more frequently today, merely their family names. A judge may, however, have been knighted previously for public services.

---

[1] See further Mackay's *Practice*, Chap. 3. Though designated Senators of the College of Justice the judges are officially addressed, *e.g.*, in petitions, as Lords of Council and Session, a title reflecting the origins of the court.

[2] The appointment is made by the Queen on the nomination of the Prime Minister, who doubtless consults the Secretary of State for Scotland and the Lord Advocate.

[3] Of the present (1963) sixteen, five had held the offices of Lord Advocate or Solicitor-General; six those of Dean of Faculty or Vice-Dean; and five were promoted from the senior Bar, and of these three had previously been Advocates-Depute.

[4] There were one or two cases of this in the eighteenth century but in those days professorships were not full-time posts. Appointment of an academic jurist has occasionally been made in America.

[5] Judges promoted to be Lords of Appeal in Ordinary, *i.e.*, to the House of Lords, receive a life peerage, and occasionally a Lord of Session receives a peerage: instances are Lord President Balfour (1899–1905), created Lord Kinross in 1902, and Lord President Cooper (1947–55), created Lord Cooper of Culross in 1954.

There is now a retiring age of seventy-five. All judges have the same rank and title and promotion to the Inner House from the Outer House is by seniority on a vacancy occurring and no judge is appointed direct or promoted to the Inner House over his brethren,[6] except in the cases of the chairs of the two divisions.

Appointment as Lord President [7] or Lord Justice-Clerk [8] is usually made direct from the Bar, usually by the promotion of a Law-Officer. Only occasionally has the Lord Justice-Clerk been promoted Lord President,[9] and it is rare for a judge already on the bench to be promoted Lord President or Lord Justice-Clerk.[10] It is apparent that promotion to the Bench is commonly the reward for parliamentary service, though it is fair to say that the system has brought to the Bench and to the offices of Lord President and Lord Justice-Clerk many outstanding lawyers whose contributions to the development of Scots law have been of permanent value.[11]

Appointment as a sheriff or sheriff-substitute is made from Q.C.s, advocates or solicitors of at least five years' standing, and sheriff-substitutes are sometimes moved from one town to another. Retirement on pension is now compulsory at seventy-two.

Legal practitioners

In Scotland the legal profession is sharply divided into advocates and solicitors,[12] each body having exclusive functions, rights and

6 In these respects the court differs markedly from the High Court and Court of Appeal in England.

7 Thus in the present century Alexander Ure, Lord Strathclyde (1913–20), was Lord Advocate 1909–13; James Avon Clyde (1920–35) was Lord Advocate 1916–20 and also Dean of the Faculty of Advocates; Wilfrid Guild Normand (1935–47) was Lord Advocate 1933–35; Thomas Mackay Cooper (1947–54) was Lord Advocate 1935–41 and Lord Justice-Clerk 1941–47; James Latham Clyde (1955–) was Lord Advocate 1951–55. A list of Lords President is in *Introduction to Scottish Legal History*, Appx. 2, and 1958 S.L.T.(News) 243.

8 *e.g.*, L.J.C. Aitchison (1933–41) was Lord Advocate 1929–33; L.J.C. Cooper (1941–47) was Lord Advocate 1935–41; L.J.C. Moncrieff (1947) was promoted from the Bench; L.J.C. Thomson (1947–62) was Lord Advocate 1945–47; L.J.C. Grant (1962–) was Lord Advocate 1960–62. A list of Lords Justice-Clerk is in *Introduction to Scottish Legal History*, Appx. 3, and 1958 S.L.T.(News) 243. See also Malcolm, "The Lord Justice-Clerk of Scotland" (1915) 27 J.R. 342, 375.

9 The only instances are: Charles Hope (L.J.C. 1804–11, L.P. 1811–41); Boyle (L.J.C. 1811–41, L.P. 1841–52); Inglis (L.J.C. 1858–67, L.P. 1867–91); Cooper (L.J.C. 1941–47, L.P. 1947–55).

10 Duncan McNeill (later Lord Colonsay) was appointed in 1851, promoted Lord President in 1852 and elevated to the House of Lords as Lord Colonsay in 1867; Alexander Moncrieff, appointed in 1926, was promoted Lord Justice-Clerk in 1947.

11 See also Wilton, " The Scottish Judiciary " (1923) 35 J.R. 73.

12 This division of the profession is not found in the U.S.A. nor in some Commonwealth countries. It is arguable whether division or fusion is theoretically better: see Walker, " Fusion of the Profession " (1956) 72 S.L.R. 25; Jackson, *Machinery of Justice in England*, Chap. 4.

privileges in certain respects and concurrent functions and rights in others. While an individual may move from the one branch to the other, no one may belong to or practise simultaneously in both.[13] The two branches of the profession have developed separately [14] and each has its own governing body, qualifications for entry, *esprit de corps* and etiquette. As compared with countries where the legal profession is undivided, the terms " counsel " (both denoting the singular and as a collective noun) and " the Bar " are properly used in United Kingdom countries of advocates and their counterparts only, and not of the whole legal profession.

The distinction between the two branches is broadly that between the specialist or consultant and the general adviser. The advocate specialises in advice on complicated issues of law, the framing of pleadings and the conduct of proceedings, oral and written, before courts and tribunals on behalf of the client. The solicitor alone comes into personal contact with the client and concerns himself generally with advice, business negotiations, taxation questions, conduct of the legal formalities relating to the sale and transfer of property, the drawing up of wills, and pleading in the inferior courts as well as much preliminary work in cases coming before superior courts. The solicitor is to a large extent the general legal practitioner, the adviser, the negotiator and the man of business, whereas the advocate is called in in cases of difficulty, for advice in tricky or important business, and in all cases where there is litigation of any consequence in prospect or in train. The two branches of the profession call for slightly different training, and appeal to different types of men. The advocate has to be the legal expert, the quick thinker, the fluent and persuasive debater, usually involved in matters of controversy, whereas the solicitor has much more routine work to do and spends much time in consulting clients, negotiating and carrying through business, frequently non-contentious, and attending to everyday affairs. Many solicitors are employed by other solicitors, by local authorities, and by large commercial and industrial concerns, to attend to business having legal connections and implications.

Advocates

The Faculty of Advocates is the Scottish Bar [15] and members of Faculty have a status corresponding to that of barrister in England

---

[13] It is, of course, also incompetent to be a Scottish solicitor and an English barrister simultaneously and vice versa, though one may be enrolled simultaneously in the *same* branch of the profession in two or more countries of the United Kingdom.

[14] See further Henderson Begg, *Treatise on Law Agents*, Chap. 1.

[15] The Society of Advocates in Aberdeen is a local body of solicitors and quite distinct from the Faculty.

or Northern Ireland.[16] With the exception of a party to the cause, the only person permitted to appear and plead a case in the superior courts in Scotland is an advocate.[17] They also have the right, equally with barristers, to appear before the House of Lords, Privy Council and Parliamentary Committees. Advocates and barristers are not, however, interchangeable in that neither may in general appear before the courts of the other country unless he has qualified in the other system of law and been called to the Bar in the other country also.[18] Advocates have the right of audience, unless it is expressly excluded by statute, before every court, civil, criminal and ecclesiastical, and before all tribunals, courts of special jurisdiction and quasi-judicial bodies in Scotland. In the inferior courts, however, and before special tribunals the right of audience is concurrent with that of solicitors. Most papers and pleadings in the Court of Session must be signed by counsel; the most important exception is a summons, which is signed by a solicitor, but it is customary to have all papers and pleadings for the superior courts prepared or revised by counsel.

The Faculty is by prescriptive right an autonomous corporation and as such dates from at least the early sixteenth century, having its origin in the group of pleaders who regularly appeared before the courts which preceded the foundation of the Court of Session.[19] Admission is by election after the intrant has petitioned the court, paid certain fees, and satisfied the Faculty Examinators as to his qualifications in both General Scholarship and in Law.[20] The principal officer of the Faculty is the Dean, who takes precedence over all members of the Bar except the Lord

---

[16] In England persons are called to the Bar, *i.e.*, become barristers-at-law, after passing examinations and " keeping terms " at one or other of the four Inns of Court (Lincoln's Inn, The Middle Temple, The Inner Temple and Gray's Inn). In Northern Ireland there is an Inn of Court of Northern Ireland. On the Inns see further Jackson, *Machinery of Justice in England*, Chap. 4, and generally Halsbury's *Laws of England*, tit. " Barrister."

[17] *Longworth* v. *Yelverton* (1867) L.R. 1 Sc.App. 218, 220. A firm (*Macbeth & Maclagan* v. *Macmillan*, 1914 S.C.(J.) 165) and a company (*Equity and Law Life Assce. Socy.* v. *Tritonia, Ltd.*, 1943 S.C.(H.L.) 88) must always be represented by counsel.

[18] Some advocates do in fact possess the additional qualification of barrister-at-law and could therefore appear in both Scottish and English courts. Apart from that a barrister cannot appear in the Court of Session or an advocate in the High Court in England.

[19] The right of advocates to plead was secured by law in the time of Alexander III: A.P.S. I, 425; and there is frequent mention in records from the thirteenth century onwards of forespeakers (*prolocutores* or *praelocutores*) and advocates. See, *e.g.*, Acts 1318, c. 17 and c. 18; 1320, c. 28; 1425, c. 45; 1429, c. 125; Bankton IV, 3, 1 *et seq.*; Mackay's *Practice of the Court of Session*, I, 102 *et seq.*; Henderson Begg, *Treatise on Law Agents*, 5 *et seq.*

[20] Much information about " devilling," as pupillage is miscalled in Scotland, about the formalities of call to the Scottish Bar, and life and work thereat, is in Lord Macmillan's *A Man of Law's Tale*, 26 *et seq.*

Advocate for the time being.[21] He is assisted by a Vice-Dean [22] and other officers, all being elected annually at the anniversary meeting of the Faculty held in January, and in practice usually re-elected so long as they are willing to serve. The Dean and his Council of senior members of Faculty exercise strict control over the professional discipline and etiquette of all members of Faculty and may censure or even dis-bar a member guilty of professional or other serious misconduct.

The Law Officers

The Crown has two official advisers or Law Officers for Scotland, the Lord Advocate and the Solicitor-General for Scotland.[23] Nowadays they are appointed by the Prime Minister and go out of office with the Government. Either or both may be M.P.s and, if in the House, assist the Secretary of State for Scotland in handling government business. They advise the Crown and represent it in civil cases and the Lord Advocate is the head of the system of public prosecution in the criminal courts, and he or the Solicitor-General appears for the Crown in important cases. He has full power over and complete discretion in the prosecution of crimes in any court in Scotland.

To assist him in the ordinary business in the High Court the Lord Advocate appoints four Advocates-Depute (one for each of the four circuits). One of these, the " Home Depute," is a Q.C., and deals with Edinburgh cases. The others are normally junior counsel, normally resign office if they take silk, and exchange circuits every six months so as to share the work evenly. He appoints also an Extra Advocate-Depute for the Glasgow circuit, and, sometimes, an Advocate-Depute for the Sheriff Court. These appointments fall when the Lord Advocate goes out of office.

Various advocates are also appointed to be standing junior counsel to various government departments and boards, and act as advisers to and counsel for these offices. These appointments are non-political, but a standing counsel resigns office when he takes silk.

Senior and Junior Counsel

An advocate or junior counsel remains a junior from the date of his call to the Bar until he becomes a Queen's Counsel, otherwise known

---

21　A list of Deans of Faculty from 1698 is in 1958 S.L.T.(News) 245.

22　A list of Vice-Deans of Faculty from 1754 is in 1958 S.L.T.(News) 245.

23　Their English counterparts are the Attorney-General and the Solicitor-General. Lists of the holders of the offices of Lord Advocate and Solicitor-General are in 1958 S.L.T.(News) 244 and in Milne, *The Scottish Office*, 218–221. See also Mackay, *Practice*, I, 119; Omond, *The Lord Advocates of Scotland*, 3 vols.; Green's *Encyclopaedia*, s.v. Criminal Administration; " Law Officers of Scotland," 1924 S.L.T.(News) 43; Malcolm, " The Solicitor-General for Scotland " (1942) 54 Jur.Rev. 67, 125; *Dumfries C.C.* v. *Phyn* (1895) 22 R. 538; *McBain* v. *Crichton*, 1961 J.C. 25; *Hester* v. *Macdonald*, 1961 S.C. 370.

as senior counsel.[24] Senior counsel thus consist of such members of the Bar as have, after a number of years of practice and the acquisition of considerable experience and legal skill, been appointed by the Queen, on the recommendation of the Lord Justice-General, to the rank and dignity of Her Majesty's Counsel learned in the law.[25] Queen's Counsel take precedence *inter se* according to the dates of their respective patents, except that the Lord Advocate for the time being has precedence over all others and is entitled to a seat " within the Bar," *i.e.*, in the well of the court, at the clerk's table on the right side. The Dean of Faculty ranks next in precedence and has his seat at the centre of the Bar. The Solicitor-General for the time being ranks third and has his seat within the Bar, at the left side of the clerk's table. Thereafter rank ex-law officers of the Crown and other Q.C.s according to the dates of their patents. As in England, a Q.C. wears a silk gown,[26] and he is entitled in court to lead any other counsel not of that rank, whatever may be his date of call to the Bar. A Q.C. may not draw or revise pleadings, nor appear in any court, nor before a Provisional Order Inquiry, or a Royal or Parliamentary Commission, unless accompanied by a junior counsel. Accordingly a party who wishes to instruct a Q.C. *must* instruct a junior as well, and this is customary in the House of Lords, the Inner House and in all cases of importance. In exceptional cases several counsel may be instructed for one party, but there must always be at least one junior among them. In some cases two juniors are instructed, one of whom acts as senior counsel, or a senior counsel may be assisted by two juniors. The rule requiring that a junior be instructed along with a Q.C. does not apply to arbitrations, nor to written opinions.

It was originally the rule, at least in England, that senior counsel must not be employed against the Crown without special licence, which was refused only if the Crown desired to be represented by the Q.C. concerned.[27]

Counsel is also frequently consulted in matters not, or not yet, the subject of litigation, as when he is asked to give his opinion on certain documents or issues. This opinion may be accepted as a basis for action or as settling a controversy without litigation. In such cases a Memorial

---

[24] In England also sometimes called " leading counsel," or " leaders."

[25] A roll of Queen's Counsel in Scotland was created only in 1897; till then the dignity was conferred only on Law Officers and the Dean of Faculty. For the full story, see " The Faculty of Advocates and Queen's Counsel " (1896) 4 S.L.T. 47, 51, 55, 60, 143, 169, 254.

[26] Hence the phrase " taking silk," signifying promotion to the rank of Q.C.

[27] With the great increase in litigation against the Crown and Crown Departments in modern times this rule was abrogated in 1920, and Q.C.s were granted a general dispensation to appear against the Crown without a licence. For the development of the status of Q.C. in England, where it originated in the 16th century, see Plucknett, *Concise History of the Common Law*, 5th ed., 230; Holdsworth, " Rise of the Order of King's Counsel " (1920) 36 L.Q.R. 212.

is prepared by a solicitor, setting out the facts which raise the legal problem, and sent with all the relevant documents and information to one or more counsel with certain questions formulated to which answers are desired. The answers are returned in the form of a written Opinion, which deals *seriatim* with the questions, usually giving reasons for the answers with references to cases and statutes.

Relations between Counsel

No form of partnership or sharing of work or profits is permitted among counsel, so that every counsel, both junior and senior, works entirely independently, and is dependent for his income on his own exertions and ability. Hence there is no such thing as standing partnerships between any two or more counsel, or between senior and junior. The collaboration which exists between a senior and the junior instructed by a party in one case subsists in respect of that case only, and the two counsel may simultaneously be instructed to appear on opposite sides in another case. Hence every counsel is alone personally and solely responsible for the whole work of his practice and for every opinion, note or pleading which he writes. It says much for the sense of honour and *camaraderie* of the Bar that such a system works smoothly and is not productive of personal enmities. The settled tradition is that disagreement and opposition are confined to the court room and are never carried over into personal relationships.

In the conduct of a litigation the junior counsel is responsible for all drawing and adjusting of pleadings,[28] incidental motions and procedure, and advice on evidence, and generally all steps leading up to the trial of the action, though on all matters he may consult with his senior, and the senior will frequently in complicated cases revise the pleadings before they are finally closed. At a hearing in court the senior counsel normally conducts the examination and cross-examination of most of the witnesses and certainly of all the important and difficult witnesses, while the junior counsel is noting the substance of the evidence, taking care that his senior is supplied with any maps, books or documents to which he may be referring, and trying to ensure that no point of substance is overlooked in the examination. There are, however, no rigid rules about the apportionment of work at a hearing and the two counsel may divide it as they choose.

[28] Hence in Scotland prior to the introduction of a roll of Queen's Counsel an advocate was said to " give up writing " (*i.e.*, pleadings) when he began to undertake only senior practice.

Instruction of Counsel

A client may instruct counsel only through an enrolled solicitor, and if he has a consultation with counsel the solicitor will be present.[29] The choice of counsel lies with the client, but he normally leaves the choice to the solicitor, who is usually better acquainted with the personality and experience of the different counsel in practice and with their special experience in particular fields. Instructions should always be in writing and counsel is not bound to appear unless properly instructed.

An advocate is presumed to have a mandate to appear for a person from the bare fact of his appearance [30] and this can be rebutted only by a disclaimer.[31] He is not responsible for the consequences if he acts on the instructions of a practising solicitor.[32] Once he has accepted instructions to act in a case he must remain free to act according to his judgment and discretion [33] so that he may take a particular course of action or even abandon or compromise a claim on his own responsibility,[34] unless he has been expressly instructed not to, though it is advisable to consult the client before taking any drastic step. " The nature of an advocate's office makes it clear that in the performance of his duty he must be entirely independent and act according to his own discretion and judgment in the conduct of the cause for his client. His legal right is to conduct the case without any regard to the wishes of his client, so long as his mandate is unrecalled, and what he does bona fide according to his own judgment will bind his client and will not expose him to any action for what he has done, even if the client's interests are thereby prejudiced." [35]

Special rules apply to " retainers," *i.e.*, to instructions with reference to any particular cause (special retainer), or retainer by virtue of instructions to draw or revise pleadings or to appear for a party in court (implied retainer), or retainer whereby the services of a particular counsel are secured in all cases in Scottish courts, but not in arbitrations or in the House of Lords, in which the person retaining him is concerned as a party (general retainer). Detailed rules have been formulated from time to time by the Dean of Faculty.[36]

Since mutual confidence is of the essence of the professional relationship, the client remains free to instruct another counsel and the counsel

---

[29] A country agent may put before counsel a memorial for opinion without the intervention of an Edinburgh agent: *Journal of Jurisprudence*, XIV, 148, 206.
[30] Ersk., III, 3, 33; Maclaren's *Practice*, 16; *Ballantine* v. *Edgar* (1676) Mor. 348; *Marchmont and Morison* v. *Home* (1715) Mor. 358.
[31] *Ogston* v. *Turnbull* (1875) 13 S.L.R. 69.
[32] *Wallace* v. *Miller* (1821) 1 S. 40.
[33] *Batchelor* v. *Pattison and Mackersy* (1876) 3 R. 914.
[34] *Mackintosh* v. *Fraser* (1860) 22 D. 421; *Duncan* v. *Salmond* (1874) 1 R. 329; *Ballach* v. *Kelly* (1900) 8 S.L.T. 52. *Cf. Strauss* v. *Francis* (1866) L.R. 1 Q.B. 379.
[35] *Batchelor* v. *Pattison and Mackersy* (1876) 3 R. 914, 918.
[36] Printed in *Parliament House Book*, Division A.

to return his papers at any stage in the course of employment. The advocate is not bound to disclose information which he has obtained in the course of the employment, unless the client waives the privilege.

An advocate is not liable in damages for wrong advice in law, negligence, mistake, indiscretion, error of judgment, or the mismanagement of a cause,[37] unless in case of an express agreement, or if he has acted fraudulently or treacherously [38]; nor is a solicitor liable who acts upon the advice of counsel in matters connected with the conduct of a suit.[39]

Solicitors

The other branch of the legal profession in Scotland consists of solicitors, formerly known as writers or law agents.[40]   While many solicitors practise individually or in partnership, many also are employed by large businesses or public or local authorities, as full-time employees, to conduct their legal transactions, or in managerial or secretarial capacities.[41]   Admission to the Roll of Solicitors kept by the Registrar of Solicitors is by petition following a period of practical training with a practising solicitor, and the taking of a law degree at a Scottish university or the passing of professional examinations in lieu thereof.[42] A solicitor in practice must take out a practising certificate annually.[43]

The professional organisation is the Law Society of Scotland, established in 1949, which comprises all practising solicitors in Scotland, conducts the professional examinations, acts as Registrar of Solicitors, and controls the Legal Aid Scheme.   In addition there are various smaller professional societies of considerable antiquity and high professional status of which the principal are the Society of Writers to the Signet, the Society of Solicitors in the Supreme Courts, the Royal Faculty of Procurators in Glasgow, and the Society of Advocates in Aberdeen (which last is a body of solicitors and is not to be confused with the Faculty of Advocates).[44]

[37] *Purves* v. *Landell* (1845) 12 Cl. & F. 91, 103; *Burness* v. *Morris* (1849) 11 D. 1258; *Batchelor* v. *Pattison and Mackersy* (1876) 3 R. 914; *Swinfen* v. *Lord Chelmsford* (1860) 5 H. & N. 890. Cf. *Fell* v. *Brown* (1791) 1 Peake 131.
[38] *Swinfen, supra*, at p. 920.
[39] *Megget* v. *Thomson* (1827) 5 S. 275; *Dixon* v. *Rutherford* (1863) 2 M. 61.
[40] Some individuals and firms adhere to the older designations but since the Solicitors (Scotland) Act, 1933, " solicitor " has been the correct term.   On the history of the profession see Henderson Begg, *Treatise on Law Agents*, Chap. 1. See also Cooper, " The Future of the Legal Profession," in *Selected Papers*, 153.
[41] See further Lynex, "The Role of the Employed Lawyer in Industry " (1954) 2 J.S.P.T.L.(N.S.) 214.
[42] See Admission as Solicitor (Scotland) Regulations, 1960, printed in *Parliament House Book*, Section D.
[43] See Solicitors (Scotland) Acts, 1933 to 1958, and Solicitors (Scotland) Practising Certificate Rules, 1951, printed in *Parliament House Book*, Section D.
[44] On these bodies see further Mackay, *Practice*, I, 128 *et seq.*

The employment of a solicitor is regulated by the general principles of the law of agency and a formal mandate is seldom necessary.[45] The extent of the solicitor's authority depends on the kind of work he has been instructed to perform.[46] He is entitled to a measure of discretion in the conduct of litigation, subject to the directions of counsel where one has been retained,[47] though he may not abandon a claim without authority from the client,[48] and various extraordinary steps, such as entering into a judicial reference, require express authority. His actings are binding on the client so long as they do not go beyond what is necessary for the accomplishment of the work he was employed to perform, or what is usual in the exercise of the authority conferred.[49]

By accepting employment solicitors undertake to perform the business entrusted to them with due diligence and skill [50] and will be liable in damages for loss sustained by the client in consequence of breach of this duty.[51] There are many decisions on what constitutes professional negligence in various circumstances.[52] A solicitor will not, however, be held liable in damages for giving incorrect advice on a doubtful point of law where there has been no clear rule or practice, since that is properly the function of counsel.[53] Nor will he be held liable if he follows the usual course of practice even if it should be held in the end to be incorrect.[54] Advice on doubtful or difficult matters of law is properly the province of counsel and the proper course in such a case is to submit such points to counsel in a Memorial containing a full and accurate statement of facts and to act upon the opinion obtained. Neglect to obtain counsel's opinion may in some cases be enough to render a solicitor liable in damages for breach of duty and he is protected against such a claim by bona fide reliance on counsel's opinion, at least in matters which do not fall within the exclusive province of the solicitor.[55]

The Crown Agent

The Crown Agent is head of the Crown Office, Edinburgh, solicitor to the Lord Advocate's department and chief permanent official of the

[45] For the cases where one is necessary, see Begg on *Law Agents*, pp. 75–78.
[46] See further Begg, *op. cit.*, Chaps. 8 and 9.
[47] *Buchanan* v. *Davidson & Stevenson* (1877) 14 S.L.R. 233.
[48] *Thoms* v. *Bain* (1888) 15 R. 613.
[49] *Sanderson* v. *Campbell* (1833) 11 S. 623.
[50] *Frame* v. *Campbell* (1839) McL. & Rob. 595; *Bell* v. *Ogilvie* (1863) 2 M. 336; see Bell's *Prin.*, §§ 153–154.
[51] *Evans* v. *Stool* (1885) 12 R. 1295; *Stewart* v. *McLean, Baird & Neilson*, 1915 S.C. 13.
[52] See Begg on *Law Agents*, Chap. 18; cases in *Faculty Digest, s.v.* " Agent and Client," and in *Scots Digest, s.v.* " Agency." See also Eddy, *Professional Negligence*.
[53] *Cooke* v. *Falconer's Reps.* (1850) 13 D. 157; *Blair* v. *Assets Co.* (1896) 23 R.(H.L.) 36.   [54] *Hamilton* v. *Emslie* (1868) 7 M. 173.
[55] Mackay's *Practice of the Court of Session*, I, 138. The practical aspects of conveyancing are possibly the only subject which is peculiarly the solicitor's province.

system of criminal administration. To his office come reports from procurators-fiscal in each sheriffdom and in reply go instructions, requests and general guidance on prosecutions.

Notaries Public

The office of notary public is very ancient and has survived as a distinct office in some legal systems.[56] In Scotland his functions were and are the authentication of various categories of formal deeds, particularly in relation to the title to heritable property, notes of which were formerly made in his protocol book.[57] In mercantile matters the noting and protesting of bills of exchange, the execution of maritime protests, and the swearing of affidavits in bankruptcy, are all notarial business, while deeds executed in Scotland for use abroad have frequently to be executed before and authenticated by a notary public. In modern times, in consequence of legal changes, his services have increasingly been dispensed with and the powers conferred also on enrolled solicitors, while since 1896 admission to the roll of notaries public has been restricted to enrolled solicitors. Admission is by petition to the First Division of the Court of Session.

Professional Fees

An advocate's fees are, as in the Roman law, regarded as honoraria, not as fees, and are presumed to have been paid at the time he is instructed.[58] The proper practice is for the solicitor to send the appropriate fee with each letter instructing a particular step to be taken,[59] but fees are sometimes noted and paid in a lump sum afterwards.[60] It follows that there are no fixed scales of fees for counsel though in practice the fees for various standard types of business are conventionally fixed within limits, depending largely on the value and importance of the cause, on its complexity, and on the time involved.[61] It is always open to a client to pay counsel more than the conventional fee though a successful

---

[56] See *Ars Notariatus; or the Art and Office of a Notary Public as practised in Scotland* (1740–1821); Murray, *Law of Scotland relating to Notaries Public* (1890); Brown, " Origin and Early History of the Office of Notary " (1935) 47 J.R. 201, 355; " The N.P.," 1923 S.L.T.(News) 103; " Mottoes of Notaries Public," 1926 S.L.T. (News) 54; see also *Sources and Literature of Scots Law* (Stair Society), 289–300.
[57] These accordingly frequently contain valuable information about lands, families and legal practice and some have been edited and published by the historical clubs.
[58] *Batchelor* v. *Pattison and Mackersy* (1876) 3 R. 914.
[59] Mackay's *Practice*, I, 115.
[60] See also Faculty Rules as to counsel's fees: 1958 S.L.T.(News) 18.
[61] For examples, see cases in *Faculty Digest, s.v.* " Expenses." It should be observed that, over all, counsel are not highly paid for their work and much of it, particularly of the kind given to young junior counsel, is very poorly remunerated, and there are many instances where counsel gets no fee at all, or only a token fee. See also Lord Macmillan, *A Man of Law's Tale*, pp. 130–140 (an exceptionally successful advocate).

litigant, if awarded expenses against his opponent, will be allowed by the Auditor of Court to recover from his opponent not what he may have paid but what was reasonably necessary in the circumstances to secure the services of competent counsel.[62]

Fees cannot be recovered by action since they are honoraria,[63] unless in the exceptional case where a solicitor has received payment of his professional account from the client and has failed to transmit counsel's fee to him,[64] or in the case of a salary as standing counsel, which may be sued for.[65] An advocate is probably entitled to retain a fee sent to him even though he has not had to render any services.[66] It is illegal to take a proportion of the subject of a litigation in lieu of a fee, or to buy up any debatable rights which are still in dependence,[67] but quite legitimate to act on the basis that there will be no remuneration unless in the event of success.[68]

In the case of the solicitor on the other hand fees are in the same category as the fees of other professional men in that the fact of employment implies an undertaking by the client to pay professional fees at the ordinary rate [69] and they may be recovered by action.[70] Fees in most cases are regulated by the Table of Fees for Conveyancing and General Business of 1952,[71] the Fees for Solicitors in the Supreme Courts of Scotland, 1948,[72] and the Fees of Solicitors and Others in the Sheriff Court [73] which are based generally, in the case of conveyancing and property transactions, on a percentage of the value of the property concerned, and in the case of litigious business, on the complexity and time occupied. The client is always entitled to have the account remitted for taxation to the Auditor of the Court of Session or of the local Sheriff Court before paying it. Solicitors are also, of course, entitled to recover all outlays and expenses properly incurred on account of the client.[74] A solicitor may charge less than is permitted by the Table of Fees and

---

[62] See *Elas* v. *Scottish Motor Traction Co.*, 1950 S.C. 570; *Macnaughton* v. *Macnaughton*, 1949 S.C. 42.

[63] *Batchelor* v. *Pattison and Mackersy* (1876) 3 R. 914.

[64] *Cullen* v. *Buchanan* (1862) 24 D. 1132; *Keay* v. *A.B.* (1837) 15 S. 748n.

[65] *McKenzie* v. *Town of Burntisland* (1728) Mor. 11421.

[66] Mackay, *Manual of Court of Session Practice*, 28.

[67] Act 1594, c. 220.

[68] *X Insurance Co.* v. *A. and B.*, 1936 S.C. 225, 238–239, 250–251.

[69] Bell, *Pr.* § 226; *Manson* v. *Baillie* (1855) 2 Macq. 80; *Goodsir* v. *Carruthers* (1858) 20 D. 1141; *Bell* v. *Ogilvie* (1863) 2 M. 336; *Winton* v. *Airth* (1868) 6 M. 1095.

[70] *Bell* v. *Ogilvie* (1863) 2 M. 336.

[71] Printed, as later revised, in the *Parliament House Book*, Section A, and separately.

[72] A.S. July 1, 1948, and subsequently increased: printed in *Parliament House Book*, Section A.

[73] A.S. May 7, 1935, and subsequently increased: printed in *Parliament House Book*, Section A.

[74] *Carrick* v. *Manford* (1854) 16 D. 410; *Dingwall's Trs.* v. *Earl of Kintore* (1862) 24 D. 427.

he may act gratuitously for a poor client, taking his chance of recovering his fees and outlays from any award of damages and expenses made against the opposite party.

It is doubtful whether the Roman law rule of *pactum de quota litis* (the prohibition on a legal adviser taking as fee a share of the property in dispute) is applicable in Scotland,[75] but the principle seems to be followed, as the practice is highly undesirable.[76] But a non-professional man may advance money to carry on a litigation on the basis of receiving a share of any sum recovered.

Transacting with Clients

A solicitor is not debarred from transacting with a client so long as he is not acting as legal adviser in that same transaction, but he must show that he made full disclosure and gave full value,[77] and it is desirable to have the client separately advised by a completely independent solicitor. A bequest in a will to the solicitor who drew up the will is valid [78] but the onus is on the solicitor to show that the testator was in full possession of his faculties and made the bequest freely and in knowledge of its effect.[79] If a solicitor has been instructed by a client to find a purchaser for property, he may not purchase himself without the client's express authority and without divesting himself of the character of agent for sale.[80] The same applies in a case of agency to purchase. Again the notarial execution of a will by a solicitor on behalf of a client is invalid if the solicitor or a partner of his takes any benefit thereunder or is nominated as executor or trustee.[81]

All these limitations arise from the policy of the law that there must be no conflict of interest between legal adviser and client and there must be no suspicion of the one gaining improper benefit for himself at the other's expense.[82]

Accounts

Solicitors are under strict obligations with regard to the care of clients' money which comes into their hands in the course of their actings on behalf of the clients. Under the Solicitors' (Scotland) Accounts Rules,

---

[75] Contrast Stair I, 10, 8; Bell, *Pr.* § 36; with *Johnston* v. *Rome* (1831) 9 S. 364.
[76] *Farrell* v. *Arnott* (1857) 19 D. 1000; Act, 1594, c. 220.
[77] *McPherson's Trustees* v. *Watt* (1877) 5 R.(H.L.) 9; *Cleland* v. *Morrison* (1878) 6 R. 156; *Gillespie & Sons* v. *Gardner*, 1909 S.C. 1053; *Aitken* v. *Campbell's Trustees*, 1909 S.C. 1217.
[78] *Rooney* v. *Cormack* (1895) 22 R. 761.
[79] *Weir* v. *Grace* (1899) 2 F.(H.L.) 30; *Rigg's Exrx.* v. *Urquhart* (1902) 10 S.L.T. 503; *Stewart* v. *Maclaren*, 1920 S.C.(H.L.) 148.
[80] *Cunningham* v. *Lee* (1874) 2 R. 83.
[81] *Ferrie* v. *Ferrie's Trustees* (1863) 1 M. 291; *Finlay* v. *Finlay's Trustees*, 1948 S.C. 16.
[82] See further cases discussed in Begg on *Law Agents*, Chap. 21.

1952,[83] made by the Law Society of Scotland, money in excess of £50 received from or held on behalf of a client must be paid into a client account, and books and accounts must be kept showing all dealings with the money of each separate client. The Law Society is empowered to institute the investigation of any solicitor's books by an accountant to ensure whether the rules are being complied with.

Regular and accurate books must be kept and business accounts, which should be rendered periodically or, in the case of employment for one transaction, at the conclusion of that transaction, must be fair transcripts of the entries therein,[84] and give all the information necessary to enable the client and the auditor to examine it.[85]

The Law Society has power [86] to withdraw the practising certificate of a solicitor who is failing to comply with the Accounts Rules, and [87] to require every solicitor in practice to deliver periodically to the Society an accountant's certificate for the purpose of ensuring that he is complying with the Accounts Rules, except in certain specified cases.

Provision is made [88] for a guarantee fund from which to compensate persons who suffer pecuniary loss by reason of dishonesty on the part of a solicitor.

Solicitors' Discipline Committee

The Solicitors' Discipline (Scotland) Committee consists of five, six, or seven solicitors recommended by the Law Society as representative of the profession throughout Scotland, and appointed by the Lord President.[89] It investigates complaints of professional misconduct by a solicitor, and may strike a solicitor off the roll of solicitors or suspend him from practice, or fine or censure him. An appeal against the decision of the Discipline Committee lies to the Court of Session. Convictions of solicitors in the criminal courts for fraud or dishonest appropriation of property are reported to the Committee for consideration. Complaints may be lodged by a client, the Council of the Law Society, the Lord Advocate, judges, sheriffs and auditors of court. A solicitor struck off the roll may subsequently petition to be restored and may be restored to the roll on proof of a substantial period of trustworthy conduct subsequent to the offence for which he was struck off. Apart from the

---

83 Printed in *Parliament House Book*, Section D.
84 *Stewart* v. *Scott* (1844) 6 D. 889.
85 *Grant* v. *Alcock* (1870) Guthrie's Sel.Shf.Ct.Cas. 11.
86 Solicitors (Scotland) Act, 1958, s. 3.
87 *Ibid.*, s. 13 (section not yet brought into force).
88 Solicitors (Scotland) Act, 1949, s. 22, and Scottish Solicitors' Guarantee Fund Rules, 1951, printed in *Parliament House Book*, Section D.
89 Solicitors (Scotland) Act, 1933, ss. 24–40, as extended by Solicitors (Scotland) Act, 1949, ss. 20 (3), 25 (3). See also Rules made by the Solicitors' Discipline (Scotland) Committee, printed in the *Parliament House Book*, Section D.

statutory jurisdiction the Court of Session probably still has a common law jurisdiction *ex proprio motu* to censure or suspend a solicitor for misconduct.[90]

Expenses in Litigation

Every civil court has an inherent common-law discretionary right to award expenses in any cause which comes before it, unless that right has been qualified or abrogated by statute.[91] In practice a pursuer usually includes an express conclusion for expenses in his summons, the justification for this being that he has been put to the expense and trouble of litigation by the defender's failure spontaneously to satisfy the pursuer's requests. The award of expenses is in the discretion of the court and accordingly, while an appeal may be taken on the question of expenses, an appellate court will not interfere unless it be shown that the judge making the award had erred in principle.

While the award of expenses is always in the discretion of the court, the court usually exercises its discretion in accordance with principles worked out in previous cases, and a large volume of case-law has developed on the subject.[92] Expenses can be awarded even if not claimed. Counsel moves for an award of expenses when judgment has been given after any hearing.

Accordingly as a rule expenses will be awarded to the successful party against the unsuccessful party, but sometimes expenses are modified or refused, sometimes no expenses are found due to or by either party and, commonly in cases arising out of a will or the disposal of an estate, all parties' expenses are made payable out of the estate. There are many special rules affecting particular categories of litigants and particular kinds of cases.

To say, however, that the court may award the successful party expenses does not mean that he will be reimbursed by the unsuccessful party to the full extent of his expenditure in the litigation. Where expenses are awarded the solicitor for the party awarded expenses must make up his itemised account and submit it to the Auditor of the Court of Session [93] for taxation. The purpose of taxation is to strike out and disallow all items of expenditure considered to have been unnecessary or excessive for the prosecution of the claim. Hence, if a party chooses to employ an unnecessary number of counsel, or pay higher fees than are warranted by ordinary practice, the extra expense will not be allowed against the other party. The auditor will allow only such expenses as are necessary for conducting litigation in a proper manner but with due regard to economy.

---

[90] Maclaren, *Court of Session Practice*, 28–29.
[91] *Rooney* v. *Cormack* (1895) 23 R. 11; *Thomson* v. *Kerr* (1901) 3 F. 355.
[92] See Maclaren on *Expenses*, and cases in the Digests *sub voce* " Expenses."
[93] Or, in the sheriff court, the Auditor of the Sheriff Court.

Parties' solicitors may attend before the auditor and contend that certain items of expenditure were justifiable, and appeal may be taken to the court against the auditor's decision.

In taxing an account, the auditor may proceed on any one of three bases, expenses as between party and party,[94] which allows only such expenses as are absolutely necessary for conducting the litigation in a proper manner with due regard to economy; expenses between solicitor and client chargeable against the opposite side, which is rather more generous; and expenses between solicitor and own client, which is still more generous and allows all expenses reasonably incurred by the solicitor for the protection of his client's interest, even though such expenses could not be recovered from the opposite party, and any extraordinary expenses specially authorised by the client.[95]

Legal Aid

A system of free legal aid for the poor has existed in Scotland since 1424. Latterly the practice was for the Faculty of Advocates annually to appoint a number of advocates as counsel for the poor, while the W.S. and S.S.C. Societies appointed agents for the poor. A committee of reporters on *probabilis causa litigandi* considered applications, which had to be supported by certificates of poverty, and could admit to the benefit of the poor's roll, which conferred the privileges of obtaining the services of counsel and solicitors for the poor gratuitously and the right to litigate without payment of any court dues.[96]

This scheme was superseded in the civil courts by the establishment of the Legal Aid Scheme in 1950,[97] intended to make legal aid more readily available for persons of small or moderate means. The general administration of the scheme is in the hands of the Law Society of Scotland, which acts through a Central Committee as supervisory and accounting body, a Supreme Court Committee of advocates and solicitors which determines whether applicants have a *probabilis causa* for litigation in the Court of Session and what contribution to the expenses they must themselves pay, and a number of Local Committees of solicitors which have similar functions in respect of their

[94] When expenses are awarded without qualification by the court, the taxation is between party and party.
[95] Apart from the question of paying another party's expenses, every client is entitled to have his solicitor's account of judicial expenses taxed by the auditor and need not pay any more than the taxed amount.
[96] See further Maclaren, *Court of Session Practice*, 274 *et seq.*; Dobie, *Sheriff Court Practice*, 491.
[97] Legal Aid and Solicitors (Scotland) Act, 1949, amended by Legal Aid Act, 1960. The Acts, the Legal Aid (Scotland) Scheme, 1958 (replacing the 1950 Scheme), the Legal Advice (Scotland) Scheme, 1959, the Legal Aid (Scotland) (Section 5) Scheme, 1960 and the Legal Aid (Scotland) (House of Lords) Scheme, 1960, made thereunder, are printed in the *Parliament House Book*, Section E, and in the Law Society of Scotland's *Compendium of Legal Aid and Advice* (3rd ed., 1960).

local sheriff courts. The various committees maintain lists of counsel and solicitors who hold themselves as willing to act for assisted persons in various types of cases. No counsel or solicitor need participate in the scheme but nearly all do.

An applicant for assistance must have his " disposable income " and " disposable capital," both of which are defined by regulations, assessed by the National Assistance Board, which fixes a maximum contribution to be required of him. He must also show to the satisfaction of the appropriate committee that he has a *probabilis causa litigandi*. If the committee is satisfied that he has a statable case it fixes the actual contribution required and issues a legal aid certificate, which entitles him to the services of counsel (if authorised) and solicitor as an " assisted person." The litigation proceeds in the normal way but all papers are marked to the effect that the party is an assisted person, and moneys payable to an assisted person under any judgment, settlement or agreement must be paid into the Legal Aid (Scotland) Fund and only the receipt of the Law Society is a good discharge. The Law Society retains any sum due to the fund in respect of the assisted person's liability to the fund and pays him the balance.

Expenses in a legal aid case are awarded and taxed according to the ordinary rules and as between solicitor and client. The solicitor recovers his fees from the Legal Aid Fund and must pay counsel, counsel's clerk and other outlays. Counsel and solicitors receive as fees 90 per cent. of the amount of fees allowed by the Auditor on taxation. An unsuccessful legally aided litigant is responsible for any award of expenses made against him, though the court in making such an award must have regard to his means, and even if successful, the balance of the expenses of the proceedings, so far as not covered by any contribution made by him or by any award of expenses from his opponent, will be deducted from the money payable to him. The scheme is accordingly one for the assistance of litigants and is not intended to be " free."

In criminal matters the Legal Aid Scheme does not yet apply.[97a] It was enacted in 1587 that those accused of crime should be represented by counsel and solicitors. In each sheriff court a number of young solicitors are appointed to the Poor's Roll and are responsible for advising and defending those who cannot afford to instruct a solicitor in the normal way. The Faculty of Advocates continues to appoint, at each anniversary meeting, six young advocates to act as counsel for the poor, who give their services without remuneration. It is the tradition of the Faculty that all advocates of less than three years' standing put down their names for circuits, volunteering to go to the circuit towns if required to defend

---

[97a] Provision for its extension to criminal cases is made by the Criminal Justice (Scotland) Act, 1963.

poor persons, and the solicitors for the poor in the circuit towns get in touch with juniors attending the circuit as required. Until recently counsel for the poor undertook these duties entirely at their own expense, or for a purely nominal fee, but in recent years the Exchequer has paid the railway fare to the trial town and the overnight hotel expenses at a prescribed rate, but no fee for the work done.

In the case of murder trials, the solicitor approaches junior counsel, whose duty it is to approach the senior Bar and to ascertain from a roster which Q.C.s are next for duty in work of this kind. Only if the Q.C. approached is actually involved in a case extending into the period in which the murder trial would be held is he excused. If the junior cannot find a Q.C. who is available, the Dean of Faculty will assign a senior counsel to the case and may even take it himself. It is an obligation of honour on the Faculty that senior and junior counsel will be found to defend a person thus accused.

It is now possible to obtain legal advice in matters not involving litigation from solicitors participating in the Legal Advice Scheme.[98]

The Legal Aid Scheme has not been applied yet to tribunals, and only recently to the provision of legal advice and to House of Lords appeals, and in some cases poor persons must still rely on legal clinics and dispensaries and citizens' advice bureaux or on the voluntary kindness of some lawyer.

Professional Ethics and Etiquette

Both branches of the legal profession have a profound *esprit de corps* and regard for the ethics of the profession, and also a distinct code of professional etiquette. Most of these rules are rules dictated by prudence and the desire that justice should, so far as humanly possible, both be done and be manifestly seen to be done. Some matters of professional etiquette, relating to the relations between the two branches of the profession, have already been touched on. No comprehensive code of professional ethics exists and much of it is simply absorbed by experience [99]; nevertheless the administration of justice depends in large part on the integrity and honour of the profession.

---

[98] Legal Advice (Scotland) Scheme, 1959.

[99] The American Bar Association has adopted a code of Canons of Professional Ethics for the guidance of its members and in some states an oath must be taken on admission to the Bar to observe the highest moral principles in the practice of the profession. The " Canons of Professional Ethics " are printed in Moreland, *Equal Justice Under Law*. The Annual Statements of the [English] Bar Council, summarised in *Current Law Year Books*, contain many rulings on points of ethics and etiquette. See also Lord Macmillan, " The Ethics of Advocacy," in *Law and Other Things*, p. 36; Stone, *Law and its Administration*, 162–165; Rogers, " Ethics of Advocacy " (1899) 15 L.Q.R. 259; Boulton, *Conduct and Etiquette at the [English] Bar*, 1961.

It is difficult to generalise but the overriding consideration, applicable equally to both branches of the profession, is that an advocate or solicitor, if consulted or instructed, must invariably apply his whole mind and devote his fullest energies to the business entrusted to him, and seek to use his ability, ingenuity and knowledge towards achieving by honest means a fair and just conclusion of the issue without regard to his personal advantage or belief. He must retain his own professional integrity and opinions and not subordinate them to the client's opinions or interests, and if a client should insist on doing what the legal adviser believes is imprudent or wrong or unjust or illegal he must be free to withdraw from the employment; he is not bound to aid in some foolish or wrongful escapade, still less to advise or abet some unjust or illegal enterprise. "An advocate in undertaking the conduct of a cause in this court enters into no contract with his client, but takes on himself an office in the performance of which he owes a duty, not to his client only, but also to the court, to the members of his own profession, and to the public. . . . The position of an agent is somewhat different. There is a contract of employment between him and his client, by virtue of which the client, for certain settled rates of remuneration, is entitled to require from the agent the exercise of care and diligence, and professional skill and experience. . . . The agent, of course, cannot be asked to follow the client's instructions beyond what is lawful and proper. For the agent, as well as the counsel, owes a duty to the court. . . . He is also bound by that unwritten law of his profession which embodies the honourable understanding of the individual members as to their bearing and conduct towards each other." [1]

Duties to the Court

A lawyer owes to any court of law or tribunal a duty to treat it with proper respect and to make any criticisms in a moderate and respectful manner. Disrespectful or insulting conduct in face of a court is punishable as contempt of court. Any attempt to exert personal influence on the court, or even to discuss privately with a judge any pending matter is very improper.

The lawyer, moreover, is present in court not merely to present his client's case but to assist the court, by argument and criticism of opposing contentions, to arrive at a just and legally correct decision. Hence his conduct must be characterised by candour and fairness. It is professionally disgraceful to resort to or be a party to any fraud, deception or trickery,[2] such as fabricating documents or deliberately withholding evidence, or

---

[1] *Batchelor* v. *Pattison and Mackersy* (1876) 3 R. 914, 918, *per* Lord President Inglis.
[2] *Cf.* Annual Statement of the [English] Bar Council, 1953, p. 16, quoted in [1954] C.L.Y. 2514.

knowingly to misquote the substance of a document, a witness's testimony, an opposing argument, or a decision or textbook. An advocate is bound to bring to the notice of the court authorities known to bear on the subject of a debate, whether or not they are in his client's favour.[3] He must not cite a decision known to have been overruled or a statute repealed or amended, nor assert as fact what has not been proved. Nor should pleading or argument include any scandalous or irrelevant matter [4] or matter merely prejudicial or statements designed to sway a jury emotionally or on grounds other than legal.

Both the court and the other parties must be able to rely on the honesty and to trust the word of legal advisers. Moreover in some cases issues are decided on the *ex parte* statements of one party,[5] so that it is important that only such statements be made as are true to the best of the adviser's belief and knowledge. It is quite improper to assert in argument a personal belief in the innocence of the client or the justice of his cause.

It is part of the duty to the court to treat opposing parties and witnesses with fairness and consideration, and not to indulge in abuse, to suggest improprieties, or to make any personal attack, even at the instance of the client, except in so far as any such conduct may be necessitated by the circumstances of the case. Thus sometimes one has to put to the other side's witnesses the suggestion that they are lying.

When initiating proceedings in court counsel and solicitors owe a duty to the court and also to the other party involved to consider seriously whether there is any prospect of success. It is professional misconduct, at least on a solicitor's part, to raise and maintain an action without belief that it has any reasonable prospect of success,[6] but counsel and agents need not go so far as to be fully convinced of the rightness or substantial justice of the client's case.[7] So, too, in presenting appeals to the High Court from conviction by a jury it has been observed that where counsel considers there are no statable grounds of appeal, he acts properly in performance of his duty to the court as well as to his client, in refusing to act further in the case.[8]

Counsel or procurator-fiscal engaged in conducting a criminal prosecution has the primary duty not of securing a conviction but of assisting the court and trying to secure that justice is done. Hence he must not

[3] *Glebe Sugar Refining Co.* v. *Greenock Harbour Trustees,* 1921 S.C.(H.L.) 72.
[4] See *Wardrope* v. *Hamilton* (1876) 3 R. 876; *A.* v. *B.* (1895) 22 R. 402; *H.* v. *P.* (1905) 8 F. 232; *M.* v. *S.,* 1909, 1 S.L.T. 192; *A.* v. *C.,* 1922 S.L.T. 34.
[5] *e.g.,* the granting of *interim* interdict.
[6] *X Insurance Co.* v. *A. and B.,* 1936 S.C. 225.
[7] So too a litigant is not liable in damages to his opponent for judicial proceedings which are unsuccessful or unfounded so long as there is no malice or fraud: *Ormiston* v. *Redpath* (1866) 4 M. 488; *Davies* v. *Brown* (1867) 5 M. 842; *Kinnes* v. *Adam* (1882) 9 R. 698.
[8] *Scott, J.N.* v. *H.M. Advocate,* 1946 J.C. 68.

press the prosecution case unduly and may properly afford the defence reasonable facilities to prepare their defence.[9] " The Crown counsel is a representative of the State, ' a minister of justice '; his function is to assist the jury in arriving at the truth. He must not urge any argument that does not carry weight in his own mind, or try to shut out any legal evidence that would be important to the interests of the person accused. ' It is not his duty to obtain a conviction by all means; but simply to lay before the jury the whole of the facts which compose his case, and to make these perfectly intelligible, and to see that the jury are instructed with regard to the law and are able to apply the law to the facts.' [10] ' It cannot be too often made plain that the business of counsel for the Crown is fairly and impartially to exhibit all the facts to the jury. The Crown has no interest in procuring a conviction. Its only interest is that the right person should be convicted, that the truth should be known, and that justice should be done.' [11] " [12]

When defending on a criminal charge a lawyer is entitled to act independently of his personal opinion as to the guilt of the accused and he is entitled and even bound to present every legal defence which he can reasonably rely on, so that no person shall be convicted save after due process of law and after guilt has been satisfactorily proved by competent evidence, to a competent tribunal. As regards confessions of guilt, if the confession is made before proceedings have commenced, no harm can be done by requesting the accused to retain another advocate. But if the confession is made during proceedings, the advocate should continue and must continue the defence by all legitimate means, though he may not set up an affirmative case inconsistent with the confession as by suggesting that another person committed the crime.[13]

Duties to the Profession

A lawyer owes it to his profession, to the abstract idea of Law and all that it stands for, and to the ideal of Justice, that he does nothing in his professional practice of which a moral, skilful, diligent and upright man need be ashamed. Advertisement, direct or indirect, is forbidden, though this does not extend to the insertion of names and addresses in the recognised Law Lists, nor giving name and qualifications as the author of legal books and articles, but it does cover articles in the press or broadcasts in which the person is named or given his professional designation.[14]

---

[9] *Cf. Smith* v. *H.M. Advocate*, 1952 J.C. 66.
[10] Sir J. Holker, Att.-Gen. (*The Times*, Feb. 25, 1880).
[11] Lord Hewart C.J., 25 Cr.App.R. at p. 115.
[12] Kenny, *Outlines of Criminal Law*, 16th ed., 504–505.
[13] Annual Statement of the [English] Bar Council, 1915, p. 14, approved by the then Attorney-General.
[14] Annual Statement of the [English] Bar Council, 1954, p. 21.

It is a duty to the profession to take a share in assisting individuals in need of legal assistance even though they may be unable to pay, or may require Legal Aid,[15] and to accept instructions in a cause from the first person who tenders instructions to him with the customary fee, even though he might prefer to act on the other side or not to be involved in that case at all. The duty to defend on a criminal charge takes priority over a competing engagement in a civil case.[16]

Other members of the profession must be treated as gentlemen of honour and not abused, ridiculed or condemned, and undertakings, promises and assurances given one to another must be fulfilled. Thus if counsel's fees are paid by the client to the solicitor it is a debt of honour to remit them to counsel. Again any ill feeling between parties should not be allowed to affect or influence their advisers in their conduct towards one another or the parties.

Duties to the Client

The lawyer's first duty to his client is to perform with requisite skill and due diligence the business entrusted to him [17] and the solicitor, though not the advocate, will be liable to the client in damages for breach of duty, negligence, or gross ignorance or want of professional skill.[18] Beyond the general duty to perform business with due diligence it is difficult to state duties in detail.

It is not, however, a lawyer's duty to do whatever may enable him to win his client's case, but only to utilise any remedy, claim or defence which is permitted by law and which may be used honourably and honestly, and he is entitled, and indeed bound, to prevent his client from taking any action which he himself ought not to do, such as fabricating or suppressing evidence or suborning witnesses. If a client does anything disgraceful or improper the lawyer should terminate his employment.[19]

The fiduciary character of the relationship between solicitor and client necessarily imposes restrictions on their transacting one with another in view of the possible conflict of interests. Contracts between them are liable to reduction, as contrary to public policy, and in any such transaction the client should be advised by another and independent solicitor.[20] Even gifts [21] or bequests [22] to the solicitor are scrutinised closely and

---

[15] On Legal Aid, see p. 233, *supra*.
[16] *Cf.* Denning, *The Road to Justice*, 53
[17] *Bell* v. *Ogilvie* (1863) 2 M. 336. For details, see Begg on *Law Agents*, Chaps. 18 and 24.
[18] *Landell* v. *Purves* (1845) 4 Bell 46; 12 Cl. & F. 91.
[19] Bankton, IV, 3, 13.
[20] *McPherson's Trustees* v. *Watt* (1877) 5 R.(H.L.) 9.
[21] *Long* v. *Taylor* (1824) 2 Sh.App. 233
[22] *Grieve* v. *Cunningham* (1869) 8 M. 317.

suspiciously while he may not make any secret profit at the client's expense in dealing with third parties.[23] So too if a solicitor acts as a trustee he may not, unless expressly authorised by the trust deed or all the beneficiaries,[24] take any remuneration for his services. Nor may a lawyer divulge secrets or confidences obtained during employment or act subsequently for others utilising knowledge gained in a previous professional connection.

Again it is quite improper to accept instructions from a client if there is any conflict of interest between that client and another client. Accordingly one advocate or solicitor should not act for two persons whose interests do, or even may, conflict.[25] Thus it is bad practice for one solicitor to act for both buyer and seller of property; he can properly protect the interests of one or other only. He cannot act for both in settling the price.[26] If he acts for both lender and borrower (which is undesirable) he is responsible to both parties for any failure in duty [27] and may be liable for recommending a security which turns out inadequate, quite apart from any failure in the legal validity of the security.[28]

Privilege

Neither advocate nor solicitor can be obliged to disclose information obtained by him in his professional capacity unless the client consents,[29] and it is a breach of professional confidence to do so voluntarily. Memorials to and the opinions of counsel are protected.[30] But anything which is part of the events in a crime or fraud is not protected.[31] The privilege certainly covers communications having reference to a contemplated action or an action in progress and probably also all communications made in a professional capacity, whether or not any dispute has yet arisen.[32]

Advocates and solicitors are absolutely privileged in their written and oral pleading in court, in commenting on the evidence and the conduct

---

23 *Tyrrell* v. *Bank of London* (1862) 10 H.L.C. 26.
24 *Lewis's Trustees* v. *Pirie*, 1912 S.C. 574. This even extends to the solicitor-trustee's partner: *Mitchell* v. *Burness* (1878) 5 R. 1124.
25 *Oastler* v. *Dill, Smillie & Wilson* (1886) 14 R. 12; *McClure, Naismith, Brodie & McFarlane* v. *Stewart* (1887) 15 R.(H.L.) 1; *Ellis's Trustees* v. *Ellis* (1898) 1 F. 4, (two parties to a special case); *Stewart* v. *McLean, Baird & Neilson*, 1915 S.C. 13; *Dunlop's Trustees* v. *Farquharson*, 1955 S.L.T.(Notes), 80.
26 *McPherson's Trustees* v. *Watt* (1877) 5 R.(H.L.) 9.
27 *McLeod* v. *McDonald* (1835) 13 S. 287; *Haldane* v. *Donaldson* (1840) 1 Rob.App. 226; *Oastler, supra.*
28 *Cleland* v. *Brownlie, Watson & Beckett* (1892) 20 R. 152; *Wernham* v. *McLean, Baird & Neilson*, 1925 S.C. 407.
29 *Forteith* v. *Earl of Fyfe* (1821) 2 Mur. 467; *Noble* v. *Scott* (1843) 5 D. 723; *Hay* v. *Edinburgh & Glasgow Bank* (1858) 20 D. 701.
30 Bell, *Prin.* § 2254; *Thomson's Trustees* v. *Clark* (1823) 2 S. 262; *Clark* v. *Spence* (1824) 3 Mur. 454.
31 *McCowan* v. *Wright* (1852) 15 D. 229, 494.
32 *Ibid.*; *Munro* v. *Fraser* (1858) 21 D. 103

of parties and in all other matters relevant to the cause,[33] while litigants have qualified privilege only and will accordingly be liable to an action for defamation if personal malice can be proved.[34] But counsel and solicitors are liable to censure for improper or insulting conduct in court and the Court of Session may punish by censure, suspension or even deprivation of the office of advocate.[35] Counsel and agent are also privileged in respect of matters alleged or put in pleadings with the authority and on the instructions of the client so long as pertinent to the matter in issue.[36]

FURTHER READING

Boulton: *Conduct and Etiquette at The Bar*, 3rd ed.
Drinker: *Legal Ethics.*
Forsyth: *Hortensius: Historical Essay on the Duties of An Advocate.*
Halsbury's *Laws of England*, tit. " Barrister."
Hannay: *The College of Justice.*
Henderson Begg: *Treatise on Law Agents*, 2nd ed.
Hilbery: *Duty and Art in Advocacy.*
Keeton and Lloyd: *The British Commonwealth*, Vol. I, 1—England.
Law Society of Scotland: *Compendium of Legal Aid and Advice*, 3rd ed.
Mackay: *Practice of the Court of Session*, Vol. I.
Muirhead: " From Attorneys to Solicitors," 68 S.L.R. 25.
Singleton: *Conduct at The Bar and some problems of Advocacy.*
Smith: *Short Commentary on the Law of Scotland.*
W.S. Society: *History of the Society of Writers to H.M. Signet*, 1936.

---

[33] *Drew* v. *Mackenzie* (1862) 24 D. 649, 662; *Williamson* v. *Umphray and Robertson* (1890) 17 R. 905.
[34] *Williamson, supra.*
[35] A.S., Dec. 21, 1649; July 26, 1699; June 23, 1756.
[36] *Ramsay* v. *Nairne* (1833) 11 S. 1033. *Cf. Bayne* v. *Macgregor* (1862) 24 D. 1126; (1863) 1 M. 615.

w.—16

CHAPTER 7

THE ELEMENTS OF LEGAL CONTROVERSY

A LEGAL controversy arises whenever two or more parties are at issue on any matter of fact or of law which affects their legal rights and duties. Such controversies may sometimes be resolved by compromise or agreement or by accepting the view of counsel or other third party. But in the last resort legal controversies can be resolved only by application to the appropriate court or tribunal for a ruling. Such applications are regulated by the several bodies of law of procedure, civil, criminal and administrative, and the principles of pleading and the principles of the law of evidence are accessory thereto. These subjects are too complicated to discuss here in detail. The following pages merely indicate in very broad outline the course of procedure followed in the commoner kinds of cases to obtain an authoritative ruling on matters in controversy and the main ways in which effect may be given to such rulings. An understanding of procedure is also important in that to understand the law stated in reported decisions it is necessary to understand how the issue had been raised before the court and what stage it had reached.

In civil or administrative proceedings, where the individual has a grievance or claim, he must initiate and press the claim himself, because the failure to satisfy his grievance or claim is a harm to him alone, but in the case of conduct stigmatised as criminal, it is prejudicial to the general welfare of the community and the claim to have the wrongdoer punished will be taken up and pressed by a public officer on behalf of the community. In a few cases a question of choice may arise, but normally the questions of who is to initiate the claim, and by what procedure, civil, criminal or administrative, will depend on the nature of the claim involved and its legal classification.

I.—CIVIL PROCEEDINGS

Before proceedings are initiated many preliminary problems have to be decided. Such problems include that of jurisdiction, *i.e.*, which court or tribunal is appropriate and can issue a valid decree against the defender or otherwise deal with the case; that of choice of law, *i.e.*, whether Scots or some other system of law falls to determine the rights and duties of parties; that of competency, whether that court can take account of the claim, or by way of the kind of proceedings contemplated; and that of choice of remedy.

242

Civil proceedings are undertaken to obtain a civil remedy. Civil remedies may be classified according to their purposes into:

(i) declaratory judgments, whereby the court declares that particular rights do or do not exist, without making any order as to consequential action, as where it declares that a pretended marriage was null;

(ii) prevention, whereby the court can stop a threatened legal wrong, or the continuance of the perpetration of a legal wrong or some illegality, before any, or any further, harm is done to the pursuer, as where it issues an order of interdict against a nuisance;

(iii) enforced performance, whereby the court gives redress by compelling the doing of what should have been done voluntarily by the defender in performance of his legal duty, as by ordering payment, delivery or other action;

(iv) damages, or substitutional redress in the shape of pecuniary compensation for loss caused or injury or harm done by the failure to implement some legal duty owed to the pursuer by the defender, as where the court awards damages in compensation for loss caused by breach of contract or by personal injuries resulting from the defender's fault;

(v) consistorial remedies, as where it judicially separates two spouses or decrees dissolution of a marriage on the ground of the commission of a matrimonial offence; and

(vi) administrative remedies, as where the court appoints a judicial factor, or new trustees, or sequestrates an estate.

COURT OF SESSION PROCEEDINGS

Court of Session proceedings are usually initiated in the Outer House by *summons*, occasionally by petition and more rarely by other forms of application to the court. A summons [1] is a writ running in the name of the Queen and passing the Royal Signet, prepared by the pursuer's legal advisers, setting out the demand of one party, the *pursuer*, against another, the *defender*, and summoning the defender to appear in court to answer the pursuer's demand, with the warning that the pursuer may proceed to take decree in absence against the defender if he does not appear to defend.

After the formal introduction stating the parties and summoning the defender to appear, the summons contains *conclusions*, or brief statements of the remedies claimed,[2] a *condescendence*, or statement

---

[1] For form see *Rules of Court*, 1948, Appx. form 1.
[2] See *R.C.* Appx. form 2, for specimens.

in numbered paragraphs of the facts on which the pursuer relies for his claim (but not of the evidence thereof nor of arguments on the relevant law), and *pleas-in-law*, which are brief propositions of law, stating the legal principles on which the pursuer rests his case.[3]

The summons is signeted at the court offices, and *citation* of the defender is effected by serving a copy of the summons on him by post or personally. The summons is then *called* by being published in the Rolls of Court and at the same time various papers known collectively as *the process* are lodged for the use of the court.

If the defender ignores the summons, the pursuer may take *decree in absence* against him. If he wishes to defend, he must *enter appearance* and lodge *defences*, which must answer, statement by statement, every material allegation in the pursuer's condescendence, and which are completed by *pleas-in-law for the defender*. The defences may be defences on the facts, in the form of statements contradictory of the pursuer's narrative in his condescendence, or defences in point of law, in the form of pleas-in-law challenging the legal basis of the pursuer's claim, or the defences may be both as to fact and law. A defender may also lodge a counterclaim with his defences.

An *open record*[4] is now made up, a duplicated pamphlet reproducing the summons, conclusions, paragraphs of the pursuer's condescendence followed each by the corresponding paragraph of the defences, the pleas-in-law for the pursuer and the pleas for the defender. Counsel now *adjust the record*[4] by each making alterations in their written pleadings to meet points made by the other, so as to narrow down the matters in dispute and focus clearly the matters of disagreement. New statements may be added to condescendence and defences, or existing statements altered, and pleas-in-law added or deleted. The pursuer may, for example, add a plea challenging the legal basis of the defences. The careful framing of written pleadings is an essential preliminary to proof or trial and proof will be limited to issues raised in the pleadings and of which the defender has thereby been given fair notice, so as to enable him to prepare his defence.

When counsel have completed their adjustments, or earlier if delay is taking place, the Lord Ordinary will pronounce an interlocutor[5] *closing the record*[4] and appointing further procedure. This completes the written pleadings. A *closed record*[4] is then made up, embodying all

---

[3] For specimens of summons, see *Encyclopaedia of Scottish Legal Styles, sub voce* " Action."

[4] In this sense pronounced " recórd." After the record has been closed alterations to the pleadings may be made only by Minute of Amendment.

[5] An interlocutor is an order made by a judge giving effect to his ruling on any matter, and disposing of the whole or any part of a case.

the adjustments made on the open record, and copies are duplicated.[6] The next step depends on whether the parties are at issue as to law, or fact, or both. If parties are at issue on a question of fact only, the court will order a *proof* (*i.e.*, trial by judge alone) or *jury trial*,[7] so that the facts can be determined. If parties are at issue on law, or on both fact and law, the court will order legal debate on Procedure Roll or Debate Roll, depending on what pleas-in-law raising legal points have been tabled in the pleadings.

This legal debate proceeds by way of legal argument only, and the party challenging the legal sufficiency or basis of the other's case must, for the purposes of argument, accept as true his opponent's narrative of the facts. His contention is that, even if the facts can be proved to be as the other party has alleged, the other is not entitled in law to succeed. The debate may discuss whether the pursuer has a *title to sue* for the remedy sought, the legal *competency* of the remedy sought, the *jurisdiction* of the court to grant the remedy in the circumstances, the *specification* or adequacy of the averments or allegations of either party, or the *relevancy* or sufficiency in law of the averments of one party or the other to justify his claim or establish his defence, on the assumption that the facts stated by him are true.[8] After the debate the judge will rule on the points of law raised and, if the parties were at issue on law alone, grant the pursuer decree (if he holds that the defences, even if proved, would not be adequate in law), or dismiss the action, as being incompetent, or because the court has no jurisdiction to deal with the claim, or the pursuer no title to sue for it, or because it has been inadequately stated, or because it is irrelevant, *i.e.*, insufficient in law, even if the facts were proved to be as stated. But if the parties were at issue on both law and fact, he will rule as to the law and order either a *proof* or *jury trial* to enable the pursuer to try to prove the facts he has averred, on the basis of which the judge has ruled as to the law, or he may order a *proof before answer*, if he cannot rule on the law without knowing the facts more fully and wishes to reserve all points of law, which will thus still be open for argument after the facts have been elucidated.[9]

---

[6] Portions of pleadings from the closed record are frequently reprinted in reported cases.

[7] Jury trial is competent only on defined and limited grounds. The institution is much criticised.

[8] See *Jamieson* v. *Jamieson*, 1952 S.C.(H.L.) 44, 50, 63; Walker, " The Theory of Relevancy " (1951) 63 J.R. 1; and on the theory of pleading Michael and Adler, " The Trial of an Issue of Fact " (1934) 34 Col.L.R. 1224. A famous example of a debate on relevancy is *Donoghue* v. *Stevenson*, 1932 S.C.(H.L.) 31, where it was held that, if the pursuer's averments were proved true, she was entitled to the remedy claimed. In fact the case was compromised, so that the pursuer never required to prove by evidence that her narrative was in fact true, and it remains unknown whether the narrative could have been proved or not.

[9] See *Forbes* v. *Forbes's Trs.*, 1957 S.C. 325.

Proof

When the case is called in court on the date fixed for the diet of proof, counsel for both parties appear, and counsel for the pursuer proceeds at once to call his witnesses. Each is in turn sworn by the judge, examined by counsel, cross-examined by defender's counsel, and, if thought necessary, re-examined by pursuer's counsel. After all the witnesses for the pursuer have been heard the defender's witnesses are in turn sworn, examined by the defender's counsel, cross-examined, and re-examined. The rules of evidence determine what must be proved, and by what means, and incidental argument may arise as to the admissibility or pertinency of some of the evidence. Leading questions, *i.e.*, questions so framed as to indicate the answer desired, are allowed only in cross-examination. The evidence is recorded by a shorthand writer and the judge makes notes for his own use. At the conclusion of the evidence, or at an adjourned *hearing on evidence*, counsel make their submissions to the judge on the effect of the evidence and what inferences should be drawn from it. The judge may give judgment at once or make *avizandum*,[10] in which case the cause is called again a few days later for judgment, when junior counsel attend, the judge reads his judgment and, on the motion of counsel, awards or reserves expenses. While the judge's opinion contains his reasons, the operative part of his judgment is the *interlocutor*, which sustains and gives effect to one or more of the pleas in law for one party and repels contrary pleas, or the *decree* which he pronounces, determining the cause, granting the pursuer the remedy sought, dismissing the action, or assoilzieing[11] the defender. Procedure where proof before answer has been allowed is the same, save that legal issues are kept open for argument when counsel is heard on the evidence.

Jury Trial

Jury trial is normally done with Issues. An *Issue* is a problem of fact precisely formulated in writing by the pursuer as a question or questions for the jury to answer; there may also be a *Counter-Issue* for the defender.[12] The jury numbers twelve and both sexes are usually represented. The members are drawn by lot from a larger number cited for the purpose.

The jury are sworn and junior counsel for the pursuer makes an

---

[10] *i.e.*, take the case for private consideration; the word is derived from medieval Latin *avizare*, to consider.

[11] The " z " is not pronounced. The word means " absolving " and the decree is called " absolvitor."

[12] For specimens, see *Hayden* v. *Glasgow Corpn.*, 1948 S.C. 143; *McLean* v. *The Admiralty*, 1960 S.C. 199.

opening speech to the jury outlining the case.[13] Evidence for the pursuer is then led as in a proof. At the conclusion of the pursuer's case counsel for the defence may submit that there is no case to answer and that the case should be withdrawn from the jury.[14] Unless this is acceded to, the defence case is opened by junior counsel and evidence for the defence led in the same way. As at a proof, the evidence is recorded in shorthand and the judge makes his own notes.

After the conclusion of the evidence senior counsel for the pursuer and for the defender successively address the jury, each trying to commend his client's case to the jury. Each counsel must, after addressing the jury, make any special requests or submissions in law to the judge, such as requests for a particular direction to the jury in point of law.

The judge then charges the jury; he instructs them that they are sole masters of the facts and judges of the credibility of witnesses, of the cogency, value and weight to be attached to their evidence, and of the inferences which may be drawn from conduct, circumstantial evidence or the absence of evidence or explanations. He will explain to them as simply as possible the points of law which are involved [15]; he will indicate the main points in the evidence, to assist the jury to have the evidence clearly before their minds; he must point out the necessity for corroborative testimony. Lastly he will indicate what elements have to be taken into account if the jury come to consider damages, and what principles should be followed in their assessment, and he will refer to the Issue, and Counter-Issue, if there is one, indicating the possible answers according to the possible views of the evidence.

If counsel for either party objects to any part of the charge or wishes any further or other direction to be given to the jury, he must say so at the end of the charge. The jury is directed to withdraw and counsel addresses the judge, indicating the direction desired, and if the judge refuses to give it, counsel must there and then tender a *Note of Exceptions*, formulating the exception taken by him or the direction desired and this note, recording the judge's determination thereon is certified by him.[16] The judge may accept counsel's proposition and give further or other directions to the jury in the sense requested.

At the conclusion of the charge the jury may at once give its verdict but usually retires to the jury room to deliberate before doing so. They may return to court to request further directions from the judge on any

---

13 On this speech see *Robertson* v. *Federation of Iceland Co-operative Societies*, 1948 S.C. 565; *Lawrie* v. *Glasgow Corpn.*, 1952 S.C. 361.
14 *McDonald* v. *Duncan*, 1933 S.C. 737; *Grant* v. *W. Alexander & Sons*, 1937 S.L.T. 572.
15 The jury must accept his view of the law: *Gelot* v. *Stewart* (1871) 9 M. 957.
16 For an example, see *Power* v. *Central S. M. T. Co.*, 1949 S.C. 376; see also *Robertson* v. *Federation of Iceland Co-operative Societies*, 1948 S.C. 565; *Bain* v. *Fife Coal Co.*, 1935 S.C. 681.

point, or to request that some portion of evidence be read over to them from the notes.

The verdict may be given unanimously or by a majority at any time, but if after three hours the jury has been unable to agree upon some verdict, the judge may order them to be discharged and order the case to be tried afresh with another jury. The verdict is normally a General Verdict, *i.e.*, such answers to the Issue, and Counter-Issue, if any, as amount to a general finding for or against the pursuer, but do not answer specific points as to grounds of liability or otherwise. A Special Verdict, *i.e.*, a series of answers to specific questions formulated by the trial judge, is competent but rare. The verdict is recorded and the jury discharged. Subsequently the party favoured by the verdict moves the court to apply the verdict, *i.e.*, convert it into a decree, and to deal with expenses.

Petitions

Petition is the proper mode of approaching the court and seeking its authority for some action, or some administrative remedy, or some appointment which only the court can make. Petitions are frequently non-contentious and uncontested. Thus a petition is appropriate for the appointment of a judicial factor, for the appointment of new trustees, to obtain power for trustees to sell heritage, to wind up a company or effect an arrangement between a company and its creditors and in various other cases.

Some petitions are presented to the Outer House, some to the Inner House. The authority of the court is necessary before the petition is served or advertised or otherwise intimated. If no answers are lodged by the respondents called, the petition appears on the rolls, counsel appears before the court and may have his petition granted at once. In some cases the court remits to a member of the Bar or to a solicitor of experience [17] to inquire into the facts alleged and report before it disposes of the petition. In other cases a proof is ordered, which proceeds in the same way as the proof in an action.

If the petition should be opposed, *Answers* are lodged and the court may hear parties, have a proof, or remit to a reporter and hear parties on his report before disposing of the application. A party affected by the petition but not desiring to oppose it may lodge a Minute and crave to be heard on some point.

Appeal to the Inner House—Reclaiming Motion

The decision of a judge pronounced in the Outer House may be appealed by way of *reclaiming motion*, which brings under the review of

---

[17] See, *e.g.*, *Scotstown Moor Children's Camp*, 1948 S.C. 630; *City Property Investment Trust Corpn., Ltd.*, 1951 S.C. 570.

the Inner House the whole or any part of the cause as decided down to that point. Only exceptionally need the leave of the Outer House judge be obtained. Copies of the pleadings and documents used in the Outer House are lodged for the court, and, where appropriate, prints of evidence extended from the shorthand-writer's notes, and of the Lord Ordinary's opinion. In due course the case appears in the rolls assigned to either the First or the Second Division and is argued. Evidence which has been heard in the Outer House is not reheard but the judges and counsel have duplicated copies of the shorthand-writer's transcript of the evidence and this, or the relevant parts of it, is read to the court. Junior counsel for the reclaimer opens the case and is replied to by junior counsel for the respondent. Thereafter senior counsel for the reclaimer and for the respondent respectively address the court. The reclaiming motion may equally be from the decision of an Outer House judge on a point debated in Procedure or Debate Roll, in which case there is purely legal argument on the pleadings, there being no evidence. In this case the Lord Ordinary's opinion is read and criticised by the reclaimer and supported by the respondent.

The Division before which the case is heard has power, if equally divided or in doubt as to a matter of complexity and difficulty, to consult the judges of the other Division,[18] or to order a rehearing before five [19] or seven judges,[20] or even before the whole court.[21]

At the end of the hearing judgment may be given at once. One of the judges delivers extempore a leading opinion and the others concur or add short opinions. In more difficult cases the court will make avizandum, *i.e.,* reserve the case for consideration, in which event the case will be called on a later date for " Advising," when judgment will be given, each judge reading the opinion he has prepared. Any judge may dissent in whole or in part from his brethren. The decision of the court will subsequently be translated into an interlocutor, which will be signed by the presiding judge. At advising, expenses fall to be dealt with on counsel's motion. The decision normally takes the form of adhering to the Lord Ordinary's interlocutor, *i.e.,* refusing the appeal, or of recalling his interlocutor and pronouncing a fresh one in different terms, *i.e.,* allowing the appeal in whole or in part.

The case may now be at an end, or there may be a further appeal to the House of Lords, or it may be remitted to the Outer House for further procedure.[22]

---

[18] *e.g., Connell* v. *Connell,* 1950 S.C. 505.
[19] *e.g., Houston* v. *Buchanan,* 1937 S.C. 460.
[20] *e.g., Yuill's Trustees* v. *Thomson* (1902) 4 F. 815; *Brodie* v. *Ker,* 1952 S.C. 216.
[21] *e.g., Lang* v. *Bruce* (1832) 10 S. 777; see also *Baird* v. *Stevenson,* 1907 S.C. 1259.
[22] Thus in *Bourhill* v. *Young,* 1941 S.C. 395, the pursuer's claim was dismissed as irrelevant in the Outer House (p. 398), reclaimed to the Inner House which

Motion for New Trial

After a jury trial has taken place a party dissatisfied with the verdict may make a motion in the Inner House for the granting of a new trial on specified and limited grounds. The court will not grant the motion for a new trial simply because it disagrees with the jury's verdict but only if the verdict is so flagrantly wrong that no reasonable jury, discharging their duty honestly under proper direction, would have given it.[23] The jury is accordingly allowed considerable latitude and its verdict will not be interfered with if there is some evidence on which a reasonable jury could have reached the verdict complained of, or unless its award of damages is grossly excessive or inadequate.[24]

The case is heard before either of the Divisions of the Inner House, and the judge who presided at the jury trial in the Outer House usually sits with the Division for the hearing of the motion. As in the case of reclaiming motions, any evidence necessary is read from the shorthandwriter's transcript. While two counsel are usually instructed, only one speech is heard from either side.

The court delivers judgment in the usual way, allowing or refusing a new trial and remitting the case to the Outer House for the verdict to be entered up, or to have a fresh jury summoned and the case retried.[25] Sometimes, by consent of parties, the court itself decides the issue instead of allowing a new trial, and in certain circumstances it may set aside the verdict and enter judgment for the party unsuccessful at the trial.[26]

Appeals from the Sheriff Court

Appeals from the sheriff court are heard and disposed of in very much the same way as reclaiming motions. The case appears in the rolls of either Division of the Inner House and the judges have before them prints of the sheriff court record, the interlocutors of the sheriff, and of any evidence heard and documents produced in the sheriff court. Argument is heard from one or two counsel on each side and the sheriff's

---

allowed a proof before answer (p. 403), dismissed after proof in the Outer House (p. 405), and this was affirmed in the Inner House (p. 407), and, on appeal, in the House of Lords (1942 S.C.(H.L.) 78). In *Boyd and Forrest* v. *G.S.W. Ry.* the action was thrice before the Inner House (1911 S.C. 37 and 42, 1914 S.C. 472) and twice before the House of Lords (1912 S.C.(H.L.) 93 and 1915 S.C.(H.L.) 20).

23 *Campbell* v. *Scottish Educational News Co.* (1906) 8 F. 691; *McGinley* v. *Pacitti*, 1950 S.C. 364.

24 *Elliot* v. *Glasgow Corpn.*, 1922 S.C. 146; *McKinlay* v. *Glasgow Corpn.*, 1951 S.C. 495.

25 Sometimes a third trial is necessary, and there is theoretically no limit, but the court rarely grants a third trial and there seems to be no record of a fourth ever being granted: see *McKnight* v. *General Motor Carrying Co.*, 1936 S.C. 17.

26 Jury Trials (Scotland) Act, 1910, s. 2: *Mills* v. *Kelvin & White*, 1913 S.C. 521; *Collum* v. *Carmichael*, 1957 S.C. 349. For an unusual example of practice, see *Moyes* v. *Burntisland Shipbuilding Co.*, 1952 S.C. 429.

interlocutor appealed from may be adhered to, or recalled and a different interlocutor substituted, or the court may make different or additional findings in fact or in law. The appeal may thus be allowed or dismissed, and the action may, if necessary, be remitted to the sheriff court. The court may order additional proof to be heard.

Other Inner House Appeals

Other Inner House appeals brought under particular statutes commonly proceed in the same general manner as appeals from the sheriff court. In some cases, particularly appeals to the Court of Session as Court of Exchequer, the appeal is by way of *stated case*, in which procedure the parties frame a case setting forth the facts found or agreed and formulating certain questions of law for the opinion of the court thereon.[27] Legal argument is heard in the usual way and the court delivers opinions containing answers to the questions of law raised by the case.

Special Cases

Apart from those petitions which are presented direct to the Inner House, the most important business originating in the Inner House is the *special case*. The essential feature of the special case is that the parties are in agreement as to the facts and are submitting differences only as to law for the opinion, or opinion and judgment, of a Division of the Court. The case is settled by counsel for the parties and sets out all the relevant facts, printing any relevant documents in an Appendix, and formulating several *questions in law* for the court, which raise the legal difficulties which they wish to have determined. The special case is commonly used where parties are in doubt or dispute as to the interpretation of a will, or trust deed, *e.g.*, has the legacy to B been revoked, is Y's share to be divided into two or three shares in the circumstances, and so on? Many important questions in the law of wills and succession are accordingly decided in special cases.[28]

Appeal to the House of Lords

Appeal to the House of Lords is competent, unless expressly excluded by statute, against most Inner House judgments and, as a rule, without leave of the Inner House.[29] Appeals may be taken on grounds of fact or of law, though appeals on fact are not viewed with favour and the House

---

[27] For an example see *Inland Revenue* v. *Glasgow Police Athletic Association*, 1952 S.C. 102 (reversed by H.L., 1953 S.C.(H.L.) 13).

[28] For an example see *Gillies* v. *Glasgow Royal Infirmary*, 1960 S.C. 438.

[29] Leave is necessary in the case of an interlocutory judgment (*i.e.*, one which does not finally dispose of the action) if the Division was unanimous. Application for leave to appeal is made by petition. See further Procedure and Standing Orders applicable to Appeals to the House of Lords, in *Parliament House Book*.

is disinclined to differ on an issue of fact from the views of the judge who saw and heard the witnesses.[30]

An appeal takes the form of a petition to the House of Lords praying that an interlocutor, set out in the schedule to the petition, may be reversed, varied or altered, so that the petitioner may have such relief as may seem right. It must be signed by two counsel as being a proper case to be heard by way of appeal. Each party lodges a printed case, or a joint case with reasons *pro* and *con*, and the appellant lodges an Appendix of all the documents in the case, including pleadings, interlocutors, correspondence, etc. The opinions of the judges in the courts below are also printed or, if the case has been reported, copies of the report are lodged. Copies of the printed cases are exchanged between the agents and copies bound in a volume containing both cases.

The case is heard by at least three, and usually by five, Law Lords sitting in the same legislative chamber as is used by the full House of Lords. Only the Lord Chancellor on the Woolsack is robed. The argument is normally sustained by one senior counsel on each side (who for this appearance wear full-bottomed wigs), but in cases of great length and complexity the argument on each side is divided, one counsel arguing certain points, the other following on other topics. Not more than two counsel will be heard on each side. Counsel for the appellant opens, and may reply briefly after the respondent has made his submissions.

The House usually takes time to consider and gives judgment later. Since the sitting is nominally a sitting of the House as a legislative body, the question is put and the peers present (*i.e.*, the Law Lords who heard the appeal) speak for or against the motion.

After judgment in the House the case returns to the Inner House, which *applies the judgment*, but if the judgment of the Inner House has not been simply affirmed, a petition must be presented to the Inner House craving it to apply the judgment of the House of Lords and to deal with expenses.

SHERIFF COURT PROCEEDINGS

Ordinary Causes

The main principles of the procedure already discussed in relation to the Court of Session apply also to the sheriff court, with certain variations of terminology and practice. Thus, for example, an action is commenced by an Initial Writ, Petition or Summons [30a] but it cannot be served on the defender without a warrant obtained from the sheriff-clerk: it does not pass the Signet. But the principles of pleading, the

---

[30] *Flower* v. *Ebbw Vale Steel Co.* [1936] A.C. 206, 220; *Thomas* v. *Thomas*, 1947 S.C.(H.L.) 45.

[30a] There is no fixed name for the first writ in a sheriff court action; it is sometimes called Initial Writ and sometimes Summons or Petition or Statement of Claim.

Open and Closed Records, the hearings on Procedure or Debate Roll and the conduct of proof follow closely Court of Session procedure. Jury trial in the sheriff court is very limited and is uncommon. The sheriff must append a note to all interlocutors, except those of a formal nature, setting forth the grounds on which he has proceeded, and in a final judgment on the merits he must set out his findings in fact and in law separately.

Summary Causes

More material variations arise in respect of summary causes, that is, actions where the value of the cause does not exceed £50, or where the parties consent to summary trial. A summary cause is commenced by the ordinary form of Initial Writ but thereafter the sheriff orders such procedure as he thinks fit. Formal defences are usual but not essential; the record is not usually made up or closed; and the evidence is not usually recorded. The procedure is intended to be carried through without delay, and the case may be heard and decided within a very short time. There is appeal to the sheriff on fact and law only if the evidence is recorded, but otherwise on law only, and further appeal is competent only with the sheriff's leave.

Small Debt Causes

Claims not exceeding, or restricted to, £20 may be pursued in the Sheriff's Small Debt Court, which deals only with the recovery of debts, demands and penalties, and a few other special kinds of cases.[30]

A small debt action is commenced by completing the blank portions of a printed form, giving a brief statement of the claim and the grounds for it. The form is signed by the sheriff-clerk, who thereby grants warrant for its service on the defender and assigns a date for the defender to appear [31]: it is served personally or by registered post. A copy of any statement of account issued is attached to the summons.

On the trial date the cases are called in succession and decree commonly passes in absence. The proceedings are summary, and the only record is that made in the statutory book of causes. Judgment is pronounced orally but the case may be adjourned for judgment. The decree is usually endorsed on the summons form and signed by the sheriff-clerk. Written defences may be ordered and such a case is then automatically transferred to the Ordinary Court roll.[32]

---

[30]b See Dobie, *Sheriff Court Practice*, Chap. 22.

[31] In the larger sheriff courts the Small Debt Court is held once or twice each week and numerous cases come up at each court. The *induciae* (period of notice) is usually six days, so that the defender will be cited to appear at the first court more than a week ahead.

[32] *Allardice* v. *Wallace*, 1957 S.L.T. 225.

Judgments in the small debt court are appealable only to the High Court of Justiciary on the grounds of corruption, malice or oppression on the sheriff's part, deviation from the due form, or incompetency of the proceedings (which includes defect in jurisdiction). There is no appeal in the normal sense of that term on the ground either of fact or of law.

Appeal from Sheriff-Substitute to Sheriff

Appeal is competent from the judgment of the sheriff-substitute to the sheriff-principal in many cases, including all final judgments, without leave, and in other cases with the leave of the sheriff-substitute. There is no appeal in Small Debt cases.

The sheriff hears oral argument on behalf of parties, based on the Record and transcript of evidence, if any, and may allow amendment of the Record, or further proof in the action. He will dispose of the appeal by adhering to the interlocutor of the sheriff-substitute, or recalling it and pronouncing a fresh one. As in the case of the sheriff-substitute, the sheriff must append to his interlocutor a note setting forth the grounds on which he has proceeded.

Appeal from Sheriff Court to Court of Session and House of Lords

Appeal to the Court of Session has already been mentioned. Further appeal to the House of Lords is competent, but only on grounds of law, and that even if further proof has been heard in the Court of Session.

DILIGENCE

When one party obtains a decree against another, as for payment of money as debt or damages, the decree may not be satisfied voluntarily, in which case resort must be had to one or more of the forms of diligence. Some forms of diligence may be used at an early stage in an action to force a debtor to appear, or to compel him to find security for the sum claimed against him pending the decision of the action, but diligence is most commonly used in execution of a judgment. The forms of diligence vary according as it is done against the person or the property of the debtor and according to the kind of property.

The usual basis for diligence is an extract of the decree of court, containing a warrant for execution, but diligence may also follow on any writ containing a clause of consent to registration for execution and recorded in the books of a court, which is equivalent to an extracted decree.

Imprisonment for civil debt or failure to obey a decree is the only form of diligence against the person and is now very limited in application.

Moveable property in the hands of a third party may be attached by *arrestment* and may be taken by a subsequent action of *furthcoming*. Moveable property in the debtor's own hands may be taken in satisfaction of a decree by *poinding* [33] followed by sale by auction. As a preliminary to poinding the defender must receive a *charge*, or formal requisition to pay, served by a messenger-at-arms (for a Court of Session decree) or sheriff-officer (for a sheriff court decree).

Adjudication is the means of attaching heritable property and requires a special action in the Court of Session. Other forms of diligence which are less common are *inhibition*, which prevents a party transacting to the creditor's prejudice, *poinding of the ground*, [33] which attaches moveables on land belonging to the proprietor of the lands; *mails and duties*, which attaches the rents payable by a debtor's tenants to him, and *sequestration for rent* which entitles a landlord to have a tenant's goods sequestrated, valued and sold. Bankruptcy (or more properly *sequestration*) is not strictly a form of diligence but may be resorted to by a creditor who presents a petition for the sequestration of the debtor as a means of exacting payment of at least part of a claim. It is the legal process whereby a person who is unable to pay his debts in full may surrender, or have all his property transferred by the court, to a trustee, who realises the property and pays creditors proportionately to their claims, after certain preferential claims have been met.

II.—CRIMINAL PROCEEDINGS

The salient feature of criminal proceedings in Scotland is that public prosecution is the rule and private prosecution uncommon,[34] except in such cases as factory inspectors, who are prosecuting in the public interest.[35] Government departments do not prosecute but in case of need the Lord Advocate acts on their behalf. Nor do the police conduct prosecutions, but transmit information to the procurator-fiscal with a view to prosecution by him.

The purpose of criminal proceedings is not so much to obtain a remedy for an injured person as to vindicate and enforce law and order, to maintain minimum standards of conduct and to prevent and suppress unsocial, amoral or other detrimental conduct by punishing those who have infringed the code of conduct maintained by the criminal law.

The system of public prosecution is directed by the Lord Advocate [36]

---

[33] Pronounced " pinding."
[34] *J. & P. Coats* v. *Brown*, 1909 S.C.(J.) 29 and the account thereof by Lord Macmillan (who was counsel in the case) in *A Man of Law's Tale* at pp. 110–114; *McBain* v. *Crichton*, 1961 J.C. 25.
[35] *e.g.*, *Griffith* v. *Ferrier*, 1952 J.C. 56.
[36] On powers and duties, see *Dumfries C.C.* v. *Phyn* (1895) 22 R. 538. See also Normand, " The Public Prosecutor in Scotland " (1938) 54 L.Q.R. 345.

who is assisted by the Solicitor-General for Scotland and six Advocates-Depute appointed by the Lord Advocate from members of the Bar. There is a small permanent staff in the Crown Office in Edinburgh, headed by the Crown Agent, and permanent officials, the procurators-fiscal, are appointed in each sheriffdom to be responsible for the investigation and prosecution of crime in the sheriffdom, subject to the over-riding control of the Crown Office.[37] It is ultimately the responsibility of the Lord Advocate in practically all cases to decide whether to prosecute, in what court, and on what charge, though most minor offences can be dealt with without need to refer to him for instructions. Cases reported by procurators-fiscal are sent to the Crown Office and there is a code of instructions issued to all P.F.'s to secure uniformity of practice, and all High Court indictments are prepared in the Crown Office.

Solemn and Summary Procedure

The important distinction in criminal proceedings is that between solemn procedure (trial on indictment before a judge of the High Court of Justiciary and a jury, or before a sheriff and jury) and summary procedure (trial on complaint before a sheriff, or magistrate, or bench of justices of the peace, in each case without a jury). This distinction depends mainly on the gravity of the particular crime in question. Some serious crimes are triable on indictment only, but many may be tried in either manner depending on the circumstances and gravity of the case. Crimes created by statute are frequently prescribed as being " punishable on summary complaint " or " punishable by a court of summary jurisdiction " only. The course of procedure followed and the measure of punishment competent differs in the two cases.

The High Court has exclusive jurisdiction in cases of treason, murder, rape, incest, deforcement of messengers and breach of duty by magistrates, and may try all crimes unless its jurisdiction is expressly or impliedly excluded by statute. Other serious crimes may be tried in the High Court or before a sheriff and jury. The sheriff court has jurisdiction over all crimes not within the exclusive competence of the High Court. Other inferior criminal courts may try cases only if jurisdiction is expressly or by implication conferred on them.

Citation and Apprehension

A person normally law-abiding and with a known residence is normally cited to appear before an appropriate court at a specified time. In other cases, particularly of more serious crimes, the accused is apprehended by the police. The police have common law and statutory powers of arrest

---

[37] On the privileged position of Lord Advocate and procurators-fiscal in conducting prosecutions see *Hester* v. *Macdonald*, 1961 S.C. 370.

without warrant or may arrest on the authority of a warrant granted by a court.

Solemn Procedure

A person arrested on a serious criminal charge must be brought before a magistrate, usually a sheriff-substitute, as soon as possible. The charge is read and he is cautioned. Normally he makes no declaration but, if he does, it is taken down and signed. He may then be committed to prison for further examination, or committed for trial, or released on bail. The case is reported to the Crown Office and the suitable mode of trial ordered, and an *Indictment* [38] is then prepared specifying the charge.[39] An accused who wishes to plead guilty and have the disposal of his case expedited may do so by letter to the Crown Agent.[40] The accused may then be sentenced.

A person indicted must appear at two diets of trial, the first or pleading diet and the second or trial diet. At the first the accused may object to the competency of the proceedings or to the legal relevancy or sufficiency of the charge. He may tender a *plea in bar of trial*, such as insanity, and any *special defence*, such as alibi, which he wishes to rely on.[41]

At the trial diet, unless the panel, as the accused is now called, pleads guilty, a jury of fifteen is empanelled and sworn, and the substance of the indictment read to it. There is no opening speech and Crown counsel proceeds at once to examine his witnesses in turn. Each is cross-examined by defence counsel and, if need be, re-examined by Crown counsel.

At the conclusion of the Crown case the presiding judge may withdraw the case from the jury but otherwise the defence witnesses are called and examined by defence counsel, cross-examined and, if need be, re-examined. If the panel gives evidence, he usually does so first, and from the witness-box, on oath. The evidence is recorded by a shorthand writer and the judge makes notes for his own use.

Thereafter prosecuting and defence counsel successively address the jury, and the judge charges the jury, instructing them in the relevant law and on the points in issue.[42]

At the conclusion of the charge the jury may give a verdict at once, or retire to consider it. The jury verdict may be returned by a majority and may, unless they have been specially directed in law that one or another is not open to them, be any one of "guilty," "not guilty,"

---

[38] Pronounced "inditement."

[39] Specimen form in Renton and Brown, *Criminal Procedure*, 3rd ed., 462.

[40] Criminal Procedure (Scotland) Act, 1887, s. 31.

[41] On preparation for trial and the practice of the Crown to give a measure of assistance to the defence, see *Smith* v. *H.M. Advocate*, 1952 J.C. 66.

[42] For specimens of presiding judge's charge to a jury, see, *e.g.*, *Bird* v. *H.M. Advocate*, 1952 J.C. 23; *H.M. Advocate* v. *Kidd*, 1960 J.C. 61.

or "not proven." Some jurors may vote for each of these possible verdicts,[43] but the panel is convicted only if at least eight jurors vote for "guilty." [44] The verdict is recorded, read over to the jury and their assent to its terms recorded. Thereafter the verdict cannot be amended.[45] If there are several counts in the indictment the jury must bring in a verdict on each count.

If the verdict is one of "not guilty" or "not proven" the accused is at once assoilzied from the charge and discharged. If the verdict is one of "guilty" prosecuting counsel moves his Lordship to pass sentence, without which no sentence can be passed,[46] and, if any previous convictions are relied on, lays before the presiding judge a copy of the notice of previous convictions previously served on the accused. If these are disputed they will have to be proved. Defending counsel may make a plea in bar of sentence, such as that the verdict is ambiguous, or that the accused has become insane. He then makes a few remarks in mitigation of punishment and the presiding judge pronounces sentence. He may adjourn the case, but not for more than three weeks at a time, to consider what sentence is suitable or to permit of inquiries being made as to the accused's physical or mental condition or his suitability for particular kinds of punishment or treatment. If the trial has been before a sheriff and jury the sheriff may remit the panel to the High Court for sentence if he thinks that any sentence which he may pronounce is inadequate.

Appeal

A person convicted on indictment in the high court or sheriff court [47] may appeal to the High Court of Justiciary sitting as Court of Criminal Appeal.[48] Appeal may be taken (a) without leave, against conviction on any question of law alone, or (b) with the leave of the High Court or upon the certificate of the judge who presided at the trial that it is a fit case for appeal, on a ground of fact or of mixed fact and law or on any other ground which appears to the court or the trial judge to be a sufficient ground of appeal, or (c) with the leave of the court, against sentence, unless the sentence is fixed by law.[49] The appeal is initiated by completing and lodging within ten days a printed form of appeal [50] stating the grounds of appeal. A prima facie ground of appeal must

---

43 See *Lord Advocate* v. *Nicholson*, 1958 S.L.T.(Sh.Ct.) 17.
44 *McPhelim* v. *H.M. Advocate*, 1960 J.C. 17, 22.
45 *McGarry* v. *H.M. Advocate*, 1959 J.C. 30.
46 See *Noon* v. *H.M. Advocate*, 1960 J.C. 52.
47 *i.e.*, after trial before a sheriff and jury.
48 Criminal Appeal (Scotland) Act, 1926.
49 This applies only to capital crimes.
50 The forms are specified in the Schedule to Act of Adjournal, October 27, 1926, and printed in Renton and Brown's *Criminal Procedure*, 3rd ed., 527–535.

be stated and not merely a vague objection to the conviction. The appellant may be released on bail pending the appeal but such applications are not regarded favourably. If released on bail the period of liberation is not counted towards his period of sentence.

Sessions of the High Court are held in Edinburgh every few weeks for the disposal of appeals and the Bench normally consists of the Lord Justice-General or Lord Justice-Clerk and two other Lords Commissioners of Justiciary, though a larger Bench may be convened to hear cases of particular importance.[51] The appellant may present a written case but usually oral argument is presented by counsel. The appellant may be present in court, in the custody of two warders, except in the case of appeals on law alone. The Crown is represented by one or more of the Advocates-Depute and sometimes by one of the Law Officers.

The court have before them the trial judge's notes and his report giving his opinion on the case or on any point arising therein and, if necessary, a transcript of the shorthand writer's notes of the evidence and proceedings at the trial. They may order the production of documents or the attendance of further witnesses for examination, so long as the witnesses could not have been examined at the trial.[52] If fresh evidence is admitted the court must consider whether the jury verdict would necessarily have been different if it had heard both the evidence now adduced and that put before it at the trial.

Where the appeal is on a matter of law alone and leave is consequently not required, counsel for the appellant proceeds at once with his argument, after which Crown counsel replies. But where leave to appeal is required counsel must first outline the circumstances of the case down to its present stage and satisfy the court that there is a prima facie case or an arguable point before they will grant him leave to develop his argument in full.[53] In considering any criticism of the trial judge's charge the court will have regard to the whole of it, not merely to some phrase.[54]

Where the appeal is against sentence counsel's statement applying for leave to appeal is treated as the hearing of the appeal, and in practice Crown counsel do not exercise their right of reply, unless called on by the court.

The court is empowered[55] to allow the appeal if they think that the verdict of the jury should be set aside on the ground that it is unreasonable

51 A notable instance is *Sugden* v. *H.M. Advocate*, 1934 J.C. 103.
52 As, for example, when it has only later been discovered that those witnesses had any knowledge of the facts in issue. See further *Lowson* v. *H.M. Advocate*, 1943 J.C. 141; *Lennie* v. *H.M. Advocate*, 1946 J.C. 79; *Gallacher* v. *H.M. Advocate*, 1951 J.C. 38.
53 *Leighton* v. *H.M. Advocate*, 1931 J.C. 1; *Fox* v. *H.M. Advocate*, 1950 J.C. 64.
54 *Reynolds* v. *H.M. Advocate*, 1928 S.N. 103; *McEwan* v. *H.M. Advocate*, 1939 J.C. 26; *McPhelim* v. *H.M. Advocate*, 1960 J.C. 17.
55 Criminal Appeal (Scotland) Act, 1926, s. 2 (1).

or cannot be supported having regard to the evidence,[56] or that the judgment of the trial court should be set aside on the ground of a wrong decision of any question of law,[57] or that on any ground there was a miscarriage of justice.[58] In other cases they dismiss the appeal, and the court may dismiss the appeal even if of the opinion that the point raised in the appeal might be decided in favour of the appellant, if they consider that no substantial miscarriage of justice has actually occurred.[59] The court may also allow an appeal but substitute a verdict of guilty of another charge, and impose a sentence therefor.[60]

SUMMARY CRIMINAL PROCEDURE

Summary criminal procedure is followed by all courts in Scotland having criminal jurisdiction, other than the High Court of Justiciary,[61] when criminal jurisdiction is exercised by the sheriff or other inferior judge sitting alone and without a jury.[62] The sheriff court has jurisdiction to try all common law offences, and also statutory offences except where that jurisdiction is expressly or impliedly excluded,[63] and certain crimes must be tried by the sheriff. Apart from that principle and from the provisions of any relevant statute, it rests with the Lord Advocate and the procurators-fiscal to decide in which court a summary prosecution is to commence.

Complaint

Summary criminal proceedings are instituted by the service of a complaint [64] and, in the case of a statutory offence, a relative notice of the

---

[56] This covers cases where the jury convicted on inadequate evidence, *e.g.*, *Morton* v. *H.M. Advocate*, 1938 J.C. 50. The test is not whether the court agrees or disagrees with the jury's verdict, but whether the jury's verdict was so flagrantly wrong and unreasonable that no reasonable jury acting honestly under proper direction could have given it: *Webb* v. *H.M. Advocate*, 1927 J.C. 92.

[57] This includes irrelevancy of the indictment, wrongful admission or exclusion of evidence, and misdirection of the jury by the presiding judge, as by laying down the wrong rule of law, or failing to direct them on some matter.

[58] Under this head the appellant must show that but for the irregularity complained of, it is reasonably probable that the jury would not have convicted him. *Cf.* *Scott (A. T.)* v. *H.M. Advocate*, 1946 J.C. 90. It covers cases of improper evidence being admitted, and other irregularities such as allegations that a witness had talked to a juror.

[59] This is known as " the proviso." It is intended to prevent convictions having to be quashed because of some trivial objection, which is valid, but does not at all disturb the rightness of the conviction.

[60] *McKenzie* v. *H.M. Advocate*, 1959 J.C. 32.

[61] These courts are the sheriff court; J.P. courts; burgh courts, including the Glasgow stipendiary magistrate's court; police courts; and the court of the Bailie of the River Clyde. Procedure is uniform for all these courts.

[62] The main procedural statute is the Summary Jurisdiction (Scotland) Act, 1954, replacing earlier Acts in similar terms. Young offenders are tried in accordance with the Children and Young Persons (Scotland) Act, 1937, as amended.

[63] *Wilson* v. *Hill*, 1943 J.C. 124.

[64] For specimen see Renton and Brown, 476–487.

penalties to which the accused is liable on conviction. This runs in the name of the procurator-fiscal or other prosecutor and states the substance of the charge against the accused, adding, in the case of a statutory contravention, that it is contrary to a specified section of a particular Act. If previous convictions are being founded on as aggravations of the charge, notice is served separately of those which it is intended to rely on, and this is not disclosed to the judge till after conviction. The complaint is signed by the prosecutor.

Trial

When the complaint is called in court, the accused must plead to it, if he has not already done so by letter, and the trial may take place then but, as a rule, if he pleads not guilty, an adjourned diet is fixed for trial.

Prior to pleading the accused may state objections to the competency or relevancy of the complaint, or pleas in bar of trial. The complaint may accordingly be dismissed or amended at this stage.

At the trial the proceedings are conducted informally and summarily and only brief notes are taken by the sheriff and the clerk of court. The witnesses are called for the prosecution and examined, cross-examined and re-examined in the usual way. Then the accused himself, if he wishes, and any witnesses for the accused are heard. Thereafter procurator-fiscal and counsel or solicitor for the accused address the court. Objections to evidence may be taken in the course of the trial and must be noted, if requested, so as to be available for appeal. No previous conviction may be disclosed, even by implication, until the judge is satisfied that the charge has been proved.[65]

The judge normally pronounces his finding at once; if not guilty or not proven, the accused is liberated at once; if guilty, the accused or his counsel or solicitor may address the court before sentence is pronounced.

The sentence is usually one of fine or imprisonment, and a fine is not infrequently paid on the spot. The court may in its discretion fix any punishment within the limits of its competency, or may dismiss with an admonition, or without recording a conviction, or may release on probation.

Review of Summary Trial Verdicts

There are six methods whereby the proceedings of courts of summary criminal jurisdiction may be reviewed. Of these two are

---

[65] *Bryce* v. *Gardiner*, 1951 J.C. 134; *McGregor* v. *Macdonald*, 1952 J.C. 4; *Clark* v. *Connell*, 1952 J.C. 119.

obsolete,[66] two uncommon [67] and only two regularly employed. These are appeal by Stated Case, and Bill of Suspension.

Either party may, on the final determination of a summary prosecution, apply to the court to state a case for the opinion of the High Court of Justiciary. A stated case may be obtained on very varied grounds, so as to cover every question likely to be raised on appeal, including objections to competency, jurisdiction, relevancy, the admission or rejection of evidence, irregularities in procedure, and the competency of sentence (but not the amount of sentence).

Review does not cover questions of fact but only questions of law (which includes legal inferences drawn from findings in fact). It is competent for either party to ask for a stated case, so that the prosecutor may appeal against an acquittal. The party dissatisfied with the legal determination of the court applies to the judge to state and sign a case for the opinion of the High Court of Justiciary. The applicant, unless he is a person prosecuting in the public interest or obtains a dispensation from the judge, must find caution [67a] for or consign a sum of money fixed by the judge.

The stated case [68] is prepared by the clerk of court [69] and each party may intimate any adjustments desired, the case being finally settled by the judge. The case narrates the circumstances and what facts the judge found to be admitted or proved,[70] and states the judge's decision and disposal of the case on the basis of these findings of fact. It then states for the opinion of the High Court one or more questions of law [71] such as: " On the facts stated was I entitled to convict the accused? " or " On the facts stated was I entitled to reject the evidence of . . .? " The question whether the inferior court was *right* in convicting is not a question of law for appeal, but a matter for the inferior court to determine on the facts.

Stated cases are heard by the High Court of Justiciary, similarly composed as for a sitting as Court of Criminal Appeal.[72] The appellant

---

66 Appeal to the Circuit Court under the Heritable Jurisdiction (Scotland) Act, 1746; and Appeal to Quarter Sessions of the Peace.
67 Appeal to the Court of Session as Court of Exchequer (competent only in Customs and Excise prosecutions); and Advocation, appropriate to the review of irregularities in the preliminary stages. It is usually resorted to by the prosecution: see *McFadyean* v. *Stewart*, 1951 J.C. 164.
67a *i.e.*, security: pronounced " kayshun."
68 For specimen see Renton and Brown, 502.
69 In the sheriff court it is done in practice by the sheriff-substitute himself.
70 It is incorrect, as is sometimes done, to narrate some of the evidence; the inferior court should have made up its mind on what it held on the evidence to have been established.
71 See *Drummond* v. *Hunter*, 1948 J.C. 109.
72 In practice the judges of one or other of the Divisions of the Inner House of the Court of Session sit as High Court for about a week, hearing first criminal appeals under the 1926 Act, and then stated cases and bills of suspension under the 1954 Act.

is represented by counsel and the procurator-fiscal by one or more Crown counsel. Legal argument is heard from both sides, one speech on each side, and the court usually disposes of the case at once. It may, however, remit the case with an opinion, or for amendment or clarification of the findings or the point in issue.

The High Court has wide powers,[73] to affirm, reverse, or alter the decision of the inferior court, to substitute a fine for imprisonment, to reduce either fine or imprisonment, to convict and sentence an accused or remit the case to the inferior court with instructions to convict and sentence, to quash the conviction, and so on.

Suspension is the procedure whereby an illegal or improper warrant, conviction or judgment issued by an inferior judge acting under summary criminal procedure [74] may be reviewed and set aside by the High Court. If the complainer is in custody the process becomes one of suspension and liberation. It is a remedy open to the person accused or convicted only and not to the prosecutor.[75] It is not a means of having reviewed the rightness of a conviction but a means of having stopped proceedings in excess of jurisdiction, illegal or unwarrantable, or where there is oppression or injustice or irregularity in the proceedings.[76]

The Bill of Suspension runs in name of the aggrieved party as complainer against the prosecutor as respondent and resembles a civil petition in form, having a prayer for the suspension of the sentence complained of, and, where appropriate, for liberation from prison, a statement of facts in numbered paragraphs, and pleas in law.[77] The prosecutor normally lodges answers in the form of corresponding paragraphs and pleas in law. The facts in the Bill must aver relevantly grounds on which the sentence is challenged, and it is competent even though the sentence has been carried out.

The Bill is put out for hearing by three or more members of the High Court of Justiciary and legal argument is heard from counsel for the suspender and from Crown counsel. The facts are not investigated except so far as admitted by the respondent but a remit may be made to the inferior court to report on some matter. It is not a suitable process to challenge the sufficiency of the evidence for conviction or the admissibility of evidence, or otherwise to challenge the merits of a conviction, but only a means to object where some miscarriage of justice is alleged.

The High Court may pass the Bill, suspend the sentence and order

---

73 Summary Jurisdiction (Scotland) Act, 1954, s. 71.
74 It has no application to trials on indictment.
75 The prosecutor's remedy is by advocation, though this may be invoked by both parties.
76 Full list of grounds in Renton and Brown, 319–320: see also *Henderson* v. *Forster*, 1944 J.C. 91; *Blair* v. *Hawthorn*, 1945 J.C. 17; *Gray* v. *Morrison*, 1954 J.C. 31.
77 For specimen, see Renton and Brown, 505.

repayment of any fine paid, or repel the reasons of suspension, refuse the Bill and let the sentence take effect, or amend the conviction and sentence and, if necessary, remit the case to the inferior court. Expenses may be awarded, in full or modified.

Juvenile Courts

Special provision is made for the treatment of young offenders.[78] These are divided into children, aged from ten to fourteen, and young persons, aged from fourteen to seventeen. A child under ten cannot in law be guilty of any offence. Persons over seventeen are dealt with in the ordinary criminal courts but there are limitations on and special provisions affecting punishment.

Special courts of summary jurisdiction have to be established in any area appointed by the Secretary of State to hear charges against children and young persons.[79] A juvenile court consists of at least three justices of the peace, including at least one from either sex, drawn from a panel of specially qualified justices, who must ordinarily not be over sixty-five. The juvenile court has the jurisdiction of a sheriff sitting summarily but the power of punishment of a J.P. court only. If no such juvenile court has been set up any court of summary jurisdiction may deal with juveniles, but it does so under the juvenile court procedure. If the charge is against a juvenile jointly with a person over seventeen the case cannot be heard in the juvenile court, and the Lord Advocate has power to order proceedings to be taken in the High Court or sheriff court in any cases.

A juvenile court must sit in a different room or building from other courts, or on different days, and proceedings are in private. The procedure is commenced by complaint by the prosecutor of the court and follows as nearly as may be that provided for summary cases generally. No newspaper report of the proceedings may, unless the court or the Secretary of State orders otherwise, reveal the name or other personal particulars of a person concerned in the proceedings, nor publish any picture of him, and the proceedings may be held *in camera*.

The court must have regard, in dealing with a child or young person, to its welfare and shall in a proper case take steps to remove him from undesirable surroundings and to secure that proper provision is made for his education and training. A parent or guardian may be required

---

[78] The provisions are contained in the Children and Young Persons (Scotland) Act, 1937, the Children Act, 1948, and the Criminal Justice (Scotland) Act, 1949. On the serious spread of juvenile delinquency see Mack: *Crime*, in *The Scottish Economy* (ed. Cairncross), 227 and on crime in Glasgow see *Third Statistical Account of Scotland*, Vol. 5, *Glasgow*, Chap. 20. In fact few juvenile courts have been established in Scotland, and most juveniles come before the sheriff court or the police courts, according to the gravity of the offence.

[79] They have been established in Aberdeen and the counties of Ayr, Renfrew and Fife.

to attend the court at all stages of the proceedings. When an offence
is charged, notice must be given to one of the area probation officers
and he must investigate and make available to the court information
on the home surroundings which may be of assistance to the court,
and obtain from the education authority a report on the school record,
health and character of the child or young person and, in proper cases,
as to the availability of approved schools.

PUNISHMENT AND TREATMENT OF CRIMINALS

Many changes have been made in the methods of punishment and
treatment in recent years and experiment and change is constantly going
on,[79a] the emphasis being now on training and reformation of criminals,
not on mere punishment.[80]

The sentence of death can be imposed only by a judge of the High
Court on a person convicted of treason or capital murder.[81] The sentence
will not be pronounced on a pregnant woman nor on a person under
eighteen, and capital cases are always reviewed by the Secretary of State
for Scotland, who may recommend reprieve and commutation of sentence,
or pardon.[82] Where a sentence is commuted to life imprisonment, the
prisoner may be released on licence at any time. Persons under eighteen
convicted of capital murder are sentenced to be detained during Her
Majesty's pleasure. Life imprisonment is also the sentence for non-
capital murder.

Imprisonment [83] may be imposed for such period as the court thinks
fit or such period as may be authorised by any relevant statute. A sheriff
acting under solemn procedure may not imprison for more than two
years and, in summary procedure, unless statute authorises more, the
maximum sentence is of three months' imprisonment. There are
restrictions on imprisonment of adult first offenders and of young persons

[79a] Further changes are being made by the Criminal Justice (Scotland) Act, 1963.
[80] In 1959 a new Scottish Advisory Council on the Treatment of Offenders was
set up to advise and assist the Secretary of State for Scotland. There is also a
Standing Advisory Council on Employment of Prisoners, appointed by the
Home Secretary and the Secretary of State for Scotland. The Department of
Criminal Science at Cambridge University has been developed into an Institute of
Criminology to study the causes and prevention of crime while research is also
pursued in various universities and by the Home Office Research Unit.
[81] As defined by the Homicide Act, 1957.
[82] On the factors taken into account see *Report of the Royal Commission on Capital
Punishment* (Cmd. 8932, 1953), paras. 36–49, 597 *et seq.*; Milne, *The Scottish
Office*, 153. See also Marshall, " The Prerogative of Mercy," 1948 *Current Legal
Problems*, 104.
[83] Transportation, penal servitude and imprisonment with hard labour have been
abolished. Scottish prisons are at Aberdeen, Dumfries, Edinburgh, Glasgow,
Greenock, Inverness, Perth and Peterhead, with an " open " prison at Newton
Stewart. There is a detention centre for young persons at Perth and Dumfries
Prison is being set aside as a young offenders' institution.

under twenty-one and a prohibition on imprisonment of persons under seventeen. Corrective training and preventive detention are special forms of imprisonment for persistent offenders.[84] There is also provision for supervision of prisoners after release. Youths aged between sixteen and twenty-one may be sentenced to undergo Borstal training for a period of not more than three years.[85] This is followed by a period of supervision.

Pecuniary fines are commonly imposed in addition to, or instead of, imprisonment; there are fixed scales of periods of imprisonment for failure to pay fines. The amount of any fine is within the court's discretion save that, unless statute otherwise authorises, the sheriff court may not impose a fine of over £25 and other inferior criminal courts not over £10.

A probation order may be made, requiring the offender to be under supervision for a period of from one to three years, to be of good behaviour and to conform to the directions of the probation officer. He may be required to reside in a specified place, or to submit to mental treatment.

Children and young persons may be put on probation, fined, committed to the care of a fit person, or have their parent or guardian fined. In more serious cases they may be detained during Her Majesty's pleasure, detained in a remand centre,[86] detention centre, or remand home,[87] committed to an approved school,[87] to a Borstal institution, or committed to the care of a fit person.

Minor penalties include forfeiture of instruments, being ordered to find caution for good behaviour, and admonition. A court may also defer sentence or admonish or discharge an accused absolutely.

III.—Proceedings in Special Courts and Administrative Tribunals

It is impossible to discuss briefly and generally the characteristic features of proceedings before special courts and administrative tribunals since they differ so very much *inter se*. They vary from special courts such as service Courts-Martial and the Scottish Land Court, which have formal rules of procedure, to tribunals where the greatest informality prevails. In every case the rules and practice of the particular judicial body must be looked for and followed.

---

[84] See Criminal Justice (Scotland) Act, 1949, s. 21.

[85] For the development of the system see Fox, *The English Prison and Borstal Systems*, 327 *et seq*. The Scottish Borstals are at Castle Huntly, Cornton Vale, Dumfries Prison and Polmont, and in a separate section in Barlinnie Prison, Glasgow, and for girls at Greenock prison.

[86] A remand centre is to be built in the Glasgow area.

[87] Remand homes and approved schools are provided by local authorities.

FURTHER READING

Court of Session
Mackay: *Practice of the Court of Session*, 2 vols.
    Manual of Practice in the Court of Session.
Maclaren: *Court of Session Practice.*
Thomson and Middleton: *Manual of Court of Session Procedure.*
Annual Reports: *Civil Judicial Statistics (Scotland).*

Sheriff Court
Dobie: *Sheriff Court Practice.*
    Sheriff Court Styles.
Lees: *Handbook of Pleading in the Sheriff Court.*
Lewis: *Sheriff Court Practice.*

Diligence
Graham Stewart: *Law of Diligence.*

Expenses
Maclaren: *Expenses in the Court of Session and Sheriff Court.*

Legal Aid
Law Society of Scotland: *Legal Aid (Scotland) Compendium.*
Annual Report of the Law Society of Scotland on the Legal Aid Scheme.

Solemn Criminal Procedure
Renton and Brown: *Criminal Procedure According to the Law of Scotland.*

Summary Criminal Procedure
Trotter: *Summary Criminal Jurisdiction.*

Punishment and Treatment
Fox: *The English Prison and Borstal System.*
Howard Jones: *Crime and the Penal System.*
HMSO: *Prisons and Borstals.*
    The Probation Service in Scotland.
King: *The Probation Service.*
Annual Reports: *Criminal Statistics, Scotland.*
    Prisons in Scotland.

Administrative Tribunals
Allen: *Administrative Jurisdiction.*
Robson: *Justice and Administrative Law.*
Annual Reports of the Council on Tribunals.

CHAPTER 8

THE SOURCES OF THE LAW

THE term " sources of the law " has several meanings which have to be carefully distinguished.[1] There are, firstly, historical sources, which are the events and incidents in legal history which have given rise to the rule or principle in question. Thus historical sources of various rules may be that the rule was laid down by Justinian and adopted into Scots law, or enacted by Parliament in response to certain needs of that time, or developed by the courts over a particular period.[2] Every principle and rule of law has a historical source somewhere, even though it may not be known, but the rule or principle does not draw its validity or binding force from that source. The historical source merely explains when and how that rule came to be established. It frequently helps also to explain why the rule took a particular form. Secondly, every rule and principle has a social, political, economic, moral or religious source in that some fact or set or state of facts, moral, political, economic and so on, have provoked or give rise to that rule. Thus some rules of law were enacted or developed for political reasons, such as the law regulating trade unions, others for economic reasons, such as the law of bills of exchange, others for moral reasons, such as those relating to punishment of cruelty and neglect of children, and so on. Again, every rule and principle has such a theoretical source, though it may be forgotten or difficult to discover, but the theoretical source also does not give the rule any legal validity but merely gives the justification for the rule, and that justification, moreover, may later disappear or seem unsound or inadequate to a later generation, but the rule is not thereby abrogated.[3] Thirdly, the enactments, ideas, decisions, books, documents and usages of persons from which a court may derive a principle for the decision of a case are sometimes spoken of as sources, and again every rule has such a source, but these are better described as the materials for formulating a decision and which determine the content of a principle or rule.

It would be better if the term " sources " were not used in these senses and instead one talked of historical origins of rules, philosophical bases

---

[1] See further Salmond, *Jurisprudence*, Chap. 6; Allen, *Law in the Making*, Introduction; Pound, *Jurisprudence*, Chap. 16; Smith, " Sources of Scots Law " (1904) 16 J.R. 375; Dove Wilson, " Sources of Scots Law " (1892) 4 J.R. 1.

[2] Many examples of historical sources of the latter two kinds may be found in Chap. 3.

[3] See further Dicey, *Lectures on the Relation between Law and Public Opinion in the Nineteenth Century*, passim.

of rules and material foundations of rules. The only true " sources " of legal principles and rules are the legal sources. Legal validity and authority accordingly belong to a rule or principle of law only by virtue of its being drawn from a legal source, a repository recognised by the legal system itself as an authoritative source of valid and binding rules and principles of law, and it is with these authoritative sources that this chapter is concerned. It is to these legal sources only that one may resort to find a rule or principle of law for the application to and solution of a legal controversy or problem raised by certain facts.

The ultimate source of all Scots law, that which confers authority on all rules and principles to make them determinative of rights and decisive of controversies, is the power of the state, that is, of the legally organised community of the United Kingdom. The state acts through its legislature and courts, and the immediate practical sources of rules and principles recognised in Scots law as legally authoritative are the statutes of the Imperial Parliament, and of the former Parliaments of Scotland and of Great Britain, subordinate legislation authorised by such statutes, judicial decisions of the superior courts of the United Kingdom, books of recognised authority, accepted customs, and decisions founded on equity or certain extraneous sources. No other sources give rise to rules and principles having authority recognised by the courts of this country, and these are the recognised forms of law in Scotland, legislation, case-law, recognised books, customs, and principles drawn from equity and extraneous sources. The facts that rules of statute-law and case-law themselves have historical origins, philosophical bases, and material foundations are matters of interest and concern to historical and theoretical legal study but do not by themselves confer any validity or authority on the rules. Hence the condemnation of the slave trade gave rise to valid and authoritative rules of law only because Parliament proscribed it by statute, not because of the historical steps towards or the moral justifications for the abolition of slavery. The legal sources, moreover, are the only sources from which new rules or principles can be added to the body of law.

These legal sources must be sharply distinguished from legal literature, the books of the law. Books are, in general, *not* authoritative sources of the law but only means of our knowledge of the law, to which we turn to discover not what the principles of law are, but what the author of the book believes the principles and rules to be, having regard to the statutes and cases which appear to him applicable to his subject-matter. Certain books, as will appear later, are in a rather more privileged position, and may be distinguished as literary sources of law, as distinct from legal literature (textbooks, periodicals, legal histories, etc.), but in general any court may quite freely ignore what is written in a text-book.[4] The function of the textbook is to collect and present in logical form a statement, drawn from the authoritative sources, of the rules of law on a given topic, the relevant statutes and scattered cases, and to suggest their effect and how they appear to the author to apply in different circumstances. Textbooks are of great value for their statement of the rules drawn from legal sources and for their criticism of rules and their conjectures of suitable developments to solve problems which have not yet arisen. If a court accepts the view of a text-writer that view becomes authoritative, not because the text-writer wrote it but because the court has adopted and approved it, and it thereby acquires the authority of case-law; in future the rule is authoritative because of the case and the judicial adoption, and not because of being in the book. The courts and Parliament are always entirely free to ignore formulations of legal principle or doctrine in a textbook, however highly esteemed it or its learned author may be. Textbooks are, in general, only secondary authorities and useful in so far as they completely and accurately present the primary authorities, *i.e.*, the statutes and cases, on any topic.

Having determined what are the recognised sources of legally authoritative rules of law it will be evident that two problems exist in relation to each class of legal source, namely, how and where to recognise and find the expressions of rules of law which come from these various sources, and, secondly, how to interpret the statements therein as to draw from them a rule suitable for the resolution of the particular problem or controversy which is in issue.

I.—LEGISLATION

Statute Law

A statute is an authoritative declaration of the will of the Queen in Parliament as to some matter of law, usually prescribing some general rule for the future regulation of conduct. It may, however, be specific and relate to only one or a few limited cases only. The body of statute law which is of relevance in Scotland comprises the body of statutes or Acts of the Scottish Parliaments down to 1707, of the Parliament of Great Britain from 1707 to 1800, and of the Parliament of the United Kingdom since 1801, in all cases so far as these statutes are still in force and have been amended but not repealed or cancelled by subsequent legislation.

At the present time a projected piece of legislation during its passage

---

[4] Lord Wrenbury, who when still young Mr. Buckley at the Bar had written a book on Companies, once remarked from the Bench when Buckley's *Companies Acts* was cited to him: " You must not substitute for the judgments of the court the irresponsible conjectures of a textbook writer." This emphasises that textbooks are not infrequently written by comparatively young and inexperienced men, and may contain statements which are tentative, conjectural or even simply wrong.

through Parliament is called a Bill,[5] and these may be of three kinds, each being subject to different procedure in Parliament. These are (*a*) public Bills which relate to matters of public policy generally, alter the general law and apply generally to the members of the public who fall within their scope: most of these are Government Bills introduced by Ministers on behalf of the Government in pursuance of the Government's policy and thereby assured of the general support in Parliament of the supporters of the Government; some public Bills are, however, introduced by private members in the limited time made available to them. These private members' Bills are not sponsored or supported by the Government and may even be contrary to its policy, though they may on the other hand be adopted later by the Government and their passage facilitated.[6]

(*b*) Private Bills, which are for the particular interest or benefit of any person or body and are solicited by the parties concerned, and deal with local or personal matters such as giving special power to a local authority, or dealing with private estates, names, peerage or status. Private Bills are brought in on petition and are usually referred to private Bill committees, before whom the promoters have to establish their case for obtaining the parliamentary powers they seek.

(*c*) Hybrid Bills, which are introduced as public Bills but affect private interests in much the same way as private Bills, and have a special procedure.[7]

There should also be noted provisional order confirmation Bills which are Bills introduced to have confirmed by Parliament orders and schemes made by Ministers. Local authorities and private bodies frequently obtain statutory powers in this way. Their proposals are made to the Secretary of State for Scotland who, if satisfied as to their desirability, and if necessary after a public inquiry, issues a provisional order confirming the scheme and later introduces (as a public Bill) a Bill confirming the provisional order and giving it statutory effect.[8] This avoids the expense of private Bills.

---

[5] Bills are drafted by Parliamentary Counsel to the Treasury or, if applicable only to Scotland, by the Legal Secretaries and Parliamentary Draftsmen of the Lord Advocate's Department in London. On drafting and the early stages of a Bill see Ram, " Improvement of the Statute Book," 1951 J.S.P.T.L. 442.

[6] Notice that private members' Bills and private Bills are completely different things; the one is introduced by a private member, rather than a Minister, but is a public Bill; the other is sponsored to affect private interests, not general to the whole country.

[7] See Erskine May, *Parliamentary Practice*, Chap. 21.

[8] The procedure is regulated by the Private Legislation Procedure (Scotland) Act, 1936. For an example see Dunoon Burgh Order Confirmation Act, 1954 (2 & 3 Eliz. 2, c. xxiii). In England procedure by provisional order has been largely superseded by procedure under the Statutory Orders (Special Procedure) Act, 1945, (also applicable to Scotland) on which see Molson in (1950) 3 *Parliamentary Affairs*, 458 and Erskine May, *Parliamentary Practice*, Chap. 31.

Acts

When Bills have passed through all their stages and received the Royal Assent they become Acts of Parliament or Statutes. Acts are now [9] classified as public or private [10] and as general or local or personal. A public Act is one which is judicially noticed, whereas a private Act is one the existence and terms of which have to be proved by the party founding on it in any court in which it is founded on. Every Act passed since 1850 is now deemed public in this sense, and to be judicially taken notice of as such, unless the contrary is expressly provided and declared by the Act.[11] A public Bill may be general, local or personal in nature, but always emerges as a public Act; a private Bill may be local or personal in nature, but emerges as a public Act in the former case and a private Act in the latter. The main distinction is accordingly between public and general Acts on the one hand and public and local and personal on the other. This distinction has been described [12] as follows: "A general Act prima facie is that which applies to the whole community. In the natural meaning of the term it means an Act of Parliament which is unlimited both in its area and as regards the individual in its effects. And as opposed to that you get statutes which may well be public because of the importance of the subjects with which they deal and their general interest to the community, but which are limited in respect of area—a limitation which makes them local—or limited in respect of individuals or persons—a limitation which makes them personal."

The classification adopted in Queen's printer's editions of the statutes is now:

(1) Public General Statutes, *i.e.*, judicially noticed and of general application.

(2) Local (formerly local and personal), either
    (*a*) public, *i.e.*, judicially noticed, but of a local character, or
    (*b*) not public, *i.e.*, declared " not to be deemed a public Act."

(3) Personal, *i.e.*, relating to individuals' personal affairs, either
    (*a*) printed by the Queen's printer, or
    (*b*) not so printed (now almost obsolete).[13]

---

[9] There were formerly other classifications at different times, for which see Craies' *Statute Law* (5th ed.), 53–54; Erskine May, Chap. 35.

[10] This classification, it should be noted, does not correspond with the classification of Bills in Parliament into public and private.

[11] Interpretation Act, 1889, s. 9.

[12] *R. v. London County Council* [1893] 2 Q.B. 454, 462, per Bowen L.J.

[13] Examples, taken from the 1893 statutes, are : The Rules Publication Act, 1893 (56 & 57 Vict. c. 66) (Public general); The East Fife Central Railway Act, 1893 (56 & 57 Vict. c. cxcvi) (Local); Ryland's Estate Act, 1893 (56 & 57 Vict. c. 1) (Private—printed by the Queen's Printer); and Fleming's Divorce Act, 1893 (Private—not printed).

Some other terms applied to Acts are merely descriptive and not strictly classificatory. Thus an Act may be called *declaratory* if passed to explain and declare the pre-existing law on some particular subject, to remove doubts thereon, and frequently to set aside what Parliament believes to have been an erroneous interpretation or judicial mistake.[14] A *codifying Act* is passed to reduce to the form of a code the whole of the existing statute-law and case-law on a given subject,[15] and thus to state the whole law on that topic in codified form, and a *consolidating Act* to bring together into one Act provisions previously contained in a number of statutes,[16] usually with corrections and minor improvements, but not effecting major changes of substance. Consolidating Acts may, exceptionally, profess to consolidate with amendments, but these are comparatively rare. Consolidating Acts are presumed not to change the law but simply to re-enact it in convenient consolidated form.[17] *Statute Law Revision Acts* are passed periodically to remove from the Statute Book spent, obsolete and unnecessary enactments.[18] *Clauses Acts*, common in the mid-nineteenth century, contained " common form " clauses and provisions intended to be incorporated by reference in common kinds of private Bills, so as to promote uniformity and reduce the length of such Bills.[19]

Long Title and Short Title

Most statutes have a formal long title which appears at the commencement and indicates the scope and purpose of the Act. Thus, *e.g.*, " An Act for codifying the Law relating to the Sale of Goods." Old Acts have in many cases a very full and cumbrous long title setting out the purpose of the Act at some length.

It has also long been the practice to provide in a section of each Act, usually near the end, for a short title, by which name the Act is usually known and cited. Thus section 64 of the above-mentioned Act provides: " This Act may be cited as ' The Sale of Goods Act, 1893 '." In 1896 the Short Titles Act was passed, which thus christened a large number of older Acts to facilitate their citation, and the Statute Law Revision Act, 1948,

---

[14] *e.g.*, Territorial Waters Jurisdiction Act, 1878, passed to overrule the decision in *R. v. Keyn* (1876) 2 Ex.D. 63.
[15] *e.g.*, Bills of Exchange Act, 1882; Partnership Act, 1890; Sale of Goods Act, 1893; Marine Insurance Act, 1906.
[16] *e.g.*, Titles to Land Consolidation Act, 1868; Companies Act, 1948. Consolidating Acts do *not* seek to incorporate the substance of case-law as do codifying Acts. But it must be noted that the terms " codifying " and " consolidating " are sometimes used carelessly and incorrectly, rather than with their strict connotation.
[17] Much consolidation of statute law has been done since 1945, mostly under the authority of the Consolidation of Enactments (Procedure) Act, 1949.
[18] *e.g.*, Statute Law Revision Act, 1960.
[19] *e.g.*, Railways Clauses Consolidation Act, 1845; Lands Clauses Consolidation (Scotland) Act, 1845.

w.—18

continued the process. The 1896 Act also gives collective titles to many groups of statutes relating to the same subject-matter.

In the case of amending Acts or further Acts on a topic already dealt with by legislation, it is commonly provided that the Act and the prior Acts may be cited together by a collective title, *e.g.*, the Merchant Shipping Acts, 1894 to 1960.

By the Interpretation Act, 1889, s. 35, an Act may be cited in any Act, instrument or document either by its short title or by reference to the regnal year and chapter.

Apart from these official titles many Acts have acquired popular titles by which, though entirely unofficially, they are commonly known in the profession and often cited in books, such as the Montgomery and Rutherford Entail Acts, so called from the Lord Advocates who sponsored them.[20]

Preamble

Statutes sometimes have a preamble setting out the facts or state of the law for which Parliament is proposing to legislate.[21] Most modern statutes have a brief preamble or none at all. Private Bills must have preambles. In modern times the preamble is often superseded in the case of public Bills by a memorandum or White Paper explaining the object of the Bill.

Schedules

Schedules are sometimes appended to Acts, containing matter which cannot conveniently be put into the body of the text, such as forms, lists of previous Acts repealed or affected, and matters of detail. The Schedule is part of the enactment and effect may have to be given to something in a Schedule as against an earlier provision in the body of the Act, but the enactment cannot be restrained or limited by the terms of a mere form inserted for convenience in a Schedule. Schedules are numbered and divided into paragraphs and sub-paragraphs, not sections. They may also be divided into parts consisting of groups of paragraphs.

Citation of Statutes

The Acts of the Scottish Parliament are cited by the year and chapter number or by the volume, page, and chapter number of the Record edition, *e.g.*, Act 1449, c. 17; A.P.S. II, 127, c. 3. The latter is more common in historical than in legal texts, and the same Act does not always bear the same number in both the Record and the Glendook duodecimo editions.[22]

---

20 A list of such popular titles is printed in Craies on *Statute Law*, 5th ed., Appx. A.
21 A famous modern preamble is that to the [English] Matrimonial Causes Act, 1937.
22 See McN[eill], " Citation of Scots Statutes," 1959 S.L.T.(News) 112.

Statutes of the British and United Kingdom Parliaments prior to 1963 are cited by an antiquated and clumsy method which must, however, be understood. Each Act when it received the Royal Assent was given a number whereby it became a chapter of the session's legislation; the numbers ran consecutively within each session of Parliament; each session of Parliament was numbered according to the regnal year or years of the sovereign during which it sat. Confusion arose from the fact that the sovereign's regnal years did not coincide with calendar years, and sessions of Parliament did not coincide with either.[23]

It may be explained as follows: George VI came to the throne on December 11, 1936, so that the year till December 10, 1937, was 1 Geo. 6, and so on. The period from December 11, 1951, till his death on February 6, 1952, was therefore 16 Geo. 6. On his death Elizabeth II succeeded and the year to February 5, 1953, was accordingly 1 Eliz. 2, and so on.[24] Each of these regnal years, it will be noted, covers parts of two calendar years. Now the session of Parliament [25] normally commences with the state opening by the sovereign about November each year, and continues with occasional adjournments till prorogation the following autumn, but sessions may be longer or shorter than this and so may fall into one, or be spread over two, or even run into a third, regnal year.[26] A new session also starts when Parliament assembles after a General Election.

When the session started it bore the number of the sovereign's regnal year in which the opening took place, say, 3 Eliz. 2, and this continued till the anniversary of her accession when the session became 3 & 4 Eliz. 2; if the same session should have run past the next anniversary of the accession, it would have become 3, 4 & 5 Eliz. 2. The statutes numbered within that session accordingly started as, *e.g.*, 3 Eliz. 2, c. 15, and after the anniversary of the accession became renumbered retrospectively as 3 & 4 Eliz. 2, c. 15. It was, however, possible, if a parliamentary session

---

[23] See further Plucknett, " Legal Chronology " in *Handbook of Dates for Students of English History* (ed. Cheney: Royal Hist. Socy. 1945).

[24] A table of regnal years is printed in Sweet & Maxwell's *Where to Look for Your Law.*

[25] A session is the period between the opening of Parliament by the Queen and its prorogation (which ends the session, but not the Parliament) or dissolution (which ends the life of that Parliament and requires a General Election). During a session Parliament may adjourn, and normally does so over Christmas, Easter and the summer: adjournment does not end the session. On prorogation and dissolution (but not on adjournment) all Bills in progress lapse and must be reintroduced in the next session and debated afresh.

[26] Thus the parliamentary session 1948–49 extended into three regnal years and the citation is 12, 13 & 14 Geo. 6, though prints of Acts issued at the start, when it was not certain that the session would extend into the second regnal year, would originally be numbered 12 Geo. 6, and later, but before it was known that the session would extend into the third regnal year, would be renumbered 12 & 13 Geo. 6, and only finally get their definitive numbering. This was followed by a shorter session in 1950 which all fell within one regnal year and is consequently cited as 14 Geo. 6. The next session (1950–51) was 14 & 15 Geo. 6.

was held wholly within one regnal year (as in 1950) and another session started in the same regnal year and carried on into the next, to have two *different* statutes of the same calendar year (1950), which are cited, *e.g.*, 14 Geo. 6, c. 3, and 14 & 15 Geo. 6, c. 3.[27] It also follows from this system that the attribution to a statute of a short title, *e.g.*, the ―― Act, 1938, does not give a certain indication of which volume of statutes the particular Act may be found in; it might be in the 1937–38 volume or the 1938–39 volume.[28] Till 1940 volumes contained the Acts of the parliamentary session, but since 1939 they contain those of the calendar year.

Commencing in 1963 United Kingdom statutes are cited by the calendar year and chapter serial number of that year, *e.g.*, 1963, c. 15.[29]

It should also be noted that public general statutes are numbered in arabic numbers, *e.g.*, c. 19, local Acts in small Roman numbers, *e.g.*, c. xxvi, and personal Acts by italicised arabic numbers, *e.g.*, c. *53*.[30] The numbering of statutes as chapters arose, at least in England, from the fact that at one time all the Acts passed in one session were called a " statute," and the chapters were on distinct topics, but the word " statute " has now for long been used to denote a separate Act and not a collection of Acts, but it is still technically called a chapter.[31]

Statutes are divided into sections, subsections and paragraphs; thus the Companies Act, 1948, s. 10 (2) (*a*) (ii), means sub-paragraph (ii) of paragraph (*a*) of subsection (2) of section 10 of the Act. The correct mode of citing the various divisions and subdivisions of legislative instruments should also be noticed. It is as follows:

Bill (before Parliament); clause; subsection; paragraph.

Act of Parliament; section; subsection; paragraph.

Schedule to Act; paragraph; sub-paragraph.

Order in Council; article; paragraph; sub-paragraph.

Regulations; regulation; paragraph; sub-paragraph.

Rules; rule; paragraph; sub-paragraph.

Commencement

Since 1793 it has been the rule that an Act comes into force on the date on which it receives the Royal Assent and this date is on printed

---

27 See further Carr, " Citation of Statutes," in *Cambridge Legal Essays*, 72, and (1940) 56 L.Q.R. 460.

28 Take the case of the Finance Act, 1955 (3 & 4 Eliz. 2, c. 15); the Finance (No. 2) Act, 1955 (4 Eliz. 2, c. 17); and the Finance Act, 1956 (4 & 5 Eliz. 2, c. 54). Despite the dates the latter two belong to the same parliamentary session and the former of them was later renumbered as 4 & 5 Eliz. 2, c. 17.

29 Acts of Parliament Numbering and Citation Act, 1962.

30 For examples, see p. 272, *supra*, note 13.

31 The lengthy Income Tax Act, 1952 (15 & 16 Geo. 6 & 1 Eliz. 2, c. 10), is divided into 26 parts, each containing several chapters. This is analogous to the division of a textbook into parts and chapters and is a different and modern use of the term in the statutory connection.

copies set on the first page, immediately below the long title. Hence the phrase " the passing of this Act " means the date of the Royal Assent and not any date fixed by the Act at which it or parts of it are to come into operation.[32] But modern Acts commonly provide for the Act or parts of it coming into force on a specified date, or provide that a particular Minister of the Crown or other person may, by statutory instrument, bring the Act into force on a date selected by him, usually called " the appointed day," and may provide for his bringing different parts of the Act into force on different dates. Hence a statute may have been passed and yet not be, or be only in part, in force, and further research is frequently necessary to discover whether, and what parts of, an Act have been brought into force. Once passed, however, it continues in force, whether or not it has been brought into operation in whole or in part, until repealed.

Application

A statute passed by the United Kingdom Parliament prima facie applies to the whole of the United Kingdom. If it is intended not to apply to Scotland this is frequently expressly stated, usually at the end of the Act. If it is intended to apply to Scotland only, this is stated in the Act and the word (Scotland) is included in the title.[33] If parts only of an Act are intended to apply to Scotland this should be stated expressly in an " application to Scotland " section. But too frequently such matter is left in doubt and an Act may be held not to be applicable to Scotland if it is expressed as an amendment of a statute from which Scotland was expressly excluded,[34] or if expressed in technical terms of English law without any mention of their Scottish counterparts.[35] Statutes applicable to the United Kingdom as a whole are usually drafted with English conditions in view and in the terminology of English law, but with an " application to Scotland " section which provides that, in the application of the Act to Scotland, particular Scottish terms are to be read for the English terms used in the body of the Act. This is a clumsy expedient since one legal system can never be translated to suit other conditions in this way and the technical terms of one system are never the exact equivalents of those of the other. The only justification is that it saves parliamentary time, but it is productive of much inconvenience when seeking to read and understand the Act under Scottish conditions.

---

[32] *Tomlinson* v. *Bullock* (1878) 4 Q.B.D. 230; *R.* v. *Weston* [1910] 1 K.B. 17.

[33] *Cf.* the National Health Service Act, 1946 [England and Wales], and the National Health Service (Scotland) Act, 1947.

[34] *Westminster Fire Office* v. *Glasgow Provident Investment Socy.* (1888) 15 R.(H.L.) 89, 94; *Levy* v. *Jackson* (1903) 5 F. 1170; *Bell* v. *Mitchell* (1905) 8 F.(J.) 15.

[35] *Scottish Drug Depot* v. *Fraser* (1905) 7 F. 646. But see *Perth Water Commrs.* v. *McDonald* (1879) 6 R. 1050; *Dunlop* v. *Goudie* (1895) 22 R.(J.) 34.

Amendment

Any statute, once passed by Parliament, may be amended or altered in any respect and to any extent by any later statute, and the amendments may in turn be amended or repealed. Hence some Acts have accumulated a great accretion of subsequent changes, the tracing of which may be a matter of difficulty. Amendment may be express, as where a later statute provides that some word or passage or section of a prior Act is to be extended or limited or modified in a stated respect, or that some new words or sections are to be added, or to be substituted for something in the original Act; or amendment may be implied from the occurrence in later legislation of a provision which is in some respect inconsistent with an existing statutory provision and which must take effect instead, as it has to be presumed to represent the later view of the legislature on the matter in issue.[36] All statutory provisions on one topic must be considered together and read as one so that in case of inconsistency the later must have effect and the earlier must give way.

Repeal

A statute, or any part thereof, may be repealed by any subsequent statute. The effect of repeal is complete obliteration of the statute or part affected and it must be considered as if it had never been, except so far as concerns proceedings begun and carried through whilst it was the existing law.[37] A statute may be repealed as regards England and Wales, and remain in force as regards Scotland, or conversely.[38] If a repealing Act or section is itself later repealed the previously repealed statute or section is not thereby revived unless there are express words reviving it.[39] Unrepealed statute-law and case-law is, of course, not affected by the subsequent repeal of a statute which had itself repealed only other parts of the statute-law. Similarly if a principle of common law is altered or abrogated, a repeal of the Act affecting it does not revive the former principle unless a contrary intention appears.[40] Repeal does not, however, affect the validity of anything done under the repealed Act while it was in force.[41] In some cases the effect of a repeal is consequently to produce some doubt as to what the surviving law really is.

Express repeal is effected by a definite statement in a statute that particular prior statutory provisions, frequently listed in a schedule, are

[36] *Mount* v. *Taylor* (1868) L.R. 3 C.P. 645.
[37] *Kay* v. *Goodwin* (1830) 6 Bing. 576, 582; Interpretation Act, 1889, s. 38 (2).
[38] Thus the Sexual Offences Act, 1956 (applicable to England only) repealed the Criminal Law Amendment Act, 1885, but left it in force in Scotland.
[39] Interpretation Act, 1889, s. 11 (1). For an example of revival see Trade Disputes and Trade Unions Act, 1946, s. 1, repealing Trade Disputes and Trade Unions Act, 1927, reviving "every enactment and rule of law amended or otherwise affected by that Act . . . as if the Act of 1927 had not been passed."
[40] *Ibid.*, s. 38 (2).   [41] *Ibid.*, s. 38 (2) (*b*).

repealed. To ascertain whether any statute or section has been expressly repealed reference must be made to the *Chronological Table to the Statutes*, the *Index to the Statutes in Force*, to the Table showing the Effect of the Year's Legislation appended to each annual volume of statutes, and to the Statute Citator in *Current Law*. The *Statutes Revised* print statutes with the omission of sections repealed by later legislation down to the end of 1948. A great deal of obsolete law is also periodically expunged by Statute Law Revision Acts which effect wholesale repeal of spent and obsolete legislation which has hitherto escaped express repeal.

Implied repeal is effected when a later Act is so plainly repugnant to and contradictory of an earlier one that the two cannot stand together, in which case the earlier gives way and the later rules.[42] It may be difficult in particular cases to say whether a later provision is consistent with an earlier, or so inconsistent as to take precedence over the earlier. The court is, however, loth to imply a repeal in this way.[43] So, too, a special Act is not repealed by a general Act unless there is some express reference to the previous legislation or unless there is a necessary inconsistency in the two Acts standing together.[44]

Desuetude

In Scotland prior to 1707 the doctrine of desuetude was accepted, whereby non-use for a substantial time was held to cancel an Act and imply repeal thereof. It applies now only to pre-1707 Scots Acts. The doctrine required not merely antiquity of the Act, but that there should be no recent instance known in which the Act had been given effect to, that it should have been long disregarded in practice, or that its provisions were out of line with modern conditions.[45] A large number of obsolete Scots Acts were repealed in 1906 [46] and there is a presumption, which is, however, rebuttable, that any Scots Act left in force thereby is still in observance and not in desuetude.[47]

The modern rule is that post-1707 legislation cannot be abrogated by non-use or even practice to the contrary and there is probably no authority for the application of desuetude to English or United Kingdom statutes of any period.[48]

---

[42] *Kutner* v. *Phillips* [1891] 2 Q.B. 267, 272; *Lang* v. *Munro* (1892) 19 R.(J.) 53; *Ross* v. *Ross* (1894) 22 R. 174.

[43] *Bain* v. *Mackay* (1875) 2 R.(J.) 32; *Dobbs* v. *Grand Junction Waterworks Co.* (1882) 9 Q.B.D. 151.

[44] *Aberdeen Suburban Tramways Co.* v. *Aberdeen Magistrates*, 1927 S.C. 683, 689.

[45] *McAra* v. *Magistrates of Edinburgh*, 1913 S.C. 1059; *Brown* v. *Magistrates of Edinburgh*, 1931 S.L.T. 456.

[46] Statute Law Revision (Scotland) Act, 1906.

[47] See generally Smith, " Desuetude " (1895) 7 J.R. 173; Philip, " Some Reflections on Desuetude " (1931) 43 J.R. 260.

[48] *See* Winfield, *Chief Sources of English Legal History*, 78–81.

Duration

Apart from the few cases to which desuetude applies the rule is accordingly that a statute endures with full force and effect, even though it be not applied or enforced, until it is repealed. Some statutes, however, are passed for a limited period only and lapse automatically at the end of that period, though each year some such Acts are continued in life for a further period by an Expiring Laws Continuance Act. Some Acts again may be expressed to lapse on a specified future date unless previously renewed, while others may be expressed to continue in force until the occasion which has given rise to them is declared to be at an end by Order in Council. Even of the permanent Acts a few, such as those conferring some privilege or immunity, can be repealed subsequently by a Statute Law Revision Act as being " spent."

Prerogative Legislation

Apart from legislation passed by Parliament with the Royal Assent, the Crown still retains a residual power in a limited class of cases of issuing Orders in Council, Letters Patent or Proclamations in the exercise of the royal prerogative.[49] At least in peacetime these powers are not of great importance, since they relate chiefly to the constitutions of overseas territories of the British Commonwealth, appeals to the Judicial Committee of the Privy Council, and matters of colonial currency. The power is also used in wartime to regulate trade, commerce, reprisals and contraband. Such orders are not numerous, nor are they an important source of law within the United Kingdom, but their existence remains possible.

Subordinate or Delegated Legislation

Subordinate legislation [50] consists of the body of rules, orders, regulations, by-laws proceeding from any body other than, and usually lower than, Parliament, such as a Minister of the Crown or a Government Department, to which Parliament has delegated power to issue such subordinate legislation, and which in the exercise of this power remains subject to the control of Parliament. Difficult questions may arise whether certain instructions issued by a Minister or Department of State are truly legislative, *i.e.*, laying down general rules, or executive, *i.e.*, dealing with a particular case, applying law rather than making it. The purpose

---

[49] For procedure see Morrison, " The Privy Council Today " (1948) 2 Parliamentary Affairs, 10. Such prerogative Orders in Council must be distinguished from Orders in Council which are used under the delegated legislative power contained in a statute, as a means of delegated legislation. These latter are discussed in the next paragraph.

[50] On the development of the practice of delegating a rule-making power see Report of the Committee on Ministers' Powers (Cmd. 4060), 13–15; Allen, *Law and Orders*, Chap. 2; Sieghart, *Government by Decree*, Part I; Craies, *Statute Law*, 5th ed., 268.

of subordinate legislation is to amplify parliamentary legislation, to provide for matters of detail, and so give effect in particulars to the general purpose and policy of the Act. The majority of the items of delegated legislation are required to be registered, numbered and published, formerly under the Rules Publication Act, 1893, and now under the Statutory Instruments Act, 1946. Power conferred on a Department is deemed to have been conferred on the Minister of the Crown in charge of the Department. Delegated legislation, if validly made and within the powers of the delegating Act, has the same force and effect as if it were contained in the Act itself. The chief forms of subordinate legislation are:

(1) *Orders in Council.* Some Orders in Council, as has been mentioned, are issued by the Queen in Council in the exercise of the prerogative power, but Parliament also frequently by statute authorises Her Majesty in Council to make Orders in Council and Orders of this class are properly subordinate legislation. Orders of this latter class are usually drafted in one or other of the Government Departments and while the Order in Council is usually reserved for the most important and national purposes, there is no strict rule as to whether the subordinate rule-making function is to be exercised by Order in Council or by other means.[51] It depends on how the empowering provision in the parent Act directs that the delegated legislative power is to be exercised.

(2) *Ministerial or departmental rules, orders and instruments.* This is the most numerous and common kind of delegated legislation, and power to make rules, orders and instruments is regularly conferred by statute on Ministers or Departments of the Crown. Prior to 1948 instances of such legislation were variously called rules, regulations and orders, but by virtue of the Statutory Instruments Act, 1946, power conferred on a Minister or Department is now exercisable by statutory instrument and such departmental legislation after 1947 is accordingly called Statutory Instruments.[52] Statutory instruments may relate to any topic at all, as may be authorised by the Act which delegates the legislative power, but subjects commonly covered by statutory instruments are matters of detail, specific requirements for certain purposes of the Act, and lists of items, goods or commodities

[51] Thus the power of making Defence Regulations under the Emergency Powers (Defence) Acts of 1939 and 1940 was to be exercised by Order in Council.
[52] Statutory Instruments are defined by the Statutory Instruments Regulations, 1947, in a very clumsy and obscure fashion.

affected for the time being by statutory provisions.[53] Thus a Minister may be empowered to prescribe by statutory instrument which places or categories of items are affected by some requirement or prohibition in the Act, and he may by further statutory instrument add to or reduce the list of places or categories, or substitute a new list, without the need for further legislation by Parliament.

(3) *Local Authority By-laws.* Power to make by-laws for their own particular area is conferred on local authorities such as town and county councils by general legislation, such as the Local Government (Scotland) Act, 1947,[54] and the Public Health Acts, and also by special private Acts obtained by particular local authorities. A municipal by-law has been defined judicially [55] as " an ordinance affecting the public or some portion of the public imposed by some authority clothed with statutory powers ordering something to be done or not to be done and accompanied by some sanction or penalty for its non-observance. Further, it involves this consequence, that if validly made it has the force of law within the sphere of its legitimate operation." By-laws can have force only within the area of the local authority in question and different local authorities may have different powers and may make different by-laws in the exercise thereof.

(4) *Public Corporations' Regulations.* Public corporations, such as the British Railways Board, are empowered by the Acts constituting them to make by-laws and other regulations regulating the performance of their functions and the rights and duties of the public when dealing with the corporation, and these by-laws, if validly made, similarly have the force of law in the places and circumstances and over the persons to which they apply.

(5) *Acts of Sederunt and Rules Committees' Rules.* Power is conferred by various statutes on various judicial committees to make rules for procedure in court. This power is exercised in the Court of Session and Sheriff Court by the passing of an Act of Sederunt,[56]

---

[53] The Index to the Statutes lists rule-making powers contained in the legislation on various subjects. The Statute Citator of *Current Law* also indicates whether regulations have been made under any statutory powers.

[54] s. 300 gives a general power to town and county councils to make by-laws for the good rule and government of the council's area of authority. Ss. 301–303 provide a code of procedure for making by-laws, and authorise penalties for infringement of them.

[55] *Kruse* v. *Johnson* [1898] 2 Q.B. 91, 94.

[56] The Rules Council (Court of Session) is authorised by the Administration of Justice (Scotland) Act, 1933, s. 18, and it recommends to the court changes in the Rules of Court. The power of the court to make Acts of Sederunt was conferred at the foundation of the court (Act 1532, c. 36) but modern Acts of Sederunt are usually passed under specific authority of some particular statute.

which is an ordinance made by the court for the regulation of judicial procedure under powers conferred on the court at its foundation and repeatedly recognised by statutes since. The High Court of Justiciary similarly has powers conferred on it by various statutes to make by Act of Adjournal rules regulating procedure in that and the inferior criminal courts. Similarly in England procedure is regulated by the Rules of the Supreme Court made under the authority of the Judicature Acts. These rules again have the force of law in the circumstances to which they apply. Their practical importance is great, since the details of litigation and court procedure are regulated by them more than by Acts of Parliament.

(6) *Autonomous Bodies' Rules.* Autonomous bodies such as professional associations, trade unions, societies and clubs may issue rules which bind their members, but these rules are binding on the individual only by agreement and by reason of his contractual membership of the body in question. A person who joins submits himself to the rules of that body by the contract of membership. Such rules are accordingly not legislation at all and have no force or effect on individuals who are not members.

Publication of Subordinate Legislation

The law on this matter is in a confused and unsatisfactory state. The substance of it can now [57] be stated as follows:

(1) If in an Act passed *before 1948* (a) power to *make* subordinate legislation is conferred on a rule-making authority,[58] or (b) power to *confirm or approve* subordinate legislation is conferred on a rule-making authority to be exercised by Order in Council or Order, or (c) power to *confirm or approve* subordinate legislation is conferred on a rule-making authority, and that legislation has to be laid before Parliament or the House of Commons, *and* the power is exercised *after 1947* in a document which is legislative rather than executive in character, then the document is a statutory instrument.[59]

(2) If in an Act passed *after 1947*, power to *make, confirm or approve* subordinate legislation is conferred on a rule-making authority, which may be exercised by Order in Council or statutory instrument, and the document is either legislative or executive in character, then the document is a statutory instrument.[60]

---

[57] Prior to 1948 the law depended on the now repealed Rules Publication Act, 1893.

[58] Defined by s. 4 of the Rules Publication Act, 1893, as including every authority authorised to make statutory rules.

[59] Statutory Instruments Act, 1946, s. 1 (2), as amplified by Statutory Instruments Regulations, 1947, reg. 2 (1) and Statutory Instruments (Confirmatory Powers) Order, 1947.   [60] Statutory Instruments Act, 1946, s. 1 (1).

Statutory instruments as so defined [61] must be sent to the Queen's Printer, numbered, and, unless otherwise provided by statute or regulations made under the Act of 1946, copies must be printed and put on sale to the public. But, however legislative in character a document issued under authority of a post-1947 Act may be, if the power of issue is not expressed to be exercisable by Order in Council or by statutory instrument, the document is not a statutory instrument within the meaning of the Act or liable to be published as such.

Publication of other Subordinate Legislation

The foregoing arrangements for publication of statutory instruments clearly do not cover all categories of subordinate legislation. Many schemes and orders emanating from Ministers or other authorities are executive rather than legislative and many circulars and instructions issued are intended as guidance and not as binding or laying down general rules of law. Such subordinate legislation other than statutory instruments may be published under particular statutory requirements or by custom and practice, but it may not, and in at least some cases ministerial circulars or letters may have legislative force yet need not be published. [62]

Amendment and Repeal of Subordinate Legislation

A power in a statute to make subordinate legislation includes, unless the contrary intention is apparent in the Act, a power to rescind, revoke, amend or vary the subordinate legislation, and the latter power is exercisable in the same manner as the original power. [63] A specific power of revocation or amendment is usually conferred by empowering statutes.

Subordinate legislation normally remains in force indefinitely until revoked or superseded. If the empowering Act is repealed the delegated legislation will fall with it but rules may be expressly saved by the repealing Act and continued in force under it, with the same force and effect as under the former Act.

Sub-delegated Legislation

In the normal case legislation effected by Parliament authorises subordinate legislation by its delegate only. But in some cases sub-delegation arises where the " parent " Act is very general, giving rise to

[61] The definitions are constructed from the Statutory Instruments Act, 1946, and the Statutory Instruments Regulations, 1947, made thereunder. They came into force on January 1, 1948. See further Griffith and Street, *Principles of Administrative Law*, 44–59; Allen, *Law and Orders*, 2nd ed., 118–137; Craies, *Statute Law*, 5th ed., 275–276.

[62] *Blackpool Corpn.* v. *Locker* [1948] 1 K.B. 349; *Patchett* v. *Leathem* (1948) 65 T.L.R. 69. See de Smith " Subdelegation and Circulars " (1949) 12 M.L.R. 37.

[63] Interpretation Act, 1889, s. 32 (3).

general delegated legislation and more specific sub-delegated legislation. Thus under the Emergency Powers (Defence) Act, 1939, passed at the outbreak of war, Defence Regulations were made; under these Regulations orders were issued; under the orders directions appeared and these in turn authorised the issue of licences in particular and specific cases, so that there were five levels in the hierarchy of legislation. In consequence while the immediate authority for a piece of subordinate legislation is normally an Act of Parliament it may be found in something which is itself an exercise of delegated power, such as the Regulations made under an Act.

It is a disputed question whether documents containing sub-delegated legislation are statutory instruments or not. The practice seems to have been to publish some sub-delegated legislation as statutory instruments [64] though the view has been expressed that the 1946 Act does not apply to sub-delegated legislation.[65]

A question which may also arise in a particular case is whether the delegate of Parliament has been authorised to sub-delegate all or any part of his subordinate legislative powers. It probably depends in each case on the generality of the main statute and the terms in which the delegates' powers are defined as against which may be adduced the fundamental common-law maxim *delegatus non potest delegare*.[66] The presumption is accordingly against any power to delegate further a delegated legislative power.

Administrative Quasi-legislation

In addition to these recognised forms of legislation and subordinate legislation, various administrative Departments sometimes issue notices, circulars, practice notes and other literature which sometimes state the way in which the Department concerned proposes to apply or interpret certain statutes or orders or as to certain arrangements made as to the operation of various matters of law. Some such statements may be of general application and affect in material degree the working of the law,[67] but they are not strictly legislative at all and would be unenforceable in the courts.[68] Yet, without having any legal force, these

[64] The orders made under the Defence Regulations, which were made under the Emergency Powers (Defence) Act, 1939, were so published.
[65] *Blackpool Corporation* v. *Locker* [1948] 1 K.B. 349, 369, *per* Scott L.J. Contrary views have been expressed: *Lewisham B.C.* v. *Roberts* [1949] 2 K.B. 608; see also *Falmouth Boat Construction Co.* v. *Howell* [1950] 2 K.B. 16, 25; *Simms Motor Units, Ltd.* v. *Minister of Labour* [1946] 2 All E.R. 201, 204.
[66] See further Griffith and Street, *Principles of Administrative Law*, 63–69; Willis, " Delegatus non potest delegare " (1943) 21 Can.Bar Rev. 257; Garner, " Delegation of Administrative Discretion " (1949) 27 *Public Administration*, 115.
[67] Thus the Inland Revenue periodically announce " concessions," that some item or other will not be counted or valued at its full value for taxation purposes.
[68] See further Megarry, " Administrative Quasi-Legislation " (1944) 60 L.Q.R. 125, 218; Allen, *Law and Orders*, 2nd ed., 221.

modifications may in practice have an important effect, an effect not really distinguishable from that of delegated legislation.

Construction or Interpretation of Legislation

The process of construction [69] or interpretation is that whereby a legal adviser or a court seeks to discover, in a particular factual context, whether a given statutory provision is applicable to the set of facts, and, if so, what meaning and effect has to be given to it. It is in essence the problem of finding the meaning of certain statutory expressions in the context of certain circumstances. This is a problem which arises very frequently, raises many and difficult issues, and is one of the most thorny with which any adviser or court can be faced. It is always a question of law, not of fact, to be decided by the court not the jury, to be decided after legal argument, not on evidence.[70] It arises frequently, not only in contentious proceedings in court, but in the course of advising or deciding on the legality or competency of some projected course of action, and in seeking to predict the legal consequences of certain action, past or proposed. A considerable volume of principles of construction, presumptions and guides has grown up in practice and much depends on which is followed, since the application of different guides may produce diametrically opposite consequences.[71] As has been observed : " The English language is not an instrument of mathematical precision. Our literature would be much poorer if it were. This is where the draftsmen of Acts of Parliament have often been unfairly criticised. A judge, believing himself to be fettered by the supposed rule that he must look to the language and nothing else, laments that the draftsmen have not provided for this or that, or have been guilty of some or other ambiguity. It would certainly save the judges trouble if Acts of Parliament were drafted with divine prescience and perfect clarity. In the absence of it, when a defect appears a judge cannot simply fold his hands and blame the draftsman. He must set to work on the constructive task of finding the intention of Parliament, and he must do this not only from the language of the statute, but also from a consideration of the social conditions which gave rise to it and of the mischief which it was passed to remedy and then he must supplement the written word so as to give force and life

---

[69] From the verb " construe," not from " construct."
[70] *Mason* v. *Bibby* (1864) 2 H. & C. 881.
[71] The principal guides are Craies' treatise on *Statute Law* (5th ed., 1952); Maxwell on *The Interpretation of Statutes* (11th ed., 1961) and Odgers, *The Construction of Deeds and Statutes* (4th ed., 1956). See also Willis, " Statute Interpretation in a Nutshell " (1938) 16 Can.Bar Rev. 1; Davies, " Interpretation of Statutes in the Light of Their Policy by the English Courts " (1935) 35 Col.L.R. 519; Friedmann, " Statute Law and its Interpretation in the Modern State " (1948) 26 Can.Bar Rev. 1277.

to the intention of the legislature." [72]   It has to be remembered that
Parliament in enacting any provision, or a Department or local authority
in enacting subordinate legislation, cannot foresee every contingency
or set of circumstances which may arise, and may never have considered
at all the kind of case which has arisen, so that it is not surprising that
the language used seldom fits every possible case. Indeed the perversity
of circumstances is such that, as soon as a carefully phrased piece of
legislation comes into force, a case seems to arise which the words do
not seem particularly apt to cover. Thus it is an offence to be in charge
of a vehicle while under the influence of drink.[73] Do the words " in charge
of" cover a drunken person put in the back seat of his car in a car-park,
the car having been immobilised,[74] a drunken person in the front passenger
seat while another person, who held only an expired provisional licence,
had started the engine,[75] a drunken person in the driving seat of a station-
ary car but who had arranged for another person to drive it to that person's
garage,[76] or a drunken person sitting beside a "learner" who was driving?[77]

The two Approaches to Interpretation
There are two general approaches or attitudes discernible in statutory
interpretation, the one favouring a literal, strict or narrow construction,
and the other a more liberal or broader construction. The choice
between them is a matter for the individual judge and much depends
on his general attitude to the law and legal development, and more
particularly on his subjective view of the case and the Act and on
whether he thinks that the statute should cover the circumstances of
the case before him or not. This renders prediction of the court's
attitude to a particular provision difficult, may give rise to inconsistencies
between similar cases or similar statutory provisions, and has given
rise to accusations of judicial bias against certain kinds of legislation,
as of giving an unduly narrow construction to some social welfare
legislation. These criticisms seem quite unjustified, but the analysis
of this belongs to jurisprudence, and need not be pursued further here.

The Literal Approach
The literal approach stresses the need for close and careful scrutiny
of the actual words enacted by the legislature and has little regard for
anything but the relevant words or phrases, the context and any other
relevant provision of the Act itself. The general effect of adopting this

[72] *Seaford Court Estates, Ltd.* v. *Asher* [1949] 2 K.B. 481, 499, *per* Denning L.J.,
criticised on appeal ([1950] A.C. 508, 530) as stated much too widely.
[73] Road Traffic Act, 1960, s. 6 (2) (formerly Road Traffic Act, 1930, s. 15).
[74] *Dean* v. *Wishart*, 1952 J.C. 9.
[75] *Winter* v. *Morrison*, 1954 J.C. 7.
[76] *Macdonald* v. *Kubirdas*, 1955 S.L.T.(Sh.Ct.) 50.
[77] *Clark* v. *Clark*, 1950 S.L.T.(Sh.Ct.) 68.

approach is that an Act will not be held to affect, or to be intended to have affected, anything not dealt with expressly or by clear implication even if the result of this attitude may be obviously absurd or inconsistent with the common-sense idea of what Parliament meant to do.[78] This approach is frequently buttressed with such arguments as that if Parliament had meant to cover this case it could and should have said so, that it is not for the courts to legislate or to usurp the function of Parliament or to speculate what Parliament might have intended and to write this into the Act. For example, at common law a wife was entitled to exact a share of her husband's moveable estate, called *jus relictae*, when he died or she divorced him. The Married Women's Property (Scotland) Act, 1881, gave a husband a corresponding right of *jus relicti*, but it was held exigible only on death, not on divorce, because the Act says "the husband of any woman who may *die*," [79] and the court declined to apply the fiction that divorce had the same effect as death in view of the literal terms of the Act, though this was commonly quoted as the basis for the wife's claim. The result is a legal anomaly; it is likely that Parliament had merely overlooked the case of divorce and did not intend to exclude it.

The Liberal Approach

The liberal approach lays stress on the need for the courts to try to appreciate the overriding intention of the legislation, the general policy behind the Act, and the need to further remedies and not to take refuge in pettifogging verbal objections. The discovery of the general purpose and intention of legislation is, however, difficult and subject to two serious handicaps. The court can most easily and readily discover Parliament's intention from what Parliament has enacted, that is, from an examination of the literal form and wording of the enactment, and, secondly, the court is not at liberty to read into a statute phrases or provisions which are quite clearly not there, however much the general policy might seem to render them desirable. Thus in *Taff Vale Ry.* v. *A.S.R.S.*,[80] the House of Lords examined the policy of successive Trade Union Acts as a means of deciding that Parliament must have meant that trade unions could be sued in their registered names for tort.

The desire to give effect to the general policy expressed in literal terms in the Act underlies what is sometimes called " the golden rule " of statutory interpretation. " The only rule for the construction of Acts of Parliament is that they should be construed according to the intent of the Parliament which passed them. If the words of the statute

[78] *Glasgow Court House Commrs.* v. *Lanarkshire C.C.* (1900) 3 F. 103.
[79] *Eddington* v. *Robertson* (1895) 22 R. 430.
[80] [1901] A.C. 426.

are in themselves precise and unambiguous, then no more can be necessary than to expound these words in their natural and ordinary sense. The words themselves alone do in such case best declare the intention of the lawgiver." [81] " It is a very useful rule in the construction of a statute to adhere to the ordinary meaning of the words used, and to the grammatical construction, unless that is at variance with the intention of the legislature to be collected from the statute itself or leads to any manifest absurdity or repugnance, in which case the language may be varied or modified so as to avoid such inconvenience, but no further." [82] It remains of course difficult in many cases to say what the intention of Parliament seems to have been, and it may well be a matter of opinion whether the ordinary meaning does or does not lead to absurdity or repugnance, so that this rule does not take the discussion much further.

Interpretation Act

Some guidance is given by the Interpretation Act, 1889,[83] which assigns meanings to a number of words commonly found in statutes and provides, for example, that words importing the masculine shall include the feminine, that words in the singular shall include the plural and vice versa, that " person " includes any body of persons corporate or unincorporate, and so on. These definitions, however, may always have to give way to contrary indications in the context of a particular Act, and this Act is accordingly far from providing a comprehensive code of interpretation. Its only real value is in fact to abbreviate statutes by permitting the omission of such phrases as " he or she," " person or persons or body of persons."

Interpretation Sections

In many modern Acts there is, usually near the end, an interpretation section which gives definitions of certain words used in the Act and provides that they shall have in the Act the particular meaning thereby assigned to them, which may be wider or narrower than the ordinary dictionary meaning of the word.[84] The section may provide that certain words shall " mean " something, which explains, defines and limits the words used, or it may provide that certain words shall " include " or " exclude " particular cases, in which case the definition is extensive or restrictive of the usual meaning. The meanings thus statutorily assigned

[81] *Sussex Peerage Case* (1844) 11 Cl. & F. 85, 143, *per* Tindal C.J.
[82] *Becke* v. *Smith* (1836) 2 M. & W. 191, 195, *per* Parke B. *Cf. Caledonian Ry.* v. *N.B. Ry.* (1881) 8 R.(H.L.) 23; *Campbell's Trs.* v. *O'Neill,* 1911 S.C. 188.
[83] Printed as an appendix to Craies' *Statute Law,* and to Maxwell, *Interpretation of Statutes.* The whole Act should be read carefully.
[84] For these see the *Index to Statutory Definitions,* and Stroud's *Judicial Dictionary.*

to particular words hold for that Act only, though subsequent legislation may refer back to that definition by providing in another context that a word shall bear the meaning assigned to it in a specified prior Act. An interpretation section which extends the meaning of a word does not thereby abolish the ordinary, popular and natural sense of the word where that is properly applicable but merely enables the word, when there is nothing in the context or subject-matter to the contrary, to be applied to some things to which it would not ordinarily be applicable.[85] Moreover the interpretation section is not to be taken as defining the terms mentioned in all circumstances but only as defining what may be comprehended by the term where the circumstances require that it should be so comprehended.[86]

Subsidiary Principles

It is apparent that courts get little assistance in the task of interpretation from the Interpretation Act and any interpretation section in the Act under consideration and that they have to draw a meaning out of the statutory passage in the circumstances which have given rise to the controversy primarily by reference to the words enacted and also to what the court or judge thinks, on a consideration of the whole legislation in issue, Parliament intended. Sometimes one factor rather than the other weighs more with the court. But numerous subsidiary principles have been developed to assist the court in its scrutiny of the language employed.

In the first place the usual dictionary meaning of a word is taken, as at the time when the statute was passed, and if the word has a technical connotation the usual technical meaning is taken. Parliament is presumed to be familiar with, and to use, the ordinary and, if applicable, usual technical meanings of words.[87] Any unusual or restricted or extended sense of a word calls prima facie for a mention in the interpretation section. Words which are permissive or empowering may be shown in particular circumstances to be really imperative, and it has been said that prima facie where powers are conferred by statute for the public benefit they must be exercised.[88]

Secondly, the usual meaning is taken subject to the context in which the word is used, so as to attribute to the word or phrase a meaning consistent with the rest of the section and even of the whole Act or series of Acts on the subject.

[85] *Robinson* v. *Barton Eccles Local Board* (1883) 8 App.Cas. 798.
[86] *Meux* v. *Jacobs* (1875) L.R. 7 H.L. 481; *Strathern* v. *Padden*, 1926 J.C. 9.
[87] *Clerical Assurance Co.* v. *Carter* (1889) 22 Q.B.D. 444.
[88] *Walkinshaw* v. *Orr* (1860) 22 D. 627; *Julius* v. *Bishop of Oxford* (1880) 5 App.Cas. 214; *Black* v. *Glasgow Corpn.*, 1958 S.C. 260.

Reference to Context

The fact that a particular word or phrase has to be construed does not justify ignoring the verbal context in which the word is used and three principles have been recognised in this connection:

(a) *Noscitur a sociis,* that is, a vague word takes a shade of meaning from the accompanying words; thus in the context of " houses for public refreshment, resort and entertainment," the last word was held to be limited to physical and not mental gratification,[89] because that meaning, it was felt, agreed better with the earlier part of the phrase than the other or wider meaning which might have covered a theatrical or musical performance.

(b) *Expressio unius est exclusio alterius.* Under this the express mention of one thing or category and not of another similar or related thing or category tends to indicate the implied exclusion of the latter. But the exclusion of the other may be the result of inadvertence or accident, so that the principle cannot be rigidly applied,[90] and is indeed of very limited value.

(c) *Ejusdem generis.* Where several things or specific items are enumerated, all of the same kind or having some distinct characteristic in common, and this enumeration is followed by general words such as " or otherwise," " or other things," " or other person," it has to be presumed that the general words are limited to other things or items or persons having the same common characteristic or of the same kind or class or category as the items specifically mentioned.[91] It is clear accordingly that the rule has no application where the specific words have no common category or characteristics,[92] or if the concluding general words are so very general as to include every other case or, at least, the case under discussion, *e.g.,* " any other place *whatsoever.*" Thus in a provision that traffic signs should include " all signals, warning signposts, direction posts, signs or devices," it was held that " devices " must be *ejusdem generis* with the previous words and could not cover a painted white line.[93] A prohibition on " all houses and every other building whatever " did not extend to a low parapet wall and iron railing.[94] Before the rule can be applied, accordingly, one must be able to discover a *genus* common to all the specific words and also to

[89] *Muir* v. *Keay* (1875) L.R. 10 Q.B. 594.
[90] *Stevenson* v. *Hunter* (1903) 5 F. 761. *Cf. Dean* v. *Wiesengrund* [1955] 2 Q.B. 120.
[91] *Mortimer* v. *Samuel B. Allison, Ltd.,* 1959 S.C.(H.L.) 1.
[92] *e.g., Crichton Stuart* v. *Ogilvie,* 1914 S.C. 888.
[93] *Evans* v. *Cross* [1938] 1 K.B. 694.
[94] *Partick Police Commrs.* v. *G.W. Steam Laundry Co.* (1886) 13 R. 500; see also *Moss' Empires* v. *Glasgow Assessor,* 1917 S.C.(H.L.) 1.

assign a meaning to the concluding general words consistent with
their limitation to that same *genus*.

Reference to Whole Act

Interpretation must have regard, moreover, not merely to the
immediate verbal context, but to the whole of the Act in which the phrase
under construction appears, because regard to the whole Act may reveal
an underlying scheme or legislative purpose which helps to give a
meaning to a particular phrase. Sections of Acts frequently refer back
and forward to other sections and even without express reference one
interpretation of a word may be more consistent with another section of
the Act than is the alternative interpretation. Thus if one section provides
for notice being " given " and another for the notice being " served on
or left with " a person, it is apparent that written notice was contemplated and that this meaning will fit both sections while oral notice
would fit only the earlier section; one does not " serve " or " leave " an
oral notice with a person. Reference to the whole Act, or at least the
whole of that part of the Act, will therefore tend to give an interpretation
consistent with the rest of the Act. Moreover where there is a series of
Acts dealing with the same subject-matter they should be looked at as
a continuous code.[95]

Further indications of the appropriate shade of meaning to give to a
word may sometimes be gathered from one or more of two sets of
indications, which are distinguished as internal and external aids to
construction.

Internal Aids to Construction

Internal aids are those indications which may be drawn from the
statute under construction itself to assist in arriving at a true interpretation of its provisions.

   (a) *Title.* It is now accepted that the title is part of an Act and
       may legitimately be used to assist in interpreting the Act as a
       whole and in ascertaining its scope.[96] The short title cannot be
       used as an aid to construction.[97]

   (b) *Preamble.* This again is part of the Act and may be resorted
       to, to explain the meaning of an Act.[98] But a preamble cannot

[95] *Hamilton* v. *N.C.B.*, 1960 S.C.(H.L.) 1.
[96] *Fielden* v. *Morley Corpn.* [1899] 1 Ch. 1, 3; *Fenton* v. *Thorley* [1903] A.C. 443, 447;
     Millar & Lang v. *Macniven & Cameron* (1908) 16 S.L.T. 56; *Vacher* v. *London Socy.
     of Compositors* [1913] A.C. 107, 128; *Mags. of Buckie* v. *Dowager Countess of
     Seafield's Trs.*, 1928 S.C. 525.
[97] *Re Boaler* [1915] 1 K.B. 21.
[98] *L.C.C.* v. *Bermondsey Bioscope Co.* [1911] 1 K.B. 445, 451; *Vacher, supra*; *Ren-
     frewshire C.C.* v. *Orphan Homes of Scotland* (1898) 1 F. 186.

cut down or control or qualify a clear and unambiguous provision in the body of the Act.[99]

(c) *Headings.* Headings prefixed to groups of sections or parts of an Act may, like preambles, be taken as a guide but only for the purpose of explaining doubtful expressions or ambiguities in the body of the sections or part of the Act.[1]

(d) *Marginal Notes.* These are not part of a statute and the courts cannot look at them.[2]

(e) *Punctuation.* Modern statutes are punctuated, but punctuation is regarded not as forming part of the statute but rather as a kind of *contemporanea expositio*.[3] Sometimes it has been referred to,[4] but punctuation is not authoritative.

(f) *Schedules.* These are part of the Act and may be looked at to resolve ambiguities,[5] though mere forms contained in a schedule cannot limit or qualify words of enactment in the Act.

External Aids to Construction

External aids are those sources of information outside the Act under construction which may be sought to be invoked to assist interpretation. The principal external aids are:

(a) *Prior state of the law.* Parliament must be presumed to know the state of the law existing when the Act in question was passed, and the intention of the later legislation may sometimes be discovered by examination of the previous state of the law. This includes the previous common law, any prior Acts, and the known defects of the previous state of the law.[6] This is sometimes comprehensively called the parliamentary history of the Act. Only prior statutes *in pari materia* relating to the same subject-matter can be regarded, so closely related that they can fairly be said to form one system of legislation, and not other statutes or other statutes vaguely relating to kindred

---

[99] *Powell* v. *Kempton Park Racecourse Co.* [1899] A.C. 143, 157, 184; *Att.-Gen.* v. *Prince Ernest of Hanover* [1955] Ch. 440; [1957] A.C. 436.

[1] *Martins* v. *Fowler* [1926] A.C. 746, 750; *Buckie Magistrates* v. *Seafield's Trustees*, 1928 S.C. 525; *R.* v. *Surrey (N.E. Area) Assessment Committee* [1948] 1 K.B. 28, 32.

[2] *Nixon* v. *Att.-Gen.* [1930] 1 Ch. 566, 593.

[3] *Duke of Devonshire* v. *O'Connor* (1890) 24 Q.B.D. 468, 478; *I.R.C.* v. *Hinchy* [1960] A.C. 748.

[4] *Alexander* v. *Mackenzie*, 1947 J.C. 155.

[5] *Ellerman Lines* v. *Murray* [1931] A.C. 126; see also *Jacobs* v. *Hart* (1900) 2 F.(J.) 33.

[6] *Bank of England* v. *Vagliano* [1891] A.C. 107, 144; *Re Mayfair Property Co.* [1898] 2 Ch. 28, 35; *Eastman Photographic Co.* v. *Comptroller-General of Patents* [1898] A.C. 571, 575; *Macmillan* v. *Dent* [1907] 1 Ch. 107, 120; *Keates* v. *Lewis Merthyr Consolidated Collieries* [1911] A.C. 641, 642; *Avery* v. *N.E. Ry.* [1938] A.C. 606, 612, 617.

topics.[7] Reference to prior statutes is particularly appropriate in the cases of a group of Acts relating to one topic, such as housing or merchant shipping, where the legislation is practically a code in itself.[8] Even subsequent legislation *in pari materia* may be looked at in the same way.

(b) *Earlier statutes repealed and consolidated by statute under construction.* Prior statutes repealed but reproduced in substance in consolidated form may be looked at [9] and judicial decisions on a repealed statute are treated as applicable to substantially identical provisions in the repealing Act.[10] This is justifiable on the basis that consolidation and re-enactment are both designed to restate rather than to change the law. Earlier legislation is of much less value as an aid to construction if the later legislation is professedly amending or clearly makes extensive changes, since there is then no presumption that Parliament intended the earlier interpretations to be continued.

(c) *Subsequent Acts.* Subsequent legislation may be looked at in order to find the proper construction to be put on an earlier and ambiguous Act [11] since Parliament may in a later Act on the same subject-matter expressly give a meaning to what was doubtful in an earlier Act, or may, more commonly, do so by implication, as by making further provision which is consistent with or inconsistent with the construction of the earlier Act proposed by the court.

(d) *Cases.* Decided cases which construe the words of an Act of Parliament [12] establish principles and rules of law whereby its scope and effect may be interpreted.[13] This principle is not without its defects as some statutory provisions have been interpreted in many cases, and the task in a subsequent case may be more obscured by the quest for a meaning consistent with the earlier cases than helped by them. But it is only if the actual words under construction have been previously construed in the same or a closely analogous statute that there

---

7 *Sharp* v. *Morrison*, 1922 S.L.T. 272.

8 *Lord Advocate* v. *Sprot's Trustees* (1901) 3 F. 440.

9 Thus in interpreting the Companies Act, 1948, reference may be made in many cases to decisions on similar sections of the 1929, 1908 and earlier Companies Acts.

10 *Smith* v. *Baker* [1891] A.C. 325; *Boyle* v. *Wilson* [1907] A.C. 45, *sub nom. Walsh* v. *Pollokshaws Magistrates*, 1907 S.C.(H.L.) 1.

11 *Att.-Gen.* v. *Clarkson* [1900] 1 Q.B. 156, 163; *Re Macmanaway* [1951] A.C. 161; *Att.-Gen.* v. *Prince Ernest Augustus of Hanover* [1957] A.C. 436.

12 Many of the interpretations put in past cases on particular words in particular statutory and factual contexts are collected in Stroud's *Judicial Dictionary*, Burrows' *Words and Phrases Judicially Defined* and in *Current Law*, *s.v.* "Words and Phrases."

13 *Re Aeronautics in Canada* [1932] A.C. 54, 70.

is any scope for case-law doing any more than lay down general principles. Reference to cases where a similar question has arisen on Acts differently framed is of little value, since they merely illustrate a general principle.[14] Moreover, when Parliament uses in an Act a term which has already received judicial interpretation in a case, it is presumed that the term is used in the sense in which it has been judicially interpreted, unless a contrary intention appears.[15] But while a court will be slow to differ from a decision when Parliament has re-enacted a statutory provision in the same terms, it may do so, and is not *bound* to apply the same meaning as before.[16] This presumption has been heavily criticised by some judges and is not very strong.[17]

In connection with cases interpreting particular statutory words and phrases it should be noted that the courts take the view that statutes common to Scotland and England should be interpreted to the same effect in both countries, so that cases from the other jurisdiction are relevant guides to interpretation. So too a phrase in a Scottish Act may sometimes be elucidated by a case construing the corresponding provision in the equivalent English Act, though here there may be more room for diversity, but English cases construing the same word or phrase in a statute not also applicable to Scotland and not the counterpart of the Scottish provision may be of very little value indeed. The value of interpretative cases from the other jurisdiction is greatest in such matters as taxation, where parity of application throughout the United Kingdom is clearly desirable.[18]

(e) *Usage and Contemporanea Expositio.* Where it appears that a statutory provision has long been understood and acted upon in a certain sense the court will adopt that sense unless it appears manifestly wrong.[19] If the meaning of the statute is clear no usage to the contrary will prevail [20] and any such understanding or practice or usage must have been generally accepted, not merely

---

14 *Reid* v. *Reid* (1886) 31 Ch.D. 402, 405.
15 *Barras* v. *Aberdeen Steam Trawling Co.*, 1933 S.C.(H.L.) 21; Winder, " Interpretation of Statutes subject to Case Law " (1946) 58 Jur.Rev. 93.
16 *Royal Crown Derby Porcelain Co.* v. *Russell* [1949] 2 K.B. 417.
17 *Paisner* v. *Goodrich* [1955] 2 Q.B. 353, 358; [1957] A.C. 65.
18 *Income Tax Commrs.* v. *Pemsel* [1891] A.C. 531; *Lord Advocate* v. *Earl of Moray's Trs.* (1905) 7 F.(H.L.) 116; *Inland Revenue* v. *Glasgow Police Athletic Assocn.*, 1953 S.C.(H.L.) 13.
19 *Gorham* v. *Bishop of Exeter* (1850) 15 Q.B. 52, 73; *Migneault* v. *Malo* (1872) L.R. 4 P.C. 123; *Welham* v. *D.P.P.* [1961] A.C. 103.
20 *Magistrates of Dunbar* v. *Duchess of Roxburghe* (1835) 3 Cl. & F. 335, 354; *Northam Bridge Co.* v. *R.* (1886) 55 L.T. 759; *Walker Trs.* v. *Lord Advocate*, 1912 S.C.(H.L.) 12.

prevalent.[21] These aids are particularly relevant to the construction of ancient statutes but have much less weight in more modern statutes.[22] The principle is accordingly relevant in the construction of old Scots Acts.[23]

(f) *Textbooks.* A statement in an established textbook as to the meaning of a statutory provision has no binding force on any court but if there is doubt and the view of the text-writer has been accepted as law for a substantial period of time the court will probably accept it as correct. This is particularly true of very old statutes commented on by text-writers of high repute.[24]

(g) *Dictionaries.* In case of doubt as to the ordinary scope or sense of particular words standard dictionaries may be consulted. Their definitions are not authoritative but are valuable evidence of the ordinary and accepted connotation of particular words and accordingly may be of assistance, but the court is quite free to hold that Parliament has used a word with another meaning than that which is usual.[25]

(h) *Royal Commission and other Reports.* Reference may not be made to Royal Commission or other Reports, on the subject-matter of the legislation, since these are merely proposals put before Parliament and there is no certainty that Parliament has accepted the recommendations in whole or in part or intended to accept or enact any part of the suggestions. Parliament has sometimes accepted a minority report and rarely accepts and enacts everything exactly as recommended by a Commission or Committee.

(j) *Hansard, White Papers, etc.* Similarly no reference is permitted to Hansard (the Parliamentary Debates), or to White Papers [26] or memoranda circulated in Parliament, since these have no authoritative verbal form, nor do they necessarily represent the finally agreed will of Parliament, while, particularly in the case of Hansard, the volume of words is considerable, there is no certainty which speech could be taken as authoritative since

---

[21] *Bank of Ireland* v. *Evans' Charity* (1855) 5 H.L.C. 389, 405.

[22] *Clyde Navigation Trustees* v. *Laird* (1883) 10 R.(H.L.) 77.

[23] *Montrose Peerage Case* (1853) 1 Macq. 401; *Graham* v. *Irving* (1899) 2 F. 29; *cf.* *Middleton* v. *Tough*, 1908 S.C.(J.) 32.

[24] *Mayor of Newcastle* v. *Att.-Gen.* (1845) 12 Cl. & F. 402; *Bastin* v. *Davies* [1950] 1 All E.R. 1095.

[25] *Camden* v. *I.R.C.* [1914] 1 K.B. 641. *Cf. McVittie* v. *Bolton Corpn.* [1945] 1 K.B. 281. In *Lord Advocate* v. *Mirrielees' Trs.*, 1945 S.C.(H.L.) 1, when considering the words "common soldier" the House was led by the O.E.D. to discuss Shakespeare's use of the phrase.

[26] *Viscountess Rhondda's Claim* [1922] 2 A.C. 339; *McCormick* v. *Lord Advocate*, 1953 S.C. 396.

the speeches are argument rather than expression of will, and each argument can usually be matched by a counter-argument.

(k) Schemes made under authority of a statute and to give effect to it are not part of the statute and may not be consulted, except to confirm an interpretation of the words of the statute itself.[27]

Presumptions

There is also a considerable body of presumptions which can be invoked in various cases and which have greater or lesser weight depending on the statute in question and the composition of the court. These are only, be it noted, presumptions which may be applied in the absence of contrary indications but they must give way to any clear indication that they should not apply. The principal ones are:

(a) The Crown, Crown officials, and Crown Departments are not bound by statute unless that is expressly laid down.[28] Hence some modern statutes provide that the Act shall bind the Crown.[29]

(b) It is presumed that fundamental principles of constitutional law or of the common law of the land will not be altered by implication but only expressly.[30] It is difficult to say what are "fundamental principles" in this sense and it might be more helpful to phrase the presumption in the form that extensive and far-reaching changes in the law require to be made expressly, or that there is a presumption against interference with existing common law rights.[31]

(c) It is to be presumed that a British statute does not intend to infringe international law.[32] It may do so, but for reasons of international peace and comity the presumption is to the contrary.

(d) It is presumed that the jurisdiction of the ordinary courts applies and that an individual aggrieved may resort thereto and bring

---

[27] *Howgate* v. *Att.-Gen.* [1951] 1 K.B. 265.

[28] *Cooper* v. *Hawkins* [1904] 2 K.B. 164; *Tamlin* v. *Hannaford* [1950] 1 K.B. 18; *Somerville* v. *Lord Advocate* (1893) 20 R. 1050; *Schulze* v. *Steele* (1890) 17 R.(J.) 47; *Edinburgh Magistrates* v. *Lord Advocate*, 1912 S.C. 1085.

[29] e.g., Crown Proceedings Act, 1947; Road Traffic Act, 1960, s. 250. *Cf. Salt* v. *MacKnight*, 1947 J.C. 99.

[30] e.g., *Nairn* v. *University Courts of St. Andrews and Edinburgh*, 1909 S.C.(H.L.) 10 (decided when women did not have the vote and had just been admitted to university degrees, but university graduates had a vote: argued that women could be graduates, and graduates could vote, *ergo* women graduates could vote. *Held* that if Parliament meant to confer the franchise on any woman it must do so expressly); *Nokes* v. *Doncaster Amalgamated Collieries* [1940] A.C. 1014; *National Assistance Board* v. *Wilkinson* [1952] 2 Q.B. 648.

[31] *Rendall* v. *Blair* (1890) 45 Ch.D. 139; *Central Control Board (Liquor Traffic)* v. *Cannon Brewery Co., Ltd.* [1919] A.C. 744.

[32] *Mortensen* v. *Peters* (1906) 8 F.(J.) 93.

actions and appeals in the usual way.[33]   Hence if appeal to the
ordinary courts is to be limited or excluded that should be
stated expressly.

(e) Statutes are presumed to have prospective effect only and not
retrospective, *i.e.*, to deal with future cases and not past ones.[34]
A provision may, of course, be expressed to be retrospective,
or it may be held that such must have been the intention of
Parliament, and this presumption is much weaker in the case of
statutes extending remedies or rights than in the case of statutes
limiting liberty or imposing penalties.[35]

(f) A strict construction will be given to penal statutes, which
impose a prohibition or a penalty, and they will not be held to
extend to cases not clearly covered by the words used.[36] So too,
there is a presumption against any interference with individual
liberty.

(g) In penal statutes or those creating criminal offences it is presumed that *mens rea* (intention, guilty knowledge) is required
for the commission of the offence and not merely the ignorant
or inadvertent doing of the prohibited thing.[37] But the words
used frequently rebut this presumption and many modern
statutes have infringed it.

(h) A strict construction is to be given to statutes restrictive of
personal liberty or encroaching on the property rights of individuals.   This presumption is weaker in times of national
emergency [38] and weaker than it used to be in view of the impact
of social welfare legislation. So too, the intention to take away
property from an individual without compensation is not to be
imputed to Parliament unless that intention is clearly expressed.[39]

(j) A strict construction is to be given to statutory provisions
imposing taxes on the public; such imposts must be clearly
imposed, if at all,[40] though the courts are not keen to stretch
this to the length of letting evasive transactions escape if they
are within the spirit if not the exact words of the section.[41]

---

[33] *Dunbar* v. *Scottish County Investment Co.*, 1920 S.C. 210; *Chester* v. *Bateson*
[1920] 1 K.B. 829; see also *Portobello Mags.* v. *Edinburgh Mags.* (1882) 10 R. 130.
[34] *Gardner* v. *Beresford's Trustees* (1878) 5 R.(H.L.) 105.
[35] *Wilson* v. *Wilson*, 1939 S.C. 102.
[36] *I.R.C.* v. *Hinchy* [1960] A.C. 748.
[37] *Younghusband* v. *Luftig* [1949] 2 K.B. 354.
[38] *Liversidge* v. *Anderson* [1942] A.C. 206.
[39] *Central Control Board (Liquor Traffic)* v. *Cannon Brewery Co., Ltd.* [1919] A.C. 744.
[40] *I.R.C.* v. *Wolfson* [1949] 1 All E.R. 865.
[41] *Howard de Walden* v. *I.R.C.* [1942] 1 K.B. 389, 397; contrast *I.R.C.* v. *Levene*
[1928] A.C. 217, 227. See also *Ross and Coulter* v. *Inland Revenue*, 1948 S.C.
(H.L.) 1; *Edinburgh Life Assce. Co.* v. *Solicitor of Inland Revenue* (1875) 2 R. 394.

Other presumptions of greater or lesser weight are sometimes enumerated but the foregoing are the principal ones.

Conclusions on Statute Law

It will be apparent that statutory interpretation is neither a mechanical task nor an exact science. It is more of an art and many factors enter into the final decision, the inherent vagueness and inexactness of the ordinary words of the English language, grammatical difficulties, human failure to foresee all possible cases, the immense variety and complexity and unusual character of the circumstances which may arise, the temperament of the judge or court before whom the matter comes, the judges' philosophy and their social, moral and other beliefs, their sympathy or lack of it for the parties, their judicial caution in adhering to a safe interpretation or valour in boldly extending a provision to cover a new case.

Too much attention should not be devoted to so-called rules of construction since " it must be remembered that the courts have laid down, indeed, not rigid rules, but principles which have been found to afford some guidance when it is sought to ascertain the intention of Parliament," [42] and so conflicting are these in many cases that one is driven to the view that " a court invokes whichever of the rules produces a result that satisfies its sense of justice in the case before it." [43] It cannot be pretended that statutory interpretation is a satisfactory part of British law.

II.—JUDICIAL PRECEDENTS OR CASE-LAW

The reports of the decisions of judges of the superior courts in past cases are also an important source of law.[44] Every judicial decision is in the first place the determination of a litigated controversy between two parties; secondly, it is an example of the application of some principle of law to certain facts, and as such, apart from its value to students and jurists, will naturally be looked at as a guide when a court again has to deal with a similar problem, since judges naturally wish to utilise the wisdom and experience of their predecessors and to give decisions consistent with those previously given in like cases. Thirdly, under the modern system of precedent, discussed later, it may in certain circumstances provide an authoritative ruling on the law which *must* be applied in a subsequent case raising a similar problem of law. The acceptance of even single decisions as binding and settling the law is, in Scotland, a

[42] *Cutler* v. *Wandsworth Stadium* [1949] A.C. 398, 410, *per* Lord du Parcq.
[43] Willis, " Statute Interpretation in a Nutshell " (1938) 16 Can.Bar.Rev. 1, 16.
[44] See generally Gardner, *Judicial Precedent in Scots Law*; and " Judicial Decisions as a Source of Scots Law " (1941) 53 J.R. 33; Smith, *Judicial Precedent in Scots Law.*

modern development under English influence, superseding the native rule that a train of decisions was very persuasive but that one decision was merely an example.[45]

Previous decisions in similar cases on questions of fact are not precedents, because the facts of every case are unique and must be examined individually,[46] but decisions on matters of fact, such as the sum of damages which may reasonably be awarded, are sometimes assisted by the citation of other decisions where similar injuries have been sustained.[47] So, too, previous decisions as to criminal penalties may give guidance, but are never binding authorities which have to be followed. A jury verdict on certain facts is never a precedent, even where very similar facts recur. Earlier cases on similar facts can only show how a basic rule has been applied to situations of a particular class.[48]

The use of judicial precedents as a source of law depends on several factors, the general practice in the superior courts, at least in cases of any difficulty or complexity or legal interest, of the judge or judges not merely issuing a decision but delivering an opinion explaining how and why they have reached their decision and what rules or principles of law they have applied[49]; the existence of a system of publishing reliable reports of the decisions of the superior courts; and the existence of a settled hierarchy of courts, in which the decisions of the higher courts carry greater weight than those of the lower.

Reports

There is no official series of law reports, though *Session Cases* in Scotland and the *Law Reports* in England enjoy a rather more favoured status than do other series in that the printed opinions are revised by the judges, which is not always the case with other reports. There is nothing, however, to prevent other reports being published or cited in court[50] and sometimes reports in other series are preferable or include

---

[45] Smith, *Judicial Precedent in Scots Law*, 1–14.
[46] *Qualcast (Wolverhampton), Ltd.* v. *Haynes* [1959] A.C. 743, 757–759; *Cavanagh* v. *Ulster Weaving Co.* [1960] A.C. 145; *Brown* v. *Rolls Royce, Ltd.*, 1960 S.C.(H.L.) 22.
[47] *Waldon* v. *War Office* [1956] 1 W.L.R. 51.
[48] *Hazell* v. *B.T.C.* [1958] 1 W.L.R. 169.
[49] Note that in the sheriff court in civil cases, the sheriff-substitute is bound by the Sheriff Courts Act, 1907, Sched. I, rule 82, to make findings in fact and in law separately, and to add a note giving his reasons. For examples see the Sheriff Court Reports. In higher courts the practice is only customary. Note also that in the Privy Council the single speech is couched in the form of advice from the Privy Council to Her Majesty to dismiss or allow the appeal. See Privy Council cases in the volumes of *Appeal Cases*. Cf. *Jacobs* v. *L.C.C.* [1950] A.C, 361, 369: " While it is the primary duty of a court of justice to dispense justice to litigants, it is its traditional role to do so by means of an exposition of the relevant law."
[50] *Renshaw* v. *Dixon* [1911] W.N. 40; Megarry, " Reporting the Unreported " (1954) 70 L.Q.R. 246; Allen, *Law in the Making*, 6th ed., 257, 355.

cases or points omitted from the main series.[51] Not all cases are reported; probably on average only about 5 per cent. to 10 per cent. of decided cases [52] so that an unreported decision can sometimes be found useful.[53] At least in England there is a salutary rule that only reports prepared and initialled by a member of the Bar may be cited [54] but there are instances of cases being cited from newspapers,[55] textbooks,[56] a shorthand report of the judgment,[57] and the personal recollection of the judge.[55] Mere notes of cases are of little use.[58]

The Form of Reports

The standard modern form of report consists of several parts. There are first certain head-words or catch-words chosen to indicate very briefly by reference to recognised legal headings and sub-heads what legal topics are dealt with in the case, mentioning first the principal ones and then the subordinate or more detailed matters,[59] and what statutes have been discussed or interpreted in the case. This is followed by the rubric or headnote, which is a concise statement of the facts, of the point of law in issue, and of the court's decision, which last element is usually preceded by the word " Held." There is also an indication of any dissenting or divergent opinions by particular judges and of any specially noteworthy remarks or observations, and sometimes a mention of the attitude adopted to certain previous cases.[60] It has to be noticed that the head-words and rubric are compiled by the reporter under the supervision of the editor of the series of reports, and they have no authority

---

[51] Thus *Robertson's Tutor* v. *Glasgow Corpn.* is reported in 1950 S.C. 502, but not in S.L.T.; *Donnelly* v. *Glasgow Corpn.* is in 1949 S.L.T. 362 and not in S.C.

[52] Walker, " The Mass of Reports " (1953) 69 S.L.R. 222.

[53] The proportion of cases decided by a single judge in the Outer House or in the Sheriff Court and not reported is much higher: so also in England. In *Leighton* v. *Harland & Wolff*, 1953 S.L.T.(Notes) 36, it was observed that it was counsel's duty to refer the court to unreported as well as reported cases on the point in issue.

[54] *Rivoli Hats* v. *Gooch* [1953] 1 W.L.R. 1190; *Birtwistle* v. *Tweedale* [1954] 1 W.L.R. 190.

[55] *R.* v. *Labouchere* (1884) 12 Q.B.D. 320, 328; *Barras* v. *Aberdeen Steam Trawling Co.*, 1933 S.C.(H.L.) 21; *Overstone, Ltd.* v. *Shipway* [1962] 1 All E.R. 52; but on the dangers of this see *Mahon* v. *Osborne* [1939] 2 K.B. 14.

[56] *Bush* v. *Whitehaven Trustees*, reported only in Hudson on *Building Contracts*, cited in *Davis Contractors, Ltd.* v. *Fareham U.D.C.* [1956] A.C. 696; *Cowe* v. *Millar*, reported only in Connell on *The Agricultural Holdings Act*, cited in *Smith* v. *Grayston Estates, Ltd.*, 1960 S.C. 349, 354.

[57] *Renshaw* v. *Dixon* [1911] W.N. 40.

[58] *Birtwistle* v. *Tweedale* [1954] 1 W.L.R. 190 (*Estates Gazette* rejected); *Rivoli Hats, Ltd.* v. *Gooch* [1953] 1 W.L.R. 1190 (*Current Law* rejected): see also *Mahon* v. *Osborne* [1939] 2 K.B. 14; *Chapman* v. *Chapman* [1954] A.C. 429.

[59] These catch-words are of great importance for determining where the case will be placed in the Digests.

[60] *e.g.*, that some precedent case has been " applied," or " followed " or " not followed " or " distinguished " or " overruled." For the significance of these terms see p. 328, *infra*.

at all. They may contain mistakes or misleading statements [61] and judges sometimes have occasion to criticise the rubric of previous reports.[62] The rubric is only the reporter's summary, his idea of what the case decided. There may be two or more sets of head-words and rubrics where the case has raised two or more distinct matters for argument and decision.

Then follows a narrative of the facts of the case and of the material steps in the litigation, sometimes with quotations from the written pleadings of the parties or from the evidence heard at an earlier stage. Sometimes this is done by incorporating the part of a judge's opinion which states the facts, or by reference to his opinion which, in the reporter's view, adequately states the facts. This information should make clear what the controversy is about, and everything that has gone before in its progress through the courts. It should, but may not, contain all factual information about the case which enables the reader to understand it and to evaluate or criticise the decision and judicial opinions. But some facts are sometimes tantalisingly omitted.

This is followed by a brief account of the arguments put forward by counsel on each side with a note of the cases, statutes and books referred to by them. Sometimes important or valuable statements are made in argument, or made by the Bench in reply to an argument. Moreover it may be very important in a later case to know whether the court was referred in argument to a particular case or statute as there have been instances of decisions arrived at in ignorance of a case or statute in point, and a decision is of lesser authority if relevant prior cases were not cited in argument.[63]

Lastly there are printed the opinions of the judges, usually in full, but sometimes with omissions. It should be noted that another series of reports may include passages omitted in one report,[64] or may give a slightly different version of a passage.[65]

The Principle of Stare Decisis

While, as has been pointed out, it is a natural and common-sense practice to have regard, when deciding a case, to reported decisions in prior cases raising the same issue of law, the modern British system

---

[61] Thus in *Victoria Laundry* v. *Newman* [1949] 2 K.B. 528 it was pointed out that the rubric in *Hadley* v. *Baxendale* (1854) 9 Ex. 341 was incorrect in a material respect.

[62] Thus in *Hamilton* v. *Hamilton*, 1954 S.L.T. 16, the report of *Robb* v. *Robb*, 1953 S.L.T. 44, was severely criticised.

[63] *Penrikyber Navigation Colliery Co.* v. *Edwards* [1933] A.C. 28.

[64] Thus the report of *Leadbetter* v. *N.C.B.* in 1952 S.L.T. 179 deals with a matter omitted from 1952 S.C. 19.

[65] Thus there are four different reports of *Holmes* v. *Mather* in 1875 (L.R. 10 Ex. 261; 44 L.J.Ex. 176; 33 L.T. 361; 23 W.R. 869) which show important verbal differences: two are set out in parallel columns for comparison in Pollock on *Torts*, 15th ed., 132.

goes further by its insistence on *stare decisis*, that is, on the principle
of abiding by authorities or decided cases, so that in certain circumstances
the doctrine derived from a precedent case or series of cases *must* be
followed and applied, even though the judge might not have been disposed
of his own accord to apply that doctrine. The habit of referring to
precedents in point and applying them has grown into the rule that a
precedent in point *must* be applied.[66]

Some reported decisions are merely instances of the application of
an existing rule of law, reported for the interest of the circumstances or
the value of the judicial expression of an old and settled principle of law,
while others are really creative of new law, as where a new rule is laid
down or an existing rule reformulated, modified, extended or limited,
or applied to a fresh set of circumstances. The former kind of cases
are merely applications of law, the latter in some measure create new
law or define or delimit the applicability of some principle or rule of
law in a sphere previously vague. Cases of the former sort may be,
but are rather unlikely to be, authoritative or binding in a future case,
but cases of the latter sort are much more likely to be authoritative in
future.

This principle of *stare decisis* may be justified on the ground that it
makes for certainty and consistency of the law, that it makes for the
disposal in the same way of similar cases (and equality of treatment is
a commonly accepted element in justice), that it tends to limit or exclude
judicial mistakes, prejudices and faulty formulations of an appropriate
rule of law to apply to the facts, and that it tends to make the law
predictable, so as to enable a legal adviser to forecast what rule a court
would probably apply to a given set of facts.

On the other hand, as will appear later, there are countervailing
disadvantages: adherence to *stare decisis* may make the law rigid, inflexible
and impervious to social change; the discovery of the doctrine enunciated
by a precedent is difficult and may be impossible; judicial distaste for,
or disinclination to be regulated by, a particular precedent produces
much verbal juggling, sophistry, casuistry and the drawing of fine, or
even invisible, distinctions; and a decision may come to depend too
much on the finding or not finding of an apt precedent in the reports.

Nevertheless this is the modern British rule [66a]: a precedent which is
both in point and binding *must* be applied; a precedent which is in point
and persuasive should be considered and may be adopted and applied;
a precedent which is not in point may be ignored. Much accordingly
depends on the criteria for deciding whether a particular precedent is

[66] See also Salmond, " Theory of Judicial Precedents " (1900) 16 L.Q.R. 376.
[66a] The rule is English in origin and has been accepted in Scotland only since 1800,
largely under the influence of the House of Lords: see Smith, *Judicial Precedent*,
10–17.

in point or not and, in the circumstances before a particular court, whether binding or merely persuasive.

When is a Precedent " in point " ?

A prior decision is a precedent in point when there was raised, argued and decided in it some issue of law as applicable to a certain set of facts which is the same issue as arises in the instant case in relation to a different set of facts of the same general kind. Similarity of facts between the precedent and the instant case is not enough and may, indeed, matter very little. One case about sale of a car may have no relation in law to another case about sale of a car. Decisions on questions of fact do not make precedents though they may give some guidance in a later case.[67] What is important is the raising in a subsequent case of the same issue of law as was decided in the precedent case, as, for example, whether artificial insemination by a donor amounts to legal adultery or not,[68] or what in law amounts to fraudulent misrepresentation inducing a contract.[69] Thus the precedent about fraudulent misrepresentation is in point in a later case of a contract of sale or of hiring, even though the precedent related to the contract to take shares in a company, but is not necessarily in point in relation to fraudulent misrepresentation inducing a marriage, since marriage is a relationship legally distinct from a commercial contract.[70]

As will be seen later, much ingenuity is sometimes devoted to arguing that a precedent is not " in point " or not " on all fours with " the instant case, on the ground that the precedent dealt with a different legal issue or that the facts are sufficiently different from those of the precedent to make the issue of law materially different. When it is remembered that facts never exactly reproduce themselves and that possible combinations of facts raising legal issues are limitless, it will be apparent that it is frequently difficult to say whether a given prior case is really in point or not, and that in most cases it is really a matter of degree, the decision being that the prior case is or is not sufficiently similar in the legal issue raised to the instant case to be treated as having raised the same point of law and accordingly to be a precedent for the decision of the instant case.

Binding and Persuasive Precedents

Even of prior decisions which are in point, not every one is binding on a subsequent court, or authoritative. Some are merely persuasive.

An authoritative or binding precedent in point is one which judges

---

[67] *Waldon* v. *War Office* [1956] 1 All E.R. 108.
[68] *MacLennan* v. *MacLennan,* 1958 S.C. 105.
[69] *Derry* v. *Peek* (1889) 14 App.Cas. 337.
[70] *Lang* v. *Lang,* 1921 S.C. 44.

in a subsequent case raising the same issue of law *must* follow and apply to the facts before them, irrespective of their views as to its soundness.

A persuasive precedent in point is one which judges in a subsequent case will take into consideration, to which they will attach such weight as they think the precedent deserves, having regard to its value, the personal eminence of the judges who decided it, the place in the judicial hierarchy from which it comes, and the extent to which it is in point in the later case, but which they are *not bound* to follow and apply. It may persuade them to apply it, but if it does so, it does so on its merits, and not because it is authoritative.

The question whether any given precedent which is " in point " is authoritative or merely persuasive in a subsequent case depends primarily on where it emanated from in the hierarchy of courts and, secondly, on certain factors affecting its evaluation. These two elements must now be considered.

The Hierarchy of Courts

The regular courts of the United Kingdom form a systematic hierarchy in which appeals generally lie from inferior courts to courts superior to them in their own line of ascent. In considering whether any given court is bound or subject to persuasion by a precedent emanating from another court in the hierarchy it is essential to have in mind the place of each court in the hierarchy. The authority of a prior decision does not depend on whether an appeal lies from the court considering the precedent to the court which issued judgment in the precedent case. It depends on the place in the hierarchy held by the court from which the precedent came relative to the place of the hierarchy held by the later court considering the precedent.

The hierarchy of United Kingdom regular courts consists of six parallel lines, comprising respectively the civil and criminal courts of Scotland, England and Wales, and of Northern Ireland. These are set out in the following table, in which courts shown on the same horizontal line are of generally corresponding standing and authority. The lowest courts can be omitted from consideration since their decisions are very seldom reported and are of negligible value as precedents.

The general principle is that any court is bound by prior decisions in point pronounced by courts superior to it in its own vertical line of authority, and that prior decisions in point of courts of equal or higher rank in other vertical lines of authority are persuasive in varying degrees. Decisions of courts of lower rank in any vertical line of authority may be ignored but may sometimes be of some persuasive value. But this general statement must now be examined in more detail in relation to the main courts since practice is not uniform in all courts. Moreover the practice in Scotland is less strict and rigid throughout than in England.

	SCOTLAND		ENGLAND & WALES		N. IRELAND
Civil	Criminal	Civil	Criminal	Civil	Criminal
H.L.		H.L.	H.L.	H.L.	H.L.
Ct. of Session (Inner Ho.)	High Court (appeals)	Ct. of Appeal [71]	Ct. of Crim. Appeal [72]	Ct. of Appeal	Ct. of Crim. Appeal
Ct. of Session (Outer Ho.)	High Court (trials)	⎧ Divisional ⎨ Court ⎩ High ⎩ Court [73]	⎧ Divisional ⎨ Court ⎩ Assizes [74]	High Court	Assizes
Sheriff-principal	Sheriff and jury		Quarter Sessions		Quarter Sessions
Sheriff-substitute	Sheriff (summarily)	County Court		County Court	

SCOTLAND

House of Lords

The House of Lords, when sitting as the final court of appeal from Scotland, sits as a Scottish court [75] and is probably absolutely bound by precedents of its own pronounced in Scottish appeals,[76] but not by its own precedents pronounced in English or Irish appeals,[77] nor by dicta on questions of Scots law raised incidentally in such appeals,[77] nor by precedents in such appeals relating to questions of general jurisprudence and not turning on specialties of English law.[78] Such precedents will, however, be persuasive.[79] Decisions of the House in English appeals on statutes common to England and Scotland are probably binding,[80] but otherwise if the statute is peculiar to England.

[71] Including the Court of Exchequer Chamber which was the predecessor of the Court of Appeal.
[72] Including the former Court for Crown Cases Reserved.
[73] Including the former separate Courts of Queen's Bench, Common Pleas, Exchequer, Admiralty and Matrimonial Causes.
[74] Including the Central Criminal Court and Crown Courts.
[75] *Concha* v. *Murietta* (1889) 40 Ch.D. 543, 550; *cf. Cooper* v. *Cooper* (1888) 15 R. (H.L.) 21; *Elliot* v. *Joicey*, 1935 S.C.(H.L.) 57.
[76] The doctrine accepted by the House for England in *London Tramways Co.* v. *L.C.C.* [1898] A.C. 375 has not been expressly accepted for Scotland, but is almost certainly the rule.
[77] *Glasgow Corpn.* v. *Central Land Board*, 1956 S.C.(H.L.) 1; and see discussion in 19 M.L.R. 427.   [78] *Orr Ewing's Trustees* v. *Orr Ewing* (1885) 13 R.(H.L.) 1.
[79] *Virtue* v. *Alloa Police Commissioners* (1873) 1 R. 285.
[80] *Inland Revenue* v. *Glasgow Police Athletic Association*, 1953 S.C.(H.L.) 13.

Decisions of the House in Scottish appeals are binding on all civil courts in Scotland, but decisions of the House in other appeals, on statutes not common to the United Kingdom, and on grounds of general jurisprudence raised in non-Scottish appeals are persuasive only, though in a high degree. It is always difficult to determine what are questions of " general jurisprudence " particularly in view of the tendency of English Lords of Appeal to assume that much English law is general, and that the same principles apply in Scotland.

Court of Session, Inner House
Either Division of the Inner House of the Court of Session is normally bound by decisions of the House of Lords in Scottish appeals, by a decision of seven or more judges, and by a previous decision of either Division.[81] In exceptional cases a precedent in point of either Division may not be followed and doubtful precedents or conflicts of precedent are normally resolved by convening a fuller court of seven or more judges.[82] There is no fixed rule that even the whole court is bound by its own previous decisions, and it is certainly not the rule that decisions of a Division have the same weight as decisions of the full court.[83] A court of seven judges may quite freely overrule a precedent of either Division.[84] There are also expressions of the view that a Division is not necessarily bound by a single decision of either Division.[85] Moreover even when a precedent is directly in point it may be disregarded if the social and economic background has so changed that the precedent is quite outmoded.[86]

Decisions of the House of Lords in English or Irish appeals are very persuasive, and of the English or Irish Courts of Appeal strongly persuasive, the degree of persuasion depending largely on the similarity of Scots to English or Irish law on the point in issue. Decisions of lower English or Irish courts are weakly persuasive.

---

[81] *e.g., Garden's Exor.* v. *More,* 1913 S.C. 285; *Heavyside* v. *Smith,* 1929 S.C. 68; *Cameron* v. *Glasgow Corpn.,* 1935 S.C. 533; *Galloway* v. *Galloway,* 1947 S.C. 330; *Marshall* v. *Scottish Milk Marketing Board,* 1956 S.C.(H.L.) 37, 39; (revd. by H.L., *ibid.,* 40–48).

[82] In *Drummond* v. *Inland Revenue,* 1951 S.C. 482, it was doubted whether it was competent for the court, when sitting as Court of Exchequer, to convene a larger court to reconsider a precedent, and the view was expressed that this should be done by the House of Lords.

[83] As is the case in England under *Young* v. *Bristol Aeroplane Co.* [1944] K.B. 718.

[84] *e.g., Cochrane's Exrx.* v. *Cochrane,* 1947 S.C. 134; *McElroy* v. *McAllister,* 1949 S.C. 110; *Smith* v. *Stewart & Co.,* 1960 S.C. 329.

[85] *Lord Advocate* v. *Young* (1898) 25 R. 778; *Earl of Wemyss* v. *Earl of Zetland* (1890) 18 R. 126, 130.

[86] *Beith's Trustees* v. *Beith,* 1950 S.C. 66. *Cf.* Lord Carmont's reasons in *Macdonald* v. *Glasgow Western Hospitals,* 1954 S.C. 453, 484, for refusing to hold the First Division bound by the First Division's decision in *Reidford* v. *Aberdeen Magistrates,* 1933 S.C. 276.

High Court of Justiciary as Court of Criminal Appeal

The High Court is not bound by decisions of the House of Lords in a criminal matter, even when dealing with a United Kingdom criminal statute, still less by the (English) Court of Criminal Appeal, though such decisions are persuasive. Nor is it bound by a previous decision of a similar quorum of the High Court, though the practice is to follow such decisions,[87] but a larger court would probably be convened to reconsider a difficult precedent.[88] There is no rule which prevents a bench of the High Court from reversing an unfortunate precedent, even of the full court, if the requirements of justice make this desirable, but normally any precedent doubted is reviewed by a larger, or even a full, bench.[89] A full bench probably can overrule a precedent decided by a prior full bench.[90]

Court of Session, Outer House

A Lord Ordinary sitting alone in the Outer House normally considers himself bound by decisions of the House of Lords in Scottish appeals, by decisions of seven or more judges, or of either Division of the Inner House. He is not bound by decisions of another Outer House judge, though he treats such decisions with respect. But he may decline to follow them, leaving it to a higher court at a later date to decide which view is right.[91] Decisions of the House of Lords in English or Irish appeals are very persuasive,[92] of the English or Irish Courts of Appeal strongly persuasive, and of the English or Irish High Courts mildly persuasive, the degree depending on the similarity of the legal systems on the point in issue.

High Court of Justiciary (as court of trial)

A single Lord of Justiciary usually accepts the law laid down previously on appeal by a bench of the High Court, but single judge rulings, though very persuasive, are not binding on other single judges.[93] Decisions of the English superior criminal courts are highly persuasive and of English trial judges mildly persuasive, if the legal systems are similar on the point in issue.

---

87 *McAvoy* v. *Cameron*, 1917 J.C. 1.
88 *Macmillan* v. *McConnell*, 1917 J.C. 43; *Marshall* v. *Clark*, 1957 J.C. 68.
89 *e.g., Kirkwood* v. *H.M. Advocate*, 1939 J.C. 36 (11 judges).
90 *Sugden* v. *H.M. Advocate*, 1934 J.C. 103.
91 *Blackwood* v. *Andre*, 1947 S.C. 333, not following *McDaid* v. *Clyde Navigation Trustees*, 1946 S.C. 462; *Blackwood* was later approved by the House of Lords in *B.T.C.* v. *Gourley* [1956] A.C. 185. *Cf. McKenzie* v. *McKenzie*, 1960 S.C. 322 and *Breen* v. *Breen*, 1961 S.C. 158, 175, 188.
92 See *Spencer* v. *Macmillan's Trs.*, 1958 S.C. 300, 303.
93 *H.M. Advocate* v. *Higgins* (1914) 7 Adam 229.

Sheriff-principal and Sheriff-substitute (civil)

Sheriffs-principal and sheriffs-substitute are not bound by decisions of the Outer House, though they treat them with respect, nor are they bound by one another, though a sheriff-substitute will usually follow the decisions of his sheriff-principal. They are, however, bound by decisions of the House of Lords and Inner House of the Court of Session and regard English and Irish decisions as persuasive in varying degrees.

Sheriff and jury; Sheriff's Summary Court (criminal)

A sheriff presiding at a trial by jury or trying a case summarily must accept law laid down by the High Court sitting as Court of Criminal Appeal but is not necessarily bound by previous rulings of a single trial judge, whether Lord of Justiciary or Sheriff.

Special Courts

In the Scottish Land Court, the court does not seem to hold itself bound by a single prior decision.[94] The Lands Valuation Appeal Court retains the power to review its own previous decisions.[95] The Courts-Martial Appeal Court follows the practice of the High Court of Justiciary as Court of Criminal Appeal. The Transport Tribunal is successor to the Railway Rates Tribunal and treats previous decisions as persuasive only.[96] The Restrictive Practices Court is empowered to discharge its own previous declarations and orders.[97]

In administrative tribunals the rules of precedent do not apply and to some extent administrative tribunals have been resorted to, to avoid this feature of British judicial technique. But where decisions are published, as of the Commissioner in National Insurance cases, there seems to be developing a tendency to have regard to prior cases in decision. Where an appeal lies from the tribunal to the ordinary courts it seems probable that the tribunals hold themselves bound by precedents in those courts. Tribunals such as the Commissioners of Income Tax in fact regard themselves as bound by reported decisions of the courts in tax cases. This was also the case with the Pensions Appeal Tribunal and in one case [97a] it was held that the English tribunal should follow a later Court of Session decision on appeal in preference to an earlier High Court decision on a similar appeal. But where there is no appeal to the ordinary courts tribunals seem to be free from the doctrine of *stare decisis*.

---

[94] See, *e.g.*, *Niven* v. *Cameron*, 1939 S.L.C.R. 23; *Chisholm* v. *Campbell Orde*, 1920 S.L.C.R. 36; *Georgeson* v. *Anderston's Trustees*, 1945 S.L.C.R. 44.
[95] *Inverness Assessor* v. *Cameron*, 1938 S.C. 360.
[96] *B.T.C.* v. *Bristow, Ltd.* (1955) 30 Traf.Cas. 217, 232.
[97] Restrictive Trade Practices Act, 1956, s. 22 (1).
[97a] *Minister of Pensions* v. *Higham* [1948] 2 K.B. 153.

ENGLAND

House of Lords

Decisions of the House of Lords when pronounced in an English appeal are binding on the House itself for the future [97b] and on all inferior English courts, civil or criminal according to the nature of the precedent, and that even though the House were equally divided so that the decision appealed against stands unreversed.[98] The decision is probably not binding if decided *per incuriam*, in ignorance of the terms of a statute or statutory instrument.[99] A binding precedent cannot be disregarded because it was inadequately argued or considered, nor because their lordships disagree with it,[1] nor even on the ground that it was based on industrial and social conditions which have changed.[2] " This House has debarred itself from ever reconsidering any of its own decisions. It matters not how difficult it is to find the *ratio decidendi* of a previous case, that *ratio* must be found. And it matters not how difficult it is to reconcile that *ratio* when found with statutory provisions or general principles; that *ratio* must be applied to any later case which is not reasonably distinguishable." [3] The House is accordingly forced in many cases to resort to " distinguishing " its own previous decisions if it wishes not to be bound to follow them.[4] It seems probable also that, if a conflict be found between two previous decisions of the House, the House could follow either and would not be bound to follow one because it was earlier or later.[5] But a dictum patently wrong and unnecessary to the decision of the precedent may be disapproved [6] and it has been suggested that when a particular precedent, even of the House, conflicts with a fundamental principle, also of the House, the latter must prevail.[7] It has also been said *obiter* [8] that there are at least three classes of cases where the House can question or limit the *ratio decidendi* of a previous House of Lords decision; (a) where it is obscure; (b) where

---

[97b] *London Tramways Co.* v. *L.C.C.* [1898] A.C. 375. On history of this see Salmond on *Jurisprudence*, 11th ed., 175–184. See also Dworkin, " *Stare Decisis* in the House of Lords " (1962) 25 M.L.R. 163.

[98] *Att.-Gen.* v. *Dean of Windsor* (1860) 8 H.L.C. 369; *R.* v. *Millis* (1844) 10 Cl. & F. 534; *Beamish* v. *Beamish* (1861) 9 H.L.C. at 338. As to other courts equally divided see *The Vera Cruz* (1884) 9 P.D. at 98.

[99] *London Street Tramways, supra,* at p. 379. " *Per incuriam* " has been said (*Morelle* v. *Wakeling* [1955] 2 Q.B. 379) to cover only decisions given in ignorance or forgetfulness of some inconsistent statutory provision or of some authority binding on the court concerned.

[1] *London Transport Executive* v. *Betts* [1959] A.C. 213.

[2] *Radcliffe* v. *Ribble Motor Services* [1939] A.C. at 245–246. But on this see Lord Evershed M.R., *The Court of Appeal in England,* p. 18.

[3] *Nash* v. *Tamplin & Sons Brewery* [1952] A.C. 231.

[4] On " distinguishing " see p. 328, *infra.*

[5] This is the rule in the Court of Appeal.

[6] *Public Trustee* v. *I.R.C.* [1960] A.C. 398.

[7] *London Transport Executive, supra,* 247, *per* Lord Denning.

[8] *Scruttons* v. *Midland Silicones, Ltd.* [1962] 1 All E.R. 1, *per* Lords Reid and Keith.

the decision is out of line with other authorities or established principles; and (c) where it is much wider than was necessary for the decision so that it becomes a question of how far it is proper to distinguish the earlier decision.

In respect of decisions pronounced in Scottish or Irish appeals the House is clearly technically not bound in a subsequent English case, but it has been suggested that it may be so bound where the Scottish case was decided in the House on the same principles as apply in English law.[9] Thus it has usually been assumed in England that *Donoghue* v. *Stevenson*[10] is binding on the House and on lower English courts, but strictly it is not. And the House can, in an English appeal, choose between previous decisions of its own in a Scottish and in an English appeal, and elect to follow the Scottish one, where the law was assumed to be the same in both countries.[11]

Court of Appeal

The Court of Appeal is bound by decisions of the House of Lords in English civil appeals. Decisions of the Court of Appeal are binding on judges of the High Court and of Assize in civil cases, on County Court judges, and on the Divisional Court in cases where an appeal lies from it to the Court of Appeal. Similar weight attaches to decisions of the former Court of Exchequer Chamber and Court of Appeal in Chancery, which were superseded by the Court of Appeal in 1875. The Court of Appeal also has held that it is bound by its own previous decisions[12] unless the prior decision was arrived at *per incuriam, i.e.,* in ignorance or forgetfulness of some inconsistent statutory provision or of some authority binding on the court,[13] or without full citation of authorities,[14] or is expressly or impliedly inconsistent with and overruled by a later decision of the House of Lords. Moreover it has the right, when referred to several conflicting previous decisions of its own, to select and follow one of them and this selection probably binds later Court of Appeal cases.[15] Full binding force attaches even to unreported decisions of the court,[16] and a full court of five judges has no greater

9 R. v. *Minister of Health, ex p. Yaffé* [1931] A.C. at 502; *Heyman* v. *Darwins, Ltd.* [1942] A.C. at 401.
10 1932 S.C.(H.L.) 31. In that case the Lords said that the principles applicable were common to Scots and to English law. But this is a dangerous doctrine.
11 *Heyman* v. *Darwins, Ltd.* [1942] A.C. 356.
12 *Young* v. *Bristol Aeroplane Co.* [1944] K.B. 718; and see Goodhart, " Precedents in the Court of Appeal " (1947) 9 C.L.J. 349; Gooderson, " Precedents in the Court of Appeal " (1950) 10 C.L.J. 432; Mason, " *Stare Decisis* in the Court of Appeal " (1956) 19 M.L.R. 136.
13 *Morelle, Ltd.* v. *Wakeling* [1955] 2 Q.B. 379.
14 *A. & J. Mucklow, Ltd.* v. *I.R.C.* [1954] Ch. 615. *Cf. Bryers* v. *Canadian Pacific Steamships, Ltd.* [1957] 1 Q.B. 134.
15 *Craddock* v. *Hampshire C.C.* [1958] 1 W.L.R. 202.
16 *Gibson* v. *South American Stores* [1950] Ch. 177; *cf. King* v. *King* [1943] P. 91.

powers than the usual court of three.[17] The court must follow its own previous decisions even though a point was less fully argued in the previous case,[18] it be argued that in the previous decision it had misunderstood a House of Lords precedent,[19] and even though another case on the same point is under appeal to the House of Lords,[20] but it can overrule one of the grounds of a prior Court of Appeal decision, leaving that decision to stand on its other ground.[21]

Court of Criminal Appeal

This court is bound by decisions of the House of Lords in English criminal appeals. Its decisions are binding on the Queen's Bench Divisional Court in criminal matters, even though no appeal lies,[22] and certainly bind Judges of Assize in criminal cases, judges of the Central Criminal Court and of the Crown Courts, and Courts of Quarter Sessions. Decisions of the old Court for Crown Cases Reserved which was the predecessor (to 1906) of the Court of Criminal Appeal are entitled to similar weight. This court also will normally follow its own decisions [23] but, since the liberty of the subject is at stake in its decisions, it may, certainly if sitting as a full court, reconsider a previous decision, if it finds that the law was misunderstood or misapplied in the earlier case.[24] Accordingly it is not always or absolutely bound by a prior decision.[25] It may also reconsider a decision which was not argued on both sides.[26]

Differences may arise between the Court of Appeal and the Court of Criminal Appeal since they are of equal status, and the same problem may arise in civil and in criminal proceedings. Thus in one case [27] the Court of Criminal Appeal held that to demand money from a member of a trade protection association as an alternative to blacklisting him was a criminal offence, but in another [28] the Court of Appeal held that an agreement by such a trader to pay a sum to have his name deleted from a blacklist was a valid contract. The House of Lords eventually held [29] that the latter view was the correct one and no crime had been committed.

17 *Morelle, Ltd.* v. *Wakeling* [1955] 2 W.L.R. 672.
18 *Critchell* v. *Lambeth B.C.* [1957] 2 Q.B. 535.
19 *Williams* v. *Glasbrook Bros.* [1947] 2 All E.R. 884.
20 *Re Yates' Settlement Trusts* [1954] 1 W.L.R. 564.
21 *Betty's Cafés, Ltd.* v. *Phillips Furnishing Stores, Ltd.* [1959] A.C. 20, 53.
22 *Ruse* v. *Read* [1949] 1 K.B. 377, 384; *Russell* v. *Smith* [1958] 1 Q.B. 27.
23 *R.* v. *Cade* [1914] 2 K.B. 209, 211.
24 *R.* v. *Taylor* [1950] 2 K.B. 368, overruling *R.* v. *Treanor* (1939) 27 C.A.R. 35. In this case seven judges sat instead of the usual three. It is not certain whether it needs the larger court to exercise this power or whether the number was summoned simply to obtain the benefit of extra opinions.
25 See Winder, " The Rule of Precedent in Criminal Courts " (1941) 5 J.Crim.L. 242.
26 *R.* v. *Ettridge* [1909] 2 K.B. at 27; *R.* v. *Norman* [1924] 2 K.B. at 322.
27 *R.* v. *Denyer* [1926] 2 K.B. 258.
28 *Hardie and Lane* v. *Chilton* [1928] 2 K.B. 306.
29 *Thorne* v. *Motor Trade Association* [1937] A.C. 797.

Divisional Courts

A Divisional Court of the High Court seems now to hold itself bound by its own decisions,[30] whether exercising civil or criminal jurisdiction, unless, probably, the prior decision was inconsistent with the decision of a higher court or obviously reached by mistake.[31] It may, however, exceptionally, depart from a previous decision.[32] The Divisional Court is certainly bound by decisions of the House of Lords and by decisions of the Court of Appeal in civil matters,[33] though it has held itself free[34] to disregard a precedent in the Court of Appeal[35] in which two prior decisions, of the House of Lords and the Privy Council respectively, had not been cited. The Divisional Court is bound in criminal matters by the Court of Criminal Appeal,[36] and by House of Lords decisions in criminal cases.

In civil matters the Divisional Court probably ranks no higher than a single judge of the High Court and its decisions cannot bind him, though only exceptionally would a single judge differ from the Divisional Court's view of the law.[37]

High Court and Assizes

Decisions of High Court judges are probably binding on county court judges in civil cases, though appeal lies not to the High Court but direct to the Court of Appeal, but a decision of one High Court judge does not bind another[38] and a High Court judge may even decline to follow a previous decision of his own.[39] It is, however, unusual, for reasons of judicial comity, to refuse to follow a decision of another High Court judge unless there seems good reason for doing so,[40] particularly in such a matter as the interpretation of a common commercial

---

30 *Huddersfield Police Authority* v. *Watson* [1947] K.B. 842 (civil); *Younghusband* v. *Luftig* [1949] 2 K.B. 354; *Russell* v. *Smith* [1958] 1 Q.B. 27 (criminal): see further Winder, " Divisional Court Precedents " (1946) 9 M.L.R. 257; Stone, " *Stare Decisis* in the Divisional Court " (1951) 14 M.L.R. 219.

31 *Melias, Ltd.* v. *Preston* [1957] 2 Q.B. 380; *Cogley* v. *Sherwood* [1959] 2 W.L.R. 781.

32 *R.* v. *Fulham Rent Tribunal* [1951] 1 T.L.R. 423.

33 *Read* v. *Joannon* (1890) 25 Q.B.D. 300, 302.

34 In *R.* v. *Northumberland Compensation Tribunal* [1951] 1 K.B. 711.

35 *Racecourse Betting Control Board* v. *Secretary of State for Air* [1944] Ch. 114.

36 In *Hawke* v. *Mackenzie* [1902] 2 K.B. 225, 232, 233 the D.C. took the view that it was bound by decisions of the former Court for Crown Cases Reserved, the predecessor of the C.C.A., and in *Russell* v. *Smith* [1958] 1 Q.B. 27 a D.C. held itself bound by the C.C.A.

37 *Chandris* v. *Isbrandtsen-Moller, Inc.* [1951] 1 K.B. 240, 243; but see *Huddersfield Police Authority* v. *Watson* [1947] K.B. 842, 848 per Lord Goddard C.J.

38 *Forster* v. *Baker* [1910] 2 K.B. 636, 638; *Green* v. *Berliner* [1936] 2 K.B. 477, 493; *Alma Shipping Co.* v. *Salgaoncar* [1954] 2 Q.B. 94, 104; *Receiver for Metropolitan Police* v. *Croydon Corpn.* [1957] 2 Q.B. 154.

39 *Andrews* v. *Styrap* (1872) 26 L.T. 704, 706.

40 *Receiver for Metropolitan Police District* v. *Croydon Corpn.* [1956] 1 W.L.R. 1113; contrast *Monmouthshire C.C.* v. *Smith* [1956] 1 W.L.R. 1132; *The Makedonia* [1958] 1 Q.B. 365.

document,[41] and that even though the previous single-judge decision has been doubted in a dissenting judgment in the Court of Appeal.[42] Even where the matter is one for the exercise of judicial discretion there is a strong tendency to conform to practice and give decisions consistent with those of other judges. In the event of one judge declining to follow another, two contradictory precedents stand in the books until a superior court in a later case resolves the conflict by approving one and over-ruling the other. Judges of the High Court are certainly bound by decisions of the House of Lords and the Court of Appeal, but probably not by Divisional Court decisions. If a single judge is faced with a series of decisions of higher courts which are difficult to reconcile, he must follow any one which is indistinguishable, failing which he must try to apply the principles which can be extracted from the reported decisions as a whole.[43]

The decisions of judges of Assize in criminal matters bind Courts of Quarter Sessions, though no appeal lies, and magistrates' courts. Decisions at Quarter Sessions apparently do not bind magistrates' courts, but in cases of any consequence appeal is usually taken by case stated from Quarter Sessions or magistrates' courts to the Queen's Bench Divisional Court for a ruling on the law. Assizes are, of course, bound by the House of Lords, the Court of Criminal Appeal, but probably not by the Divisional Court in its criminal jurisdiction.

County Courts

County court judges are bound by decisions of the House of Lords and Court of Appeal, and probably by decisions of single judges of the High Court, but probably not by other county court decisions, of which only few are reported. In practice other single-judge decisions are followed, unless they appear unsound.

Quarter Sessions

Quarter Sessions are bound by decisions in criminal cases of the House of Lords and Court of Criminal Appeal, and probably by rulings of the Divisional Courts in criminal matters and by pronouncements of single judges at Assizes.

NORTHERN IRELAND

The doctrine of binding precedent is accepted in Northern Ireland so that decisions of the House of Lords in Northern Ireland cases, of the Court of Appeal, Court of Criminal Appeal and of the High Court

41 *Alma Shipping Co.* v. *V. M. Salgaoncar E. Irmaos, Ltda.* [1954] 2 Q.B. 94.
42 *Re Cohen* [1960] Ch. 179.
43 *Re House Property and Investment Co., Ltd.* [1954] Ch. 576.

of Northern Ireland are binding on lower courts. The Court of Appeal is bound by its own previous decisions [44] under the principles laid down in *Young* v. *Bristol Aeroplane Co.*[45] Decisions of the English and Scottish superior courts have persuasive value and decisions of the Irish courts prior to 1921 have high persuasive value. Decisions of the Irish courts are entitled to the highest respect but are never binding on Scottish or English courts.[46]

PRIVY COUNCIL

Judgments of the Privy Council, except possibly in those few cases where it sits as a court of appeal from a United Kingdom court, are not binding on any United Kingdom court,[47] though highly persuasive and entitled to great weight because of the personal eminence of the lawyers who form the Judicial Committee.[48] The Privy Council is, moreover, not bound by its own previous judgments and may reconsider points decided in previous appeals to the Board.[49]

Binding Precedent

The foregoing paragraphs indicate that of prior decisions in point in a later case the category of binding precedents is determined for any given court primarily by the place of that court in the hierarchy in relation to the place held by the court which subsequently has to consider the applicability of the prior decision to a case before it.

Persuasive Precedent

The category of persuasive precedents includes all precedents other than those which may be held binding under the foregoing principles. Thus any case decided by a court in another vertical line of the judicial hierarchy will be persuasive in greater or less degree, depending on the status of the court which decided it. So will a case from a court of equivalent or even lower status, in the same or another line, though but little weight attaches in the latter case.

Other persuasive precedents include judgments of the Privy Council when sitting as the final court of appeal from the colonies, and formerly from the dominions [50]; judgments of superior courts in Ireland [51] and

---

[44] *Parkinson* v. *Watson* [1956] N.I. 1.
[45] [1944] K.B. 718.
[46] *Re Parsons* (1890) 45 Ch.D. 51.
[47] *Dulieu* v. *White* [1901] 2 K.B. 669; *Venn* v. *Tedesco* [1926] 2 K.B. 227; *Lynn* v. *Bamber* [1930] 2 K.B. 72; *Brown* v. *John Watson, Ltd.,* 1914 S.C.(H.L.) 44; *Duncan* v. *Cammell Laird & Co.* [1942] A.C. 624.
[48] *Leask* v. *Scott* (1877) 2 Q.B.D. 376, 380.
[49] *Re Transferred Civil Servants (Ireland) Compensation* [1929] A.C. 242; *Mercantile Bank of India* v. *Central Bank of India* [1938] A.C. 287; see also Raney, " The Finality of Privy Council Decisions " (1926) 4 Can.B.R. 307.
[50] *Leask* v. *Scott* (1877) 2 Q.B.D. 376, 380.   [51] *Re Parsons* (1890) 45 Ch.D. 51.

countries of the Commonwealth [52]; judgments of superior courts in America [53]; judgments of foreign courts [54]; while rather similar persuasive force attaches to judicial dicta,[55] to statements in reputable books [56] and articles in standard legal periodicals, and to the Civil [57] and Canon Laws and the opinions of the standard commentators thereon.[58] Judgments of the Scottish courts are persuasive in England and elsewhere, particularly when interpreting a United Kingdom statute or discussing a point of general jurisprudence.[59]   In matters of commercial law it is particularly desirable that there should be uniformity of decision in common law jurisdictions.[60]

Factors affecting the Evaluation of Precedents

Quite apart from the formal questions whether a precedent is authoritative and binding or merely persuasive its value as a guide in a future case is affected by various other factors which are all of relevance when one has to evaluate a precedent.   The importance of the factors affecting evaluation arises particularly when a court is trying to find a reason for not holding itself bound.

A precedent in general gains authority from its antiquity and the lapse of time since it was decided.   This is particularly so if it has been approved, followed and applied in other cases, but even if it has stood unquestioned and unreversed for a substantial time, a precedent may have acquired such authority that a later court will hesitate to overrule it, even though it could, in view of the upset to the law and to

---

52 *Chester* v. *Waverley*, 62 C.L.R. 1 (Australia) cited in *Bourhill* v. *Young*, 1942 S.C. (H.L.) 78; *cf. Hughes and Vale Pty. Ltd.* v. *State of N.S.W.* [1955] A.C. 241, 307; *Midland Silicones, Ltd.* v. *Scruttons, Ltd.* [1961] 1 Q.B. 106, 128.

53 *Castro* v. *R.* (1881) 6 App.Cas. at 249; *Scaramanga* v. *Stamp* (1880) 5 C.P.D. at 303; *Cory* v. *Burr* (1882) 9 Q.B.D. at 469; *Donoghue* v. *Stevenson*, 1932 S.C.(H.L.) 31; *Haynes* v. *Harwood* [1935] 1 K.B. at 156–157, 163, 167; *Walsh* v. *Lord Advocate* 1956 S.C.(H.L.) 126; *Midland Silicones, Ltd.* v. *Scruttons, Ltd., supra.*   But see cautions voiced in *Re Missouri* (1889) 42 Ch.D. at 330; *Fender* v. *Mildmay* [1938] A.C. at 25; *A/B Karlshamns Oljefabriker* v. *Monarch S.S. Co.*, 1949 S.C.(H.L.) 1.

54 *Sugden* v. *H.M. Advocate*, 1934 J.C. 103.

55 As to judicial dicta, see p. 325, *infra.*

56 *e.g.*, Dicey on *Conflict of Laws.*

57 *e.g.*, *Taylor* v. *Caldwell* (1863) 3 B. & S. 826; *Cantiere San Rocco* v. *Clyde Shipbuilding Co.*, 1923 S.C.(H.L.) 105.

58 *e.g.*, Pothier: *McLean* v. *Clydesdale Bank* (1883) 11 R.(H.L.) 1.

59 *Minister of Pensions* v. *Higham* [1948] 2 K.B. 153, 155; *Murdoch Lownie* v. *Newman* [1949] 2 All E.R. 783; *Newman* v. *Lipman* [1951] 1 K.B. 333, 337; *Regional Properties* v. *Frankenschwerth* [1951] 1 K.B. 631; *Cording* v. *Halse* [1954] 3 W.L.R. 625; *Trickers (Confectioners)* v. *Barnes* [1955] 1 W.L.R. 372; *Cording* v. *Halse* [1955] 1 Q.B. 63; *R.* v. *Minister of Agriculture* [1955] 2 Q.B. 140; *Watson* v. *Nikolaisen* [1955] 2 Q.B. 286; *Wiseburgh* v. *Domville* [1956] 1 W.L.R. 312; *Kahn* v. *Newberry* [1959] 2 Q.B. 1; *Abbott* v. *Philbin* [1960] Ch. 27 (revd. [1961] A.C. 352); see also *McLean* v. *Clydesdale Bank, supra.*

60 *Midland Silicones, Ltd.* v. *Scruttons, Ltd.* [1961] 1 Q.B. 106, 128.

expectations and transactions founded on the precedent.[61] If it has been considered as establishing the law and been acted upon a later court will not interfere with it.[62]

Conversely, however, an older precedent may be of small value if inadequately reported,[63] repeatedly criticised, not followed or distinguished, or if in the course of time it becomes inconsistent with modern views and doctrines or is inconsistent with or superseded by later legislation. It may thus become practically obsolete and inoperative.[64]

Something depends too on whether the court in the precedent case was unanimous or divided, and in the latter case, whether the dissents were substantial and on weighty grounds. Approval by a subsequent court, especially if a higher one, affirmation on appeal, approval by academic jurists, consultation with other judges [65] or the presence of a larger bench,[66] and the passage of a subsequent statute which does not interfere with the decision [67] all tend to strengthen it.

The personal eminence of the judges has also to be borne in mind. Some decisions can be characterised as of a " strong bench," not so much in number of judges as of high judicial quality. Other cases are of the converse.[68] In modern times judgements of Lord President Inglis,[69] Lord Dunedin (both as Lord President and later as Lord of Appeal) [70] and Lord President Cooper [71] are always entitled to especial respect. In

---

[61] *West Ham Union* v. *Edmonton Union* [1908] A.C. 1; *Baird* v. *Baird's Trs.*, 1956 S.C.(H.L.) 93, 107–108; *Brownsea Haven Properties, Ltd.* v. *Poole Corpn.* [1958] Ch. 574. *Cf. Fortington* v. *Lord Kinnaird*, 1942 S.C. 239, 266: " [The precedent] has been cited and quoted too often down to very recent times to be open to challenge."

[62] *Pugh* v. *Golden Valley Ry.* (1880) 15 Ch.D. at 334; *Smith* v. *Keal* (1882) 9 Q.B.D. at 352; *Bourne* v. *Keane* [1919] A.C. 815, 857; *Admiralty Commissioners* v. *S.S. Valverda* [1938] A.C. 173, 194; see also *Ridsdale* v. *Clifton* (1877) 2 P.D. 306; *Foakes* v. *Beer* (1884) 9 App.Cas. 630; *Queen* v. *Edwards* (1884) 13 Q.B.D. 590; *Re Wallis* (1890) 25 Q.B.D. 180; *Admiralty Commissioners* v. *S.S. Amerika* [1917] A.C. 38, 55; *Weld Blundell* v. *Stephens* [1920] A.C. 956, 987; *French Marine* v. *Compagnie Napolitaine* [1921] 2 A.C. 494, 511; *Gibaud* v. *G.E. Ry.* [1921] 2 K.B. 426, 432; *Triefus & Co.* v. *Post Office* [1957] 2 Q.B. 352.

[63] *Stirling* v. *Lauderdale* (1733), disregarded in *Glasgow Corpn.* v. *Lord Advocate*, 1959 S.C. 203, 231.

[64] *Rawlence* v. *Spicer* [1935] 1 K.B. at 435; *Matthews* v. *Kuwait Bechtel Corpn.* [1959] 2 Q.B. 57. *Cf.* also the observations in *R.* v. *Jackson* [1891] 1 Q.B. 671, that a husband's right to chastise his wife is now obsolete, and *Winchester* v. *Fleming* [1958] 1 Q.B. 259. *Cf.* also *Beith's Trustees* v. *Beith*, 1950 S.C. 66.

[65] *e.g.*, where the judges of one Division of the Court of Session consult with the other Division before giving their judgment, as in *Connell* v. *Connell*, 1950 S.C. 505.

[66] As in cases argued before seven judges.

[67] *Cf. Thorne* v. *Motor Trade Association* [1937] A.C. 797, 806.

[68] *Cf.* Kennedy, " The Second Division's Progress " (1896) 8 J.R. 268, where he criticises the Second Division of his day.

[69] See Crabb Watt, *John Inglis*, Chap. 13.

[70] " Dunedin, the greatest master of the principles of Scots Law in our time ": *per* Lord Macmillan, *Stewart* v. *L.M.S. Ry.*, 1943 S.C.(H.L.) 19, 38.

[71] See Smith, " The Contribution of Lord Cooper of Culross to Scottish Law " in (1956) 67 J.R. 249 and in Lord Cooper's *Selected Papers*, xxix.

the House of Lords judgments of Lords Cairns, Halsbury, Watson, Macmillan, Atkin and Wright have similarly had special value and are not lightly to be disregarded.

Precedents are of less value if it appears that the case was not fully argued,[72] as where only one party appeared, or if some points passed unnoticed or were not argued [73] or conceded,[74] or if it appears from the printed arguments of counsel in the report that certain relevant cases or statutes were not cited or considered in the precedent,[75] particularly if they were to a contrary effect, or if no reasoned judgments are delivered,[76] or if there are powerful dissenting judgments, or if the case were compromised or settled,[77] or if the report is defective,[78] or if the judges differ as to their reasons or if these seem defective, or if the decision has apparently been reached on some specialty, such as to avoid hardship or injustice, or on the particular terms of a deed or contract or statute.

The Technique of Handling Precedents

Decisions are cited in textbooks for various reasons, sometimes as examples, sometimes for the form of action chosen, sometimes for points which are implicit in the case, sometimes for the interest of the decision reached, and sometimes for other reasons. But all these reasons are of little or no value when the matter in issue is whether a later court is in the circumstances bound to follow or is subject to persuasion to follow the principle of law enunciated or developed in the precedent, because the importance of precedents as a source of law is that earlier cases lay down and develop principles, rules and doctrines of law capable of future application.[79] The problem is: what is it in a precedent that a later court must, or should consider carefully whether to, follow and apply?

---

[72] *R.* v. *Ettridge* [1909] 2 K.B. at 27 (C.C.A.); *Edwards* v. *Jones* [1947] 1 All E.R. 830 (D.C.); *Nicholas* v. *Penny* [1950] 2 K.B. 466. *Cf. Sagar* v. *Ridehalgh* [1931] 1 Ch. 310. In *Bell* v. *Bell*, 1941 S.C.(H.L.) 5, an undefended divorce case, in view of the importance of the principle of law in issue, the Solicitor-General appeared in the House of Lords, at the House's request, and was heard, so that the House had the benefit of argument on both sides.

[73] *Rahimtoola* v. *Nizam of Hyderabad* [1958] A.C. 379.

[74] *O'Shea* v. *O'Shea and Parnell* (1890) 15 P.D. 59, 64; *Young* v. *Sealey* [1949] 1 All E.R. 92, 108.

[75] *e.g., Racecourse Betting Control Board* v. *Secretary of State for Air* [1944] Ch. 114, not followed in *R.* v. *Northumberland Compensation Appeal Tribunal, ex p. Shaw* [1952] 1 K.B. 338.

[76] As in some old cases.

[77] *Sagar* v. *Ridehalgh* [1931] 1 Ch. 310.

[78] Some reports prior to 1800 are so brief and defective that it is not really possible to say what the basis for the decision was: such a precedent is of little value.

[79] " The only use of authorities or decided cases is the establishment of some principle, which the judge can follow out in deciding the case before him," *Re Hallett* (1879) 13 Ch.D. 696, 712, *per* Jessel M.R.; *cf. Smith* v. *Harris* [1939] 3 All E.R. 960, 965.

A reported case is of value as a precedent for guidance in future cases, whether authoritative or persuasive, only in respect of the principle of law, if any, which can be derived from it, as that on which it was decided,[80] and which must, or may, be used again to decide a later case. Not every reported case contains a statement of a principle; it may be reported for the interest of the factual situation, or simply as an example of how the court applied a particular principle in certain circumstances, or because of a ruling on evidence or pleading or procedure, or because of the application of an accepted principle to a new or unusual set of facts. Again it may not be apparent on what principle the judges proceeded, but in many cases a statement of a principle of law can be discerned as expressed or implied in the decision reached in the circumstances, and it is this statement alone which is valuable in subsequent cases. " When any tribunal is bound by the judgment of another court, either superior or co-ordinate, it is, of course, bound by the judgment itself. And if from the opinions delivered it is clear—as is the case in most instances—what the *ratio decidendi* was which led to the judgment, then that *ratio decidendi* is also binding." [81] " The inevitable first question, then, with which the court must deal necessarily is:—Is a certain general *ratio* laid down and at the root of [the precedent]; and is it to be approved and applied? " [82]

The Ratio Decidendi

This underlying principle of a judicial decision is termed the *ratio decidendi* and it is only this element of the decision which is binding upon a subsequent judge.[83] It has been defined as " the reason or ground on which a judgment is rested," [84] " the underlying principle which forms the authoritative element [of a judicial decision]," [85] or " the conclusion reached by the judges on the basis of the material facts and on the exclusion of the immaterial ones," [86] or " the proposition of law which was necessary for the decision, or can be extracted from the decision," [87] or " the enunciation of the reason or principle on

[80] " The only thing in a judge's decision binding as an authority upon a subsequent judge is the principle on which the case was decided ": *Osborne to Rowlett* (1880) 13 Ch.D. 774, 785, *per* Jessel M.R. *Cf. Craig* v. *Glasgow Corpn.*, 1919 S.C.(H.L.) 1, 10.

[81] *G.W. Ry.* v. *Owners of S.S. Mostyn* [1928] A.C. 57, 73, *per* Lord Dunedin, quoted in *Beith's Trs.* v. *Beith*, 1950 S.C. 66, 70 and *Douglas Hamilton* v. *Duke and Duchess of Hamilton's Trs.*, 1961 S.C. 205, 229.

[82] *Fortington* v. *Lord Kinnaird*, 1942 S.C. 239, 269, *per* Lord Mackay; *cf.* Lord Wark at 281.

[83] *Re Hallett* (1879) 13 Ch.D. 696, 712; *Osborne to Rowlett* (1880) 13 Ch.D. 774, 785.

[84] Bell's *Law Dictionary*, 884; *cf.* Fraser Tytler's *Memoirs of Lord Kames*, I, 114: ". . . the *ratio decidendi*, or rule of law on which the judgment rests."

[85] Salmond, *Jurisprudence*, 11th ed., 223.

[86] Paton, *Jurisprudence*, 2nd ed., 160, following Goodhart, *Essays*, 22.

[87] Dias & Hughes, *Jurisprudence*, 72.

which a question before a court has been decided is alone binding as a precedent," [88] or " that part of [any judgment of any court] . . . which is considered to have been necessary to the decision of the actual issue between the litigants." [89]   Finding the *ratio* of a case is a process of abstracting principle from a mass of allegations, facts, arguments, opinions and judgment. *Ratio* should *not* be translated as " the reason *for* the decision," because a decision yielding a sound *ratio* may be reached, overtly or tacitly, for a bad reason, *e.g.*, because the judge disapproved of the pursuer's morals, or felt sorry for him. " The reason which the judge gives for his decision is never the binding part of the precedent." [90]

The determination of the *ratio decidendi* of a precedent is the task of the judge in a subsequent case, or of the legal adviser when trying to discover the law applicable to a problem before him. He has to try to determine what general proposition of law the precedent expressly or impliedly stated, apart from the court's application of that proposition in the circumstances of the prior case to produce the court's actual disposal of the case. It is a task of extreme importance and considerable difficulty for which unfortunately no settled formula or rules of thumb can be suggested; it cannot be done mechanically; it is an art rather than a science.[91]

Finding the Ratio Decidendi

It should be noted first that the *ratio* of a decision is not necessarily contained in the rubric of the report, since that is compiled by the reporter and is not authoritative, nor is it necessarily to be found in any phrase or passage of any of the opinions delivered in the case. It is the proposition of law which is the ground or basis of the decision, or was necessary for the decision of the precedent, necessarily underlying and inherent in the decision reached on the facts alleged or found proved,[92] a generalised statement of law which justifies the decision on the facts of the

---

88 Halsbury's *Laws of England*, tit. " Judgments," para. 1682.
89 Allen, *Law in the Making*, 6th ed., 247.
90 Goodhart, " Determining the *Ratio Decidendi* of a Case " in *Essays in Jurisprudence and the Common Law*, 1, and (1930) 40 Yale L.J. 161.
91 There is a considerable periodical literature on this topic. The most important are: Goodhart, " Determining the *Ratio Decidendi* of a Case," in *Essays in Jurisprudence and the Common Law*, 1; Paton and Sawer, " *Ratio Decidendi* and *Obiter Dictum* in Appellate Courts " (1947) 63 L.Q.R. 461; Gooderson, " *Ratio Decidendi* and the Rules of Law " (1952) 30 Can.B.R. 892; Simpson, " *Ratio Decidendi* of a Case " (1957) 20 M.L.R. 413; (1958) 21 M.L.R. 155; Montrose, " *Ratio Decidendi* and the House of Lords " (1957) 20 M.L.R. 124; Montrose, " *Ratio Decidendi* of a case " (1957) 20 M.L.R. 587; Goodhart, " *Ratio Decidendi* of a case " (1959) 22 M.L.R. 117; Simpson, " *Ratio Decidendi* of a Case " (1959) 22 M.L.R. 453.
92 In Scottish practice when the precedent is of a decision on relevancy (as to which see p. 245, *supra*) the facts averred and accepted for the purposes of argument are material, but when the precedent is of a decision arrived at after proof or trial the material facts are those which have been held proved.

precedent case, neither more nor less.[93] A judgment must always be read as applicable to the facts of the case in which it was delivered and the generality of expressions used are qualified by the facts of the case and are not necessarily more widely applicable.[94]

According to Goodhart [95] one must first determine what facts were averred for the purposes of the argument (in a debate on pleadings) or were found to have been proved (in a decision after proof) and segregate these facts into facts necessary for or material to the decision and facts immaterial to the decision. It is impossible to lay down in the abstract what facts or averments can be treated as immaterial. Any fact or averment may be material but normally such facts or averments as the name, age, sex, status or condition of the parties, time, date, place, or weather conditions of the happenings, and all merely coincident and concomitant circumstances will be immaterial, though in particular cases any one or more of these factors may be material. If the judge treats any factor as material, either expressly or impliedly, in his opinion, then it must be accepted as material. The material facts or averments must then be set down in relation to the actual decision of the court and the *ratio* formulated in terms of a general proposition of law which takes account of all, but no more than, the material facts or averments and of the ultimate decision. Thus the *ratio* of *Donoghue* v. *Stevenson* [96] might be expressed as follows: A person who claims to have suffered injury in consequence of drinking a bottled drink containing an impurity is entitled to claim damages direct from the manufacturer thereof where there was no reasonable possibility of intermediate inspection of the product between manufacture and consumption.

The more facts or averments are held to be material and therefore

---

[93] In logic, of course, an indefinitely large number of general propositions can be thought of all of which would justify the particular decision on the actual facts of the precedent. No general proposition can be deduced from one particular proposition. But in fact the possible general propositions are limited by the court's opinion and by the accepted context of that branch of the law and other cases on related points. On this point see further Stone, *The Province and Function of Law*, 186 *et seq.*; Patterson, *Jurisprudence*, 306 *et seq.*

[94] *Quinn* v. *Leathem* [1901] A.C. 495, 506, *per* Lord Halsbury.

[95] " Determining the *Ratio Decidendi* of a Case," *supra.*

[96] 1932 S.C.(H.L.) 31. It has to be remembered that *Donoghue's* case was decided, even in the House of Lords, on the basis of facts averred to have happened, and not proved to have taken place. The main averments were that Mrs. D. was bought a ginger-beer (manufactured and put out in an opaque bottle by S.) by a friend in a café. She drank some of it and when emptying the rest of the bottle into her glass, the remains of a decomposed snail floated out of the bottle. She was shocked and made sick, and sued S. for damages. In law, could she recover? This was the question for debate, it being necessarily assumed for the purposes of that debate, that Mrs. D. could, if called on, prove by evidence that there had in fact been a decomposed snail in the bottle. As the case was finally settled by agreement, Mrs. D. was never called on to try to prove the existence of the snail, and that it had caused her sickness. The case is familiarly known as the " Snail in the bottle " case.

necessarily incorporated in the *ratio,* or the more narrowly they are stated, the narrower will be the resulting *ratio* and the more limited its scope of application in future cases.[97] Conversely the fewer the essential material facts or averments, or the more broadly they are stated, the wider will be the principle and the more readily available for later cases.

It follows also from this insistence on material facts that a case may yield a *ratio* even if there is only a judgment on certain facts with no opinion delivered and no reasons given. This technique of seeking to determine material facts and elicit a *ratio* therefrom may also tend to produce a statement of a *ratio* which is very closely related to the facts of a case and dependent on its specialties. Also, relating the *ratio* so closely to the material facts of a case means that the *ratio* is not strictly applicable to any future case unless it has the same material facts or averments, and this theory of *ratio* may produce a state in which every case has its own *ratio,* which is not necessarily applicable to any other case.

Alternatively one can approach the problem by searching the opinions of the judges for a statement of principle which that judge held to subsume and to justify his decision on the facts or averments of the case before him. This depends on a close analysis of the opinions and no more detailed guidance than that can be given. On this basis examination of the opinions in *Donoghue* v. *Stevenson* shows that Lord Macmillan considered the case to fall within this principle: " A person who for gain engages in the business of manufacturing articles of food and drink intended for consumption by members of the public in the form in which he issues them is under a duty to take care in the manufacture of these articles," and Lord Atkin under this: " A manufacturer of products which he sells in such a form as to show that he intends them to reach the ultimate consumer in the form in which they left him with no reasonable possibility of intermediate examination, and with the knowledge that the absence of reasonable care in the preparation or putting up of the products will result in an injury to the consumer's life or property, owes a duty to the consumer to take that reasonable care."

This kind of approach to the problem of finding the *ratio* implies that there is no *ratio* where a case is decided without opinions being expressed,[98] and it tends to produce *rationes* which are broader than

---

[97] Thus a *ratio* which starts " A married person . . ." is narrower than one starting " A person . . ." and one including the fact of sex, *e.g.* " A married female person . . ." is narrower still. A formulation of the *ratio* of *Donoghue* which says " a bottled drink " is narrower than one which says " food or drink," and narrower still than one which says " manufactured product " (which could include clothing, vehicles, etc.).

[98] Lord Dunedin in *G.W. Ry.* v. *S.S. Mostyn* [1928] A.C. 57, 73 suggested that in such a case the judgment on the facts might be binding, apart from any *ratio* or principle discoverable. So too if there are opinions delivered which do not seem to yield any clear statement of the principle on which the case was decided.

required for, or sometimes justified by, the circumstances of the case argued and decided, and which may in literal terms cover sets of circumstances never contemplated by the judges, since judges commonly express their opinions more generally than the facts of the case demand. In fact, even if no opinions are delivered, a *ratio* may exist and can be inferred from the facts taken along with the actual judgment or disposal of the case. It is essential to remember that no proposition can ever be said to be the *ratio* if the court's actual decision and disposal of the case is not consistent with or does not follow from that proposition.

Any formulation of the *ratio* of a precedent must moreover be construed in the light of cases subsequent to the precedent and what may appear to be, or even be clearly indicated as, part of the *ratio*, may have been explained in later cases as inaccurate or unnecessary.[99]

Multiple Rationes

It is, of course, apparent that one precedent may contain decisions and rulings on several separate points of dispute, and any one of these separately may be a valuable precedent in a later case, even though the other points decided in the precedent may have no relevance. Thus if a precedent contains rulings on (i) the jurisdiction of the court, (ii) a matter of pleading, (iii) the merits of the claim, (iv) the kind of remedy, and (v) the expenses of the cause, the *ratio* on point (iii) may be extracted and used in a subsequent case for which the precedent is in point, even though the other points argued and decided in the precedent did not arise in the subsequent case. One case may, that is, be authority for several points of law on different topics, and may consequently be referred to in a textbook in several different contexts.

But even on a single point a judge sometimes gives two or more reasons for his decision or formulates his ruling on the law in two or more ways. Each formulation is regarded as a separate *ratio decidendi* and both are binding; a later court cannot pick one and ignore the other [1]; but one may be *obiter* or merely tentative, and merely tentative indications of opinion do not amount to *ratio*.[2] One ground of decision may subsequently be overruled, leaving the decision to rest on the other ground.[3] It is also difficult where a judge discusses several possible grounds of decision and finally, looking at the case as a whole, arrives at a decision without making clear which ground is really the basis of decision. Probably in such a case a subsequent court must accept each

---

[99] See, *e.g.*, the explanation of the *ratio* of *Barwick* v. *English Joint Stock Bank* (1866) L.R. 2 Ex. 259 in *Lloyd* v. *Grace, Smith & Co.* [1912] A.C. 716.

[1] *Behrens* v. *Bertram Mills Circus, Ltd.* [1957] 2 Q.B. 1, 24.

[2] *Jacobs* v. *L.C.C.* [1950] A.C. 361, 369. " There is no justification for regarding as *obiter dictum* a reason given by a judge for his decision because he has given another reason also." *Cf. London Jewellers* v. *Attenborough* [1934] 2 K.B. 206, 222.

[3] *Betty's Cafés, Ltd.* v. *Phillips Furnishing Stores, Ltd.* [1959] A.C. 20, 53.

of the grounds of decision as being the *ratio* of the case. " It is well established that if a judge gives two reasons for his decision, both are binding. It is not permissible to pick out one as being supposedly the better reason and ignore the other one; nor does it matter for this purpose which comes first and which comes second. But the practice of making judicial observations *obiter* is also well established. A judge may often give additional reasons for his decision without wishing to make them part of the *ratio decidendi*; he may not be sufficiently convinced of their cogency as to want them to have the full authority of precedent, and yet may wish to state them so that those who later may have the duty of investigating the same point will start with some guidance. This is a matter which the judge himself is alone capable of deciding and any judge who comes after him must ascertain which course has been adopted from the language used and not by consulting his own preference." [4]

A rather similar problem arises in the event of discrepancy or conflict between the opinions delivered and the interlocutor pronounced as the operative part of the court's decision. On principle the *ratio* has to be consistent with the operative decision, whatever the opinions may appear to say.[5]

Ratio in Appellate Courts

It is likewise obviously a problem of great difficulty to determine the *ratio* of the decision of an appellate court, where several opinions may be delivered (apart from any dissents), and different judges may formulate principles differently or proceed on the basis of different facts being material. It is possible for several judges of an appellate court each to arrive at the same decision and to concur in the disposal of the case but for different reasons, and each judge's opinion may yield a quite distinct *ratio*, possibly inconsistent with the others.[6]

If the *ratio* common to all, or at least to the majority, of the judges is obscure, a subsequent court is probably entitled to consider itself influenced by the decision itself and to choose for itself the *ratio* of the precedent.[7]

Cases where there is no useful Ratio

There are some few cases which are decided entirely on their own facts and which are not authority for anything more than the particular

---

4 *Behrens* v. *Bertram Mills Circus* [1957] 2 Q.B. 1, *per* Devlin J.
5 See, however, *Pollok School* v. *Glasgow Town Clerk*, 1946 S.C. 373 and 1947 S.C. 605. 6 *e.g.*, *Republica de Guatemala* v. *Nunez* [1927] 1 K.B. 669.
7 *G.W. Ry.* v. *S.S. Mostyn* [1928] A.C. 57, 73, where the House of Lords abandoned the attempt to discover the *ratio* of *River Wear Commrs.* v. *Adamson* (1877) 2 App.Cas. 743. See further Paton and Sawer, " *Ratio Decidendi* and *Obiter Dictum* in Appellate Courts " (1947) 63 L.Q.R. 461. See also the observations of L.-P. Cooper in *Macdonald* v. *Glasgow Western Hospitals*, 1954 S.C. 453, 474 on *Reidford* v. *Aberdeen Magistrates*, 1933 S.C. 276.

decision of that case. Among such cases are decisions on matters of fact, on the sentence or measure of damages appropriate in the circumstances, on the way judicial discretion is being exercised in the particular case, or those decided on the terms of a particular trust deed or will, or on the precise terms of particular pleadings, or in the precise factual circumstances of a particular case. They are decisions on their own facts and do not purport to lay down any general rules or principles, and are unlikely to be of any value at all as precedents unless in the very unlikely event of precisely similar circumstances arising again. The decisions are merely choices between one of two or more possible interpretations of words or facts and proceed on no legal basis capable of wider application. Every such case has, of course, its own individual *ratio* but it is so special to the terms and circumstances of that case that it is of little or no use as a precedent for the future. Thus in *Mair's Trustee* v. *Aberdeen Royal Infirmary*[9] a testatrix made certain bequests and directed finally that " what money is left over " was to go to a charity. It was held that, while the word " money " might sometimes cover heritable property, it did not do so *in the will under construction,* and accordingly that a bequest of heritage which had lapsed did not fall under this residuary bequest of " money."

There is again no useful *ratio* where the judgments delivered are so unclear that a subsequent court cannot find the *ratio,*[10] and where a case has been so frequently distinguished or doubted that it cannot be taken as more than a decision on its own special facts.[11]

Ratio and Obiter Dictum

All statements by the judges which are outwith the *ratio* or are not necessary for the *ratio* fall to be classed as *obiter dicta.* Such dicta thus include all statements of law which go beyond the occasion, as where a rule is laid down for " animals " in a case dealing with a horse; or which lay down a rule irrelevant to the problem before the court, as where in the case of a limited company a judge says " It would be competent for a local authority . . ."; or which are stated as analogies, as where a judge remarks, " Similarly in cases of . . . the same would apply "; or which deal with the opposite case, as where a judge remarks, " Conversely, the rule would not apply to . . ."; or which deal with hypothetical

---

[9] 1946 S.L.T. 88.
[10] The famous example is *River Wear Commrs.* v. *Adamson* (1877) 2 App.Cas. 743; in *G.W. Ry.* v. *S.S. Mostyn* [1928] A.C. 57, the House of Lords abandoned the attempt to find its *ratio.*
[11] Thus *McLachlan* v. *McLachlan*, 1945 S.C. 382, has been distinguished in *Swan* v. *Swan* [1953] P. 258, *Jamieson* v. *Jamieson*, 1951 S.C. 286; *Scott* v. *Scott*, 1960 S.C. 36 and *Breen* v. *Breen*, 1961 S.C. 158 and can now be regarded as limited to its own special circumstances, if not indeed wrongly decided.

cases, as where a judge states the law " if the pursuer had proved . . . then I should have been prepared to hold that . . ."; or which are mere observations made in the course of argument.[12] There can be no complete catalogue of what will be dicta rather than part of the *ratio* and these are only examples. Subsequent judges sometimes condemn as mere dicta statements which others have thought were part of the *ratio* of prior decision.

Dicta are of varying weights and varying value, from mere casual observations, possibly unconsidered, possibly even erroneous, to carefully considered statements which are not, however, part of the *ratio* as going outside or beyond the circumstances of the case before the court.[13] They may be highly important as persuasive precedent in future,[14] but they are never binding.[15]

Drawing the distinction between *ratio* and *obiter dictum* is clearly also an art rather than a science; different men may differ as to what is *ratio* and what is dictum in a precedent, and while to stigmatise something as merely dictum is one of the easiest ways to avoid being bound by an inconvenient precedent, that is not always practicable. All that can be said is that the *ratio* is the central and essential part of the decision while the dicta are collateral and inessential, but in certain cases have to be weighed and regarded carefully. Cross [16] sums it up as follows: " The *ratio decidendi* of a case is any rule of law expressly or impliedly treated by the judge as a necessary step in reaching his conclusion, having regard to the line of reasoning adopted by him, or a necessary part of his direction to the jury. In arriving at it regard must be had to the facts of the case, the issues raised by the pleadings and arguments, and the previous state of the law. Further guidance may sometimes be obtained from the observations in prior and subsequent cases by judges who were members of the court in the case the *ratio decidendi* of which is to be determined. It is open to question whether the decision of any issue in a case in favour of the party against whom the court order is made can constitute part of the *ratio decidendi* of that case. The *ratio decidendi* of a case is generally the proposition of law for which that case may be cited as authority but it is the practice of the judges to interpret a decision in the light of the facts of the case and the decisions in other cases. Accordingly, in order to ascertain the proposition of law for which a case is authority at a later date, regard must be had to subsequent cases in which it has been considered."

---

[12] Practice Note [1942] W.N. 89.
[13] *Slack v. Leeds Industrial Co-operative Society* [1923] 1 Ch. 431, 451.
[14] *Cf. Re House Property and Investment Co.* [1953] 3 W.L.R. 1037.
[15] " A dictum of a judge of first instance is not binding even upon himself ": *Kwei Tek Chao v. British Traders and Shippers* [1954] 3 W.L.R. 496, *per* Devlin J.
[16] *Precedent in English Law*, pp. 75–76.

Ratio and Principles of Law

The *ratio* of a case is accordingly the proposition of law necessary to the decision of the case. It is not the same as a general principle of law but is an example and application of such a principle and general principles of law have in fact been, particularly in England, largely built up by the generalisation from a number of specific *rationes* or principles of particular cases whereas in Scotland *rationes* have also been frequently deductions from overriding general principles of law. The *ratio* or principle of a case is thus related to but distinct from those broader and more general principles. Thus to say that a man is entitled to recover damages from one who has caused him loss, injury or damage without legal justification is a general principle from which may be deduced, in the circumstances of an actual case, the *ratio* that if a defender has caused another person loss and damage by knocking him down with his car, an action lacking legal justification, the other person may recover damages from the defender. The *ratio* of *Donoghue* v. *Stevenson* [17] is distinct from, and a specific instance of, the more general principle that a person is liable in damages to another if it was foreseeable that his act or omission might cause injury to that other, and if his act or omission has actually so caused injury.

The possibility exists of conflict between a binding precedent and a fundamental principle, in which case it has been said that the fundamental principle must prevail,[18] but this involves the difficult task of formulating verbally the fundamental principle as well as the *ratio* of the precedent.

The Application of Precedents in Later Cases

When a precedent is cited in a later case the later court has several things to do before it can accept and apply it or reject it. It has to decide first of all what the *ratio* of the precedent is and then, comparing the material facts of the precedent with those of the instant case, to decide whether the precedent is in point or not. If it is not in point, if the material facts do not coincide in all respects, the precedent is not exactly in point and is not decisive, though it may remain highly persuasive. Now it has to be accepted that precedents are hardly ever absolutely in point, exactly on all fours, agreeing in all material facts. They will always differ, if only in point of time, and usually in some other respects too, from the instant case, and this question comes to be whether a particular precedent is, if not exactly, at least sufficiently closely in point to be treated as relevant. Secondly, the court must consider from what place in the judicial hierarchy the precedent has come and whether it is binding under the rules of *stare decisis* or merely persuasive, and in the latter case,

[17] p. 321, *supra*.
[18] *London Transport Executive* v. *Betts* [1959] A.C. 213, *per* Lord Denning.

how highly persuasive it is, having regard to the status of the court and the other factors affecting evaluation. Thirdly, the court must decide how far the precedent is to be influential in their decision. Is the later court going to accept it as binding and apply it to the case before the court or to try to avoid that course?

The court may *apply* the precedent by accepting the *ratio*, if it is binding on that court, and applying it to the material facts of the instant case, in effect saying that the rule of case X (the precedent) shall govern the present facts also.[19] Or the court may *follow* the precedent, if it is merely persuasive, applying it by analogy or by extension to the instant case, or adopting its reasoning as leading to the decision of the instant case.

A court may also *not follow* a precedent. This can be done only in the case of a precedent which is not binding or proceeds from a court of co-ordinate jurisdiction.[20] It is a plain indication that the second court has serious doubts about the correctness of the precedent. In such a case the precedent and the later case both stand in the reports as representing divergent views as to the law and this divergence can be solved only by a later superior court accepting one and overruling the other decision,[21] or possibly by reconciling both by means of an explanation or formula which allows each to stand as correct in its own circumstances.

Alternatively, the court may *distinguish* the precedent by pointing to differences between the precedent and the instant case in certain material facts. It may decline on that ground to consider the precedent to be in point and to be either binding or even persuasive. The technique of distinguishing is much resorted to where a judge or court does not in fact wish to be bound by or to follow or apply a particular precedent.[22] It tends to produce hair-splitting distinctions when courts point to slight or even imaginary differences in facts to avoid being required to follow the precedent.

If a court *approves* a precedent, the precedent must have been one accepted on its merits as a valuable guide though not binding, either because it comes from an inferior court or one in a different line of descent.[23] If the court *disapproves* a precedent, the precedent must be one

---

[19] See, *e.g.*, *Lockhart* v. *Barr*, 1943 S.C.(H.L.) 1.

[20] Thus in *Blackwood* v. *Andre*, 1947 S.C. 333 a judge of the Outer House did not follow another judge of the Outer House in *McDaid* v. *Clyde Navigation Trustees*, 1946 S.C. 462.

[21] In *British Transport Commission* v. *Gourley* [1956] A.C. 185, *McDaid* was approved and *Blackwood* disapproved.

[22] See, *e.g.*, *Donoghue* v. *Stevenson*, 1932 S.C.(H.L.) 31, Lord Atkin at pp. 49–56, Lord Macmillan at pp. 65–69.

[23] Thus the Inner House might approve an Outer House precedent or an English precedent but it is not for the Inner House to " approve " a House of Lords decision, whether it is binding or not, since it comes from a superior court. It could only apply it or follow it or distinguish it.

not binding in the circumstances and not so closely in point as to require the court either not to follow or to overrule it.[24] Weaker than disapproval is the action of a court when it *doubts* a precedent, which can be done only in the case of a merely persuasive precedent, or one not sufficiently in point to be binding but on an analogous point. The effect of this is to suggest that the doubted case may not be good law.

Other modes of dealing with precedents, as where they are *considered, explained, discussed, questioned, observed upon* or *commented on*, are self-explanatory; all are appropriate to precedents which are not in the circumstances both in point and binding.

Lastly, a superior court may *overrule* a precedent of a lower court in the same line of descent by declaring expressly or impliedly that the precedent is bad law and no longer of any authority on the point in question.[25] A precedent overruled becomes null and void for the future so far as concerns the *ratio* on which it has been overruled, but other points decided in the same case may still continue to be accepted as good law.

A court is sometimes faced with the difficult task of *reconciling* precedents, and trying to derive from two or more binding precedents a doctrine which subsumes them both or all. " What is the duty of a judge when he is confronted with a series of decisions which are difficult to reconcile? In my judgment it depends: if there is a decision which cannot be distinguished from the case before him, even if it is a decision of a judge of first instance, *a fortiori*, of course, if it is a decision of the Court of Appeal or House of Lords, he ought to apply it—expressing maybe his doubts whether it is still good law, but leaving a superior tribunal to overrule it." [26] Sometimes it is possible to reconcile, some-times one decision or group of decisions can be distinguished and the other followed, sometimes one can be set aside as inconsistent with a later decision of a superior court, but sometimes a court or judge may be faced with two equally binding precedents of equal status which cannot be reconciled, in which case the only course open is to follow what appears the better or preferable.[27]

---

[24] Thus the Court of Session may disapprove an English Court of Appeal decision, and conversely. See, *e.g., Dempster's Trs.* v. *Dempster*, 1949 S.C. 92.

[25] Thus *Horn* v. *N.B. Ry.* (1878) 5 R. 1055 was overruled in *McElroy* v. *McAllister*, 1949 S.C. 110. Notice that overruling a precedent is quite distinct from reversing a prior decision of the instant case (not the precedent) by a lower court. Also overruling a precedent does not affect the decision of the earlier case as between the parties to it, since it was decided on what was then believed to be the law, but is now found to have been an incorrect statement of the rule. Old cases cannot be reopened on this ground. In *Davie* v. *New Merton Board Mills* [1959] A.C. 604, the House of Lords, in an English appeal, purported to overrule *Donnelly* v. *Glasgow Corpn.*, 1953 S.C. 107. This is, strictly, a misstatement; all that the House could do in an English appeal was to disapprove a Scottish case.

[26] *Re House Property Investment Co.* [1953] 3 W.L.R. 1037.

[27] See, *e.g., Angus's Executrix* v. *Batchan's Trs.*, 1949 S.C. 335, where one prior decision was followed and the other overruled.

Conclusions on Case-law

Possibly even more than with statutory law it will be apparent that the handling of case-law is an art rather than a mechanical process. Lord Wright, indeed, observed that it was partly intuition.[28] Such rules as there are are not by any means settled nor unchanging. In the last resort a great deal depends on judicial temperament, on whether the judge agrees with and cares to follow a precedent or whether he disagrees with it, wants to avoid it, and can find a way of avoiding being bound, on whether he values more highly consistency of decisions or what he conceives to be the requirements of justice in the circumstances. It is undoubtedly true that the rigidity of some of the modern rules leads to much casuistry, narrow verbal distinctions, excessive refinements of rules and doctrines and hypocrisy in " distinguishing " cases when the truth is that the later court does not wish to apply the rule of the precedent. Nevertheless despite the rules there is still considerable scope for judicial discretion and the creative function of the judge, developing the law according to current trends, beliefs and policies.

But while these difficulties arise in marginal cases it has to be remembered that principles worked out and laid down in cases of the higher courts suffice for the decision of hundreds of cases in lower courts, in which those precedents are accepted as undoubtedly in point and equally undoubtedly authoritative, and, on the whole, the advantages of consistency, certainty and predictability of the law justify in large measure the existence of the rule of *stare decisis*. What is, however, very doubtful is whether the House of Lords at least, and possibly also the Inner House and corresponding courts, should not have the power to overrule their own previous decisions, and whether any binding force should ever attach to a single decision of a single judge. But the discussion of this belongs to jurisprudence.

III.—LITERARY SOURCES—BOOKS OF AUTHORITY

Statements as to the law made by legal writers have varying degrees of authority, but always less than that of statute or case-law in that in case of conflict the rule laid down by statute or worked out by the courts has undoubtedly to be given effect to, notwithstanding anything in the books. The highest degree of authority attaches to the writings of a small number of writers, all of bygone ages, who all treated in their works of the whole law of Scotland, or at least of very large tracts of it. These are known as the institutional writings, and a statement in one of them, in default of other authority, will almost certainly be

---

[28] " Precedents," 8 Camb.L.J. 138.

taken as settling the law.[29] Among the institutional writers are *always included*[30] Sir Thomas Craig (*Jus Feudale*, 1655); Viscount Stair (*The Institutions of the Law of Scotland*, 1681); Lord Bankton (*An Institute of the Laws of Scotland*, 3 volumes, 1751–53); Professor John Erskine (*An Institute of the Law of Scotland*, 2 volumes, 1773); and Professor George Joseph Bell (*Commentaries on the Law of Scotland and the Principles of Mercantile Jurisprudence*, 1800, and *Principles of the Law of Scotland*, 1829).

To these are sometimes added Sir George Mackenzie (*The Institutions of the Law of Scotland*, 1684) and Henry Home, Lord Kames (*Principles of Equity*, 1760), but not all authorities concede the privileged status of institutional writings to these works.

In criminal law, Baron David Hume (*Commentaries on the Law of Scotland respecting Crimes*, two volumes, 1797), Sir George Mackenzie (*The Laws and Customs of Scotland in Matters Criminal*, 1678) and, probably, Archibald Alison (*Principles of the Criminal Law of Scotland*, 1832, and *Practice of the Criminal Law of Scotland*, 1833) are also regarded as institutional writers.

The authority of a statement by an institutional writer [31] is probably about equal to that of a decision of either Division of the Inner House. It has been said,[32] " Stair, Erskine and Bell are cited daily in the courts, and the court will pay as much respect to them as to a judgment of the House of Lords, though it is bound to follow a judgment of the House of Lords whatever the institutional writers may have said." The authority of institutional writings does not, however, extend automatically to all the writer's works, so that Erskine's *Principles*, written as a textbook for students, is not institutional, and Hume's *Lectures on Scots Law*,[33] not finally revised or published by him, are not entitled to the same weight as his *Commentaries on Crimes*.[34] These other works are merely legal literature though valuable specimens of it in view of the personal eminence of the writer. The institutional writings have been immensely influential in the past and have guided many past decisions of the courts, so that their

---

[29] " When on any point of law I find Stair's opinion uncontradicted I look upon that opinion as ascertaining the Law of Scotland ": *Drew* v. *Drew* (1870) 9 M. 163, 167, *per* Lord Benholme. See also *Kennedy* v. *Stewart* (1889) 16 R. 421, 430, on Kames.

[30] The dates given are of the first publication of the books in question.

[31] A distinction may have to be taken between what the writer himself wrote and what a later editor may have added. Hence reference to the last edition *by the author* is sometimes made.

[32] Lord Normand, *The Scottish Judicature and Legal Procedure* (Holdsworth Club, Birmingham, address, 1941).

[33] *Ed.* Paton, Stair Society, 6 Vols.

[34] *Fortington* v. *Kinnaird*, 1942 S.C. 239, 253; see also *Pettigrew* v. *Harton*, 1956 S.C. 67; *MacLennan* v. *MacLennan*, 1958 S.C. 105; *Thomson* v. *St. Cuthbert's Cooperative Assocn., Ltd.*, 1958 S.C. 380, 394, 398; *N.C.B.* v. *Thomson*, 1959 S.C. 353, 383; *Purden's C.B.* v. *Boyd*, 1962 S.L.T. 180.

importance is not confined to the somewhat spasmodic reference to them today.

IV.—CUSTOM

Among other sources mention must be made of custom, which now plays a much smaller part as a source than it formerly did, in that many older customs have now been embodied in legislation or cases or books of authority. Many general customs have accordingly been incorporated long ago in the common law of Scotland. Thus the " legal rights " of spouses on death and the common-law rules of landlord and tenant are based on very old customs. But apart from these customs, now absorbed into the law, custom may still be alleged in a particular case and, if proved, will be a valid source of a new rule of law. Such a custom must be (*a*) in some sense an exception to or qualification of the ordinary rule of law yet not run completely counter to or be contradictory of an already established rule of statute or case-law. It must, that is, be an exception to, yet still consistent with, the existing general body of law.[35] It may, for example, be confined to a locality. Also it must be (*b*) definite and certain. It cannot be a custom if it is not known what it is, or is vague or if it is not habitually observed. It must further (*c*) be fair and reasonable; hence a claim for an exaction by a landlord for which nothing was given in return has been held unreasonable.[36] (*d*) It must have been generally accepted for so long as to justify the inference that it has long been accepted as law, as the binding rule. No particular period of time must be proved.[37]

The basis on which the court in an appropriate case will enforce the custom as law is that it has been shown to have been so certain, settled and established that it was in fact accepted as law and treated as binding, even though it had not previously been before the courts or obtained express judicial recognition. If it is proved that a particular custom is accepted as law it will rule notwithstanding that either party is ignorant of it; *ignorantia juris neminem excusat*.[38] The importance of this kind of custom as a source of new rules of law is clearly limited.

Quite distinct from this kind of custom is the kind of custom or usage, sometimes sought to be proved, particularly in mercantile matters, to assist in interpreting a contract or implying a term into one. In this case evidence may be allowed to explain or supplement a mercantile contract, not on the basis that the custom is a rule of law, but on the

---

[35] *Walker Trustees* v. *Lord Advocate*, 1912 S.C.(H.L.) 12.
[36] *Bruce* v. *Smith* (1890) 17 R. 1000.
[37] Ersk., I, 1, 44; *secus* in England.
[38] *Learmonth* v. *Sinclair's Trustees* (1878) 5 R. 548.

ground that parties must have known of and must be taken to have intended to act in accordance with some particular trade usage. Since the basis for this kind of custom is implied agreement of parties to be bound by the custom, notice to or knowledge of the usage on the part of the person against whom it is pleaded must be proved.[39] Such a usage must be reasonably fair [40] and at least generally recognised in the trade in question.[41] Thus under this rule it has been proved that by the custom of the rabbit trade " one thousand " means 1,200,[42] or that a provision in a contract for oil for the reference of disputes to " arbitration in Glasgow " meant, by the custom of the oil trade, a reference to an arbiter appointed by each party with an oversman chosen by them.[43] Moreover unless a contract is made expressly subject to some usage, proof of usage is not permitted to contradict the plain meaning of express words in the contract. Thus a contract to supply " the whole of the steel for [a bridge], the estimated quantity to be 30,000 tons," was held to be a contract for the whole amount of steel, despite an alleged usage of the steel trade that the words meant 30,000 tons only.[44]

Parties may also contract in general terms by reference to, *e.g.*, the custom of a particular port, and in that case they will be bound by the custom even though they did not know of its precise terms.[45]

The importance of this kind of custom as a source of law is considerable and in many cases mercantile contracts still have to be interpreted in accordance with customs and usages of particular ports, or particular trades.

V.—EQUITY

Scottish courts have always administered an undivided system of law and equity [46] and many of the principles commonly applied by the

---

[39] *Holman* v. *Peruvian Nitrate Co.* (1878) 5 R. 657.
[40] *Devonald* v. *Rosser* [1906] 2 K.B. 728.
[41] *Hogarth* v. *Leith Cottonseed Oil Co.*, 1909 S.C. 955; *Dick* v. *Cochrane & Fleming*, 1935 S.L.T. 432.
[42] *Smith* v. *Wilson* (1832) 3 B. & Ad. 728.
[43] *United Creameries Co.* v. *Boyd & Co.*, 1912 S.C. 617.
[44] *Tancred, Arrol & Co.* v. *Steel Co. of Scotland* (1887) 15 R. 215; (1890) 17 R.(H.L.) 31; *MacLellan* v. *Peattie's Trustees* (1903) 5 F. 1031. *Cf. Affreteurs Reunis* v. *Walford* [1919] A.C. 801.
[45] *Strathlorne S.S. Co.* v. *Baird*, 1915 S.C. 956; revd. 1916 S.C.(H.L.) 134. *Cf. Forget* v. *Baxter* [1900] A.C. 467.
[46] Until 1875 England had courts of common law which administered law and courts of equity which gave equitable remedies. The distinction still persists in some Commonwealth countries. Since 1875 all courts in England may give both legal and equitable remedies but it is doubtful how far law and equity have been merged; the merger is still incomplete. On English Equity see further Levy-Ullmann, *The English Legal Tradition*, Part 3; Plucknett, *Concise History of the Common Law*, 675 *et seq.*; Potter, *Historical Introduction to English Law*, 4th ed., 569 *et seq.*; Allen, *Law in the Making*, Chap. 5.

courts are as much equitable as legal in origin and justification.[47] Many doctrines of Scots law have been modified by equity, in the sense of the force of reason and natural justice, to rectify or avoid an excessive strictness or rigidity. In many fields of law this influence has so exercised itself in the past that the legal and equitable elements in the modern doctrine have been completely blended and the boundary is not perceptible. But equity remains a valid and unexhausted source of Scots law in that it is still open to a court to delimit a rule or interpret a principle in the light of what seems consistent with reason and natural justice.

Apart from instances where the rule of law has been modified by equitable ideas in the course of its development, the Court of Session and, to some extent, the High Court of Justiciary retain an ultimate residuary equitable power to provide a remedy where justice requires it and to intervene to prevent unduly rigorous law working injustice. This power, the *nobile officium*, has of late come to be much restricted and is, as a rule, exercised now only in circumstances for which there is precedent or analogy.

Moreover, in many fields of law a judge is expressly or impliedly enjoined to keep equitable considerations, the concepts of what is reasonable and conform to natural justice, in mind. He is endowed with discretion, which has to be exercised consistently with these principles and not arbitrarily, though in practice the exercise soon tends to become limited by the ways in which the exercise has been done in past cases, and repeatedly he finds that he has to do what is " just and reasonable " or " fair," or otherwise finds a standard fixed which has to be applied to the facts of the case having in mind the equitable considerations of providing a remedy for any obvious wrong, of avoiding the injustice of excessively rigid application of law, and of rewarding care, diligence and honesty.

VI.—EXTRANEOUS SOURCES

Extraneous sources include all those other sources to which a judge may resort, in default of guidance from the sources already discussed, and from which he may draw or adapt a principle or rule to apply to a new problem before him.

Other Systems of Law

If the sources from which rules and principles of Scots law are normally drawn, those already discussed, yield nothing or nothing very satisfactory, it is permissible and proper to look at other systems of law in which the

---

[47] See further Walker, " Equity in Scots Law " (1954) 66 Jur.Rev. 103; art. " Equity " in Green's *Encyclopaedia*; Lord Murray, "The Law of Nature" in (Stair Society) *Sources and Literature of Scots Law*.

problem may have arisen and which may, accordingly, be able to suggest a suitable rule. Among other systems regard should first be had to Roman law, particularly in questions of obligations and moveable property. Roman law has long been, and may still be, a good quarry for the material of legal decisions and it would be consistent with the tradition of Scots law if resort were made to the Roman law more instead of always running to the English books.[48] Modern systems of law which have drawn heavily on the Roman law, such as the Roman-Dutch law of South Africa, and later commentators on the Roman law, such as Voet, may also usefully be referred to.

In consistorial matters the old Roman Canon law and the great mass of learned commentaries thereon is likewise a traditional, and still valuable and highly reputable, source.

Especially in matters of commercial and industrial law, the laws of England, the Commonwealth countries, and the United States may usefully be looked at. But one has always to keep in mind the very different history, development and working-out of English rules and doctrines. In particular the different approaches of common law and of equity to the same problems prior to 1875, and the continuing results of that dichotomy since then, make English law a very unsafe guide unless in the hands of a scholar who understands both systems. Immense harm has been done to Scots law by the uncritical culling from English law of decisions which appear applicable equally to Scotland but which have really been misunderstood. Moreover, the more remote the legal system from which guidance is being sought, the greater the danger of failing to appreciate the background of the decision or the rule and of importing an unsound principle. Continental law is also occasionally referred to.[49]

Dissenting judgments, *obiter dicta*, and argument by analogy from principles accepted in other contexts may also give assistance.

Legal Literature

Writers on law, whose writings are legal literature rather than literary sources of the law, are technically not authorities at all and, according to

---

[48] Ersk. I, 1, 41, speaks of the Roman law as " of great weight in all cases not fixed by statute or custom, and in which the genius of our law will suffer us to apply it."
[49] For examples of reference to foreign law, see, *e.g., Donoghue* v. *Stevenson,* 1932 S.C.(H.L.) 31 (English and U.S. cases); *A/B Karlshamns Oljefabriker* v. *Monarch S.S. Co.,* 1949 S.C.(H.L.) 1 (U.S. case); *Drummond's J.F.* v. *H.M. Advocate,* 1944 S.C. 298 (English and French law); *Cantiere San Rocco* v. *Clyde Shipbuilding Co.,* 1923 S.C.(H.L.) 105; *Glasgow Corpn.* v. *Lord Advocate,* 1959 S.C. 203; (Roman law); *Sugden* v. *H.M. Advocate,* 1934 J.C. 103 (Dutch jurists, French and Roman law); *Collins* v. *Collins* (1884) 11 R.(H.L.) 19; *Purves' Trustees* v. *Purves* (1895) 22 R. 513; *Annan* v. *Annan,* 1948 S.C. 532; *Imre* v. *Mitchell,* 1958 S.C. 439, 464 (all Canon law); *Walsh* v. *Lord Advocate,* 1956 S.C.(H.L.) 126 (U.S. case); *Breen* v. *Breen,* 1961 S.C. 158 (Roman and Canon law).

the older view, cannot be quoted during their lifetimes,[50] unless possibly they are elevated to the Bench, and even then their writings are of less weight than their judgments.[51] Their writings are secondary and not primary sources of the law. Such writings can only be " adopted " in argument as representing part of the speaker's contention as to the law. " The law books give no assistance because the work of living authors, however deservedly eminent, cannot be used as authority, although the opinions they express may demand attention." [52] But in fact in modern practice many writers are nowadays cited in argument notwithstanding that they are neither dead nor on the Bench. While many such books are referred to in argument and even sometimes quoted in judgments they are only statements of what the jurist in question *believes* the law to be, what he submits is the result of the statutes and decided cases, and any court is quite free to differ from him and to lay down the true rule otherwise.[53] Such books do not state the law authoritatively, in the way institutional writings do, but are only persuasive and state what the writer thinks is the law, on a particular subject. Many books are in fact highly regarded and their views usually accepted and followed, and approval of a decision by the text writers may be taken as supporting its soundness,[54] or disapproval as shaking its authority [55] but it is important to remember that they do not impose law on the Bench, but merely may be voluntarily accepted for their clarity of statement. The precise degree of regard paid to a particular book depends on the writer's reputation, the esteem in which the book is held in the profession, and its age, for all books tend to become out of date, and if not revised may become practically valueless by the passage of time and the progress of the law, as new statutes and cases arise.

Legal literature, of course, serves an invaluable purpose in presenting, either for student or practitioner or judge, a connected, coherent and

---

[50] Hence Lord Wright, speaking of (the then still-living) Sir Frederick Pollock's *Law of Torts*, called it " fortunately not a work of authority ": *Nicholls* v. *Ely Beet Sugar Factory* [1936] 1 Ch. 343, 349.

[51] A distinction may also be taken between a work written by a judge when he was young and an inexperienced advocate at the Bar and a work written in the days of his maturity.

[52] *Donoghue* v. *Stevenson*, 1932 S.C.(H.L.) 31, 35, *per* Lord Buckmaster.

[53] See, *e.g.*, *Bell* v. *Blackwood Morton & Sons, Ltd.*, 1960 S.C. 11, 23, disapproving passage in *Glegg on Reparation*. *Cf. Bastin* v. *Davies* [1950] 2 K.B. 579, where Lord Goddard C.J. said " If a statement has appeared in a well-known textbook for a great number of years and has never been dissented from by a judicial decision, it would be most unfortunate to throw doubt on it after it had been acted on . . . for so long." For criticisms of statements in textbooks see also *Re H. L. Bolton Engineering Co., Ltd.* [1956] Ch. 577; *Beevis* v. *Dawson* [1957] 1 Q.B. 195, 207.

[54] *Cf. Dempster's Trs.* v. *Dempster*, 1949 S.C. 92, 95, *per* Lord Jamieson, "The decision . . . has been accepted by the text writers as settling the law."

[55] Thus *Machado* v. *Fontes* [1897] 2 Q.B. 231 has been almost universally condemned by the text writers: see *McElroy* v. *McAllister*, 1949 S.C. 110, 135 where L.-P. Cooper noted this consensus of disapproval.

systematic account of the law on its topic, and in collecting in its text and footnotes references to the main statutes, cases and other primary sources of the rules of law on the subject. Many textbooks have done much to clarify and systematise the law and by constructive suggestions, generalisations from cases, examination of terms and doctrines, criticism of unsatisfactory decisions and interpretations of statute, and indications of desirable developments have influenced courts and judges in subsequent cases.[56]

In the present century the influence of legal literature has extended also to the chief legal periodicals; courts and judges have shown themselves sensitive to criticism by academic jurists in these journals, and have with increasing frequency considered and paid respect and attention to opinions expressed therein. Everything depends on the personal standing and reputation of the writer, without which matter in a legal journal carries no weight.[57]

Ideals of Justice

In default of all other sources the judge is thrown back on his own moral conscience, his beliefs as to what is fair and right and reasonable in the circumstances, in short, on his idea of what justice requires.[58] In the House of Lords it has been said [59]: " In the end and in the absence of authority binding this House, the question is simply: ' What does justice demand in such a case as this ? ' " Failing other authority the broad principles of justice, as the judge sees it, are not a bad basis for decision, and such principles can also sometimes be appealed to in support of a conclusion based also on another ground. Thus conduct has been stigmatised as " morally and socially wrong," [60] or it has been held that something was " contrary to natural justice," [61] or " opposed to the fundamental principles of justice." [62]

Akin to ideals of justice, and indeed only facets of justice under other names are those considerations of morality and public policy sometimes invoked to justify a decision, reflecting the fact that an important characteristic of any acceptable system of law is that it will promote what is generally beneficial and good and discourage the contrary.[63]

---

[56] Thus the completely unofficial *Restatement of the Law*, published by the American Law Institute, has considerable influence: it was cited in, *e.g.*, *McPhail* v. *Lanark C.C.*, 1951 S.C. 301.
[57] For an example of the influence of periodicals see *Haynes* v. *Harwood* [1935] 1 K.B. 146.   [58] See further Cardozo, *Nature of the Judicial Process.*
[59] *National Bank of Greece and Athens S.A.* v. *Metliss* [1958] A.C. 509, 525, *per* Viscount Simonds.   [60] *Wilson* v. *Glossop* (1888) 20 Q.B.D. 354.
[61] *Valentini* v. *Canali* (1889) 24 Q.B.D. 166.
[62] *Robinson* v. *Continental Insurance Co.* [1915] 1 K.B. 155.
[63] For cases where considerations of morality and public policy have been in issue, see, *e.g.*, *R.* v. *Bourne* [1939] 1 K.B. 687; *Steel* v. *Glasgow Iron & Steel Co.*, 1944 S.C. 237; *Fender* v. *Mildmay* [1938] A.C. 1; *Beresford* v. *Royal Insurance Co.* [1938] A.C. 586.

Conclusions

These, then, are the sources, and it will be seen that the legal adviser must sometimes have to search long and deeply for the basis for his advice, and the judge at least as far and widely for the ground of his decision and its justification in the eyes of critical jurists and subsequent judges. Frequently no ready-made proposition of law can be found directly applicable to the facts in issue, and the search must be for the materials with which the court may fashion a proposition for application to those facts. Increasingly, moreover, the courts in their decisions put the stamp of authority on propositions which in part they work out and formulate themselves, but in large part they select and develop from doctrinal writings. New problems keep on turning up and every now and then a case arises which raises some quite fundamental point and requires for its solution long and careful research in these sources and sometimes outward from them into history or social science or some other branch of learning which might at first sight appear remote from the law. The inevitable conclusion is that nothing can be ignored by the lawyer as irrelevant to his main study and that the wider his background knowledge the better. Moreover even when matter bearing on the problem can be found in the statutes or cases or books the matter must be interpreted to see what light it casts on the problem, and to decide whether it supplies the answer or merely a guide to the answer.

FURTHER READING

Sources Generally
Allen: *Law in the Making.*
Gray: *Nature and Sources of the Law.*
Holdsworth: *Sources and Literature of English Law.*
Holland: *Jurisprudence*, Chap. 5.
Paton: *Jurisprudence*, Chaps. 6–10.
Patterson: *Jurisprudence*, Chaps. 9–11.
Pound: *Jurisprudence*, Chap. 16.
Salmond: *Jurisprudence*, Chaps. 5–9.
Stair Society: *Sources and Literature of Scots Law.*
Sweet and Maxwell: *Guide to Law Reports and Statutes.*

Legislation
Allen: *Law and Orders.*
Carr: *Delegated Legislation.*
Craies: *Treatise on Statute Law.*
Davies: " Interpretation of Statutes in the light of their policy by the English courts " (1935) 35 Col.L.R. 519.
Erskine May: *Treatise on the Law, Privileges, Proceedings and Usages of Parliament.*
Friedmann: " Statute Law and its Interpretation in the Modern State " (*Law and Social Change*, Chap. 2).
Graham-Harrison: " Criticisms of the Statute Book," 1935 J.S.P.T.L. 9.

Griffith and Street: *Principles of Administrative Law.*
Ilbert: *Legislative Methods and Forms*, 1901.
　　Methods of Legislation, 1911.
Jennings: *Parliament.*
Maxwell: *The Interpretation of Statutes.*
Thring: *Practical Legislation.*
Willis: " Statute Interpretation in a Nutshell " (1938) 16 Can.B.R. 1.

Case-Law
Cross: *Precedent in English Law.*
Daniel: *History and Origin of the Law Reports.*
Ellis Lewis: " History of Judicial Precedent " (1930) 46 L.Q.R. 207, 341; (1931)
　　　　47 L.Q.R. 411; (1932) 48 L.Q.R. 230.
Frank: *Courts on Trial.*
　　　Law and the Modern Mind.
Gardner: *Judicial Precedent in Scots Law.*
　　　" Judicial Precedent in American and Scots Law " (1940) 52 J.R. 144.
Gibb: *Law from over the Border.*
Goodhart: " Precedent in English and Continental Law " (1934) 50 L.Q.R. 40.
Jensen: *The Nature of Legal Argument.*
Levi: *Introduction to Legal Reasoning.*
Moran: *The Heralds of the Law.*
Ram: *The Science of Legal Judgment*, 1871.
Smith: *Judicial Precedent in Scots Law.*
Stone: *The Province and Function of Law*, Chaps. 6 and 7.
Wallace: *The Reporters*, 4th ed., 1882.
Wambaugh: *Study of Cases*, 2nd ed., 1894.

Institutional Writings
Black: " The Institutional Writers " in (Stair Society) *Sources and Literature of
　　　Scots Law.*
Cooper: " Some Classics of Scottish Legal Literature " in *Selected Papers.*
Fifoot: *Judge and Jurist in the Reign of Queen Victoria.*

Custom
Institutional writers.

Equity
Kames: *Principles of Equity.*

Extraneous Sources
Cardozo: *Nature of the Judicial Process.*
Frank: *Courts on Trial.*
Mackintosh: *Roman Law in Modern Practice.*
Oliver: " Roman Law in Modern Cases," in *Cambridge Legal Essays*, 243.

CHAPTER 9

THE REPOSITORIES OF THE LAW

A DISTINCTION has been drawn between the legally authoritative sources of the law and legal literature, or books about the law, which are sources of our knowledge of the law, setting out only the author's view of what the law is on the subject discussed in his work. Legal literature has no binding authority at all and is only a secondary source of the law, though some books may in fact enjoy a high reputation and exercise an influence not much inferior to that of a judicial decision. The whole corpus of books which contain the written law, both the authoritative sources, and the unauthoritative books about the law or literary or secondary sources, forms the repositories of the law, to which the inquirer must resort to search out the law applicable to some precise point. A knowledge of these repositories is essential; the lawyer must know where to and how to look for the law.[1]

PRIMARY OR AUTHORITATIVE SOURCES

Statutes

Scots Acts prior to 1707 are to be found in *The Acts of the Parliaments of Scotland*, 1124–1707,[2] and also in Murray of Glendook's *Laws and Acts of Parliament*, 1424–1681,[3] while Scots Acts still in force in 1908 were reprinted in *Scots Statutes Revised*, 1424–1707.[4]

Statutes of the Parliament of England prior to 1707 are contained in the *Statutes of the Realm*, 1225–1713,[5] and in various editions of the *Statutes at Large*.[6] Legislation during the Interregnum is collected in the *Acts and Ordinances of the Interregnum*, 1642–60.[7]

[1] Every lawyer and student should become familiar with the Legal Bibliographies and Reference Books listed on pp. 351–352.
[2] ed. Thomas Thomson and Cosmo Innes, 11 vols. in 12, and Index Vol., 1814–75, cited, *e.g.*, A.P.S. II, 345.
[3] folio, 1681; duodecimo, 1682; cited, *e.g.*, Act 1449, c. 18.
[4] 1908.
[5] Published by the Record Commissioners, 9 vols. in 10, larger folio, 1810–22, with alphabetical index, 1824, and chronological index, 1828. It includes private Acts to 1539 and the titles of private Acts thereafter.
[6] The best are Ruffhead's (1215–1764) in 9 vols. with 9 supplementary vols. covering 1763–1800; Runnington's new edition of Ruffhead (1215–1785) in 10 vols. with 4 supplementary vols. covering 1785–1800; Tomlins and Raithby's (1215–1800) in 10 vols. quarto, or 20 vols. octavo, continued by a Queen's Printer's edition 1801–69 in 29 vols.; and Pickering's (1215–1761) in 24 vols., continued to 1806 by 22 supplements.
[7] ed. Firth and Rait, 3 vols., 1911.

Acts of the Parliaments of Great Britain, 1707–1800, and of the Parliaments of the United Kingdom since 1801 are also in the *Statutes at Large*. There is also an edition of statutes 1806–69 in 63 volumes, and since 1831 the Queen's Printer has published annually the *Public General Statutes*.

The most convenient modern editions are the *Statutes Revised*, third edition (1235–1948) [8] which prints, in chronological, not classified, order, the statutes so far as still in force and as amended to the end of 1948. Each volume has its subject and chronological index which lists all Acts of the period and gives the reason for omissions. This is continued by annual volumes of *Public General Statutes*. The *Scots Statutes Revised* [9] includes only Acts applicable to Scotland, as amended to the date of each volume. This is continued by *Scots Statutes* [10] and *Scottish Current Law Statutes*.[11] There are other editions, such as the Blackwood edition [12] while reprints of statutes were issued with the *Scots Law Times* from 1901 to 1948 and with the [English] *Law Reports* since 1865.

Halsbury's *Statutes of England* [13] contains the public general Acts applicable to the United Kingdom and to England, classified under alphabetical subject-headings, and annotated. There are also various books containing statutes relevant to particular topics, and annotated editions of particular Acts.

None of the foregoing includes local or private Acts.

There is a separate annual volume of *Local and Personal Acts* (with tables and index) and some cities have published volumes containing their own local Acts.

Subordinate Legislation

Orders in Council and Statutory Rules and Orders have been issued since 1904 in annual volumes, collected under the same headings of legal subjects as in the *Indexes to the Statutes in Force*. Since 1948 the annual volumes have been entitled *Statutory Instruments*.

The *Statutory Rules and Orders and Statutory Instruments Revised* [14] reprints all S.R. & O.s and S.I.s of a permanent nature and still in force, as amended, arranged, not numerically or chronologically, but under subject-headings. The last volume contains a list of subject-headings, a numerical table, and a table of effects.

[8] (1235–1948) 32 vols.
[9] (1707–1900) in 10 vols.
[10] (1901–1948) in 12 vols.
[11] (1949–   ), annual volumes.
[12] (1707–1847) in 3 vols., and annual vols. 1848–1947.
[13] 2nd ed., 27 vols. and supplements.
[14] (1904–1948) 25 vols., continued by annual volumes of S.I.s.

Halsbury's *Statutory Instruments* [15] also collect the orders and instruments under subject-headings and include annotations but neglect purely Scottish matters, so that they must be used only cautiously.

Acts of Sederunt passed by the Court of Session to regulate procedure are collected in various older collections [16] but the *Codifying Act of Sederunt* of 1913 [17] collected those relative to procedure then in force, and was itself superseded by the *Rules of Court*, 1936, revised edition, 1948.[18] Modern Acts of Sederunt are published in the *Scots Law Times* and *Parliament House Book*. Acts of Adjournal passed by the High Court of Justiciary to regulate criminal procedure are also published in the *Scots Law Times* and *Parliament House Book*.[19]

Indexes to Legislation

Statutes can be traced through the *Index to the Statutes in Force, 1235-*,[20] and the *Chronological Table of Statutes, 1235-*.[21] The Index is alphabetical and analytical within each heading, and provides a subject-matter index to every provision in any Act of Parliament in operation at the present time; it has to be noticed that some headings are duplicated, such as Education (England) and Education (Scotland), where there are two distinct bodies of statute-law referring to the two countries. Headings are not duplicated where the statute-law is entirely or largely common to the two countries. The Chronological Table gives a list of public general Acts (other than Scots Acts) from 1235 to the date of the edition in chronological order showing, for repealed Acts, by what Act they were repealed, and, for Acts still in operation, the effect on each section of all subsequent amendments and modifications, both by Act of Parliament and by statutory instrument.

There is a separate *Index to Local and Personal Acts, 1801-1947*, continued by the tables and index of the annual volumes thereof.

Subordinate legislation can be traced by recourse to the *Guide to Government Orders*,[22] the *Numerical Table, S.R. & O.s and S.I.s as at*

---

[15] 24 vols. and supplements.
[16] See Sweet and Maxwell's *Legal Bibliography*, Vol. 5, for details. They are cited, *e.g.*, A.S. 9th March 1951.
[17] Cited by book, chapter and section, *e.g.*, C.A.S., A, ii, 2.
[18] Reprinted, as amended to date, in the annual *Parliament House Book*: cited by book and number, or by number alone, *e.g.*, R.C. II, 134 or R.C. 134.
[19] Cited, *e.g.*, A.A. 2nd February 1921.   [20] 2 volumes, annually.
[21] Annually. These volumes act as the general Table and Index of the *Statutes Revised*, as continued by the annual *Public General Statutes*.
     There is also published annually *Annotations to Acts*, a volume of notes by means of which the effect of each year's legislation can be noted up briefly on any set of statutes to keep them up to date, and this includes gummed printed sheets, called " annexes," for lengthier entries, which can be stuck in at the appropriate places.
[22] H.M.S.O. Published in alternate years. This acts as Index to the *S.R. & O.s and S.I.s Revised*, as continued by the annual *Statutory Instruments*.

December 31, 1952,[23] and the *S.I. Effects.*[24] The *Guide* shows all statutory powers to make subordinate legislation, under classified sub-headings with the references of the enabling Acts and of all amending Acts. There are cross-references and a Table of Statutes. With each power are given particulars of all instruments under it current at the stated date of the volume, showing the date, title and number of the instrument and a reference to where it can be found in the *S.R. & O.s and S.I.s Revised, 1948,* by volume and page or (in the case of post-1948 exercise) to the annual volume and page of S.I. The *Numerical Table* shows in chronological order, with the exception of certain categories, the titles, numbers and volume references of all *S.R. & O.s and S.I.s* then in operation. The annual Supplement thereto lists the new instruments made during the year and still current and those earlier ones which fall to be deleted from the Table as now revoked or spent.

Parliamentary and Command Papers

Parliamentary papers include documents, such as reports of Parliamentary committees, ordered to be printed by either or both Houses of Parliament and are known, according to the colour of the cover, as Blue Books and White Papers.[25] They include many documents important for the study of the law. Other official documents, such as Reports of Royal Commissions, Departmental Committees and Law Reform Committees, are presented to Parliament by command of Her Majesty and are published in blue or white covers as Command Papers.[26] Many of these official papers contain valuable information about the working of government and of the law, interesting criticisms and proposals for amendment of the law, and they are sometimes the basis for legislation.

Case-Law—Scottish Reports

Down to the eighteenth century the only reports were notes of cases made by private individuals for their own use and subsequently

---

23 H.M.S.O., 1953, with annual Supplements.
24 H.M.S.O., annually. This volume comprises a table showing the effect of the statutory instruments of the year on previous statutory rules and orders and statutory instruments, showing which have been revoked or amended, and which have become spent or have ceased to operate. It does not cover instruments made under emergency legislation.
25 They are cited by the title, followed by, in brackets, the year, the House concerned and the serial number, *e.g.* (1950: H.C. 178). They are catalogued in the annual *Government Publications.*
26 They are cited by title, followed by, in brackets, the year, series and number therein. Command papers have been issued in five series, identified and numbered as follows: 1833–69, numbered 1 to 4222; 1870–99, C. 1 to C. 9550; 1900–18, Cd. 1 to Cd. 9239; 1919–56, Cmd. 1 to Cmd. 9889; November 1956 to date, Cmnd.1 onwards. Some are commonly known by the name of the chairman of the committee reporting, *e.g.,* the Beveridge Report is the *Report on Social Insurance and Allied Services* (1943: Cmd. 6404). A list of the reports commonly thus known is in *Where to Look for your Law.*

published. These private reports are cited by volume and page with an abbreviation of the reporter's name. Lists of the various series of older reports can be found in the (Stair Society) *Sources and Literature of Scots Law*, pp. 47–53, and in the *Parliament House Book*. Brief reports are also found in the published volumes of Practicks.

In 1705 the Faculty of Advocates first appointed a reporter of decisions.[27] There were issued three series of their reports, known as the *Faculty Collection*, namely, the Old Series in fourteen volumes (1752–1808), the New Series in seven volumes (1808–25) and the Octavo Series in sixteen volumes (1825–41). The first two series are cited by the date of the decision with the letters F.C. added, *e.g.*, 10th Jan., 1793, F.C., and the Octavo Series by volume and page, *e.g.*, 9 Fac.Dec. 123.[28]

Most of the older cases are reprinted in Kames' and Woodhouselee's *Dictionary* (five vols. covering cases 1540–1796 and cited Fol.Dic. or K. & W. Dic.) and in Morison's *Dictionary of Decisions* (twenty-two vols.)[29] with Morison's *Synopsis* 1808–16 (two vols.) and *Indexes* (one vol.) and Tait's *Index* (one vol.).[30] Brown's *Supplement* in five volumes (1622–1794) includes most of the cases omitted by Morison and is cited, *e.g.*, 3 B.S. or Brown's Supp. He also published in four volumes Brown's *Synopsis of Cases, 1540–1827*, contained in Morison's *Dictionary*, Brown's *Supplement* and in some other series down to 1827.

Session Cases

From 1821 to 1906 five series of *Session Cases* were issued, distinguished by the initial letter of the editor or chief reporter's name. These are:

First Series—	Shaw	16 vols.	1821–38 *e.g.*, 5 S. 399.[31]
Second Series—	Dunlop	24 vols.	1838–62 *e.g.*, 7 D. 436.
Third Series—	Macpherson	11 vols.	1862–73 *e.g.*, 10 M. 124.[32]
Fourth Series—	Rettie	25 vols.	1873–98 *e.g.*, 17 R. 931.
Fifth Series—	Fraser	8 vols.	1898–1906 *e.g.*, 4 F. 297.

[27] The Faculty reporters were in succession Forbes (later Professor of Law at Glasgow) (1705–13), Bruce (1714–15), Edgar (1724–25) and Falconer (1744–51), and from 1714 to 1744 the work was very inadequately done, but the collections of Lords Elchies, Kames and Kilkerran and of Clerk Home supply the defects.

[28] Halkerston's *Compendium* (1819, and Supplement 1820) contains indexes of the decisions in Faculty Collection 1752–1817.

[29] Vols. 20 and 21 consist of a Synopsis or Digest of the cases in the previous 19. This is distinct from Morison's Synopsis 1808–16. Vol. 22 is a Supplemental volume. The Appendix to the Dictionary is usually bound into it, each title after the title in the Dictionary, but sometimes bound as two separate volumes. It is paginated consecutively throughout the work and cited, *e.g.* (1540) Mor. 5932 or (1714) M. 12345.

[30] The notes at the end of Tait's *Index* supply much valuable bibliographical information about the older Scottish reports and reporters.

[31] There are two editions of the early volumes of Shaw which do not coincide in pagination.

[32] Distinguish this reference from Morison's *Dictionary*. These volumes are sometimes cited Macph.

From 1907 the *Session Cases* were issued by the Faculty of Advocates. In 1957 the Scottish Council of Law Reporting was formed to take over the responsibility for publishing *Session Cases*. They are cited by the year and page of the annual volume, *e.g.*, 1935 S.C. 475.[33]

House of Lords Cases

The older House of Lords decisions in Scottish appeals are in private reports. These are similarly listed in the *Sources and Literature of Scots Law*, pp. 55–56, and in the *Parliament House Book*.

From 1850 House of Lords decisions are reported and bound in with the annual volumes of *Session Cases* but separately paginated,[34] as follows:

Dunlop	12 vols.	1850–62	(1850) 13 D.(H.L.) 5.
Macpherson	11 vols.	1862–73	(1862) 1 M. (or Macph.) (H.L.) 3.
Rettie	25 vols.	1873–98	(1873) 1 R.(H.L.) 10.
Fraser	8 vols.	1898–1906	(1898) 1 F.(H.L.) 6.
Session Cases		1907–	1950 S.C.(H.L.) 20.

Some Scottish appeals are also reported in the English volumes covering the same period, in Law Reports (*Appeal Cases*) and *All England Reports*.[35]

Justiciary (Criminal) Cases

Some early criminal reports have been published independently. Separate series of criminal reports by private reporters appeared from 1819 to 1916. They also are listed in the *Parliament House Book* and are cited by the editor's name, volume and page.

From 1874 Justiciary cases have also been published in the annual volumes of *Session Cases* but paginated separately,[34] as follows:

Rettie	25 vols.	1874–98	(1874) 1 R.(J.) 10.
Fraser	8 vols.	1898–1906	(1898) 1 F.(J.) 20.
Session Cases	11 vols.	1907–16	1907 S.C.(J.) 15.[36]
Justiciary Cases		1917–	1917 J.C. 5.[36]

[33] Where the date is an essential part of the reference to the volume (*i.e.*, since 1906), it is *not* in brackets. Where the date is not essential (*i.e.*, before 1907), it is put, if at all, in round brackets. Square brackets are *never* used in references to Scottish but only in references to English reports, for which see *infra*.

[34] It follows that since 1874 volumes of Scottish reports contain three sets of reports, each separately paginated (House of Lords, Justiciary and Court of Session). Hence 1958 S.C.(H.L.) 1; 1958 J.C. 1 and 1958 S.C. 1 are all different reports, in different series, but contained in the one volume.

[35] Information on which of the older series of English House of Lords cases contain Scottish appeals may be found in Stair Society, *Sources and Literature of Scots Law*, pp. 57–58.

[36] The change in the abbreviated citation after 1916 should be noted.

Since 1917 these Justiciary cases, as well as being bound in with *Session Cases*, are sometimes found bound separately, five years to a volume. The citation remains the same.

Collateral Reports and Reprints

At various times other series of reports have been issued and are frequently of value in reporting other cases and supplying information on matters omitted from the reports already mentioned. These include Murray's *Jury Court Reports* (five vols., 1815–30) and McFarlane's *Jury Court Reports* (one vol., 1838–39), Shaw's *Teind Court Decisions* (one vol., 1821–31), Deas and Anderson's reports (five vols., 1829–33), Fergusson's *Consistorial Cases* (one vol., 1811–17) and Stuart, Milne and Peddie's *Reports* (two vols., 1851–53). More important are the *Scottish Jurist* (forty-five vols. and five parts, 1829–73, cited Sc.Jur.), the *Scottish Law Reporter* (sixty-one vols., 1866–1924, cited S.L.R.),[37] and the *Scots Law Times*, since 1893. This last is cited from 1893 to 1908 by volume, *e.g.*, (1900) 7 S.L.T., and thereafter by the year only.[38] The last two include House of Lords, Justiciary and Court of Session cases, while the S.L.T. has also separately paginated sections of reports of Sheriff Court cases, Lyon Court cases, and notes of recent decisions.[39] Some Scottish appeals to the House of Lords are also reported in current English series of reports.

The *Scots Revised Reports* includes in forty-five volumes a reprint of the principal decisions down to 1873, as follows: Morison's *Dictionary*, two vols.; *Faculty Collection*, 1807–25, two vols.; House of Lords Appeals, ten vols.; Shaw, six vols.; Dunlop, thirteen vols.; Macpherson, eleven vols.; cases reported only in the *Scottish Jurist*, vols. 1–37 (1829–65), one vol.

Selected sheriff court cases are found in Guthrie's *Select Cases in the Sheriff Courts*,[40] Sheriff Court Reports printed in the *Scottish Law Review*,[41] and sheriff court cases in the *Scots Law Times*.[42]

Decisions of the Scottish Land Court are published as a Supplement to the *Scottish Law Review*.[43]

Decisions of Scottish courts of special jurisdiction and administrative tribunals are only sometimes reported: some may be found in the ordinary series, some in the Administrative Law Reports published

---

[37] Distinguish references to the *S.L. Reporter* from those to the *S.L. Review*, which contains the Sheriff Court reports (1885 to date).
[38] From 1909 to 1916 there are two volumes in each year, cited, *e.g.*, 1912, 1 S.L.T.— and 1912, 2 S.L.T.—.
[39] These notes are frequently but not always superseded by a full report issued in a later part.   [40] Two vols., 1861–78 and 1879–85.
[41] 1885 to date: cited, *e.g.* (1954) 70 Sh.Ct.Rep.—.
[42] Latterly these are separately paginated and cited, *e.g.*, 1955 S.L.T.(Sh.Ct.)—.
[43] 1913 to date: cited, *e.g.* (1951) 40 L.C.— or 40 S.L.C.R.—.

in the *British Journal of Administrative Law* (now *Public Law*) and others in series published by the Government.

English Reports

The practice of noting cases began early in England [44] and from the later twelfth century to 1536 there is a series of Year Books, notes made in law-French of points of procedure and pleading, probably for the writer's own information, but later copied and printed. Reports proper begin in the sixteenth century. Down to 1865 reporting was in the hands of private reporters and the reports vary greatly in value [45]; they were usually printed some time afterwards, sometimes from inaccurate or even stolen notes. Round about 1800 the practice developed of judges revising copies of their judgments and even supplying copies to the reporters, and one reporter in each court tended to be favoured as the " authorised " reporter, though this was never official, and the practice of revising judgments was extended to other series also. The various series of private reports are usually cited by initials or abbreviations of the reporters' names, though in some instances other abbreviations, sometimes confusing, are used.[46] Two reprints of the older reports have to be noticed: *The Revised Reports* (1785–1865) in 149 volumes (plus Table of Cases (one vol.) and *Index-Digest* (two vols.)), which omits some obsolete cases, and the *English Reports* (1220–1865) in 178 volumes, which is a literal reprint with a few annotations.[47] Both are generally reliable and very useful.

[44] On the older English reports and reporters see Holdsworth, *Sources and Literature of English Law*, 74–104, and " Law Reporting in the Nineteenth and Twentieth Centuries " in *Essays in Law and History*, 284; Winfield, *Chief Sources of English Legal History*, 145–199; Bolland, *The Year Books*; Pollock, *First Book of Jurisprudence*, Chap. 5; Veeder, " The English Reports " in (1901) 15 Harv.L.R. 1, 109, reprinted in part in *Select Essays in Anglo-American Legal History*, II, 123; Daniel, *History and Origin of the Law Reports*. On reporting see also Moran's *Heralds of the Law*; Goodhart, " Reporting the Law " (1939) 55 L.Q.R. 29; O'Sullivan, " Law Reporting " (1940) 4 M.L.R. 104.

[45] This has given rise to many stories about reports and reporters, some of which can be read in Williams' *Learning the Law* and in Allen's *Law in the Making*.

[46] Lists of these abbreviations can be found in Sweet and Maxwell's *Where to Look for your Law*, in Sweet and Maxwell's *Guide to Law Reports and Statutes* and prefaced to Halsbury's *Laws of England*, vol. I., any volume of the *English and Empire Digest*, or to Green's *Encyclopaedia of Scots Law*, vol. I. The date is not an essential of the reference to a pre-1865 report, but if inserted it is put in round brackets, *e.g.* (1842) 10 M. & W. 546.

[47] A chart supplied with the set in a slim volume to itself shows in which volume is to be found any particular volume of the old reports. The spine of each volume of the E.R. lists which of the older volumes are reprinted within. This chart is not perfect and some of the old reports are known under variant names; this can be found in *Where to Look for your Law*. Volumes 177–178 contain a complete index of cases under the names of the parties. Lists in *Where to Look for your Law* and the *Guide to Law Reports and Statutes* indicate in which volumes of Revised Reports and/or English Reports private reports are reprinted. Another table in the *Guide* shows what volumes of what series relate to particular calendar years from 1810 onwards.

In 1866 the Incorporated Council of Law Reporting began to publish the *Law Reports*, and these quickly superseded all the old private reporters though not the series of reports issued by various legal journals. The *Law Reports* have no exclusive privilege of citation but are usually preferred for purposes of citation and references.[48]   They have been issued in three series, 1866–75, 1876–90, 1891 to date.[49]

Other series

Other series of reports now discontinued are the *Law Times Reports* (New Series, 177 volumes, 1859–1947, cited, *e.g.* (1934) 150 L.T. —), the *Law Journal Reports* (127 volumes, 1822–1949, cited, *e.g.* (1930) 99 L.J. —),[50] *The Times Law Reports* (71 volumes, 1884–1952, cited, *e.g.* (1910) 26 T.L.R. —),[51] and *Commercial Cases* (46 volumes, 1895–1941, cited, *e.g.* (1941) 46 Com.Cas. —).

Other series now current are the *All England Law Reports* (since 1936,[52] cited, *e.g.* [1950] 2 All E.R. —) and the *Weekly Law Reports* (since 1953, cited, *e.g.* [1953] 1 W.L.R. —), which replaced the earlier *Weekly Notes* (1865–1952, cited, *e.g.* [1945] W.N. —)[53] while brief

48   See *Fairman* v. *Perpetual Investment Building Socy.* [1923] A.C. 74; Practice Note [1931] W.N. 121.
49   The series comprise the following: First Series: Admiralty and Ecclesiastical (4 vols.); Crown Cases Reserved (2 vols.); Common Pleas (10 vols.); Chancery Appeals (10 vols.); English and Irish Appeals [House of Lords] (7 vols.); Equity (20 vols.); Exchequer (10 vols.); Privy Council Appeals (6 vols.); Probate and Divorce (3 vols.); Queen's Bench (10 vols.); Scotch and Divorce Appeals (2 vols.). These are cited, *e.g.* (1875) L.R. 7 H.L.—; (1875) L.R. 10 Q.B.—.
      Second Series: Appeal Cases (15 vols.); Chancery Division (45 vols.); Common Pleas Division (5 vols.); Exchequer Division (5 vols.); Probate Division (15 vols.); Queen's Bench Division (25 vols.). These are cited, *e.g.* (1890) 15 App.Cas.—; (1890) 25 Q.B.D.—.
      Third Series: Appeal Cases; Chancery Division; Queen's (King's, 1901–1952) Bench; Probate Division. These are cited, *e.g.* [1959] A.C.—. Sometimes there is more than one volume for each court in one year, *e.g.* [1958] 2 Q.B.—.
      In 1958 a series of reports of the Restrictive Practices Court commenced (cited (1959) L.R. 1 R.P.—).
      For correct abbreviations see *Where to Look for your Law* and *Guide to Law Reports and Statutes*.
      Note that L.R. precedes the volume number in the First Series only, and that D. after Q.B., Ch., C.P., Ex., and P. is found only in the Second Series.
      Prior to 1891 the date is not an essential of the reference to the Law Reports and goes in round brackets. After 1890 the year is essential and is put in square brackets.
50   From 1947 the volumes were cited, *e.g.* [1949] L.J.R.—.   Many volumes of *Law Journal* are separately paginated within the volume for the different courts, *e.g.*, for L.J.C.P. and L.J.Ch.
51   The 1950 volume was cited 66 T.L.R. Part 1 and Part 2, and the 1951 and 1952 volumes [1951] 1 T.L.R. and 2 T.L.R.
52   Reports of selected cases 1843–1935 are now being published by All E.R. in a series called *All E.R. Reprints*.
53   On the authority of *Weekly Notes* see *Re Loveridge* [1902] 2 Ch. 859; *Re Smith's Settlement* [1903] 1 Ch. 373.

reports and notes are to be found in many of the legal journals and periodicals.

Special series of reports and Irish and Commonwealth Series may be traced through *Where to Look for your Law* and *Guide to Law Reports and Statutes*.

Digests of Case-Law

The finding of case-law is greatly facilitated by the Digests of case-law which arrange the reported cases under main and subordinate subject-headings on an analytical basis, the main headings being arranged in alphabetical order. Each entry gives a brief account of the case and the legal propositions which can be inferred from it but the entries are so brief that they are not a substitute for the full reports. It is usually necessary to follow up a point by searching the relevant headings in the main part of the Digest and then in each supplementary volume down to the latest published. There is considerable variation in the headings and sub-headings used [54] so that a search must frequently be made under several different headings but experience greatly increases familiarity with the system used.

The older Scottish cases are mostly to be found, grouped under alphabetical subject-headings, in Morison's *Dictionary of Decisions*, 1540–1808, five supplementary volumes known as *Brown's Supplement*, and Tait's *Index* (one volume). Shaw's *Digest of Cases* (three volumes) contains House of Lords decisions from 1726 to 1868 and decisions of the Scottish superior courts from 1800 to 1868. This is carried on by the *Faculty Digest* from 1868.[55] The *Scots Digest* contains House of Lords cases from 1707–1944 and cases from the Scottish superior courts from 1800–1944.[56] The *Sheriff Court Digest* covers 1885–1944 in five volumes dealing with consecutive periods, and there is a *Digest of Sheriff Court Cases reported in S.L.T.*, 1893–1943.

English cases are digested in Mews' *Digest of English Case-law* (which includes a selection of Scottish cases),[57] in the *English and Empire Digest* which contains English cases from early times with Scottish and

---

[54] Thus the *Faculty Digest* includes all criminal cases under the heading Justiciary; Shaw's *Digest* puts such cases under the heading Crime. There are, of course, many cross-references to assist the searcher but much ingenuity and some luck is sometimes requisite for the search. Of course there may not be any cases closely in point: the *Digest* only contains what has been reported in the main series of reports.

[55] 1868–1922, 6 vols., supplementary volumes 1922–30, 1930–40, and 1940–50, and annual supplementary parts thereafter.

[56] 1800–1873, 4 vols.; 1873–1904, 2 vols.; supplementary volumes 1904–14, 1914–23, 1923–30, 1930–37, 1937–44, and supplementary parts to 1947. Superseded by *Scottish Current Law* thereafter.

[57] Second ed., 24 volumes (to end of 1924) and supplementary volumes.

Commonwealth decisions in footnotes on each page,[58] and in the *Law Reports Digest of Cases*, 1865–1950 [59]

Modern Digests also contain such additional reference tools as an index of statutes, showing in what cases statutory provisions have been interpreted, an index of cases commented on in later cases, an index of words and phrases discussed in particular cases, and an index of parties' names whereby a case known by name can be traced to its classified subject. Very recent cases are found in *Current Law*.[60]

Institutional Writings

The standard editions in modern use are:

Craig's Jus Feudale and the Books of the Feus, translated by J. A. (Lord President) Clyde, 2 vols., 1934; Stair's *Institutions*, new (fifth) edition, with notes by Professor J. S. More,[61] 2 vols., 1832 [62]; Bankton's *Institute*, only edition, 3 vols., 1751–53 [62]; Erskine's *Institute*, new (eighth) edition, with notes by J. Badenach Nicolson,[63] 2 vols., 1871 [62]; Bell's *Commentaries*, seventh edition, by John (later Lord) McLaren, 2 vols., 1870 [64]; and Bell's *Principles*, tenth edition by Sheriff William Guthrie, 1899.[65]

On criminal law the standard editions are: Mackenzie's *Laws and Customs*, second edition, 1699, and in his collected *Works* (2 vols., 1716–22); Hume's *Commentaries*,[66] fourth edition with supplement by B. R. Bell, 2 vols., 1844 [64]; and Alison's *Principles* and *Practice*, only editions, 1832 and 1833.[64]

SECONDARY SOURCES—LEGAL LITERATURE

These sources comprise all commentaries, books and other writings about the law or any topic thereof, other than institutional writings, which may give a court, or an enquirer, valuable guidance on where to find the authoritative primary sources of a principle of law relevant to the problem before him, on the interrelation of several relevant primary

---

[58] 48 volumes, with supplements.
[59] Twelve volumes, covering 1866–1950, continued by *Index to Law Reports*, 1951–60.
[60] On this see further p. 363, *infra*.
[61] In *Fortington* v. *Kinnaird*, 1942 S.C. 239, 265, Lord Justice-Clerk Cooper attached importance to the views expressed in More's Notes and Lord Mackay (at p. 276) said that the Notes " carries almost the authority of a separate Institution."
[62] These books are cited by Book, title and section, *e.g.*, Stair, I, 1, 16.
[63] In *Fortington*, *supra*, Lord Cooper attached importance also to Lord Ivory's Notes to Erskine, which are printed in Lord Ivory's (sixth) edition of Erskine, and reprinted in Badenach Nicolson's edition.
[64] These books are cited by volume and page.
[65] This book is cited by the section number.
[66] In *H.M. Advocate* v. *Grant* (1848) J. Shaw 17, 92, Lord Justice-Clerk Hope spoke of Hume as of great authority; see also Paton's Biography of Baron Hume (*Lectures* (Stair Society) VI) at 350.

sources, such as several statutes and cases, and on the interpretations which have hitherto been placed by the courts on the primary authorities. Legal literature is also valuable as giving a coherent account of all the law on a topic, with the legislation, case-law, views of the institutional writers, and later comment and criticism brought together into a related whole and presented, so far as possible, as a reasoned and systematic body of related principles and rules.

The writings of legal literature, of commentaries and treatises on the law and various branches of it, has from the time of Gaius been an important function of the academic jurists. The literary sources are the essential means of legal study, of research for the answer to some problem, and of obtaining a general conspectus of the law on any topic.

Some books are written expressly for students, or for different groups of students, others for legal practitioners as reference books and guides through the tangle of statutes and cases. A knowledge of what books there are on each subject and what they cover, their relative sizes and values, their standing, is a necessary part of a lawyer's knowledge, and with these books his investigation of any problem starts.[67]

The following list of books includes those which are reliable guides on their various subjects. The classification is systematic, corresponding to the systematic division of the Law of Scotland previously set out.[68] On every topic the distinction between Scottish and English books must be kept in mind, since the latter do not usually cite statutes applicable to Scotland or Scottish cases, ignore specialties of Scottish procedure, and are all, to a greater or less degree, depending on whether the topic is one on which Scots and English law diverge much or little, unreliable guides in Scottish practice. But many English books have to be considered, if only *faute de mieux*, in default of any, or any modern, Scottish book.[69]

GENERAL BOOKS

Legal Bibliographies and Reference Books
Institute of Advanced Legal Studies: *Bibliographical Guide to U.K. Law.*
Manual of Legal Citations, Part I.

---

[67] See further Chap. 10, *infra.*
[68] Chap. 4, *supra.*
[69] The list does not include books written wholly or primarily for students. Books written from the English standpoint but useful, if care be taken, in Scotland are listed with " E " prefixed to the title. There are very many other English books some of which may be useful on particular points in Scottish practice but which are not listed because they have no general utility in Scotland. This list does not attempt to deal with related social sciences, background legal subjects, international or supranational law, nor with books which are obsolete or of mainly historical interest, nor with the considerable literature of biography, legal essays, collected papers, studies in honour of distinguished jurists, famous trials, etc. These must be looked for in the legal bibliographies.

Stair Society: *Sources and Literature of Scots Law.*
Sweet & Maxwell, Ltd.: *Guide to Law Reports and Statutes,* 4th ed., 1962.
      Where to Look for Your Law, 14th ed., 1962.
      Legal Bibliography of the British Commonwealth—
          Vol. 1—*English Law to* 1800.
          Vol. 2—*English Law* 1800–1954.
          Vol. 5—*Scots Law and Roman Law, to* 1955.
Price and Bitner: *Effective Legal Research* (U.S.A.).

Dictionaries
    Bell: *Dictionary and Digest of the Law of Scotland.*
E Wharton: *Law Lexicon.*
E Jowitt: *Dictionary of English Law.*

Maxims
    Trayner: *Latin Maxims and Phrases.*
E Broom: *Legal Maxims.*

Words and Phrases
    Index to Statutory Definitions, 2nd ed., 1936.
    Gibb and Dalrymple: *Scottish Judicial Dictionary.*
E Stroud: *Judicial Dictionary of Words and Phrases,* 3rd ed., 4 vols.
E Burrows: *Words and Phrases Judicially Defined,* 5 vols.

Encyclopaedias and General Textbooks
    Green's *Encyclopaedia of the Laws of Scotland,* 16 vols. and suppls.
E Halsbury's *Laws of England,* 3rd ed.
    Erskine: *Principles of the Law of Scotland,* 21st ed., 1911.
    Gloag and Henderson: *Introduction to the Law of Scotland,* 6th ed., 1956.
    Smith: *Scotland* (The British Commonwealth Series, Vol. 11).[69a]
    Smith: *Short Commentary on Scots Law.*[69a]
    Lillie: *Mercantile Law of Scotland.*
    Gow: *Mercantile and Industrial Law of Scotland.*

Older Books, not Institutional, but still Valuable [70]
Balfour: *Practicks; or System of the More Ancient Law of Scotland,* 1754 and
        (Stair Society) 1962–63
Dallas, George, of St. Martins: *Stiles of Writs,* 1697, 1774.
Dirleton (Sir J. Nisbet, Lord): *Doubts and Questions in the Law.* 1698.
Forbes, Prof. Wm.: *Institutes of the Law of Scotland,* 2 vols., 1722–30.
Hermand, George Fergusson, Lord: *Consistorial Decisions* (ed. Walton, Stair
        Society), 1940.[71]
Hope, Sir Thomas: *Minor Practicks,* 1726 and 1734.
          Major Practicks (ed. Lord Clyde, Stair Society), 1937–38.
Hume, Prof. (later Baron), David: *Lectures on the Law of Scotland* (ed. Paton,
    Stair Society) 6 vols., 1939–58.[72]

[69a] The text of these books is identical.
[70] The dates given are those of first publication and, where applicable, of a modern edition. In some cases there were several early editions, for which see the bibliographies.
[71] On the authority of this, see *Fortington* v. *Kinnaird,* 1942 S.C. 239, 277.
[72] On the authority of Hume's *Lectures,* see *Fortington* v. *Kinnaird,* 1942 S.C. 239, 253, 265.

Kames (Henry Home, Lord) [73]: *Elucidations respecting the common and statute law of Scotland*, 1777.
Historical Law Tracts, 1758.
Principles of Equity, 1760.
Statute Law of Scotland Abridged, 1757.
Mackenzie, Sir George: writings contained in his *Works*, 2 vols., 1716–22.
More, Prof. J.S.: *Lectures on the Law of Scotland*, ed. McLaren, 2 vols. 1864.
Regiam Majestatem, ed. Skene, 1597, 1609, 1774 and (ed. Cooper, Stair Society) 1947.
Skene, Sir John: *De Verborum Significatione*, 1597.[74]
Spotiswoode, Sir Robert: *Practicks of the Law of Scotland*, 1706.
Stuart, Gilbert: *Observations concerning the Public Law of Scotland*, 1779.
Stuart, Sir James, of Goodtrees: *Answers to Dirleton's Doubts and Questions in the Law of Scotland*, 1715.
Wallace, George: *System of the Principles of the Law of Scotland*, Vol. I, 1760.[75]

PUBLIC LAW

CONSTITUTIONAL LAW

General
    Fraser: *Outline of Constitutional Law.*
E Dicey: *Introduction to the Study of the Law of the Constitution.*
E Jennings: *The Law and the Constitution.*
E Hood Phillips: *Constitutional and Administrative Law.*
E Wade and Phillips: *Constitutional Law.*
E Ridges: *Constitutional Law.*
E Campion: *British Government since 1918.*
E Halsbury's *Laws of England*, Vol. 7.

The Crown
E Anson: *Law and Custom of the Constitution*, Vol. 2.

The Executive
E Jennings: *Cabinet Government.*
E Keith: *The British Cabinet System.*
E Mackintosh: *The British Cabinet.*
E Wheare: *Government by Committee.*

The Legislature
E Jennings: *Parliament.*
E   *Party Politics*, 3 vols.
E Anson: *Law and Custom of the Constitution*, Vol. 1.
E May: *Parliamentary Practice.*
E Schofield: *Parliamentary Elections.*

The Judicial System
E Kiralfy: *The English Legal System.*
E Jackson: *The Machinery of Justice in England.*

---

[73] Kames also published various volumes of essays and decisions.
[74] Reprinted in Skene's *Lawes and Acts of Parliament*, 1597, and in R. Bell's *Dictionary of the Law of Scotland.*
[75] No more ever published. On the authority of this book, see *Kerr* v. *Martin* (1840) 2 D. 752, 776, 792.

The Civil Service
E   Mackenzie and Grove: *Central Administration in Britain.*

The Armed Forces
   HMSO: *Queen's Regulations and Admiralty Instructions for the government of Her Majesty's naval service.*
   Manual of Military Law.
   Queen's Regulations and War Office Instructions.
   Manual of Air Force Law.
   Queen's Regulations and Air Council Instructions for the RAF.

Established Churches
   Mair: *Digest of Church Laws.*
   Cox: *Practice and Procedure in the Church of Scotland.*
   Black: *Parochial Ecclesiastical Law of Scotland.*
   Buchanan: *Law of Scotland on Teinds or Tithes.*
   Connell: *Law of Scotland respecting Parishes.*
        Law of Scotland regarding Tithes and Stipends, 2 vols.
   Elliot: *Teinds or Tithes, and Procedure in the Court of Teinds.*

Public Revenue and Taxation
E   Wheatcroft (ed.): *British Tax Encyclopaedia,* 5 vols.
E   Simon: *Income Tax,* 6 vols.
E   Dymond: *Death Duties.*
E   Green: *Death Duties.*
E   Alpe: *Law of Stamp Duties.*

Nationality and Citizenship
E   Jones: *British Nationality Law and Practice.*
E   Parry: *Nationality and Citizenship Laws of the Commonwealth*

Rights and Liberties of Citizens
        See books on Constitutional Law—General.

Commonwealth, colonial and foreign relations
E   Halsbury's *Laws of England,* Vol. 5.
E   Jennings: *Constitutional Laws of the Commonwealth.*
E   Wheare: *The Statute of Westminster and Dominion Status.*
E   McNair: *Law of Treaties.*

ADMINISTRATIVE LAW
General
E   Griffith and Street: *Principles of Administrative Law.*
E   Wade: *Administrative Law.*
E   Robson: *Justice and Administrative Law.*

Central Departments
E   Mackenzie and Grove: *Central Administration in Britain.*
E   Chester: *Organisation of British Central Government.*
   Milne: *The Scottish Office.*
   HMSO: *Handbook on Scottish Administration.*

Local authorities
  McLarty: *Source-Book and History of Administrative Law in Scotland.*
  Miller: *Outline of Administrative and Local Government Law in Scotland.*
  HMSO: *Local Government in Scotland.*
  Muirhead and Guest: *Law and Practice relating to Police Government in Burghs in Scotland,* 3 vols.
  Whyte: *Local Government in Scotland.*
  Hutton: *Local Government (Scotland) Act,* 1947.
  Taylor: *Local Authority Meetings.*
  Purves: *Scottish Licensing Laws.*
  Gordon: *Law of Housing in Scotland.*
  Armour: *Law of Valuation in Scotland.*
  Guest: *Law of Valuation and Rating in Scotland.*
  Campbell: *The Town and Country Planning (Scotland) Act,* 1947.
E Chester: *Central and Local Government: Financial and Administrative Relations.*
  Mill: *The Scottish Police.*
E Schofield: *Local Government Elections.*

Public Corporations
E Robson: *Nationalised Industry and Public Ownership.*
E Dalton: *The Electricity Act,* 1947.
E Stemp and Wing: *The Gas Act,* 1948.

Delegated Legislative Powers
E Allen: *Law and Orders.*
E Sieghart: *Government by Decree.*

Delegated Judicial Powers
E Allen: *Administrative Jurisdiction.*

Control of Powers
E Schwarz: *Law and the Executive in Britain.*
E Robinson: *Public Authorities and Legal Liability.*
E Street: *Governmental Liability.*
E Bickford Smith and Middleton: *The Crown Proceedings Act.*
E de Smith: *Judicial Review of Administrative Action.*
E Kersell: *Parliamentary Supervision of Delegated Legislation.*

Social Services
E Hall: *Social Services of Modern England.*
E Ormrod and Walker: *The National Health Service.*
E Speller: *The National Health Service Act,* 1946.
E Steele: *The National Assistance Act,* 1948.
E Potter and Stansfeld: *National Insurance.*
E Potter and Stansfeld: *National Insurance (Industrial Injuries) Act,* 1946.
E Vester and Cartwright: *Industrial Injuries,* 2 vols.

CRIMINAL LAW AND PROCEDURE
Prosecution
  Gross: *Criminal Investigation.*
  Mill: *The Scottish Police.*

356 The Scottish Legal System

Jurisdiction and Procedure
Alison: *Practice of the Criminal Law of Scotland.*
Renton and Brown: *Criminal Procedure according to the Law of Scotland.*
Trotter: *Summary Criminal Jurisdiction.*
E   Archbold: *Pleading, Evidence and Practice in Criminal Cases.*

Liability
Hume: *Commentaries on the Law of Scotland respecting Crimes,* 2 vols.
Alison: *Principles of the criminal law of Scotland.*
Mackenzie: *Laws and Customs of Scotland in matters criminal.*
Burnett: *Treatise on various branches of the criminal law of Scotland.*
Anderson: *Criminal Law of Scotland.*
Macdonald: *Practical Treatise on the Criminal Law of Scotland.*
Angus: *Dictionary of Crimes and Offences.*
E   Kenny: *Outlines of Criminal Law.*
E   Williams: *The Criminal Law; The General Part.*
E   Russell on *Crimes,* 2 vols.

Punishment
E   Fox: *The English Prison and Borstal System.*
E   HMSO: *Prisons and Borstals—England and Wales.*

PRIVATE LAW
GENERAL

Sources and Literature
See Chap. 8, *supra.*

General principles
See General Books, *supra.*

Lapse of Time
Millar: *Prescription.*
Napier: *Prescription.*

Personal Bar
Rankine on *Personal Bar and Estoppel.*

INTERNATIONAL PRIVATE LAW
Jurisdiction
Gibb: *International Law of Jurisdiction.*
Duncan and Dykes: *Principles of Civil Jurisdiction as applied in Scotland.*
Maclaren: *Court of Session Practice.*

Concepts, Classification, Choice of Law and Foreign Judgments
E   Graveson: *The Conflict of Laws.*
E   Schmitthoff: *The English Conflict of Laws.*
E   Cheshire: *Private International Law.*
E   Dicey: *Conflict of Laws.*

LAW OF PERSONS
Natural persons
Fergusson: *Consistorial Law.*
Lothian: *Consistorial Actions.*

Fraser: *Treatise on Husband and Wife*, 2 vols.
Walton: *Handbook of Husband and Wife*.
Fraser: *Treatise on the Law of Scotland relative to Parent and Child and Guardian and Ward*.
Trotter: *Law as to Children and Young Persons*.
Cowan: *Children and Young Persons (Scotland) Act*, 1932.
E Eversley: *Law of Domestic Relations*.
E Bromley: *Family Law*.
Begg on *Law Agents*.

Unincorporated Associations
E Lloyd: *Law relating to unincorporated associations*.
E Keeling: *Trusts and Foundations*.
Clark: *Treatise on the Law of Partnership and Joint-Stock Companies*.
E Pollock: *Digest of the Law of Partnership*.
E Lindley: *Treatise on the Law of Partnership*.
E Vester and Gardner: *Trade Union Law and Practice*.
E Citrine: *Trade Union Law*.
E Fuller: *Law of Friendly Societies and Industrial and Provident Societies*.
E Daly: *Club Law and Unregistered Friendly Societies*.

Juristic Persons or Corporations
E Arnold: *Municipal Corporations*.
Wilton: *Company Law and Practice in Scotland*.
Palmer's *Company Law*, 20th ed. with Scottish suppt.
E Gower: *Principles of Modern Company Law*.
E Pennington: *Principles of Company Law*.
E Gore-Brown: *Handbook on Joint-Stock Companies*.
E Buckley on *The Companies Acts*.
E Halsbury's *Laws of England*, Vol. 6.
E Wurtzburg: *Law relating to Building Societies*.
E Street: *Ultra Vires*.

LAW OF OBLIGATIONS
Law of Contract generally
Gloag: *Law of Contract*.
Walker: *Law of Damages in Scotland*.
E Anson: *Principles of the English Law of Contracts*.
E Cheshire and Fifoot: *Law of Contract*.
E Pollock: *Principles of Contract*.
E Chitty: *Contracts*, 2 vols.
E Mayne and Macgregor: *Law of Damages*.

SPECIFIC CONTRACTS
Agency
E Fridman: *Law of Agency*.
E Powell: *Law of Agency*.
E Bowstead: *Digest of the Law of Agency*.

Banking Contracts
Wallace and McNeil: *Banking Law*.
E Paget: *Law of Banking*.
E Hart: *Law of Banking*.
E Gutteridge: *Law of Bankers' Commercial Credits*.

E   Megrah: *Bankers' Commercial Credits.*
E   Davis: *Law relating to Commercial Letters of Credit.*
E   Sheldon and Drover: *Practice and Law of Banking.*

Carriage
Deas: *Railways.*
E   Macnamara: *Law of Carriers by Land.*
E   Kahn-Freund: *Law of Carriage by Inland Transport.*
E   Leslie: *Law of Transport by Railway.*
E   Chorley and Giles: *Shipping Law.*
E   Temperley: *Merchant Shipping Acts.*
E   Maclachlan: *Treatise on Merchant Shipping.*
E   Carver: *Carriage of Goods by Sea.*
E   Scrutton: *Contract of Affreightment as expressed in charter-parties and bills
        of lading.*
E   Kennedy: *C.I.F. Contracts.*
E   Sassoon: *F.O.B. Contracts.*
E   Tiberg: *Law of Demurrage.*
E   Kennedy: *Treatise on the Law of Civil Salvage.*
E   Norris: *Law of Salvage.*
E   Chalmers: *Marine Insurance Act.*
E   Stevens & Sons: *British Shipping Laws*, 14 vols.
E   Arnould: *Law of Marine Insurance and Average*, 2 vols.
E   Lowndes and Rudolf: *Law of General Average.*
E   Marsden: *Law of Collisions at Sea.*
E   McNair: *Law of the Air.*
E   Shawcross and Beaumont on *Air Law.*
E   Cheng: *Law of International Air Transport.*

Caution and guarantees
Gloag and Irvine on *Rights in Security and Cautionary Obligations.*
E   Rowlatt: *Principal and Surety.*

Custody and Deposit
E   Paton: *Bailment in the Common Law.*
E   Beven: *Negligence*, Vol. 2.

Employment
Fraser: *Law of Master and Servant.*
Umpherston: *Law of Master and Servant.*
Smith: *Law of Master and Servant.*
E   Batt: *Law of Master and Servant.*
E   Diamond: *Law of Master and Servant.*
E   Munkman: *Employer's Liability.*
E   Samuels: *Factory Law.*
E   Redgrave: *Factories and Truck Acts.*
E   Bowen: *The Mines and Quarries Acts.*
E   Temperley: *The Merchant Shipping Acts.*
E   Haslam: *Law relating to Trade Combinations.*
E   Flanders and Clegg: *System of Industrial Relations in Great Britain.*
E   Sharp: *Industrial Conciliation and Arbitration in Great Britain.*
HMSO: *Industrial Relations Handbook.*

Hiring
E Paton: *Bailment in the Common Law.*
E Beven: *Negligence,* Vol. 2.

Hire-Purchase
    Gow: *Law of Hire-Purchase in Scotland.*
E Goode: *Hire-Purchase Law and Practice.*

Insurance
E Preston and Colinvaux: *Insurance.*
E Macgillivray on *Insurance Law,* 2 vols.
E Houseman: *Law of Life Insurance.*
E Welford and Otter-Barry: *Law relating to Fire Insurance.*
E Welford: *Law relating to Accident Insurance.*
E Shawcross on *The Law of Motor Insurance.*
E Arnould on *Marine Insurance,* 2 vols.

Lease
    See under PROPERTY—Corporeal Heritable.

Loan
E Paton: *Bailment in the Common Law.*
E Beven: *Negligence,* Vol. 2.

Moneylender's Contracts
E Stone and Meston: *Law relating to Moneylenders.*

Partnership
    See under PERSONS—Unincorporated Associations.

Pledge and pawn
E Paton: *Bailment in the Common Law.*
E Beven: *Negligence,* Vol. 2.

Sale of incorporeal rights
    See books on PROPERTY—Incorporeal Moveable Property.

Sale of land
    See books on PROPERTY—Conveyancing.

Sale of moveables
    Brown (M.P.): *Treatise on the Law of Sale.*
    Brown (R.): *Sale of Goods Act.*
E Chalmers: *Sale of Goods Act.*
E Schmitthoff: *Sale of Goods.*
E Benjamin: *Treatise on the law of sale of personal property.*
E Wilberforce, Campbell and Elles: *Restrictive Trade Practices and Monopolies.*

Securities
    Gloag and Irvine: *Rights in Security and Cautionary Obligations.*

Works
E Hudson on *Building Contracts.*
E Emden and Watson on *Building Contracts and Practice.*

Law of Quasi-Contract or restitution
Gloag on *Contract*, Chap. 18.

Law of Delict or Reparation generally
Glegg: *Law of Reparation in Scotland.*
Guthrie Smith: *Law of Damages.*
Walker: *Law of Damages in Scotland.*
E   Salmond: *Law of Torts.*
E   Winfield: *Textbook of the Law of Tort.*
E   Pollock: *Law of Torts.*
E   Street: *Law of Torts.*
E   Clerk and Lindsell: *Law of Torts.*
E   Williams: *Joint Torts and Contributory Negligence.*
E   Mayne and Macgregor: *Law of Damages.*

Specific delicts
E   Beven: *Negligence in Law*, 2 vols.
E   Charlesworth: *Law of Negligence.*
    Borthwick: *Law of Libel and Slander in Scotland.*
    Cooper: *Law of defamation and verbal injury.*
E   Gatley: *Libel and slander in a civil action.*
E   Gibb: *Law of Collisions on Land.*
E   Bingham: *Motor Claims Cases.*
E   Marsden: *Collisions at Sea.*
E   Munkman: *Employer's Liability at Common Law.*
    Broun: *Law of Nuisance in Scotland.*

LAW OF PROPERTY
Classification and divisions of property
E   Adkin and Bowen: *Law of Fixtures.*

Corporeal heritable property
    Rankine: *Law of Landownership in Scotland.*
    Ferguson: *Law of Water and Water Rights in Scotland.*
        Law of roads, streets and rights of way.
    Stewart: *Laws and rights of fishing in Scotland.*
    Tait: *Game and fishing laws of Scotland.*
    Sandford: *History and Law of Entails.*
    Ross: *Law of Entail in Scotland.*
    Dobie: *Manual of the Law of Liferent and Fee.*
    Gloag and Irvine: *Rights in Security.*
    Rankine: *Law of Leases in Scotland.*
    Hunter: *Landlord and Tenant*, 2 vols.
    Connell and Johnston: *Agricultural Holdings (Scotland) Acts.*
    Scott: *Law of Smallholdings.*
    Stewart: *Law relating to Mines, Quarries and Minerals in Scotland.*
    Fraser: *Rent and House-Letting Acts in Scotland.*
E   Megarry on *The Rent Acts.*

Incorporeal heritable property
    Gloag and Irvine: *Rights in Security.*
    Hewlett: *Jurisdiction in Scottish Peerage Cases.*
    Riddell: *Law and Practice in Scottish Peerages.*

Innes: *Scots Heraldry.*
Stevenson: *Heraldry in Scotland,* 2 vols.
Wallace: *Nature and Descent of Ancient Peerages.*

Corporeal moveable property
Dobie: *Liferent and Fee.*
Gloag and Irvine: *Rights in Security.*
E   Vaines: *Personal Property.*
E   Goodeve: *Personal Property.*
E   Paton: *Bailment in the Common Law.*
        also books on sale, hiring, etc.

Incorporeal moveable property
Hamilton: *Bills of Exchange Act,* 1882.
McNeil: *Bills of Exchange, Cheques and Promissory Notes.*
E   Chalmers on *Bills of Exchange.*
E   Byles on *Bills of Exchange.*
E   Copinger and Skone James on the *Law of Copyright.*
E   Kerly: *Law of Trade Marks and Trade Names.*
E   Terrell and Shelley: *Law of Patents.*
E   Blanco White: *Patents for Inventions.*
E   Russell Clarke: *Copyright in Industrial Designs.*
E   Moulton and Langdon-Davies: *Law of Merchandise Marks.*
        For shares, see books on companies.

Succession and Executors
McLaren: *Law of Wills and Succession,* 2 vols. and Supp. Vol. by Dykes.
Walker: *Intestate Succession in Scotland.*
Murray: *Law of Wills in Scotland.*
Henderson: *Principles of Vesting in the Law of Succession.*
Macmillan: *Law of Bona Vacantia in Scotland.*
Currie: *Confirmation of Executors in Scotland.*

Trusts, Trustees and Judicial Factors
Menzies on *Trustees.*
Mackenzie Stuart on *Trusts.*
Thoms: *Judicial Factors.*
Irons: *Judicial Factors.*

Bankruptcy
Goudy: *Treatise on the Law of Bankruptcy in Scotland.*
Wallace: *Law of Bankruptcy in Scotland.*

Conveyancing
Burns: *Handbook of Conveyancing.*
        Conveyancing Practice.
Montgomery Bell: *Lectures on Conveyancing,* 2 vols.
Menzies: *Lectures on Conveyancing.*
Wood: *Lectures on Conveyancing.*
Hendry: *Manual of Conveyancing.*
Craigie: *Scottish Law of Conveyancing—Moveable Rights.*
                                    Heritable Rights.
Ross: *Lectures on Conveyancing,* 2 vols.

LAW OF ACTIONS
Jurisdiction
 Gibb: *International Law of Jurisdiction.*
 Duncan and Dykes: *Principles of Civil Jurisdiction.*

Civil Procedure
 Parliament House Book.
 Maclaren: *Court of Session Practice.*
 Maclaren: *Bill Chamber Practice.*
 Thomson and Middleton: *Manual of Court of Session Procedure.*
 Mackay: *Manual of Practice in the Court of Session.*
  Court of Session Practice, 2 vols.
 Lewis: *Sheriff Court Practice.*
 Dobie: *Sheriff Court Practice.*
 Irons: *Law and Practice in the Dean of Guild Court.*
 Macdonald: *Scottish Justices Manual.*

Pleading
 Lees: *Handbook of pleadings in the sheriff court.*

Evidence
 Lewis: *Manual of the Law of Evidence in Scotland.*
 Dickson: *Treatise on the Law of Evidence in Scotland.*
 E Cross: *Evidence.*
 E Phipson: *Treatise on the Law of Evidence.*

Civil Remedies
 Burn-Murdoch: *Interdict in the Law of Scotland.*
 Walker: *Law of Damages in Scotland.*
 Rankine: *Law of personal Bar and Estoppel.*

Diligence
 Graham Stewart: *Law of Diligence.*

Expenses
 Maclaren on *Expenses in the Supreme and Sheriff Courts.*

Legal Aid
 Law Society: *Legal Aid and Advice Compendium.*

Arbitration
 Bell: *Law of Arbitration in Scotland.*
 Irons and Melville: *Law of Arbitration.*

There are also many books of forms and precedents to assist in the framing of pleadings and the drafting of every kind of legal document, and forms are appended to some treatises.

Legal Periodicals
 Periodicals have various functions, to keep the jurist, practitioner and student acquainted with recent changes and developments in the

law, and to enable him to bring his search for any matter of law right up to date, to keep members of the profession in touch with changes affecting them and matters of common interest, and to serve as an outlet for academic thinking and a forum for the discussion of doctrines and critical analysis of developments.

The first function is performed primarily by *Current Law*. This publication appears in pamphlet form each month and each monthly part contains, digested under subject-headings, notes of all British statutes, statutory instruments, cases and articles published during the previous month.[76] The indexes are cumulative, including references to matter included in any of the monthly parts for the current year. It has to be noted that all matters applicable to the United Kingdom generally are included in the English section of *Current Law*, so that the Scottish lawyer cannot ignore that section of the publication entirely.

Each Spring the matter contained in the twelve monthly parts of the previous calendar year's *Current Law* is brought together, reprinted and issued in consolidated form as the *Current Law Year Book*.[76] There are indexes of cases, statutes and subjects. The volumes for 1956 and 1961 (Master Volumes 1948–56 and 1957–61) contain cumulative references to matters covered in detail in the annual volumes 1948–56 and 1957–61.

The *Current Law Citator Volume* lists all statutes passed, amended, applied, repealed or otherwise affected by legislation in the period 1948– , together with statutory instruments made under rule-making powers contained in statutes, and cases and articles relating to the statute. It also lists separately for England and for Scotland all the reports of each decided case and indicates by reference to paragraph numbers in what other cases the case under consideration was applied or distinguished or otherwise treated, or discussed in the periodicals. The references in the *Citator Volume* are to the *Current Law Consolidation* volume 1947–51,[77] which contains United Kingdom and English matter only, and for matters subsequently to 1951 to the annual volumes of the *Scottish Current Law Year Book*. The monthly parts of *Current Law* enable research

[76] There are two editions of both monthly parts and Year Book, the Scottish and the English. The Scottish is a complete reprint of the English edition with the addition of pages printed on green paper in the monthly parts, of exclusively Scottish material. The English pages contain (a) exclusively English matter, and also (b) United Kingdom matter also applicable in whole or in part to Scotland. Both sets of pages must accordingly be looked at.

[77] *Current Law* began in England in 1947 and in Scotland in 1948. The *Current Law Consolidation* deals with matter in the English *Current Law*, 1947–51, and has no Scottish equivalent, but United Kingdom and English matters for 1948–51 are found in the U.K. and English sections of the *Scottish Current Law Year Books*, 1948–49–50–51, and a paragraph reference to the C.L.C. (unless it relates to 1947) can be traced through the indexes to these years of the *Scottish Current Law Year Book*. The preface to each volume gives guidance on the use of these volumes.

to be continued from the date of the *Citator Volume* used down to the time of search.

The second function of the periodical, that of the professional journal, is performed by several journals many of which include also notes, or full reports, of cases and reviews of legislation.[78] Articles and notes in periodicals of the third kind, *fora* for scholarly discussion, may be persuasive authority and may have considerable influence on judicial thinking; articles vary from highly theoretical to very practical but the general theme is of scholarly analysis, discussion and criticism. There are many journals of this kind, both general [79] and specialised,[80] and a few of the major U.S. and other foreign periodicals also sometimes contain matter of interest in this country.

Articles in legal periodicals can be traced through the special indexes thereto.[81]

Apart from periodicals there are various annuals which frequently contain valuable information and articles [82] and many volumes of collected essays and studies, sometimes by one author, sometimes by several, and sometimes contributed by many hands to make a volume in honour of a distinguished jurist.[83]

---

[78] The main ones are the *Scots Law Times* (1893–   ); the *Scottish Law Review* (1885–   ); the *Scottish Law Gazette* (1933–   ); the *Journal of the Law Society of Scotland* (1956–   ) and the *Conveyancing Review* (1957–   ). In England there are the *Law Journal* (1822–   ); the *Law Times* (1843–   ); the *Solicitors' Journal* (1857–   ) and the *Law Society's Gazette* (1904–   ).

[79] The principal are the *Juridical Review* (1888–1955); the *Juridical Review: The Law Journal of the Scottish Universities* (1956–   ), and in England, the *Law Quarterly Review* (1885–   ); the *Cambridge Law Journal* (1921–   ); the *Modern Law Review* (1937–   ); the *Journal of the Society of Public Teachers of Law* (1924–38 and, New Series, 1947–   ).

[80] The principal are *Public Administration* (1923–   ); the *British Journal of Administrative Law* (1954–57) merged with *Public Law* (1956–   ); *Justice: The Journal of the International Commission of Jurists* (1958–   ); the *Journal of Planning and Property Law* (1948–   ); the *British Tax Review* (1956–   ); the *Journal of Criminal Law* (1937–   ); the *Journal of Criminal Science* (1948–   ); the *Criminal Law Review* (1954–   ); the *British Journal of Delinquency* (1950–60) incorporated in the *British Journal of Criminology* (1960–   ); the *Howard Journal* (1921–   ); the *Medico-Legal Journal* (1901–   ); *Medicine, Science and the Law* (1960–   ); the *Business Law Review* (1954–   ); the *Journal of Business Law* (1957–   ); the *Industrial Law Review* (1946–   ); the *Conveyancer and Property Lawyer* (1936–   ); the *Journal of Comparative Legislation and International Law* (1896–1951), combined with the *International Law Quarterly* (1947–51) into the *International and Comparative Law Quarterly* (1951–   ); also the annual *British Yearbook of International Law* (1921–   ); and *Current Legal Problems* (1948–   ).

[81] See Jones-Chipman *Index to Legal Periodical Literature*, 1803–1937, 6 vols.; *Index to Legal Periodicals* (1908–   ); *Index to Foreign Legal Periodicals* (1960–   ); *International Index to Periodicals*, 1907–55 (now *International Index*, 1955–   ); and *Subject-Index to Periodicals* (1915–   ).

[82] The chief are the *U.N. Yearbook*; the *European Yearbook*; and the *Yearbook of World Affairs*.

[83] These are more common in Germany and Italy where they are known as *Festschriften* and *Studi*.

CHAPTER 10

LEGAL METHOD

THE problem of legal method consists in ascertaining what methods should and can best be adopted to find the principles of law relevant to the solution of some legal difficulty. It has to be remembered that in many cases there is no ready-made proposition of law applicable to the legal problem in question, and the search must be for the materials from which to develop a proposition of law, one which, in the last resort, the courts would hold to be properly applicable to the case. As in other sciences, systematic inquiry is essential, though the difficulties thereof in legal contexts are numerous, frequently arising from uncertainty as to the precise state of the facts for which a rule of law is required. The task is essentially the same, whether the purpose of the search is to advise, on the basis of a prediction of what the court seems likely to do, the task of the legal adviser; or to find the material to persuade a judge or arbiter, the task of the pleader; or to reach and justify a decision, the task of the judge; or to state and systematise the law, the task of the jurist.

Analysis of Problem

The first step is to analyse the factual situation and diagnose the legal difficulty it discloses. The facts must be discovered as fully and accurately as possible, though it may be necessary initially to assume some facts and formulate a legal answer on the basis that certain facts, still unknown or doubtful or unproved, can yet be discovered or proved. Frequently further factual information must be sought before an answer to the legal difficulty can be attempted. It has also to be remembered that one set of facts may contain several legal problems and that a particular answer to one problem may affect the answers to the others.

The facts known or believed, or at least stated and assumed for the purposes of inquiry to exist should be set down in chronological order and checked for discrepancies by reference to all other sources of information available, such as documents or other witnesses' evidence. Irrelevant facts and details should be eliminated, though what is irrelevant may depend on the particular legal issue involved; there is no invariable standard of relevancy of facts and only legal knowledge can enable one to say what is relevant or irrelevant in a particular context.

The factual situation can best be stated under five headings, as follows: (i) the parties to the controversy, any peculiarities of status or capacity

attaching to them, and any legal relationship between them; (ii) the
events giving rise to the controversy; (iii) the remedy sought or other
object of the legal quest; (iv) the legal basis for claiming the remedy, or
proponing the defence; and (v) the point or points in doubt or dispute,
which may relate to any one or more of the previous four heads. Only
legal study and experience enable a person to recognise what elements
in a factual situation give rise to doubt or difficulty. The trained legal
mind sees difficulties not apparent to the layman. Thus in a simple
matrimonial case the problem might be analysed thus:

    (i) W (Scot) and H (French), married in London on ——;
   (ii) W left H on ——; H friendly with X; suspicious circumstances;
  (iii) divorce of H;
  (iv) adultery by H;
   (v) Have Scottish courts jurisdiction to grant divorce?
      Is W justified in leaving H, or herself in desertion?
      Evidence of H's adultery?

Classification

The next stage is to classify each point of difficulty in terms of the
legal concepts and categories involved under such legal headings and
sub-heads as the legal encyclopaedias, indexes, digests and other reference
books deal with particular topics, as if the factual situation were having
to be fitted into place in one of these publications.[1] Categorisation should
be done by reference to main subject of law, branch thereof and sub-head,
e.g., contract—formalities, need for writing—sale of heritage. This
indicates both where to look and the means of narrowing down the search
to the precise point in issue. This categorisation is by far the most
important element in the legal analysis of a problem.[2] It requires extensive
knowledge of the logical system of the law, of the classification of its
rules and principles and of the most likely heads under which topics
may be discussed. It is essential to note that the classification is by
legal categories, *e.g.*, divorce, hiring, defamation, etc., and that the
factual element is subsidiary, though not irrelevant since, *e.g.*, sale of a
house and sale of a car depend to a substantial extent on different rules.

Finding the Law—Primary and Secondary Authorities

In searching for correct principles and rules of law to apply to the
problems formulated the distinction between primary and secondary
authorities is important. Primary authorities are those books which
state rules and principles of law in authoritative form: such are statutes,

---

[1] These are the headings and sub-heads used in Chaps. 4 and 9, though the reference
and search books break headings down into a much finer sub-classification.
[2] It is particularly important and difficult in cases raising issues of International
Private Law.

statutory instruments and other legislation, binding cases and judicial opinions, and passages in institutional writings. A statement of a rule by one of these authorities, if in point, may be binding or will be, at least, persuasive. Secondary authorities are those sources of information in which individuals of greater or less eminence and experience, state with a greater or lesser degree of authority *their view* of what rules and principles of law are relevant to various topics: such are passages in legal encyclo-paedias, dictionaries, and textbooks, articles in legal periodicals, and other expressions of opinion of suggestions as to the law. Secondary authorities are always of lesser authority than primary authorities, though some of them, such as some highly respected textbooks have weight not far short of binding judicial opinions; but statements by one of these authorities, however much in point, will never be binding on a court.

Consulting the Secondary Sources

If the subject-matter of the problem is relatively unfamiliar it is advisable to start by reading the most general secondary authorities and proceeding only later to more detailed and specific secondary authorities and thence to primary authorities, proceeding, for example, from an article in the encyclopaedia or a general textbook, to a book more specifically related to the subject of inquiry alone, thence to relevant statutes and cases.[3] If the subject-matter is familar in general terms, one may go at once to the specific detailed textbook, or even direct to the statutes and cases which may be remembered from previous study as relevant.

It is always proper to start with these secondary authorities since reference to the relevant articles and chapters will tend to refresh the mind as to the branch of law involved, or if the topic is unfamiliar, it will place the problem in perspective in relation to and against a back-ground of the rest of the law on that topic. This general scrutiny of the background sometimes uncovers hitherto unsuspected pitfalls and difficulties, such as the requirement of any proceedings being taken within a limited period or in a particular form. Every legal adviser is constantly discovering in this way points he was unaware of or had forgotten.

In searching secondary sources the proper approach is to work from the more general to the more particular and from that in turn to the specific statutes and cases, that is, from secondary authorities to primary authorities. The reason for this approach is that primary authorities such as statutes, statutory instruments and cases do not, in themselves, give any guide or indication to later changes or develop-ments of the law, to other statutes or cases in point, to the amending,

---

[3] For the main secondary authorities, see Chap. 9.

repealing or overruling effect of later legislation or cases, to the way in which the statement of law in question has been interpreted in the courts, nor to the explanations or criticisms of jurists. Only in the systematic treatise can one find a synthetic picture of the law, admittedly as understood by one particular legal writer, but taking account of all the statutes, amendments, orders, cases, discussion, criticism and so on down to the date at which he wrote. Even then text-writers are fallible and may overlook or misstate some points.

Accordingly research in a secondary authority in the first place is likely, quite apart from any guidance or statements of principle by the text-writer, to yield a list of statutes, orders and cases which seem relevant to the topic which embraces the instant problem. Research to ascertain the solution of a legal difficulty must *never*, however, stop at the text-books or other secondary authorities because these represent merely what some legal scholar *thinks* is the legal position resulting from the various statutes and cases, and his view may be mistaken. Passages in encyclopaedias and textbooks are sometimes criticised by judges as being inaccurate or mistaken.[4]

Even if a sentence in a textbook appears exactly to fit the circumstances of the instant problem the basis in statutes and cases for the writer's view *must* be examined to see if they appear to justify his view. If they do, the statutes and cases are the primary material for solving the instant problem and the text-writer's view is purely supplementary and confirmatory.

Method of Searching Secondary Authorities

The relevant secondary authorities must be searched systematically and the following principles should be followed in order: (i) search the table of contents of the volume for headings which may be relevant, having in mind both the legal categories involved and the salient facts of the problem-situation, *e.g.*, divorce—cruelty—kicking, or negligence —car (automobile, vehicle, road traffic)—skidding; (ii) search the subject-index similarly; (iii) if any relevant case is already known, trace from the index of cases whether it is cited in the volume, and read each page whereon it is cited; (iv) if any relevant statute is known, check the index of statutes similarly; and (v) if any significant word or phrase is involved, check any index of words and phrases discussed, and follow up any leads given thereby. Lastly, note the date of the edition being used, or the date stated in the preface as that down to which the writer has been able to take account of changes in the law, because information about subsequent changes must be sought elsewhere.

---

[4] *e.g.*, *Bell* v. *Holmes* [1956] 1 W.L.R. 1359; *Sinclair* v. *Juner*, 1952 S.C. 35, 43, *per* L.P. Cooper.

As each secondary authority is examined a brief note should be made of any passages which appear helpful and of all references given to primary authorities, so that these clues can be followed up, these notes being segregated according to the legal problem to which they seem to indicate an answer.

With any luck this process should accordingly yield, under the heading of each problem, a list of text-writer's statements, and references to institutional writings, relevant cases, statutes and other points.

Research into Primary Authorities

Research into the secondary authorities in the way already discussed may be expected to yield at least some references to primary authorities which must next be followed up. It may, however, yield little or nothing, in which case equally the search must be carried to the primary authorities, and in any event a search must always be made for primary authorities which have come into being since the date of publication of the textbook or other secondary authority, such as new cases, statutes or orders, and for primary authorities which have been overlooked or omitted from the textbooks.[5]

References culled from the encyclopaedias and textbooks should be followed up first and read carefully, since these are likely to be the most important statutes and cases on the subject and they will probably themselves contain other references backwards leading the inquiry to other statutes and cases. Beyond that comes the search in the primary authorities by means of the Indexes to legislation and Digests of case-law. The *Index to the Statutes in Force* must be searched under all topic-headings which it is thought might conceivably cover any statute relevant to the problem. This Index groups " under titles which are descriptive of recognised branches of the law,[6] index entries setting out in general terms the subject-matter of the enactments which constitute those branches. Against those entries are inserted regnal year citations of the current enactments which support each proposition indexed." [7] These citations lead to the relevant provisions (in any edition of the

---

[5] Even the most diligent compiler of a textbook may overlook some decision or other point and textbooks and encyclopaedias do not guarantee to, and, in many instances, do not even attempt to, refer to all the statutes and cases. They try as a rule to mention all the more interesting and important ones. It is the function of the textbook to explain the state of the law, not to list all the cases, and it is always open to argument whether particular cases are sufficiently relevant or important to be cited on a particular point.

[6] While these branches and headings correspond generally to the branches and headings used in Chaps. 4 and 9 hereof, there are some " catch-all " titles, such as Animals.

[7] *Index to the Statutes in Force*, Preface. The whole Preface should be read for information on how to use the Index.

statutes). Most titles are divided and subdivided, dealing with substantive law, adjective law, and miscellaneous provisions, or following the layout of the principal Act.

The *Digests* of case-law must similarly be searched using successively the analytical or topic-heading approach, which is similarly based on recognised branches, headings and sub-headings,[6] the table of cases approach (where any analogous case is known), the table of statutes approach (where any relevant statute is known), and the index of words and phrases approach (where any word or phrase may have previously been discussed). This must be done for the main body of each Digest used, and for each supplement in turn.[8]

The institutional writers should be searched in succession, using the tables of contents and the general indexes to the standard editions, and the older non-institutional writings should also be searched. This is less necessary where the subject of inquiry is a matter of entirely modern law.

Bringing Research up to date

It must be kept in mind that research in even the latest published edition or volumes of these tools of primary research can bring the statement of law down, at best, to a period a few months back, or sometimes a year or two back.[9] The search must be carried on by the use of *Current Law.*

The *Scottish Current Law Year Books*, the *Citator Volume*, and the monthly parts of *Current Law* enable search to be continued from the date of the authorities consulted down to the time of search.

Utility of English and Foreign Authorities

In many cases it is desirable and even necessary to have recourse to authorities, both secondary and primary, which are not Scottish, most commonly to English authorities, such as Halsbury's *Laws of England,* or English textbooks. On many topics the law is in a general way common to Scotland and to England, while on others rules applicable to Scotland have very similar English counterparts. In topics of the former kind it is useful and indeed necessary to look at the English books, subject always to the caution that peculiarities of Scottish practice, of courts and procedure are seldom discussed, that purely Scottish primary authorities are frequently not cited, and that one must always

---

[8] The *Faculty Digest* Index volume contains a subject-index, indexes of cases referred to in other cases, of statutes commented on, of words defined, and of cases in the *Digest.* This last leads from a known case to the heads under which it appears and hence to similarly classified cases.

[9] The time-lag required to print and publish these books alone makes them not quite up to date even when they are freshly published.

consider whether any statement made in the book is consistent with the general body of law and practice of Scotland; much harm has been done in the past by too-ready and uncritical acceptance of principles laid down in English books, even though they may appear to be entirely applicable in Scotland.[10] In topics of the latter kind resort to English books is much more difficult and dangerous and they should not be searched save in default of any Scottish authority. On other topics again the laws of Scotland and of England are quite different and reference to English authorities is of little or no value.

Periodicals

Articles, discussion and criticism in legal periodicals [11] are of increasing importance and it is desirable to check the relevant periodicals to see if there are any articles on the subject and if any relevant cases have been criticised therein. These may be found through the *Index to Legal Periodicals* and *Current Law*.

Synthesis of Materials

The next step is to effect a synthesis of materials bearing on each problem under investigation in the case. In all but the simplest cases it should be done on paper by noting down in summary form all the relevant materials which have been discovered, in chronological order, thereby seeing how far each new factor affects the earlier ones.[12] This inevitably involves at every stage taking decisions on interpretation of statutory provisions, on the *rationes* and evaluation of cases and on the applicability and weight of passages in institutional writers and lesser authorities.

In thus working towards an answer to any problem the weight to be given to the various sources of law is important. If there is a statutory provision which appears to cover the case, or as interpreted in other cases has been held to do so, that must rule. In default of statutory provision, if there is a *ratio* discoverable from a judicial precedent which is both in point and binding, that must rule. In default of statute or binding precedent, the answer may be supplied or suggested by a passage in an institutional writer, a passage in a textbook of greater or less authority, the *ratio* of a merely persuasive precedent, or of one not directly in point though closely analogous, an *obiter dictum* in a precedent, suggestion or criticism in a legal periodical, or other indication.

---

[10] *Cf.* Lord Cooper's warning in *McLaughlan* v. *Craig*, 1948 S.C. 599, of the dangers of reliance on English authorities in negligence cases.

[11] For these see Chap. 9, *supra*.

[12] For examples in judicial opinions of the tracing out of a long series of cases see *Donoghue* v. *Stevenson*, 1932 S.C.(H.L.) 31, *per* Lord Atkin, *Candler* v. *Crane, Christmas & Co.* [1951] 2 K.B. 164, and *Re Diplock* [1948] Ch. 465. For examination of institutional writers and cases see *Fortington* v. *Kinnaird*, 1942 S.C. 239.

Failing all else, an answer may be suggested by common sense, reason and personal ideas of the requirements of equity and justice.

This process of synthesis of materials determines the net consequence of all the various legal factors which are elements in making up the answer to the problem under consideration. The process is not an exact science but a difficult process of balancing and weighing, depending on tentative interpretation of possibly obscure and conflicting statutory phrases and provisions, on eliciting the *rationes* of cases and on the evaluation of materials from secondary sources. The synthesis in fact demands a prediction, a prophecy, a guess at what a court would decide on these materials. Sometimes no clear or decided view can be arrived at, but only a formulation that something " appears to be the law " or is " thought to be the rule."

It has to be noticed that in the case of some problems the answer may be wholly negative, in that each possibility is negatived, or the answer may contain two positive alternatives, in that each of two possible courses may be legally competent.[13] In this case the choice of which course to adopt may be determined by other factors, such as the availability of evidence, and the general convenience of making one claim rather than another.

The process in operation

One brief example may show how this process of finding the law applies. Suppose the problem is: a coalman supplied a bag of coal which contained an explosive and when some of the coal was put on the fire an explosion took place damaging the room. *Quid juris*? Analysis and classification suggest that the problem is Contract—sale of goods— goods of defective quality—coal. Search in the general books suggests as relevant the Sale of Goods Act, 1893, s. 14 (1) of which imports an implied warranty of fitness of goods sold for a particular purpose in certain cases. The books on sale in discussing this section mention *Duke* v. *Jackson*, 1921 S.C. 362, which seems almost exactly to fit these facts but to lead to an odd result, inconsistent with the common-sense interpretation of the section of the 1893 Act. The index of statutes commented on in the *Faculty Digest* leads also to this case as the closest in point of several on that section. The *Current Law Case Citator*, under Scottish cases, reveals that this case was distinguished in a virtually identical Scottish case in 1948, where the opposite conclusion was reached, and that there was an article discussing the case of *Duke* in 1954 S.L.T., which in turn reveals that *Duke's* case was severely criticised in the

---

13 Thus investigation into whether divorce is possible for adultery or for desertion on certain facts may reveal that both are competent, as where a husband deserts and lives in adultery with someone else. After three years' desertion divorce is open on either ground or on both.

English Court of Appeal in another exactly similar case [14] in 1954. The *Current Law Case Citator*, under English cases, indicates that *Duke* was " not followed " in the 1954 English case, and also indicates several comments on this English case in the periodicals, which, when read, seem to favour it as a true application of section 14 (1) and to condemn *Duke*. The *Current Law Statute Citator*, under the heading of the 1893 Act, s. 14 (1), lists various other cases but none when examined is any more closely in point.

Synthesis of these materials thus suggests that the answer to the problem is given by section 14 (1), as interpreted in the English case, and that *Duke* should not be followed but distinguished.

Formulation of Solution

The materials discovered for answering each issue in doubt having been thus assembled, and a provisional view formed on each point, it remains to put them together and see how far, if at all, a complete legal answer has been found to the whole problem posed by the facts. Inconsistencies may be found, discrepancies or doubtful points, and much may have to be left on a hypothetical basis, depending on the view taken on some prior issue. The answer to one problem may exclude some possible answer on another problem, or may depend on the answer adopted to some logically prior problem.

The last stage in formulating the solution is to put it into shape for use, possibly drafting an opinion on the state of the law for information and future reference, possibly framing advice on what should be done immediately, possibly drafting a summons or petition or other pleading so as to obtain a remedy from a competent court.

It is important that a systematic process of research be undertaken at an early stage into all the legal problems which are apparent, as not infrequently in practice a view is formulated, advice is given or a claim made without considering subsequent difficulties, such as that of proving allegations made in a summons. It is not possible to foresee or take precautions against every eventuality, every defence, or every unexpected point which may emerge later, but every difficulty visible or readily foreseeable should be taken into account from the start, since there is no point in embarking on a course of legal action if there appears to be substantial danger of not being able to take it through all its stages.

Testing the Solution

The only real test for a legal adviser's solution for any legal difficulty or problem in issue is to have the matter decided by the court, which can be done only if there is truly a controversy. The courts will not

[14] *Wilson* v. *Rickett, Cockerell & Co.* [1954] 1 Q.B. 598.

answer academic problems, where the rights of individuals are not affected by their decision. But, while the court's decision of any legal problem settles the matter as between the parties and may, under the doctrine of precedent, settle the law for the future, it does not follow that the court's decision is necessarily right. For there are many reported cases which have been subsequently overruled as wrongly decided, or have been so criticised and distinguished or not followed as to be devoid of authority and little regarded. The judgment of the court has, however, to be accepted as the answer and there is no other way of testing or verifying the solution, and the acid test of any legal advice comes when the conduct based on that advice is scrutinised by the court. This does not mean that every time a court action fails the legal adviser has been wrong, because actions which involve any issue of evidence or fact may, independently of the law and legal advice, fail if the evidence does not measure up to expectations, or if it does not impress the judge or jury as accurate, or if judge or jury decline to draw any desired inference from it. In these respects very much depends on the manner and demeanour of witnesses, and the whole way in which the evidence comes out and the impact which it makes on the tribunal of fact. But in a purely legal issue, such as the debate on a plea to the relevancy of pleadings, an appeal on a point of law, or a stated case or special case, the court's decision, right or occasionally wrong, is the only real test of the validity of the legal advisers' solution to his problem.

FURTHER READING

Bell: *Dictionary and Digest of the Law of Scotland* (ed. Watson).
Broom: *Legal Maxims.*
Cardozo: *Nature of the Judicial Process.*
Craies: *Statute Law* (5th ed.).
Gibb and Dalrymple: *Scottish Judicial Dictionary.*
Index to Legal Periodicals, 1908 to date.
Institute of Advanced Legal Studies: *Bibliographical Guide to United Kingdom Law.*
Jowitt: *Dictionary of English Law.*
Maxwell: *Interpretation of Statutes* (11th ed.).
Price & Bitner: *Effective Legal Research* (*U.S.A.*).
Stair Society: *Sources and Literature of Scots Law*, 1936.
Stroud: *Judicial Dictionary* (3rd ed., 4 vols.).
Sweet & Maxwell: *Where to Look for Your Law.*
                Guide to Law Reports and Statutes (4th ed.).
Trayner: *Latin Maxims and Phrases* (4th ed.).
Wharton: *Law Lexicon* (13th ed.).
Words and Phrases Judicially Defined (5 vols.).

INDEX

BENTHAM, 126
BILL CHAMBER, 92
BILL OF SUSPENSION, 182, 183, 185, 262–263
BILLS (before Parliament), 270
BLOOD-FEUD, 48
BLUE BOOKS, 343
BOARD OF TRADE Shipping Inquiries, 203
BORSTAL TRAINING, 266
BOSWELL, JAMES, 94
BRACTON, 48
BREVIARIUM ALARICIANUM, 113, 115
BRIEVES, 46–47
BURGH COURTS, 41
BURGH PROSECUTOR, 182
BURGHS, 40, 76, 84–85
  of barony, 40
  of regality, 40
BURGHS, Convention of Royal, 40, 42
BURGHS, Four, 38, 41–42
BURLAMAQUI, 127
BY-LAWS, municipal, 282
BYNKERSHOEK, 127

CALLING of summons, 244
CANON LAW, 44, 46, 100, 121–123
CAPACITY, 150
CARRIAGE, contract of, 153
CASE,
  special, 178–179, 251
  stated, 179–182, 183, 185, 188, 189, 251, 262
CASE-LAW. See JUDICIAL PRECEDENTS.
CASES as guide to interpretation, 294
CATEGORIES of legal thought, 366
CAUSATION, 15
CAUTION, 262, 266
CELTIC LAW, 35–36
CENTRAL GOVERNMENT, 76, 82
CERTIORARI, 206
CHAMBERLAIN, 41, 42, 44
CHANCELLOR, 56, 57
CHANCERY, 46, 48, 205
CHARGE to jury, 247, 257
CHARGE to pay, 255
CHIEF BARON, 91
CHIEF JUSTICE, LORD, 206, 212
CHURCH and State, 82, 140
CHURCH OF SCOTLAND, 190
CIRCUITS, 184, 206, 211, 222
CITATION of defender, 244, 256
CITATION of statutes, 274
CIVIL OR ROMAN LAW, 111. See also ROMAN LAW.
CIVILIANS, French and Dutch, 89, 92, 117–118
CLASSIFICATION, 106, 366
CLAUSES ACTS, 273
CLEMENTINAE, 122

CLIENTS, solicitors transacting with, 230
COCKBURN, Henry, 94
CODE NAPOLEON, 118
CODEX,
  Gregorianus, 112, 113
  Hermogenianus, 112, 113
  New, 114
  Old, 114
  of Canon Law, 122
  Theodosianus, 112, 113
CODIFYING ACTS, 273
COLLECTIVE BARGAINING, 166
COLLEGE OF JUSTICE, 56–58, 218
  Senators of, 57, 218
COMMAND PAPERS, 343
COMMENCEMENT of Acts, 276
COMMENTATORS, 116
COMMERCIAL LAW, 164–165
COMMISSARIES, 58, 91
COMMISSION FOR GRIEVANCES, 62
COMMISSION OF ASSIZE, 211
COMMISSIONERS OF SUPPLY, 76, 77
COMMITTEE FOR CAUSES, 50, 52, 54
COMMITTEE OF ARTICLES, 50, 51
COMMON LAW, 136
  not altered by implication, 297
COMMON MARKET, 130
COMMON PLEAS, Court of, 205
COMMON SERGEANT, 211
COMMONWEALTH, 63, 140
COMPANIES, law of, 98
COMPARATIVE LAW, 123
COMPARATIVE METHOD of legal study, 6
COMPLAINT, criminal, 260
COMPURGATION, 47
CONCEPTS, legal, 29
CONCLUSIONS of summons, 243
CONCORDIA DISCORDANTIUM CANONUM, 121
CONDESCENDENCE, 243
CONFLICT OF LAWS, 115, 148
CONGREGATION OF CARDINALS, 122
CONSISTORIAL CAUSES, 58
CONSISTORIAL REMEDIES, 243
CONSOLATO DEL MARE, 102
CONSOLIDATING ACTS, 273
CONSTABLE, 38
CONSTITUTION, law of the, 140–141
CONSTITUTIONAL HISTORY, 110, 141
CONSTRUCTION of statutes, 286–299
CONTEMPORANEA EXPOSITIO, 295
CONTEXT, reference to, in interpretation, 291
CONTRACT, 153
CONTROVERSY, LEGAL, 242
CONVENTION OF ESTATES, 51
CONVENTION OF ROYAL BURGHS, 40, 42
CONVENTIONS OF CONSTITUTION, 140
CONVEYANCING, 161

380 Index

JACOBITE REBELLIONS, 74, 77
JEFFREY, Francis, 94
JUDGE-ADVOCATE, 192
JUDGE OF POLICE, 182
JUDGES, 218
  English, 205
  Irish, 213
  Scottish, 174–177, 218
  temperament of, 27
JUDGES-DELEGATE, 45
JUDGMENT, moral, 25
JUDICIAL FACTOR, 160
JUDICIAL FUNCTION, 172
JUDICIAL KNOWLEDGE, 163
JUDICIAL POWERS, review of, 143
JUDICIAL PRECEDENTS,
  application of, in later cases, 327
  as sources of law, 299–330
  binding and persuasive, 304, 315
  discovering ratio of, 319–330
  evaluating, 316
  hierarchy of courts and, 305–315
  in English courts, 310
  in Irish courts, 314
  in Scottish courts, 306
  method of finding, 349
  technique of handling, 318, 327
  valuable elements in, 319
  when " in point," 304
JUDICIAL SYSTEM, 172–217
JURA IN RE ALIENA, 156–158
JURA IN RE PROPRIA, 156–158
JURIES. See JURY TRIAL
JURISDICTION, 148, 162, 175, 183, 185, 188, 242, 256, 260
JURISPRUDENCE,
  analytical, 109
  definitions of, 107
  different senses of the word, 4, 12, 15
  historical, 109, 110
  philosophical, 108
  sociological, 109
JURISTS, writings of, 67, 79, 93, 331, 350
JURY COURT, 90
JURY TRIAL, 47, 178, 181, 202, 204, 245, 246–247, 250, 257
JUS
  civile, 111, 134
  gentium, 111
  honorarium, 111
  praetorium, 111, 134
JUSTICE, College of, 56, 64, 72
  origins of, 53
JUSTICE, Ideals of, as source of rules, 337
JUSTICE, International Court of, 128
JUSTICE-AYRES, 39, 60, 66
JUSTICE-CLERK, 66, 178, 184, 219
JUSTICE-GENERAL, 39, 65, 66, 184
JUSTICES OF THE PEACE, 60–61, 73, 77, 208

JUSTICIARS, 39
JUSTICIARY, HIGH COURT OF, 39, 65–66
  Lords Commissioners of, 66
JUSTINIAN, 114–115
  legislation of, 114
  reconquest of Italy by, 113

KAMES, Henry Home, Lord, 80, 331, 353
KING'S BENCH, Court of, 205
KING'S COUNCIL, 50, 55
KING'S COUNSEL, 223
KIRK SESSIONS, 77, 190

LABOUR ORGANISATION, International, 128
LAND COURT. See COURTS.
LAND TENURE, feudal, 36, 100
LANDLORD AND TENANT, 157
LANGUAGE and law, 31
  importance of, 31
LATERAN COUNCIL, 47
LAUDER, Sir John, of Fountainhall, 68
LAW,
  adjective, 137
  administrative, 137
  agricultural, 164, 166
  and anthropology, 10
  and economics, 7
  and history, 9
  and philosophy, 13
  and politics, 6
  and psychology, 11
  and sociology, 8
  as a social science, 2, 5
  as command, 18
  as rules for achieving justice, 19
  as social control, 19
  books of authority in, 330
  Canon. See CANON LAW.
  choice of, 242
  Civil. See ROMAN LAW.
  civil, 131, 134
  classification of, 106, 132
  commercial, 165–166
  common, 136
  Communist, 125
  comparative, 123
  constitutional, 137, 140
  consuetudinary, 136
  criminal, 134, 137
  customary, 332
  definitions of, 3, 12, 15, 18–19
  distinguished from legal system, 20
  English, 102
  extraneous sources of, 334
  facts and, 22
  families of, in world, 124
  family, 150